EVALUATING
FAMILY PROGRAMS

MODERN APPLICATIONS OF SOCIAL WORK

An Aldine de Gruyter Series of Texts and Monographs

James K. Whittaker, Series Editor

EVALUATING FAMILY PROGRAMS

Heather B. Weiss
Francine H. Jacobs
Editors

ALDINE DE GRUYTER
New York

ABOUT THE EDITORS

Heather B. Weiss has been the Director of the Harvard Family Research Project since its inception in 1983. The Project provides information about the development, implementation, and evaluation of family support and education programs to policymakers, program directors, and evaluation researchers. Dr. Weiss and other Project members are currently investigating state-sponsored family support initiatives and are compiling data on model programs sponsored by schools, churches, and other community groups.

Francine H. Jacobs is Assistant Professor of Child Study at Tufts University. Prior to this appointment, she was the Associate Director of the Harvard Family Research Project. Dr. Jacobs has served in public health and child services agencies, has directed child care and early intervention programs, and is an evaluation consultant to numerous organizations.

ALDINE DE GRUYTER
A Division of Walter de Gruyter, Inc.
200 Saw Mill River Road
Hawthorne, New York 10532

Library of Congress Cataloging-in-Publication Data

Evaluating family programs.

(Modern applications of social work)
Bibliography: p.
Includes index.
1. Family social work—United States
—Evaluation.   2. Child welfare—United States
—Evaluation.   3. Family allowances—United
States—Evaluation.   4. Evaluation research
(Social action programs)—United States.
I. Weiss, Heather Bastow.   II. Jacobs, Francine
Helene.   III. Series.
HV699.E85   1988   362.8'28'0973   88-920
ISBN 0-202-36047-4
ISBN 0-202-36048-2 (pbk.)

Printed in the United States of America
10 9 8 7 6 5 4 3 2 1

CONTENTS

FOREWORD

The diverse composition of American families, and the changing ways of raising our children, have become subjects of intense scrutiny by researchers and policymakers in recent years. Shifting demographics and work patterns, growing numbers of women in the work force, teenage pregnancy, single-parent families, and the deinstitutionalization of the elderly, disabled, and mentally ill—all these trends significantly affect family life.

The two-parent family, with one breadwinner and one homemaker, which was regarded as the norm when today's young parents grew up, is now atypical of most families. One in five children now lives in a single-mother home; in the majority (61%) of families with children under the age of 16, there is either a single parent or two working parents; 22% of all children born in 1985 were born to an unwed mother; 21% of American children (13 million) live below the poverty line.

Accompanying these demographic changes have been grave stresses, and the emergence of heightened demands for often inadequate supportive services. The House Select Committee on Children, Youth, and Families was created in 1983 to ascertain for policymakers the nature of the changes affecting America's families, and to weigh public policies in response to those needs. In nearly 50 hearings, we have heard poignant accounts of futile searches for affordable, quality child care, research about the pressures of caring for multiply handicapped children, and the dramatic impact of a pregnancy on the life of an adolescent.

While parents, policymakers, and researchers share common aspirations for families—economic security, emotional stability, opportunity—these profound changes in family life have been accompanied by a growing divisiveness about the appropriate nature of public and private involvement in supporting families. The extensive research reviewed by the Select Committee demonstrates conclusively that calls for self-reliance on the part of overburdened families, and volunteerism on the part of charities and the overextended private sector, cannot match the beneficial outcomes attributed to well-designed and conscientiously operated programs supported jointly by the community, the private sector (including charities and religious organizations), and government.

Increasingly, legislators, social service providers, and program administrators have come to rely upon program evaluation as a guide in their attempts to recognize needs and to provide services to meet them. In recognition of the need for high-quality evaluation resources for family support programs, the Harvard Family Research Project has collected a broad range of experiences and recommendations from child and family specialists, program directors, and evaluation experts.

The resulting volume, *Evaluating Family Programs,* effectively bridges the gap between researchers and practitioners in order to bring practical, understandable advice to the providers of family programs, and to program funders and policymakers. The authors have moved outside the traditional approaches of their disciplines to create new models for delivering and evaluating services. This volume sets a mood of genuine inquiry and excitement about successful aspects of programs while maintaining openness about the limitations of both research and practice.

Evaluating Family Programs reminds us that in order to develop sound family policy we must look at children and families in context. We will fail in our attempts to help children if we ignore the reciprocal influences of extended family, culture, community, and social institutions. It urges that those who advocate program accountability understand that not all types of evaluations are always appropriate for all programs, and it notes that limitations in current evaluation technologies make it difficult to fully evaluate all outcomes. As policymakers, program administrators, and informed citizens come to rely more upon the results of program evaluations, we must improve our evaluation methods while not losing sight of the limitations of evaluation.

Evaluating Family Programs is a thought-provoking contribution to the efforts of those who seek to support the American family with compassion, understanding, and realism.

> *George Miller*
> Chairman, Select Committee on
> Children, Youth, and Families,
> U.S. House of Representatives

Every once in a while, a book comes along that through its synthesis of disparate bodies of knowledge and sheer scope of analysis helps to define a new area of inquiry. In developmental research, Bronfenbrenner's minor classic *The Ecology of Human Development: Experiments by Nature and Design* comes immediately to mind. Such works are, by their nature, written in broad strokes and leave the practitioner hungry for the details of "how to." Heather Weiss and Francine Jacobs (Harvard Family Research Project) have addressed this need with a rich and detailed summary of the state of family intervention research.

In examining the analytic, conceptual, methodological, and organizational issues attendant to family-oriented research in the community, the contributors have demonstrated that, in family support research at least, one need not trade methodological rigor for programmatic relevance. They have also shed considerable light on what an ecological perspective actually means both for program developers *and* evaluators. In fact, a thread that runs through the many excellent chapters in this impressive volume are the notions that program development and evaluation ought to be thought of as organically related, and that such "mission-oriented" research is relevant to a wide range of demonstration efforts designed to reduce the risk of adverse developmental outcomes for children and families. Whatever the differences in population, presenting problems, and agency settings among the intervention programs reported here, the creative interplay of research and practice is evident throughout. Much of the merit of this book, in fact, lies in its potential for technology transfer—from preschool programs to parent education efforts and from maternal and child health to child abuse and neglect—both with respect to the technology of intervention and the technology of evaluation. Social work practitioners and other human service providers will discover rich material in this book on family stress and coping, social supports, practitioner roles, and organizational issues related to programmatic research. There is a wealth of detail on practical problems in conducting family evaluative research in social service and educational settings and an equally rich compilation of solutions for overcoming them. This is, at once, an utterly practical and deeply speculative book about family

support research and intervention. Students and practitioners will find many helpful suggestions, as well as excellent presentations and analysis of central issues within its covers.

Perhaps the most important contribution of Weiss, Jacobs, and their colleagues is the underlying perspective they provide on families: throughout, the authors hold a nondeficit, nonpathological view of family functioning and child development. An emphasis on family strengths abounds. Stress, coping patterns, environmental resources, and personal skills are viewed in complex interaction, not as isolated entities. Criterion measures extend beyond individual child and parent outcomes to community measures. Over and over, through specific program examples, a new relationship is unveiled between parent and professional, as indeed between researcher and practitioner.

If (and I would fervently hope, when) public policymakers sense the urgency of shoring up the most basic unit of the nation's social infrastructure, the lessons gleaned from the scores of programs described in this volume will do much to chart the future course of action.

James K. Whittaker
Professor of Social Work
The University of Washington

PREFACE

The Harvard Family Research Project was established in 1983 to collect, review, synthesize, and disseminate information about the effectiveness and evaluation of a burgeoning and promising set of preventive programs: those designed to provide support and education to families with young children. Our initial review indicated that program design was substantially ahead of the evaluation of these diverse grass roots programs and that there was considerable unmet demand for both evidence of effectiveness and sensitive evaluation strategies. With this diagnosis of the state-of-the-art in mind, we outlined this volume, and commissioned essays from innovative program evaluators, directors, and researchers. Each author deserves our thanks for a stimulating contribution, for cooperation in conforming to our volume's length restrictions, and for patience and responsiveness during the editorial process.

Since *Evaluating Family Programs* grows out of the Harvard Family Research Project, it reflects the work of many hands. The HFRP was established with a grant from the Charles Stewart Mott Foundation. While we are solely responsible for the work herein, we are particularly grateful to Marilyn Steele, Program Officer, and to Willard Hertz, Vice President, for their unswerving enthusiasm and support of the Project and this volume. Dr. Steele's commitment to evaluation strategies that respond to the needs of community-based programs stimulated our thinking about appropriate ways to assess family programs. The volume was completed with grants to the Project from the Carnegie Corporation of New York and the Ford Foundation. We would especially like to thank Dr. Barbara Finberg, Vice-President, and Dr. Vivien Stewart, Program Officer, of Carnegie Corp., and Dr. Oscar Harkavy, Chief Program Officer, at the Ford Foundation for providing both financial and non-financial support at a critical time in our work.

We would like to acknowledge the contributions of several important members of our early childhood and family policy community. The work of Urie Bronfenbrenner, Jacob Gould Shurman Professor of Human Development and Family Studies, Cornell University, on the ecology of human development has been a theoretical lodestar for this volume.

The ecological perspective on human services which James K. Whittaker, Professor of Social Work, University of Washington, has promoted also has enriched this work. Ann Rosewater, Staff Director to the Select Committee for Children, Youth, and Families has provided helpful comments and encouragement at numerous points in this process; Ann also was among the first policy analysts to push for *reasonable* strategies to determine the effectiveness of these programs. And, of course, the integrity and vision of the Select Committee's work has reinforced our own. Finally, Deborah Klein Walker has been an invaluable friend and a source of critical perspective throughout.

Project staff members and colleagues have provided needed social support in the production of this book. Margaret Herzig, our editor and Project manager, has gone the mile with us; her gentle but tenacious organizational skills, editorial wisdom, and style have been simply invaluable in bringing the book to fruition. As Project administrator, Laura Stephens-Swannie focused her great capacity for hard work with unbelievable equanimity—coordinating drafts and manuscripts, word processing, and keeping the overall effort synchronized. Charles Gerlach, research assistant par excellence, compiled and checked the accuracy of the listings in the instrument source list (Appendix A); it was a monumental task which he tackled with characteristic thoroughness, efficiency, and amiability. We are very much indebted to Carole Upshur, Associate Professor, College of Public and Community Service at the University of Massachusetts, Boston, for preparing the clear and detailed Glossary of Research and Evaluation terms. Her ability to explain and illustrate complex concepts has contributed substantially to our goal of demystifying the process of evaluation and reaching a broader audience.

As an editorial consultant in the book's final stages of preparation, Constance Putnam helped in the difficult job of shortening the manuscript. Her editorial skills were akin to those of a surgeon in their delicacy and attention to preserving the chapters' organic structure. We would also like to thank Mark Meterko, Survey Research Coordinator, Harvard Community Health Plan; Amy Richman of Work/Family Directions; and Donna Karl, Director of the Neighborhood Support Systems for Infants, for their helpful suggestions on the Glossary.

The Project's research assistants have proofread, done word processing, checked references, and the like with great care. They include Lisa Brown, Beth Gamse, Charles Gerlach, Fatima Lee, Joe Parker, Kris Puopolo, Susan Shepherd, Joan Test, Andrew Untch, and Lily Wiatrowski. Jane Tyler-Guild helped with early manuscript preparation; Martha Learner also assisted with word processing. Steve and Julie Hite provided critical technical assistance with word processing throughout.

Harvard University and the Graduate School of Education have given us a congenial home, rich resouces, and ready administrative support.

Finally, we would like to thank Trev Leger and Sheila Johnston at Aldine for their ongoing support and creative editorial advice.

Heather B. Weiss
Francine H. Jacobs

Introduction: Family Support and Education Programs— Challenges and Opportunities

Heather Bastow Weiss and Francine H. Jacobs

Contemporary American families, like earlier ones, are driven by the powerful urge to do the best for their children. However, they face many stresses as they attempt to build fulfilling, growth-promoting family lives. These stresses reverberate through everyday family life and stem from many sources, including: work-related pressures (on both single- and dual-worker families), increased mobility and isolation, economic problems from under- and unemployment, and changes in family structure such as single and teen parenthood. Increased recognition of these stresses and their possible long-term negative consequences, coupled with knowledge about the powerful and interrelated roles played by the family and its social support system in human development, have gradually forced more public consideration of how to provide support, education, nurturance, and reinforcement to child-rearing families. As a result, a new breed of community-based preventive programs that provide social support to young families has been growing up around the country.

These programs, which we group under a family support and education label, build on parents' desires to do the best for their children by building strong families in supportive communities. Public policy-makers and professionals who work with children are showing increasing interest because of the possibility that these programs can enhance and strengthen families, and because diagnoses of many current social problems—from infant morbidity to school failure—point to breakdowns in parenting and family functioning and to a weak social infrastructure of community support for young families. Taken together, these diverse and promising programs constitute a significant and growing movement that could have a major positive impact on the health, development, and well-being of American children and their families.

Evaluating Family Programs was designed to stimulate and reinforce this movement by addressing two interrelated questions: what is known to date about program effectiveness, and what strategies can be employed to learn how to strengthen these programs and to document their effectiveness? Thus, the volume represents an effort to capture both the fruits of past evaluation practice and the most current and creative thinking about future directions. It is our belief that this is an auspicious time to encourage discussion about these programs because policymakers' demands for and receptivity to information about effective family support and education programs are greater than they have been in some time (see Weiss, Chapter 1, this volume). As a result, programs that have documented their implementation and effectiveness have a good chance of finding increased public interest and support as policymakers reconsider what service and family income-generating strategies are necessary to address major family-related social problems.

In this introduction we describe the basic characteristics of family support and education programs, highlighting those features that pose special challenges to evaluators. We then briefly explain how our understanding of the literature about program effectiveness and appropriate evaluation strategies led to the book's content and structure.

THE DEFINING CHARACTERISTICS OF FAMILY SUPPORT AND EDUCATION PROGRAMS

Thousands of programs (from income-support programs to the provision of quality child care or intensive family counseling services) can legitimately be placed under the rubric of family support and education. This volume's focus is on the design and evaluation of a narrower set of direct service programs for families with preadolescent children. [See Part III of this book and Zigler, Weiss, and Kagan (1983) for examples of specific programs.] This subset shares the following defining characteristics.:

1. They demonstrate an *ecological approach* to promoting human development in that they foster child and adult growth by enhancing *both* the family's child-rearing capacities and the community context in which childrearing takes place.

2. They are community-based and sensitive to local needs and resources, even when they have a federal or state sponsor.

3. They provide services in each of the domains typically included within the concept of social support (see Cleary, Chapter 8, this volume): They supply *information* (e.g., child health and development and parenting information), *emotional and appraisal support* (e.g., empathy, feedback, and reinforcement to adults in parenting roles and access to other parents) and *instrumental assistance* (e.g., transportation and referrals to other services.)

4. They emphasize *primary* and *secondary prevention* of various child and family dysfunctions.

5. They have developed innovative and multilateral (as opposed to exclusively professional) approaches to service delivery through such means as peer support, creative use of volunteers and paraprofessionals, and the promotion of informal networks.

6. They underscore the *interdependent* relationship between family and community (including both formal and informal supports) while at the same time framing this relationship so as to reinforce and respect the family's role and prerogatives.

This set of characteristics defines a broad range of programs across many professional areas; we have chosen to be deliberately inclusive for several reasons. First, these characteristics are, in fact, found in programs operating under many different auspices (e.g., community organization, early childhood and education, medicine, mental health, social work). These programs have been mounted by different agencies to prevent a wide variety of social problems that are felt to be related to a lack of support and education for parents and families. As a result, programs that may seem dissimilar because they are under different auspices, serve different populations, or are addressed to social problems "owned" by another agency, on closer examination turn out to employ similar means to achieve similar or overlapping ends. For example, Cohn (1981) suggests seven types of services, from perinatal support to parent education, in a paper outlining a general approach to the prevention of child abuse and neglect. Many of these same services are also prominent in infant development or family-oriented early childhood programs. Second, given similar goals, objectives, and services, these different programs are likely to have at least some common short-term outcomes (such as enhanced parenting skills, reduced social isolation, or richer and developmentally appropriate parent–child interaction), although some of their longer term outcomes (such as reduced rates of abuse and neglect or fewer repeat pregnancies) would necessarily differ.

The book is guided by this more inclusive definition, rather than by one defined more narrowly by discipline, child's age, or some other limiting criterion, because we hope to encourage more programmatic cross-fertilization, recognition of common evaluation issues, and more interdisciplinary efforts to assess these complex programs. Therefore, the authors examine measurement and evaluation issues common to a wide range of programs, and the volume includes case studies of evaluations of programs created to prevent abuse and neglect, teen parenting problems, infant morbidity, school failure, and developmental delay.

Several additional characteristics distinguish these programs from more traditional and treatment-oriented health, social, and educational services. Social policies and programs for children and families often originate in efforts to prevent social problems rather than in efforts to promote or enhance health or well-being. Both rationales underlie the family support and education movement. Regardless of rationale, however, these programs report that they attempt to build on family strengths to empower parents, and that they incorporate a nondeficit service delivery philosophy whereby providers do things *with*, not *to*, families. They have tried to reconceptualize the relationship between families and their sources of assistance, moving from a model where parents are viewed as passive recipients of didactic professional or scientific expertise to a model where the parent, other parents, and professionals all have expertise and support to share. Parents are both recipients and providers of support through peer support and informal helping arrangements. Redefinition of the role of the professional is thus one of the hallmarks of these programs.

The role of program participants is also redefined in these usually voluntary programs in that parents have considerable latitude in determining the amount and nature of their program involvement. Many programs individualize their services in accord with each family's strengths and needs; some include drop-in and other discretionary services, and most are structured to allow both program and parental input into the content of a home visit or group meeting. These characteristics can make it difficult to define the "treatment" families receive and hence to use evaluation procedures that assume a uniform treatment (Hewett and DeLoria, 1982; see Jacobs, Chapter 2, this volume).

Contemporary programs also reflect a number of recent general trends and changes within human service delivery systems. These include distrust of some professionals; the incorporation of nonprofessional service providers, volunteers, and self-help groups; an increased emphasis on service access, case coordination, and information and referral services; and a movement toward more ecological intervention strategies. The latter is reflected in the shift from a focus on changing the individual parent or child, to an emphasis on strengthening the relationship and interaction between them, and, increasingly, on reinforcing the relationship between the family and both formal and informal supports within the community. Information about the most frequently provided services from a recent national survey of family support and education programs confirms this shift. The three services provided most frequently were parent and child development education, informal networking among parents, and information and referral to other community services (Hite, 1985).

By and large these programs are family-oriented, not family-focused, an important distinction made by Kahn and Kamerman (1982) regarding family service programs in general. They are family-oriented in that staff work with parents (often mothers) and children together or they provide support and reinforcement to adults in their parent and family roles. Fewer of these programs are family-focused, that is, few design their services to include all family members or assess their possible impact on the family as a system. We note this distinction here because the book aims both to provide tools for the examination of each type of program and to encourage programs to address the question of what aspects of both individual and family functioning may be affected by program participation.

Although we make no attempt at an historical overview here, we would be remiss not to point out that while the majority of these contemporary programs originated within the past 20 years (Hite, 1985), they have deep roots in the past (Schlossman, 1983). They are part of a long American tradition that began in the colonial period when community leaders provided advice on how to rear a moral and religious child. As the following far from exhaustive list indicates, this tradition of support and community concern for families continued with: nineteenth-century, church-based maternal associations and independent child study groups based on peer support models (Kuhn, 1947; Sunley, 1955); turn-of-the-century home visit programs to families of immigrant kindergartners (Lazarson, 1971); progressive era settlement house programs (Weissbourd, 1983); the parent education efforts of the 1920s and 1930s (Brim, 1959; Schlossman, 1976, 1983); more recent War on Poverty Programs including Head Start and its experimental Child and Family Resource Programs (Zigler and Valentine, 1979; Zigler and Weiss, 1985; Nauta and Hewett, Chapter 17, this volume) and other experimental early childhood programs designed to promote child development through parent education and support (Lazar and Darlington, 1982; Tivnan, Chapter 9, this volume).

We have argued that these diverse programs have sufficient common characteristics to warrant our grouping them together to consider the common challenges they pose for program designers and evaluators. However, while we here emphasize the commonalities and similarities, differences among the programs should not be minimized. Because of their different professional auspices and grounding in local needs and resources, these programs vary on many dimensions, including goals and auspices, setting, funding level and sources, client and staff characteristics, number and types of service delivery mechanisms, curriculum, philosophy of child and family development, program size, duration and intensity, and parental roles. One of the principal strengths

of the larger family support movement is the recognition that just as there is no one type of American family, there can be no one type of universally effective family support and education program.

Another important point of diversity that gives strength to the overall family support movement while challenging evaluators is the fact that many programs are not time-limited, large-scale, well-funded research and demonstration programs. While large research and demonstration programs can serve as flagships offering theoretically based intervention models and state-of-the-art evaluation strategies, the bulk of the program fleet consists of small, service-oriented, state or locally funded programs without access to substantial evaluation expertise.

One challenge for those intent on encouraging better testing and documentation of the effectiveness of these programs lies in developing differentiated evaluation strategies. We must assess the fleet of community programs as well as the flagship research and demonstration projects, convey the lessons learned by more experienced evaluators to less experienced ones, and devise technical assistance strategies and networks to help local programs conduct the best possible evaluations (Weiss 1983; Jacobs, 1984). This volume was designed in response to these challenges and in light of our assessment, outlined below, that the evaluation of family support and education programs requires both conceptual and methodological departures from previous evaluation practice.

The Framework of the Book

We began to examine the literature on family support and education programs and their evaluation in 1983 in an era of growing disillusionment with 1960s-style social programs aimed at eliminating poverty, promoting equal opportunity, and enhancing human development (Murray, 1984). In the midst of this disillusionment, the fact that this period left a substantial and pertinent legacy of hard-won knowledge about how to design, implement, and evaluate preventive programs for children and families received little attention.

Looking back, we found the immediate precursors of contemporary family support and education programs in programs developed in the 1960s. At that point program developers and policymakers confronted an important choice about the design of interventions to improve the chances of school success for poor children: Should they serve only the child or, in addition, the parents and/or family? (Weiss, in press). A number chose the latter option and implemented early childhood and/or infant/toddler programs that worked with parents to enhance child development, obtain needed social services, and in some cases,

provide peer support. Support and education services were provided to parents through home visits, parent groups, and information and referral to other community services. These programs, together with several Head Start experimental programs, focused attention on more family-centered approaches and began a still-continuing cycle of program-development, evaluation, feedback, and revision.

Our review of this legacy and of evidence about various later family support and education programs yielded mixed results: Metaphorically speaking, we found a cup that is both half-full and half-empty (Weiss, 1984). It is half-full because there are several mutually reinforcing longitudinal evaluations that have demonstrated the positive impact of more family-oriented early childhood programs on children's subsequent development and performance. Indirect evidence about the importance of formal and informal social supports for positive child and family functioning has also been accumulating from program evaluations and social and psychological research. Finally, there is a recent set of innovative evaluations that have addressed some of the conceptual and methodological problems of earlier efforts and which point to some promising new directions for future evaluations. (See the case study section of this volume for prime examples.)

The cup is half-empty because relatively few programs have been evaluated systematically, and of those that have, very few of the family-oriented programs have assessed their effects on anyone but the child (Jacobs, 1984). Complex programs designed to strengthen aspects of the child's familial and community context (including parenting skills, aspects of parent–child interaction, and familial use of formal and informal social supports) rarely tested whether they in fact did so, only whether the overall program had enhanced the child's cognitive development. Programs premised on ecological theories of development rarely examined the implications of these theories for these programs' evaluation. Until recently, few have taken the opportunity these programs offer to test and expand ecological theories of human development.

Furthermore, the concept of useful and systematic evaluation has been narrowly defined; most evaluations have not included assessment of program processes or implementation. As a result, there is very little pertinent information for policymakers or program designers about what programs work for whom, when, how, and why (Weiss, 1983). Program development was substantially ahead of program evaluation. As a National Academy of Sciences panel convened earlier in the decade to address issues in the evaluation of early childhood intervention programs noted: "There is an overarching need to test the basic assumptions of these programs, that the most effective way to create and sustain benefits for the child is to improve his or her family and community environment" (Light and Travers, 1982, p. 23). Therefore, we concluded that while these programs were promising, any definitive judgments about family-oriented approaches were premature.

By the early 1980s the demand for evidence of program effectiveness was also increasing. There were two reasons for this. First, public and private groups were struggling with questions about how to allocate scarce human service dollars to support young children and families. Second, the publication of dramatic results from several careful longitudinal studies suggesting the cost effectiveness of early childhood programs encouraged some policymakers to expect documentation of effectiveness from other programs (Lazar and Darlington, 1982; Berreuta-Clement, Schweinhart, Barnett, Epstein, and Weikert, 1984).

This book is designed in accordance with the above overall appraisal and with our desire to encourage and provide some tools for more useful family support and education program evaluation. It is our view that future evaluations should be designed both for purposes of program improvement and to test this seemingly positive set of approaches to strengthening families as contexts for development. Part I is comprised of two chapters. To help programs implement our recommendation that evaluation move beyond child outcomes to assess a range of effects and causal processes, Chapter 1 summarizes what is known about program effectiveness across an ecological continuum from child to community. This chapter also assesses the place of family support and education programs within the larger context of policy debates about how to prevent damage to children and families.

Integrating some of the methodological and conceptual lessons learned from previous program evaluations, Chapter 2 outlines a broad conception of evaluation, one that is particularly useful for family support and education programs because it takes into consideration the needs and resources of the "small fleet" as well as the "large flagship" programs. Given our broad conception of evalution and our view that all programs should conduct some form of it, Appendix B contains a glossary of technical terms used in the volume to assist readers less familiar with evaluation terminology.

In line with the foregoing argument for the application of a broader set of process and outcome measures, the chapters in Part II review and recommend measures to assess changes in: the child, parent–child interaction, the parent, the family system, family stress and coping, and social support. An instrument source list appears as Appendix A to assist readers interested in obtaining each of the measures discussed in the chapters.

Part III presents case studies of the evaluations of 10 different programs written by the programs' directors or evaluators. We chose these cases to cover a wide range of programs serving different populations.

The evaluations are instructive because, taken together, they address many of the current issues involved in the design and implementation of family support and education program evaluation. They also describe efforts to measure a broad range of outcomes, examine program processes and implementation, and suggest new directions for future evaluators. Several of the chapters describe efforts to provide cross-site technical assistance in evaluation to networks of small programs, a strategy we think is especially appropriate given the nature of the family support movement.

Part IV moves from discussions of measures and programs to examine broader theoretical and policy issues relevant to family support and education programs. The first chapter discusses the advantages and limitations of cost-analyses to measure program effectiveness. The second describes meta-analysis, a relatively new technique for quantitative review of the effects of multiple research studies. The third chapter explores the implications of racial and ethnic diversity for program design and evaluation. Finally, because ecological theories of human development and family functioning implicitly or explicitly underlie most family support and education programs, the section's last chapter critiques and extends two such theories, comparing Bronfenbrenner's (1979) ecology of human development and Minuchin's (1974) theory of family systems, and probes the implications of these theories for more family-focused programming. The book's concluding chapter recommends questions, methods, and directions that evaluators should consider in order to move from the current situation in which these programs are regarded as "promising" to one in which the full potential of strong programs becomes more effectively demonstrated.

References

Berreuta-Clement, J., Schweinhart, L., Barnett, W., Epstein, A., and Weikert, D. (1984). Changed lives: The effects of the Perry Preschool Program on youths through age 19. *Monographs of the High/Scope Educational Research Foundation, 8*, 1–210.

Brim, O. (1959). *Education for child-rearing*. NY: Russell Sage.

Bronfenbrenner, U. (1979). *The ecology of human development: Experiments by nature and design*. Cambridge, MA: Harvard University Press.

Cohn, A. (1981). An approach to preventing child abuse. National Committee for the Prevention of Child Abuse, 332 S. Michigan Ave., Suite 950, Chicago, IL.

Hewett, K., and DeLoria, D. (1982). Comprehensive family service programs: Special features and associated measurement problems. In

R. Light and J. Travers (Eds.), *Learning from experience: Evaluating early childhood demonstration programs* (pp. 203–254). Washington, D.C.: National Academy Press.

Hite, S. J. (1985). *Family support and education programs: Analysis of a national sample.* Cambridge, MA: Unpublished doctoral dissertation, Harvard Graduate School of Education.

Jacobs, F. (1984). The evaluation of family support and education programs: A Five-Tiered Approach. In H. Weiss and F. Jacobs (Eds.), *Final report to the Mott Foundation: The effectiveness and evaluation of family support and education programs* (pp. 54–98). Cambridge, MA: Harvard Family Research Project.

Kahn, A. J., and Kamerman, S. B. (1982). *Helping America's families.* Philadelphia, PA: Temple University Press.

Kuhn, A. L. (1947). *The mother's role in childhood and childhood education: New England concepts, 1830–1860.* New Haven, CT: Yale University Press.

Lazar, I., and Darlington, R. (1982). Lasting effects of early education: A report from the Consortium for Longitudinal Studies. *Monographs of the Society for Research in Child Development, 47,* (2–3, Serial No. 195).

Lazerson, M. (1971). *Origins of the urban school.* Cambridge, MA: Harvard University Press.

Light, R., and Travers, J. (1982). *Learning from experience: Evaluating early childhood demonstration programs.* Washington, D.C.: National Academy Press.

Minuchin, S. (1974). *Families and family therapy.* Cambridge, MA: Harvard University Press.

Murray, C. (1984). *Losing ground: American social policy 1950–1980.* NY: Basic Books.

Schlossman, S. L. (1976). Before Home Start: Notes toward a history of parent education in America, 1897–1929. *Harvard Educational Review, 46*(3), 436–467.

Schlossman, S. L. (1983). The formative era in American parent education: overview and interpretation. In R. Haskins and D. Adams (Eds.), *Parent education and public policy.* Norwood, NJ: Ablex.

Sunley, R. (1955). Early nineteenth-century American literature on child rearing. In M. Mead and M. Wolfenstein (Eds.), *Childhood in contemporary cultures* (pp. 150–167). Chicago, IL: University of Chicago Press.

Weiss, H. (1983). Strengthening families and rebuilding the social infrastructure: A review of family support and education programs. A State-of-the-Art paper for the Charles Stewart Mott Foundation.

Weiss, H. (1984). The effectiveness of family support and education programs. In H. Weiss and F. Jacobs, *The effectiveness and evaluation of family support and education programs.* A Final Report to the Charles Stewart Mott Foundation. Cambridge, MA: Harvard Family Research Project.

Weiss, H. (in press). Family support and education in early childhood programs. *Family support programs: The state-of-the art.* New Haven, CT: Yale University Press.

Weissbourd, B. (1983). *The family support movement: Greater than the sum of its parts.* Paper presented at a Conference on Family Support Programs: The State-of-the-Art. Sponsored by the Bush Center in Child Development and Social Policy, Yale University, New Haven, CT. May, 1983.

Zigler, F., and Valentine, J. (Eds.) (1979). *Project Head Start: A legacy of the War on Poverty.* NY: Free Press.

Zigler, E., and Weiss, H. (1985). Family support systems: An ecological approach to child development. In R. Rapoport (Ed.), *Children, youth, and families: The action–research relationship* (pp. 166–205). Cambridge, MA: Cambridge University Press.

Zigler, E., Weiss, H., and Kagan, S. (1983). *Programs to strengthen families.* New Haven, CT: Bush Center in Child Development and Social Policy.

LIST OF CONTRIBUTORS

James T. Bond, Director, National Council of Jewish Women, Center for the Child, New York, NY

Paul D. Cleary, Assistant Professor, Department of Social Medicine and Health Policy, Harvard Medical School, Boston, MA

Carmen P. Cortez, Director of Programs, AVANCE Education Programs for Parents and Children, San Antonio, TX

Ruth W. Crocker, Family Consultant, Weight Control Program, The Children's Hospital, Boston, MA

Carl J. Dunst, Director, Family, Infant and Preschool Program *and* Senior Research Associate, Human Development Research and Training Institute, Western Carolina Center, Morganton, NC

Barry Dym, Director, Family Institute of Cambridge, Cambridge, MA

Ann Ellwood, Executive Director, Minnesota Early Learning Design, Minneapolis, MN

Robert Halpern, Senior Research Associate, High/Scope Educational Research Foundation, Ypsilanti, MI

Penny Hauser-Cram, Eliot-Pearson Department of Child Study, Tufts University, Medford, MA

Kathryn Hewett, Staff Psychologist, Dana Farber Cancer Institute, Boston, MA

Gail A. Howrigan, Research Associate, Center for Behavioral Development and Mental Retardation, Division of Psychiatry, Boston University School of Medicine, Boston, MA

Francine H. Jacobs, Assistant Professor of Child Study, Tufts University, Medford, MA

Marty Wyngaarden Krauss, Assistant Professor, Florence Heller Graduate School for Advanced Studies in Social Welfare, Brandeis University, Waltham, MA *and* Director of Social Science Research, Eunice Kennedy Shriver Center, Waltham, MA

Shelby H. Miller, Former Director, Adolescent Parents Project, Child Welfare League of America, Washington, D.C. *and* Program Officer, Urban Poverty Program, Ford Foundation, New York, NY

Anita M. Mitchell, Senior Scientist, Southwest Regional Laboratory, Los Alamitos, CA

Marrit J. Nauta, Vice President, Abt Associates, Inc., Cambridge, MA

David Olds, Assistant Professor of Pediatrics, University of Rochester, Rochester, NY

Douglas R. Powell, Associate Professor, Department of Child Development and Family Studies, Purdue University, West Lafayette, IN

Gloria G. Rodriguez, Executive Director, AVANCE Education Programs for Parents and Children, San Antonio, TX

Jack P. Shonkoff, Associate Professor of Pediatrics, University of Massachusetts Medical School, Worcester, MA

Diana T. Slaughter, Associate Professor of Education, Human Development and Social Policy Program, Northwestern University, Evanston, IL

Terrence Tivnan, Assistant Professor, Harvard Graduate School of Education, Cambridge, MA

Carol M. Trivette, Research Associate, Child Development Laboratory of the Family, Infant and Preschool Program, Western Carolina Center, Morganton, NC

Carole C. Upshur, Associate Professor, University of Massachusetts College of Public and Community Service, Boston, MA *and* Associate in Pediatrics, University of Massachusetts Medical School, Worcester, MA

Deborah Klein Walker, Associate Professor of Human Development, Harvard School of Public Health, Boston, MA

Heather B. Weiss, Director, Harvard Family Research Project, Harvard Graduate School of Education, Cambridge, MA

Karl R. White, Co-Director, Early Intervention Research Institute, Utah State University, Logan, UT

part I

THE STATE OF OUR KNOWLEDGE ABOUT PROGRAM EFFECTIVENESS

FAMILY SUPPORT AND EDUCATION PROGRAMS: WORKING THROUGH ECOLOGICAL THEORIES OF HUMAN DEVELOPMENT

Heather B. Weiss

INTRODUCTION: PROMISING PROGRAMS AT A CROSSROADS

Family support and education programs are at a crossroads. Previously, the family support and education field could be characterized as a set of two dozen or so flagship research and demonstration programs and a larger grass roots fleet of small and fledgling community-based programs. Both the fleet and flagship programs have had uncertain credibility and funding and little visibility, particularly among policymakers and human service professionals. Now these programs are moving out of relative obscurity to become the focus of substantial attention at all levels of government. This is reflected in the fact that the programs and the trends they reflect—the movement from treatment to preventive early intervention, from services for children to support for children in the context of family and community, and from top-down to community-based human service programs—are frequently discussed both in general debates about efforts to strengthen families, and in more specific debates about the role of the family in welfare reform, education reform, child welfare reform, and in abuse and neglect prevention efforts. Moreover, the larger political climate is changing from wariness and reluctance about getting involved with the so-called family business to more support of preventive interventions. This is indicated by the increasing number of local, state, and federal officials who are funding pilot and sometimes more extensive systems of family support and education programs. Now that they have entered into the human service mainstream, pressures will mount for them to prove themselves both as effective programs and as vehicles or contributors to larger public policy efforts to enhance the well-being and life chances of children and families.

As many analysts of social policy have pointed out (Cronbach and Associates, 1980; C. Weiss, 1983; Hayes, 1982; Moynihan, 1985), evidence of program effectiveness alone does not drive or determine policy. Yet certain types of evaluation information now have a critical role to play both in the development and in the proliferation of strong programs and policies. Evaluations need to be designed not only to document individual program implementation and effectiveness—to determine whether a program "works"—but also to address collectively and cumulatively the larger and more differentiated questions now on the minds of policymakers: Which family support and education programs work for *whom, how, when, where, and why.* If strong programs *and* policy-relevant evaluations can be designed and implemented, family support and education programs may not evolve into just another short-lived and faddish panacea for social ills. Instead, they may be able to serve as central building blocks for a human service system realigned around prevention and the promotion of family health and well-being.

This is a particularly opportune time to examine what is known about program effectiveness, for two reasons. First, the family support and education field has achieved increased visibility partly because of promising results from several flagship research and demonstration programs. Second, as policymakers' interest grows, there is an increasing demand for information about proven program models and for evidence about the differential effectiveness of family as opposed to strictly child-centered programs. In this chapter I will review the evidence about effectiveness, raise questions about the roles and content of evaluation for flagship and fleet programs in this newly emerging policy and service arena, and suggest evaluation strategies that may prove to be particularly useful in the future.

The chapter begins with a critical overview of past evaluation practice and then discusses the utility of describing and evaluating family support and education programs in accord with ecological theories of human development. These programs, whether in the form of relatively simple parent support groups or more complex, comprehensive, multiservice programs, attempt to influence many aspects of the interactions between children, their families, and the larger environment. But relatively few evaluations have attempted to assess either short- or long-term effects of these programs on other than the child's cognitive abilities. Therefore, in accord with the argument that more differentiated and ecologically oriented assessments are necessary and useful, the chapter's third section reviews evidence from flagship programs that ventured beyond such limited child measures. This evidence is arrayed along a five-part ecological continuum from the child to the formal and informal supports for the family in their community. The next section summarizes what we know about these programs in terms of the questions policy makers ask about them and suggests a set of research and policy questions for the future. Finally, an argument is made that while promising evidence about program effectiveness and grass roots program popularity are factors driving policymakers' current interest, the way certain program assumptions and features harmonize with diverse political interests and ideologies is also a critical factor in placing families and children on policymakers' agendas (Weiss, 1986). The chapter's final section examines the integrative role these programs may play in the broader context of current debates about diverse social reform efforts and lays out a set of cautions and challenges for the next round of family support and education program evaluation.

THE HALF-EMPTY CUP AND THE EMERGING CONSENSUS ON FUTURE DIRECTIONS FOR PROGRAM EVALUATION

As noted in the introduction to this volume, the cup of knowledge about program effectiveness is both half-full and half-empty. At the risk of beating a dead horse, some of the reasons why it is half-empty bear repeating and additional reasons deserve mention. This discussion will indicate the contours of the emerging consensus about the past evaluation problems of these programs and will suggest several areas program evaluators should address. Few systematic summative evaluations of programs in the larger fleet of grass roots community-based programs have been conducted, so assessments of the experiences of flagship research and demonstration programs are reviewed here. This is not to suggest that the fleet should not conduct evaluation (see Jacobs, Chapter 2, this volume). Rather it will be argued throughout that there should be a division of labor between fleet and flagship programs because evaluations of each can answer many pressing evaluation questions.

There is widespread agreement that the evaluation of family support and education programs has been straining and stimulating measurement and evaluation technology. These programs are predicated on the assumption that the provision of information, emotional support, and instrumental assistance to families will help parents reduce stress and enhance their coping and child-rearing capacities, and thereby positively affect the child's development. But until the recent past, measurement of program effects has been a Procrustean bed. Possible effects on everything but the child's cognitive development were lopped off not least because of the serious and persistent problem of inadequate alternative child measures (see Gray and Wandersman, 1980; Hauser-Cram and Shonkoff, Chapter 3, this volume) never mind the lack of conceptually and psychometrically adequate and culturally sensitive measures to assess parental or familial functioning.

The results of these limitations are threefold. First, many programs have been reluctant to conduct evaluations out of concern that what they do will not be fairly assessed by such narrow outcomes. They have been in a "Catch-22" situation: Evaluate with inappropriate measures and risk no results, or evaluate with unproved and sometimes suspect measures and risk both credibility and results (see Ellwood, Chapter 13, this volume).

Second, understanding of the full range of possible program effects—can they promote sustained adult as well as child development, for example—has been limited. Some argue (H. Weiss, 1983; Zigler and Weiss, 1985; Seitz, Rosenbaum, and C. Apfel, 1985) that these programs deserve the attention of policymakers because they produce positive and policy-relevant outcomes for parents as well as children. More evidence collected with broader measures of program impact are necessary to sustain such an argument.

Third, it is now clear that some programs do produce meaningful and sustained gains for children, but limited measurement has restricted understanding of the process by which programs achieve their effects. Measurement of changes in intermediate or mediating variables thought to be affected by program participation would help in building and testing causal models of how these programs lead to enhanced development (see Dunst and Trivette, Chapter 14; Olds, Chapter 10, this volume). Many hypothesize, for example, that these programs change parents and families in ways that have both direct and indirect benefits for the child (Bronfenbrenner, 1979, 1984). Zigler and Berman (1983), for example, suggest direct benefits through an enhanced educational process and indirect ones by virtue of enhanced parental self-esteem, happiness, or sense of control. Clarke-Stewart and Fein (1983), however, caution that some evidence suggests that changes in the child may precede those in the parents, and they question whether family as opposed to child-centered early childhood interventions are warranted. Broader measures and longitudinal examination of the relationship between changes in parents and children are necessary to understand the complex and nonlinear causal processes underlying these programs and to help resolve the larger policy question of whether early childhood programs that work with families are as or more powerful than those that focus only on the child.

A broad consensus is now emerging that more differentiated assessment is necessary in the evaluation of these programs, despite the risks entailed (Gray and Wandersman, 1980; Travers and Light, 1982; Weiss, 1983; Ramey, Bryant, Sparling, and Wasik, 1984; and this volume, Section II). The risks stem from the lack of psychometrically proven measures, the scanty theoretical and empirical base now available on which to base decisions about *which* of many possible aspects of the child's interpersonal and material environment to assess, and the temptation to measure an unwieldy number of possible outcomes. In many cases, the program's goals demand that evaluators focus on areas of assessment for which only relatively untested measures exist (e.g., parental knowledge or social support). To facilitate their choices, some means of sharing information about relatively untested measures in areas of potential program impact—would be invaluable. Individual programs are well-advised to take some calculated measurement risks by using less proven measures in conjunction with more standard measures of known reliability and validity. As the National Academy of Sciences Panel on Outcome Measurement in Early Childhood Demonstration Programs (Travers and Light, 1982) has argued, measure development is not fairly or primarily a job for evaluators but is one for basic researchers. Nonetheless, both fleet and flagship programs could and should serve as useful laboratories to test and refine appropriate measures.

Conceptions of what adequate program evaluation entails have also changed considerably in the past 20 years, at least in part as a result of challenges and experience gained from efforts to evaluate early childhood education programs for disadvantaged children in the 1960s and 1970s (Light and Travers, 1982; Hewett, 1982). The simple treatment-black box-outcome conception of evaluation has given way to a much more complex model and to understanding of the difficulties inherent in the implementation of both programs and their evaluations (see Jacobs, Chapter 2, this volume; C. Weiss, 1983; Light and Travers, 1982). While evaluators are far from achieving consensus on issues such as whether or not experimental design with random assignment is a *sine qua non* for evaluation, there are nonetheless some emerging areas of agreement about important evaluation components and about the problems likely to be encountered during the evaluation process. Many of these problems of evaluation design and implementation (e.g., threats to internal validity, differential attrition, treatment diffusion, limits imposed by sample size, missing data on repeated measures) are described in detail in the case studies in Section III of this volume, so only a few of those bearing on the issue of how we can gain more relevant broad-based knowledge about program effectiveness will be summarized here.

The importance of systematically gathering information about program implementation and program processes—of unpacking the black box—is one arena of growing consensus in evaluation practice (Campbell, 1974; Cronbach and Associates 1980; C. Weiss, 1981). At this juncture, knowledge about family support and education program effectiveness is not only narrow, due to restricted outcomes, but it is also shallow due to few efforts to unpack the black box of treatment. The sparsity of data limits what can be said about commonly occurring implementation problems among these programs. As a result, there are presently several areas in which information about implementation and treatment are especially needed if evaluators are to be responsive to the needs of policymakers interested in the utility and practicability of these programs.

First, more attention needs to be paid to program participation data; there is now relatively little information to answer questions about who is attracted to and who remains in what type of programs. Such data would help resolve several current debates about policy-relevant issues such as whether or not low-income parents can be reached through parent groups (see Miller, Chapter 16, this volume; Slaughter, 1983). It would also help address the larger policy question of whether or not these programs can attract and maintain participation by hard-to-reach, very poor, at-risk families (Blank, 1987).

Similarly, future policy and program development would benefit from a better understanding of the personal and environmental factors that condition program participation. The examination of participation patterns and an ethnographic study of implementation by the Child and Family Resource Program evaluators (see Nauta and Hewett, Chapter 17, this volume, and Travers, Nauta, Irwin, Goodson, Singer, and Barclay, 1982), for example, showed that some programs were caught in a dilemma relevant to contemporary debates about how to support both parenting and financial independence among mothers on welfare: Should they encourage mothers to gain training or employment to achieve financial independence and face inevitable attrition, or discourage it because it would mean lower program participation by tired and extremely time-pressed mothers? More research on how parents' social networks and personal characteristics affect participation would be extremely useful in determining what kinds of programs are appropriate for what kinds of families (see Powell, Chapter 11, this volume; Kessen and Fein, 1975). In sum, even relatively simple and carefully collected information from flagship and fleet programs about participation now can inform both policy debates and program planning.

The lack of emphasis in the past on program processes and implementation also has left the family support and education field short on cross-program knowledge gleaned from program practice. This lack is acute now that state and local policymakers want not only data on outcomes, but detailed information about how to design and implement programs. More emphasis should be placed on efforts to collect and share practice-based information about implementation issues such as staff recruitment, training and supervision; outreach strategies; staff turnover and burnout; use of volunteers; and meshing evaluation and service delivery needs. Such information is useful in understanding the pattern of program outcomes (see Nauta and Hewett, Chapter 17, this volume) as well as for future program development. Collection of in-depth information about parents' perceptions and experiences with the program is also useful in understanding underlying causal processes and outcomes, as well as in identifying especially important program components or negative consequences of participation (Weiss, 1979; Gray and Wandersman, 1980; Andrews, Blumenthal, Johnson, Kahn, Ferguson, Lasater, Malone, and Wallace, 1982). Again, this is an area where both fleet and flagship programs have important roles to play in collecting relevant information.

Now that public interest in family programs is increasing, there are two other areas where pertinent knowledge is thin and where future evaluations can make major contributions. By virtue of the fact that many past evaluations were not designed to unravel what program components or service configurations (e.g., home visits, parent groups, health and developmental screening) produced what outcomes or to examine relationships between program comprehensiveness, intensity and outcomes, cost-conscious planners of new programs have little to go on when building new programs. This is an especially difficult situation because many planners are confronting the problems of the "demonstration-dilution" dilemma. To wit, much of our current knowledge about program effectiveness comes from single-site, un-replicated, and costly research and demonstration programs that con-ducted carefully controlled field experiments. However, some poli-cymakers and program planners indicate they cannot afford to replicate such a model widely, if it means providing services at the same cost level as the original demonstration. Unfortunately, researchers have little to offer them as guidelines for determining what cost-cutting re-visions, *if any,* will preserve outcomes.

Two studies of programs for low-income families that contrasted dif-ferent intensities and types of treatment have indicated that reduced levels *may not* produce so many significant effects, and that fairly com-prehensive and intensive services are needed to benefit low-income families regarded as at-risk for poor developmental outcomes (see Olds, Chapter 10, this volume; Ramey *et al.,* 1985). Evaluation designs that vary the types, duration, and intensity of treatment and field trials that test variations, including less costly replications of tested programs, could make a major contribution to policymakers grappling with the complex issues inherent in the demonstration-dilution dilemma. Research on program replication and adaptation processes that is akin to that now being done on the diffusion of innovative prevention programs (Price, 1986) would also help both programs and policymakers.

Past single-site research and demonstration programs have tended to focus their efforts on creating research designs that minimize threats to internal validity, thereby ensuring that changes can be attributed to the program and not to some other factor. There has been considerably less attention paid to questions of external validity or the generalizability of the program to other sites and populations.[1] Replications of models that test positive at one site are important in establishing the strength and importability of a program; more widespread replication may help to determine if the program can be implemented successfully on an even wider scale. However, exclusive reliance on replicating proven models may be an inappropriate strategy for program proliferation in the family support and education area. Given the demonstration-dilution dilemma, the paucity of proven models, and the likely importance of the programs' community base and of local pride to program success, a strategy that combined dissemination of proven models with support for developing and testing the effectiveness of many locally developed models may be more appropriate at least in the short run.

This combined strategy would mean support and testing not only of theory-based flagship research and demonstration programs, but also stable and promising community-based service programs. This strategy has the additional benefit of reflecting the current reality of how programs are developed in that few state or local ones are full replications of existing models; some do, however, adapt parts of model programs developed elsewhere (Weiss and Hite, 1976). Finally, such a combined strategy is important because a disproportionate amount of evidence of effectiveness comes from flagship programs, and it may or may not be generalizable to similar community-based programs. The latter need to generate their own evidence. One mechanism to facilitate such evaluation of community-based programs is the development technical assistance network; two versions of which are described in Section III of this volume (see Bond and Halpern, Chapter 15; and Walker and Mitchell, Chapter 18, this volume).

The Half-Full Cup: Promising Evidence of Effectiveness

Family support and education programs attempt to strengthen various aspects of the child's context to promote development; as such, they are in line with and have stimulated larger trends within child

---

[1] The plan for the cross-site Parent Child Development Center evaluation (Andrews *et al.*, 1982) called for eventual replication to test the exportability of the programs, but that stage was never reached.

development and family research that emphasize more ecological efforts to understand development (Bronfenbrenner, 1979; Sameroff, 1983; Maccoby and Martin, 1983). In their examination of the history of environmental models in developmental research, Bronfenbrenner and Crouter (1983) write of "creative theorists" and "theory translators." The latter they describe as "able to transform new, highly general and often strange theoretical ideas into delimited, researchable problems and corresponding operational definitions" (p. 371). Family support and education programs represent a new group of "practice translators" of ecological theories of child development. As such, they offer fertile ground for theory translators—ecologically oriented evaluators—who use them to plumb ecological theory and to discover its empirical bases (see Olds, Chapter 10; Dunst and Trivette, Chapter 14, this volume; Ramey, Bryant, Sparling, and Wasik, 1984).

Because of their philosophical and practice base in efforts to strengthen the context for a child's development, it is useful to describe these programs and evidence about their effectiveness in terms of an ecological schematic such as the following five-level one: child, parent, parent–child, family functioning, and informal and formal supports. This schematic is useful in charting what aspects of child development or context particular program components are designed to change. (See Table 1.1 for an example of a chart designed to summarize program goals and measures such an ecological framework.) Such a schematic can be used not only to describe program components and goals, but also as a device to organize goals into a causal framework. Such a framework can help array critical aspects of context likely to be affected by the program and can thereby facilitate choices about what aspects of the child or of his or her context to measure as covariates or as mediating and short- and long-term outcome variables (see Olds, Chapter 10, and Bond and Halpern, Chapter 15, this volume, for excellent examples of such causal frameworks). Ecological diagramming can also help to alert evaluators to the *nonprogram* contextual factors that may independently affect development or interact with the program to affect participation or outcomes (see Olds, Chapter 10; Dunst and Trivette, Chapter 14, this volume), some of which the evaluator may want to take into account. Wahler (1980), for example, has found that characteristics of a mother's social network affected the maintenance of effects of a parent training program and Powell (Chapter 11, this volume) has investigated how network characteristics affect program participation.

A possible risk associated with using such frameworks and organizing devices, particularly in their simpler forms, is that they will make dynamic programs seem static and encourage linear as opposed to reciprocal, nonlinear, multicausal analyses of program processes and outcomes. Using such ecological diagrams in conjunction with person-process-context research designs (Bronfenbrenner and Crouter, 1983), which emphasize developmental processes, the interconnections among environmental levels and the possibility of multiple and reciprocal influences on development, would help to minimize those risks.

Turning to examine differentiated evidence on program effectiveness, Table 1.1 presents information on the goals and measures of more than a dozen programs on the five-part ecological schematic. It illustrates the evolution of evaluations from nearly exclusive emphasis on the child's cognitive development to inclusion of changes in parentsand parent–child interaction and, more recently, to changes in informal and formal social support. Notice that the child column on the table has an entry for every study with one exception; the other columns have more entries as their dates become closer to the present. The table is in chronological order by publication date, not by dates of service delivery. Some listed at the middle are longitudinal reports about the effects of programs delivered as early as the late 1960s, and as such their outcomes tend to emphasize the child level. With a few exceptions (BEEP Mother–Child Home Program, New Parents as Teachers, Prenatal and Early Infancy Project) participants in these flagship research and demonstration programs were exclusively low-income families.

As will be clear, the evidence about these programs is scattershot; it comes from programs with different goals, service components, populations, settings, and evaluation strategies. This makes it very difficult to make overall generalizations about effectiveness. The evidence, therefore, needs to be read not as definitive but as suggestive of the larger potential of these programs and as indicative of the need for further program evaluation.

PROGRAM EFFECTS ON THE CHILD

Much of the early evidence on child effects comes from early intervention programs of the 1960s and 1970s designed to enhance the early development of poor children. Many of these programs worked not only with the child (for example, in a preschool program) but also with the family through services such as home visitors, parent groups and service brokering. Examples include the Perry Preschool Project, The Family-Oriented Home Visiting Program, the Mother–Child Home Program, and the Institute for Developmental Studies program, and others described in Table 1.1. Early evaluations of these programs and of others which did *not* substantially involve families indicated such programs could achieve short-term positive cognitive outcomes for children. But questions about the differential effectiveness of programs working with families and about longer term maintenance of gains were raised. These questions set two broader research efforts in motion: summary reviews of programs' effects and a stream of longitudinal research.

Two influential reviews in the mid-1970s reinforced family-oriented approaches when they came to the *tentative* conclusion that a parent component did result in a more successful intervention measured in terms of cognitive gains for the child (Bronfenbrenner, 1974; Goodson and Hess, 1975). Bronfenbrenner hypothesized that programs that stress reciprocal mother–child interaction around a joint task or activity early in the child's life reinforce the mother–child system and that the system then develops its own momentum with positive implications for subsequent interaction and longer term impact. As the parent and parent–child columns of Table 1.1 suggest, by the late 1970s and early 1980s there were a few evaluations designed to examine if and how changes in the parent and parent–child interaction affected child development.

To address questions about maintenance of gains and longitudinal effects on children, a few individual programs conducted longer term follow-ups of program and control children, and some banded together into the Consortium for Longitudinal Studies (Lazar and Darlington, 1982) for similar purposes. In addition to tracking cognitive performance, the Consortium also found positive effects on two additional policy-relevant outcomes: assignment to special education and retention in grade. Evidence based on subsequent school performance was important because the pattern of cognitive effects across many programs suggested they did not so much enhance achievement as "prevent or slow the declines from average intellectual performance" (Ramey *et al.*, 1983).

Subsequently, several individual programs continued longitudinal follow-up (see Tivnan, Chapter 9, this volume) and one, the Perry Preschool Project, has found some dramatic effects. This is a program that provided center-based preschool education and weekly home visits by teachers to families of low income black children between 1962 and 1967. At age 19, the program, as opposed to control group youth, were more likely to be employed or pursuing their education, less likely to have had a teenage pregnancy or to have been arrested or in detention, and to have performed better on a test of functional competence (Berreuta-Clement, Schweinhart, Barnett, Epstein, and Weikert, 1984). These results were reinforced by similar ones from a longitudinal evaluation of a New York program (Jordan, Grallo, Deutsch, and Deutsch, 1985).[2]

---

[2] One recent reanalysis of the effects of a Consortium program, the Mother–Child Home Program, however, found smaller IQ gains than originally reported; the authors hypotheses about why this is the case are worthy of consideration by contemporary evaluators (Madden, O'Hara, and Levenstein, 1984).

TABLE 1.1. Program Evaluation Goals and the Dependent Measures Used to Assess Them[a]

Studies	Child		Parent	
Informal and formal	Goals	Measures	Goals	Measures
Perry Preschool Project (Weikart, Bond, and McNeil, 1978)	Child intellectual development Social–emotional development Academic success	a. Stanford–Binet Scale b. Lieter International Performance Scale c. Peabody Picture Vocabulary d. Illinois Test of Psycholinguistic Abilities e. California Achievement Test f. Pupil Behavior Inventory g. Ypsilanti Rating Scales	Child–rearing attitudes Provision of stimulation Home environment	Maternal Attitude Inventory[b] Cognitive Home Environment Scale
Family-Oriented Home Visiting Program (Gray and Ruttle, 1980)	Child intellectual development Sibling development	a. Bayley Scales of Infant Development b. Stanford–Binet Scale c. Receptive Language Test a. Slosson Intelligence Test b. Gilmer Test of Basic Concepts	Maternal child-rearing behavior and attitudes	a. HOME Inventory b. Maternal Teaching Strategy Instrument (MTSI)
Consortium for Longitudinal Studies (Lazar and Darlington, 1982)[c]	Academic success Intellectual development School competence Attitudes and values	a. Iowa Test of Basic Skills or Metropolitan Achievement Test or Wide Range Achievement Test or California Test of Basic Skills and Stanford Achievement Test a. Stanford-Binet Scale b. Peabody Picture Vocabulary Test c. WISC-R a. Grade retention b. Assignment to special classes a. Achievement orientation b. Self-evaluation	Maternal attitudes	a. Satisfaction with child's school performance b. Aspirations for child's future
Child and Family Resource Program (Travers et al., 1982)	Intellectual development Child health	a. Bayley Scales of Infant Development b. Preschool Inventory c. High/Scope Pupil Observation Checklist d. Schaefer Behavior Inventory a. Physical growth b. Child medical checkups c. Child dental checkups	Maternal functioning, coping skills Maternal health Maternal attitudes and teaching skills	a. Interview questions: Independence, coping b. Parental locus of control Utilization of services Strom's Parent-as-a-Teacher Inventory

Parent–child		Family functioning		Informal and formal social support	
Goals	Measures	Goals	Measures	Goals	Measures
None specified	N/A	None specified	N/A	None specified	N/A
None specified	N/A	None specified	N/A	None specified	N/A
None specified	N/A	None specified	N/A	Family use of community services	Reports from child welfare agencies
Parent–child interaction	Carew Toddler and Infant Experiences System (30 parents)	Family economic situation	a. Employment and training b. Reliance on wages c. Different sources of income	None specified	N/A

(*continued*)

TABLE 1.1. (*continued*)

Studies	Child		Parent	
	Goals	Measures	Goals	Measures
Birmingham Parent-Child Development Centers (Andrews *et al.*, 1982)	Cognitive development	a. Bayley Mental Scale of Infant Development b. Stanford-Binet Scale c. Concept Familiarity Index	Maternal behavior and attitudes	a. Mother's behavior in waiting room situation b. Mother's behavior in nonsocial stress situation c. Mother's behavior in teaching situation d. HOME Inventory e. Problem-solving interview at graduation
	Social development	a. Child's behavior in waiting room situation b. Child's behavior in nonsocial stress situation c. Child's behavior in teaching situation		
Houston Parent-Child Development Center (Andrews *et al.*, 1982)	Cognitive development	a. Concept Familiarity Index b. Bayley Scales of Infant Development c. Stanford-Binet Scale	Maternal behavior and attitudes	a. Mother's behavior in teaching situation b. HOME Inventory
	Social development	a. Child behavior in teaching situation		
New Orleans Parent-Child Development Centers (Andrews *et al.*, 1982)	Cognitive development	a. Bayley Scales of Infant Development b. Stanford-Binet Scale c. Uzgiris-Hunt Scales of Infant Ordinal Development d. Pacific Test Series e. Concept Familiarity Index f. Ammons Full-Range Picture Vocabulary Test g. Purdue Self-Concept Scale (follow-up study) h. Effectance Motivation (follow-up study)	Maternal behavior and attitudes	a. Mother's behavior in waiting room situation b. Mother's behavior in teaching situation
Yale Child Welfare Research Program (Rescorla *et al.*, 1982)	Cognitive development	a. Yale Revised Developmental Schedules b. WISC-R c. Child Assessment Scale	Child-rearing practices Utilization of program components	Mother Interview Scale Project Utilization Scale
Yale Child Welfare Research Program 5-Year Followup Study (Trickett, Apfel, Rosenbaum, and Zigler, 1982)	Academic achievement	a. Peabody Picture Vocabulary Test b. Peabody Individual Achievement Tests c. School records	None specified	N/A
	Achievement motivation and attitudes	a. Box Maze b. Sticker Game c. Locus of Control Scale		

Parent–child		Family functioning		Informal and formal social support	
Goals	Measures	Goals	Measures	Goals	Measures
None specified	N/A	None specified	N/A	None specified	N/A
None specified	N/A	None specified	N/A	None specified	N/A
None specified	N/A	None specified	N/A	None specified	N/A
None specified	N/A	Family economic self-sufficiency	a. Educational advancement b. Rate of subsequent births c. Employment rate d. Quality of Life Scale	None specified	N/A
None specified	N/A	None specified	N/A	None specified	N/A

(continued)

TABLE 1.1. (*continued*)

| Studies | Child | | Parent | |
	Goals	Measures	Goals	Measures
United Charities of Chicago Parent Education Programs (Slaughter, 1983)	Child intellectual development	a. Cattell Infant Scales b. Peabody Picture Vocabulary Test c. McCarthy Scales of Mental Ability	Child-rearing attitudes Maternal personality	Attitude questionnaire a. Loevinger Scale of Ego Development b. Self-esteem scale c. Inventory of Expressed Values
AVANCE (Rodriguez, 1983)	None specified	N/A	Knowledge of child development Maternal attitudes and behavior	Pre/post questionnaire Pre/post questionnaire
Brookline Early Education Project (BEEP) (Pierson, Bronson, Dromey, Swartz, Tivnan, and Walker, 1983; Pierson, Walker, and Tivnan, 1984)	Functioning in school Developmental status Health status	a. Executive Skill Profile b. Teacher ratings a. McCarthy Scales b. Pediatric Developmental Assessment a. Diagnostic monitoring	Parent involvement and attitudes	a. Parent interview b. Record of parent–teacher contacts
Mother-Child Home Program (Madden *et al.*, 1984)	Cognitive development Social development	a. Cattell Developmental and Intelligence Scale b. Stanford-Binet Scale c. Peabody Picture Vocabulary Test d. Program Achievement Test e. Wide Range Achievement Scales (Reading and Arithmetic Scales) f. Teacher ratings of school performance) a. Child's behavior traits (teacher rating)	None specified	N/A
Perry Preschool Project Long-Term Follow-up (Schweinhart and Weikart, 1980; Berrueta-Clement *et al.*, 1984)	Intellectual performance Academic achievement Academic motivation Social development Self-sufficiency	a. WISC b. California Achievement Test a. Grades b. Grade retention a. Value of schooling b. School motivation a. Delinquent behavior b. Self-concept questionnaire c. Peer relations/network d. Leisure time questionnaire e. Parent-child relationship f. Teenage pregnancy a. Employment b. Earnings c. Adult Performance Level Survey	None specified	N/A

Parent–child		Family functioning		Informal and formal social support	
Goals	Measures	Goals	Measures	Goals	Measures
Parent–child interaction and maternal teaching skills	a. Maternal teaching style b. Child verbal play c. Child non-verbal play	None specified	N/A	None specified	N/A
None specified	N/A	None specified	N/A	Utilization of social supports	a. Knowledge of social agencies b. Perceived social support questionnaire
None specified	N/A	None specified	N/A	None specified	N/A
Positive mother–child interaction	Maternal Interactive Behavior Record (Coded behavior observation)	None specified	N/A	None specified	N/A
None specified	N/A	None specified	N/A	None specified	N/A

(continued)

TABLE 1.1. (*continued*)

| Studies | Child | | Parent | |
	Goals	Measures	Goals	Measures
Institute for Developmental Studies Long-Term Follow-up (Deutsch, Jordan, and Deutsch, 1985; Jordan et al., 1985)	Educational attainment Employment status Verbal ability Self-concept Motivation for academic tasks Sense of control of academic outcomes	Educational Expectations Scale Biographical Youth Interview (3-point index) Vocabulary Subtest of WAIS a. Rosenberg's Self-Esteem Scale b. Self-Concept Ability Scale Need for Academic Competence Questionnaire Intellectual Achievement Responsibility Scale	None specified	N/A
Missouri New Parents as Teachers (Pfannenstiel and Seltzer, 1985)	Child cognitive ability Child language ability Child social development Child hearing	Kaufman Assessment Battery for Children Zimmerman Preschool Language Scale a. Personal–Social Subscale of Battelle Development Inventory b. Ratings by psychometrists during cognitive testings a. Parent interview b. "Whisper test"	Parent knowledge	Parent Knowledge Survey Instruments
Project CARE (Ramey et al., 1985; Bryant, Ramey, and Burchinal, 1982; Bryant and Ramey, 1984)	Child cognitive development	a. Bayley Scales of Mental Development b. Stanford–Binet Scale	Maternal caregiving behaviors Maternal knowledge of infant development	HOME Inventory Knowledge of Infant Development Scale (KIDI)
Yale Child Welfare Research Program 10-Year Follow-up Study (Seitz et al., 1985)	Academic performance Need for special school services	a. Peabody Individual Achievement Tests b. WISC-R c. Teacher ratings Teacher report	Parental attitudes	a. Involvement in child's school b. Perceived satisfaction as a parent
Prenatal and Early Infancy Project (Olds, Henderson, Chamberlin, and Tatelbaum, in press)	Intellectual development	a. Bayley Scales of Infant Development b. Cattell Scales	Child-rearing attitudes	a. Infant Temperament Q-Sort b. HOME Inventory

---

[a] Studies are arranged in chronological order by publication date.

[b] Some measures listed under parent column also could go under the parent–child column.

[c] Measures vary across individual programs.

Parent–child		Family functioning		Informal and formal social support	
Goals	Measures	Goals	Measures	Goals	Measures
None specified	N/A	None specified	N/A	None specified	N/A
None specified	N/A	None specified	N/A	None specified	N/A
Mother–child interaction	a. Mother and child free play behaviors coded using Reciprocal Control Category System b. Ainsworth Strange Situation	Live events stress Maternal and child high risk status	Holmes and Rahe Schedule of Recent Experience Revised High Risk Index	Maternal social support	a. Social Support Interview Schedule b. Sociogram c. Community Interaction Checklist
None specified	N/A	Family economic self-sufficiency	a. Maternal education b. Family size c. Socioeconomic status	None specified	N/A
Prevent child abuse Parent–child relationship	a. Clinical reports b. Emergency room visits a. Reports of conflict with infant b. Reports of scolding infant c. Avoidance of restriction and punishment	Economic self-sufficiency	a. Educational attainment b. Obtaining employment c. Length of time on public assistance d. Repeat pregnancies	Utilization of medical resources Utilization of social supports	a. Number of sick-child visits b. Number of child hospitalizations a. Child-care help for family and friends b. Relationship with boyfriend

The gradual accumulation of mutually reinforcing longitudinal evidence about positive and policy-relevant behavioral changes in program participants has sparked new interest in early childhood programs, setting off a new round of state initiatives, and has usefully reoriented thinking about appropriate child outcomes. But it has not resolved the central question of when and whether family-oriented programs are as good as, or superior to, child-focused ones. Or, it may be for example, that a family-oriented intervention for children 0–3 followed by a child-centered preschool program at 4 and 5 and strong parent involvement programs in the school years produces the strongest and most enduring gains for children. Attaining greater clarity on this issue of working with families directly through evaluations designed to compare the two approaches and indirectly through the accumulation of evidence about family-oriented programs is one of the foremost challenges facing programs and evaluators. The evaluation of Project Care (Ramey *et al.*, 1985), which contrasted treatments (home visits and a combination of center care and home visits) is one good example of a design for tests of contrasting treatments.

PROGRAM EFFECTS ON THE PARENT AND PARENT-CHILD INTERACTION

The Head Start experimental programs (Parent Child Development Centers [PCDC] and Child and Family Resource Programs [CFRP]) designed to assess parent and family-oriented early childhood programs mark the start of a more explicit effort to achieve program impact on parents per se and thus also on parental factors that might mediate child outcomes. As Table 1 shows, more recent programs have examined their effects on parents in their parental and their adult roles; illustrative results are noted here to indicate some of the possible areas of change. Generalizations about overall parental effects are premature, because as Table 1.1 illustrates, so few programs have measured changes in this area, and among those that have, few use comparable measures. The labels parent and parent–child reflect more the future directions for evaluation in this area than actual practice insofar as all the research reported here is about mothers, not fathers or parents.

Through interviews, behavior inventories, attitude and knowledge questionnaires, and in a few instances, through actual observations of mother-child interaction, programs have documented a variety of parental changes that *may* promote enhanced child development (see Chapters 4 and 5, this volume). They include: increased knowledge of child development (Rodriguez and Cortez, Chapter 12, this volume; Pfannenstiel and Seltzer, 1985), increased recognition of the parent's role as the childs' teacher (Travers *et al.*, 1982; Slaughter, 1983); better caregiving behaviors as illustrated by better control techniques, more elaborate verbal interchanges, better maternal teaching strategies, more initiation of contact with the childs' teacher (see Andrews *et al.*, 1982; Gray and Ruttle, 1980; Slaughter, 1983; and Hauser-Cram, 1983); and less restrictive behavior and less use of severe punishment (Olds, Henderson, Chamberlin, and Tatelbaum, in press; Rodriguez, 1983). Because so much of the data comes from parental self-report or brief observations it is unclear how much they reflect actual or enduring changes in parental behavior. Knowledge of program effects within this domain will be strengthened when individual studies use cross-corroborating measures of parent change and test them against other outcomes thought to relate to better parenting (see Olds *et al.*, in press, for such a research design and analysis strategy).

A few programs have also examined their effects on adult characteristics and behaviors that are hypothesized to have indirect positive benefits on the child. Those measures and the studies showing positive effects include: greater sense of control (Travers *et al.*, 1982); enhanced self-esteem and coping (Travers *et al.*, 1982; Slaughter, 1983); and enhanced problem-solving (Andrews *et al.*, 1982). It is unclear as yet whether and how these changes eventually promote enhanced child development. The CFRP program, for example, showed positive parent outcomes in several of these areas but did not simultaneously show gains for participating children. Perhaps such changes are more likely to show up in longitudinal assessments or with other school and life performance-based measures of child development.

Evaluating the evidence on early childhood interventions, Clarke-Stewart and Fein (1983) argue that some evaluations show that changes in the child precede those in parents and they suggest that this throws family-oriented programs open to question. However, even if this is the order of one sequence of change, the fact that parents do change may mean they are more supportive of the child's growth subsequently; more ecological and longitudinal research is required to test such propositions.

Three programs have demonstrated the utility of examining relatively straightforward and policy relevant behavioral indications of adult development. Together, their positive results suggest that these programs (albeit fairly intensive ones) can have dramatic effects on parents' capabilities and personal development. Specifically, Olds *et al.* (in press) report that their nurse-home visited mothers were more likely to have completed or returned to school and to have expressed concern about finding employment. Travers *et al.* (1982) found CFRP was an effective social service program that "succeeded in moving families into new jobs, schools or vocational training and enhanced their prospects for achieving economic self-sufficiency" (p. 132). The longitudinal assessment of the Yale Child Welfare Research Project (Rescorla, Provence, and Naylor, 1982; Seitz *et al.*, 1985) suggested that the program's major contribution was its long-term impact on family patterns—specifically in terms of limitations on family size, improvements in residence, educational advancement, economic self-sufficiency, and quality of life. The Yale evaluators hypothesize that the program enhanced self-esteem and coping capacities and enlarged parents' personal aspirations, which then had positive consequences for adult development, family functioning and the quality of the parent–child relationship.

These studies also have important implications for the inclusion of family support and education programs in welfare reform and other efforts aimed at maximizing current and future economic self-sufficiency. They suggest that through intensive family support and education programs it may be possible to promote both child and adult development, although the CFRP evaluation suggests that tension may surface between the child development and adult and social service goals if they are not kept in balance and supplied with sufficient resources for their accomplishment. At a minimum, these programs' results suggest the importance of going beyond child outcomes and assessing a set of outcomes that are both policy relevant and helpful in explaining how programs help build a family climate that promotes human development.

Program Effects on Family Functioning

It is noteworthy that none of the programs in Table 1.1 has examined their impact on family functioning when it is defined in terms of enhanced family cohesion, communication, or joint problem-solving. This may reflect the lack of consensus about appropriate family dimensions to measure and the underdeveloped state of measurement in this area (see Walker and Crocker, Chapter 6, this volume). It also reflects the lack of explicit program goals in this area, yet there is now some evidence that the larger fleet of family support and education programs have begun to attend explicitly to couple and family-level concerns and goals. A recent survey of 217 such programs that provide parenting and child development education, for example, indicated that 75% cover family communication skills and 72% cover family management and problem solving skills in their curricula (Maciuika and Weiss, 1987). This suggests that the evaluation of family functioning should emerge as an important area for evaluators. This is another area where programs are ahead of evaluators. The lack of attention to family influences and outcomes parallels a similar lack in developmental research on socialization. Until recently, attention there, too, has focused on parent-child interaction, skipped or at least minimized the family dynamics and relationships, and emphasized extrafamilial social support and the way it affects development (see Dym, Chapter 22, this volume; Maccoby and Martin, 1983).

While, as Table 1.1 indicates, one could argue that parental changes leading to improved family economic circumstances, better parental problem solving, and reduced dependence on public assistance signal or promote better family functioning, some exploration of improved interpersonal family functioning nevertheless is warranted, both to understand the full range of program effects and underlying causal processes. Efforts to understand interfamilial changes are also important, because some recent research on the effects of maternal stress and support on parenting behavior suggests the central role support from the father or another adult can play (Crnic and Greenberg, in press; Belsky, 1984). This is an area especially worth inquiry by flagship research and demonstration programs that offer family-level services because initial work in this area will have to grapple with especially complex conceptual and measurement issues. It is also an area in which more than child development expertise is required; interdisciplinary collaborations with family sociologists and family-oriented clinicians with assessment expertise is critical. Many family support and education programs purport to strengthen families; one of the major challenges facing evaluators now is to define what that means and to test the attendant propositions.

EFFECTS ON INFORMAL AND FORMAL SUPPORT

Driven by Brontenbrenner's emerging theories about the ecology of human development (1979) and concurrent research on social networks and social support (Cochran and Brassard, 1979), developmental researchers have been examining the effects of intra- and extrafamilial social support on child development and family functioning. While this is an area that suffers from conceptual and measurement confusion (see Cleary, Chapter 8, this volume), researchers have shown that various aspects of social support appear to play a crucial if largely uncharted role in family coping, well-being, and in child development. It has been shown, for example, to be related to maternal–infant attachment (Crockenberg, 1981) and to the adjustment of children following divorce (Hetherington, 1981). Researchers have examined both direct effects of support and the ways support moderates stress to promote development (see Krauss, Chapter 7, this volume; Crnic and Greenberg, in press). Given that family support and education programs provide services rightfully labeled as social support, it is surprising that so few evaluations have measured it as either a mediating or outcome variable (see Powell, Chapter 11, this volume). Many programs feel that benefits derived from interpersonal support and informal networking are central for many participants, but few have tested the consequences of this for such areas as child-rearing strategies, parent–child interaction, or parental or personal well-being. As with family functioning, this may stem from a program's uncertainty about what areas of social support and/or stress to measure and how to measure them.

As Table 1.1 indicates, some programs have begun to examine their impact on parents' knowledge and use of community services (Rodriguez, 1983; Ramey *et al.*, 1985) and on changes in parents' perceptions of availability and use of informal support (Olds, Chapter 10, this volume). At this juncture, it may be appropriate for flagship programs to examine how social support moderates stress and affects development and for fleet programs to focus on more simply defined and measured changes in amount or perceptions of support as one of several mediating or possibly outcome variables. Both are important to explore, but the former may involve more hair-tearing conceptual, measurement, and analysis issues. Both fleet and flagship programs could usefully team up with researchers with a theoretical interest in social support in a mutually beneficial action research collaboration (Zigler and Weiss, 1985; Rook and Dooley, 1985). Previously, the bulk of the work on relationships among stress, support, and various health and developmental outcomes has been correlational; evaluations of family support and education interventions offer the possibility of exploring causal relationships.

Finally, with the exception of one early Head Start evaluation (Kirschner Associates, 1970) no one has systematically examined the impact of these programs on the services available in their communities nor the obverse, the way community services affect program operations. This is an aspect of the child's developmental context that developmentalists rarely study, but those who have suggest that neighborhood and community variables play a critical direct and indirect role in family and child development (Garbarino and Sherman, 1980; Bronfenbrenner, 1984). Better understanding of these relationships may pay off with answers to policy as well as developmental questions; specifically: in better targeting of programs (for example, to at-risk neighborhoods, not individuals); better understanding of how programs can build positive relationships with other community agencies; and in better networking and brokering for individual clients.

This discussion indicates that the further one travels on this ecological continuum, the less is known, but looking at Table 1.1 in terms of rows, not columns, it is clear that there is a trend toward flagship evaluators building more complex research designs to understand the effects of these multifaceted programs. It should also be evident that programs in the fleet have important roles to play in addressing some of the questions raised herein, for example, through documentation of participation and qualitative studies of program implementation as well as through studies of program-induced changes in children, families, and communities (see Jacobs, Chapter 2, this volume). Evidence from both sorts of programs will be necessary to respond to the complex questions posed by a new audience for these programs—public policymakers.

PUBLIC POLICY QUESTIONS AND CONSIDERATIONS

Given the heightened interest of public policymakers in family programs, it is important for evaluators to begin considering how to address the questions these decision makers raise as they consider more widespread implementation of family programs. The preeminent question that public policymakers ask is: Do these programs prevent major social problems such as school failure, delinquency, public dependency, and other problems of children and families? Do they advance positive social goods such as equal educational opportunity, individual opportunity to develop to the fullest, and reinforce a community's sense of cohesion and responsibility for all its members? The previous review suggests that the answers may be positive but that considerably more evidence is needed to substantiate this. As the longitudinal results from the Perry Preschool Project and the results of several studies that have examined the effects of these programs on adults suggest, they may make very important and lasting changes in the lives of children and families. "Given the limitations of our assessment methods and the difficulties inherent in running a support program," as Tivnan (this volume) notes, however, "the actual measured effects are likely to be small, difficult to detect, and unevenly distributed across participants. They are also likely to vary across different outcome areas, many of which have yet to be addressed by more than a few studies. Some of the questions that evaluators must be prepared to address in the coming decade are:

• *Will these programs save money and wasted lives?* With the exception of the Perry Preschool Project, no programs have done sophisticated cost-effectiveness analyses, and few keep useful records of actual program costs. Cost analyses are very difficult to do (see White, Chapter 19, this volume). But at a minimum, programs need to gather better information about the actual cost of service provision.

• *What works, how, when, where, and why?* Policymakers want to know what kinds of program components and what levels of duration and intensity are appropriate for particular populations. As noted earlier, evaluations designed to answer these questions will provide critical knowledge to future program planners. Further, as these programs become more widespread, the issue of sensitivity to different cultural values and styles of parenting will also come more to the forefront; therefore research on the sensitivity of different program models to different cultural styles will become increasingly important (see Slaughter, Chapter 21, this volume).

• *What models are exportable and should be exported or adapted for implementation more broadly?* Should the process of proliferating family support and education programs be one of replication of proven models, partial adaptation, or of the development of more home-grown, grass-roots programs? If the latter, what kinds of structures should be set up to honor local initiatives but avoid continual re-invention of the wheel? At present, knowledge about program implementation and replication is very thin, so these are particularly difficult questions to answer. Furthermore, it is unclear what the relationship is between a program and its context; knowledge about this issue will influence decisions about exportability. Former Congressman Tip O'Neill is known for the remark that all politics are local; in the end, this may hold for programs, too, in that some sense of local ownership, even of models developed elsewhere, may be important to program success.

• *Will these programs be able to reach the most needy and hard-to-reach families?* Data from flagship programs about participant attrition suggests that some of these programs have a fairly high dropout rate, and as noted earlier, there is little systematic data on program participation to counter concern on this issue. Further, some people argue that family support and education programs are a creature of the middle class. The evidence reviewed here suggests otherwise, but cross-program participation data is also necessary to address this claim systematically and empirically. Further, many argue that these programs are needed because of changing family demographics—more working mothers, more single parents, etc.; these very factors may also make it very difficult for these programs to reach and serve families. This is an issue that also needs to be addressed by both program developers and future evaluators.

• *How will these programs fit in with already established human service programs in health, education, and social services?* This question will require research both in local communities and at the level of state and national policy for families. Should these grass-roots programs that are typically developed outside of traditional services be added on to existing systems or substitute for other programs? As they are incorporated into the social service mainstream, how can their new ways of doing business with families be maintained in the context of organizations that may be less responsive to families? At this point, the answers to these questions are largely speculative. If careful consideration is not given to such issues, we face such risks as program cooptation and the development of a diverse set of categorical and sometimes competing primary prevention programs (Weiss, Resnick, and Hausman, 1987).

• *Should programs be targeted to at-risk populations or open to everyone?* Some argue that instead of targeting, policymakers should work toward the development of community prevention systems which provide services, albeit sometimes different ones, for all families, not simply those regarded as at-risk (Zigler and Weiss, 1985; Chamberlin, 1983). At this juncture, policymakers appear to prefer the strategy of targeting high-risk groups, if for no other reason than it helps in the allocation of scarce resources. Advocates for and against this strategy need better evidence about the effects of these different strategies on children, families, and communities to make their respective cases.

• Finally, public policymakers, particularly those reluctant to provide publicly financed programs for families, ask: *Can family programs harm a family, abridge family privacy, or create family dependence?* These are complex issues to address, but at a minimum evaluators should always be on the lookout for negative unintended consequences of their interventions.

Reflecting back on many years of social program evaluation, Cronbach and Associates (1980) observe that no single evaluation has ever addressed all of the important questions. That is the case in the field of family program evaluation as well. But if many programs keep their sights on preceding questions, over time, programs and evaluators may be able to assess the effectiveness of individual programs and also contribute to our cumulative understanding of these larger policy questions. There is now a new window of opportunity for programs for young children and families that is arguably, at least, partly the result of evidence of program effectiveness gathered by many of the earlier programs described herein. The current generation of programs launched in this time of renewed interest in turn should be building their legacy for the next generation through careful examination of program processes and effects.

Family Support and Education Programs: A Middle Ground for Family Policy

Studies of the forces driving public policy usually have a humbling effect on program evaluators; they reveal that action in the public arena is a function of the complex interplay of political interests, ideologies, values, and, finally, of information. Political interest in the family is high once again, and as debates about the future of the family and its role in a revised welfare state evolve, many are acknowledging the central role that values as well as information play in shaping programs and policies. "It is neither possible nor desirable to attempt to construct a family policy on the basis of presumed social science knowledge," wrote U.S. Senator Moynihan in 1985; rather, "family policy must reflect shared values" (p. ii). There is widespread agreement about the pivotal role the family plays in child development and in the creation and maintenance of the sense of community necessary for societal survival. The fact that there is growing interest in family support and education programs may be in good part because they reflect a set of values and an approach to strengthening families that has a broad bipartisan and public appeal.

Specifically, underlying these programs is a complex and integrative diagnosis of why children, youth, and families are perceived by many to have more problems. Some recent commentators argue that these problems are simply a function of parents shirking their responsibility to care for and nurture their children. Others suggest the larger community has failed families because services are underfunded, have deteriorated, are misdirected, or nonexistent. The ideology and design of family support and education programs suggest that problems lie not only with families but in the deterioration of relationships between families and the formal and informal supports within the community. This more complex diagnosis helps to integrate two usually separate policy questions: What should government or the community do for families? and What should families do for themselves? into one: What can government and community institutions do to enhance the family's capacity to help itself and others? Because these programs reflect an integration of values, they have gotten bipartisan support from legislators in several states who see in them ways to strengthen families that are consistent with their values (Hausman, Weiss, and Gerlach, 1987). These programs are also negotiating their way through tough issues related to family privacy and public responsibility for families. Because of these factors, they may form a basis on which more policymakers can build new and reform old programs and policies for families.

Those interested in and providing family support and education programs may now be in a position similar to the one that the planners of Head Start were in at the outset of the War on Poverty some 20 years ago. Then, as now, there was a broad political consensus about the importance of early education in efforts to promote the life chances of children, particularly poor ones. Then, as now, researchers and program planners are acutely aware of the limitations of available knowledge and of policymakers' demands for evidence and for assistance in mounting new policy initiatives. If one waits for better evidence, there is a risk that the necessary political momentum may be lost. Perhaps the Head Start solution should be tried again. As Zigler (1979) has noted, Head Start represented a "calculated risk" for the original planning committee. Rather than trying to design one ideal model, they worked out a flexible program that would allow for community input and program variation. Such a plan would be in keeping with some of the most important strengths of existing family support and education programs. Head Start also illustrates the importance of building in credible program evaluations so that when there is less interest in these programs, evidence of program effectiveness can help sustain them.

We are now in a different position from Head Start's planners because much more evidence about effectiveness and the possible pitfalls of programs is available to help in the design of strong programs. We are in a position to learn from past mistakes. For example, we know that we should avoid overselling programs, as that will only make them into yet another failed social panacea. We know, furthermore, that there is not going to be a cheap programmatic magic bullet but that sustained and costly programs are necessary to support development of children and families, especially those who are disadvantaged for economic and other reasons. We know program directors, evaluators, and policymakers must work together to unravel the complex influences on positive child and family development and to bring this knowledge to bear in their efforts to create and support programs that enhance the life chances of our nation's families. This collaborative journey will be long and, at times, arduous. It will, no doubt, reveal new pitfalls. But most would agree that few journeys are so worth taking.

REFERENCES

Andrews, S. R., Blumenthal, J. B., Johnson, D. L., Kahn, A. J., Ferguson, C. J., Lasater, T. M., Malone, P. E., and Wallace, D. B. (1982). The skills of mothering: A study of parent-child development centers. *Monographs of the Society for Research in Child Development, 47*(6, serial no. 198). Chicago, IL: University of Chicago Press.

Belsky, J. (1984). The determinants of parenting: A process model. *Child Development, 55,* 83–96.

Berreuta-Clement, J., Schweinhart, L., Barnett, W., Epstein, A., and Weikert, D. (1984). Changed lives: The effects of the Perry Preschool Program on youths through age 19. *Monographs of the High/Scope Educational Research Foundation* (no. 8). Ypsilanti, MI: High/Scope Press.

Blank, S. (January 1987). *Contemporary parenting education and family support programs: Themes and issues in an emerging movement.* New York: Foundation for Child Development.

Bronfenbrenner, U. (1974). Is early education effective? *Columbia Teachers College Record, 76*(2), 274–303.

Bronfenbrenner, U. (1979). *The ecology of human development.* Cambridge, MA: Harvard University Press.

Bronfenbrenner, U. (1984). The ecology of the family as a context for human development: Research perspectives. *Developmental Psychology.*

Bronfenbrenner, U. and Crouter, A. (1983). The evolution of environmental models in developmental research. In P. Mussen (Ed.)., *Handbook of child psychology.* NY: J. Wiley and Sons.

Bryant, D. and Ramey, C. (March, 1984). *Results from Project Care: An Early Intervention Comparison Study.* Paper presented at the Gatlinburg Conference, Gatlinburg, Tennessee.

Bryant, D., Ramey, C. T., and Burchinal, M. (March, 1982). *Intervention effects on mother-child interactions.* Paper presented at the International Conference on Infant Studies, Austin, Texas.

Campbell, D. (September, 1974). *Qualitative knowing in action research.* Paper presented at the meeting of the Society for the Psychological Study of Social Issues, New Orleans.

Chamberlin, R. (1983). Strategies for disease prevention and health promotion in maternal and child health: The "ecologic" versus the "high risk" approach. *Journal of Public Health Policy, 5,* 185–197.

Clarke-Stewart, K., and Fein, G. (1983). Early childhood programs. In P. Mussen, (Ed.), *Handbook of child psychology: Infancy and developmental psychobiology* (Volume 2). NY: Wiley.

Cochran, M., and Brassard, J. (1979). Child development and personal social networks. *Child Development, 50*(3), 601–616.

Crnic, K., and Greenberg, M. (in press). Maternal stress, social support, and coping: Influences on the early mother-infant relationship. In Z. Boukydis (Ed.), *Research on support for parents and infants in the postnatal period.* Norwood, NJ: Ablex.

Crockenberg, S. (1981). Infant irritability, mother responsiveness, and social support influences on the security of infant-mother attachment. *Child Development, 52,* 857–865.

Cronbach, L. and Associates. (1980). *Toward reform of program evaluation.* San Francisco, CA: Jossey Bass.

Deutsch, M., Jordan, T. J., and Deutsch, C. P. (1985). *Long-term effects of early intervention: Summary of selected findings.* Mimeograph. New York University, Institute for Developmental Studies.

Garbarino, J., and Sherman, D. (1980). High-risk neighborhoods and high-risk families: The human ecology of child maltreatment. *Child Development, 51,* 188–198.

Goodson, B., and Hess, R. (1975). *Parents as teachers of young children: An evaluative review of some contemporary concepts and programs.* Unpublished manuscript, Stanford University.

Gray, S. W., and Ruttle, K. (1980). The family-oriented home visiting program: A longitudinal study. *Genetic Psychology Monographs, 102,* 299–316.

Gray, S., and Wandersman, L. (1980). The methodology of home-based intervention studies: Problems and promising strategies. *Child Development, 51,* 93–109.

Halpern, R. (1984). Lack of effects for home-based early interventions? Some possible explanations. *American Journal of Orthopsychiatry, 54*(1), 33–42.

Hauser-Cram, P. (1983). A question of balance: Relationships between parents and teachers. Doctoral dissertation, Harvard Graduate School of Education.

Hausman, B., Weiss, H., and Gerlach, C. (1987). *The choices of the states: Family support and education programs.* Unpublished manuscript. Harvard Family Research Project, Cambridge, MA.

Hayes, S. (Ed.). (1982). *Making policies for children: A study of the federal process.* Washington, D.C.: National Academy Press.

Hetherington, M. (1981). Children of divorce. In R. Henderson (Ed.), *Parent–child interaction.* NY: Academic Press.

Hewett, K. (1982). (assisted by D. DeLoria). Comprehensive family service programs: Special features and associated measurement problems. In R. Light and J. Travers (Eds.), *Learning from experience: Evaluating early childhood demonstration programs.* Washington, D.C.: National Academy Press.

Jordan, T. J., Grallo, R., Deutsch, M., and Deutsch, C. (1985). Long-term effects of early enrichment: A 20-year perspective on persistence and change. *American Journal of Community Psychology, 13*(4), 393–415.

Kessen, W., and Fein, G., and others. (1975). *Variations in home based infant education: Language, play, and social development.* Final report: OCD-CB-98. Office of Child Development, Department of Health, Education, and Welfare, Washington, D.C.

Kirschner Associates. (1970). *A national survey of the impact of Head Start centers on community institutions.* Albuquerque, NM: Author.

Lazar, I., and Darlington, R. (1982). Lasting effects of early education: A report from the Consortium for Longitudinal Studies. *Monographs of the Society for Research in Child Development, 47*(2-3) (Serial No. 195).

Light, R., and Travers, J. (1982). *Learning from experience: Evaluating early childhood demonstration programs.* Washington, D.C.: National Academy Press.

Maccoby, E., and Martin, J. (1983). Socialization in the context of the family: Parent-child interactions. In P. Mussen (Ed.), *Handbook of child psychology,* (volume IV). NY: Wiley.

Maciuika, L., and Weiss, H. (1987). Issues and trends in parent education. Unpublished manuscript. Harvard Family Research Project, Harvard Graduate School of Education.

McLaughlin, M. (1980). Evaluation and alchemy. In J. Pincus (Ed.), *Educational evaluation in the public policy setting.* Santa Monica, CA: Rand.

Madden, J., O'Hara, J., and Levenstein, P. (1984). Home again: Effects of the mother-child home program on mother and child. *Child Development, 55,* 636–647.

Moynihan, D. P. (1985). *Family and nation.* Cambridge, MA: Harvard University Press.

Olds, D., Henderson, C., Chamberlin, R., and Tatelbaum, R. (in press). Preventing child abuse and neglect: A randomized trial of nurse home visitation. *Pediatrics.*

Pfannenstiel, J. and Seltzer, D. (1985). *New Parents as Teachers Project.* Evaluation report prepared for the Missouri Department of Elementary and Secondary Education, Jefferson City.

Pierson, D., Bronson, M., Dromey, E., Swartz, J., Tivnan, T., and Walker, D. (1983). The impact of early education: Measured by classroom observations and teacher ratings of children in kindergarten. *Evaluation Review, 7*(2), 191–216.

Pierson, D., Walker, D., and Tivnan, T. (1984). A school-based program from infancy to kindergarten for children and their parents. *The Personnel and Guidance Journal, 62*(8), 448–455.

Price, R. H. (1986). Education for prevention. In M. Kessler, and S. Goldston, (Eds.), *A Decade of Progress in Primary Prevention.* Hanover, NH: University Press of New England.

Ramey, C., Bryant, D., and Suarez, T. (1983). Preschool compensatory education and the modifiability of intelligence: A critical review. In D. Detterman (Ed.), *Current topics in human intelligence.* Norwood, NJ: Ablex.

Ramey, C., Bryant, D., Sparling, J., and Wasik, B. (1984). A biosocial systems perspective on environmental interventions for low-birth weight infants. *Clinical Obstetrics and Gynecology, 27*(3), 672–692.

Ramey, C., Bryant, D., Sparling, J., and Wasik, H. (1985). Project CARE: A comparison of two early intervention strategies to prevent retarded development. *Topics in Early Childhood Special Education, 5*(12), 12–25.

Rescorla, L., Provence, S., and Naylor, A. (1982). The Yale Child Welfare Research Program: Description and results. In E. Zigler and E. Gordon (Eds.), *Daycare: Scientific and social policy issues.* Boston, MA: Auburn House.

Rodriguez, G. G. (1983). *Final Report: Project CAN PREVENT.* San Antonio, TX: Avance.

Rook, K., and Dooley, D. (1985). Applying social support research: Theoretical problems and future directions. *Journal of Social Issues, 41,* 5–28.

Sameroff, A. J. (1983). Development systems: Contexts and evolution. In P. Mussen (Ed.), *Handbook of child psychology: History, theory, and methods* (volume I). NY: Wiley and Sons.

Schweinhart, L., and Weikart, D. (Eds.). (1980). Young children grow up: The effects of the Perry Preschool Program on youths through age 15. *Monographs of the High/Scope Educational Research Foundation* (no. 7). Ypsilanti, MI: High/Scope Press.

Seitz, V., Rosenbaum, L., and Apfel, N. (1985). Effects of family support intervention: A ten-year follow-up. *Child Development, 56,* 376–391.

Slaughter, D. (1983). Early intervention and its effects on maternal and child development. *Monographs of the Society for Research in Child Development, 48*(4) (serial no. 202).

Travers, J., and Light, R. (1982). *Learning from experience: Evaluating early childhood demonstration programs.* Washington, D.C.: National Academy Press.

Travers, J., Nauta, M. J., Irwin, N., Goodson, B., Singer, J., and Barclay, C. (1982). *The effects of a social program: Final report of the Child and Family Resource Program's infant-toddler Component.* Cambridge, MA: Abt Associates, Inc.

Trickett, P., Apfel, N., Rosenbaum, L., and Zigler, E. (1982). A five-year follow-up of participants in the Yale Child Welfare Research Program. In E. Zigler and E. Gordon (Eds.), *Day care: Scientific and social policy issues.* Boston, MA: Auburn House.

Wahler, R. (1980). The insular mother: Her problems in parent-child treatment. *Journal of Applied Behavior Analysis, 13*(2), 207–219.

Wandersman, L., Wandersman, A., and Kahn, S. (1980). Social support in the transition to parenthood. *Journal of Community Psychology, 8,* 332–342.

Weikart, D., Bond, J. T., and McNeil, J. (Eds.) (1978). The Ypsilanti Perry Preschool Project: Preschool years and longitudinal results through fourth grade. *Monographs of the High/Scope Educational Research Foundation* (No. 3). Ypsilanti, MI: High/Scope Educational Research Foundation.

Weiss, C. (1981). Doing science or doing policy? *Evaluation and Program Planning, 4* (3 and 4), 397–402.

Weiss, C. (1983). Ideology, interests, and information: The basis of policy positions. In D. Callahan and B. Jennings (Eds.), *Ethics, the social sciences, and policy analysis.* NY: Plenum.

Weiss, H. (1979). *Parent support and education: An analysis of the*

Brookline Early Education Project. Unpublished doctoral dissertation, Harvard Graduate School of Education.

Weiss, H. (1983). Strengthening families and rebuilding the social infrastructure: A review of family support and education programs. Paper prepared for the Charles Stewart Mott Foundation, Flint, Michigan.

Weiss, H. (1986). Testimony presented before the U.S. House of Representatives Select Committee on Children, Youth, and Families, Hearings on Family Strengths, February 25.

Zigler, E., and Berman, W. (1979). Head Start: Not a program but an evolving concept. In E. Zigler and J. Valentine (Eds.), *Project Head Start: A Legacy of the War on Poverty.* NY: Free Press.

Zigler, E., and Berman, W. (1983). Discerning the future of early childhood intervention. *American Psychologist, 38*(8), 894–906.

Zigler, E., and Trickett, P. (1978). IQ, social competence, and evaluation of early childhood intervention programs. *American Psychologist, 33*(9), 789–798.

Zigler, E., and Weiss, H. (1985). Family support systems: An ecological approach to child development. In R. Rapoport (Ed.), *Children, youth, and families: The action-research relationship.* Cambridge: Cambridge University Press.

chapter 2

THE FIVE-TIERED APPROACH TO EVALUATION: CONTEXT AND IMPLEMENTATION

Francine H. Jacobs

I remember my initial response to the Westinghouse Learning Corporation evaluation of Head Start (1969), which I read about as a day care director in the early 1970s. I was surprised at the results as reported, which implied that Head Start was ineffective at achieving any important long-term benefit to children. These findings ran counter to my own practical experiences in the field, to observations I had made in Head Start programs, and to my beliefs about child development. I was concerned that support for the national program would be undermined and that fewer children would be served as a result. But my predominant feeling at the time was one of amazement at how far afield the evaluation seemed to have been from the real concerns, goals, and dreams of program personnel and participants. How had evaluation, a scientific (and I thought, precise) endeavor, missed by so much?

My reaction was common in the early childhood community, and for many, this amazement soon turned to disappointment and anger, hardening into strong, generalized, antievaluation sentiment. Much has changed in the intervening 15 years: The design and conduct of evaluation have improved; early childhood programs have matured and diversified, increasingly embracing an ecological view of child development; the family-support movement has gained visibility and respect. And in the past few years, program directors and policymakers have expressed renewed interest and belief in program evaluation; they are joined by numbers of legislators, funders, and public and private agency administrators. In responding to this heightened receptivity to our trade, we evaluators must remain mindful of the hard-learned lessons of the past lest, regardless of our increased technical sophistication, we "miss" again.

This chapter first offers a brief personal analysis of how evaluation in its early days could have been so "off-base" and a summary of the lessons from that period. It then presents a five-tiered approach to program evaluation as an attempt to build those lessons into a graduated model of evaluation.

LESSONS FROM THE PAST

Most commentators date modern program evaluation history back to the 1960s, when the young industry was pressed into service to evaluate the nation's War on Poverty social programs for children. The roots of this field, however, date back centuries, to age-old arguments pitting reason against intuition, science against art. Thus program evaluation, relying most heavily on "the basic research fields that emphasize formal design and quantitative analyses—statistics, economics, experimental psychology, survey research in sociology, and political science" (Travers and Light, 1982, p. 48), represents a relatively recent, but decisive, triumph of "empiricism over contemplation" (Shils, 1980).

The Promise of Science

In America, the early twentieth century was a watershed period in this struggle (Shonkoff, 1983). Since the key to obtaining "truth" in the natural world was seen to be rigorous logic and empirical study, science held the promise of unlocking the mysteries of every other sphere of life, including human development (Shils, 1980). The cornerstones of this approach were: reductionism (the dissection of all phenomena into the smallest unit for manageable study); controlled experimentation (creating neutral, uncontaminated laboratory conditions); and careful measurement (Anastasiow, 1985; Hawkridge, 1970). Advances in defense and space technology and in the medical sciences reinforced this belief and investment in scientific research (Hawkridge, 1970).

Human behavior and character, however, presented some knotty problems. Theories of human development had existed for centuries untested through scientific method, and early twentieth century theorists such as John Dewey, Horace Mann, and Jane Addams were horrified at attempts to do so. Their cautions, however, fell victim to "the prospect of a genuine science of human behavior on the model of the enormously successful modern natural sciences" (Bellah, 1983, p. 45), and the social sciences were inaugurated (Guba and Lincoln, 1981; Shils, 1980). There was increasing momentum in the 1930s and 1940s for making educational practice scientific and not intuitive. Similarly, the establishment of child study as a "science" in the late 1940s and early 1950s was seen to grant legitimacy to interest in the first years of life and to the developing field of early childhood education (Braun and Edwards, 1972).

To realize these promises, early investigators had three central tasks: They needed to isolate important units of human character that were "pure variables"—devoid of contextual influences. They needed instrumentation to measure these constructs. And they needed a framework for controlled study in which manipulation of these variables would yield cause-and-effect truths, that is, general laws of human development (Gardner, 1983; Mishler, 1979).

The Allure of Measurement. Intelligence became the first, and remains the most popular, element of human character studied in this manner, perhaps because intelligence was seen as unrelated to spirituality or morality, dimensions of life too controversial to attack with science. Its assumed immutability—preordained through genetic imperative and fixed at birth—also made it well suited for scientific inquiry. Finally, it was already the subject of spirited debate and curiosity in Europe (Gardner, 1983; Gould, 1981). Theorists of the early 1900s sought to measure intellectual powers and compare individual intelligences based on uniform criteria. In 1908, Alfred Binet produced a set of "reasoning" tasks, scaled by complexity, which became known as the first test of intelligence. Until recently the IQ test was seen as "psychology's greatest achievement, its chief claim to social utility, and an important scientific discovery in its own right" (Gardner, 1983, p. 16).

IQ tests were put to immediate and widespread uses other than those for which Binet had intended them: He had devised a scale to identify children whose poor performance required special education; instead, his tests were transformed into a method to "label in order to limit" (Gould, 1981, p. 152)—to *deny* those same children academic opportunities. Further, given the class and cultural biases inherent in IQ test items, poor children suffered disproportionally from the test's popularity. Yet the resulting scores were seen to represent both present intelligence and future capacity, making educational intervention foolhardy. Industrial America of the 1920s and 1930s embraced this hereditarian, noninterventionist position (Condry, 1983; Lazerson, 1983). Needing factory workers, in essence it schooled its children along social class lines; poor or minority children, seen to be of limited intelligence, were steered into the unskilled labor force.

As with other grand philosophical theses, eventually the antithetical position—first proposed by Binet, Piaget, Montessori, Dewey, and others and later by Bloom (1964), Hunt (1961), and Bruner (1960), among many—gained prominence. Built on a fuller, more interactive view of early development, intelligence was seen as malleable, reflective of environment as well as heredity, and thus responsive to intervention, the earlier the better.

The social utility of this position was apparent in postwar America, when intellectual contributions to Cold War competitions, not factory work, were needed from its youth (Grubb and Lazerson, 1982). A growing dissatisfaction among minorities with unequal educational opportunities and the rediscovery of conscience in the middle class regarding the conditions of poor Americans (Murray, 1984) no doubt provided additional incentives for championing "nurture over nature." Central to this discussion, however, is that through the 1960s—whether one stood on the side of heredity or environment, the maintenance of class structure or social mobility, early education or later schooling—researchers remained devoted to measuring intelligence with IQ tests. This devotion continued despite mounting testimony to the serious limitations of both the construct of intelligence and the available standardized instruments (see, for example, Cole, 1985; Mercer and Richardson, 1976; Senna, 1973).

Other standardized assessment tools for use with young school-aged children also became and remained popular, although they suffered similar shortcomings. For example, achievement tests, while more explicitly designed to assess the content rather than the potential for knowledge, have been criticized for measuring only a narrowly defined set of information and failing to assess such larger order skills as analysis and synthesis. Like IQ tests, they are also susceptible to class and cultural bias (Bligh, 1979).

Finally, the allure of measurement dazzled even those caring for the "diaper set," and developmental tests for infants and toddlers appeared in the 1920s and 1930s. Arnold Gesell, an early researcher–pediatrician, developed instruments to document "normal" development for this age group; Nancy Bayley's scales were designed to allow for predictions of later intelligence (Horowitz, 1982). These and other efforts reflected the hereditarians' view of infant development as an inevitable unfolding of natural capacities, "a reasonably stable, predictable, linear process" (Shonkoff, 1983, p. 31).

Accumulated experiences with these measures and an increasingly sophisticated understanding of early development have highlighted their limitations in achieving these original purposes (Hauser-Cram and Shonkoff, Chapter 3, this volume; Shonkoff, 1983). Yet paradoxically, with the proliferation of early intervention programs for disabled children, infant assessments using these standardized instruments are, if anything, more popular in the past decade than they were previously.

The Neglect of Context. A fundamental tenet of empirical study is that phenomena exist in pure, protean forms, uncontaminated by environment; indeed, efforts to delineate and quantify intelligence using standardized measures were initiated in accordance with this ideal. As research from the 1930s onward has demonstrated, however, the influences on a child's development of family, community, culture, educational and social institutions, are impossible to ignore (Bronfenbrenner, 1979; Consortium for Longitudinal Studies, 1983; Weiss, Chapter 1, this volume). Attempts to create laboratory conditions by holding these factors constant during the intentional manipulation of the variable under examination often yielded cumbersome, narrow studies of limited validity and utility. Further, it became increasingly clear that researchers themselves were open to contextual contamination in their selection of measures and interpretation of results. Nonetheless, many respected researchers have persisted in applying "context-stripping methods of investigation" (experimental design, standardized measurement, and statistical analysis) to their studies (Mishler, 1979).

Why has this occurred? Webb, Campbell, Schwartz, and Sechrest (1966) have argued that shrinkage in focus and methods was a necessary evolutionary step for the social sciences. In becoming a legitimate science, the field advanced by subtracting knowledge previously gained by subjective means, primarily by intuition, introspection, and the use of nonscientific qualitative methods. In the early stages of this process, a developing science should be expected to take halting, careful, self-conscious steps. As early as 1959, however, sociologist David Reisman voiced concern about this narrowing of vision, suggesting that "the scientific ego had become too harsh" (Webb *et al.*, p. 171), creating a serious mismatch between the richness of what could be studied and the paucity of acceptable techniques.

Evaluation necessarily followed suit. In its early years, "evaluation and measurement were virtually interchangeable . . . both . . . inextricably tied to the scientific paradigm" (Guba and Lincoln, 1981, p. 2). Eventually the concept of evaluation was broadened to include the assessment of a particular intervention on a variety of behaviors, although intelligence and individual achievement remained ascendant among them. Experimental methods were, of course, preferred.

The continued denial of context in much of the research conducted through the 1960s testifies to science's formidable hold on that generation's imagination. In fact, Mishler (1979) contends that the older generation of researchers currently perpetuate this approach in their senior faculty roles as the "gate-keepers" at academic institutions: "We have all had students and younger colleagues complain that they cannot find the right methods to study the problems in which they are interested. All too often we help them reshape their problem so that available methods can be used. In the process, the original problem is often lost" (pp. 17–18).

Coming into the 1960s

A stunning social optimism characterized America in the early 1960s. The economy was burgeoning; American troops, in theory, were not fighting abroad. The country could now attend to its serious domestic problems. The Great Society was initiated, and Congress "proceeded to enact the stockpile of social programs that reformers had unsuccessfully been advocating for decades" (Weiss, 1983a).

Head Start and Title I of the Elementary and Secondary Education Act (ESEA) contained the early childhood components of this historic multipronged attack on poverty, and as such they represented the federal government's first large-scale investment in young children. Desiring to protect this investment, Congress made the ESEA one of the first pieces of reform legislation to require program accountability through evaluation (Patton, 1978; Tavris, 1976). A young evaluation field, primarily composed of classically trained social science researchers and evaluators, was called into action on short notice. Its "bag of tricks" was meager for the task at hand: a number of standardized child-focused measures of intelligence and achievement, a commitment to experimental study of program impact, and little time for conceptualizing a feasible design (Gordon, 1979; Rivlin and Timpane, 1975).

Early evaluation planning of Head Start revealed "a constant tension between the desire to bring to bear upon this large-scale 'field experiment' the techniques of small-scale controlled laboratory research and the more realistic pressures to apply flexible strategies" (Gordon, 1979, p. 399). Ultimately, acknowledgment of the "sloppy" field conditions produced some flexibility in data collection techniques which was tolerated rather than embraced. The impulse to "protect the prevailing scientific paradigm" (Minuchin, 1985, p. 294) was satisfied.

Evaluation of both Head Start and Follow Through took many forms over a 15-year period. Datta (1979) identifies three distinct waves in the Head Start case. In the first, from 1965–1968, a relatively modest study suggested that the program had immediate short-term and perhaps long-term benefits. In the second wave, from 1969–1974, the findings created a "winter of disillusion." Specifically, findings from the Westinghouse Learning Corporation evaluation (1969)—considered the first major evaluation effort—were interpreted by many to indicate that while immediate benefits accrued, they "washed out" by early elementary school age. Datta characterizes the third wave, from 1975 onward, as a hopeful period, during which reanalyses of earlier work shed new light on Head Start effects, and subsequent demonstration projects such as Home Start and the Parent Child Development Centers incorporated innovations in service and evaluation (see Hewett and DeLoria, 1982; Affholter, Connell, and Nauta, 1983).

The second wave of findings had a pervasive and somewhat chilling impact on the American public (Ianni and Orr, 1979; MacRae, Jr. and Haskins, 1981), presenting it in one fell swoop with the failures of both science and broad-based social interventions. The Westinghouse evaluation's (1969) methodology was roundly and appropriately criticized, although some critics also displayed a tendency to "kill the messenger" attempting to deliver as ordered (Weiss, 1983a). Other critics blamed the architects of the national program, pointing to its intensely political nature, the haste with which local programs were implemented, the unrealistic expectations many held for dramatic effects from relatively weak interventions, and legislators' naive understandings of the role of evaluation research in public policy formation. Placing blame is far less important to us than describing the impact of these findings and critiques on the public's view of evaluation and on its practice. These provide lessons for current efforts.

The news that Head Start achieved few of its intended benefits caused widespread disappointment and discouragement. Some commentators claim the American public interpreted these findings as evidence of the intractability of domestic poverty and withdrew its support for social programming when quick solutions seemed impossible. Others argue that disinterest in the plight of other people's children is characteristically American, and thus Americans were simply returning to form (Grubb and Lazerson, 1982). For whatever reasons, it appeared that these findings contributed to a temporary, but real, erosion of support for the Great Society's early childhood agenda (Weiss, 1983a; Zigler and Valentine, 1979).

Early childhood program personnel also appeared markedly affected by these results. In interviews I conducted on this topic in the early 1970s, sentiment fell into two camps: A number of staff members were profoundly demoralized, questioning their "total child" approach, which had not yielded results according to test scores. Others dismissed the evaluation itself, claiming that it, not the program, was responsible for the negative findings. In particular, they railed against the use of achievement tests which did not reflect their programs' goals. Neither group was eager to participate in future evaluations.

Policymakers were disappointed as well, often faulting the social scientists who had undertaken this and other evaluation studies. Senator Patrick Moynihan (1969) disparaged the then current intervention research, finding it "fragmented, contradictory, incomplete" (p. 191). Regarding social science research, he suggested that "enough snake oil has been sold in this Republic to warrant the expectation that public officials will begin reading labels" (p. 191) prior to funding such efforts. Senator Mondale also criticized policy research for its inability to marshall evidence that is validated by all or even most researchers. In a

1971 address, he represented his "confused and disheartened" Congressional colleagues who found that: "For every study, statistical or theoretical . . . there is always another, equally well documented, challenging the assumptions or conclusions of the first. No one seems to agree with anyone else's approach. But more distressing: no one seems to know what works" (Light and Pillemer, 1984, p. viii).

Finally, a number of social scientists and evaluators echoed these sentiments, although the flawed national evaluations catalyzed and highlighted, rather than *caused,* their critical views of classical evaluation (Cronbach and Associates, 1980; Filstead, 1979; Guba and Lincoln, 1981). For example, Guba (1972) noted: "Innovations have persisted in education . . . not because of the supporting evidence of evaluation but despite it." He described such a program in New York City: "Test data failed to affirm what supervisors, teachers and clients insisted was true—that the program was making a difference so great that it simply could not be abandoned" (Guba, 1972, p. 251). In their retrospective study of early childhood demonstration program evaluations, Travers and Light (1982) disparage the "pursuit of spurious rigor. . . . There is nothing scientific about adherence to forms and techniques that have proved their usefulness elsewhere, but fail to fit the phenomena at hand" (p. 48).

Thus the next generation of program evaluators were forced to work under far less hospitable conditions: The love affair with science had dissipated, leaving program directors warier, policymakers more suspicious, and the public increasingly disillusioned with both social programs and social science. Belief in evaluation had been undermined, as the field experienced the "lethal consequences of overpromising and underdelivering" (Datta, 1983, p. 469).

Lessons from the Battlefield. With the luxury of hindsight, however, one can see how "failing big" has benefited the field, forcing a retreat into modesty that might otherwise not have occurred. The limits of scientific inquiry, applied to an increasingly complex set of programs for young children and their families, have become more generally acknowledged. This has opened the door to integrating research techniques long popular in the "softer social sciences" of anthropology, clinical psychology, and sociology (Firestone and Herriott, 1983; Goetz and LeCompte, 1984; Patton, 1980). For example, qualitative data collection strategies such as participant and key informant interviews, structured program observations, ethnographic community studies, document and case reviews have been added to the evaluator's accepted repertoire. Often they are viewed as supports rather than substitutes for quantitative techniques (Travers and Light, 1982). Nonetheless, the popularity of mixed-method inquiry has muted the earlier generation's debate of "quantitative versus qualitative," suggesting a hard-won appreciation of program context (Bryk, 1978; Hatch, 1983; Reichardt and Cook, 1979; Rist, 1980). Given the power of the scientific ideals, these compromises are not trivial.

A somewhat more enlightened approach to outcome measurement has been adopted. One of the most often cited limitations to past evaluations has been their reliance on child measures of cognition and achievement (Jacobs, 1984). Arguably, these had been reasonable indicators of success in the experimental, cognitively oriented early intervention programs of the early 1960s (Travers and Light, 1982), but they had not translated well as measures of effectiveness in the multipurposed Head Start and Title I. This position has been integrated into current evaluation practice.

The call for multiple-measures that tap a range of child developmental areas came early on (e.g., see Rivlin and Timpane, 1975; Walker, 1973) and has continued to develop momentum. The additional recommendation that outcome measures reflect the increasingly ecological focus of programs has been acknowledged in theory (Hewett and DeLoria, 1982; Travers and Light, 1982). However, as the chapters on measurement in this volume attest, the absence of standardized measures capable of assessing the ecological continuum has made application of the ecological approach difficult; few researchers are willing to abandon standardized measures altogether in favor of program-specific impact measures.

Program evaluation has moved away from serving primarily a summative function—that is, answering the question: Is the program effective? It is now used increasingly to answer a variety of questions posed by a diverse set of concerned parties. To some of these "stakeholders" (Weiss, 1983b), documenting internal program process, profiling participants and their communities, monitoring legislative requirements for programming, describing initial program implementation and subsequent program replication, and maintaining service utilization data, all fall under the definition of program evaluation. So while summative evaluation remains the preferred mode, many other genres have been offered (Nevo, 1983; Patton, 1978, 1982).

It is unlikely that evaluators in the near future will be called upon to design a summative evaluation of a large-scale federal initiative such as Head Start; there are simply too many political and social purposes to accommodate into a reasonable design. Further, we now know that such programs will "work" for certain children and families in certain locales and not for others. The task, then, is to avoid inappropriate pressures to answer the *broad* questions (e.g., "fund/no fund"), and concentrate instead on teasing out differentiated effects within a single program or across a manageable number of like-minded ones to explain why those effects occurred (see Bond and Halpern, Chapter 15, this volume; Walker and Mitchell, Chapter 18, this volume). Of course, to be done properly, evaluators must document and credit the complexity in individual programs (Nauta and Hewett, Chapter 17, this volume).

Evaluation can describe program process and document services delivered and client satisfaction with them; it can measure impact on participants and offer hypotheses about why such benefits occurred (or failed to occur); it can draw comparisons across programs. These endeavors generate useful data and insight with applications for policy; but evaluations rarely, if ever, create public policy (Gallagher, 1981; Pettigrew, 1985; Weiss, 1983a) and should not be expected to do so: Policy decisions are essentially moral or political ones made through a complex democratic process (Zigler, 1979).

Programming and Politics in the 1980s

Program evaluation has evolved not only through internal process, but also in interaction with a new set of programs developing in a markedly different political climate. Early childhood programs increasingly have become ecological in orientation (Bronfenbrenner, 1979); it is widely believed that parents should be involved with their children's early schooling, and that parent and community support for learning is at least as important as the particular skills children may develop.

Family support programs represent a further statement of the ecological position: Since young children live primarily within families, promoting the well-being of family members and the family unit is viewed as necessary to a child's healthy development. Thus, parents and other family members receive direct services in addition to, or exclusive of, their children (Weissbourd, 1983; Weiss and Jacobs, Introduction to this volume). These programs often are preventive rather than remedial, offering a range of voluntary activities such as parent education classes, parent–child play groups, and mothers' discussion groups. The bulk of family support programs are small, young, grassroots operations. According to a recent national program survey (Hite, 1985; Weiss and Hite, 1986), an estimated 30% had initiated services within the prior 2 years, with more than half having begun within the past 5 years. The typical annual budget was $7000, with over 70% relying to some degree on volunteer staffing. (See Weiss and Jacobs, this volume, for a more detailed discussion of program characteristics.)

The political milieu for these and the more traditional family-oriented social services also has changed dramatically. The widespread public support for social programming of the 1960s and early 1970s has dissipated, whereas political struggle over the family and its private responsibilities has intensified. At one end of the continuum, families are seen as collections of individuals who, due to the exigencies of modern life, are often beleaguered and isolated, and therefore need public recognition and support. At the other end, families are seen as self-sustaining units of parents and offspring. To the extent that they have difficulty meeting obligations to their children, it is primarily because not enough time and energy is invested in home life, the moral structure of society is collapsing, and/or the government is meddling in private family relationships—those between husband and wife, parents and children (Lasch, 1977; White House Conference on Families, 1980).

The more conservative, laissez-faire attitude seems to have prevailed at the federal level of government. Public support for children and families—be it financial, educational, or social in nature—has eroded in the past several years (Preston, 1984); the increase in poverty rates among children since 1979, (see "Children and families in poverty," 1985; Sidel, 1986;) and the Reagan Administration's repeated attempts to dismantle a number of the federal legislative entitlements for children and families (Children's Defense Fund, 1986) are two often cited examples. State and municipal governments have successfully and innovatively filled part of this gap; there remains, however, concern about program availability, accessibility, and eligibility across communities.

Thus there is little agreement about how much of what kind of support to families is appropriate. Images of family support and education programs as interfering, ineffective, or fostering public dependence abound. Program advocates often find themselves poorly defended against such accusations, since evidence of program effectiveness or even program utilization is scarce or inaccessible. To be sure, the bulk of family support programs has a limited vision of their role in this national policy debate.

Evaluation in the 1980s: "These Are the Times that Try Our Souls. . . ."

Evaluation in the 1980s enjoys improved technology and practice. Yet it is challenged both by the new genre of grassroots programs and by a decidedly more conservative political climate. This situation presents both great opportunities and dangers. Hopefully, the lessons of modesty and restraint discussed earlier will be brought to bear as evaluators meet these challenges.

An evaluation must be tailored to the program under investigation: What are its age and developmental stage, the concerns and dreams of its clients and staff, its data collection capabilities? Outcome measures must reflect program goals rather than the evaluator's desire to use only those instruments with sound psychometric properties. Perhaps most importantly, evaluators must not promise to answer questions for which their tools and techniques are underdeveloped or inappropriate; recent calls for cost–benefit studies of family-oriented programs to legitimate their public support is a case in point, presenting an eerie parallel to the demands for impact evaluation of the 1960s (Bellah, 1983; Maling and Keepes, 1985).

Many family support programs, by their nature, resist experimental and quasi-experimental study. They are too young to have an articulated set of goals and too inexperienced or overworked to collect even basic service utilization data. Veteran programs present other challenges: They often are committed to multiple outcomes for many individuals who partake differentially of the services offered. And they are some-times wary of evaluators and disinclined to be scrutinized. Yet neither set of family programs can be absolved of their responsibility to be accountable to participants, funders, and community supporters. Apart from an ethical obligation to provide the best services possible, pro-grams must see themselves as part of a national movement that needs evidence to support its broad-based appeal and to document its ef-fectiveness. Given the tenor of the times, future public support for programs to strengthen and support families may hang in the balance. And undoubtedly, trust in evaluation would be greatly undermined by another cycle of inappropriately designed efforts. Thus an approach to evaluation that is broad enough to encompass the range of family programs is in order.

Clearly the evaluations of seasoned, well-funded programs bear dif-ferent burdens from those of the smaller, less experienced programs. Often these demonstration programs elect, or are required, to conduct impact evaluations. These are critical to informing policy, advancing our understanding of child and family development and of interven-tion effects, and aiding in the development of a more responsive and responsible evaluation technology. Evaluations of the remaining programs—in fact, the current majority—should be oriented toward helping programs maintain a satisfied clientele, documenting services delivered for community and national program justification, describing program implementation to aid in program improve-ment and replication, and assessing, if possible, immediate program effects.

The case studies in this volume represent evaluations of the former type (see Introduction to Section III). The remainder of this chapter presents a framework for evaluating family programs of the latter variety. While this Five-Tiered Approach has implications for flagship evalua-tions, it is designed to be particularly responsive to the needs of the larger fleet—those local, low-budget programs that need to be intro-duced to the potential benefits of evaluation. Therefore, it focusses on the earlier levels of this schema.

The Five-Tiered Approach to Family Program Evaluation

Several basic assumptions about the role and value of program evaluation underlie this graduated approach:

Evaluation should be viewed as the systematic collection and analysis of program-related data that can be used to understand how a program delivers services *and/or* what the consequences of its services are for participants (see Cronbach, 1982; Travers and Light, 1982). Thus, for our purposes, it is both descriptive and "judgmental" of program merit, with the emphasis on designing an evaluation that fits the program.

Evaluation is a necessary component to every program, regardless of its size, age, and orientation. The foregoing definition allows for a wide range of activities under the rubric of evaluation and assumes that all programs should engage in some of those activities. At a minimum, programs should be able to identify their beliefs at the beginning of their operation, to describe changes in orientation as they occur, and to document the services delivered. These data can provide feedback to improve individual program effectiveness. They also can generate information for the general public about the need and value of the program within the community. Simple evaluations can and should be movement-builders.

There are numerous legitimate purposes for evaluation. Programs must be committed to providing an effective service, but not all evaluation should attempt to determine program impact per se. Programs have natural life cycles (Cronbach, 1982; Pincus, 1980); thus, for example, it would be foolish to push an outcome evaluation onto a young program still searching for a well-defined set of goals and services. Donald Campbell (1983) presumably was speaking to this situation when he urged us to "evaluate no program until it is proud."

There are also many legitimate audiences for an evaluation. Program evaluations serve many masters; the audience for a particular evaluation will not only influence decisions concerning data collection and analyses but also study dissemination. For example, an evaluation initiated by program personnel to improve the quality of their own services should differ from one undertaken at the behest of funders interested in the extent of community acceptance of the program. Neither audience is more or less legitimate; both are "stakeholders" with information needs (Cronbach and Associates, 1980; Patton, 1982). The goal of an evaluation should be to be used by its intended audience, not to conform to an ideal that will gain it entry into "some evaluation heaven where the souls of virtuous studies ascend" (Patton, 1978, p. 24).

Evaluation activities should not detract from service delivery. Many family support programs feel they cannot afford to divert funds and staff time toward evaluation. Yet often they are required, or feel compelled, to attempt the costly impact evaluations demanded by funders or community supporters. These demands should not simply be accepted; they must be negotiated both within programs (among staff and between staff and clients) and between the program and the "outside." (See Bond and Halpern, Chapter 15; Ellwood, Chapter 13; Miller, Chapter 16, this volume.) These negotiations will allow for the proper allocation of resources between service and evaluation.

IMPLEMENTING THE FIVE-TIERED APPROACH

The Five-Tiered Approach organizes evaluation activities at five levels, each requiring greater efforts at data collection and tabulation, increased precision in program definition, and a greater commitment to the evaluation process. At each level, corresponding sets of purposes and audiences are presented (see Table 2.1). Although these tiers appear in sequence, programs can and should engage in several levels of evaluation at the same time and should return to previous levels when appropriate. For example, an established early intervention program for families with handicapped children should return to the preimplementation phase if it considers serving families with able-bodied children. Similarly, if a community's character changes, forcing a veteran program to reassess its target population and service modalities, that program should return to an earlier level of evaluation.

Level One: The Preimplementation Tier

The first level, the preimplementation tier, creates the conditions for all subsequent evaluation efforts. This set of activities has been called the needs assessment stage (Upshur, 1982; Walker and Mitchell, Chapter 18, this volume) or the planning period for evaluation, when the program's evaluability is determined (Wholey, 1977). Defining these activities as a most basic form of evaluation may help programs to see these necessary tasks in the larger evaluation context, easing them into the process.

In theory, all operating programs have negotiated this level successfully, since they have convinced funders to finance them, families to use them, and communities to support them. In truth, however, sometimes programs—even good ones—are established quickly for political reasons, for example, because of the special interests of powerful community leaders. These programs are not always compelled to think through their definitions of the problems to be addressed, their organizational structures, and their chances for success in dealing with these problems.

Programs should resist the short-sighted impulse to "take the money and run," for it is likely that at some point in a program's natural life, information from this initial tier will be requested. This material will offer modest protection for the program from the sometimes poor memories and shifting loyalties of funders; it also allows for the broadest range of future evaluation options by providing the necessary baseline data.

Let us use a child abuse and neglect prevention program as a hypothetical case and outline briefly its evaluation at Level One. The program initiators believe that child abuse and neglect is a problem in their community and need to support this contention with evidence. They might:

1. Locate statistical data that describe their community, highlighting those sociodemographics thought to correlate with child abuse and neglect. These could include, for example, the overall census in the potential service area; racial composition of the community; income distribution among resident households; unemployment figures; local rates of child abuse and neglect.
2. Research any local press coverage of the problem in recent years.
3. Identify several community leaders (e.g., the Mayor, Commissioner of Human Services, day care directors, clergy) to interview on the subject. Do they feel the rates are increasing? Why? What are the effects on the community? Written interview notes should be kept.
4. Describe their proposed (or actual) program, in writing, including reference to:
   a. The specific target population (e.g., court-referred cases or families at-risk? How will it define at-risk?)
   b. Ideas about how families change (e.g., when they receive peer support).
   c. Description of the services to be offered (e.g., parent support groups and 24-hour hotline); by whom (e.g., volunteer social workers; veteran parents); at what anticipated cost per family (e.g., $500/year).
   d. What are the intended benefits (e.g., increased parental self-esteem; more appropriate discipline)?

Often this information is included in a grant proposal for program support; I recommend that all programs, whether they already have funding or are seeking it, engage in these activities.

TABLE 2.1. Summary of Five-Tiered Approach to Program Evaluation

Evaluation level	Title of evaluation tier	Purpose of evaluation	Audiences
Level 1	Preimplemention tier	1. To document the need for particular program within community 2. To demonstrate the fit between community needs and proposed program 3. To provide "data groundwork"	1. Potential funders 2. Community/citizen groups

Level 2	Accountability tier	1. To document program's
		  a. utilization
		  b. entrenchment
		  c. penetration into target population
		2. To justify current expenditures
		3. To increase expenditures
		4. To build a constituency
			1. Funders, donors
			2. Community leaders, media

Level 3	Program clarification tier	1. To provide information to program staff to improve the program	1. Program staff 2. Program participants
Level 4	Progress toward objectives tier	1. To provide information to staff to improve program 2. To document program effectiveness	1. Staff members 2. Program participants 3. Funders 4. Other programs

Tasks	Types of data to collected/analyzed
1. Detail basic characteristics of proposed program 2. Conduct community needs assessment to support establishment of such program 3. Revise proposed program coordinated to assessed needs	1. Locally generated statistics that describe populations and needs for service (including public/personal costs of not providing the program) 2. Interviews with community leaders on seriousness of problem 3. Interviews or survey data from prospective participants

1. Describe accurately program participants and services provided
2. Provide accurate cost information per unit of service
	1. Client-specific monitoring data
	2. Service-specific monitoring data
	3. Case material
	  a. Data from interviews with clients indicating clients' needs and responses
	  b. Community (nonuser) reactions to program

1. Question basic program assumptions: what kinds of services for whom and by whom? 2. Clarify and restate program's mission, goals, objectives, and strategies	1. Content of staff meetings, supervision sessions, interviews with staff 2. Observation by staff of program activities and staff process 3. Previously collected staff and service data 4. Interview data from parents on desired benefits to program 5. Client satisfaction information
1. Examine outcome (short-term) objectives 2. Derive measurable indicators of success for a majority of the outcome objectives 3. Decide on data analysis procedures 4. Assess differential effectiveness among individual clients 5. Assess community awareness among individual clients	1. Interview material regarding individual client's progress toward objectives 2. Standardized test scores for clients, where applicable 3. Client-specific information from criterion-referenced instruments 4. Client satisfaction data 5. Evidence of support/resistance to program in community

(*continued*)

TABLE 2.1. *(continued)*

Evaluation level	Title of evaluation tier	Purpose of evaluation	Audiences
Level 5	Program impact tier	1. To contribute to knowledge development in the substantive fields of child development, family process, organizational theory, and/or to the refinement of evaluation practices 2. To produce evidence of differential effectiveness among alternative program approaches 3. To suggest program models worthy of replication	1. Academic and research communities 2. Policymakers at federal, state, and local levels 3. General public, through the media 4. Potential program directors and funders

Level Two: The Accountability Tier

The second level, the accountability tier, involves the systematic collection of client-specific and service-utilization data, often considered a program monitoring function. Most evaluators assume that programs routinely collect these data. However, results from a recent national program survey (Hite, 1985) and personal experience providing technical assistance in the field indicate the contrary: Over 20% of those survey respondents keep *no* service utilization figures at all, and there is wide variation on the types of client background data collected (see Table 2.2). So, while many programs collect *some* information on clients and *some* information on service, these data are often sporadically or unsystematically gathered. As a result, it is difficult for these programs to report (and support with evidence) the numbers of people they serve, a description of their model family, what portion of the needy population they have reached, which families are getting which services, how staff members spend their time, and the like.

According to the foregoing program survey, low-budget programs

Tasks	Types of data to collected/analyzed
1. Delineate specific impact objectives that are to be achieved, presumably through the accretion of short-term objectives' success	1. Quantifiable client-specific data, including standardized test results collected over time (longitudinal client data)
2. Identify measure(s) that can assess enduring and/or lifestyle changes among participants	2. Control group data or comparison group standards
3. Develop evaluation plan that reflects common understandings among evaluator(s), program personnel, contractor (if different from program)	3. Qualitative client data, including record reviews, client interviews, etc.
	4. Cost-effectiveness information, necessary for planning program replication

TABLE 2.2. Percentages of Family Support Programs Collecting the Following Types of Background Data on Their Clients[a,b]

Type of information	Percentage of programs collecting information
Family income	46.0
Mother's education	48.0
Father's education	46.0
Marital status	74.0
Ages of children in family	89.0
Race	48.5
Mother's age	58.0
Father's age	55.0
Number of family members	85.0

[a]From Jacobs and Weiss (1985).
[b]Data source: Harvard Family Research Project National Program Survey, 1984 ($N = 387$).

are less likely than others to engage in systematic record-keeping, which is not surprising: Major funders tend to require these monitoring data, so programs with monies from county or state agencies or from larger private foundations usually *do* document service utilization. Further, smaller programs often do not know what information to collect or how to set up an easy, efficient data system, and they may not appreciate the benefits of collecting this information altogether (Condelli and Plantz, 1985; Walker and Mitchell, Chapter 18, this volume).

Low-budget programs can benefit greatly from evaluation at this level for several reasons: First, these grassroots programs "stay close" to their intended constituencies, so it is likely that client data would demonstrate that the target population indeed *was* enrolled. Second, these programs tend to rely heavily on paraprofessionals and volunteers, which in theory should yield a greater penetration into both the needy population and the general community than can be achieved by programs with comparable budgets staffed solely by professionals. Third, well-designed, thoughtful programs should be encouraged to experiment with the types and number of services offered and clients involved; additional funds for such activities generally cannot be secured without the previously mentioned documentation.

This level is called the accountability tier because the data to be collected are necessary for the program to be minimally accountable to funders (whatever the investment), to participants, and to the larger community. A program, however small, should be able to report that, in a particular time period, X number of families were provided Y amount of service at a cost of Z. Evaluation at this tier does not require documentation of success in attaining the client-related goals and objectives detailed at Level One. Nor does it demand that program staff use the information collected to modify the program in dramatic ways, although presumably, utilization figures and case material will raise issues to be addressed regarding service delivery. Second tier evaluation simply documents what exists—client characteristics, service/intervention descriptions and costs—and it may be the correct place to stop to allow newly organized programs "to catch their breath."

Congress' Select Committee for Children, Youth, and Families has successfully raised day care to national prominence through amassing and reporting day care utilization figures and airing consumer and provider testimony (case material) on the issue, which in our schema, constitutes evaluation activity at the second tier (see, e.g., Select Committee on Children, Youth, and Families, 1984). The family support movement should undertake a similar process. Indeed, if all programs could reach this level of evaluation, a visible national constituency for family support programs could be established.

Level Three: The Program Clarification Tier

The third level, the program clarification tier, helps programs make use of the information generated in previous stages while encouraging them to draw on staff and participant feedback to monitor and improve program operation. Often this is the most useful genre of evaluation, with many data collection and analysis options open to younger, low-budget programs. At this level, program staff rely primarily on their own "collective wisdom" to answer the question of "how can we do a better job serving our clients?"

At this stage original program material defining the program's orientation and organization is reviewed critically, integrating the lessons that have been learned during implementation. For example, the target population for an early intervention program as described in its proposal may be "children at risk for developmental delays because of biological or family factors." Upon reviewing the client-specific data, a program may find that all their children and families are biologically (constitutionally) at-risk; none is at-risk because of family problems. This finding suggests that either the definition of target population needs to be amended to reflect the actual client composition, or that the program needs to improve outreach to environmentally at-risk families. However, it also may be that staff members are uncomfortable with their original charge, and in this case further discussion, not vigorous case-finding, would be in order.

Program goals and objectives should be scrutinized as well. Walker and Mitchell (this volume, Chapter 18) offer a typology of program objectives as a starting point for this examination. They suggest that programs organize objectives as follows: process objectives (what staff will do—how members will behave—to reach program goals); product objectives (what staff will develop, such as curricula or implementation reports, to support these intentions); outcome objectives (how participants will change in the short term); and impact objectives (what differences these changes will make in the long term).

This typology stimulates precise thinking about what a program hopes for clients to achieve and the intervention strategies for achieving these ends. For example, a program working with families of chronically ill children adopts as its primary impact objective (agreed on by parents as well) that families will encourage children to become self-reliant and feel more competent. The typical intervention combines daytime home visiting with weekly mothers' support groups held in the evenings. Evaluation here might raise the question, "How can we expect *families* to become less overprotective if our intervention is directed solely at the mother and child?" Confronting this issue, the program may redefine its target to the mother–child dyad or may revise its intervention, visiting during the evenings when father and siblings are present.

Programs must push toward consensus on both their broad-ranging goals and more specific objectives; philosophical biases and inter-professional competitions may surface and must be addressed. Through this sometimes painful process much of the growth in programs occurs, and an opportunity for this discussion should be built into each pro-gram's annual schedule.

How can a program be reasonably certain, even if there is staff con-sensus, that the chosen set of services is appropriate for the individual family/client or for the target population as a whole? Additional activities may include:

1. *Case management of individuals or families.* Staff members across disciplines should assess the fit between client needs and services pro-vided. Observations of direct service by fellow staff are often helpful, as is clinical supervision by "outside" practitioners. These techniques help to validate or modify intervention approaches.

2. *Client satisfaction surveys.* Well-designed client satisfaction questionnaires may yield valuable participant feedback for program improvement. Undertaking such a survey will require additional staff time (to help develop the questionnaire, tabulate and analyze the re-sponses) and resources (for typing and printing the survey and for post-age), and in most cases an external evaluator should be consulted at this point. Programs without the means for this modest investment can convene participant forums to elicit feedback from clients (Upshur, 1982). Of course, program participants must be assured that no aversive responses will accrue from expressed criticisms or concerns.

In addition to these clearly formative evaluation activities, programs should be encouraged to collect and maintain process and implemen-tation data. Program process data describe how the program operates: what services are offered and used and by whom; which staff members provide specific program components; how program policy decisions are made; what participants and staff members observe and experience day-to-day. Such information, often written in informal journals, is helpful not only for improving the program, but also for understanding *why* certain services seem to be effective for, or are preferred by, certain clients. It also documents the program's internal organization should others be interested in replicating it.

Implementation data, similar to process information, are useful in establishing whether the intended service is actually being offered (Fil-stead, 1979; McLaughlin, 1980; Morris and Fitz-Gibbon, 1978; Patton, 1978). For example, in describing parent education home visits, Clarke-Stewart (1981) suggests that regardless of training to standardize interventions, home visitors may be implementing their personalized versions of the curriculum. This is an important piece of information to help understand why the program affected certain recipients differentially, an issue critical to evaluation at subsequent levels.

Evaluation at this tier is rich and varied, and in many respects, this third tier's activities are the most reliable for current family support programs. The options for evaluation activities are numerous, and programs may need help in setting evaluation priorities and/or analyzing the data collected. This information often can be put to immediate use, and evaluation here remains close to the program, reflecting the ever-changing beliefs and behaviors of the real people who work there and participate in it. Evaluations aiming to improve individual program effectiveness cannot avoid engagement at this level.

Level Four: The Progress-toward-Objectives Tier

The fourth level, the progress-toward-objectives tier, focuses on program effectiveness but must first incorporate the fuller evaluation activities of previous tiers. Programs engaged at this level often are longer lived, more experienced, and relatively secure financially; therefore they have the time, resources, and interest to collect and analyze the necessary information. Evaluation here pushes programs to articulate short-term objectives with behavioral indicators of their attainment. Further, it seeks to understand which participants achieved which of these proximate objectives; are there differential program effects based on participants' ages, races, or expressed opinions about, for example, discipline or optimal family communication?

Thus at Level Four, the evaluation landscape shifts dramatically. First, there is a move toward objective measurement of program effects. Second, accountability for client progress (or lack of it) as distinct from accountability for service provision (as at Level Two) is emphasized. Third, activities are staff and resource intensive: Staff members are required to help formulate measurable indicators of success, collect various new types of data, and maintain written documentation of the units of service delivered. Programs often enlist professional evaluators to help design and implement these evaluations, since the demands for data collection training and data analysis generally exceed the capabilities of individual programs. Finally, issues of program and evaluation dissemination become important, especially if the program is "proud" (à la Campbell) and eager to replicate (see Ellwood, Chapter 13; Rodriguez and Cortez, Chapter 12, this volume).

According to this model (see *Tasks* in Table 2.1), the first step is to organize objectives by some outcome schema, assuring that if, for ex-

ample, the program intends to increase a family's sense of connectedness in its neighborhood, an objective of that genre is present under
"family-community" outcomes. To continue the example, staff and
clients next need to achieve consensus on a behavioral measure of
success for that objective. What kinds of activities might serve as indicators that the family has made progress in this regard? One indicator
could be report of attendance at three or more housing project tenants'
meetings during a 6-month period, or regular involvement in program
activities.

Let us use the parent–child outcome objective of "disciplining children appropriately for their age and developmental stage" in a preventive child abuse program as another example. Staff can use the program's drop-in center to observe parents and children in an informal
atmosphere; the indicator of success for the first 6 months might be
three separate half-hours of mother–child interaction without physical
punishment. Once this objective is achieved (and documented), increasingly difficult short-term objectives should be set. Several behavioral indicators may be generated for each objective. (See Howrigan,
Chapter 4, this volume, for cautions about participant observations.)

Many programs that evaluate at this level use standardized tests to
measure client progress. The vast majority of those standardized (norm-
referenced) instruments focus on *child* outcomes, and, more specifically, on cognitive development (see Hauser-Cram and Shonkoff,
Chapter 3; Weiss, Chapter 1, this volume), since among other reasons,
current measurement technology at other ecological levels of development remains quite primitive (see Cleary, Chapter 8; Krauss, Chapter
7; Walker and Crocker, Chapter 6, this volume). While the appeal of
standardized instruments with sound psychometric properties is understandable, sole reliance on them in evaluating family support programs, with their multiplicity of desired outcomes, is indefensible. A
combination of measurement strategies, including the development of
program-specific (criterion-referenced) instruments, is critical (Bryk,
1978; Patton, 1978).

Analyses of these data must include the examination of differential
short-term effects. Does the program seem to work better with families
configured in a certain way, or with particular cultural groups? For example, does an early intervention program appear more effective for
families with handicapped children as opposed to those considered
environmentally at-risk? or with single teen mothers rather than two-
parent older families? These analyses help programs improve services
and provide the bases for developing replication strategies.

As with developing a client-satisfaction survey, constructing program-
specific instruments—including observation scales and parent/family
interview schedules (and their coding conventions)—often cannot be
done by program personnel alone, unless the program director is also

a researcher (see Dunst and Trivette, Chap. 14; Olds, Chap. 10, this volume). External evaluators generally enter the process here. Programs sometimes are unsure of how to find an evaluator, although the human resources for these efforts exist in most communities. For example, innovative collaborative arrangements between programs and university-based evaluators (and their students) have appeared in many localities, and a greater number of independent consulting firms have become involved with these programs. Whomever the contractor, the key to a successful evaluation is establishing a respectful, dynamic partnership between evaluator and program. "Action research," originally proposed by Kurt Lewin (1946) and revived in the recent past (see Bond and Halpern, Chapter 15, this volume; Rapoport, 1985), is one appropriate model for implementing this synergistic relationship.

Finally, evaluation at Level Four often involves a reorientation toward the outside world. Programs may be considering whether to replicate and may want to test the waters of broader community acceptance and support. If programs decide to replicate or otherwise broaden their bases of support (e.g., solicit more funding for additional service components), evaluators can assist them in producing evidence of their place and value in the community and in presenting their effectiveness data in a proper form for dissemination.

Level Five: The Program-Impact Tier

At this final program-impact tier both the program and its evaluator have committed themselves to an experimental or quasi-experimental methodology, seeking to identify and measure long- and/or short-term impacts on children or families using random assignment or comparison groups or standards. These evaluations are often multiyear efforts, with intensive and complex data collection and treatment requirements. While occasionally these evaluations provide direct feedback and information to programs, more often they are externally directed, meant to contribute more broadly to developmental theory and clinical or evaluation practice. Only a fraction of family support programs at present conduct such evaluations, which seems appropriate given the nature of these programs and the demands of these evaluations.

In order to "qualify" here, evaluations not only must "do science well," but also must contain evidence of sincere engagement at earlier levels. That is, these evaluations should truly reflect the expressed goals and objectives of their programs, however complex and inconvenient. Program process and implementation data should be included, as should direct participant feedback. Evaluation reports should describe the audiences for the evaluation, the trade-offs among various techniques and measures, and the strengths and weaknesses in the design.

The evaluation's "story," as well as its results, should be told. The majority of case studies in this volume exemplify Level Five evaluations.

CONCLUSIONS

The primary intent of this chapter has been to argue the case historically, conceptually, and pragmatically for a broadened notion of program evaluation technology" (Hobbs *et al.*, 1984, p. 267). Second, the current level of evaluation appears sufficient: "Evidence of accessibility, use, and parents' satisfaction perhaps is all that is possible and shoestring, demonstration and local, proud and floundering. The time is ripe for a reasoned and calibrated approach that satisfies the needs of program directors, researchers, funders, and evaluators.

A decade of evaluation of Minnesota's pilot Early Childhood Family Education programs demonstrates such a reasoned approach: Evaluation activities have included a range of assessment strategies, but have stopped short of measuring program impact on participants for two reasons: These parent education programs have such broad ranging goals that "demands for measurable effects would push the limits of program evaluation technology" (Hobbs *et al.*, 1984, p. 267). Second, the current level of evaluation appears sufficient: "Evidence of accessibility, use, and parents' satisfaction perhaps is all that is possible and all that should be required. That evidence is available, and it is uniformly positive" (Hobbs *et al.*, 1984, p. 267). This example of common sense and restraint is commendable. (See Minnesota Department of Education, 1986.)

We must remember that we are conducting program evaluation at a curious moment in American history: While national politics appear quite conservative, there is a growing awareness, expressed at the local and state levels of government and by local citizenry, that some preventive public and private investment in families is warranted. If we maintain our vows of modesty, promising only as much as we can deliver, family support program evaluations can nurture this budding community support by helping local programs document, improve and expand services. The scientists among us, at the same time, should be encouraged to launch flagship evaluations, the results of which will be needed for future programming. A "paradigm of choices" (Patton, 1980) may well serve us best.

REFERENCES

Affholter, D. P., Connell, D., and Nauta, M. (1983). Evaluation of the child and family resource program: Early evidence of parent–child interaction effects. *Evaluation Review*, 7(1), 65–77.

Anastasiow, N. J. (June, 1985). *A qualitative method of evaluation and a critique of the hypothetico-deductive model's application to educational research.* Paper presented at the Mailman Foundation meeting, New York, N.Y.

Bellah, R. N. (1983). Social science as practical reason. In D. Callahan and B. Jennings (Eds.), *Ethics, the social sciences and policy analysis* (pp. 37–64). NY: Plenum Press.

Bligh, H. F. (April, 1979). *Achievement testing—A look at trends.* Paper presented at the 1979 convention of the National Council on Measurement in Education, San Francisco. (ERIC Document Reproduction Service No. ED 177 221).

Bloom, B. S. (1964). *Stability and change in human characteristics.* NY: John Wiley & Sons.

Braun, S. J., and Edwards, E. P. (1972). *History and theory of early childhood education.* Worthington, OH: Charles A. Jones.

Bronfenbrenner, U. (1979). *The ecology of human development: Experiments by nature and design.* Cambridge, MA: Harvard University Press.

Bruner, J. S. (1960). *The process of education.* Cambridge, MA: Harvard University Press.

Bryk, A. S. (1978). Evaluating program impact: A time to cast away stones, a time to gather stones together. *New Directions for Program Evaluation, 1,* 31–58.

Campbell, D. (May, 1983). *Threats to validity added when applied social research is packaged as "program evaluation" in the service of administrative decision making.* Paper presented at the Conference on Family Support Programs: The State-of-the-Art. Sponsored by the Bush Center in Child Development and Social Policy, Yale University, New Haven, CT, May 1983.

Children and families in poverty: Beyond the statistics. (November, 1985). *Proceedings and Debates of the 99th Congress, First Session, 131*(152).

Children's Defense Fund. (1986). *A children's defense budget: Annual of the children's defense fund FY 1987.* Washington D.C.: Author.

Clarke-Stewart, K. A. (1981). Parent education in the 1970s. *Educational Evaluation and Policy Analysis, 3*(6), 47–58.

Cole, M. (1985). Mind as a cultural achievement: Implications for IQ testing. In E. Eisner (Ed.), *Learning and teaching the ways of knowing* (pp. 218–249). Chicago, IL: National Society for the Study of Education.

Condelli, L., and Plantz, M. C. (1985). Investments in evaluation: Evaluation grants funded under the H.D.S. coordinated discretionary funds program FY 1982—FY 1984.

Condry, S. (1983). History and background of preschool intervention programs and the Consortium for Longitudinal Studies. In the Consortium for Longitudinal Studies (Ed.), *As the twig is bent: Lasting effects of preschool programs* (pp. 1–32). Hillsdale, NJ: Lawrence Erlbaum Associates.

Consortium for Longitudinal Studies (1983). *As the twig is bent: Lasting effects of preschool programs.* Hillsdale, NJ: Erlbaum.

Cronbach, L. J. (1982). *Designing evaluations of educational and social programs.* San Francisco, CA: Jossey-Bass.

Cronbach, L. J., and Associates. (1980). *Toward reform of program evaluation: Aims, methods, and institutional arrangements.* San Francisco, CA: Jossey-Bass.

Datta, L. (1979). Long-term gains from early intervention: Findings from longitudinal studies. In E. Zigler and J. Valentine (Eds.), *Project Head Start: A legacy of the War on Poverty* (pp. 433–466). NY: Free Press.

Datta, L. (1983). Epilogue: We never promised you a rose garden but one may have grown anyhow. In the Consortium for Longitudinal Studies (Ed.), *As the twig is bent: Lasting effects of preschool programs* (pp. 467–480). Hillsdale, NJ: Erlbaum.

Filstead, W. J. (1979). Qualitative methods: A needed perspective in evaluation research. In T. D. Cook and C. S. Reichardt, *Qualitative and quantitative methods in evaluation research* (pp. 33–48). Beverly Hills, CA: Sage.

Firestone, W. A., and Herriott, R. E. (1983). The formalization of qualitative research: An adaptation of "soft" science to the policy world. *Evaluation Review, 7*(4), 437–466.

Gallagher, J. J. (1981). Models for policy analysis: Child and family policy. In R. Haskins and J. J. Gallagher (Eds.), *Models for analysis of social policy: An introduction* (pp. 37–77). Norwood, NJ: Ablex.

Gardner, H. (1983). *Frames of mind: The theory of multiple intelligences.* NY: Basic Books.

Goetz, J. P., and LeCompte, M. D. (1984). *Ethnography and qualitative design in educational research.* NY: Academic Press.

Gordon, E. W. (1979). Evaluation during the early years of Head Start. In E. Zigler and J. Valentine (Eds.), *Project Head Start: A legacy of the War on Poverty* (pp. 399–404). NY: Free Press.

Gould, S. J. (1981). *The mismeasure of man.* New York: W. W. Norton.

Grubb, W. N., and Lazerson, M. (1982). *Broken promises: How Americans fail their children.* NY: Basic Books.

Guba, E. G. (1972). The failure of educational evaluation. In C. Weiss (Ed.), *Evaluating action programs: Readings in social action and education* (pp. 3–28). Boston, MA: Allyn & Bacon.

Guba, E. G., and Lincoln, Y. S. (1981). *Effective evaluation.* San Francisco, CA: Jossey-Bass.

Hatch, J. A. (1983). Applications of qualitative methods to program evaluation in education. *Teaching and Learning, 59,* 1–11.

Hawkridge, D. G. (1970). Designs for evaluative studies. In American Institute for Research, *Evaluative research: Strategies and methods* (pp. 24–47). Pittsburgh: American Institute for Research.

Hewett, K., and DeLoria, D. (1982). Comprehensive family service programs: Special features and associated measurement. In J. R. Travers and R. J. Light (Eds.), *Learning from experience: Evaluating early childhood demonstration program* (pp. 203–253). Washington, D.C.: National Academy Press.

Hite, S. J. (1985). *Family support and education programs: Analysis of a national sample.* Cambridge, MA: Unpublished doctoral dissertation, Harvard Graduate School of Education.

Hobbs, N., Dokecki, P., Hoover-Dempsey, K., Moroney, R., Shayne, M., and Weeks, K. (1984). *Strengthening families.* San Francisco, CA: Jossey-Bass.

Horowitz, F. D. (1982). Methods of assessment for high-risk and handicapped infants. In C. T. Ramey and P. L. Trohanis (Eds.), *Finding and educating high-risk and handicapped infants* (pp. 101–118). Baltimore, MD: University Park Press.

Hunt, J. M. (1961). *Intelligence and experience.* NY: Ronald Press.

Ianni, F. A., and Orr, M. T. (1979). Toward a rapprochement of quantitative and qualitative methodologies. In T. D. Cook and C. S. Reichardt (Eds.), *Qualitative and quantitative methods in evaluation research* (pp. 87–98). Beverly Hills, CA: Sage.

Jacobs, F. (1984). The state-of-the-art in family program evaluation. In H. Weiss and F. Jacobs (Eds.), *Final report to the Mott Foundation: The effectiveness and evaluation of family support and education programs* (pp. 64–98). Cambridge, MA: Harvard Family Research Project.

Jacobs, F., and Weiss, H. (1985). Evaluating Family Programs. Workshop presented at the National Association of Young Children Annual Conference, New Orleans, Louisiana, November 14.

Lasch, C. (1977). *Haven in a heartless world: The family besieged.* NY: Basic Books.

Lazerson, M. (1983). The origins of special education. In J. G. Chambers and W. T. Hartman (Eds.), *Special education politics* (pp. 15–47). Philadelphia, PA: Temple University Press.

Lewin, K. (1946). Action research and minority problems. *Journal of Social Issues, 2,* 34–46.

Light, R. J., and Pillemer, D. B. (1984). *Summing up: The science of reviewing research.* Cambridge, MA: Harvard University Press.

McLaughlin, M. W. (1980). Evaluation and alchemy. In J. Pincus (Ed.), *Educational evaluation in the public setting* (R-2502-RC, pp. 41–47). Santa Monica, CA: Rand Corporation.

MacRae, D., Jr., and Haskins, R. (1981). Models for policy analysis. In R. Haskins and J. J. Gallagher (Eds.), *Models for analysis of social policy: An Introduction* (pp. 1–36). Norwood, NJ: Ablex.

Maling, J., and Keepes, B. (1985). Educational research and evaluation. In E. Eisner (Ed.), *Learning and teaching the ways of knowing* (pp. 265–286). Chicago, IL: National Society for the Study of Education.

Mercer, J. R., and Richardson, J. G. (1976). "Mental retardation" as a social problem. In N. Hobbs (Ed.), *Issues in the classification of children.* Vol. 2 (pp. 463–496). San Francisco, CA: Jossey-Bass.

Minnesota Department of Education, Division of Development and Partnership (March 1986). Evaluation Study of Early Childhood Family Education: Report to the Legislature.

Minuchin, P. (1985). Families and individual development: Provocations from the field of family therapy. *Child Development, 56,* 389–302.

Mishler, E. G. (1979). Meaning in context: Is there any other kind? *Harvard Educational Review, 49,* 1–19.

Morris, L. L., and Fitz-Gibbon, C. T. (1978). *How to measure program implementation.* Beverly Hills, CA: Sage.

Moynihan, D. P. (1969). *Maximum feasible misunderstanding: Community action in the War On Poverty.* NY: Free Press.

Murray, C. (1984). *Losing ground: American social policy 1950–1980.* NY: Basic Books.

Nevo, D. (1983). The conceptualization of educational evaluation: An analytical review of the literature. *Review of Educational Research, 53*(1), 117–128.

Patton, M. Q. (1978). *Utilization-focused evaluation.* Beverly Hills, CA: Sage.

Patton, M. Q. (1980). *Qualitative evaluation methods.* Beverly Hills, CA: Sage.

Patton, M. Q. (1982). *Practical evaluation.* Beverly Hills, CA: Sage.

Pettigrew, T. (1985). Can social scientists be effective actors in the policy arena? In R. L. Shotland and M. M. Mark (Eds.), *Social science and social policy* (p. 121–134). Beverly Hills, CA: Sage.

Pincus, J. (1980). The state of educational evaluation: Reflections and a summary. In J. Pincus (Ed.), *Educational evaluation in the public policy setting* (R-2502-RC, pp. 1–10). Santa Monica, CA: Rand Corporation.

Preston, S. H. (May 1984). *Children and the elderly: Divergent paths of America's dependents.* Presidential address to the Population Association of America, Minneapolis, Minnesota.

Rapoport, R. N. (Ed.) (1985). *Children, youth, and families: The action-research relationship.* NY: Cambridge University Press.

Reichardt, C. S., and Cook, T. D. (Eds.) (1979). *Qualitative and quantitative methods in evaluation research.* Beverly Hills, CA: Sage.

Rist, R. C. (1980). Blitzkrieg ethnography: On the transformation of a method into a movement. *Educational Researcher,* 8–10.

Rivlin, A. M., and Timpane, P. M. (1975). Planned variation in education: An assessment. In A. M. Rivlin and P. M. Timpane (Eds.), *Planned variation in education: Should we give up or try harder?* (pp. 1–22). Washington, D.C.: The Brookings Institute.

Select Committee of Children, Youth, and Families. (1984). *Families and child care: Improving the options.* Washington, D.C.: U.S. House of Representatives.

Senna, C. (1973). *The fallacy of I.Q.* NY: The Third Press.

Shils, E. (1980). *The calling of sociology.* Chicago, IL: The University of Chicago Press.

Shonkoff, J. P. (1983). The limitations of normative assessment of high-risk infants. *Topics in Early Childhood Special Education, 3*(1), 29–43.

Sidel, R. (1986). *Women and children last: The plight of poor women in affluent America.* NY: Viking.

Tavris, C. (September 1976). Compensatory education: The glass is half full. *Psychology Today,* 63–74.

Travers, J. R., and Light, R. J. (Eds.) (1982). *Learning from experience: Evaluating early childhood demonstration programs.* Washington, D.C.: National Academy Press.

Upshur, C. (1982). *How to set up and operate a non-profit organization.* Englewood Cliffs, NJ: Prentice-Hall.

Walker, D. (1973). *Socioemotional measures for preschool and kindergarten children: A handbook.* San Francisco, CA: Jossey-Bass.

Webb, E. J., Campbell, D. T., Schwartz, R. D., and Sechrest, L. (1966). *Unobtrusive measures: Nonreactive research in the social sciences.* Chicago, IL: Rand McNally.

Weiss, C. H. (1983a). Ideology, interests, and information. In D. Callahan and B. Jennings (Eds.), *Ethics, the social sciences, and policy analysis* (pp. 213–245). NY: Plenum Press.

Weiss, C. H. (1983b). The stakeholder approach to evaluation: Origins and promise. In A. S. Bryk (Ed.), *Stakeholder-based evaluation* (pp. 3–14). San Francisco, CA: Jossey-Bass.

Weiss, H., and Hite, S. (1986). Evaluation: Who's doing it and how? *Family Resource Coalition Report, 5*(3), 4–7.

Weissbourd (1983) *The family support movement: Greater than the sum of its parts.* Paper presented at a Conference on Family Support Programs: The State-of-The-Art. Sponsored by the Bush Center in Child Development and Social Policy, Yale University, New Haven, CT, May 1983.

Westinghouse Learning Corporation/Ohio University (April 1969). *An evaluation of the effects of Head Start experience on children's cognitive and affective development (Preliminary Draft).* Author.

White House Conference on Families (October 1980). *Listening to*

American families: Action for the 1980s: The report to the President, Congress, and families of the nation. Washington, D.C.: Author.

Wholey, J. S. (1977). Evaluability assessment. In L. Rutman (Ed.), *Evaluation research methods: A basic guide* (pp. 39–56). Beverly Hills, CA: Sage.

Zigler, E. (1979). Project Head Start: Success or failure? In E. Zigler and J. Valentine (Eds.), *Project Head Start: A legacy of the war on poverty* (pp. 495–507). NY: Free Press.

part II

MEASURING CHILD, PARENT, AND FAMILY OUTCOMES

Family support programs present a unique set of challenges to program evaluators. Their diversity of target populations, service models, program size and resources, their attitudes toward research activity, and their insistence on an ecological view of child development demand creative and practical evaluation strategies. The chapters in this section, taking seriously the field's commitment to ecological intervention, suggest measures and methods to assess program processes and impacts along an ecological continuum including children, parents, parent–child dyads, families and social support networks. In our view it is only with such diverse means of measurement that we can increase our understanding of program impacts and the means by which they are achieved.

Evaluations to date have focused primarily on child-oriented outcomes, relying often on measures of intelligence and achievement. Hauser-Cram and Shonkoff detail the limitations of this approach and recommend that evaluators assess a wider range of functional domains, considering both long-term and short-term child impacts. For example, they suggest a shift toward studying the effects of interventions on social competence and individual adaptation, an orientation that validates gains made by children with atypical as well as typical developmental patterns.

While the ultimate goal of many family support programs is to improve child functioning, many programs seek to enhance parent–child interactions as the primary route toward this end. Howrigan discusses the limitations of current theory and methodology in this area of research, then recommends consideration of observational measures of interaction. Howrigan identifies the most common obstacles and pitfalls to observational evaluation research and discusses the merits of both standardized and nonstandardized measures.

Often parents by themselves are the intended beneficiaries of family support programming, although sometimes they are not acknowledged as such in evaluation designs. Upshur distinguishes those interventions meant to change parents in their parenting roles (e.g., those that enhance knowledge of child development) from interventions meant to affect some aspect of their general adult status (e.g., those that provide employment counseling). She suggests that both sets of goals are legitimate for these programs and proposes a range of measures and procedures to assess program impact in these domains.

Walker and Crocker begin the discussion of measuring family-level impacts, which is continued by Krauss. Walker and Crocker maintain that many family support programs are misnamed, dealing not so much with the family as with subgroupings within it. Hence, many do not expect or cannot document family-level effects to their interventions. Nonetheless, to the extent that programs seek to improve family functioning, they should consider a family systems orientation for their services and for the design of their evaluations. Walker and Crocker do not recommend any single global measure in this domain but review several acceptable instruments that address key aspects to family functioning.

Krauss explores a particular type of impact felt at the family level: the amelioration of stress experienced by young families. She argues convincingly for consideration of this outcome in the evaluation of family support programs, especially those dealing with at-risk or troubled families. She concludes, however, that theoretical frameworks for understanding stress and coping and the clinical practice of such interventions outstrip the capacities of current instrumentation and suggests a partnership among researchers, program personnel, and evaluators in the development and refinement of relevant measures.

Many family support programs seek to enhance the relationship of participant families to their larger community, including neighbors, extended family members, and other potential providers of formal and informal social support. Cleary outlines the many ways in which social support has been conceptualized and measured, and he reviews a number of measures available to tap these various aspects of social support. He suggests that there are a plethora of social support instruments—including a number with sound psychometric properties— but that their direct relevance to any given family program may be limited; thus, programs may be required to develop their own instrumentation.

In our work at the Family Research Project we have become aware that program directors and evaluators can benefit not only from the kind of conceptual help provided in these chapters, but also from practical help in gathering information about measures and in procuring measures from their authors or publishers. Therefore we have compiled a list of all the measures described in this section (Appendix A) and have identified their sources as a practical contribution to our readers.

RETHINKING THE ASSESSMENT OF CHILD-FOCUSED OUTCOMES

Penny Hauser-Cram
Jack P. Shonkoff

For the past 20 years the thinking of social policy planners and evaluators of family support and education programs has been dominated by assessments of IQ, school readiness, and cognitive achievement. Other areas of child performance (e.g., social competence) have been examined less frequently, and effects on parents, family, or community systems have been virtually ignored. Increasingly, however, those who seek to assess the value of intervention services acknowledge the need to examine a wider range of program effects.

The growing attention to broader, more ecologic domains presents an exciting opportunity for reconceptualizing the child-oriented impacts of family services. As the burden of demonstrating program effectiveness is distributed more evenly across multiple dependent variables, opportunities arise for greater creativity in assessment. This chapter provides a brief overview of traditional approaches to child-focused outcome evaluations, explores contemporary assessment issues, and suggests an agenda for further investigation.

Traditional Approaches to Child-Focused Outcomes

Supportive and educational services for families with young children are designed to serve a wide spectrum of needs. Most attempt to prevent developmental attrition (i.e., "falling behind") in young children whose vulnerability is defined primarily by risk factors associated with poverty or social disorganization. Head Start centers are a classic ex-

ample of this type of service (Zigler and Valentine, 1979). Other programs providing early intervention services aim at ameliorating adverse
impacts and preventing secondary handicaps in children with specific
developmental disabilities related to biological vulnerability, such as
cerebral palsy or sensory impairment. Prototypes of such service programs include a variety of projects supported by the Handicapped
Children's Early Education Program and approved by the Joint Dissemination Review Panel of the United States Department of Education
(White, Mastropieri, and Casto, 1984). Despite marked variations in
service models, target populations, and the methodological quality of
program evaluations, the primary focus on child-oriented cognitive
outcomes has been striking.

Countless philosophical debates and political battles have been
waged over the goals and objectives of early childhood programs, but
promoting individual cognitive development has rarely fallen far from
the top of the list. For example, despite the mandate of Head Start to
influence a broad range of outcomes, including the health status of
children and the level of community involvement demonstrated by
participating parents, more than half of its effectiveness studies have
focused primarily on children's IQ scores (Jacobs, Chapter 2, this volume; Zigler and Valentine, 1979). Similarly, in a meta-analytic review
of 31 studies of early intervention services for biologically impaired
infants and young children, we (Shonkoff and Hauser-Cram, in press)
found IQ/DQ (developmental quotient) or age equivalence to be the
unit of effectiveness reported in the majority of the studies.

NORMATIVE SCALES OF DEVELOPMENT/INTELLIGENCE

Standardized developmental scales for infants and intelligence tests
for older preschoolers have been the most frequently employed measures of effectiveness of early childhood programs. Their well-documented psychometric properties and relative ease of administration
have contributed much to their appeal. As children approach school
age, the increasing validity of the IQ as a predictor of academic performance strengthens its salience for policymakers who view success
in school as the foremost socially desirable outcome for youngsters in
a competitive society. Despite their widespread use, however, standardized cognitive tests have important limitations as measures of program efficacy.

Infant and Toddler Instruments

For infants and toddlers under 2 years of age, more than 100 instruments are available to evaluate developmental status (Johnson and

Kopp, 1980). Although most assessment measures for this age group are adaptations of the Gesell Developmental Schedules (Gesell, Halverson, Thompson, Ilg, Castner, Ames, Amatruda, 1940), relatively few have supportive data regarding their reliability or validity. In fact, the Gesell Schedules themselves are best considered as a detailed observational record of a child's developmental status, rather than as an instrument with secure psychometric properties (Meisels, 1987).

The best standardized and most frequently employed measure is the Bayley Scales of Infant Development (BSID) (Bayley, 1969). The BSID consists of a Mental Scale of 163 items and a Motor Scale of 81 items. The range of skills assessed on the Mental Scale includes sensory–perceptual discriminations, acquisition of object permanence, memory, problem-solving strategies, learning facility, verbal communication, and ability to classify objects and make generalizations. The Motor Scale consists of items related to gross body control (e.g., lateral head movements, sitting, walking) and fine motor activities (e.g., use of a pincer grasp). The BSID was normed on a sample of 1262 children aged 2–30 months. Although its test items cover a wide range of domains, even those that appear to be tapping cognitive abilities are heavily reliant on motor skills. Separation of the scale into motor and mental components therefore can be misleading. Indeed, the correlation between standard scores on the Mental and Motor Scales is high for the younger ages ($r = .75$ at 6 months) and tends to decrease with age. The BSID is not unique in its reliance on motor skills. Other popular instruments, such as the Cattell Infant Intelligence Scale (Cattell, 1940) or the Griffiths Mental Development Scale for Testing Babies from Birth to Two Years (Griffiths, 1951) suffer from the same drawbacks. The assessment of cognitive abilities in infants or toddlers with significant motor impairment remains a major unresolved dilemma.

Instrument selection for measuring developmental progress in infants and toddlers demands a clear recognition of the domains of early childhood evaluation. Standardized developmental tests for infants generally tap perceptual and perceptual–motor skills whose relationship to later cognitive functioning is tenuous, even though they are often characterized as cognitive assessment measures. When such normative instruments are used to assess infants of minority cultural groups or those whose atypical development is related to biological vulnerability or frank central nervous system dysfunction, their diagnostic and prognostic value becomes even more limited. In fact, seemingly pathological responses on normative infant testing may reflect alternative adaptive behaviors that can be understood only in the context of an individual child's unique characteristics and the environment in which he or she lives (Shonkoff, 1983). The withdrawal reaction of a premature baby when presented with moderate visual or auditory stimulation is an example of such a behavior.

Preschool IQ Measures (2–6 Years)

Standardized IQ tests have dominated the evaluation of preschool children. The oldest established instrument for assessing IQ in children as young as 2 years is the Stanford–Binet Intelligence Scale (Form L-M) (Terman and Merrill, 1937). It consists of 142 items that assess both verbal and nonverbal intelligence, including such factors as memory, conceptual thinking, reasoning, numerical competence, language, visual–motor skills, and social understanding. Because the test is constructed so that task presentation ceases when a child fails items at a certain level, most children are presented only 18 to 24 tasks. The generation of a single test score—the overall IQ—rather than a profile reflecting different aspects of a child's functioning is a major shortcoming except for programs that focus on IQ status as a specific goal.

The Wechsler Preschool and Primary Scale of Intelligence (WPPSI) (Wechsler, 1967) is another popular standard preschool IQ instrument. It assesses mental skills in children from the ages of 4 to 6.5 years and consists of eleven subtests: six verbal (information, vocabulary, arithmetic, similarities, comprehension, and optional sentence) and five performance (animal house, picture completion, mazes, geometric design, and block design). Unlike the Stanford–Binet, the WPPSI yields performance, verbal, and full-scale IQ scores, thus providing an intellectual profile as well as an overall index of "intelligence." Like the Stanford–Binet, it is best suited as an outcome measure for programs aimed at changing IQ status.

A third and increasingly popular measure for assessment of preschoolers is the McCarthy Scale of Children's Abilities (McCarthy, 1970). Although on some subtests this scale suffers from requiring failure on a specified number of items before testing ceases, it provides assessment of the 2.5- to 8.5-year-old child across a wide range of domains of development. A "general cognitive" score, which can be derived from a combination of item scores, has been shown to correlate at .71 with the WPPSI Full Scale IQ and at .81 with the Stanford–Binet (Form L-M) IQ.

The Peabody Picture Vocabulary Test-Revised (PPVT-R) (Dunn and Dunn, 1959) is another commonly employed measure, with a more narrow focus. This test requires little special training and little time for administration. The examiner reads a stimulus word, the child points to the picture best illustrated by that word. The items are arranged in ascending order of difficulty, and the test is continued until six failures out of eight consecutive responses are recorded. Although an IQ score can be derived from this test, the PPVT-R clearly taps only one aspect of mental activity-receptive vocabulary. Its use as an outcome measure for a program designed to have impact in other areas would be inappropriate.

The value of any single test for assessing a child's progress in a program is of course dependent on the program's goals. Critics have pointed out that, although IQ scores certainly reflect a child's basic cognitive abilities, they are affected by past experiences as well as by individual personality variables and motivation in a formal testing session. In fact, Zigler and Trickett (1978) charge that IQ shifts resulting from preschool intervention programs are more often reflective of motivational factors that influence test performance than changes in a child's intrinsic cognitive functioning. The cultural biases of standardized intelligence tests have been well described and debated vigorously in both the scholarly literature and popular media (Gardner, 1983; Gould, 1981; Hafner and White, 1981; Kamin, 1974; Mercer, 1974; Oakland, 1977). Although an IQ score remains a strong predictor of school achievement, it accounts for only half of the variance and reflects an inadequate sampling of the skills and competencies of low-income children (Zigler and Trickett, 1978). As one of several outcome measures, an IQ score can be very useful. As the only measure of program effectiveness, an IQ score may be inappropriate and misleading.

Instruments for the School-Age Child

In addition to traditional cognitive measures, numerous instruments are available for assessing development in the school-age years. One popular area of focus for child-oriented outcomes in program evaluation has involved the concept of screening for school readiness. In general terms, this refers to the identification of developmentally appropriate skills and behaviors that are presumed to be prerequisites for successful performance in the early elementary grades. A multitude of screening batteries and diagnostic instruments have been employed to evaluate individual function in such areas as gross and fine motor abilities, receptive and expressive language competence, perceptual discrimination, visual–perceptual–motor skills, mastery of simple math concepts, and behavioral characteristics related to the development of selective attention.

A widely used screening measure for children about to enter either kindergarten or first grade is the Metropolitan Readiness Test (Nurss and McGauvran, 1933). This instrument yields four scores: reading readiness, number readiness, draw-a-man (optional), and total readiness. It appears to have adequate predictive validity, at least in determining those children who will be at either end of the scale in reading skills after several months of instruction. The Denver Developmental Screening Test (DDST) (Frankenburg and Dodds, 1967) is another commonly employed preschool screening instrument. It assesses four areas of development: personal–social, fine motor–adaptive, language, and gross motor. Although often administered at the time of school entry, the DDST can also be used with younger children, including infants or toddlers.

The proper use of screening instruments is to identify children who may have problems in certain areas of development, so that school personnel can be alerted to those youngsters who may not optimally benefit from traditional instruction or who may need additional services. Such measures do not generate a diagnosis or represent a complete evaluation of a child's skills. Because screening tests often fail to indicate a child's strengths sufficiently, they should be used only as a first step to further evaluation, not as an outcome measure (Hauser-Cram, 1979).

A second area of performance scrutinized by traditional outcome evaluations of school-age children is the measurement of academic achievement. This may involve multidimensional assessments as well as the specific evaluation of individual content areas. One instrument often used to measure overall academic progress is the Wide Range Achievement Test (WRAT) (Jastek and Jastek, 1965). This test yields three measures of achievement: reading, including pronunciation of visually presented unrelated words; arithmetic, including the solution of written and orally presented problems; and spelling, involving the dictation of single words. There are many other popular and similar achievement tests, including the California Achievement Tests: Forms C and D (CTB/McGraw-Hill, 1970), Iowa Tests of Basic Skills (Hieronymous, Lindquist, and Hoover, 1955), and the Metropolitan Achievement Test (Durost, 1961). Subtests of these instruments are often used to measure achievement in specific skill areas. The use of such tests as outcome measures is most appropriate for programs designed to improve academic performance. Because standardized achievement tests allow comparisons to be made across schools, they can be useful components in an evaluation battery.

Summary of Current Practice

The popularity of standardized IQ tests, formal screening of preschool readiness skills, and documentation of academic achievement are well entrenched in our culture. Although extensive training of examiners is required, such measures are fairly quick and easy to administer, and conventional statistical analyses can be used to compare a group's performance to the larger population for which mean scores and the standard deviation are known.

Given the advantages of conventional child outcome measures, why is it necessary to reconsider our reliance on such instruments? First, IQ and achievement tests are narrow in their focus; programs typically aim to change behavior in many domains (such as socialization and motivation) that are not adequately tapped directly by such traditional tests. Particularly in programs for preschool children, the focus of intervention may be on learning strategies rather than acquisition of new information. Second, traditional measures by themselves yield few compelling policy implications. What, for example, is the social significance of improving IQ scores by 5 points? Does it mean that children will perform better in school or achieve greater productivity in later life? Will the school system be spared additional costs for these youngsters? Policymakers often demand outcomes that can be linked to school and life success, as well as to societal costs. Programs that can demonstrate cost-savings, as well as long-term success, certainly improve their chance to win political support.

An overwhelming emphasis on standardized cognitive outcomes to measure the effects of early education and family-support programs is clearly problematic. The narrow scope of such measures fails to tap the breadth and richness of program impacts on children. The traditional focus on "the mean" undermines an appreciation of alternative developmental pathways and individual differences within the "normal" population. The pass/fail orientation to the assessment of task-oriented skills often does not identify competence that is not reflected in subtest or summary scores. The cultural biases against ethnic minorities and economically disadvantaged groups often confuse the stigmatizing concept of "abnormality" with the very different problem of competitive disadvantage within a specific social system. Finally, the inevitable devaluation of atypical developmental patterns of children with discrete disabilities precludes the recognition that some deviance may be quite adaptive. The temperamentally passive child whose information-processing style is more intuitive than sequential, for example, and the youngster of average ability whose disorganized family life has provided minimal models for planning task completion, may each perform poorly on a standardized test (and, indeed, may be at risk for problems in school) without being "abnormal." Similarly, neither the child with cerebral palsy who will never speak clearly but has learned the use of a communication board, nor the blind infant who is delayed in mastering the challenges of mobility, will have his or her abilities reflected adequately through a standardized cognitive measure. The need is clear to shift from insistence on conformity to traditional test norms toward a greater focus on social competence and individual adaptation.

EXTENDING THE BASE OF CHILD-FOCUSED OUTCOMES

Demands for accountability in the use of public resources and recognition of the limitations of conventional cognitive instruments demand a critical reassessment of child-oriented outcomes and their measurement. An obvious starting point is the clarification of specific program goals and objectives.

Early childhood family-oriented programs have traditionally served two related yet distinct populations. One group includes children for whom normative development is an achievable goal. Such youngsters are free of significant constitutional limitations and live within poor or disorganized families that present a mix of risk factors (e.g., parental stress, poor nutrition) and protective factors (e.g., high parental aspirations for child) that contribute to child developmental outcomes. For these children the program goals are to maintain optimal progress and prevent developmental or behavioral attrition despite environmental constraints.

The second group is composed of children for whom atypical development is inevitable. Such youngsters have specific biological disabilities that preclude normal development (e.g., spina bifida, Down syndrome) and receive environmental supports of varied quality (e.g., strong parent–child attachment, maternal depression). For these children, program goals focus on facilitating adaptive behavior and functional competence within the limits determined by each child's individual deficits and strengths. The exclusive use of normative instruments for such youngsters condemns them to automatic failure.

The dependent variables and outcome measures for these two intervention groups clearly do not overlap entirely. Clarifying their essential differences highlights the inappropriateness of using a single test or uniform battery of tests to evaluate child-oriented effects in all family programs. Instead, evaluators must select individualized measures powerful and sensitive enough to detect meaningful changes predicted by program objectives. If dependent variables are too globally defined, it may be difficult to design measures of sufficient sensitivity to reflect the more subtle yet important changes that occur as a result of a specific intervention. For example, a therapeutic program for children with cerebral palsy may have a significant effect on the quality of a child's coordination but not influence the age of onset of walking (as reflected in a global gross motor score). The selection of outcome variables and measurement instruments must be tailored to the specific goals and objectives developed for each distinct target population.

Only in relation to program goals can the relative merits of quantitative measures compared to ethnographic or descriptive techniques of data collection be assessed and evaluation strategies be developed. For some programs, the benefits of the analytic opportunities offered by quantitative data will outweigh the richness and depth provided by qualitative information. For others, it will work the other way around. When programs require the assessment of variables for which tests with well-developed psychometric properties are not available, multiple measures offer greater validity. In attempting to evaluate attentional factors in a preschool child, for example, one might use questionnaires to elicit teacher and parent ratings in conjunction with observational measures taken in both naturalistic and controlled laboratory settings.

Several logistical caveats must be kept in mind when considering the assessment of young, vulnerable children. For example, the test administrator's ability to elicit optimal performance may have an impact on the results. Where the test is administered—at home or in a clinical setting—may also affect a young child's responses. Similarly, characteristics of the examiner, such as gender and race, can influence children's test-taking behaviors (Sheehan and Keogh, 1981). In the assessment of handicapped children some researchers (Fuchs, Fuchs, Power, and Dailey, 1985) have found that examiner unfamiliarity had a negative impact on the child's test performance. Such situational factors must be considered and controlled for in research design and analysis.

Finally, child-focused outcomes must be defined in terms of both short-term/immediate effects and long-term/persistent or "sleeper" effects. The former typically address specific skill areas (e.g., motor skills, language performance, cognitive abilities) and have been the most frequently studied impacts of intervention programs; long-term outcomes, on the other hand, have been less well studied. They present greater analytical challenges and offer exciting opportunities to document more substantive and far-reaching program effects. Persistent long-term impacts might include sustained improvement in self-esteem and task motivation. Sleeper effects may be reflected in less need for special education services, more frequent completion of high school, avoidance of delinquency, and successful employment in adult life. Long-term outcomes are frequently emphasized as important policy-relevant variables (e.g., see Berrueta-Clement, Schweinhart, Barnett, Epstein, and Weikart, 1984; Lazar and Darlington, 1982). The policy implications of short-term developmental outcomes, on the other hand, should not be devalued; they may be of particular interest to researchers interested in developmental transactions. Short-term child gains may be critical determinants of the kind of change in parental aspirations and behaviors that lead to sustained impacts on the parent–child relationship, with subsequently improved outcomes for both.

Assessment of a broad range of both short- and long-term impacts is likely to satisfy the information needs of a diverse audience. The discovery of unanticipated outcomes (both positive and negative) also requires broad assessments. A program that encourages a great deal of parent–child interaction, for example, may result in a child's enhanced linguistic skills but unanticipated increased dependence on the mother. The relative salience of individual variables and the availability of assessment instruments will vary considerably.

In summary, evaluations must assess a wider range of functional domains than traditional verbal and motor areas and must address both
short- and long-term outcomes that have broad significance beyond
the results of academically oriented achievement tests. Differential
evaluation formats are essential for handicapped and atypical children
to assess developmental progress and adaptation within the framework
of the individual child's assets and liabilities.

NEW DOMAINS OF EVALUATION

This section explores two related developmental domains that program evaluators might consider in expanding the scope of child-focused
outcome assessments: social competence and self-regulatory behaviors. The purpose of this discussion is to suggest areas that deserve a
closer look in assessing the impact of family programs rather than to
endorse any one instrument. Health indexes, although often included
as important outcomes for programs serving young children and families, require extensive elaboration and will not be addressed in this
chapter.

Many dimensions of child function are worthy of consideration as
outcome measures for family programs; social competence and self-
regulatory behaviors are particularly salient. Despite the fact that no
universally accepted definitions of their underlying constructs have
emerged, these two related dimensions represent aspects of child development that many programs attempt to influence. Debates continue
regarding those variables that define the parameters of these child
characteristics; not surprisingly, the instruments available to tap them
lack the psychometric properties of more conventional measures.
Nevertheless, gathering meaningful data about the benefits and drawbacks of family programs requires an expanded view of child outcomes.
The following section is intended to establish a framework for this wider
perspective by suggesting measures that represent promising new approaches to evaluation.

Social Competence

Despite the attractiveness of individual social competence as a measure of a program's success, even some of its strongest advocates (e.g.,
Zigler and Trickett, 1978) admit that its definition is vague and elusive.
Most agree, however, that social competence is expressed both within
and outside of the school context. In fact, academic achievement is
not strictly tied to social competence. A child may be successful academically but demonstrate poor peer relationships or, conversely, have

difficulty meeting school requirements but get along well socially with peers and adults.

Schools frequently judge successful students through the use of standardized achievement tests. While scores on such tests certainly have value as outcome measures and allow comparisons to be made between schools and across school districts, other variables are also important, as they allow for comparisons of a range of domains of social competence within the constraints of a particular school environment. These include school grades, promotion or graduation, and the need for special education, counseling, or tutorial services. Furthermore, some of these variables can be used in analyses of costs and benefits (see White, this volume, Chapter 19). If, for example, a school saves on tutorial expenses as a result of a specific early prevention program, school officials may view that program as more successful (and more worthy of continued support) than one that raises the mean achievement scores of average students by a few points. Especially in times of reduced public resources, evaluators must include outcomes that yield measurable economic benefits, even if such outcomes do not allow easy comparisons across settings.

Another set of school-related social competence measures relates to students' commitments and attitudes. Such measures as rates of absenteeism, completion of homework, teacher and student ratings of classroom behavior, attitudes toward school, and aspirations for the future are likely to correlate highly with assessments of academic achievement; when combined with formal performance measures, they produce a fuller picture of school success.

Social competence measures of school function and commitment have been employed in several well-known program evaluations. In one of the first published documents to focus on global measures of school success as a reflection of program impact, Lazar and Darlington (1982) pooled data from fifteen studies on early education projects and performed secondary analyses using measures such as assignment to special education, retention in grade, student ratings of school performance, and maternal attitudes toward a child's school performance. Seitz, Rosenbaum, and Apfel (1985) developed a similar combined index of school adjustment in their 10-year follow-up evaluation of a support and intervention program for impoverished families with young children. Their index assessed the following: poor achievement (a year or more below the actual grade level), absenteeism (20 or more absences during the school year), classroom behavior problems based on teacher ratings, and reception of school services related to remediation or school adjustment.

Berrueta-Clement *et al.* (1984) developed yet another set of school-competence measures to assess the impact of the Perry Preschool Project on youth through 19 years of age. They included items such as mean number of days absent per year, mean number of grades repeated, percentage of children classified as handicapped, percentage of time spent in special education placement, percentage of children receiving special services, and number of failing grades obtained per year. Students were also interviewed about their aspirations, attitudes toward services, and time spent on homework. Furthermore, outcomes were linked to an economic analysis of costs expended or saved, based on the assumption that successful school performance saves money for schools and society.

A similar battery of school competence measures could be modified for the evaluation of handicapped children. Absenteeism, for example, is as important for atypical populations as it is for nondisabled populations. Although retention in grade may be a less meaningful measure for the handicapped child, extent or type of special education and related services is clearly important. In such cases, analyses of cost savings could include estimates of reductions in needed services and prevention of more restrictive placements as a result of specific interventions.

Although social competence in childhood is tied closely to the demands of school, it applies broadly to the realm of interpersonal relationships. Dimensions that may be worthy of measurement include collaborative interaction, sharing materials, combining resources with others, and asserting rights appropriately; important interactions with adults include using them as resources, following directions, and accepting limits and responsibilities. One method of assessing peer interactions involves observation of children in a natural setting, like a classroom. The Executive Skills Profile (Bronson, 1975) is one tool that provides just such an opportunity to measure a child's ability to successfully influence others with appropriate and effective "cooperative strategies" such as using words rather than force. This instrument was used in the evaluation of the Brookline Early Education Project (Pierson, Walker, and Tivnan, 1984) and has demonstrated sensitivity to change in the preschool and young elementary age group. Like other observation measures, however, it is rather expensive to administer because of the need to train observers and to analyze voluminous data.

An alternative type of social competence measure that is quicker and less costly to administer involves ratings made by teachers or parents. Compared to direct observations, this approach is prone to greater bias since it taps perceptions rather than samples of behavior. However, programs often aim to change perceptions as well as behavior. Perhaps the best known and most rigorously standardized behavioral rating scale is the Child Behavior Checklist (CBCL) developed for children between the ages of 4 and 16 years (Achenbach and Edelbrock, 1981). The CBCL consists of 118 behavior problems (such as "argues a lot," "too dependent") and 20 social competence items, and includes school-related questions about academic performance, special class placement, and grade retention. The CBCL is constructed so that changes in behavioral status can be analyzed either by specific categories of problems or by the total number of problems listed. The unavailability of norms for children under 4 years of age or youngsters with handicaps, however, limits its applicability for evaluating the effects of many family programs.

An alternative instrument for evaluators interested in the social competence of younger or atypical children is the restandardized Vineland Adaptive Behavior Scales (Sparrow, Balla, and Cicchetti, 1984). This 577 item questionnaire is divided into five domains with eleven sub-domains: communication (retentive, expressive, written); daily living skills (personal, domestic, community); motor skills (fine, gross); socialization (interpersonal, play and leisure time, coping skills); and maladaptive behavior. Normative data were obtained from a representative national sample of 3000 individuals, with approximately 100 in each of 30 age groups between birth and 18 years, 11 months. The Vineland yields an Adaptive Behavior Composite score that can be derived from the responses of parents, teachers, or service providers. The revised Vineland is too new to have been used extensively, but it appears most promising.

Self-Regulatory Behaviors

Many programs for families with young children aim to promote the development of the child's problem-solving skills, focusing on approaches taken to tasks, rather than on the attainment of correct solutions or the acquisition of new knowledge. However, as Miller and Dyer (1975) pointed out, few measures of self-regulatory behavior have been developed with adequate reliability and predictive validity; this observation remains true today for attention, motivation, and curiosity.

Attention. The most frequently studied behavioral characteristic that could be described as self-regulatory is attention. Volumes of work in cognitive psychology have focused on different aspects of this developmental trait. Generally, attention has not been conceptualized as a unitary construct but, rather, as consisting of several elements including a selective process (that allows discrimination between relevant and irrelevant information), an intensive process (that allows the amount of focused attention to vary), and a sustaining process (that permits heightened or prolonged receptivity to a specific input) (Parasuraman and Davies, 1984). Although considerable laboratory research has been conducted on attentional processes, investigation in applied settings has been much less frequent (Hale and Lewis, 1979). Furthermore, measures of attention have rarely been included in family program evaluation batteries, because of the paucity of measures with adequate validity and utility in applied settings.

Three types of measures have been developed to assess attention:

1. *Parent or teacher checklists,* such as those devised by Conners (1969, 1970) are designed to facilitate the identification of "hyperactive" children. They are of limited value in assessing subtle differences among normal children.

2. *Direct observation measures* for use in a school setting typically employ time-sampled or event-sampled assessments of children's classroom activities, with coding of such parameters as task persistence, task involvement, and frequency of inattention, along with a wide range of behaviors and activities (Coller, 1972; Schaefer and Aaronson, 1967; Stallings, 1972). Stallings (1972) used such a measure in an assessment of the Head Start and Follow Through Programs and demonstrated its utility as an evaluation instrument.

3. *Vigilance tasks,* such as the Matching Familiar Figures Test, distinguish between two cognitive styles that relate to attention: "reflective" children, who focus on parts of presented stimuli, and "impulsive" children, who respond to a gestalt impression instead of individual selection of relevant features (Siegelman, 1969). Differences in these styles were shown to correlate with differences in reading achievement in elementary school children (Kagan, 1964), but the validity of this test as an evaluation instrument has yet to be determined.

Motivation and Curiosity

Other self-regulatory behaviors, such as motivation and curiosity, have been studied less extensively by developmental researchers but occasionally have been included in evaluation batteries. Such qualities include seeking out variation in response to a repetitive task and relying on internal resources rather than external cues in problem solving.

Two measures of motivation were used by Trickett, Apfel, Rosenbaum, and Zigler (1982) as part of an evaluation battery for the Yale Child Welfare Research Project. One task, "The Box Maze" (Harter and Zigler, 1974), involved scoring the number of unique paths the child creates in completing a maze. This measure was found to discriminate between institutionalized and noninstitutionalized retarded individuals and among children of different socioeconomic groups. Achenbach and Zigler (1968) measured the degree to which children imitated a model in completing a picture using stickers and were able to discriminate reliably between normal and retarded children.

A more comprehensive selection of tasks, The Cincinnati Autonomy Test Battery (CATB) (Banta, 1970), generates test scores on fourteen variables including, among others, curiosity, innovative behavior, impulse control, reflectivity, incidental learning, intentional learning, persistence, resistance to distraction, and curiosity verbalization. Details of the tasks related to each of the fourteen variables, intercorrelations among performances on those various tasks, and correlations with Stanford–Binet IQ scores have all been reviewed by Banta (1970). Miller and Dyer (1975) selected those tasks with the highest reliability ratings and used them to analyze the effects of four different preschool programs. They found that these measures (which include the child's tendency to explore, manipulate, and investigate novel materials) to varying extents differentiated among preschool programs. Although these measures were developed for research purposes, further elaboration of these and similar measures may be promising for outcome evaluation.

Few tests of self-regulatory behavior have been developed to assess infants and toddlers. One measure that has received increased attention in the child-development literature, however, is the Infant Behavior Record of the Bayley Scales of Infant Development, which Matheny, Dolan, and Wilson (1974) found to contain two clusters of intercorrelated items. One cluster relates to primary cognition and includes sensorimotor skills, task alertness, persistence at tasks, and reaction to new stimuli. Another cluster relates to extraversion and includes verbal behavior (during the second year of life), social orientation to the examiner, cooperation, and emotional tone. Although these scales were not designed to measure change as a result of an intervention, they have been used successfully as part of an evaluation battery to assess program impacts (Goldberg, Brachfeld, and DeVitto, 1980).

Assessment of functional play behavior illustrates perhaps the most promising approach to analyzing changes in infant and toddler self-regulatory behaviors. Rubin, Fein, and Vandenberg (1983) emphasize the value of examining behaviors during unstructured play but stress that there are no universally accepted definitions of what to observe. Most schemes for analyzing play activity share a theoretical focus based on Piagetian notions of the development of symbolic activity. Ungerer, Zelazo, Kearsley, and Kurowski (1979), for example, devised a scheme for recording four different categories of play: stereotypical (e.g., mouthing, banging); relational (e.g., use of two objects together in a nonfunctional manner); functional (use of objects in a functionally appropriate way); and symbolic, with three types of symbolic play noted (substitution of one object for another; use of an inanimate object as an independent agent; and use of imaginary objects). Hill and McCune-Nicolich (1981) demonstrated the utility of assessing unstructured play and its relationship to cognitive development in young children with Down syndrome using a five-level scale. A more elaborate assessment of infant play, developed by Belsky and Most (1981) and refined by Belsky, Hrncir, and Vondra (1983), involves a 14-step sequence that has mouthing of objects at its lower end and double substitution of objects (e.g., to treat a shell as a bowl and a stick as a spoon, and stir in the shell with the stick) at its upper end. Children play with two sets of toys for 10 minutes each and their highest level of performance is recorded. This scale has yet to be used with handicapped children or as an outcome measure for evaluating an intervention program, but one should note that changes in play behavior assessed by similar instruments are often more closely linked to program goals than are changes in IQ scores.

Finally, some promising measures of mastery motivation have been developed for infants (Messer, McCarthy, McQuiston, MacTurk, Yarrow, and Vietze, 1986) and toddlers (Morgan and Harmon, 1984). These measures derive from theoretical work on the relationship between motivation and competence (Bruner, 1973; White, 1959, 1963). The assessment procedure is somewhat comparable for infants and toddlers, with observational ratings of children's exploration and persistence in several types of tasks (e.g., cause-and-effect tasks, means-end tasks, combinatorial tasks). These measures have been used with both normally developing youngsters (Yarrow, McQuiston, MacTurk, McCarthy, Klein, and Vietze, 1983) and with mentally retarded children (Schwethelm and Mahoney, 1986). In addition, Morgan and his colleagues (Morgan, Maslin, Powers, and Harmon, 1986) have developed a questionnaire for parents about their child's mastery and enjoyment of tasks. It consists of four scales: general persistence at tasks, mastery pleasures, independent mastery during challenging play, and competence. The sensitivity of this battery of motivation measures in detecting changes due to intervention has yet to be fully demonstrated. However, the further refinement of such measures is encouraging, as motivation is an aspect of child development that many programs hope to affect. Researchers and service providers alike will benefit from a better understanding of the relationship between motivation and other important dimensions of child growth.

SUMMARY

Traditional measures of IQ, preschool readiness skills, and academic achievement have shouldered the burden of demonstrating the efficacy of early childhood intervention programs during the past two decades. Some evaluators now point to the need for greater attention to family and community program impacts; others emphasize the importance of a broader approach to the assessment of child-focused effects.

We have discussed two dimensions of function representative of this shifting orientation: social competence and self-regulatory behavior. Each domain requires considerable creative thought to achieve construct refinement, measurement conceptualization, and the development of valid and reliable instruments. We selected specific tests and protocols to illustrate potentially fruitful assessment strategies; none of them is without important limitations, and preferable alternatives may emerge.

Instrument development is a task that requires careful and arduous work. However, the assessment of program effects on children cannot await the completion of that task. In fact, limited public resources have made the need for careful measurement of program impacts more compelling than ever. The first responsibility of a careful evaluator should be to assist programs in defining their specific goals for families and children in measurable terms. Only then can instruments be considered that will accurately assess program accomplishments and shortcomings.

In seeking instruments that address program goals, evaluators must remain aware of the specific limitations and distinctions among diagnostic/prescriptive tools, screening tests, and legitimate developmental outcome measures. Diagnostic/prescriptive protocols, such as the Hawaii Early Learning Profile (HELP) (Furono, O'Reilly, Hosaka, Inatsuka, Allman, and Zeisloft, 1979) are useful to service providers for designing an appropriate child-oriented educational plan; screening tools like the Denver Developmental Screening Test, however, merely indicate areas of potential weakness that require further assessment. Neither type of test was designed to be used as an outcome measure of children's progress. On the other hand, standardized instruments that tap well-defined developmental domains and yield an interpretable score, like the Bayley Mental and Motor Scales, are appropriate choices for outcome measures. In the evaluation of a specific program, however, their value is dependent on the degree to which they test areas of development that the program is designed to affect. Even then, important limitations of such measures must be acknowledged, particularly when administered to atypical groups.

A useful strategy in program evaluation is to consider pairing standardized instruments with additional measures that assess children's skills in specific domains or in more natural settings. Using multiple measures to document change may be particularly rewarding for handicapped children because it allows evaluators to approach the assessment of specific competencies in a variety of ways, thereby increasing the likelihood that a given skill can be tapped. In this regard, program evaluators need not avoid developing their own measures of program impacts, as long as they recognize their limitations and take them into account in the analyses of findings. In such cases, problems will be minimized if emphasis is placed on describing changes in performance or behavior rather than on diagnostic labeling or assigning meaningless or misleading numerical scores.

There is a critical need for carefully validated instruments to measure a wide range of developmental and behavioral changes in children. The design and refinement of such measures must not occur in isolation from ongoing discussion of the meaning and underlying constructs of the target behaviors and developmental functions. Service providers and recipients must help to articulate the specific goals and objectives of individual programs and welcome their assessment. Program evaluators must consider the value of multifaceted approaches to assessing child-focused outcomes and be willing to employ imperfect measures, while acknowledging that imperfection. Child development researchers must continue to develop new instruments with rigorous psychometric properties. In addition, policy planners must understand the technical limits of measurement in human development. Past approaches to assessing program impacts on children focused on attributing importance to what was measurable. Future efforts must be directed more toward measuring what is important.

ACKNOWLEDGMENTS

The authors wish to acknowledge support for work related to this chapter by the Division of Maternal and Child Health, U.S. Public Health Service, and the Jessie B. Cox Charitable Trust.

REFERENCES

Achenbach, T., and Edelbrock, C. (1981). Behavioral problems and competencies reported by parents of normal and disturbed children aged four through sixteen. *Monographs of the Society for Research in Child Development, 46,* Serial No. 188.

Achenbach, T., and Zigler, E. (1968). Cue-learning and problem learning strategies in normal and retarded children. *Child Development, 39,* 827–848.

Banta, T. J. (1970). Tests for the evaluation of early childhood education: The Cincinnati Autonomy Test Battery (CATB). In J. Hellmuth (Ed.), *Cognitive studies-1.* NY: Brunner/Mazel.

Bayley, N. (1969). *Bayley Scales of infant development.* NY: The Psychological Corporation.

Belsky, J., and Most, R. (1981). From exploration to play: A cross-sectional study of infant free play behavior. *Developmental Psychology, 17*, 630–639.

Belsky, J., Hrncir, E., and Vondra, J. (1983). *Manual for the assessment of performance, competence, and executive capacity in infant play.* Unpublished manuscript.

Berrueta-Clement, J. R., Schweinhart, L. J., Barnett, W. S., Epstein, A. S., and Weikart, D. P. (1984). *Changed lives: The effects of the Perry Preschool Program on youths through age 19.* Ypsilanti, MI: High/Scope Educational Research Foundation.

Bronson, M. B. (1975). Executive competence in preschool children. Paper presented at the meeting of the American Educational Research Association, Washington, D.C., April.

Bruner, J. S. (1973). The organization of early skilled action. *Child Development, 44*, 1–11.

Cattell, P. (1940/r1960). *Cattell Infant Intelligence Scale.* NY: The Psychological Corporation.

Coller, A. R. (1972). Overview snapshot observational technique (OSOT): Administration manual. Gainesville, FL: Institute for Development of Human Resources.

Conners, C. K. (1969). A teacher rating scale for use in drug studies with children. *American Journal of Psychiatry, 126*, 884.

Connors, C. K. (1970). Symptom patterns in hyperkinetic, neurotic and normal children. *Child Development, 41*, 667.

CTB/McGraw-Hill (1970). *California Achievement Tests: Forms C and D.* Monterey, CA: Publishers Test Service.

Dunn, I. M., and Dunn, L. M. (1959). *Peabody Picture Vocabulary Test.* Circle Pines, MN: American Guidance Service.

Durost, W. M. (Ed.). (1961). *Metropolitan Achievement Tests.* NY: Harcourt, Brace & World.

Frankenburg, W., and Dodds, J. (1967). The Denver Developmental Screening Test. *The Journal of Pediatrics, 71*, 181–191.

Fuchs, D., Fuchs, L. S., Power, M. H., and Dailey, A. M. (1985). Bias in the assessment of handicapped children. *American Educational Research Journal, 22*(2), 185–198.

Furono, S., O'Reilly, K., Hosaka, C., Inatsuka, T., Allman, T., and Zeisloft, B. (1979). *Hawaii Early Learning Profile.* Palo Alto, CA: VORT Corporation.

Gardner, H. (1983). *Frames of mind.* NY: Basic Books.

Gesell, A., Halverson, H. M., Thompson, H., Ilg, F. L., Castner, B. M., Ames, L. B., and Amatruda, C. S. (1940) *The first five years of life.* NY: Harper and Row.

Goldberg, S., Brachfeld, S., and DeVitto, B. (1980). Feeding, fussing, play: Parent–infant interactions in the first year as a function of early medical problems. In T. Field, S. Goldberg, D. Stern, and A. Sostek

(Eds.), *Interactions of high risk infants and children*. NY: Academic Press.

Gould, S. J. (1981). *The mismeasure of man*. NY: W. W. Norton.

Griffiths, R. (1951; revised 1955). *The Griffiths Mental Development Scale for Testing Babies from Birth to Two Years*. Author.

Hafner, A. L., and White, D. M. (1981). Bias in mental research. An essay review of *Bias in mental testing*. *Harvard Educational Review, 51* (4), 577–586.

Hale, G. A., and Lewis, M. (Eds.). (1979). *Attention and cognitive development*. NY: Plenum Press.

Harter, S., and Zigler, E. (1974). The assessment of effectance motivation in normal and retarded children. *Developmental Psychology, 10*, 169–180.

Hauser-Cram, P. (1979). *Developmental screening: A review and analysis of key issues*. Cambridge, MA: The Huron Institute.

Hieronymous, A. N., Lindquist, E. F., and Hoover, H. D. (1955/revised 1979). *Iowa Tests of Basic Skills, Forms 7 and 8*. Chicago, IL: Riverside.

Hill, P., and McCune-Nicolich, L. (1981). Pretend play and patterns of cognition in Down's syndrome children. *Child Development, 52*, 611–617.

Jastek, J. F., and Jastek, S. R. (1965/revised 1976). *The Wide Range Achievement Test*. Wilmington, DE: Guidance Associates.

Johnson, K., and Kopp, C. (1980). A bibliography of screening and assessment measures for infants. Project REACH. University of California, Los Angeles.

Kagan, J. (1964). Reflection–impulsivity and reading ability in primary grade children. *Child Development, 36*, 609–628.

Kamin, L. (1974). *The science and politics of I.Q.* Potomac, MD: Erlbaum.

Lazar, I., and Darlington, R. (1982). Lasting effects of early education. *Monographs of the Society for Research in Child Development, 47*, 2-2, Serial No. 195.

McCarthy, D. (1970, revised 1972). *McCarthy Scales of children's abilities*. NY: The Psychological Corporation.

Matheny, A. P., Dolan, A. B., and Wilson, R. S. (1974). Bayley's Infant Behavior Record: Relations between behavior and mental test scores. *Developmental Psychology, 10*, 696–702.

Mercer, J. (1974). A policy statement on assessment procedures and the rights of children. *Harvard Educational Review, 44*, 125–141.

Meisels, S. J. (1987). Uses and abuses of developmental screening and school readiness testing. *Young Children, 42*(2), 4–6; 68–73.

Messer, D. J., McCarthy, M. E., McQuiston, S., MacTurk, R. H., Yarrow, L. J., and Vietze, P. M. (1986). Relation between mastery behavior in infancy and competence in early childhood. *Developmental Psychology, 22*(3), 366–372.

Miller, L. B., and Dyer, J. L. (1975). Four preschool programs: Their dimensions and effects. *Monographs of the Society for Research in Child Development, 40,* 5–6, Serial No. 162.

Morgan, G., and Harmon, R. J. (1984). Developmental transformations in mastery motivation: Measurement and validation. In R. N. Emde and R. J. Harmon (Eds.), *Continuities and discontinuities in development* (pp. 263–291). NY: Plenum.

Morgan, G., Maslin, C. A., Powers, J. M., and Harmon, R. J. (May, 1986). The dimensions of mastery questionnaire: Its reliability, factor structure, and validity. Paper presented at the biennial conference of the Developmental Research Group, Estes Park, CO.

Nurss, J. R., and McGauvran, M. E. (1933; revised 1976). *The Metropolitan readiness tests.* NY: The Psychological Corporation.

Oakland, T. (Ed.) (1977). *Psychological and educational assessment of minority children.* NY: Brunner/Mazel.

Parasuraman, R., and Davies, D. R. (Eds.). (1984). *Varieties of attention.* Orlando, FL: Academic Press.

Pierson, D. E., Walker, D. K., and Tivnan, T. (1984). A school-based program from infancy to kindergarten for children and their parents. *Personnel and Guidance Journal, 62* (8), 448–455.

Rubin, K. H., Fein, G. G., and Vandenberg, B. (1983). Play. In P. H. Mussen (Ed.). *Handbook of child psychology.* 4th Edition. NY: John Wiley & Sons.

Schaefer, E. S., and Aaronson, M. (1967). *Classroom behavior inventory: Preschool to primary.* Rockville, MD: National Institute of Mental Health.

Schwethelm, B., and Mahoney, G. (1986). Task persistence among organically impaired mentally retarded children. *American Journal of Mental Deficiency, 90*(4), 432–439.

Seitz, V., Rosenbaum, C. K., and Apfel, N. H. (1985). Effects of family support intervention: A ten-year followup. *Child Development, 56,* 376–391.

Sheehan, R., and Keogh, B. R. (1981). Strategies for documenting progress of handicapped children in early education programs. *Educational Evaluation and Policy Analysis, 3*(6), 59–67.

Shonkoff, J. (1983). The limitations of normative assessments of high risk infants. *Topics in Early Childhood Special Education, 3,* 29–43.

Shonkoff, J., and Hauser-Cram, P. (1987). Early intervention for disabled infants and their families: A quantitative analysis. *Pediatrics, 80*(5), 650–658.

Siegelman, E. (1969). Reflective and impulsive observing behavior. *Child Development, 40,* 1213–1221.

Sparrow, S., Balla, D., and Cicchetti, D. (1984). *Vineland Adaptive Behavior Scales: Expanded Form Manual.* Circle Pines, MN: American Guidance Service.

Stallings, J. (1972). *Training manual for classroom observation.* Menlo Park, CA: Stanford Research Institute.

Terman, L. M., and Merrill, M. A. (1937). *Revised Stanford-Binet scale.* Chicago, IL: Riverside.

Trickett, P. K., Apfel, N. H., Rosenbaum, L. K., and Zigler, E. F. (1982). A five-year follow-up of participants in the Yale Child Welfare Research Program. In E. Zigler and I. Gordon (Eds.), *Day care: Scientific and social policy issues.* Boston, MA: Auburn House.

Ungerer, J. A., Zelazo, P. R., Kearsley, R. B., and Kurowski, K. (1979). Play as a cognitive assessment tool. Paper presented at the UAP-USC Ninth Annual International Interdisciplinary Conference on Piagetian Theory and its Implications for the Helping Professions, Los Angeles, February 2–3.

Wechsler, D. (1967). *Wechsler Preschool and Primary Scales of Intelligence.* NY: The Psychological Corporation.

White, K., Mastropieri, M., and Casto, G. (1984). An analysis of special education early childhood projects approved by the Joint Dissemination Review Panel. *Journal of the Division of Early Childhood, 9,* 11–26.

White, R. W. (1959). Motivation reconsidered: The concept of competence. *Psychological Review, 66,* 297–333.

White, R. W. (1963). Ego and reality in psychoanalytic theory. *Psychological Issues, 3,* 1–40.

Yarrow, L. J., McQuiston, S., MacTurk, R. H., McCarthy, M. E., Klein, R. P., and Vietze, P. M. (1983). Assessment of mastery motivation during the first year of life: Contemporaneous and cross-age relationships. *Developmental Psychology, 19*(2), 159–171.

Zigler, E., and Trickett, P. K. (1978). IQ, social competence, and evaluation of early childhood intervention. *American Psychologist, 33,* 789–798.

Zigler, E., and Valentine, J. (Eds.). (1979). *Project Head Start—A legacy of the war on poverty.* NY: Free Press.

EVALUATING PARENT–CHILD INTERACTION OUTCOMES OF FAMILY SUPPORT AND EDUCATION PROGRAMS

Gail A. Howrigan

Parent education and support programs are predicated on the notion that interventions with children in isolation from the family context often lack impact and staying power. Interventions designed to help parents help their children, however, can benefit both parents and children. The parent becomes an agent of change for the child—or in traditional terms—socializes the child.

Family programs that seek to alter and evaluate interactions between parent and child rely heavily on the theories of socialization that have arisen over the last six decades. In this chapter I will discuss some limitations of those theories and of early attempts at measuring parent–child interaction. I will then discuss the current state of the art of measuring parent–child interaction and conclude with both recommendations and caveats for program directors and evaluators.

EARLY SOCIALIZATION THEORY

The early literature on socialization reflects a number of theoretical biases and methodological approaches. These include: a unidirectional model of influence; exclusive focus on the mother and child; cultural absolutism; the deficit model; and nonobservational methods of measurement. As discussed in the following, all of these characteristics have been criticized in recent years.

Unidirectional Model of Influence

Early "social mold" theories of socialization sought to elucidate "the processes by which the actions of an asocial infant are assimilated to the complex demands of society" (Hartup, 1978, p. 25) and to explain behavior in terms of constructs such as "achievement," "aggression," and "dependency." These theories, drawn largely from the fields of psychoanalysis and learning theory, paid little attention to the child's role in socialization.

Exclusive Focus on the Mother and Child

This focus is a product of Freudian theory, of animal studies concerned with stimulation of the young organism, and, perhaps, of a long history in the Western world of religious veneration and secular romanticization of the maternal role. Although there has been a recent spate of interest in father–child interaction (Lamb, 1981), less attention has been paid to siblings or other family members, and there have been few attempts at a polyadic approach (Dunn and Kendrick, 1982; Lewis and Feiring, 1979; Parke, Power, and Gottman, 1979).

Cultural Absolutism

A third limitation of socialization theory stems from its failure to integrate findings from cross-cultural and subcultural research. This failure is particularly serious in intervention research where the subjects typically come from racial, ethnic, and economic subgroups that differ maximally from the populations on which most developmental theory has been based. Cultural bias "results not so much from the imposition of the researcher's own cultural values as from reliance on theoretical models that do not acknowledge culture at all" (Harkness, 1980, p. 12).

We now have ample evidence that the demands and practices of culture affect many aspects of development, such as cognition, social development, physical development and functioning, and language (Blurton-Jones, 1972; Cole and Scribner, 1974; Leiderman, Tulkin, and Rosenfeld, 1977; Munroe and Munroe, 1975; Munroe, Munroe, and Whiting, 1981; Schwartz, 1976; Snow, De Blauw, and Van Roosmalen, 1979; Super, 1981; Triandis and Heron, 1981; Werner, 1979; Whiting, 1980). There is disagreement about the size and exact causes of inter- and intracultural differences in socialization (Zigler, Lamb, and Child, 1982), but it seems clear that parental expectations socialize children to fulfill parents' ideals of adult behavior (Barry, Child, and Bacon, 1959; Kohn, 1969, 1976, 1979; LeVine, 1974; Lewis and Freedle, 1977; Miller and Swanson, 1958; Whiting and Whiting, 1975). For example, the white middle-class model of parenting stresses the notion of parental efficacy and includes lavish use of parental attention and praise, intended to produce self-confident adults who can master their work environments (LeVine, 1980). Children of this group respond with a degree of adult attention-seeking and competitiveness that is striking when seen in cross-cultural perspective (Whiting and Whiting, 1975). This serves them well in school achievement, a necessary step to occupational success in the present American economy.

Those involved in intervention must recognize that white middle-class child-rearing practices in the United States represent one possible adaptation to *a particular set* of economic demands and expectations. Trying to change mothers' interactional styles and children's cognitive functioning without considering whether other aspects of families' settings can support the changes is unproductive. In fact, parents of all groups tend to rear their children pragmatically. As a result, interventions are unlikely to have large effects if they are not accompanied by large-scale institutional change in society (Hinde, 1983; Laosa, 1979, 1981; Ogbu, 1981).

The Deficit Model

A fourth, related, limitation of socialization theory as it informs intervention is its domination by the deficit model, which portrays poor children and the children of some subgroups in the American population as less successful in school than the offspring of the white middle class and attributes this lack of success to improper socialization. This assumption leads back to the mother and looks to her behavior with her child as the source of "the problem." To a striking degree, developmental researchers' interest in parent–child interaction has been narrowly focused on two issues related to the deficit model: the role of parent–child interaction as mediator of the child's cognitive development; and parent–child interaction as an index of the quality of the parent–child bond, which is thought to be at risk in "disadvantaged" populations.

Nonobservational Methods of Measurement

Questionnaires, self-reports, and retrospective accounts dominated the methodology of early socialization research (Wright, 1960). However, as investigators began to add systematic observations in naturally occurring settings (Barker, 1963; Kagan and Moss, 1962), discrepancies emerged between what parents *said* they did and what they *actually* did (Smith, 1958; Yarrow, Campbell, and Burton, 1968). Parents could not always tell investigators about their own and their children's behavior. For example, they tend not to report what they do *not* do (such as failing to respond to infant distress); when faced with a contradiction between actual behavior and group norms, they frequently report the latter as the former (Patterson, 1977; Whiting and Whiting, 1970).

RECENT TRENDS

Each of these limitations of early socialization theory and methodology has been addressed in recent literature. Unfortunately, however, intervention research and evaluation methods have yet to be significantly affected by these critiques.

The *unidirectional model of influence* gradually gave way to new insights in ethology, psychiatry, environmental psychology, social policy, and family sociology. In the decade following Bell's (1968) seminal article, the issue of the direction of effects in parent–child relations attracted the attention of many researchers (Lewis and Rosenblum, 1974), and consideration of the child's contribution is still very evident in mainstream developmental research.

This idea seems to have been taken less seriously in intervention research, perhaps because it runs counter to the notion of mother as teacher. While the term "interaction" is invoked constantly, a close look suggests that in many cases little attention is paid to bidirectional interaction. Clarke–Stewart and Fein (1983) point out that only a few such studies have employed designs that allow examination of direction of effects. None of those has provided strong support for the accepted view, and several point instead to the child as the more likely source of change in the parent–child relationship in intervention research. Moreover, while current theoretical thinking about parent–child interaction increasingly includes an interest in individual variations in children, and in how such variations contribute to interaction (Dunn and Kendrick, 1980; Walters and Walters, 1980), research on intervention tends to gloss over individual differences, assuming that all children need, or should elicit, the same input from their caregivers.

With regard to the *mother–child focus* and to the *cultural context of the child,* some progress has been made in promoting an "ecological" perspective in the theory and practice of intervention (see Dym, Chapter 22; Dunst and Trivette, Chapter 14; Jacobs, Chapter 2; Walker and Crocker, Chapter 6; Weiss, Chapter 1, all in this volume). But evaluation methodology still lags behind theory, paying scant attention to the broader social–ecological context (Harkness, 1980; Harkness and Super, 1980; Whiting, 1980). While background information is often used in analyses, study designs rarely incorporate the broader cultural and social factors that shape child-rearing strategies and settings. Data consist almost exclusively of the specific actions and vocalizations that mothers and children direct to each other or of qualitative ratings of the tone of such interaction, without reference to a larger context (what time of day it was, how occupied the mother was, what the physical space available to the child was like, etc.). 236968.

Interaction research also gives little consideration to other important people in the lives of the mother and child. Assessments based exclusively on mother–child interaction may underestimate the amount of social and cognitive stimulation children experience, especially in families that do not approximate the small nuclear family model (Stack, 1974). Better ecological description of what occurs in the households of children served by family support programs would also enable those programs to better suit their interventions to the families' actual situations.

Critics of the *deficit model of intervention* have proposed a "difference" model as an alternative (Howard and Scott, 1981; Laosa, 1979, 1981; Ogbu, 1981). However, intervention research has failed to explore whether and how the interactive behavior of mother and child may be adaptive in their own terms.

The 1960s saw a dramatic expansion of *observational methodology* (Lytton, 1971). Along with observation in natural contexts, investigators observed parents and children in a variety of contrived and controlled settings. These early studies laid the groundwork for our present understanding of the consequences of different styles of parent–child interaction within our own society (Baumrind, 1967; Baumrind and Black, 1967; Clarke-Stewart, 1973; Hess and Shipman, 1965; White and Watts, 1973). During the 1970s, observational research in child development was refined methodologically and applied to a wider age range and a great variety of focal behaviors. Simultaneously, researchers came to understand that observational and self-report data were not interchangeable alternatives, but complementary strategies that could provide both objective descriptions of behavior and a basis for interpreting those descriptions with information on parental attitudes and knowledge (Maccoby and Martin, 1983; Messick, 1983).

MEASURING PARENT–CHILD INTERACTION

Reviewers of intervention studies noted, as late as 1978, a lack of interactive data from evaluations of family programs (Ramey, Farran, and Campbell, 1979). Bronfenbrenner's influential review of intervention results, which pointed to a key role for mothers in motivating and sustaining the child's interest in challenging tasks, helped to change that situation (Bronfenbrenner, 1974). Since then, many program evaluations have included parent–child interaction measures.

Table 4.1 lists some representative studies, the type of intervention offered, program goals, and the interactive measures used to assess effects. In addition to providing the theoretical basis for parent–child interventions and a methodology for evaluating their results, interactive measures have been used to carry out clinical or diagnostic assessments (Bromwich, 1976; Patterson, 1977; Roberts and Forehand, 1978) and as a teaching tool and source of feedback in programs that attempt to alter directly the way parents deal with their children (Musick, Clark, and Cohler, 1981; Musick, Stott, Cohler, and Dincin, 1981).

The Range of Measures

Interaction measures vary on a number of dimensions; choice of measures will depend on the age of the children, the behaviors of interest, and the resources available to investigators. Several recent evaluations have strengthened their analyses by assessing interaction with more than one measure and in more than one setting (see Table 4.1). Far from representing duplication of effort, such strategies serve a variety of purposes. They can increase confidence in findings, and they can be used to address two crucial questions: whether treatment mothers *can* interact with their children in the desired manner (structured tasks) and whether they in fact *do* use the desired styles in everyday dealings with the child (unstructured observations). Finally, multiple measures can provide important insights into data; for example, is the mother's tendency to organize her interaction with her child around objects (home or laboratory observation) a function of the availability of toys in the home, or is it independent of their availability (Caldwell and Bradley, 1984)?

To aid interpretation of data on parent–child interaction, a number of researchers have developed their own measures or employed established measures to capture parental attitudes, perceptions, and knowledge concerning child rearing. Examples include Field's developmental milestone questionnaire (Field, Widmayer, Stringer, and Ignatoff, 1980); Bee and colleagues' measure of the accuracy of mothers' expectations for infant behavior (Bee, Barnard, Eyres, Gray, Hammond, Spietz, Snyder, and Clark, 1982); Kessen and Fein's list of maternal activity choices (Kessen and Fein, 1975); the Weikart group's Ypsilanti Picture Sorting Inventory to measure maternal perceptions and expectations for child development (Lambie, Bond, and Weikart, 1974), and their interviews on "childmindedness," (Epstein and Weikart, 1979); Broussard's Neonatal Perception Inventory (Broussard and Hartner,

1970); and Slaughter's (1983) and Baldwin, Cole, and Baldwin's (1982) postobservation interviews to elicit mothers' assessments of how closely the interaction in the observation resembled that which took place at home. A measure that seems not to have been used in this context is an infant or child temperament rating (Buss and Plomin, 1984; Carey and McDevitt, 1978; Fullard, McDevitt, and Carey, 1984). Such ratings could contribute to our understanding of how and why parents and children behave with each other as they do.

Methodological Issues: Initial Considerations

In their recent review of design and analysis in developmental psychology, Appelbaum and McCall (1983) warn that social interaction research, "even in its simplest form, may be the most complicated and difficult methodologically and statistically of any major endeavor in the discipline" (p. 465). Those involved in evaluating family programs are therefore well advised to consider whether their data can be collected by nonobservational means (Hinde, 1983; Whiting and Whiting, 1970). If observational research is warranted, there must be full awareness that pitfalls await (Parke, 1978). We have only recently become aware of some of those pitfalls, and do not yet have adequate solutions to many of them. Nevertheless, the face validity of direct observation of behavior, as opposed to methodologically tighter but less direct measures, keeps investigators and methodologists on the job. (For an overview of observational methodology see Hutt and Hutt [1970]; Weick [1968].)

Design

Theoretical considerations and availability of resources influence decisions about research design. A local program with limited resources will probably choose a single measure—one that is neither especially labor-intensive nor technically demanding. Large-scale demonstration efforts will probably opt for multiple measures.

Whenever possible, researchers are urged to combine the strengths of different points on the field–laboratory continuum. Naturalistic observations have much to tell us about how the behaviors of interest function in the real world, but questions of causation cannot readily be addressed without some use of experimental manipulation. Parke (1979) suggests a number of design variants for combining field and laboratory in intervention and assessment. One design, for example, would employ both methods, but not with all subjects. Observations might be done only for a subsample to see whether the mothers who

TABLE 4.1. Summary of Representative Intervention Studies Using Interactive and Related Measures.

Reference Project name	Sample description	Program goals	Intervention	Interactive and related measures
Berrera et al. (1986)	38 experimental infants (low birthweight) 21 controls (low birthweight) 24 controls (normal birthweight) Ages during program: 4–14 months corrected age Wide range of SES and demographic characteristics Subjects matched on key variables	"To teach parents to use problem-solving strategies to cope with the challenges of parenting"	Home visits (mean of 23 visits over 12 months) Two treatment groups: 1. Focus on improving child's level of functioning 2. Focus on improving quality of parent-child interaction	All groups: A. Videotaped observations of 10-minute period of free play in home at 4 and 16 months • Focus on responsiveness of both mother and infant • Observers blind B. Caldwell-Bradley HOME at 4, 8, 12 and 16 months NB: Authors considered HOME a measure of home environment, not interaction
Bromwich and Parmelee (1979) (UCLA Infant studies Program)	30 experimental infants 33 control infants Both groups were high-risk preterm infants with varied SES and demographic characteristics	"To enhance parents' enjoyment of and sensitivity and responsiveness to their infants and thus to increase their motivation and ability to provide opportunities and	Individualized education through home visits over 14 months (frequency not specified)	A. Parent Behavior Progression—rating scales based on informal home observations and parent reports, does not take infant's behavior into account—fo-

Study	Sample	Goal	Treatment	Measures
	Ages during program: 10–24 months Groups matched on SES, race and ethnicity, and severity of risk factors	experiences that would further the infant's development"		cuses on the mother B. Play Interaction Measure—method of scoring not specified, based on videotaped 10–minute observations of structured play situation in laboratory; assesses contributions of both mother and child
Dickie and Gerber (1980)	10 treatment families 9 control families All white, middle-class families with normal infants; treatment included fathers, mothers, and infants, 4–12 months old	"To improve parent-infant competence . . [by increasing] contingency experience"	16 hours of training over 8 weeks with focus on child development, individual infant variation, effect of infant on parent, and contingent responding	A. Naturalistic home observation—2 hours, ratings based on Baumrind • Focus on home modification for infant, parent-infant interaction, and infant responsiveness • Observers blind B. Videotape in home of 10 minutes of free play, 5 minutes with each parent engaged in play

(continued)

103

TABLE 4.1. (*continued*)

Reference Project name	Sample description	Program goals	Intervention	Interactive and related measures
				• Ratings based on Moss (see Dickie and Gerber, 1980) • Raters blind C. Parent ratings of own and spouse's parental competence
Falender and Heber (1975) (Milwaukee Project)	21 experimental dyads 18 control dyads Low SES black children whose mothers had low IQs. Ages 6 months–5 years	To "prevent cultural–familial mental retardation" of "high-risk" children; authors hypothesized that "changes induced in the child by extrafamilial stimulation" would induce "changes in the mother's behavior in her interactions with the child"	Full-day, year-round program of environmental stimulation with a cognitive–language orientation, provided to children from 6 months to 5 years	Videotaped observations done in a van equipped as a lab A. Block Sort maternal teaching task adapted from Hess and Shipman (1965) B. Mother and child cooperate on Etch-a-Sketch task On both tasks behaviors coded as rating scales with an adaptation of Caldwell's AP-PROACH system

Fields *et al.* (1980)

60 preterm infants of adolescent mothers
  30 assigned to treatment
  30 controls
30 full-term infants of adolescent mothers
30 preterm infants of adult mothers
30 full-term infants of adult mothers
All subjects were black, low SES
Age 0–8 months

"To [teach] developmental milestones and child-rearing practices, . . . age-appropriate stimulation and to facilitate mother-infant interactions"

Biweekly ½-hour home visits by a trained interventionist and a teenage, black, female, student to explain and demonstrate caretaking practices, stimulating exercises, and developmental milestones

In perinatal period:

  A. Perinatal Anxieties and Attitudes scale
  B. Mother's Assessment of the Behavior of her Infant (adapted from Neonatal Behavioral Assessment Scale)
  C. Maternal Developmental Expectations and Child-Rearing Attitudes Survey

At 4 months:

  D. Carey Infant Temperament Questionnaire
  E. Videotaped observations of feeding and face-to-face play interactions

At 8 months:

  F. Carey Infant Temperament Questionnaire
  G. HOME

(continued)

TABLE 4.1. (continued)

Reference Project name	Sample description	Program goals	Intervention	Interactive and related measures
Gray and Ruttle (1980) (The Family-Oriented Home Visiting Program)	27 experimental children 20 control children All families were low-income, equal proportions black and white, and had 2 children under age 5. Ages during program: 17–33 months Treatment apparently assigned randomly	"[To enable low-income] mothers to become more effective educational change agents for their children under kindergarten age"	Home visits with materials, by professional and paraprofessional visitors, 30 visits over 9 months; focuses included: •Improving mothers' teaching styles •Increasing mothers' and children's reciprocal talk.	A. Caldwell-Bradley HOME B. Maternal Teaching Style Instrument (MTSI), adapted by Sandler from Hess & Shipman NB: Authors consider both measures to be assessments of the mother, not of interaction between mother and child
Madden et al. (1984) (Mother-Child Home Program)	112 experimental children (considered "at risk" educationally) 54 control children (similar background) Ages during program: 2–4 years;	"To enable low-income mothers to prevent later educational disadvantage . . . by initiating and maintaining a cognitively stimulating mother-child interaction in the home"	Home visits (approximately 75 visits over 2 years) Two treatment groups: 1. Toys and books given, but no modeling of their use provided (VISM)	All groups: Videotaped observations of 10-minute, semi-structured play session (location not specified) at end of treatment (Maternal Interactive Behavior Record)

106

	All low-income, urban, predominantly black Treatment assigned randomly		2. Toys and books given, demonstrator models interaction around them	• Focus on behaviors closely related to program goals • No information on observers
Whitt and Casey (1982)	15 experimental mother–infant dyads 17 control dyads All first-born, low-income, racially mixed Ages 2–27 weeks	"To enhance the affective interaction between mother and infant and to stimulate the infant's cognitive development by prompting mother's awareness of social nature of infant behavior and encouraging responsiveness. . . . improving . . . understanding of normal infant development . . . , and enhancing maternal feelings of confidence and competence	During 6 half-hour well-baby visits to pediatrician at 2, 4, 8, 15, 21 and 27 weeks, discussion and modeling with mother: 1. For treatment group, focus was on issues of development, responsiveness, etc. 2. For control group, focus was on accident prevention and nutrition	Both groups: Laboratory observation in "naturalistic" setting—21 minutes at 27 months Observer blind to treatment group; observation scored three ways: A. Behavior counts of mother and infant behaviors B. 2-item responsive behavior chains C. Ratings of affective characteristics

in laboratory observations of a structured task exhibit higher levels of desired behaviors also do so at home.

Recruitment and Training of Observers

Two key considerations in recruiting observers often conflict with one another. The first is rapport with the families to be assessed and familiarity with the subculture to which they belong. Being the subject of observation is unnerving under any circumstances, but parents and children will be most "themselves" in the presence of someone they know and have grown to trust, with someone with whom they share values and other important aspects of identity. As a result, some studies have had home visitors carry out observations on the families they serve. This practice raises the second consideration, that of bias and halo effects in the observer. Recent large-scale evaluations have taken pains to assure that their observers are "blind" to the treatment condition of their subjects (Andrews, Blumenthal, Johnson, Kahn, Ferguson, Lasater, Malone, and Wallace, 1980; Whitt and Casey, 1982). "Blindness," on the one hand, and sharing the subjects' subculture, on the other, are especially important if the data entail a high degree of inference, as in rating scales (Cairns and Green, 1979). Available evidence indicates that behavior counts, however, are not significantly affected by observers' expectations (Patterson, 1977).

Observers must be trained to achieve acceptable levels of reliability. Since this is a long and tedious task, investigators need to allow plenty of time for it (Lytton, 1973). A good practice is to start training observers with videotapes of the kinds of interaction they will be observing. This allows observers and instructors to review a sequence several times, until understanding and agreement are reached. A next step is to move training to a live pilot context similar to that in which real data will be collected—since coding from the stream of behavior in real time is a very different activity. Finally, the various forms of reliability should be checked frequently over the course of data collection. We now know that there is very likely to be "drift" over time, both of the judgments of observers from each other and of the observers as a group vis-à-vis objective reality; familiarity in this instance breeds inattention and changed standards (Cairns, 1979; Cicchetti, 1984; Hollenbeck, 1978; Yarrow and Waxler, 1979).

Observation Methods

There are to date very few standard observation measures, that is, ones with well-established psychometric properties and for which there are adequate norms. Most investigators devise their own instruments or make modifications to existing ones, in accord with theoretical dictates and practical necessity. In the following sections I will briefly discuss the major considerations involved in observational measurement of parent–child interaction.

Focus. The first step is to identify the behaviors of interest, for example, the discrete acts of mother and infant during feeding or play (look, touch, smile); children's reactions to strangers; aggressive behavior; parental control or teaching strategies; the range of children's social contacts, and the quality of their relationships. The major considerations concerning choice of focus are *theoretical justification* (which should be closely connected to program goals), *opportunity* (How difficult will it be to see these behaviors?), and *feasibility* (Is the behavior frequent enough to be statistically analyzable? Is it too subtle to be captured reliably?). It is important at this stage to think about how the focal behavior can be operationalized. We no longer attempt to measure directly such elusive constructs as "dependency" or "aggression." (See Patterson [1979] for an account of how he and his colleagues broke down "aggression" into component behaviors that could be recorded reliably and made theoretical sense.)

Setting. The field versus laboratory setting debate seems to be the methodologists' counterpart to the theoreticians' nature–nurture conflict and shows as little hope of imminent resolution (Beckwith, 1976; Bell, 1964; Clark-Stewart, 1981; Lytton, 1971; Rheingold, 1979). Several considerations guide the investigator's choice of settings for observation: *theoretical concerns* (What behaviors are of interest? What contexts are likely to elicit them?); *ecological validity* (Is the observation setting representative of, or generalizable to, the class of settings about which the investigator wishes to make inferences?); *comparability across groups and settings* (Is the setting equally familiar to and ecologically valid for all subject groups?); and *frequencies* (Will the chosen settings produce an analyzable quantity of the behaviors of interest in a reasonable period of time?)

Again, unfortunately, desiderata may be in conflict with one another, as, for example, when ecological validity considerations lead to unstructured observations in a naturally occurring context, which may provide enough instances of the focal behaviors only after many hours. Parke (1979) suggests that, in analyzing potential interaction settings, the investigator should consider the physical setting, the immediate stimulus field, and the cast of social agents.

There is accumulating evidence that choice of settings is anything but trivial. Psychologists have long operated on the assumption that there is a large "person component" in behavior, that is, a stable tendency for a given individual to behave similarly in different contexts.

Recent reviews, however, have argued that we have probably over-estimated trait stability, and that individual behavior is, instead, quite labile across contexts (Bronfenbrenner, 1979; Hess, 1981; Maccoby and Martin, 1983). Further, the same behavior may have different meanings in different contexts, especially for older children. Approaches to the problem include: *establishing a behavioral baseline* (Hess, 1981), either by making observations in a number of settings and collapsing data across all settings, or by having a skilled person make ratings based on observations in a variety of settings; and *using only one setting for observations, but making certain that the setting represents accurately the behaviors about which the investigator wishes to make inferences.* In the latter case, if a contrived event is used to represent usual be-havior, preliminary work will have to be done to show that there is, in fact, a good correlation between the two. Bronfenbrenner's (1979) analysis of how laboratory settings affect subjects is particularly im-portant in evaluating family intervention programs. Such settings, however homelike, decrease the frequency of children's positive re-actions and seem to have effects on parents (which differ by social class). Compared to rates derived from home observations, middle-class, nonminority parents react by apparently attempting to show what good socializers they are, interacting more and more positively than at home, while lower SES and minority parents, seemingly intimidated by the unfamiliarity of the setting, display fewer and less positive in-teractions with their children than they do at home.

A further problem for evaluators of parent education programs is that the demand characteristics of laboratory settings and tasks may be perceived and understood very differently by different treatment groups (Yarrow and Anderson, 1979). It seems likely that treatment mothers will recognize a teaching task as another in a class of situations in which they have been trained to act in a specified way, whereas the com-parison mothers may find such a test setting puzzling at the least, and probably threatening as well (see Madden, O'Hara, and Levenstein, 1984).

In general, we need more home observations in evaluations of parent education and early childhood intervention programs (Carew, 1979; Gray and Wandersman, 1980). As noted, there are hazards in assuming that surrogate settings are adequate stand-ins. However, a review of evaluation studies will show that very few have employed naturalistic home observations. (The few exceptions have, for the most part, used the HOME [Caldwell and Bradley, 1984], which, as will be further dis-cussed below, can provide a rough estimate of mother–child relations but is not a substitute for sustained, systematic observations.) Using laboratory settings and structured tasks to test whether treatment mothers in intervention programs have learned new ways of interacting with their children recalls the "competence-performance" distinction used by linguists. Looking at mother–child interaction in such contexts seems only to answer the question of competence—Can they do it when artificial conditions call for it?—and not to speak to the more important issue of everyday performance—Have the mothers (and children) really incorporated new interactional styles into their regular behavioral repertoires (see Bromwich and Parmelee, 1979)? Both Carew (1979) and Bronfenbrenner (1979) argue persuasively that, because the consequences of research in social policy areas are so much greater than those of purely academic research, social policy researchers bear a special responsibility for making their investigations as rigorous and accurate as possible.

Task. Whether interaction to be observed takes place around a specific task or in a highly structured situation is usually considered part of the setting. Here I treat it separately only to emphasize that the task (and the issue of whether there is to be one at all) can be quite independent of the setting (Parke, 1979). For example, home observations can be structured by the investigator, who might ask the parent to interact with the child around a game or toy supplied by the investigator (see Mrazek, Dowdney, Rutter, and Quinton, 1982, for an example), or who might achieve a kind of standardized context by arranging to conduct observations in all households during the same care routine or part of the day, such as feedings or bedtime. Ethnographic spadework in the form of preliminary interviews with a number of families about their daily routines will help to identify comparable periods or routines (Whiting, Child, and Lambert, 1966). Similarly, observations in laboratory settings may impose minimal structure, as when parent and child are left in a room arranged to look like a living room, with several toys, and are given instructions to interact as they would at home. In this case, however, investigators may accept too readily the apparent similarity of laboratory setting to a naturally occurring one, overlooking the effect on the subjects of the unfamiliarity of the laboratory setting (Yarrow and Waxler, 1979).

Researchers choosing a task or structure for observations also need to keep in mind age-appropriateness and the relevance of the task to the intervention being evaluated. Careful choices of setting and structure can serve both to minimize the negative effects on subjects of unfamiliarity and to maximize efficiency in data collection and "control" in the research design sense.

Data and Recording Systems. Having settled on focal behaviors and settings to elicit them, investigators must then make a series of practical decisions about the form they wish their data to take and how to record those data.

Quantitative and qualitative data. Researchers must decide whether the data are to be quantitative, qualitative, or both. Rating scales (widely used in the early years of child development research) fell for a time into disfavor for a number of valid reasons (Cairns and Green, 1979; Hinde, 1983; Maccoby and Martin, 1983; Walker, 1973). Recently, however, interest in ratings has revived; they apparently tap interpersonal behavior at a level different from that of microanalytic techniques, and there is a need for both kinds of information. Ratings apparently represent a stable central tendency in an individual's or dyad's behavior, "averaging out the moment-to-moment changes in situations or eliciting conditions" (Maccoby and Martin, 1983, p. 24), while frequency counts and other quantitative measures are extremely sensitive to contextual influences (Cairns and Green, 1979). Numerous studies have combined ratings with quantitative methods to capture both kinds of information (Andrews *et al.*, 1982; Clarke-Stewart and Hevey, 1981; Kessen and Fein, 1975; Siegel, Bauman, Schaefer, Saunders, and Ingram, 1980; Whitt and Casey, 1982).

Ratings can be carried out on the scene or after the fact by the actual observer, or they can be done by an independent rater from behavior protocols. Because ratings represent a considerable "boiling down" of complex data, and because of questions about their accuracy, it is preferable that ratings done at the scene not be the only form in which interactional data are preserved. The greatest danger of ratings is that the rater may adjust his or her judgments in relation to an unconsciously assumed group baseline when comparing, for instance, boys and girls, or families with different socioeconomic or demographic characteristics. The only defense is to base the ratings on clear and detailed definitions of behavior, to do thorough reliability training beforehand, and to do frequent checks during the course of data collection (Walker, 1973).

Level of behaviors. Since most observational analyses will involve quantifying behaviors, investigators must decide how finely to break down behaviors in their recording scheme. Most observation codes used for parent–child interaction use mid-level variables or a combination of "molar" and "molecular" behaviors. In choosing an appropriate level for behavior variables, the investigator should aim for one that will produce usable frequencies for the behaviors of greatest interest, but it is desirable to retain a fair degree of discrimination (see Hartup [1979] for a more complete discussion of this issue).

Time intervals and length of observations. The question of appropriate time intervals for data recording continues to bedevil researchers. The difficulty is that different behaviors, having correspondingly different natural durations and frequencies, are best captured by different intervals. The usual solution has been to use the shortest interval observers find they can manage; manageability, in turn, relates to the size and complexity of the behavior code (Cairns, 1979; Maccoby and Martin, 1983). Researchers are likely to opt for short intervals if sequence of behaviors needs to be preserved, as it does for many analyses that attempt to make causal inferences about interaction. A problem with erring on the side of short intervals is that long-duration behaviors will be recorded in several sequential intervals, and it may not be possible to distinguish between a long continuous bout and repeated short instances of the same behavior.

How much observation time per subject is needed? There is little evidence on which to base an answer to this question (Clarke-Stewart and Fein, 1983). In general, the amount of time needed is dictated by frequency of behaviors and by the statistics that will be used in the analysis. Yarrow and Waxler (1979) found that a minimum of an hour was needed to obtain reasonably stable estimates for most behaviors. They warn that the single 10- or 20-minute observation per subject that is "so characteristic of child behavioral research" is, in consequence, "a flimsy platform . . . from which to launch conclusions" (p. 48). Sackett (1978) also discusses the issue of time- versus event-sampling.

Recording techniques and coding. Decisions have to be made about how data are to be recorded and/or coded. At one extreme are full audio- and video-recording of interaction for later coding; at the other, checklists with a few key behaviors to be noted as they occur. In between are techniques such as written narrative records that must be coded later and computer-ready records that are produced by event-recorders (Conger and McLeod, 1977; Simpson, 1979). Choices will depend on theoretical interests, ability of observers, sample size, and resources (See Cairns, 1979; Holm, 1978; Longabaugh, 1980; Lytton, 1971). For major evaluations it may be impractical to use a method that will require later coding; while data may be lost in precoded techniques, they are far more efficient for data-handling. If coding is done separately, it is preferable for coders to be "blind" to subjects' treatment condition. Whatever recording and coding methods are chosen, it is necessary to go through a preliminary stage of getting to know the phenomenon under study, developing a behavioral taxonomy, and eventually arriving at a code that captures what the investigators believe is important and is manageable for the observers. In addition to construct validity and observer reliability, it is important to try to foresee, insofar as is possible, the requirements of any analyses that may be attempted. (For examples of interaction studies that contain useful details on the development of behavior codes, see Bromwich [1978]; Bronson [1974]; Carew *et al.* [1978]; Clarke-Stewart [1973]; White [1979]; and Yarrow, Rubenstein, and Pederson, [1975].)

Analysis. The analysis of observational data is technically complex and resists brief description and summarization. Two particularly troublesome (and important) issues are how to handle the sequential analysis of behaviors within a single session and how to make sense of behavioral change over time in the developing child. Probably the best single brief summary of analysis issues is to be found in Maccoby and Martin (1983, pp. 18–26).

The most basic level of analysis involves calculating simple counts of frequencies and durations (including latencies) from which rate scores can be computed. The next level of complexity might include combining behaviors into more global clusters (Patterson, 1982), scaling various behaviors along a single dimension (Martin, 1981), or computing "derived" measures, for example, the proportion of vocal bids to which the caregiver responds (Hinde and Hermann, 1977). To capture a view of behavior "flowing and interlocking through time" (Maccoby and Martin, 1983, p. 19), several methods have been devised for examining sequential contingencies (Bakeman, 1978). Examples or discussion of a variety of such techniques are found in Bakeman and Brown (1977), Castellan (1979), Farran and Haskins (1980), Gottman and Bakeman, (1979), Lubin and Whiting (1977), Martin (1981), Martin, Maccoby, Baran, and Jacklin (1981), and Sackett (1978, 1979). Techniques that functionally parallel those for behavior sequences have been developed to examine longitudinal interactional data, though there continues to be a great deal of controversy about their validity and interpretation (Gottman, 1979; Gray and Wandersman, 1980; Maccoby and Martin, 1983; Nesselroade and Baltes, 1979; Parke *et al.*, 1979).

In sum, a large range of analytic possibilities is available to investigators. Researchers need to avoid violating the requirements of the underlying statistical assumptions, however, and should have access to expert consultation on these matters. Just as dissatisfaction with frequency counts has led to renewed interest in rating scales, it has also begun to produce creative thinking about how to improve the recording and analysis of interaction (Clarke-Stewart and Fein, 1983, pp. 941–942; Clarke-Stewart and Hevey, 1981; Dowdney, Mrazek, Quinton, and Rutter, 1984). Finally, I would appeal to investigators not to confine their efforts to the interactive data alone. Behavior can be most usefully explained not by reference only to itself, but in relation to its context, which includes ideological, psychological, social–structural, and physical elements (see Longfellow, Zelkowitz, and Saunders, 1982, and Zelkowitz, 1982, for an example).

Alternative Measures of Interaction

Two standardized instruments, the Caldwell and Bradley HOME and variants of the Ainsworth Strange Situation, have been used in place of or in conjunction with the methods described previously (see Table

4.1). The appropriateness of these two instruments as indexes of parent–child interaction is discussed here in light of the foregoing method-ological points and of recent criticisms in the developmental literature.

Caldwell's and Bradley's HOME. The Home Observations for Meas-urement of the Environment (HOME) (Caldwell and Bradley, 1984) is designed primarily to measure the quality of the home environment (see Upshur, this volume, for a detailed description). Because it includes subscales for "emotional and verbal responsivity," "acceptance of child's behavior," and "parental involvement with child," several family intervention studies have used this measure as the only means to assess mother–child interaction; it is to that use that the following comments are directed.

The HOME presents several problems as a measure of parent–child interaction. About half of the items for infants and toddlers (22 of 45) refer to behavior that can be construed as interactional; of those, only slightly more than half are likely to be observed directly by the home visitor. The rest would have to be scored from the caregiver's replies to probes. In addition, because the scoring criteria for many items are not clear or obvious, and the manual's instructions are not sufficiently specific, the HOME incurs all the risks associated with rating scales.

A related issue concerns the likelihood that the visit–interview rep-resents a naturalistic slice of interaction for the parent and child. The parent's engagement in responding to the interviewer is likely to in-terfere with his or her usual manner and frequency of interacting with the child; the child is also likely to react to having a visitor in the home. Observer effects are also a problem during sustained, systematic be-havior observations, but in that situation the observer does not engage members of the family in conversation and is likely to have spent enough time in the home that family members have, to some extent, become comfortable with the observer (see Mrazek *et al.*, 1982, on the importance of observer nonengagement). Further, the length of the visit, estimated by Caldwell and Bradley to be about 1 hour, allows for a rather small sample of behavior, especially given the constraints on normal interaction just described. It seems probable that there would often be no examples of some of the behaviors to be coded. A more appropriate use of the HOME is found in Olson, Bates, and Bayles (1984), where observers completed the HOME after conducting 6 hours of continuous home observation. Another important difficulty with us-ing the HOME to assess interaction is that it takes account of the child's characteristics or contributions to interaction only indirectly, in that scores on some items are dependent on the child supplying the stimulus for the caregiver's response. Given current conceptual emphasis on the child's contribution to interaction, direct assessment of the child's behavior is preferable.

Still other difficulties arise with the HOME when it is used in the evaluation of family programs. First, it places great emphasis on the provision of objects (toys and books) and on living arrangements and interactional styles that are characteristic of the middle and upper classes. It is unrealistic to expect poor, busy, stressed mothers to display such tolerance and expansiveness and to have the means to provide the materials. Thus the deficit model is reinforced.

Second, as I indicated earlier, there may be an interaction between treatment group and subjects' perception of what is called for. If treatment mothers have taken part in classes, group discussions, or home visits that included explicit instruction in how to foster their children's development, they are likely to recognize the hidden agenda of many of the items and to respond in the way they believe they should (see Barrera, Rosenbaum, and Cunningham, 1986; Bryant and Ramey, 1985).

In summary, the HOME is not a strong instrument for assessing parent–child interaction, although it may provide a reasonable gross measure of overall home stimulation.

Attachment measures. The concept of attachment (Bowlby, 1969) has had a powerful influence on theory about children's socioemotional development. Bowlby suggests that the tendency of infants and young children to seek and maintain contact with their mothers (or other primary caregivers) is part of an evolutionarily adaptive strategy to protect infants and to provide them with nurturing and a secure base from which to explore their environments. The resulting close contact and frequent interaction serves as "a facilitator, mediator, and behavioral indicator of an underlying bond, an enduring and focused relationship between the child and mother" (Clarke-Stewart and Fein, 1983, p. 945).

Following up on Bowlby's theory, Ainsworth and colleagues developed a measurement technique for assessing the quality of the mother–child bond, assumed to reflect the history of their interaction (Ainsworth, Blehar, Waters, and Wall, 1978; Belsky, Rovine, and Taylor, 1984). Three kinds of behavior are now thought of as the best indicators of attachment in children 12–24 months old: the child's interest in, and tendency to seek and maintain physical contact; reaction to separation from the mother; and response to reunion with her. The "Strange Situation" was devised to assess all three.

The procedure takes place in a setting unfamiliar to the child because Bowlby felt that the attachment system is best observed when fear and distress are activated. The assessment is divided into a series of episodes, each about 3 minutes long, in which the mother and child are alone in the room (furnished with two chairs), a stranger joins them and approaches the baby, the mother leaves the baby with the stranger, the mother returns and comforts the baby while the stranger leaves, the mother leaves again, the baby is left alone, the stranger joins the baby and offers to comfort if necessary, and, finally, the mother rejoins the baby and the stranger. Observation is done through one-way mirrors. Records of the actions of the baby and the adults are made and later rated for proximity and contact-seeking, contact-maintaining, resistance, avoidance, search, and distance interaction. Depending on their particular combination of reactions, babies are assigned to one of three major attachment classifications: "avoidant," "secure," and "resistant."

Because attachment classification is conceived as a direct measure of the quality of the mother–child relationship, it has been widely used not only in general developmental research, but also in contexts where conditions suggest there may be some peril to the relationship, for example, when the mother is emotionally impaired (Gross, 1983; Sameroff, Seifer, and Barocas, 1983), and in comparisons of children who have attended day care early in life with those who have not (see Clarke-Stewart and Fein, 1983, for a review of this issue). Some investigators have adapted the rating scales for use in naturalistic settings, such as the home or day care center (Siegel *et al.*, 1980).

There are several conceptual and methodological problems with the classic attachment paradigm. Recent critiques have been made by Campos, Barrett, Lamb, Goldsmith, and Stenberg (1983), Clarke-Stewart and Fein (1983), Hinde (1983), Kagan (1984), and Lamb, Thompson, Gardner, and Charnov (1985). To begin, attachment classifications are quite unstable over time and across attachment figures and have been shown to be affected by both the child's nature (as measured by temperament scales and the Brazelton Neonatal Behavioral Assessment Scales) and by the family's social support circumstances (Crockenberg, 1981). The relationships between attachment classification and maternal sensitivity (as assessed from observations) have been neither strong nor consistent. Critics of Ainsworth's approach have noted that the child's contribution to the natural ongoing interaction of the mother–child pair has been largely ignored in efforts to link particular styles of mothering to attachment classification.

The distribution of classifications is different in other cultures, indicating that attachment behavior may be influenced by underlying cultural ideology about child behavior and parent–child relations. Some behaviors observed in the Strange Situation paradigm may have different meanings for children of varied rearing conditions; for example, behavior that is termed "avoidant" may be truly so for children who are reared entirely at home, while it may indicate an ability to function independently for children who have spent considerable time in day care (Clarke-Stewart and Fein, 1983).

In the Strange Situation, the actions of the mother are strongly constrained by the instructions she is given beforehand, raising the possibility that the child's behavior can be explained, in part, as a response to her peculiar (from the child's point of view) behavior, rather than to the separations and reunions themselves. Clarke-Stewart and Fein raise the point that experience in day care (and probably in other treatment conditions in intervention programs) make aspects of the Strange Situation more familiar to and therefore less stressful for children in some treatment groups than in others. Finally, while Ainsworth herself has clearly distinguished between the *strength* of attachment and the *quality* of attachment (arguing that her procedure serves to assess only the latter) (Ainsworth, 1977), this distinction sometimes is lost in other investigators' hands.

Critics do not reject the concept of attachment; rather, they argue that claims for the reliability and validity of the Strange Situation and its variants are not well founded and that it is not a sensitive index of security of attachment. The paradigm may be most useful when assessing the effects of relatively extreme infant care circumstances. Investigators still need a sensitive measure of the quality of mother–child relationships. I hope that workers in both applied and pure developmental research will continue to develop methods and instruments to meet this need.

METHODOLOGICAL RECOMMENDATIONS

Planning and executing program evaluations are extremely complex endeavors. However, they present the opportunity to make real contributions to our understanding of the processes of development, *if* the research is carefully thought out as a series of steps. Each step must address clear, circumscribed questions, and be informed by the conceptual integration of the findings from foregoing steps (Gray and Wandersman, 1980; Hartup, 1978). (See Patterson's work with the families of socially aggressive boys for an excellent example of this approach.)

Investigators must seek a greater degree of ecological validity in their choices of instruments and settings than has generally been the case. While control (in the psychometric sense) is always needed, it does us no good if data are so distorted by its application that they do not represent a realistic picture of everyday behavior. Assessment situations should be *equivalent* across groups in terms of familiarity and ecological validity, rather than exactly *alike* (Harkness and Super, 1980).

Whenever possible, multiple measures in a given domain are preferable to a single one (Osofsky and Connors, 1979). The aim is not to produce equivalent data by similar means, but to approach a given behavioral issue by a process resembling triangulation, varying samples, settings, tasks, and types of data. Each instrument produces interesting data of its own, as well as shedding light on the findings of the others.

An example of this approach, and another strong recommendation for investigators interested in understanding parent–child interaction, is the use of a measure of parents' ideas and knowledge about children and child rearing. What parents do with their children becomes much more understandable when we know something about the ideology that shapes their approach to socialization and about the knowledge they bring to that process.

Behavioral definitions must be very explicit and clear, no matter what system of recording interaction is used, and reliability training and checking need to be careful and frequent. This is especially important for rating scales, which are easily subject to unconscious biases and shifting baselines. (Ratings are therefore probably best used in combination with another, more objective measure.) Similarly, careful thought needs to be given to selecting and training observers, raters, and coders. All three jobs require the capacity for rapport with subjects, perceptiveness, cultural sensitivity, consistency, objectivity, dedication, flexibility, and tolerance for hard work and boredom.

CONCEPTUAL RECOMMENDATIONS

Conceptual recommendations for parent–child interaction research cluster around two areas. First, evaluators need to design their studies and choose their instruments so as to allow fuller investigation of questions of direction of effects, both within occasions and across time, and to seek to incorporate information on individual children's characteristics and contributions to interaction. Such strategies greatly complicate the work of evaluators, but recent developmental research shows us that what goes on between parents and children is indeed very complex (Belsky, Gilstrap, and Rovine, 1984; Belsky, Rovine, and Taylor, 1984; Belsky, Taylor, and Rovine, 1984; Clarke-Stewart and Hevey, 1981; Dowdney et al., 1984; Olson et al., 1984). Until these complexities are taken into account, efforts to trace the effects of interventions will continue to produce weak and ambiguous findings.

The second area concerns cultural appropriateness of research methods (see Slaughter, this volume). Evaluators must question the universal applicability of particular mother–child interaction styles and take seriously the notion that environmental constraints and culture-specific ideologies powerfully affect how parents can and should interact with their children (LeVine, 1980). To this end, we badly need ethnographic investigation of community child-rearing goals, expectations, and theories, as well as more documentation of parent–child interaction styles and of the ecology of childrearing in various settings and subcultures. The value of such data outweighs the cost of attaining them, and they would provide a basis for guiding intervention and understanding assessment results. Another step toward strengthening intervention research might be to include community members at several stages of the intervention and research process. Older mothers and grandmothers could serve as informants for the background data-gathering described previously, as advisors during the planning and implementation of the intervention, and as collaborators in the interpretation of results. Family education professionals have lost valuable opportunities by ignoring community resources and failing to utilize methods that have proved their worth in work done outside this country.

The measurement of parent–child interaction is still at an early stage. There is a lack of uniformity across studies in the instruments chosen or devised to measure similar constructs. There is, at best, only "modest agreement" on what constitutes optimum states in the behavioral domains of interest. And finally, we lack population norms at the community, regional, and national levels to aid in interpreting measurement values (Halpern, 1984). Nevertheless, the parent education movement offers opportunities to make creative contributions to what is known about how parents and children behave together and influence one another.

REFERENCES

Ainsworth, M. D. S. (1977). Attachment theory and its utility in cross-cultural research. In P. H. Leiderman, S. R. Tulkin, and A. Rosenfeld (Eds.), *Culture and infancy* (pp. 49–67). NY: Academic Press.

Ainsworth, M. D. S., Blehar, M. C., Waters, E., and Wall, S. (1978). *Patterns of attachment.* Hillsdale, NJ: Erlbaum Associates.

Andrews, S. R., Blumenthal, J. B., Johnson, D. L., Kahn, A. J., Ferguson, C. J., Lasater, T. M., Malone, P. E., and Wallace, D. B. (1982). The skills of mothering: A study of parent child development centers. *Monographs of the Society for Child Development, 47*(6, Ser. No. 198).

Appelbaum, M. I., and McCall, R. B. (1983). Design and analysis in developmental psychology. In W. Kessen (Ed.), *Handbook of child psychology: Vol. 1. History, theory, and methods* (pp. 415–476). NY: Wiley.

Bakeman, R. (1978). Untangling streams of behavior: Sequential analyses of observation data. In G. P. Sackett (Ed.), *Observing behavior: Vol. 2. Data collection and analysis methods* (pp. 63–78). Baltimore, MD: University Park Press.

Bakeman, R., and Brown, J. V. (1977). Behavioral dialogues: An approach to the assessment of mother–infant interaction. *Child Development, 48,* 195–203.

Baldwin, A. L., Cole, R. E., and Baldwin, C. P. (1982). Parental pathology, family interaction, and the competence of the child in school. *Monographs of the Society for Research in Child Development, 47*(5, Ser. no. 197).

Barker, R. G. (Ed.). (1963). *The stream of behavior.* NY: Appleton Century-Crofts.

Barrera, M. E., Rosenbaum, P. L., and Cunningham, C. E. (1986). Early home intervention with low-birth-weight infants and their parents. *Child Development, 57,* 20–33.

Barry, H., III, Child, I. L., and Bacon, M. K. (1959). Relation of child training to subsistence economy. *American Anthropologist, 61,* 51–63.

Baumrind, D. (1967). Child care practices anteceding 3 patterns of preschool behavior. *Genetic Psychology Monographs, 75,* 43–88.

Baumrind, D., and Black, A. E. (1967). Socialization practices associated with dimensions of competence in preschool boys and girls. *Child Development, 38,* 291–327.

Beckwith, L. (1976). Caregiver–infant interaction and the development of the high risk infant. In T. Tjossem (Ed.), *Intervention strategies for high risk infants and young children* (pp. 119–139). Baltimore, MD: University Park Press.

Bee, H. L., Barnard, K. E., Eyres, S. J., Gray, C. A., Hammond, M. A., Spietz, A. L., Snyder, C., and Clark, B. (1982). Prediction of IQ and language skill from perinatal status, child performance, family characteristics, and mother–infant interaction. *Child Development, 53,* 1134–1156.

Bell, R. Q. (1964). Structuring parent–child interaction situations for direct observation. *Child Development, 35,* 1009–1020.

Bell, R. Q. (1968). A reinterpretation of the direction of effects in studies of socialization. *Psychological Review, 75,* 81–95.

Belsky, J., Gilstrap, B., and Rovine, M. (1984). The Pennsylvania Infant and Family Development Project, I: Stability and change in mother–infant and father–infant interaction in a family setting at one, three, and nine months. *Child Development, 55,* 692–705.

Belsky, J., Rovine, M., and Taylor, D. G. (1984). The Pennsylvania Infant and Family Development Project, III: The origins of individual differences in infant–mother attachment: Maternal and infant contributions. *Child Development, 55,* 718–728.

Belsky, J., Taylor, D. G., and Rovine, M. (1984). The Pennsylvania Infant and Family Development Project, II: The development of reciprocal interaction in the mother–infant dyad. *Child Development, 55,* 706–717.

Blurton-Jones, N. (Ed.). (1972). *Ethological studies of child behavior.* Cambridge, England: Cambridge University Press.

Bowlby, J. (1969). *Attachment and loss: Vol. 1. Attachment.* London: Hogarth Press.

Bromwich, R. (1978). *Working with parents and infants: An interaction approach.* Baltimore, MD: University Park Press.

Bromwich, R. M. (1976). Focus on maternal behavior in infant intervention. *American Journal of Orthopsychiatry, 46*(3), 439–446.

Bromwich, R. M., and Parmelee, A. H. (1979). An intervention program for preterm infants. In T. Field, A. Sostek, S. Goldberg, and H. Shuman (Eds.), *Infants born at risk: Behavior & development* (pp. 389–412). NY: Spectrum Publications Medical and Scientific Books.

Bronfenbrenner, U. (1974). *Is early intervention effective? A report on longitudinal evaluations of preschool programs* (Vol. 2). Washington, D.C.: Dept. of Health, Education, and Welfare.

Bronfenbrenner, U. (1979). *The ecology of human development.* Cambridge, MA: Harvard University Press.

Bronson, W. C. (1974). Mother–toddler interaction: A perspective studying the development of competence. *Merrill-Palmer Quarterly, 20,* 275–301.

Broussard, E. R., and Hartner, M. S. S. (1970). Maternal perception of the neonate as related to development. *Child Psychiatry and Human Development, 1,* 16.

Bryant, D. M., and Ramey, C. T. (1985). Prevention-oriented infant education programs. *Journal of Children in Contemporary Society, 17*(1), 17–35.

Buss, A. H., and Plomin, R. (1984). *A temperament theory of personality development.* NY: Wiley.

Cairns, R. B. (1979). Toward guidelines for interactional research. In R. B. Cairns (Ed.), *The analysis of social interactions: Methods, issues, and illustrations* (pp. 197–206). Hillsdale, NJ: Erlbaum Associates.

Cairns, R. B., and Green, J. A. (1979). How to assess personality and social patterns: Observations or ratings? In R. B. Cairns (Ed.), *The analysis of social interactions: Methods, issues, and illustrations* (pp. 209–226). Hillsdale, NJ: Erlbaum Associates.

Caldwell, B. M., and Bradley, R. H. (1984). *Home observations for measurement of the environment (HOME).* Little Rock, AR: Center for Child Development and Education, College of Education, University of Arkansas.

Campos, J. J., Barrett, K. C., Lamb, M. E., Goldsmith, H. H., and Stenberg, C. (1983). Socioemotional development. In M. M. Haith and J. J. Campos (Eds.), *Handbook of child psychology: Vol. 2. Infancy and developmental psychobiology* (pp. 783–915). NY: Wiley.

Carew, J. (1979). Commentary by Jean Carew. In A. S. Epstein and D. P. Weikart, *The Ypsilanti–Carnegie infant education project* (pp. 75–79). Ypsilanti, MI: High/Scope Press.

Carew, J. V. et al. (1978). *Toddler and Infant Experiences System Coding Manual.* Oakland, CA: TIES Project.

Carey, W. B., and McDevitt, S. C. (1978). Revision of the Infant Temperament Questionnaire. *Pediatrics, 61*(5), 735–739.

Castellan, N. J., Jr. (1979). The analysis of behavior sequences. In R. B. Cairns (Ed.), *The analysis of social interactions: Methods, issues, and illustrations* (pp. 81–116). Hillsdale, NJ: Erlbaum Associates.

Cicchetti, D. V. (1984). On a model for assessing the security of infantile attachment: Issues of observer reliability and validity. *The Behavioral and Brain Sciences, 7,* 149–150.

Clarke-Stewart, K. A. (1973). Interactions between mothers and their young children: Characteristics and consequences. *Monographs of the Society for Research in Child Development, 38*(6 and 7, Ser. No. 153).

Clarke-Stewart, K. A. (1981). Observation and experiment: Complementary strategies for studying day care and social development. In S. Kilmer (Ed.), *Advances in early education and day care* (Vol. 2, pp. 227–250). Greenwich, CT: JAI Press.

Clarke-Stewart, K. A., and Fein, G. G. (1983). Early childhood programs. In M. M. Haith and J. J. Campos (Eds.), *Handbook of child psychology: Vol. 2. Infancy and developmental psychobiology* (pp. 917–1000). NY: Wiley.

Clarke-Stewart, K. A., and Hevey, C. M. (1981). Longitudinal relations in repeated observations of mother–child interaction from 1 to 2-½ years. *Developmental Psychology, 17,* 127–145.

Cole, M., and Scribner, S. (1974). *Culture and thought.* NY: Wiley.

Conger, R. D., and McLeod, D. (1977). Describing behavior in small groups with the data-myte event recorder. *Behavior Research Methods and Instrumentation, 9*(5), 418–424.

Crockenberg, S. B. (1981). Infant irritability, mother responsiveness, and social support influences on the security of infant–mother attachment. *Child Development, 52,* 857–865.

Dickie, J. R., and Gerber, S. C. (1980). Training in social competence: The effects on mothers, fathers, and infants. *Child Development, 51,* 1248–1251.

Dowdney, L., Mrazek, D., Quinton, D., and Rutter, M. (1984). Observation of parent–child interaction with two- to three-year-olds. *Journal of Child Psychology and Psychiatry, 25*(3), 379–407.

Dunn, J., and Kendrick, C. (1980). Studying temperament and parent–child interaction: Comparison of interview and direct observation. *Developmental Medicine and Child Neurology, 22,* 484–496.

Dunn, J., and Kendrick, C. (1982). *Siblings: Love, envy, and under-standing.* Cambridge, MA: Harvard University Press.

Epstein, A. S., and Weikart, D. P. (1979). *The Ypsilanti–Carnegie Infant Education Project.* Ypsilanti, MI: High/Scope Press.

Falender, C. A., and Heber, R. (1975). Mother–child interaction and participation in a longitudinal intervention program. *Developmental Psychology, 11*(6), 830–836.

Farran, D. C., and Haskins, R. (1980). Reciprocal influence in the social interactions of mothers and three-year-old children from different socioeconomic backgrounds. *Child Development, 51,* 780–791.

Field, T. M., Widmayer, S. M., Stringer, S., and Ignatoff, E. (1980). Teenage, lower-class, black mothers and their preterm infants: An intervention and developmental follow-up. *Child Development, 51,* 426–436.

Fullard, W., McDevitt, S. C., and Carey, W. B. (1984). Assessing temperament in one- to three-year-old children. *Journal of Pediatric Psychology, 9*(2), 205–217.

Gottman, J. M. (1979). Time-series analysis of continuous data in dyads. In M. E. Lamb, S. J. Suomi, and G. R. Stephenson (Eds.), *Social interaction analysis: Methodological issues* (pp. 207–230). Madison, WI: University of Wisconsin Press.

Gottman, J. M., and Bakeman, R. (1979). The sequential analysis of observational data. In M. E. Lamb, S. J. Suomi, and G. R. Stephenson (Eds.), *Social interaction analysis: Methodological issues* (pp. 185–206). Madison, WI: University of Wisconsin Press.

Gray, S. W., and Ruttle, K. (1980). The Family-Oriented Home Visiting Program: A longitudinal study. *Genetic Psychology Monographs, 102,* 299–316.

Gray, S. W., and Wandersman, L. P. (1980). The methodology of home-based intervention studies: Problems and promising strategies. *Child Development, 51,* 993–1009.

Gross, D. (1983). How some dyads "fail": A qualitative analysis with implications for nursing practice. *Infant Mental Health Journal, 4*(3), 272–286.

Halpern, R. (1984). Lack of effects for home-based early intervention? Some possible explanations. *American Journal of Orthopsychiatry, 54*(1), 33–42.

Harkness, S. (1980). The cultural context of child development. In C. M. Super and S. Harkness (Eds.), *New Directions for child development no. 8: Anthropological perspectives on child development* (pp. 7–14). San Francisco, CA: Jossey-Bass.

Harkness, S., and Super, C. M. (1980). Child development theory in anthropological perspective. In C. M. Super and S. Harkness (Eds.),

New directions for child development no. 8: Anthropological Perspectives on Child Development (pp. 1–6). San Francisco, CA: Jossey-Bass.

Hartup, W. W. (1978). Perspectives on child and family interaction: Past, present, and future. In R. M. Lerner and G. B. Spanier (Eds.), *Child influences on marital and family interaction: A life-span perspective* (pp. 23–46). NY: Academic Press.

Hartup, W. W. (1979). Levels of analysis in the study of social interaction: An historical perspective. In M. E. Lamb, S. J. Suomi, and G. R. Stephenson (Eds.), *Social interaction analysis: Methodological issues* (pp. 11–33). Madison, WI: University of Wisconsin Press.

Hess, R. D. (1981). Approaches to the measurement and interpretation of parent–child interaction. In R. W. Henderson (Ed.), *Parent child interaction: Theory, research, and prospects* (pp. 207–233). NY: Academic Press.

Hess, R. D., and Shipman, V. C. (1965). Early experience and the socialization of cognitive modes in children. *Child Development, 34,* 869–886.

Hinde, R. A. (1983). Ethology and child development. In M. M. Haith and J. J. Campos (Eds.), *Handbook of child psychology: Vol. 2. Infancy and developmental psychobiology* (pp. 27–92). NY: Wiley.

Hinde, R. A., and Herrmann, J. (1977). Frequencies, durations, derived measures and their correlations in studying dyadic and triadic relationships. In H. R. Schaffer (Ed.), *Studies in mother–infant interaction* (pp. 19–46). London: Academic Press.

Hollenbeck, A. R. (1978). Problems of reliability in observational research. In G. P. Sackett (Ed.), *Observing behavior: Vol. 2. Data collection and analysis methods* (pp. 79–98). Baltimore, MD: University Park Press.

Holm, R. A. (1978). Techniques of recording observational data. In G. P. Sackett (Ed.), *Observing behavior: Vol. 2. Data collection and analysis methods* (pp. 99–108). Baltimore, MD: University Park Press.

Howard, A., and Scott, R. A. (1981). The study of minority groups in complex societies. In R. H. Munroe, R. L. Munroe, and B. B. Whiting (Eds.), *Handbook of cross-cultural human development* (pp. 113–154). NY: Garland Press.

Hutt, S. J., and Hutt, C. (1970). *Direct observation and measurement of behavior.* Springfield, IL: C. S. Thomas.

Kagan, J. (1984). *The nature of the child.* NY: Basic Books.

Kagan, J., and Moss, H. A. (1962). *Birth to maturity.* New Haven, CT: Yale University Press.

Kessen, W., and Fein, G. (1975). *Variations in home-based infant education: Language, play, and social development.* New Haven, CT: Yale University Press (ERIC Document Reproduction Service No. ED 118 233).

Kohn, M. L. (1969). *Class and conformity: A study in values.* Homewood, IL: Dorsey.

Kohn, M. L. (1976). Social class and parental values: Another confirmation of the relationship. *American Sociological Review, 41,* 538–545.

Kohn, M. L. (1979). The effects of social class on parental values and practices. In D. Reiss and H. A. Hoffman (Eds.), *The American family: Dying or developing?* (pp. 45–68). NY: Plenum.

Lamb, M. E. (1981). *The role of the father in child development,* 2nd ed. NY: Wiley.

Lamb, M. E., Thompson, R. A., Gardner, W., and Charnov, E. L. (1985). *Infant–mother attachment.* Hillsdale, NJ: Erlbaum Associates.

Lambie, D. Z., Bond, J. T., and Weikart, D. P. (1974). Home teaching with mothers and infants. *Monographs of High/Scope Educational Research Foundation. No. 2.* Ypsilanti, MI: High/Scope Press.

Laosa, L. M. (1979). Social competence in childhood: Toward a developmental, socioculturally relativistic paradigm. In M. W. Kent and J. E. Rolf (Eds.), *Primary prevention of psychopathology: Vol. 3. Social competence in children* (pp. 253–279). Hanover, NH: University Press of New England.

Laosa, L. M. (1981). Maternal behavior: Sociocultural diversity in modes of family interaction. In R. W. Henderson (Ed.), *Parent–child interaction: Theory, research, and prospects* (pp. 125–167). NY: Academic Press.

Leiderman, P. H., Tulkin, S. R., and Rosenfeld, A. (Eds.). (1977). *Culture and infancy.* NY: Academic Press.

LeVine, R. A. (1974). Parental goals: A cross-cultural view. *Teachers College Record, 76*(2), 226–239.

LeVine, R. A. (1980). A cross-cultural perspective on parenting. In M. Fantini and R. Cardenas (Eds.), *Parenting in a multicultural society* (pp. 17–26). NY: Longman.

Lewis, M., and Feiring, C. (1979). The child's social network: Social object, social functions, and their relationship. In M. Lewis and L. A. Rosenblum (Eds.), *The child and its family* (pp. 9–28). NY: Plenum Press.

Lewis, M., and Freedle, R. (1977). The mother and infant communication system: The effects of poverty. In H. McGurk (Ed.), *Ecological factors in human development* (pp. 205–215). NY: North-Holland.

Lewis, M., and Rosenblum, L. A. (Eds.) (1974). *The effect of the infant on its caregiver.* NY: Wiley.

Longabaugh, R. (1980). The systematic observation of behavior in naturalistic settings. In H. C. Triandis and J. W. Berry (Eds.), *Handbook of cross-cultural psychology: Vol. 2. Methodology* (pp. 57–128). Boston, MA: Allyn & Bacon.

Longfellow, C., Zelkowitz, P., and Saunders, E. (1982). The quality of mother–child relationships. In D. Belle (Ed.), *Lives in stress* (pp. 163–178). Beverly Hills, CA: Sage.

Lubin, D., and Whiting, B. B. (March 20, 1977). *Learning techniques of persuasion: An analysis of sequences of interaction.* Paper presented at the Biennial Meeting of the Society for Research in Child Development, New Orleans, Louisiana.

Lytton, H. (1971). Observation studies of parent–child interaction: A methodological review. *Child Development, 42,* 651–684.

Lytton, H. (1973). Three approaches to the study of parent–child interaction: Ethological, interview, and experimental. *Journal of Child Psychology and Psychiatry, 14,* 1–17.

Maccoby, E. E., and Martin, J. A. (1983). Socialization in the context of the family: Parent–child interaction. In E. M. Hetherington (Ed.), *Handbook of child psychology: Vol. 4. Socialization, personality, and social development.* NY: Wiley.

Madden, J., O'Hara, J., and Levenstein, P. (1984). Home again: Effects of the Mother–Child Home Program on mother and child. *Child Development, 55,* 636–647.

Martin, J. A. (1981). A longitudinal study of the consequences of early mother–infant interaction: A microanalytic approach. *Monographs of the Society for Research in Child Development, 46*(3, Ser. No. 190).

Martin, J. A., Maccoby, E. E., Baran, K. W., and Jacklin, C. N. (1981). The sequential analysis of mother–child interaction at 18 months: A comparison of microanalytic methods. *Developmental Psychology, 17,* 146–157.

Messick, S. (1983). Assessment of children. In W. Kessen (Ed.), *Handbook of child psychology: Vol. 1. History, theory, and methods* (pp. 477–527). NY: Wiley.

Miller, D. R., and Swanson, G. E. (1958). *The changing American parent.* NY: Wiley.

Mrazek, D. A., Dowdney, L., Rutter, M. L., and Quinton, D. L. (1982). Mother and preschool child interaction: A sequential analysis. *Journal of the American Academy of Child Psychiatry, 21*(5), 453–464.

Munroe, R. L., and Munroe, R. H. (1975). *Cross-cultural human development.* Monterey, CA: Brooks/Cole.

Munroe, R. H., Munroe, R. L., and Whiting, B. B. (Eds.), (1981). *Handbook of cross-cultural human development.* NY: Garland Press.

Musick, J., Clark, R., and Cohler, B. (1981). The Mothers Project: A program for mentally ill mothers of young children. In B. Weissbourd and J. Musick (Eds.), *Infants: Their social environments* (pp. 111–127). Washington, D.C.: National Association for the Education of Young Children.

Musick, J., Stott, F., Cohler, B., and Dincin, J. (1981). Post hospital treatment for psychotic depressed mothers and their children. In M. Lansky (Ed.), *Family therapy and major psychopathology* (pp. 91–121). NY: Grune & Stratton.

Nesselroade, J., and Baltes, P. (Eds.) (1979). *Longitudinal research in the study of behavior and development.* NY: Academic Press.

Ogbu, J. U. (1981). Origins of human competence: A cultural-ecological perspective. *Child Development, 52,* 413–429.

Olson, S. L., Bates, J. E., and Bayles, K. (1984). Mother–infant interaction and the development of individual differences in children's cognitive competence. *Developmental Psychology, 20*(1), 166–179.

Osofsky, J. D., and Connors, K. (1979). Mother–infant interaction: An integrative view of a complex system. In J. D. Osofsky (Ed.), *Handbook of infant development* (pp. 519–548). NY: Wiley.

Parke, R. D. (1978). Parent–infant interaction: Progress, paradigms, and problems. In G. P. Sackett (Ed.), *Observing behavior: Vol. 1. Theory and applications in mental retardation* (pp. 69–94). Baltimore, MD: University Park Press.

Parke, R. D. (1979). Interactional designs. In R. B. Cairns (Ed.), *The analysis of social interactions: Methods, issues, and illustrations* (pp. 15–30). Hillsdale, NJ: Erlbaum Associates.

Parke, R. D., Power, T. G., and Gottman, J. M. (1979). Conceptualizing and qualifying influence patterns in the family triad. In M. E. Lamb, S. J. Suomi, and G. R. Stephenson (Eds.), *Social interaction analysis: Methodological issues* (pp. 231–252). Madison, WI: University of Wisconsin Press.

Patterson, G. R. (1977). Naturalistic observation in clinical assessment. *Journal of Abnormal Child Psychology, 5*(3), 309–322.

Patterson, G. R. (1979). A performance theory for coercive family interaction. In R. B. Cairns (Ed.), *The analysis of social interactions: Methods, issues, and illustrations* (pp. 119–162). Hillsdale, NJ: Erlbaum Associates.

Patterson, G. R. (1982). *Coercive family process.* Eugene, OR: Castalia Press.

Ramey, C. T., Farran, D. C., and Campbell, F. A. (1979). Predicting IQ from mother–infant interactions. *Child Development, 50,* 804–814.

Rheingold, H. L. (1979). Mother–infant behavior: Description or explanation? In E. B. Thoman (Ed.), *Origins of the infant's social responsiveness* (pp. 291–304). Hillsdale, NJ: Erlbaum Associates.

Roberts, M. W., and Forehand, R. (1978). The assessment of maladaptive parent–child interaction by direct observation: An analysis of methods. *Journal of Abnormal Child Psychology, 6*(2), 257–270.

Sackett, G. P. (1978). Measurement in observational research. In G.

P. Sackett (Ed.), *Observing behavior: Vol. 2. Data collections and analysis methods* (pp. 25–43). Baltimore, MD: University Park Press.

Sackett, G. P. (1979). The lag sequential analysis of contingency and cyclicity in behavioral interaction research. In J. D. Osofsky (Ed.), *Handbook of Infant Development* (pp. 623–652). NY: Wiley.

Sameroff, A. J., Seifer, R., and Barocas, R. (1983). Impact of parental psychopathology: Diagnosis, severity, or social status effects? *Infant Mental Health Journal, 4*(3), 236–249.

Schwartz, T. (Ed.) (1976). *Socialization as cultural communication.* Berkeley, CA: Univ. of California Press.

Siegel, E., Bauman, K. E., Schaefer, E. S., Saunders, M. M., and Ingram, D. D. (1980). Hospital and home support during infancy: Impact on maternal attachment, child abuse and neglect, and health care utilization. *Pediatrics, 66*(2), 183–190.

Simpson, M. J. A. (1979). Problems of recording behavioral data by keyboard. In M. E. Lamb, S. J. Suomi, and G. R. Stephenson (Eds.), *Social interaction analysis: Methodological issues* (pp. 137–156). Madison, WI: University of Wisconsin Press.

Slaughter, D. T. (1983). Early intervention and its effects on maternal and child development. *Monographs of the Society for Research in Child Development, 48*(4, Ser. No. 202).

Smith, H. G. (1958). A comparison of interview and observation methods of maternal behaviors. *Journal of Abnormal and Social Psychology, 57,* 278–282.

Snow, C. E., DeBlauw, A., and Van Roosmalen, G. (1979). Talking and playing with babies: The role of ideologies of child-rearing. In M. Bullowa (Ed.), *Before speech: The beginning of interpersonal communication* (pp. 269–288). Cambridge, England: Cambridge University Press.

Stack, C. B. (1974). *All our kin: Strategies for survival in a black community.* NY: Harper & Row.

Super, C. M. (1981). Behavioral development in infancy. In R. L. Munroe, R. H. Munroe, and B. B. Whiting (Eds.), *Handbook of cross-cultural human development* (pp. 181–270). NY: Garland Press.

Triandis, H. C., and Heron, A. (Eds.). (1981). *Handbook of cross-cultural psychology* (Vol. 4). Boston, MA: Allyn & Bacon.

Walker, D. K. (1973). *Socioemotional measures for preschool and kindergarten children.* San Francisco, CA: Jossey-Bass.

Walters, J., and Walters, L. H. (1980). Parent–child relationships: A review, 1970–1979. *Journal of Marriage and The Family, 42,* 807–822.

Weick, K. E. (1968). Systematic observational methods. In G. Lindzey and E. Aronson (Eds.), *Handbook of social psychology: Vol. II* (pp. 357–451). Cambridge, MA: Addison-Wesley.

Werner, E. E. (1979). *Cross-cultural child development: A view from the planet Earth*. Monterey, CA: Brooks/Cole.

White, B. L. (1979). *The origins of human competence: The final report of the Harvard Preschool Project*. Lexington, MA: Heath.

White, B. L., and Watts, J. C. (1973). *Experience and environment: Major influences on the development of the young child*. Vol. I. Englewood Cliffs, NJ: Prentice-Hall.

Whiting, B. B. (1980). Culture and social behavior: A model for the development of social behavior. *Ethos, 8*(2), 95–116.

Whiting, B. B., and Whiting, J. W. M. (1970). Methods for observing and recording behavior. In R. Naroll and R. Cohen (Eds.), *A handbook of method in cultural anthropology* (pp. 282–315). NY: Natural History Press.

Whiting, B. B., and Whiting, J. W. M. (1975). *Children of six cultures: A psychocultural analysis*. Cambridge, MA: Harvard University Press.

Whiting, J. W. M., Child, I. L., and Lambert, W. W. (1966). *Field guide for a study of socialization*. (Six Cultures Series, Vol. 1). NY: Wiley.

Whitt, J. K., and Casey, P. H. (1982). The mother–infant relationship and infant development: The effect of pediatric intervention. *Child Development, 53*, 948–956.

Wright, H. F. (1960). Observational child study. In P. H. Mussen (Ed.), *Handbook of research methods in child development* (pp. 71–139). NY: Wiley.

Yarrow, L. J., and Anderson, B. J. (1979). Procedures for studying parent–child interaction: A critique. In E. B. Thoman (Ed.), *Origins of the infant's social responsiveness* (pp. 209–224). Hillsdale, NJ: Erlbaum Associates.

Yarrow, M. R., and Waxler, C. Z. (1979). Observing interaction: A confrontation with methodology. In R. B. Cairns (Ed.), *The analysis of social interactions: Methods, issues, and illustrations* (pp. 37–65). Hillsdale, NJ: Erlbaum Associates.

Yarrow, M. R., Campbell, J. D., and Burton, R. V. (1968). *Child rearing: An inquiry into research and methods*. San Francisco, CA: Jossey-Bass.

Yarrow, L. J., Rubenstein, J. L., and Pedersen, F. A. (1975). *Infant and environment: Early cognitive and motivational development*. NY: Wiley.

Zelkowitz, P. (1982). Parenting philosophies and practices. In D. Belle (Ed.), *Lives in stress* (pp. 154–162). Beverly Hills, CA: Sage.

Zigler, E., Lamb, M. E., and Child, I. L. (1982). *Socialization and personality development* (2nd Ed.). NY: Oxford University Press.

chapter 5

MEASURING PARENT OUTCOMES IN FAMILY PROGRAM EVALUATION

Carole C. Upshur

Those who design programs for young children and families often act on the belief that intervention directed at parents is as necessary as intervention directed at the child. Many programs provide parents with knowledge about child development, techniques for interacting with their children, advice on health and nutrition, and self-improvement options such as assistance with employment, education, and housing (see Evans and Halpern, 1981; Nauta and Travers, 1982, and Section III of this volume for descriptions of program models). Yet, despite wide-spread acceptance that such an "ecological approach" is more appro-priate than focusing solely on the child, evaluations of early childhood programs have continued to focus narrowly on outcomes in child development.

The effectiveness of early intervention is most frequently measured through the use of the intelligence quotient (IQ) test or the develop-ment quotient (DQ) test (Dunst and Rheingrover, 1982; Simeonsson, Cooper, and Scheiner, 1982; Zigler and Trickett, 1978). Impacts on child development in domains such as social competence, motivation, tem-perament, or behavior have rarely been documented. Virtually non-existent are descriptions of measures of changes in parents, siblings, or family status (see Hauser-Cram and Shonkoff, Chapter 3; Jacobs, Chapter 2, this volume).

If programs providing family support and education on the ecological model are to be fully evaluated, assessment of parent development must be incorporated into the evaluation procedure. This chapter will review evidence supporting the notion that parent and family development crucially affects the development of the child. Parent and family variables will then be discussed, and finally, specific measures and instruments that can be used in evaluating parent outcomes will be identified.

Parent and Family Roles in Child Development

The major impetus for the early childhood education movement of the 1960s and the continuing concern for providing family support and education programs to a wide range of families in the 1980s came from research linking socioeconomic status (SES) with individual intellectual development, more specifically to scores on IQ tests (Coleman, Campbell, Hobson, McPortland, and Mood, 1966; Kennedy, Van De Riet, and White, 1963; Lesser, Fifer, and Clark, 1965). Higher social class (as indicated by occupation and education of parents and type of residence) correlated positively with performance on traditional IQ tests. The relationship between SES and a child's ability to handle abstract language and thought can be detected at ages as early as 7 months (Wachs, Uzgiris, and Hunt, 1971). The dramatic clarity of these findings suggested that early "compensatory" education should be provided to disadvantaged children before they enter school to improve their school performance and academic achievement.

Despite the role of parents' SES, Head Start, the flagship of the compensatory education movement, was initially organized as a group program primarily working with children. In a seminal review, Bronfenbrenner (1974) analyzed the results of evaluations of these group programs for children and concluded that IQ gains were common in the first year of participation in a program, but that neither earlier enrollment nor increased length of enrollment produced greater IQ gains. Program participation also failed to produce long-term gains in IQ scores. Gains made in preschool years were usually lost at entry to school, although "follow-through" programs tended to stabilize gains.

Most importantly, however, parent involvement emerged as a critical discriminator between those children who retained IQ gains and those who did not. Earlier enrollment *did* make a difference if parents were involved and the gain extended to other siblings. Further, mothers themselves showed gains in confidence and self-concept, gains that were assumed to have reverberating, positive effects on the children. These findings prompted Bronfenbrenner to recommend a wide range of parent-oriented supports and services as essential to promoting significant and stable improvements in development, particularly in the domains of cognitive skill and academic achievement.

In the decade that has passed since Bronfenbrenner's review, parent involvement in intervention programs for young children has been widely promoted (Nauta and Travers, 1982; Travers and Light, 1982; Yurchak and Stix, 1980). A number of studies have shown significant improvements in children's performance based on work with parents (Goodson and Hess, 1978; Love, Nauta, Coelen, and Ruopp, 1975; Madden, Levenstein, and Levenstein, 1976; Olds, Chapter 10; Tivnan, Chapter 9, this volume; Yawkey, 1982). Yet, there is still widespread reliance on IQ or DQ measures of children as the primary method of assessing program impact. This practice has been criticized not only for its limitations in assessment of the child, but also for its failure to assess impact on the level of the family (Sheehan and Keogh, 1981; Simeonsson *et al.*, 1982; Travers and Light, 1982; Zigler and Balla, 1982).

In recent years there has been some attempt to develop and apply a wider range of measures in evaluating early intervention and family support services. A few studies have assessed early intervention program impacts on parent–child interaction, social support networks, and family stress (Bristol, 1983; Dunst, Trivette, and Cross, 1984; Field, 1977; Upshur, 1981; see also this volume, Chapter 4, Howrigan, and Chapter 17, Nauta and Hewett). However, relatively little work has been done on measuring the impact of interventions directly on parents. Using meta-analytic techniques (see Hauser-Cram, this volume, Chapter 20), White (1984) reviewed 162 early intervention studies that identified 1665 effect sizes; he noted that only 5% of all effect sizes were measures of impact on someone other than the target child.

Parent Variables

Once it is recognized as useful and important to investigate program impacts on parents, the variables most fruitfully incorporated into such investigations must be selected. I will present two categories of parent variables; *descriptive* characteristics of parents and families; and parent characteristics considered to be *targets of intervention*.

Examples of variables that are used descriptively include income, parents' education, and residence. We have seen that these characteristics often correlate with child outcomes, particularly in cognitive skill areas. Other variables that may be used descriptively, but about which little is known, include ethnicity, cultural or religious affiliations, family composition, language spoken at home, and urban or rural location.

Examples of variables used as targets of intervention, often called dependent variables, include attitudes, behavior, knowledge, and self-development. We have some evidence that these variables are mediating factors in influencing child development, beyond the seemingly powerful influence of SES. For example, Caldwell and Bradley (1984) have noted that *within* social class categories there are substantial differences in parent attitudes and behavior toward their children. They note a 1953 study by Kahl that found that within SES groups, families who valued "getting ahead" versus "getting by" were more interested in education, and that this explained more of the variance in educational achievement of children than SES alone, when children were matched for IQ. Each of these types of variables will be described in more detail in the following sections.

Attitudes and Behaviors

Several studies have examined the home environment and have found such dimensions as parental language use, presence of academic and intellectual stimulation, and amount of parent interaction with the child as important predictors of children's intellectual performance (Jones, 1972; Whiteman, Brown, and Deutsch, 1967; Whiteman and Deutsch, 1968).

Specific maternal style dimensions have been found to relate to a child's success in performing cognitive tasks. For example, Bernstein's work (1961, 1971) has linked social control types to language competence. Hess and Shipman (1965) found that maternal behavior demonstrating limited language usage, more restrictions, repetitive and reactive teaching, and less praise produced less effective behavior on the part of children.

Parenting Knowledge

Many programs seek to educate parents about child development or about specific behaviors, problems, or issues. Yurchak and Stix (1980) and Harman and Brim (1980) both cite the imparting of knowledge to parents as an important goal of family support and intervention programs (see also, Ellwood, Chapter 13, and Rodriguez and Cortez, Chapter 12, this volume). A study by Pinsker and Geoffrey (1981) in which specific parent teaching curricula were implemented and evaluated against a control group found that parent knowledge increased significantly and that there were impacts on children such as decreases in problem behavior and higher family cohesion. Minde, Shosenberg, Marton, Thompson, Ripley, and Burns (1982) reported a number of differences between parents of premature infants who participated in parent education groups and parents who did not participate. Participants reported more competency in handling their infants and behavioral differences such as visiting and stimulating their hospitalized infants; once home, program parents spent more time talking to and looking at their infants.

Personal Development

Parents who have health problems, are depressed, have poor self-concepts, feel out-of-control of their lives, or are under a variety of stresses are not likely to be able to provide optimal conditions for child development. Evans and Halpern (1981) found that teenage mothers involved in a home visit program were more likely to earn their general education diploma and enroll in vocational training; they learned more about child development, and they played and talked more with their children. Positive changes in parents' life style, self-image, and mental health thus may set the stage for more positive parent–child interaction. This, in turn, may produce positive effects on the child's development and on the family unit.

The arena for exploring program impacts on parents is large and varied. There are important reasons to investigate some or all of the foregoing variables as significant outcomes of family support and education interventions.

DESIGNING PROGRAM EVALUATIONS WITH PARENT OUTCOMES

The design of an evaluation program must take into account a number of factors unique to the program to be evaluated. These factors include: the theoretical orientation and goals of the program, the desired depth and duration of evaluation activities, and the resources available for those activities. These are discussed below. Another factor, discussed in Jacobs (Chapter 2, this volume), is the intended purpose of the evaluation (e.g., for use in fund raising, research, or public support efforts).

Clarification of program goals and theoretical orientation is prerequisite to evaluation. One can only test for effectiveness if one is clear about what one expects to effect, immediately and/or causally. Since it remains unclear what causal sequences hold among changes in knowledge, attitudes, and behavior (Harman and Brim, 1980), programs differ in the attention and primacy they attribute to intervention in each of these domains. Underlying these choices are theories, implicit or explicit, about causal sequences. For example, many family-oriented programs focus primarily on providing information and promoting skills in parents (Chrisner and Relich, 1981; Hennon and Peterson, 1981; Pinsker and Geoffrey, 1981; Reineke and Benson, 1981). These programs view positive changes in levels of skill and knowledge as effecting positive changes in the domain of the presenting problem (e.g., experienced stress, maladaptive behavior). Other programs may choose to consider parental SES as a dependent variable, that is, they may aim to promote a higher standard of living. This theoretical orientation is supported by Bronfenbrenner's work (1974) indicating that for certain families, no progress can be made in the psychological domain until basic housing and income needs are met. Work by Seigel, Bauman, Schaefer, Saunders, and Ingram (1980) also supports this view. They found, for example, that major differences in maternal attachment related more to SES variance than to participation in four different levels of home and hospital support services.

Programs differ in the extent to which they evaluate changes both in the target domain and the causally affected domain. For example, some programs providing skills and information may simply measure whether parents make use of the skills and information (Hennon and Peterson, 1981), while others will test for knowledge gain (Reineke and Benson, 1981), and still others will test for the hoped-for attitude or behavior change (Chrisner and Relich, 1981; Pinsker and Geoffrey, 1981).

In clarifying program goals, debate may be sparked about how one defines which outcomes are "good." While this debate may prove thorny, it is likely to be fruitful, not only for those attempting to design an appropriate evaluation, but for those directing the program as well. Being clear about what one hopes to accomplish generally increases the likelihood of accomplishment.

Decisions concerning amount of data to be collected and type of measures to be used in an evaluation must be made on the basis of how much staff time and effort can be devoted to the evaluation and on the basis of the time and effort available from parents. The involvement of parents in evaluation activities in terms of their time (for completing questionnaires, allowing home observations, filling out follow-up information, etc.) should be proportionate to the intensity and length of the services provided to them. Programs also need to be sensitive to the intrusiveness of repeat measures, especially months or years after the program has ended. In addition, the types of questions asked or measures used should be carefully evaluated in terms of parent reactions. Many parents will be quite anxious and fearful of attempts to test their knowledge or observe their parenting style. Yurchak and Stix (1980) suggest that such problems can be avoided by involving parents in the design and review of evaluations.

Staff involvement required by evaluation efforts can be substantial, as it is usually recommended that more than one piece of data or measure be collected for each goal area, regardless of specific goals. While some types of measures are quickly and easily administered (e.g., SES measures) others may require detailed observations and recording of events. Many staff hours and extensive training may be required to assure reliability.

Generally, more complex and multidimensional program goals require more complex and time-consuming methodologies for evaluation. In some cases, long-term follow-up may be required to demonstrate effectiveness. Face-to-face interviews are most likely to provide accurate and comprehensive data. However, they are time-consuming to conduct and analyze. Since cost factors are often of crucial importance in selecting evaluation procedures, many programs opt for an intermediate level of cost and effort as is required for the administration of questionnaires or scales assessing parental attitudes or personality dimensions. In choosing among such pencil-and-paper measures, programs must consider their complexity, length, and reading level.

Recommended Measures of Parent Variables

Once a program has identified its goals and assessed its resources, decisions must be made concerning methods of data collection and choice of measures. Reviews of the literature on evaluation of family support and parent education programs reveal that few programs have focused on parent outcomes and that few standard measures have been developed that are useful to evaluate parent education programs (Hicks and Williams, 1981). By far the most commonly used measures of program impact on parents are program-specific questionnaires dealing with parent reactions to the services and tests of parent knowledge. A few programs document specific SES variables, and some look at personality or attitude dimensions of parents, such as locus of control. In this section I will suggest methods for documenting both descriptive parent variables and variables likely to be targets of intervention.

Documentation of Descriptive Parent Variables

It is usually not very difficult to draw up a set of five to ten questions addressing basic SES and other specific characteristics of parents and families. Of greater difficulty than the design of such an evaluation tool is its presentation to parents, as they may question both its confidentiality and its subsequent use. Parents should be carefully advised of the use and confidentiality of the data and should not be coerced into reporting. Items such as income are often more easily obtained if ranges, rather than specific dollar amounts, are requested. The ranges, to be maximally useful, should correspond to ranges used by the U.S.

Census Bureau or other standard research sources. Occupations of parents should also be classified into common groups such as used by Hollingshead and Redlich (1958). Typically descriptive measures include race, income, number and ages of members in the household, mother's and father's occupation, and highest grade completed by parents.

Additional items can cover issues of importance to particular programs such as language spoken at home or religious affiliation. These items should be collected at the point of entry to a program, but they should also be monitored for change. For example, Nauta and Travers (1982), Evans and Halpern (1981), and Provence and Naylor (1983) all report as significant positive impacts of family support programs increases in mother's involvement in education, training, or employment.

Documentation of Parent Variables That Are Targets of Intervention

Only two measures of parent attitude and behavior have been used widely; the Caldwell and Bradley HOME (Caldwell and Bradley, 1984) and the Strom Parent as a Teacher (PAAT) (Strom, 1984). These two instruments will be reviewed later in this section.

While a few instruments can be identified which measure parent attitudes and behavior, there are no widely used standard measures of knowledge of child development. This is not surprising since programs have a wide variety of philosophies, cultural orientations, and goals with regard to child development. This is an area where programs are most likely to develop their own questionnaires to determine what changes in knowledge have occurred. Suggestions on developing such questionnaires are given later in this section.

Finally, as with measures of child development knowledge, there are no commonly used personality instruments or other indicators of personal change in parents. There are, however, some instruments that can be recommended. These include a relatively new and increasingly popular instrument, the Parenting Stress Index (PSI), which is used to assess a variety of dimensions of parenting (Abidin, 1983). Many of its subscales deal with child characteristics; several others, however, assess parent characteristics such as depression, sense of competence, and health. The PSI, as well as a few personality tests, will be further discussed shortly.

Caldwell and Bradley HOME

This instrument has been used in a number of research studies and evaluations of parenting programs. It requires that an interviewer/observer visit a child's home to record information about the home environment, to observe parent–child interaction, and to ask a few questions of the caregiver present. Caldwell and Bradley (1984) report that items were developed through a review of the research literature indicating what characteristics of a young child's environment foster optimum development. In its current form the instrument consists of two scales, a 45-item scale for children ages 0–3, and a 55-item scale for children ages 3–6. An experimental version of a third scale for children ages 6–10 is also included in the 1984 edition of the HOME manual. Subscales address the following dimensions: frequency and stability of adult contact, the amount of vocal and developmental stimulation; basic need gratification; emotional climate; avoidance of restrictions on exploratory behavior; availability of play materials and home characteristics indicative of parental concern for achievement. There are six subscales for the Infant and Toddler version and seven for the Preschool version. More detailed psychometric work has been completed with the Infant and Toddler version.

The scales take about 1 hour to administer. Interobserver agreement of 90% can be achieved on scoring. Each item has only a YES/NO choice for scoring, thus making observer training and reliability less complex than for more detailed observational measures. Reasonable reliability and moderate stability of the scale has been shown, although scores on the Infant and Toddler scale tend to be higher for older children because of the tendency of most families to purchase more toys as the child reaches age 1 or 2. Validation studies have investigated the correlation of HOME scores with SES variables and standardized measures of cognitive and general development (i.e., the Stanford–Binet Intelligence Scale, Terman and Merrill, 1973; and the Bayley Scales of Infant Development, Bayley, 1969). Low to moderate correlations between the HOME and SES are noted as positive indication that the HOME is more sensitive than SES inpredicting a child's cognitive development. Low HOME scores at early ages have been found to predict later problems such as malnutrition and language delay (Cravioto and DiLicardie, 1972; Wulbert, Inglis, Kriegsman, and Millis, 1975). The HOME is thus recommended primarily as a screening instrument, although a variety of intervention programs have also used it to measure impact of parent training and education.

On the Infant and Toddler scale, three subscales are oriented to measuring the parent–child interaction, while the other three are oriented to the structure of the household and the types of toys and activities the parent provides. Representing the latter category are these sample items:

- Child is taken to the grocery store at least once a week.
- Toys for literature and music.
- Child has three or more books of his/her own.

Each item is scored either "YES" or "NO" based on parent report. The Preschool scale has four subscales oriented to these same dimensions.

The HOME has the advantage of including a visit to the child's environment to obtain a more objective and accurate view of the family and parent–child interaction than self-report checklists. However, there are some problems with the use of the HOME. First, while the HOME manual attempts to explain how each item should be scored, users have found that further definitions and specific directions to observers need to be given to assure consistency and accuracy in recording results. Second, observers need to be trained carefully and their scoring decisions periodically monitored. Third, when one observer is visiting both experimental and control families, there is a great likelihood of bias in favor of the experimental families who may be more familiar to the project and may be given "benefit of the doubt." Using observers who are blind to the treatment status and histories of families is thus recommended (Halpern, 1984).

Strom Parent As A Teacher

The Parent As A Teacher (PAAT) measure is designed to assess parent attitudes toward their children and to determine feelings and values concerning child behavior. It consists of 50 items to which parents respond in one of four ways from "strong no" to "strong yes" with four points given for the most favorable response (Strom and Slaughter, 1978). Sample items include:

It is all right for my child to disagree with me.
I feel able to choose new toys for my child.
I try to praise my child a lot when we play.

The overall conceptual framework of the instrument derives from a range of child development findings but relies most heavily on work describing the nature of creative thinking and the importance of play. It is designed as a tool to help parents to understand their beliefs and attitudes and to analyze how they interact with their children. The items are organized into five subscales, as follows:

1. *Creativity:* Assesses parents' encouragement of problem solving, anxiety over disagreements, openness to new experiences, and level of sex role stereotyping.
2. *Frustration:* Assesses parents' expectations concerning children's needs and frequency with which children's needs are divergent from parents' expectations.

3. *Control:* Assesses parents' willingness to share some control with their children and acknowledgment of the need to allow for some disagreements, for spontaneity, and for privacy.
4. *Play:* Assesses parents' tolerance and encouragement of fantasy.
5. *Teaching/Learning:* Assesses parents' approach to teaching and the level of coercion used in teaching.

The scale was initially developed in 1972 and pretested on black and Mexican–American children and families in Arizona (Strom and Johnson, 1978). The subscales are not considered internally valid, and correlation among them is expected; rather, they are useful as a diagnostic or teaching tool with parents. A validity study was conducted that compared observations of families during home visit play situations with responses to the PAAT. Behavior consistent with parent self-report on the PAAT was observed for 66% of the 38 items that could be observed (Strom and Johnson, 1978). In other words, 66% of the time, parents actually behaved in ways they reported on the PAAT. In a study of Native American tribes, Strom and Hill (1979) found marked cultural differences between two tribes in parent scores on the PAAT, as well as differences depending on the child's sex and sex of the parent answering the questions. Parental level of education correlated significantly with both the total score and all subscales in this study as well as other studies of the measure.

Correlations with child development scores on the McCarthy Scales (McCarthy, 1972) have also been demonstrated in a study of families of private nursery school children (Strom, Hathaway, and Slaughter, 1981). In this study, the mother's attitude toward control (i.e., sharing control with the child and allowing spontaneity) was the best predictor of McCarthy scores.

In a study of the use of the PAAT with families having a child aged 2–12 years with Down's syndrome or other brain damage, Strom, Rees, Slaughter, and Wurster (1980, 1981) investigated the differences that might exist between parents of normal children and parents of handicapped children. Findings indicated that these parents score low on creativity and play, preferring to have very directed, specific interactions with their children and preferring not to allow the child a decision-making role. The parents of handicapped children scored high on the teaching/learning subscale, demonstrating the recognition of their important role in working with their child. Overall, the PAAT scores in this study did predict which parents would fare better in a home-based language stimulation program. High-scoring families had better attendance and better record keeping and their children showed greater success. They were also less likely to report uncertainty about whether their handicapped child would be maintained at home or institutionalized.

The PAAT is relatively easy to administer and has been used by a number of family and parenting intervention programs to measure program impact (Nauta and Travers, 1982; Strom and Slaughter, 1978; Yurchak and Stix, 1980). For parents who cannot read, Strom and Hill (1979) report a procedure for tape recording the questions and using symbols for parents to respond. The scale has also been used extensively in Spanish.

There are two major cautions associated with the PAAT's use as an evaluation tool. First, with cultural subgroups, some items generated large scores in the opposite direction of what the scale indicates is a positive attitude for child development (Nauta and Travers, 1982). Strom recommends in such cases focusing program interventions on items where there is a range of parent responses, as those items are not likely to be tied strongly to cultural patterns and may be more amenable to change. (For a discussion of intervention and cultural characteristics, see Slaughter, Chapter 21, this volume.) Second, there does not seem to be a history of controlled studies using the PAAT, although significantly positive changes in PAAT scores have been reported for a few intervention studies (Nauta and Travers, 1982; Strom and Slaughter, 1978). One can question whether positive parent reports in postprogram administrations of the PAAT are a function of social response bias. Further, the relationship between parent reporting and parent attitude change and behavior change is unclear. Positive scores on the PAAT do not necessarily indicate that parents' interactions with their children have in fact changed.

Program Questionnaires as Measures of Child Development Knowledge

Since there are no standard measures of knowledge about child development, many programs have developed their own questionnaires based on the type of information they are trying to convey (Chisner and Relich, 1981; Hennon and Peterson, 1981; Pinsker and Geoffrey, 1981; Reineke and Benson, 1981). These questionnaires are designed to "test" parents' understanding of the content of specific training sessions, dealing with behavior management, knowledge of child development, or child safety and health issues. They can also be designed to gain reactions and opinions of parents to various aspects of service delivery.

Questionnaires developed for individual programs should be seen primarily as sources for formative evaluation, that is, as tools to modify or improve programs. They should not generally be relied upon as significant indicators of program impact because programs usually do not have the time to conduct reliability and validity studies of these questionnaires—nor is the in-depth development of program questionnaires a good use of evaluation resources.

The problems in designing adequate questionnaires are many. Poorly designed questionnaires can yield an inaccurate picture of the impact of a program. For example, the bias of most parents will be to report favorably about a program whether or not they liked it, because it is polite and socially acceptable to do so. Programs need to word questions to encourage honest feedback. Some suggestions on designing these questionnaires include:

1. Make the questions and format simple, taking into account reading levels of parents. Some formats likely to obtain higher response rates than those requiring parents to write out answers are checklists, true-or-false questions, and those which use numerical ratings. Keep questionnaires short enough to be completed in 15–20 minutes.

2. Encourage frankness by preserving anonymity. This might mean not obtaining names on the questionnaires or setting up a coding system. Consider having parents fill out the forms at home. While fewer may be returned, comments will be more candid.

3. Pilot-test questionnaires with a few parents to determine which questions are susceptible to misinterpretation. If the questionnaire is used with large numbers of parents and over several years, determine which questions are consistently left blank and which are almost always answered correctly. Keep track of characteristics of parents who do not return or fill out the questionnaires; this may provide clues that your program is working only for some.

4. Administer the questionnaires both before and after parents receive services, so that the impact of the program can be documented. Preprogram questionnaires can include a specific test of knowledge plus questions on what parents expect to learn or gain from the program. Postprogram questionnaires should repeat the test of knowledge and also determine whether parent expectations were met and how satisfied they were with the program.

Personality Tests as Measures of Parents' Personal Development

While it is commonly assumed that the emotional health of the mother can play a major role in a child's development, few family support or parent education programs assess the personality of the mother. This may be because personality measures are considered too intrusive, too time-consuming, or not useful without interpretation by clinical experts. Nauta and Travers (1982), however, used a simple, five-question locus-of-control scale to assess whether parents felt in control of their lives. Those who scored high on the scale, or whose scores increased, had more positive outcomes on other dimensions, such as obtaining jobs and interacting more favorably with their children. A sample question is: "I shouldn't plan ahead because things don't usually work out." Parents were asked to check a number from one to five that represented strong agreement through strong disagreement with the statement.

Another simple locus-of-control scale, the Rotter (1966), has 29 paired statements. The parents indicate which statement they most agree with. Scoring is done by adding up the number of items indicating "lack of control." Olds (1984) has used a modified version of the Rotter in evaluating parent support programs in New York State. A copy of the scale can be found in Robinson and Shaver (1973). A sample statement is:

Many times I feel that I have little influence over the things that happen to me.

For parent intervention programs this dimension, lack of a sense of personal control, is interpreted as meaning that parents do not believe that support or stimulation of their children will produce any positive impact on a child's development, for example, they believe that how children turn out has little to do with what parents do. Changing such an attitude is obviously important for positive child rearing.

A new locus of control scale has been developed specifically to tap parents' attitudes as to what factors influence their child's development: the Child Improvement Locus of Control Scales (CILC) (DeVellis, DeVellis, Revicki, Lurie, Runyan, and Bristol, 1985). This 27-item Likert scale is a multidimensional instrument that assesses beliefs such as: one's child improves or fails to improve because of (a) chance; (b) efforts of professionals or experts; (c) child's own efforts; or (d) parents' efforts to help child. The CILC has been used in two studies, one involving parents of autistic children and one involving parents of physically ill children. Factor analyses performed on scale scores from these two studies and calculation of alpha coefficients for subscales indicated satisfactory psychometric properties. Results were also found to have face validity, that is, parents' responses correlated well to various characteristics of the parents and the particular problems of their children. While this is a new instrument, because it is designed specifically to address issues of parenting, it holds promise.

The self-concept of parents is another important variable that can be measured simply. The Rosenberg Self-Esteem Scale (1965) is a 10-item rating scale that asks simple questions concerning an individual's attitude toward him/herself and whether (s)he can identify characteristics that engender satisfaction or pride. The reader is asked to rate him/herself on a scale of 1–4, from strongly agree to strongly disagree on these questions:

1. *I feel that I am a person of worth, at least on an equal plane with others.*
2. *I feel that I have a number of good qualities.*
3. *All in all, I am inclined to feel that I am a failure.*
4. *I am able to do things as well as most other people.*
5. *I feel I do not have much to be proud of.*
6. *I take a positive attitude toward myself.*
7. *On the whole, I am satisfied with myself.*
8. *I wish I could have more respect for myself.*
9. *I certainly feel useless at times.*
10. *At times I think I am no good at all.*

The Rosenberg Scale is designed for brevity and ease of administration and has reasonable validity and reliability. It is noted as a "model short measure" in a review by Robinson and Shaver (1973).

Parenting Stress Index (PSI)

The Parenting Stress Index (Abidin, 1983) has not yet been widely used as a measure in family support or parent training programs. However, it has been used in a few studies and holds promise as a multi-faceted scale that taps several areas of parent attitudes and feelings, including personal emotional status. It was developed as a screening and diagnostic tool to identify stresses in the parent–child interactive system due to child characteristics, mother characteristics, life events, and demographic variables. Items were drawn from the research literature on child development and rated by a panel of professionals. Several stages of field testing resulted in refinement of the Index down to 101 items plus an optional 19-item *Life Events* scale. Parents answer each item by circling a number from 1–5, representing strong agreement to strong disagreement. The Index is at the fifth-grade reading level and takes 20–30 minutes to complete. Sample items are:

My child is much more active than I expected.
I feel capable and on top of things when I am caring for my child.
I feel trapped by my responsibilities as a parent.

A recent factor analysis of the PSI indicated that 58% of the total variance in the scale is accounted for by the Parent Characteristics Domain and the Child Characteristics Domain (Loyd and Abidin, 1985). Each of these domains has subscales as follows:

Child domain	Parent domain
Adaptability	Depression
Acceptability	Attachment
Demandingness	Restrictions of role
Mood	Sense of competence
Distractibility/hyperactivity	Social isolation
Reinforces parent	Relationship with spouse
	Parent health

Validity is substantiated by use of research studies to generate the items, correlational studies to eliminate items not showing a good "fit" on subscales, and by concurrent validity of PSI subscale scores with other measures of the same construct. In addition, studies of families with atypical children consistently have demonstrated the discriminate validity of the scale. Total stress scores and child domain scores discriminated between groups of parents with normal children and parents of children with retardation, cerebral palsy or developmental delay, and feeding problems. A study of abusive mothers compared to nonabusive mothers also found significant differences on all scales of the PSI (Mash, Johnston, and Kovitz, 1983).

I recommend use of the PSI with two caveats. First, some parents may react to the negative wording of most of the items. Second, despite the scale's name, only the most recent version of the scale has been designed to be administered to both fathers and mothers.

Recommendations and Conclusion

There are no simple answers as to how family support and parent education programs can measure impacts on parents. This is both because few in-depth evaluations in this area have been conducted and because the level of instrument development for this field is in its infancy. For programs that have limited resources to conduct evaluations, basic documentation of family demographic characteristics and simple program questionnaires asking for parents' opinions about the success of the project can provide some basis for program justification and improved program services.

I would recommend for programs that have specific curricula, additional documentation using a pre–post test paradigm to determine how much parents have learned from their participation. Programs with somewhat more resources and interest are encouraged to consider using the Parent As A Teacher or Parenting Stress Index, with the recognition that these measures will require more supervision in administration and analysis than internal program questionnaires. Finally, the Caldwell and Bradley HOME is recommended as a measure for those programs that can devote the time and effort required to make home visits and train observers.

It is possible that little change may be documented through use of these measures. This is neither a clear indictment of the measures nor of the program. Increased duration and intensity of participation in a program may be what is required in this case, not fundamental redesign of the program or its evaluation procedures. An intervention program may be only one small part of a parent's or family's weekly or monthly activities. Long-term family patterns, cultural preferences and attitudes, and individual personality dimensions will not change quickly or easily. Nauta and Travers (1982) found that parents who were more active and received more services from the Child and Family Resource Programs demonstrated more positive results than those less active. Harman and Brim (1980) note that changes in parents will take 1–2 years. Thus, programs should not expect dramatic changes on the measures discussed from relatively less intense and short-term activities.

In general, evaluation procedures should reflect the goals of the program. However, it is wise to look for unintended as well as intended consequences. For example, programs designed to impart knowledge of child development may also positively influence self-esteem or other aspects of quality of life. The causal connections between different aspects of change are not always clear; broad-based evaluation efforts may aid researchers in clarifying these connections. Moreover, the causal relations between parent change and child change are uncertain. Harman and Brim (1980) recommend that early education programs be judged effective only if improvements are documented in children as well as parents, as it is not certain that change in parent knowledge, behavior, or attitude effects change in children. However, they raise the possibility that change in parents alone may be an adequate effect, given the current limitations in measuring impacts, particularly long-term impacts, on children.

It is also useful to test for unintended *negative* consequences of intervention. It is possible, for example, that parents may develop an overreliance on expert opinion and feel that their own instincts are to be rejected in favor of "child development advice." Alternatively, the program may provide recommendations that contradict what may be most useful in a parent's particular cultural milieu (Howrigan, Chapter 4; Slaughter, Chapter 21, this volume). It must be remembered that all children and parents are unique and that, while we have some idea of what type of environment promotes child development, we are far from having all the answers.

A final recommendation concerns the extent to which both fathers and mothers are involved with an intervention program. While it may be true that mothers still spend more time with young children than fathers, neglecting the knowledge, attitudes, and behaviors of fathers will limit our ability to effect changes in the family system. Programs also need to acknowledge the roles played by other individuals who spend considerable time with the children (e.g., grandparents or sitters).

In conclusion, we have seen that a wide range of parent variables exist that may influence child development and that may be appropriate targets of intervention of family support and education programs. While the study of the parents' role in child development is filled with complexities and uncharted territory, it is clear that parents' knowledge, beliefs, and attitudes (as well as economic and cultural characteristics) have a great influence on the development of their children. To the extent that positive changes in these domains of parents' lives are taken as targets of intervention, it is imperative that tools continue to be developed to understand these changes and the relationships among them.

REFERENCES

Abidin, R. B. (1983). *Parenting stress index manual.* Charlottesville, VA: Pediatric Psychology Press.

Bayley, N. (1969). *Bayley Scales of Infant Development.* San Antonio, TX: Psychological Corporation.

Bernstein, B. (1961). Social class and linguistic development: A theory of social learning. In A. Halsey, J. Flood, and A. Anderson (Eds.), *Education, economy, and society.* NY: Free Press.

Bernstein, B. (1971). *Class, codes and control.* London: Routledge and Kegan Paul.

Bristol, M. (1983). *The effects of perinatal coaching on mother–infant interaction.* Unpublished doctoral dissertation, Michigan State University, East Lansing.

Bronfenbrenner, U. (November, 1974). Is early intervention effective? *Day Care and Early Education, 2,* 15–19.

Caldwell, B., and Bradley, R. H. (1984). *Home Observation for Measurement of the Environment.* Little Rock, AK: University of Arkansas.

Chisner, W. D., and Relich, S. Y. (1981). *Operation life's work.* Pennsylvania.

Coleman, J., Campbell, E., Hobson, C., McPortland, J., and Mood, A. (1966). *Equality of educational opportunity.* Washington, D.C.: U.S. Government Printing Office.

Cravioto, J., and DiLicardie, E. (1972). Environmental correlates of severe clinical malnutrition and language development in survivors from kwashiorkor or marasmus. In Pan American Health Organization, *Nutrition: The nervous system and behavior* (Scientific Publication No. 251). Washington, D.C.: Pan American Health Organization.

DeVellis, R., DeVellis, B., Revicki, D., Lurie, S., Runyan, D., and Bristol, M. (1985). Development and validation of the Child Improvement Locus of Control Scales. *Journal of Social and Clinical Psychology* 3(3), 307–324.

Dunst, C., and Reingrover, R. (1982). An analysis of the efficacy of early infant intervention programs with organically handicapped children. In *Evaluation and Program Planning,* Vol. 4. Englewood Cliffs, NJ: Pergamon Press.

Dunst, C., Trivette, C., and Cross, A. (1984). *Mediating influences of social support: Personal, family, and child outcomes.* Morgantown, NC: Family, Infant, and Preschool Program.

Evans, J., and Halpern, R. (1981). *Dissemination of the High/Scope Parent to Parent Model—A case study.* Ypsilanti, MI: High/Scope Educational Research Foundation.

Field, T. (1977). Effects of early intervention, interactive deficits, and experimental manipulation on mother–child interaction. *Child Development, 48,* 763–771.

Goodson, B. D., and Hess, R. D. (1978). The effects of parent training programs on child performance and parent behavior. In B. Brown (Ed.), *Found: Long-term gains from early education.* Boulder, CO: Westview Press.

Halpern, R. (October, 1984). *Some comments on the Caldwell HOME.* Paper presented at Child Survival/Fair Start Evaluation, Ford Foundation.

Harman, D., and Brim, O. G. (1980). *Learning to be parents: Principles, programs, and methods.* Beverly Hills, CA: Sage.

Hennon, C. B., and Peterson, B. H. (1981). An evaluation of a family life education delivery system for young families. *Family Relations, 30,* 387–394.

Hess, R. D., and Shipman, U. C. (1965). Early experience and the socialization of cognitive modes in children. *Child Development, 36,* 869–886.

Hicks, M. W., and Williams, J. W. (1981). Current challenges in education for parenthood. *Family Relations, 30,* 579–584.

Hollingshead, A., and Redlich, F. C. (1958). *Social class and mental illness.* NY: Wiley.

Jones, P. (1972). Home environment and the development of verbal ability. *Child Development, 43,* 1081–1086.

Kahl, J. A. (1953). Educational and occupational aspirations of "common-men" boys. *Harvard Educational Review, 23,* 186–203.

Kennedy, W. A., Van De Riet, V., and White, J. C. (1963). A normative sample of intelligence and achievement of Negro elementary school children in the southeastern United States. *Monographs of the Society for Research in Child Development, 28*(6).

Lesser, G. S., Fifer, G., and Clark, D. H. (1965). Mental abilities of children in different social class and cultural groups. *Monographs of the Society for Research in Child Development, 30*(102).

Love, J. M., Nauta, M. J., Coelen, C. G., and Ruopp, R. R. (1975). *Home Start Evaluation Study: Executive summary.* Ypsilanti, MI and Cambridge, MA: High/Scope Educational Research Foundation and ABT Associates.

Loyd, B. H., and Abidin, R. R. (1985). Revision of the Parenting Stress Index. *Journal of Pediatric Psychology, 10*(2), 168.

McCarthy, D. (1972). *McCarthy Scale of Children's Abilities.* San Antonio, TX: Psychological Corporation.

Madden, J., Levenstein, P., and Levenstein, S. (1976). Longitudinal IQ outcomes of the mother–child home program. *Child Development, 47,* 1015–1025.

Mash, E. J., Johnston, C., and Kovitz, K. (1983). A comparison of the mother–child interaction of physically abused and non-abused children during play and task situations. In R. R. Abidin, *Parenting Stress Index Manual* (p. 13). Charlottesville, VA: Pediatric Psychology Press.

Minde, K. N., Shosenberg, N., Marton, P., Thompson, J., Ripley, J., and Burns, S. (1982). Self-help groups in a premature nursery—a controlled evaluation. *Pediatrics, 69,* 933–940.

Nauta, M. J., and Travers, J. (1982). *The effects of a social program: Executive summary of CFRP Infant-Toddler Component.* Washington, D.C.: Administration for Children, Youth, and Families, Department of Health and Human Services.

Olds, D. (September, 1984). *Research design of the Prenatal/Early Infancy Project, Elmira, New York.* Paper presented at the Harvard Family Research Project Seminar Series, Cambridge, Massachusetts.

Pinsker, M., and Geoffrey, K. (1981). A comparison of parent effectiveness training and behavior modification parent training. *Family Relations, 30,* 61–68.

Provence, S., and Naylor, A. (1983). *Working with disadvantaged families: Scientific and practical issues.* New Haven, CT: Yale University Press.

Reineke, R. A., and Benson, P. L. (1981). *Minnesota Early Learning Design,* unpublished manuscript. Minneapolis, MN.

Robinson, J. P., and Shaver, P. R. (1973). *Measures of social psychological attitudes.* Ann Arbor, MI: Institute for Social Research, University of Michigan.

Rosenberg, M. (1965). *Society and the adolescent self image.* Princeton, NJ: Princeton University Press.

Rotter, J. B. (1966). Generalized expectations for internal versus external control of reinforcement. *Psychological Monographs, 80*(Whole No. 609).

Seigel, E., Bauman, K. E., Schaefer, E. S., Saunders, M. M., and Ingram, D. D. (1980). Hospital and home support during infancy: Impact on maternal attachment, child abuse and neglect, and health care utilization. *Pediatrics, 66,* 183.

Sheehan, R., and Keogh, B. K. (1981). Strategies for documenting progress of handicapped children in early education programs. *Educational Evaluation and Policy Analysis, 3,* 59–67.

Simeonsson, R., Cooper, D. H., and Scheiner, A. B. (1982). A review and analysis of the effectiveness of early intervention programs. *Pediatrics, 69,* 635–641.

Strom, R. D. (1984). *Parent as a teachers manual.* Bendenville, IL: Scholastic Testing Service, Inc.

Strom, R., and Hill, J. (1979). Child rearing expectations of Hopi and Navajo parents of preschoolers. *Journal of Instructional Psychology, 6,* 15–27.

Strom, R., and Slaughter, H. (1978). Measurement of child rearing expectations using the Parent As A Teacher Inventory. *Journal of Experimental Education, 46,* 44–53.

Strom, R., and Johnson, A. (1978). Assessment for parent education. *Journal of Experimental Education, 47,* 9.

Strom, R., Rees, R., Slaughter, H., and Wurster, S. (1980). Role expectations of parents of intellectually handicapped children. *Exceptional Children, 47*(2), 144.

Strom, R., Hathaway, C., and Slaughter, H. (1981). The correlation of maternal attitudes and preschool children's performance on the McCarthy Scales of Children's Abilities. *Journal of Instructional Psychology, 8,* 139–145.

Strom, R., Rees, R., Slaughter, H., and Wurster, S. (1981). Child rearing expectations of families with atypical children. *American Journal of Orthopsychiatry, 57,* 285–296.

Terman, L. M., and Merrill, M. A. (1973). *Stanford–Binet Intelligence Scale, Third Revision.* Chicago, IL: Riverside Publishing Company.

Travers, J. R., and Light, R. J. (Eds.). (1982). *Learning from experience: Evaluating early childhood demonstration programs.* Washington, D.C.: National Academy Press.

Upshur, C. C. (1981). *Final report: Evaluation of First and Affiliated*

Toddler Early Intervention Programs. Boston: University of Massachusetts.

Wachs, T., Uzgiris, I., and Hunt, J. M. (1971). Cognitive development in infants from different age levels and different environmental backgrounds: An explanatory investigation. *Merrill–Palmer Quarterly, 17,* 283–317.

White, Karl (1984). *An integrative review of early intervention efficacy research*. Logan, UT: Utah State University Early Intervention Research Institute.

Whiteman, M., and Deutsch, M. (1968). Social disadvantages are related to intellective and language development. In M. Deutsch *et al.* (Eds.), *The disadvantaged child*. NY: Basic Books.

Whiteman, M., Brown, B., and Deutsch, M. (1967). Some effects of social class and race on children's language and intellectual abilities. In M. Deutsch *et al.* (Eds.)., *The disadvantaged child*. NY: Basic Books.

Wulbert, M., Inglis, S., Kriegsman, E., and Millis, B. (1975). Language delay and associated mother–child interactions. *Developmental Psychology, 11,* 61.

Yawkey, T. (1982). Effect of parents play routines on imaginative play in their developmentally delayed preschoolers. *Topics in Early Childhood Special Education, 2*(3), 66–75.

Yurchak, M. J., and Stix, S. (1980). *Evaluating Title I programs for parents of young children*. Cambridge, MA: The Huron Institute.

Zigler, E., and Balla, D. (1982). Selecting outcome variables in evaluations of early childhood special education programs. *Topics in Early Childhood Special Education, 1*(4), 11.

Zigler, E., and Trickett, P. (1978). I.Q., social competence, and evaluation of early childhood intervention programs. *American Psychologist, 33,* 789.

chapter 6

MEASURING FAMILY SYSTEMS OUTCOMES

Deborah Klein Walker
Ruth W. Crocker

INTRODUCTION

Although it would seem obvious that family programs need to be based upon theories of family functioning and family development, many are not. Instead, the majority of such programs—for example, early intervention, adolescent pregnancy, parent support groups, family life education—are based more on child development theories and classical psychodynamic notions of treatment than on theories of family operations. The application of family theory to interventions is left primarily to "common sense."

In fact, however, family support programs affect a wide range of family members, including the child, the parents, siblings, and grandparents; these family members are either directly involved (through program participation) or indirectly involved through being part of a system in which one member has grown or changed. To deal effectively with any member of a family, one must understand the family environment and social context of that member.

Family systems theory, an outgrowth of general systems theory as postulated by von Bertalanffy (1968), Bateson (1972), and others, offers this necessary perspective by providing an explanation for why children and adults behave in certain ways, and by exploring implicit family rules for behavior, communication patterns, structures and alliances within families, intergenerational influences, and family development patterns. We will argue that knowledge of family functioning and family development over time is crucial to the design and evaluation of family programs.

Not surprisingly, professionals trained in child development seldom learn about family systems theory; most child development theory is based on theories about individual child motivation and learning. Although there has been a recent emphasis in the development literature on better understanding the environment and ecology of the individual child, few child development experts appear knowledgeable about family systems theory.

The fields of family study and family therapy, however, have made significant theoretical and methodological advances during the past 20 years (Gurman and Kniskern, 1981a; Gurman and Kniskern, 1981b; Wynne, 1983). Consequently, a growing set of instruments for assessing family functioning and family systems outcomes now exists. In this chapter we give a brief overview of family systems theory and its applications in program evaluations. We will then provide brief descriptions of the measures currently available to assess family functioning or family systems outcomes in program evaluations and make recommendations for their use in program evaluations.

Overview of Family Systems Theory

Family systems theory provides a unique lens through which to observe and decipher human behaviors and relationships. It borrows from the biological sciences and general systems theory, viewing the family as a living unit constantly accommodating to developments within its individual components and their relationships to one another and to external influences. During the past 40 years, it has grown as a body of knowledge through the contributions of both theoreticians (physical scientists, anthropologists, learning theorists, etc.) and clinicians (psychiatrists, psychologists, etc.). A family system may be defined as any social unit with which an individual is intimately involved. This unit is not limited by generational or physical boundaries. Like other living systems, families must adapt to internal and external demands for change in order to survive and thrive. But these accommodations are not always smoothly made; again like other living systems, families are most comfortable with maintaining their former, stable form and identity. Families develop interactive patterns called structures, which can become rigid or unadaptive. For example, the family that does not know how to usher its adolescent into approaching adulthood may set unreasonably restrictive curfew hours ("to keep her a child"), against which the child rebels, staying out all night. This acting-out behavior reinforces the family's position that the adolescent is too childish to be trusted. Each member of this family plays his or her part in attempting to maintain the old form—the status quo—denying that the child *is* maturing and that new rules need to be set. This inclination toward maintaining the stability of the unit is called *homeostasis*. Families are also governed by sets of "family rules," which are unique to each family. These rules may be explicitly stated or implicitly understood. Nonetheless, the individual's behavior, both within and outside the family, makes reference to the rules learned and practiced in the family.

One of the most distinctive features of family systems theory is the rejection of linear and unidirectional causality—i.e., the belief that one behavior directly causes another—in favor of a belief in *recursive causality*. In this view, children shape family life and influence parental behaviors at least as much as the family influences children (see Dym, Chapter 22; Howrigan, Chapter 4, this volume). There is no causal beginning point in behavioral sequences. There are no clearly defined perpetrators or victims. Accordingly, family systems clinicians rarely "blame" one family member for another's problems in families where maladaptive patterns emerge. Interventions are meant to help disrupt the stable system so that members are free to develop other strategies for coping with difficulties.

Another key concept of family systems theory is *nonsummativity:* The family is greater than the sum of its members. An understanding of the family cannot be gained simply by describing the individuals within it. It is critical to identify and describe the interactional patterns among members and the rules governing their behavior. The understanding and assessment of family functioning must include developmental and ecological perspectives as well. The developmental perspective reveals that families progress through a series of identifiable developmental stages; at each stage there is the possibility for successful adjustment or family dysfunction to occur. Success at one stage is dependent upon having negotiated well in a previous stage (Carter and McGoldrick, 1980; Critchley, 1982). The ecological perspective places the family in the broader context of extended families, neighborhoods, communities, and religious groups. Relationships across those interacting systems will affect the family's response to a program or treatment intervention.

Normal Family Functioning

Until recently much of the knowledge that had been gathered about families was based on studies of families "in trouble" as evidenced by a symptomatic family member—usually a child with a chronic illness or a handicapping condition. Although the characteristics of healthy families have not been investigated extensively in methodologically sound studies, there is now consensus among clinicians and theorists in characterizing normal family function. Families that work well together tend to communicate (often in a noisy fashion), clearly have well-defined generational boundaries and subsystems, demonstrate effective and efficient decision making, and are adaptive and able to cope with change (Fisher, Giblin, and Hoopes, 1982; Fisher and Sprenkle, 1978; Gantman, 1980). Many different models of family therapy are compatible in their *definitions* of normal family functioning; differences among the schools center around the *appropriate focus* for therapeutic intervention.

Recent studies utilizing family systems theory have focused on defining a range of interactional variables in families and then correlating those variables with healthy or dysfunctional behavior (Lewis, Beavers, Gossett, and Phillips, 1976; Olson, Sprenkle, and Russel, 1979). Dysfunctional families appear to be characterized by stronger parent–child coalitions (Haley, 1976; Minuchin, 1974), with weak parental coalitions and conflicted marital relationships (Farina and Holzberg, 1968; Lidz, 1973). A dysfunctional family is more rigidly organized and has difficulty managing conflict and negotiating group tasks (Solvberg and Blakar, 1975). Functional families, on the other hand, are characterized by more flexible interactional patterns with better conflict management. A stronger alliance between the parents as well as better marital adjustment is more likely, and parents clearly have more influence than the child. The family can function effectively and efficiently doing tasks together (Haley, 1976; Lewis, Beavers, Gossett, and Phillips, 1976).

Implications for Family Program Development and Evaluation

Applying family systems theory to the design and evaluation of family support programs might well provide unconventional responses to the following questions (Jacobs, 1986):

1. *Which family members should be clients?*

While many programs state that they serve "families," in truth many are designed only for children and mothers. This discrepancy underlines their nonsystemic orientation; regardless of specific program goals, focusing on only a subset of a family reduces the likelihood of success. Without understanding how the whole family operates—its rules and values, its preferred methods for coping with difficulties, and how it measures success among its members—one simply has insufficient data from which to develop interventions.

For example, an adolescent parenting program seeking to reduce repeat births among its young mothers may provide extensive services to the new mother and her baby. Yet subsequent pregnancies among some of the teens may well occur if the program does not try to involve other family members. Only with such involvement can it be determined whether the pregnancies serve an unstated function in the teen's family, as many child-expressed problems do (Wendt and Zake, 1982; see Dym, Chapter 22; Dunst and Trivette, Chapter 14, this volume).

Families attempting to promote their children's development have needs of their own. These needs are legitimized by some programs, most notably by those working with young special needs children. Such programs *assume* that to achieve success with children, the family must be nurtured, supported, and sometimes counseled; individual family plans and activities are developed toward this end (Bristol and Gallagher, 1982). Thus, the reciprocal impacts of parents and children are explicitly acknowledged and the *family* is the client.

It is not always possible to include all family members directly in a program. However, a family systems orientation requires staff to determine how supportive those other members are of the program's goals and to attempt to acknowledge their concerns within the program structure. A program designed to increase a mother's sense of competence and self-esteem, for example, should seek to understand the degree to which such goals are consistent both with the values of others (e.g., the husband or boyfriend) and with her cultural values. Without a contextual approach, well-intentioned programs that genuinely reflect *individual* family members' dreams can be undermined by larger systemic forces.

2. To which families should programs be offered?

In times of scarce resources, policymakers and program planners are forced to make difficult decisions about how to appropriate preventive program funds. In primary prevention programming, a family life-cycle perspective (Carter and McGoldrick, 1980; Garbarino, 1982) can be particularly helpful, as it suggests a focus on families in transition between life stages. It is those periods that are often particularly stressful, as they involve negotiating new family roles, rules, and expectations—changes that can often lead to family dysfunction. Thus, programming offered at critical periods may yield greater benefits than services offered at noncrisis times.

Family life-cycle information can also be helpful to programs serving families with disabled children and marginal families considered at-risk for parenting problems. A life-cycle perspective allows program staff to provide what physicians call "anticipatory guidance"—a road map for clients of what to expect in child or family development in the future (Foster, Berger, and McLean, 1981). For example, families with disabled children often experience difficulty and sadness when their children's "normal" age peers make the expected transitions whereas their children cannot (Featherstone, 1980). Being able to anticipate these periods may reduce the negative impacts associated with them. Similarly, families at-risk for child abuse or neglect may benefit from understanding that difficulties at certain life stages are normal.

3. *How should program goals and intervention strategies be developed?*

A systemic approach to defining program goals would necessarily consider the client's family goals as well as the family's cultural definitions of successful childrearing and family functioning. Ethnic and cultural norms are powerful influences in families and must be reflected in program goals and objectives (Garbarino and Sherman, 1980; see Slaughter, Chapter 21; Howrigan, Chapter 4, this volume).

Similarly, certain modes of intervention may be more consonant with some personal and cultural values than others. For example, learning about child development from a lecture or an adult education course may be an effective mode for some, while observing a home visitor interact with one's children and joining in the activities may be effective for others. One can judge the appropriateness of such modes only with knowledge of the individual participants, their families, and their cultural contexts.

Finally, family systems theory argues for individualized goal-setting and services; parents who share economic, racial, and educational characteristics are not necessarily a homogeneous group. The challenge to family programs is to capture the shared goals and preferred modes of program strategies while remaining flexible enough to tailor the program for individual families. In order to do this effectively, sociodemographic characteristics must be considered *along with* other personal and family characteristics.

4. *How should evaluations of family programs incorporate a family perspective?*

In addition to using standardized measures of family systems outcomes programs might consider enlisting the help of practitioners trained in family systems theory to collect data on family goals and processes of attainment. This more individualized approach to documenting change can serve to balance and inform interpretation of the data collected through other techniques.

FAMILY ASSESSMENT INSTRUMENTS

Planning for the Evaluation

The major purposes of the evaluation and the resources available for its implementation will dictate the overall design and the choice of specific instruments and techniques. More sophisticated family programs with staff able to conduct an outcome or summative evaluation may want to use family systems outcome measures to assess progress on a particular objective. Smaller programs will not be able to use these measures, since their use is time consuming and costly.

On the other hand, programs with few resources may use an experienced family systems therapist as an interviewer at various points in a process evaluation to give feedback to staff about the program's development and potential impact on both individual family members and the family unit. However, since clinical assessments and open-ended interviews are often not standardized or easily quantifiable, programs frequently choose traditional evaluation research design utilizing instruments that are more easily quantifiable and have better psychometric properties.

The term "family functioning" is fixed to many instruments and has many meanings: Some measures of family functioning attempt to assess only a particular dimension of family life while others attempt to measure many factors; some focus on the individuals within the family, some on the subsystems within the family, and some on the total family system. There are many more measures available in the literature to assess individual and/or subgroup (primarily mother–child and marital relations) functioning than to assess total family functioning. The selection of multifactorial measures to assess total family functioning presents more of a challenge to the program evaluator. The remainder of this chapter focuses on those multifactorial measures.

Types of Family Assessment Techniques

Several researchers have developed classification schemes of family assessment techniques (Gurman and Kniskern, 1981a; Gurman and Kniskern, 1981b; Holman, 1983; Kracke, 1981). The measures of family functioning found in an extensive literature review on measures (Buros, 1974; Filsinger, 1983; Forman and Hagan, 1983; Gersten, 1974; Johnson, 1973; Johnson and Bommarito, 1971; Kracke, 1981; Margolin and Ferrandez, 1983; National Institute of Mental Health, 1983; Robinson and Shaver, 1973; Strauss and Brown, 1978; Walsh, 1982; Walsh and Wood, 1983) are best classified into four types: (1) direct interviews including structured tasks, (2) observation/rating scales, (3) self-report scales, and (4) projective techniques. This classification is simply a device to make discussion and comparison of the various measurement types possible. In fact, they can overlap and can be used together.

Direct Interview and Structured Tasks. An interview format that may or may not involve a task-oriented procedure is frequently used in clinical assessment (Holman, 1983; Kracke, 1981). Systematic approaches to the interview's recording and content have been made by various practitioners (Holman, 1983; Leader, Burck, Kinston, and Bentovim, 1981; Watzlawick, 1966). The interview can be enhanced by using doll play, family role play (family sculpture), and structured diagrams of family relations over several generations (the genogram and the eco-map) (Hartman, 1978; Holman, 1983; Kracke, 1981; Meyerstein, 1979; Wachtel, 1982). Such family assessments, which tend to be descriptive, rather than quantitative and standardized, are most useful for clinical purposes; more structured interview formats, which use standardized items and trained interviewers, can also be successfully used in program evaluations.

Sometimes the interview is combined with giving the family a joint task. The interviewer or independent observer/rater can make a quick and efficient family process assessment when families are asked to discuss what they would like to change or how they will do something together (Beavers, 1981). Families left to do the task alone characteristically interact in their particular family patterns which reveal underlying structural patterns and dynamic relationships. In a study designed to assess the effect of different tasks on emergent patterns of family interaction in 30 families, Zuckerman and Jacob (1979) found marked consistency in family interaction across three experimental tasks; multiple studies have demonstrated that patterns of family operation are characterized by regularity and predictability across situations and over time (Alexander, 1973; Ferreira and Winter, 1966; Haley, 1976; Minuchin, Rosman, and Baker, 1978).

Observation/Rating Scales. Assessment of family functioning is best accomplished by raters uninvolved in the evaluation, unfamiliar with the family, and unaware of any hypotheses about the family or the effectiveness of the program. Raters should be trained to observe and tested to have a high level of interrater reliability. Ratings can be made at the time of the family interview or task, or later, using videotapes of the family interactions. The best known example of an observational measure of family functioning is the Beavers–Timberlawn Family Evaluation Scale (Lewis *et al.,* 1976). Other observational measures less developed to date include the Family Interaction Scales (Riskin and Faunce, 1970a, 1970b) and the Dynamics of Family Life Scale (Walsh and Wood, 1983).

There are several tradeoffs in using observation/rating scales (see Howrigan, Chapter 4, this volume). First, although they tend to be more expensive, they provide a rich source of information about the family, which can be assessed by independent judges. Observations also allow for analyses of sequential events and complex verbal and nonverbal interactions, but they are often difficult to code, score, and analyze. Observational measures can be used to validate the less expensive self-report methods (National Institute of Mental Health, 1983) and to complement their findings (Walsh and Wood, 1983).

Self-Report Scales. These are paper-and-pencil measures administered to one or more family members about their perceptions of the family's organization and functioning. Because they are easy to use and score, the large majority of evaluations of family outcomes are conducted with such instruments (Filsinger, 1983; Forman and Hagan, 1983). In addition to the five self-report scales reviewed in the next section, there are several new measures cited in the literature that may be useful in future evaluations. They include the Feetham Family Functioning Survey (Roberts and Feetham, 1982); the Family Evaluation Form (in Forman and Hagan, 1983), and the Family Assessment Measure (Skinner, Steinhauer, and Santa-Barbara, 1983; Steinhauer, Santa-Barbara, and Skinner, 1984).

Although there are administrative and cost advantages in favor of using self-report measures in program evaluations, one must be cautious in making inferences about family functioning based on the perceptions of one or more family members. Moreover, if more than one member of the family fills out the measure, there is no consensus on how the scores of the various members should be used in the final analyses (National Institute of Mental Health, 1983).

Projective Techniques. Measures of this type are based on the assumption that the characteristics of an individual or family are best understood by observing the individual or family's reaction to a particular set of stimuli. Examples of projective measures used to assess family interaction are the Family Apgar Index (Adaptation, Partnership, Growth, Affection, Resolve) (Good, Smilkstein, Schaffer, Good, and Avons, 1979; Smilkstein, 1978); the Kinetic Family Drawing (Holtz, Brannigan, and Schofield, 1980); the Family Relations Test (Kauffman, 1970); the revised Rorschach Measures of Family Interaction (Lerner, 1975); and applications of the Thematic Apperception Test (Kracke, 1981).

Overall, however, these measures are nonstandardized, have poor technical quality, and are expensive to use since trained clinicians are needed. In sum, although perhaps useful in augmenting clinical assessments, these techniques are not useful as outcome measures in program evaluation design.

Selecting Family Systems Outcome Measures

Selecting an appropriate instrument to assess family outcomes is a complex process. Recent advances in family assessment instrumentation have led to the development of a few measures for use in program evaluation, but they have been used in only a few programs so far. The following questions are useful to guide selection among these new measures:

1. *What is the administrative feasibility of the measure?* Are resources available to administer the measure? Observational tools are more costly for two major reasons: *(a)* observers must be selected and trained, and *(b)* the entire family must be assembled at once. Financial considerations must be taken into account.
2. *What is the technical quality of the measure?* Three major aspects of the instrument's technical quality must be examined: First, is the instrument reliable? In the case of observational techniques, what is the level of interrater reliability? In the case of self-report measures, what levels of internal consistency coefficients have been obtained in past studies? Second, is the instrument valid? What attempts have been made in past studies to assess the various types of validity—construct, concurrent, predictive, and content? Finally, are there well-standardized norms for the instrument on various populations of families?
3. *What scoring and analysis procedures are necessary in using the measure?* Scores generated from the measure should have direct and meaningful use in a program evaluation. For example, the constructs measured by the scores ought to be a direct measure of the desired outcomes of the program and not some theoretical construct only tangentially related to the objective.

Descriptions of Family Systems Outcome Measures

Through a comprehensive review of the current literature on family systems outcome measures (Filsinger, 1983; Forman and Hagan, 1983; Kracke 1981; Straus and Brown, 1978; Walsh, 1982; Walsh and Wood, 1983) we have identified seven of the most widely used family functioning measures. Table 6.1 lists the seven measures and indicates each measure's assessment technique, number of items, and number of scales.

Table 6.2 identifies the dimensions of family functioning captured by the instruments' subscales. The five dimensions, drawn from Fisher's (1976) schema, include structural descriptors (i.e., roles, alliances, communication patterns), controls and sanctions (i.e., dependency and power), emotions and needs (i.e., rules of affective expression, need satisfaction), cultural aspects (i.e., social position, cultural heritage), and development aspects (i.e., appropriateness to developmental stage of the family). An analysis of the seven measures described in this chapter, following Forman and Hagan (1983), reveals that about half of

TABLE 6.1. Overview of Family Functioning Measures

Instrument and authors	Assessment technique	Number of items	Number of scales
Beavers–Timberlawn Family Evaluation Scale (BTFES) (Lewis, Beaver, Gossett, and Phillips, 1976)	Observation/ rating scale	13	13 and a global health scale
Family Adaptability Cohesion Evaluation Scales (FACES II) (Olson, Portner, and Bell, 1982)	Self-report	30	14
Family Concepts Assessment Method (FCAM) (Van der Veen, 1965)	Self-report (2 versions)	80	9 and 3 global family scores
Family Environment Scale (FES) (Moos, 1974)	Self-report	90	10 and an incongruence score
Family Functioning Index (FFI) (Pless and Satterwhite, 1973)	Self-report (screening)	15	6 and a total score
Family Interaction Scales (FIS) (Riskin and Faunce, 1970)	Observation/ rating scale	6	6
McMaster Family Assessment Device (FAD) (Epstein, Baldwin, and Bishop, 1983)	Self-report (screening)	53	6 and a general functioning score

the subscales assess structural descriptors. The second most frequently assessed dimensions are controls and sanctions, and emotions and needs. None has a subscale for developmental aspects, and very few assess cultural aspects.

The following section presents brief descriptions of each of the seven measures of family functioning highlighted in Tables 6.1 and 6.2; they are listed in alphabetical order.

Beavers–Timberlawn Family Evaluation Scale (BTFES). The Timberlawn study of family functioning operationalized several of the key concepts of family systems theory. In addition, the study clarified dimensions of healthy, mid-range, and severely dysfunctional families (Beavers and Voeller, 1983; Lewis *et al.*, 1976). Lewis and his colleagues developed a schema of characteristics for several possible variants in levels of family

TABLE 6.2. Family Measure Subscales Categorized by Fisher's Schema[a,b]

Measure	Subscale	SD	C and S	E and N	CA	DA
BTFES	Overt power		X			
	Parental coalitions	X				
	Closeness			X		
	Mythology	X				
	Goal-directed negotiation	X				
	Clarity of expression	X				
	Responsibility		X			
	Invasiveness	X				
	Permeability	X				
	Range of feelings			X		
	Mood and tone			X		
	Unresolvable conflict	X				
	Empathy			X		
FACES II	Family cohesion					
	Emotional bonding			X		
	Family boundaries	X				
	Coalitions	X				
	Time	X				
	Space	X				
	Friends			X		
	Decision making	X				
	Interests and recreation			X		
	Family adaptability					
	Assertiveness		X			
	Leadership (control)		X			
	Discipline		X			
	Negotiation	X				
	Roles	X				
	Rules		X			
FCAM	Consideration versus conflict	X				
	Open communication	X				
	Togetherness versus separateness	X				
	Internal versus external locus of control		X			
	Family actualization versus inadequacy			X		
	Family loyalty			X		
	Closeness versus estrangement			X		
	Community sociability				X	
	Family ambition				X	
FES	Cohesion	X				
	Expressiveness			X		
	Conflict		X			
	Independence		X			
	Achievement orientation				X	
	Intellectual–cultural orientation				X	

(continued)

TABLE 6.2. (*continued*)

Measure	Subscale	SD	C and S	E and N	CA	DA
	Active recreational orientation				X	
	Moral–religious emphasis				X	
	Organization	X				
	Control		X			
FFI	Frequency of disagreement	X				
	Communication	X				
	Problem solving	X				
	Weekends together	X				
	Marital satisfaction			X		
	Happiness			X		
FIS	Clarity	X				
	Total continuity	X				
	Commitment			X		
	Agreement and disagreement	X				
	Affect intensity			X		
	Relationship quality			X		
FAD	Problem solving	X				
	Communication	X				
	Rules	X				
	Affective responsiveness			X		
	Affective involvement			X		
	Behavior control		X			

[a]Key to Fischer's Schema: SD: Structural descriptors; C and S: Controls and sanctions; E and N: Emotions and needs; CA: Cultural aspects; DA: Developmental aspects.

[b]Adapted from Forman and Hagan (1983, pp. 30–31).

functioning, which integrate interaction patterns both within the family and the family developmental stage. Based on the "entropy" model of family systems, the observation/rating scales assess healthy family functioning as the maintenance of a structured yet flexible balance between a family's internal and external environments. In the original study, 12 families with an adolescent hospitalized in a private psychiatric hospital and 11 matched volunteer families with no identified emotionally ill member were presented a series of tasks. The five tasks included discussing common family problems, planning a common activity, and assessing family strengths. Afterward, raters assessed films of the families using process-oriented, interactional rating scales. Beavers (1982) found that family processes correlated significantly with family capabilities and the functioning of offspring.

Moderate interrater reliability (.65–.90) in the original pilot study was established after extensive training with clinically trained observers. Discriminant validity was supported by the scale's ability to differentiate between families containing a psychiatrically impaired adolescent and healthy families, as rated by an experienced psychiatric social worker and a clinical psychologist (Lewis *et al.*, 1976). Although it is theoretically and practically appealing, this instrument needs more development before it can be used efficiently in program evaluations.

Family Adaptability and Cohesion Evaluation Scales (FACES). FACES II, a modification of the original FACES, was developed to assess the two central dimensions of cohesion and adaptability of the circumplex model developed by Olson and his colleagues (Olson, Russell, and Sprenkle, 1983b; Olson, Sprenkle, and Russell, 1979; Russell, 1979; 1980). Family cohesion assesses separateness and connectedness of family members while family adaptability assesses flexibility and ability to change. Family communication, the third dimension, is seen as facilitating movement on the other two dimensions in the model. A family is scored as representing one of four levels of family cohesion, ranging from extreme high cohesion (enmeshed) to extreme low cohesion (disengaged) and one of four levels of family adaptability ranging from extreme high adaptability (chaotic) to extreme low adaptability (rigid) (Olson, McCubbin, Barnes, Larsen, Muxen, and Wilson, 1983a; Olson and Portner, 1983; Olson, Portner, and Bell, 1982).

FACES II was designed to assess individual family members' perceptions of the family. Its seventh-grade reading level makes it accessible to both adolescents and adults. The scale is given twice to each family member, once to describe the family as it is, and once to describe how each would like it to be. Comparison of the perceived score and the ideal score for each family member provides an assessment of the level of satisfaction with the current family system. A newly developed alternative hypothesis for the circumplex model states that extreme family types will function well as long as all family members like it that way (Olson *et al.*, 1983b).

FACES II was developed from two prior editions of the scale with 90 or more items. Internal consistency reliability was .87 for cohesion, .78 for adaptability, and .90 for the total scale (Olson and Portner, 1983). Construct validity using factor analysis and discriminant and predictive validity was established using the national survey data on a sample of predominantly white Lutheran families located in the midwest ($N = 2082$ parents and 416 adolescents) (Olson and Portner, 1983; Olson *et al.*, 1982).

FACES II, which can be easily administered and quickly scored, is one of the most widely used family functioning scales. National norms are designed so that the scores can be plotted directly into the circumplex model with 16 family types. Separate norms are available for parents and adolescents, but not for males and females, since their scores are quite similar (Olson and Portner, 1983b). The authors report that the lack of agreement among family members was quite large. Although this raises unresolved issues about which view is most valid, it highlights the need for assessments from as many family members as possible (Olson and Portner, 1983). The developers' claim that the instrument is useful in clinical and research settings has been disputed by others (Beavers and Voeller, 1983; Olson *et al.*, 1983b), and both methodological and technical inadequacies of the scales have been documented in other studies (Bararowski, Dworkin, Dunn, Nader, and Brown, 1984; Bilbro and Dreyer, 1981; Bloom, 1985; Sigafoos, Reiss, Rich, and Douglas, 1985).

Family Concept Assessment Method (FCAM). There are two principal versions of the Family Concept Assessment Method: the Family Concept Q Sort (FCQS) and the multiple choice Family Concept Inventory (FCI) (Forman and Hagan, 1983). The FCQS, which was developed by Van der Veen (1965), consists of 80 items that are forced into a nine-step q-sort normal distribution ranging from "least like my family" to "most like my family." The FCI eliminates the forced response distribution and allows for each of the 80 items to be rated from 0 (least like the family) to 8 (most like the family). In addition, 21 of the original 80 items were modified in the FCI edition in order to clarify their meanings. The instrument provides an assessment of a person's perception of his/her family and its cognitive, social, and emotional structures. The FCAM generates three global scores: Family Congruence, the degree of agreement between the real and/or ideal family concepts of the various family members, either in pairs or as an entire unit; Family Satisfaction, the correlation between a person's real and ideal item scores; and Family Effectiveness, a summary score of family adjustment based upon 48 of the 80 items. Although a variety of studies using the measure in the 1960s and early 1970s showed moderate stability and validity, very few are available in published journal articles (Forman and Hagan, 1983).

Family Environment Scale (FES). The Family Environment Scale is a self-report paper-and-pencil inventory intended to assess the social climates of all types of families. It measures and describes the interpersonal relationships among family members, the directions of personal growth emphasized in the family, and the family's basic organizational structure (Moos and Moos, 1981).

The scale is easy to administer and score, has been widely used, and has moderate reliability; internal consistency estimates ranged from .64 to .79 in the original standardization sample of 285 families (Moos, 1974). It has been used in previous studies to examine the correlates of family functioning with prognosis in an alcoholism treatment program (Moos, Bromet, Tsu, and Moos, 1979) and with nutrient intake (Kintner,

Boss, and Johnson, 1981). Several studies have raised issues about the generalizability of the factor structure reported in the manual (Fowler, 1981, 1982; Robertson and Hyde, 1982). On the other hand, several studies using the FES with other family functioning measures have found it to have good technical properties. For example, Bararowski *et al.* (1984) found the FES had better reliability than FACES II. Bloom (1985) found that the three dimensions of the Moos model best described factor analyses of items from several different family systems outcome measures.

Family Function Index (FFI). This self-report scale, developed by Pless and Satterwhite (1973), was adapted from a semistructured interview schedule given to a random sample of parents of school-aged children (*N* = 399) in New York. Factor analyses of mother's responses to 15 items resulted in six scales (see Table 6.2). Correlations between these scores and the total score were computed separately for each parent and ranged widely from very low correlations for problem solving to .90s correlations for marital satisfaction for both parents. External validity was determined in several correlational studies using independent ratings of caseworkers and those of the family members. Five-year test–retest reliability was established on a randomized follow-up sample of the original sample (Satterwhite, Zweig, Iker, and Pless, 1976). Parallel forms of the FFI are available for husband and wife. The information concerning total family functioning is obtained solely from parents with no provision made for how to rate single-parent families.

Family Interactive Scales (FIS). These theoretically based observation/rating scales assess behavior in six major areas (see Table 6.2):

Clarity—whether family members speak clearly to one another
Topic continuity—whether family members stay on the same topic with one another and how they shift topics
Commitment—whether family members take direct stands on issues and feelings with one another
Agreement and disagreement—whether family members explicitly agree or disagree with one another
Affect intensity—whether family members show variations in affect as they communicate with one another
Relationship quality—whether family members are friendly or attacking one another (Kracke, 1981; Riskin, 1982; Walsh and Wood, 1983)

Scoring involves a microanalysis of the family discussion: Everything uttered is scored. Although the scale developers have shown that the instrument can be used with reliability and validity as a clinical tool, much more development of this instrument is needed before it can be used effectively in program outcome evaluations (Faunce and Riskin, 1970; Kracke, 1981; Riskin and Faunce, 1970a, 1970b).

McMaster Family Assessment Device (FAD). This instrument was designed as a screening tool to identify problem areas in family functioning in a way that is useful both to researchers and family clinicians (Epstein, Baldwin, and Bishop, 1983). Based on the McMaster Model of Family Functioning, a clinically oriented conceptualization of families (Epstein, Bishop, and Baldwin, 1982), the instrument assesses six dimensions of functioning (see Table 6.2). Each family member rates his or her agreement or disagreement with how well an item describes his or her family by selecting one of the four options from strongly agree, agree, disagree, and strongly disagree (Epstein *et al.*, 1983).

The instrument was developed on a sample of 503 individuals, 294 of whom came from 112 families, most of whom had one member in an adult psychiatric hospital, and 209 of whom were students in an introductory psychology course. Cronbach alpha reliability estimates for the total sample ranged from .72 for roles and for behavior control to .92 for general functioning. The scales were moderately intercorrelated, which suggests they were not assessing independent domains of functioning. Some evidence of validity was demonstrated by the fact that the nonclinical and clinical families' scores were significantly different. Future research using this new tool is needed to clarify its usefulness for program evaluations.

RECOMMENDATIONS

We believe that all family programs can benefit greatly from learning about family systems. Staff in family programs need to plan programs and evaluations based as much on knowledge of family development as of child development. In many cases, the success or failure of a particular intervention hinges more on the actions of subgroups and structural changes within the family system than on the quality or intensity of approaches to changing the child's behavior.

Selecting a family systems outcome measure for use in a program evaluation is difficult, not least because a global measure of family functioning that is well standardized and relatively simple to administer does not now exist and may never be developed. Moreover, relationship between complex family processes and simple behavior indexes or measures of individual and/or subgroup functioning have not been studied adequately to determine whether a simple behavioral indicator or a simple self-report measure by one family member can explain most of family functioning. From a theoretical perspective, it is hard to believe that a simple relationship between simpler indexes and a global measure of family functioning can exist in most cases. Finally, progress depends upon substantial financial support, since it can be achieved only by family systems researchers and practitioners with a wide range of knowledge and skills. We hope public and private funders will begin to pay more attention to this area of measurement development.

An astute judge of family outcomes measures realizes that many measures purporting to assess family functioning actually measure only a narrow range of family life from one family member's perspective. In some program evaluations, for example, a measure of parent–child interactions, sibling relationships, or satisfaction with marriage might be appropriate—but if such a measure is used, it should be clear that it assesses only part of the family system and not overall functioning.

In the absence of better measures, we will have to do our best with the small set currently available. The optimal family systems outcome measure for use in program evaluation should be based on a theoretical model that is testable. It should have good technical qualities, be objective and quantifiable, and be multifactorial. It should focus on the entire family, use objective observers, and be relatively simple to administer and score. The only measure currently available that meets many of these criteria is the Beavers–Timberlawn Family Evaluation Scale; the drawback to using this measure is that the collection and analysis of data is both time-consuming and costly, but with appropriate refinements and validity checks this measure could be much less costly.

The other measures currently available all rely on some form of self-report. The Family Adaptability Cohesion Evaluation Scales (FACES II) and the Family Environment Scale come closest to meeting all of the criteria. Although both have strengths and weaknesses, FACES II, which is more theoretically grounded in family systems theory, is currently used more than all the other measures in family research and evaluation. Both FACES II and FES must be used cautiously, since they rely on reports from individuals and not objective observations of the family's interactions over time. More empirical work must be done to determine the extent of the bias one can expect in self-report assessments.

A family program with little or no evaluation money will not be able to use a family systems outcome measure in a traditional outcome evaluation. As indicated previously, however, these programs could benefit from the expertise of a trained family systems consultant or staff member to review program and evaluation plans, conduct some of the interviews in the evaluation, participate in staff meetings, and review the qualitative findings collected during the evaluation. Recent promising advances in measurement development in the family systems outcome field suggest that a better measurement technology may be forthcoming. At least now there are some appropriate measures available for use, if one has time and resources. The push for program accountability and documentation of effective intervention strategies will bring the agendas of family systems therapy, family research, and family support programs closer together in the future. It is our hope that family programs will incorporate the family systems approach in both their program interventions and their evaluation designs.

ACKNOWLEDGMENTS

Partial support for this work was provided by the Mellon Foundation's awards to junior faculty at the Harvard School of Public Health.

REFERENCES

Alexander, J. J. (1973). Defensive and supportive communications in normal and deviant families. *Journal of Clinical and Consulting Psychology, 40,* 223–231.

Bararowski, T., Dworkin, R. J., Dunn, J. K., Nader, P. R., and Brown, J. (1984). *Comparative reliability of two measures of family functioning.* Paper presented at APHA, Anaheim, California.

Bateson, G. (1972). *Steps to an ecology of mind.* NY: Pallatine.

Beavers, W. R. (1981). A systems model of family for family therapists. *Journal of Marital and Family Therapy, 7,* 299–307.

Beavers, W. R. (1982). Healthy midrange and severely dysfunctional families. In N. Walsh (Ed.), *Normal family processes* (pp. 45–66). NY: Guilford.

Beavers, W. R., and Voeller, M. N. (1983). Family models: Comparing and contrasting the Olson circumplex model with the Beavers systems model. *Family Process, 22,* 85–97.

Bilbro, T. L., and Dreyer, A. S. (1981). A methodological study of a measure of family cohesion. *Family Process, 20,* 419–427.

Bloom, B. L. (1985). A factor analysis of self-report measures of family functioning. *Family Process, 24*(2), 225–239.

Bristol, M., and Gallagher, J. J. (1982). A family focus for intervention. In C. T. Ramey and P. O. Trohanis (Eds.), *Finding and educating the high-risk and handicapped infant* (pp. 137–161). Baltimore, MD: University Press.

Buros, O. K. (Ed.). (1974). *Tests in print II: A comprehensive bibliography of tests for use in education, psychology, and industry.* Highland Park, NJ: Gryphon.

Carter, E. A., and McGoldrick, M. (1980). *The family life cycle.* NY: Gardner.

Critchley, D. L. (1982). A developmental perspective for treatment of families with young children. In I. W. Clements and D. M. Buchanan (Eds.), *Family therapy: A nursing perspective* (pp. 267–276). NY: Wiley.

Epstein, N. B., Baldwin, L. M., and Bishop, D. S. (1983). The McMaster Family Assessment Device. *Journal of Marital and Family Therapy, 9,* 171–180.

Epstein, N. B., Bishop, D. S., and Baldwin, L. M. (1982). McMaster Model of family functioning: A view of the normal family. In F. Walsh (Ed.), *Normal family processes* (pp. 115–141). NY: Guilford.

Farina, A., and Holzberg, J. (1968). Interaction patterns of parents and hospitalized sons diagnosed as schizophrenic or non-schizophrenic. *Journal of Abnormal Psychology, 73,* 114–118.

Faunce, E. E., and Riskin, J. (1970). Family interaction scales: II. Data analysis and findings. *Archives of General Psychiatry, 22,* 513–526.

Featherstone, H. (1980). *A difference in the family.* NY: Basic Books.

Ferreira, A. L., and Winter, W. D. (1966). Stability of interactional variables in family decision-making. *Archives of General Psychiatry, 14,* 352–355.

Filsinger, E. E. (1983). *Marriage and family assessment: A sourcebook for family therapy.* Beverly Hills, CA: Sage.

Fisher, B., and Sprenkle, D. (1978). Therapists' perceptions of healthy family functioning. *International Journal of Family Counseling, 6,* 1–10.

Fisher, B. L., Giblin, P. R., and Hoopes, M. H. (July, 1982). Healthy family functioning: What therapists say and what families want. *Journal of Marital and Family Therapy,* 273–284.

Fisher, L. (1976). Dimensions of family assessment: A critical review. *Journal of Marriage and Family Counseling, 2,* 367–382.

Forman, B. D., and Hagan, B. J. (1983). A comparative review of total family functioning measures. *American Journal of Family Therapy, 11,* 25–40.

Foster, M., Berger, M., and McLean, M. (1981). Rethinking a good idea: A reassessment of parent involvement. *Topics in Early Childhood Special Education, 1,* 55–65.

Fowler, P. C. (1981). Maximum structure of the Family Environment Scale: Effects of social desirability. *Journal of Clinical Psychology, 38,* 285–292.

Fowler, P. C. (1982). Factor structure of the Family Environment Scale: Effects of social desirability. *Journal of Clinical Psychology, 38,* 285–292.

Gantman, C. A. (1980). A closer look at families that work well. *International Journal of Family Therapy, 2,* 106–119.

Garbarino, J. (1982). *Children and families in the social environment.* NY: Aldine.

Garbarino, J., and Sherman, D. (1980). High risk neighborhoods and high risk families: The human ecology of child maltreatment. *Child Development, 51,* 188–198.

Gersten, J. C. (1974). Measures of family functioning. In G. D. Grave and I. B. Pless (Eds.), *Chronic childhood illness: Assessment of outcome* (pp. 193–201). Washington, D.C.: Public Health Service, DHEW.

Good, M. J., Smilkstein, G., Schaffer, T., Good, B. J., and Avons, T. (1979). The family Apgar Index: A study of construct validity. *Journal of Family Practice, 8,* 577–582.

Gurman, A. S., and Kniskern, D. P. (1981a). *Handbook of family therapy.* NY: Brunner/Mazel.

Gurman, A. S., & Kniskern, D. P. (1981b). Family therapy outcome research: Knowns and unknowns. In A. S. Gurman and D. P. Kniskern (Eds.), *Handbook of family therapy.* NY: Brunner/Mazel.

Haley, J. (1976). *Problem Solving Therapy.* New York: Harper and Row.

Hartman, A. (1978). A diagrammatic assessment of family relationships. *Social Casework, 59,* 465–476.

Holman, A. M. (1983). *Family assessment: Tools for understanding and intervention.* Beverly Hills, CA: Sage.

Holtz, R., Brannigan, G. G., and Schofield, J. J. (1980). The Kinetic Family Drawing as a measure of interpersonal distance. *Journal of Genetic Psychology, 137,* 307–308.

Jacobs, F. (1986). Written communication, December.

Johnson, O. G. (1973). *Tests and measurements in child development: Handbook II* (2 vols.). San Francisco, CA: Jossey-Bass.

Johnson, O. G., and Bommarito, J. W. (1971). *Tests and measurements in child development: A handbook.* San Francisco, CA: Jossey-Bass.

Kauffman, J. M. (1970). Validity of the Family Relations Test: A review of research. *Journal of Projective Techniques and Personality Assessment, 34,* 186–189.

Kintner, M., Boss, P. G., and Johnson, N. (1981). The relationship between dysfunctional family environments and family member food intake. *Journal of Marriage and the Family, 24,* 636–641.

Kracke, K. R. (1981). A survey of procedures for assessing family conflict and dysfunction. *Family Therapy, 8,* 241–253.

Leader, P., Burcke, C., Kinston, W., and Bentovim, A. (1981). A method for organising the clinical description of family interaction: The Family Interaction Summary Format. *Australian Journal of Family Therapy, 2,* 131–141.

Lerner, P. M. (1975). Rorschach measures of family interaction: A review. In P. M. Lerner (Ed.), *Handbook of Rorschach scales.* NY: International Universities.

Lewis, J. M., Beavers, W. R., Gossett, J. T., and Phillips, V. A. (1976). *No single thread: Psychological health in family systems.* NY: Brunner/Mazel.

Lidz, T. (1973). *The origin and treatment of schizophrenic disorders.* NY: Basic.

Margolin, G., and Ferrandez, V. (1983). Other marriage and family questionnaires. In E. E. Filsinger (Ed.), *Marriage and family assessment: A sourcebook for family therapy* (pp. 317–338). Beverly Hills, CA: Sage.

Meyerstein, I. (1979). The Family Behavioral Snapshot: A tool for teaching family assessment. *American Journal of Family Therapy, 7,* 48–56.

Minuchin, S. (1974). *Families and family therapy.* Cambridge, MA: Harvard University Press.

Minuchin, S., Rosman, B., and Baker, L. (1978). *Psychosomatic families: Anorexia nervosa in context.* Cambridge, MA: Harvard University Press.

Moos, R. H. (1974). *Family Environment Scale: Preliminary manual.* Palo Alto, CA: Consulting Psychologists Press.

Moos, R. H., and Moos, B. S. (1981). *Family Environment Scale manual.* Palo Alto, CA: Consulting Psychologists Press.

Moos, R. H., Bromet, E., Tsu, U., and Moos, B. S. (1979). Family characteristics and the outcome of treatment of alcoholism. *Studies in Alcoholism, 40,* 78–88.

National Institute of Mental Health (1983). *Methods for assessing and promoting healthy family functioning: A state of the art workshop.* Final report of conference funded by National Institute of Mental Health, San Diego, California.

Olson, D. H., and Portner, J. (1983). Family adaptability and cohesion evaluation scales. In E. E. Filsinger (Ed.), *Marriage and family assessment: A sourcebook for family therapy* (pp. 299–316). Beverly Hills, CA: Sage.

Olson, D. H., Sprenkle, D. H., and Russel, C. (1979). Circumplex model of marital and family systems: I. Cohesion and adaptability dimensions, family type and clinical applications. *Family Process, 18,* 3–28.

Olson, D. H., Portner, J., and Bell, R. (1982). *FACES II: Family Adaptability and Cohesion Evaluation Scales.* St. Paul, MN: Family Social Science, University of Minnesota.

Olson, D. H., McCubbin, H. I., Barnes, H., Larsen, A., Muxen, M., and Wilson, M. (1983a). *Families: What makes them work.* Beverly Hills, CA: Sage.

Olson, D. H., Russell, C. S., and Sprenkle, D. H. (1983b). Circumplex model of marital and family systems: VI. Theoretical update. *Family Process, 22,* 69–83.

Pless, I. B., and Satterwhite, B. (1973). A measure of family functioning and its application. *Social Science and Medicine, 7,* 613–621.

Riskin, J. (1982). Research on "nonlabeled" families: A longitudinal study. In N. Walsh (Ed.), *Normal family processes* (pp. 67–93). NY: Guilford.

Riskin, J., and Faunce, E. E. (1970a). Family Interaction Scales: III. Discussion of methodology and substantive findings. *Archives of General Psychiatry, 22,* 527–537.

Riskin, J., and Faunce, E. E. (1970b). Family Interaction Scales: I. Theoretical framework and method. *Archives of General Psychiatry, 22,* 504–512.

Roberts, C. S., and Feetham, S. L. (1982). Assessing family functioning across three areas of relationships. *Nursing Research, 31,* 231–235.

Robertson, D. U., and Hyde, J. J. (1982). The factorial validity of the Family Environment Scale. *Educational and Psychological Measurement, 42,* 1233–1241.

Robinson, J. P., and Shaver, P. R. (1973). *Measures of social psychological attitudes.* Ann Arbor, MI: Institute for Social Research, University of Michigan.

Russell, C. (1979). Circumplex model of family systems: III. Empirical evaluation with families. *Family Process, 18,* 29–45.

Russell, C. (1980). A methodological study of family cohesion and adaptability. *Journal of Marital and Family Therapy, 6,* 459–470.

Satterwhite, B. B., Zweig, S. R., Iker, H. P., and Pless, I. B. (1976). The Family Functioning Index: Five year test-retest reliability and implications for use. *Journal of Comparative Family Studies, 7,* 111–116.

Sigafoos, A., Reiss, D., Rich, J., and Douglas, E. (1985). Pragmatics in the measurement of family functioning: An interpretive framework for methodology. *Family Process, 24,* 189–203.

Skinner, H. A., Steinhauer, P. D., and Santa-Barbara, J. (1983). The Family Assessment Measure. *Canadian Journal of Community Mental Health, 2,* 91–105.

Smilkstein, G. (1978). The Family Apgar: A proposal for family function test and its use by physicians. *Journal of Family Practice, 6,* 1231–1239.

Solvberg, H., and Blakar, R. (1975). Communication efficiency in couples with and without a schizophrenic offspring. *Family Process, 14,* 515–534.

Steinhauer, P. D., Santa-Barbara, J., and Skinner, H. (1984). The process model of family functioning. *Canadian Journal of Psychiatry, 29,* 77–88.

Straus, M. A., and Brown, B. W. (1978). *Family measurement techniques: Abstracts of published instruments.* Minneapolis, MN: University of Minnesota.

Van der Veen, F. (1965). The parent's concept of the family unit and child adjustment. *Journal of Counseling Psychology, 12,* 196–200.

von Bertalanffy, L. (1968). *General systems theory: Foundation, developments, applications.* NY: Braziller.

Wachtel, E. F. (July, 1982). The family psyche over three generations: The genogram revisited. *Journal of Marital and Family Therapy, 8,* 335–343.

Walsh, N. (1982). Conceptualizations of normal family functioning. In N. Walsh (Ed.), *Normal Family Processes* (pp. 3–44). NY: Guilford.

Walsh, W. M., and Wood, J. I. (July, 1983). Family assessment: Bridging the gap between theory, research, and practice. *American Mental Health Counselor Association Journal,* 111–120.

Watzlawick, P. (1966). A structured family interview. *Family Process, 5,* 256–271.

Wendt, R. N., and Zake, J. (August, 1982). *Family systems theory and school psychology: Implications for training and practice.* Paper adapted from presentation at the 90th Annual Convention of the American Psychological Association, Washington, D.C.

Wynne, L. C. (1983). Family research and family therapy: A reunion. *Journal of Marital and Family Therapy, 9,* 113–117.

Zuckerman, E., and Jacob, T. (1979). Task effects in family interaction. *Family Processes, 18,* 47–52.

chapter 7

MEASURES OF STRESS AND COPING IN FAMILIES

Marty Wyngaarden Krauss

INTRODUCTION

A diverse range of publicly and privately supported programs has been established to help young families cope with both the predictable and unpredictable stresses of parenting. For example, programs are available for single parents, for parents of premature infants, for families with children who are vulnerable to developmental delays, and for families who have children with newly diagnosed illnesses or life-long disabilities. While the goals of such programs vary depending upon population served, theoretical orientation, and program resources, many programs share the goal of promoting family and/or individual coping skills to reduce or ameliorate negative consequences of stress.

Coping refers to the cognitive and behavioral efforts used to master conditions of harm, threat, or stress when a routine or automatic response is neither readily available nor a natural part of the individual's or family's repetoire (Hill, 1949; Lazarus, 1966; McCubbin, Cauble, and Patterson, 1980b). Frequently studied coping responses include development of social and emotional support networks, dependence upon religious or spiritual beliefs, temporary or long-term denial of the stressful situation, and mastery of the situation through self-education. A considerable amount of research has focused on identifying the correlates and consequences of stress upon families (Carter and McGoldrick, 1980; McCubbin and Patterson, 1983; McCubbin, Patterson, Comeau, Joy, Cauble and Needle, 1980a; Reiss and Oliveri, 1980) and on the process by which effective coping patterns are nurtured

(Pearlin and Schooler, 1978). These studies have affected the types of services and programs provided to families and stimulated the development of instruments useful for research and program evaluation.

The purpose of this chapter is to describe the potential contribution of such measures to family program evaluation. It begins with a review of the conceptual bases on which instruments measuring stress and coping behavior are grounded. The impact of these concepts on program development and evaluation is then discussed. Measures that are particularly promising for use in family programs are then reviewed and issues related to their administration are discussed.

CONCEPTUAL FRAMEWORKS FOR EVALUATING STRESS AND COPING

Family stress as an area of sociological research can be traced to studies of the effect of economic depression on families conducted in the 1930s and to subsequent investigations of bereavement, alcoholism, war separation and reunion, and unemployment. The earliest, and most enduring conceptual foundation for research on variability in family reactions to stress is the ABCX model proposed by Hill in 1958. This model postulates that:

> A (the stressor event)—interacting with B (the family's "crisis-meeting" resources)—interacting with C (the definition the family makes of the event)—produces X (the crisis).

The import of this formulation lies in its identification of variables accounting for a family's vulnerability to an initial crisis or stressor event. What it failed to address, however, were the dynamics of coping and recovery. More recent work has focused on these dynamics and what is often called the family's regenerative power (Burr, 1973; Hansen, 1965).

Research using Hill's ABCX model has yielded four additional factors found to influence the nature of family adaptation to crisis over time:

1. The pile-up or accumulation of additional stresses and strains
2. Family efforts to marshall new resources from within the family and community
3. Revision of the definition or meaning ascribed by the family to the stressful situation
4. Family coping strategies designed to promote adaptation.

These factors were incorporated into the Double ABCX Model (McCubbin and Patterson, 1982), as presented in Figure 7.1. The components of that model are:

Precrisis Variables:

(a) (Stressor): A life event or transition that produces, or has the potential to produce, change in the family social system.

(b) (Existing resources): The family's ability to prevent an event or change in the family social system from creating a crisis.

(c) (Perception of "a"): The family's subjective definition of the stressor and its hardships and how they are affected by them.

(x) (Crisis): A continuous variable denoting the disruptiveness, disorganization, or incapacity in the family system.

Postcrisis Variables:

(aA) (Pile-up): Contributing to pile-up are: the initial stressor and its hardship, normative transitions, prior strains, the consequences of family efforts to cope, and intrafamily and social role ambiguity.

(bB) (Existing and new resources): Existing resources are already part of the family's repertoire and can be individual, family, or community-based. Expanded family resources are new resources strengthened or developed in response to the crisis.

(cC) (Perception of $Xx + aA + bB$): The meaning the family gives to the stressor believed to have caused the crisis, the added stressors and strains, old and new resources, and estimates of what is needed to restore family balance.

(xX) (Adaptation): Considered to be composed of three elements—the individual family member, the family system, and the community in which the individual and the family live. Family adaptation reflects family efforts to achieve a balance or fit between and among the demands and capabilities of reciprocal relationships.

While perceptions and internal and external resources are embedded in most conceptualizations of coping (Antonovsky, 1974; Pearlin and Schooler, 1978), coping skills have emerged as a distinct area of investigation for understanding individual and family management of stress. The Double ABCX model presents coping skills as the product of an interaction among the factors listed previously and as a predictor of the adaptability of the family to a stressful experience. It has proved useful for understanding the adaptation process of families confronted with either (or both) a discrete stressful event (e.g., birth of a first child, death of a family member) or an enduring stressful situation (e.g., parenting a handicapped or chronically ill child, being a socially isolated single parent). It acknowledges variability in internal and external coping resources. It also acknowledges that the interpretation or perception of the crisis situation represents a powerful, though changeable, force in the family's ability to cope. It thus recognizes the importance of

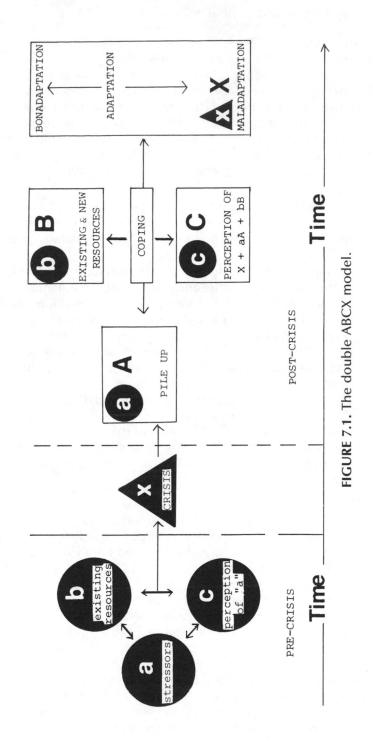

FIGURE 7.1. The double ABCX model.

both external and internal resources to a family's vulnerability and re-generative power.

The coping behaviors used by individuals and/or families also reflect available resources including: social resources (e.g., interpersonal networks), psychological resources (e.g., personality characteristics drawn upon to interpret threats to stability and well-being), and specific coping responses (e.g., behaviors, cognitive understandings, and perceptions) (Pearlin and Schooler, 1978). Distinctions among these types of resources are helpful in characterizing family situations and in designing family intervention programs.

While there is a long tradition of research on the individual psychology of coping (Lazarus, 1966; 1975), conceptualizations and research on the contribution of environmental or social factors to problem-solving skills are more recent (Beckman, 1983; Crnic, Friedrich, and Greenberg, 1983; Farber, 1970). In this discussion, *coping is defined as the overt and covert behaviors individuals use to prevent, avoid, or alleviate stressful situations* (McCubbin et al., 1980a; Pearlin and Schooler, 1978).

IMPLICATIONS FOR PROGRAM DESIGN AND EVALUATION

Most programs serving families have as either a stated or implicit goal the positive adaptations of individual family members or the family as a unit to a stressful situation. While the approaches programs take vary considerably, commonly found program characteristics are suggested by the conceptual issues discussed previously. For example, most models of stress acknowledge that a specific stressor reverberates through a family. Thus, the family as a unit, rather than its individual members, are often the focus of intervention (see Dym, Chapter 22; Walker and Crocker, Chapter 6, this volume).

By defining the basic components of adaptation to stress, the Double ABCX model also identifies possible points of effective intervention. Programs can more effectively target their services to those components (e.g., extending family resources, coping skills, perceptions) most in need of shoring up or most amenable to intervention. For example, many programs serving families with handicapped children establish parent support groups to help parents change their perception of the meaning and impact of rearing a handicapped child. Such groups also serve to broaden the parents' social support network—an external resource (see Dunst and Trivette, Chapter 14, this volume).

The Double ABCX model also acknowledges the variability in intensity with which a family reacts to a stressful event. For some families, the birth of a first child will produce an enormous upheaval that may strain internal and external resources to a dysfunctional level. For others, little stress is experienced. Professionals must, therefore, be attentive to the multiplicity of impacts that a single stressor may have.

Moreover, the model accommodates individualized and culturally determined styles of coping. These styles may have proved valuable to the family in meeting prior challenges but may not be effective for new stressors. In such cases, programs must build upon the existing strengths of the family rather than using strategies that conflict with, or are insensitive to, family coping styles.

IMPLICATIONS FOR PROGRAM EVALUATION

The conceptual framework discussed previously also has implications for the evaluation of programs aiming to reduce stress and enhance coping skills. First, given that the concepts of stress and coping are multidimensional, the choice of evaluation instruments should reflect that complexity. Either more than one instrument is needed to measure program impacts in these areas or a single "hearty" instrument with subscales tapping various dimensions should be used.

Second, because stress and coping patterns change over time, the instruments selected must be sensitive enough to detect both large and small changes. The significance attributed to small decrements of stress in a family that has experienced chronic stress over long periods of time (e.g., parenting a handicapped child, long-term child abuse or neglect), may well be equal to the significance attributed to a large decrease in stress for a less chronically stressed family. For some families, simply keeping the existing level of stress from escalating may be an important goal. In such a case, no change in the measured level of stress may signal a positive outcome.

Third, family stress and coping patterns are the product of both internal and external factors that may be exceedingly difficult to change through short-term intervention. Programs must conceptualize the anticipated level or degree of change in stress and coping patterns in light of the depth of services available and the complexity of the situations of families served.

INSTRUMENT SELECTION

Once a program decides to include measures of stress and coping among its evaluation tools, it may decide to develop its own instrument, modify an existing instrument, or use an existing instrument without modification. Developing new measures or modifying existing instruments allows programs to tailor evaluation instruments to their program and population. For example, stresses experienced by single teenage parents (e.g., social isolation, financial hardship, personal immaturity) may be different from those affecting parents of handicapped children (e.g., perceived stigma, physical demands of care). If existing instruments do not tap these specific factors, program directors may choose to develop their own instruments or adapt other instruments to meet their evaluation goal.

However, there are disadvantages to this approach. Instrument development or modification is time consuming and requires special expertise. Further, the ability to compare program effectiveness across similarly focused programs is compromised when evaluation methodologies are highly individualized (Travers and Light, 1982). Use of standardized instruments enables programs to compare their results with those of other investigators. Such comparison provides a frame of reference for interpreting findings and contributes to our general understanding of interventions designed to ameliorate stress and promote coping skills. Finally, standardized measures tend to be relatively easy and inexpensive to administer. Unfortunately, there are few measures of stress and coping appropriate for use in programs serving families with young children, and many of those that do exist are overly broad in focus and unlikely to detect significant effects of short-term or less intensive intervention.

Review of Selected Measures of Stress and Coping

The measures described in this section have all been used for various types of target populations typically served by programs serving families with young children. They are relatively easy to administer and analyze, and they are multidimensional. Measures of stress are presented first with those relevant for individuals distinguished from those relevant for families as a unit. Measures of coping are then presented. While conceptually, factors associated with stress and factors affecting individual and family styles of coping are distinct, operationally measures of stress and coping tap many similar constructs. Measures of stress generally focus on specific events or conditions that are potentially stress producing while measures of coping generally focus on ways in which individuals or families adapt to stressful conditions.

MEASURES OF STRESS

Individual Stress Measures

The Questionnaire on Resources and Stress (QRS) (Holroyd, 1974). This questionnaire measures family stress, coping, and adaptation in families with a handicapped child. The original QRS is a true–false, self-administered questionnaire at a readability level of Grade 6, composed of 285 items representing 15 nonoverlapping scales (and a lie scale). It purports to measure three broad dimensions: parent problems, problems in family functioning, and problems the parent sees in or for the child.

The original QRS was found to differentiate between married and single mothers, between mothers and fathers, and between mothers of retarded children and mothers of emotionally disturbed children (Holroyd, 1974). It has been used to compare stress levels between parents of Down syndrome and autistic children (Holroyd and MacArthur, 1976) and between families of institutionalized and noninstitutionalized autistic children (Holroyd, Brown, Wikler, and Simmons, 1975). Other studies confirm a relationship between measured stress levels using the QRS and the child's level of functioning (Beckman, 1983; Holroyd and Guthrie, 1979) and interview-based ratings of stress (Holroyd *et al.*, 1975). Its major drawbacks are its length (administration requires approximately 1 hour), lack of information on its internal reliability, and some question as to whether the 15 rationally determined scales are, in fact, distinct and valid.

Two shortened versions of the original 285-item QRS are available. Holroyd (1982) factor-analyzed data from a population of 526 cases and found 11 orthogonal factors. From these, 66 items were selected (6 per factor), with factor score correlations ranging from .64 to .90. This 66-item version is called the QRS-Short Form (QRS-SF). A study using the QRS-SF with a sample of 189 parents of handicapped and nonhandicapped children found weaknesses in the scale related to its reliability and stability of the factor analysis procedures by which it was generated. It was noted, however, that the QRS-SF retains clinical value as a general assessment tool for the measurement of stress and coping, and that used in combination with other clinical instruments, it is a useful tool for families with a handicapped member (Salisbury, 1985).

The other shortened version, the QRS-F, was developed by Friedrich, Greenberg, and Crnic (1983). Its development was based on 289 completed QRS forms from parents of children of all ages diagnosed with autism, cerebral palsy, cystic fibrosis, Down syndrome, hematological disorders, neuromuscular disease, psychiatric disorders, renal disease, and mixed developmental and/or mental retardation disorders. Using a three-step analytic procedure, 52 items from the original QRS were identified as the most reliable. Factor-analysis yielded four distinct factors: parent and family problems, pessimism, child characteristics, and physical incapacitation. The correlation of scores between the QRS and the QRS-F was .997.

The QRS, the QRS-SF, and the QRS-F are most appropriately used in programs serving families with handicapped children. Efforts have been made to stabilize psychometric properties, reduce length, and establish utility in differentiating stress and coping mechanisms between families with and without handicapped children and among families with handicapped children. Periodically, it has been "popular" with programs serving families because of its ease in administration, its suitability for diverse types of handicapping conditions, and its multiplicity of subscales that permit more precise identification of areas appropriate for intervention.

The Parenting Stress Index (PSI). This is a screening and diagnostic instrument developed by Abidin (1983) to identify parent–child systems under stress or at risk for dysfunctional parenting and the development of emotional problems in children below the age of 10 years. It is a 101-item instrument with an optional 19-item Life Events Scale which is self-administered using a 5-point Likert scale. The scale is described in more detail by Upshur (Chapter 5, this volume).

The PSI is considered appropriate for assessing stress in families with children having the following types of handicaps: mental retardation, hyperactivity, cerebral palsy, developmental delay, prematurity, otitis media, SIDS, or apnea. It is also useful for studies of "normal" families, medical utilization, family relations, and intervention. It is currently used in over 300 medical centers, mental health clinics, and programs serving families.

The Hassles Scale (Kanner, Coyne, Schaefer, and Lazarus, 1981). This scale measures the frequency of occurrence of commonly experienced daily irritants, frustrations, demands, or problems. The 117-item scale also measures the severity or intensity (rated on a 3-point scale of "somewhat," "moderate," or "extreme") of each hassle occurring during the month. The items reflect the content areas of work, family, social activities, environment, practical considerations, finances, and health.

When the Hassles Scale was administered monthly to 100 persons over a 9-consecutive-month period, the test–retest reliability for the frequency score had an average correlation of .79, while the average correlation for the severity score was .48 (Delongis, Coyne, Dakof, Folkman, and Lazarus, 1982). This suggests that people experience roughly the same number, though not necessarily the same type, of hassles month-to-month. However, the variability in the intensity scores suggests that the scale is sensitive to fluctuations in individual responses to hassles.

The scoring procedures for the scale produce two summary scores, a simple frequency of the number of items checked (ranging from 0 to 117), and an intensity score, which is obtained by summing the numbers representing the severity of the hassle (1, 2, or 3) and dividing by the frequency total. Both the frequency and intensity scores correlate with poor overall health status and with the reporting of lower energy levels. The frequency of hassles, but not their intensity, significantly correlates with a high frequency of somatic symptoms (Delongis *et al.*, 1982).

Family Stress Measures

The Family Inventory of Life Events and Changes (FILE). The inventory is a self-report instrument designed to record the normative and non-normative life events and changes in a family. Of the 71 items, 34 refer to events that are chronic and that generate a prolonged amount of stress (e.g., spouse/parent separation or divorce, child became seriously ill or injured, family member lost a job). The others refer to events within the preceding year. Each item is worded to reflect a change of sufficient magnitude to require some adjustment in the regular pattern of interaction in family members. Thus, the FILE assesses the "pile-up" of life events as conceptualized within the Double ABCX model (McCubbin and Patterson, 1983).

The FILE has a Cronbach's alpha reliability of .81 (Olson and Mc-Cubbin, 1983). It generates eleven scores—nine scale scores of recent family changes, a total recent life change score, and a total past life change score. The nine scales of recent family changes are: (1) intra-family strains; (2) marital strains; (3) pregnancy and childbearing strains; (4) finance and business strains; (5) work–family transitions and strains; (6) illness and family care strains; (7) losses; (8) transitions in and out; and (9) family legal violations.

These scales were created on the basis of factor analyses and are not recommended for use alone as reliable indicators of stress. Scale scores are obtained by summing the responses for the items in that scale. The total score for recent life changes is a sum of the scale scores. The past life changes score is a sum of responses to the 34 items in this scale.

The FILE was validated by correlating each of the nine subscales and the total scale score with the Family Environment Scale, a measure of family functioning (Moos, 1974). While the correlations were in the expected directions, the coefficients were generally only moderate in strength.

Because the focus of the FILE is the family, it is one of the few available instruments that acknowledges the social context of the individual. Further, its multidimensionality permits the identification of areas in which families may be under comparatively more stress. Despite these attributes, programs using the FILE as part of their evaluation activities have not reported significant differences in pre- and posttreatment scores for families. This has been interpreted by researchers as an indication that the FILE is not sensitive to small or subtle changes in the amount of stress families experience. The FILE is generally viewed as an appropriate measure for examining family stress from a broad, life stage perspective.

The Adolescent–Family Inventory of Life Events (A-FILE). This inventory is a 50-item self-report instrument which parallels the FILE in content and format but which focuses on those normative and nonnormative events to which an adolescent would be especially sensitive.

Measures of Coping

The most extensive work on measures of family coping has been done by McCubbin and Patterson (1981) and includes instruments designed to assess coping strategies for families facing specific situations. For example, measures have been developed for:

(1) Families experiencing prolonged separation or divorce *(The Family Coping Inventory—FCI)*
(2) Dual career families *(The Dual-Employed Coping Scales—DECS)*
(3) Two-parent families dealing with developmental and situational stressors *(The Family Crisis Oriented Personal Evaluation Scales— F-COPES)*
(4) Families caring for a chronically ill member *(The Coping Health Inventory for Parents—CHIP)*
(5) An adolescent family member coping with stress *(The Adolescent Coping Orientation for Program Experiences—A-COPE).*

Because these measures are similar in scope, content, length, and scoring procedures, CHIP will be described here as a representative measure.

The Coping Health Inventory for Parents (CHIP). CHIP is a measure of family coping behaviors manifested in response to living with a child who is chronically ill. It is based on family stress theory, social support theory, and theories on the individual psychology of coping and family medical support.

The 45-item self-report instrument is completed by parents individually and can be used to assess differences in coping behaviors between mothers and fathers, to assess intervention programs aimed at strengthening parental coping (as a pre- and posttest measure), and to aid in clinically identifying specific coping behaviors that need to be strengthened. The respondent indicates how helpful each coping behavior has been in managing the needs of the child. A 4-point rating scale is used, ranging from "extremely helpful" to "not helpful." A principal components factor analysis with iterations identified three coping patterns that accounted for 71.1% of the variance of the original correlation matrix. The three patterns are described here. CHIP scores represent a summation of scores for each of the three coping patterns.

1. *Maintaining family integration, cooperation and an optimistic definition of the situation.* This coping pattern is composed of 19 behaviors involving doing things as a family, strengthening family relationships, and developing and maintaining a positive outlook on life in general and specifically when a member has a chronic illness. Internal reliability = .79 (Cronbach's alpha).

2. *Maintaining social support, self-esteem, and psychological stability.* This coping pattern consists of 18 behaviors that focus on the parent's effort to maintain a sense of his/her own well-being through social relationships, involvement in activities that have the potential for enhancing self-esteem, and managing psychological tensions and strains. Internal reliability = .79 (Cronbach's alpha).

3. *Understanding the medical situation through communication with other parents and consultation with medical staff.* This coping pattern involves eight behaviors focusing on relationships developed with other parents who have a child with a similar illness and the relationship developed with medical personnel. It includes behaviors directed at understanding medical information and mastering the use of medical equipment in the home. Internal reliability = .71 (Cronbach's alpha).

The CHIP has been used in a study of the coping patterns of parents of children with cystic fibrosis (CF) (McCubbin, McCubbin, Patterson, Cauble, Wilson, and Warwick, 1983). Parental coping was found to be an appropriate target for primary prevention in assisting families to adapt to chronic stressors, and some families were found to be at greater risk than others for poor coping skills. Specifically, single-parent families, families with an older CF member, and/or families with limited income were identified as high-risk.

Research suggests that the CHIP is a valid and useful measure for evaluating family level coping patterns and the relationship of these patterns to specific outcomes. However, studies using the CHIP as a pre- and posttest measure have not been reported. Thus, its sensitivity to changes in family coping patterns over time and with varying intensities of service provision is unknown.

The Folkman–Lazarus Ways of Coping Checklist. This is a 68-item checklist spanning a range of thoughts and actions people use to deal with taxing events (Folkman and Lazarus, 1980). Unlike the instruments developed by McCubbin and Patterson, the Folkman–Lazarus Ways of Coping Checklist taps coping behaviors associated with ordinary stressful events in day-to-day lives rather than coping behaviors related to chronic stresses or specific life events. The checklist includes items from the domains of defensive coping (e.g., avoidance, intellectualization, isolation, suppression), information-seeking, problem-solving, palliation, inhibition of action, direct action, and magical thinking. The checklist is binary *(yes/no)* and is always analyzed with a specific stressful event in mind. It is not designed to assess coping styles or traits but rather is a process measure that, when administered over regular intervals for a unique stressor occurring in the preceding month, can yield information on the consistency (or variability) in the individual's coping mechanisms.

The checklist consists of a 27-item problem-solving-focused scale and a 41-item emotion-focused coping scale. Scores are derived by summing "YES" responses for each scale. The alpha coefficients for internal consistency of the problem-focused scale and the emotion-focused scale are estimated at .80 and .81, respectively. The scales correlate at approximately .45. These results were obtained from a 12-month study of stress, emotions, and coping for a sample of 100 respondents ages 45–64. The respondents were fairly evenly distributed by sex, were predominantly Protestant, had at least a ninth-grade level of education, and were not severely disabled (Aldwin, Folkman, Schaefer, Coyne, and Lazarus, 1980).

No studies have been reported that have used the Folkman–Lazarus Ways of Coping Checklist in clinical settings. One of its potential advantages, however, for programs serving families with young children is that it can be administered to respondents focusing on a common, specific event. This enables a program to compare coping patterns as a basis for intervention programming and follow-up. For example, if a program found that the majority of its clients utilized problem-solving coping techniques, it might focus on organizing information and knowledge-building activities.

ISSUES IN INSTRUMENT ADMINISTRATION

While the measures presented have not been widely used either in cross-sectional or program evaluation studies, they represent potentially useful tools that may be used as currently constructed or modified to suit specific program objectives. None is particularly difficult or time-consuming to administer or interpret, and the manuals available for each are adequately detailed for program use.

Programs which have conducted evaluations using measures described previously or similar tools have noted several important implementation issues. First, asking individuals to complete instruments measuring stress and coping may itself produce stress. Some questions focus directly on highly sensitive or emotionally loaded issues that may be disturbing. Thus, programs must be attentive to the need for follow-up or support to respondents during and after the questionnaire administration.

Second, programs that have used measures of stress and coping suggest that their administration always be linked to or timed with the administration of other, less charged instruments. The emotional intensity accompanying completion of questionnaires on personal and family stress can be diffused with other more objective or less personal questions. Third, many programs suggest that the questionnaires be administered in the home or wherever the respondent will feel most comfortable and relaxed. Program staff may need to remain at the home during the administration to answer questions as they arise, to help respondents cope with unresolved feelings that might surface after completing the questionnaires, and to provide meaningful feedback.

Fourth, while most measures are written in straightforward language and many are specifically designed for persons with a moderate level of education, difficulties have been noted in their use with some families with limited education and reading skills.

It is also recommended that program personnel communicate with the developers of the instruments selected for use. Most instrument developers maintain lists of programs that have used their instruments and compile summary reports regarding program findings. They welcome collaboration with users of the instrument as it enables them to revise and refine their instruments based on programmatic applications.

Summary and Recommendations

Theoretical frameworks for studying stress and coping in families are clearly more plentiful than measures available to operationalize those frameworks. However, in recent years, measures of stress and coping in evaluation studies have become increasingly important as more rigorous and comprehensive models for understanding the dynamics of family interventions have emerged. The management of stress and the promotion of adequate coping skills are now, indeed, considered to be integral dimensions of the adaptational process in families undergoing predictable and unpredictable stressful situations. Programs seeking to assist families are increasingly cognizant of their potential impact on these dimensions and are in need of reliable and valid measures.

Of the three measures of individual stress discussed in this chapter the *Questionnaire on Resources and Stress* has been the most extensively used with parents (usually mothers) of handicapped children.

This scale has been subject to revision during the last several years, and there are currently three versions in use. It has proven to be a useful measure of stress and clearly will benefit from continued refinement. The *Parenting Stress Index* is one of the most frequently used measures of stress for parents (again, usually mothers) who are "at-risk" for a variety of problems either in themselves or in their relationships with their children. Its multidimensionality and the inclusion of a variety of standard sociodemographic questions give it a comprehensiveness for data collection that is noteworthy. *The Hassles Scale* has not been widely used in programs serving families but is a potentially serviceable measure for programs tracking stress levels over short (e.g., monthly) intervals. Its sensitivity to changes in the intensity of hassles suggests that it may be useful for monitoring subjective perceptions of stress. More applied work is needed before the scale can be recommended on a widespread basis. The *Family Inventory of Life Events and Changes (FILE)* may prove to be a useful tool for programs focused at the family level when used in conjunction with other measures of stress and coping.

The measures of coping described here are appropriate for consideration by a wide range of programs serving families with young children. The numerous instruments developed by McCubbin and Patterson allow programs a number of options in selecting measures that are most appropriate for their specific needs. Results from some of the preliminary studies using the *Coping Health Inventory for Parents* (Bristol, 1984; McCubbin *et al.*, 1983) suggest that it taps salient dimensions of the coping process and that these dimensions are predictive of both child and family outcomes. These encouraging findings should prompt other programs to incorporate these measures in their evaluation plans. The *Folkman–Lazarus Ways of Coping Checklist,* like the Hassles Scale, has not benefited from extensive testing in clinical settings. It appears, however, to be a potentially useful tool in assessing individual or family level response to specific events and, if administered repeatedly over brief intervals, in identifying patterns of coping. Programs that provide highly structured, intensive services may find the Checklist sensitive to small or subtle changes in coping patterns.

The selection of measures of stress and coping discussed in this chapter is neither comprehensive nor exhaustive. Researchers are continually refining existing measures and developing new ones in order to capture more completely the often subtle but important impacts for which intervention programs can claim credit. The success of these efforts depends in large part upon incorporating the experiences and findings of programs utilizing the measures in their routine and special evaluation activities. Given the current emphasis on strengthening the family, on seeking creative ways of reducing stress, and on fostering positive coping mechanisms, it can be expected that programs will increasingly include such measures and share their findings with the professional, research, and academic communities.

References

Abidin, R. B. (1983). *Parenting Stress Index Manual*. Charlottesville, VA: Pediatric Psychology Press.

Aldwin, C., Folkman, S., Schaefer, C., Coyne, J., and Lazarus, R. S. (1980, August). *The ways of coping: A process measure*. Paper presented at the meeting of the American Psychological Association. Montreal, Canada.

Antonovsky, A. (1974). Conceptual and methodological problems in the study of resistance resources and stressful life events. In B. Dohrenwend and B. Dorehrenwend (Eds.), *Stressful life events: Their nature and effects* (pp. 245–258). NY: Wiley.

Beckman, P. J. (1983). Influence of selected child characteristics on stress in families of handicapped infants. *American Journal of Mental Deficiency, 88*, 150–156.

Bristol, M. M. (October 1984). *Families of developmentally disabled children: Healthy adaptation and the double ABCX model*. Paper presented at the Family Systems and Health Pre-Conference workshop, National Council in Family Relations, San Francisco, California.

Burr, W. (1973). *Theory construction and the sociology of the family*. NY: Wiley.

Carter, E. A., and McGoldrick, M. (Eds.). (1980). *The family life cycle: A framework for family therapy*. NY: Gardner Press.

Crnic, K. A., Friedrich, W. A., and Greenberg, M. T. (1983). Adaptation of families with mentally retarded children: A model of stress, coping, and family ecology. *American Journal of Mental Deficiency, 88*, 125–138.

DeLongis, A., Coyne, J. C., Dakof, G., Folkman, S., and Lazarus, R. S. (1982). Relationship of daily hassles, uplifts, and major life events to health status. *Health Psychology, 1*, 119–136.

Farber, B. (1970). Notes on sociological knowledge about families with mentally retarded children. In M. Schreiber (Ed.), *Social work and mental retardation* (pp. 118–124). NY: John Day.

Folkman, S., and Lazarus, R. S. (1980). An analysis of coping in a middle-aged community sample. *Journal of Health and Social Behavior, 21*, 219–239.

Friedrich, W. N., Greenberg, M. T., and Crnic, K. (1983). A short-form of the questionnaire on resources and stress. *American Journal of Mental Deficiency, 88*, 41–48.

Hansen, D. (1965). Personal and positional influence in formal groups: Compositions and theory for research on family vulnerability to stress. *Social Forces, 44,* 202–210.

Hill, R. (1949). *Families under stress.* NY: Harper.

Hill, R. (1958). Generic features of families under stress. *Social Casework, 49,* 139–150.

Holroyd, J. (1974). The questionnaire on resources and stress: An instrument to measure family response to a handicapped family member. *Journal of Community Psychology, 2,* 92–94.

Holroyd, J. (1982). *Manual for the Questionnaire on Resources and Stress.* Los Angeles: UCLA Neuropsychiatric Institute.

Holroyd, J., and Guthrie, D. (1979). Stress in families of children with neuromuscular disease. *Journal of Clinical Psychology, 35,* 734–739.

Holroyd, J., Brown, N., Wikler, L., and Simmons, J. Q. (1975). Stress in families of institutionalized and non-institutionalized autistic children. *Journal of Community Psychology, 2,* 92–94.

Holroyd, J., and McArthur, D. (1976). Mental retardation and stress on the parents: A contrast between Down's syndrome and child autism. *American Journal of Mental Deficiency, 80,* 431–436.

Kanner, A. O., Coyne, J. C., Schaefer, C., and Lazarus, R. S. (1981). Comparison of two modes of stress measurement: Daily hassles and uplifts versus major life events. *Journal of Behavioral Medicine, 4,* 1–39.

Lazarus, R. (1966). *Psychological stress and the coping process.* NY: McGraw-Hill.

Lazarus, R. (1975) The self-regulation of emotion. In L. Levi (Ed.), *Emotions: Their parameters and measurement* (pp. 47–69). NY: Raven Press.

McCubbin, H. I., and Patterson, J. M. (1981). *Systematic assessment of family stress, resources, and coping: Tools for research, education, and clinical intervention.* St. Paul, MN: University of Minnesota.

McCubbin, H. I., and Patterson, J. M. (1982). Family adaptation to crisis. In H. I. McCubbin, E. Cauble, and J. M. Patterson (Eds.), *Family stress, coping, and social support* (pp. 26–47). Springfield, IL: Charles C. Thomas.

McCubbin, H. I., and Patterson, J. M. (1983). The family stress process: The Double ABCX Model of adjustment and adaptation. In H. I. McCubbin, M. B. Sussman, and J. M. Patterson (Eds.), *Social stress and the family: Advances and developments in family stress theory and research* (pp. 7–37). NY: Haworth Press.

McCubbin, H. I., Patterson, J. M., Comeau, J. K., Joy, C. B., Cauble, A. E., and Needle, R. H. (1980a). Family stress and coping: A decade review. *Journal of Marriage and the Family, 42,* 855–871.

McCubbin, H. I., Cauble, A. E., and Patterson, J. M. (Eds.). (1980b). *Family stress, coping, and social support.* Springfield, IL: Charles C. Thomas.

McCubbin, H. I., McCubbin, M. A., Patterson, J. M., Cauble, A. E., Wilson, L. R., and Warwick, W. (1983). CHIP—Coping Health Inventory for Parents: An assessment of parental coping patterns in the care of the chronically ill child. *Journal of Marriage and the Family, 45,* 359–370.

Moos, R. H. (1974). *Family environment scale.* Palo Alto, CA: Consulting Psychologists Press.

Olson, D., and McCubbin, H. (1983). *Families: What makes them work.* Beverly Hills, CA: Sage.

Pearlin, L. I., and Schooler, C. (1978). The structure of coping. *Journal of Health and Social Behavior, 19,* 2–21.

Reiss, D., and Oliveri, M. E. (1980). Family paradigm and family coping: A proposal for linking the family's intrinsic and adaptive capacities to its responses to stress. *Family Relations, 29,* 431–444.

Salisbury, C. L. (1985). Internal consistency of the short-form of the questionnaire on resources and stress. *American Journal of Mental Deficiency, 89,* 610–616.

Travers, J. R., and Light, R. J. (Eds.). (1982). *Learning from experience: Evaluating early childhood demonstration programs.* Washington, DC: National Academy Press.

chapter 8

SOCIAL SUPPORT: CONCEPTUALIZATION
AND MEASUREMENT

Paul D. Cleary

The provision or facilitation of social support is frequently a central goal of family programs. Yet while there is clear consensus that social support is important, there is little consensus as to how it is best conceptualized and measured, or what the processes are by which it promotes the objectives of families. In this chapter I will provide a brief review of the literature on the conceptualization, measurement, and effects of social support, then offer a pragmatic guide to various approaches to the measurement of social support.

THE SOCIAL SUPPORT LITERATURE

Social Support and Family Functioning

The interrelationships among the child, his or her family, and other social contacts are critical influences on the child's well-being and eventual development (Bronfenbrenner, 1979; Zigler and Weiss, 1985). The social support that these relationships provide is important both in facilitating the normal developmental processes of childhood (Cochran and Brassard, 1979) and in ameliorating effects of stress (see Dunst and Trivette, Chapter 14, this volume). There has been relatively little research on effects of social support on development, but a growing body of research indicates that social factors have important effects on young children. Boyce (1985), for example, argues that the mutual, interactive social support that emerges from the child's earliest experiences in the family is an important determinant of health and development. Also, substantial evidence indicates that social support in pregnancy can influence such "hard" outcomes as infant birthweight (Oakley, 1985).

Social Support and Health

Many studies link social support to utilization of health services, adherence to medical regimens, recovery, rehabilitation, adaptation to illness, and mortality (Broadhead, Kaplan, James, Wagner, Shoenbach, Grimson, Heyden, Tibblin, and Gellbach, 1983; Wallston, Alagna, DeVellis, and DeVellis, 1983). Most impressive, however, are those linking social support to mortality (Berkman and Breslow, 1983; Berkman and Syme, 1979; Blazer, 1982; House, Robbins, and Metzner, 1982). Yet researchers have gained little understanding of the nature of this relationship (Cohen and Wills, 1985; Wallston *et al.*, 1983). For example, Wallston and colleagues (1983) report that although various measures of social support or quality of life have been shown to be related to the onset of illness (Bruhn, 1965; Cobb, Kasl, French, and Norstedbo, 1969; Hinkle and Wolff, 1958), the data is far from consistent, and a number of researchers have reported negative findings (Bruhn, Wolf, Lynn, Bird, and Chandler, 1968; Caplan, Cobb, French, Van Harrison, and Pinneau, 1975). Social support may act in exceedingly complex ways by affecting exposure, susceptibility, incidence, help-seeking, and disease course (Cohen and Wills, 1985). Nevertheless, the relevance of social support to a number of health-related processes is now well established.

Many studies also link social support to psychological health and psychiatric morbidity. Kessler and McLeod (1985) have reviewed this literature and conclude that being part of a social network does not, in general, buffer the impact of stressful life events on mental health. However, membership in affiliative networks may have a small effect on mental health, independent of stress, and specific types of support, such as emotional support and perceived availability of support, may buffer the impact of stressful life events. Cohen and Wills (1985) found that support appears to protect people from potentially adverse effects of stressful events when the measures used assessed interpersonal resources that were responsive to the needs elicited by stressful events. They also found an overall beneficial effect of support as defined by degree of integration in a larger social network.

Social Support in Program Evaluations

Whether a program fails or succeeds in achieving its goals, it is important to be able to identify precisely what the components of the

program were and what other factors may have conditioned participants' responses. There is enormous variability in people's responses
to events or situations. When faced with daily hassles or life-threatening
events, some people show almost no adverse consequences while others are severely affected. For example, most women respond to the
birth of a child with unparalleled joy, whereas other women experience
serious affective disorders (Brockington and Kumar, 1982). One possible
explanation for this diversity of response is that people have different
psychological and social resources available to them. Thus, "social
support" may affect how a person responds to an event or situation
and may contribute to or modify the effects of a program. To neglect
this variable is to limit the advancement of knowledge about program
effectiveness.

Family programs usually are multifaceted and offer services ranging
from straightforward information to therapeutic intervention. Program
objectives and processes are difficult to define, and program evaluations
tend to focus on such concrete questions as: Did the family use the
services, and were they satisfied with the services received? Unfortunately, because programs frequently effect people in a variety of complex ways, such evaluations may not tap important social processes
through which a program has an impact. For example, a visit to a social
worker may entail discussion about many topics, one of which may be
how to identify and mobilize existing sources of support. If specific
measures assessing use of existing sources of support are not included
in an evaluation, one loses the ability to describe this important aspect
of the program. One would not know whether to attribute the program's success to the direct services provided by the social worker, to
the client's ability to mobilize existing resources more effectively, or
to some combination of the two.

One of the most striking features of the social support literature is
the lack of overlap between the more theoretical studies and those
pertaining to family program evaluation. The theoretical literature is
characterized by relatively abstract concepts, and the importance of
social support tends to be tested using large population studies and
complicated multivariate statistical models. The majority of this literature focuses on diffuse sets of life events, minor irritants, and, to a
lesser extent, ongoing chronic problems. Family program research, on
the other hand, usually focuses on a well-defined, specific problem
(e.g., coping with a new child) and is conducted with very small samples. It often implicitly assumes that the program provides support and
addresses the more basic question of whether there is an overall difference between the experimental and control group. Rarely do evaluations attempt to disentangle the complicated effects of multifaceted
interventions.

Applied researchers are frequently frustrated by the apparent irrelevance of many of the ideas in the literature on social support. Theoretical researchers, on the other hand, are often frustrated by the apparent lack of sophistication of measurement and research design used in many program evaluations. Yet, these points of view do not represent an unresolvable conflict. Program directors and evaluators must carefully consider the ways in which social influences will cause or mediate the impact of family programs and incorporate measures of those social influences in the evaluation design. They may choose to develop measures for their particular program, but they should also consider including, when feasible, questions or scales that measure the dimensions of social support described in this chapter. An integration of the analytic tradition and the applied tradition, as well as greater collaboration between the researchers involved, would undoubtedly be mutually beneficial (Rook and Dooley, 1985). Only by tying empirical results to the theoretical dimensions posed in the literature will we be able to advance our knowledge of how social support works and how specific programs achieve (or fail to achieve) their goals.

Definitions of Social Support

There is vigorous debate about what social support is (Carveth and Gottlieb, 1979; DiMatteo and Hays, 1981; Turner, Frankel, and Levin, 1983), whether its effects are direct or indirect, whether its effects are best modeled as main effects or buffering effects, how its effects are manifest, what its dimensions are, and how best to measure it. As Cohen, Mermelstein, Kamarck, and Hoberman (1985) have observed, "there are almost as many measures of social support as there are studies" (p. 73). In assessing the impact of a program, researchers may consider degree of social support as a preexisting characteristic of a person's environment, as a component of the intervention itself, and as an outcome variable—a measure of "program impact." If degree of social support is conceptualized as the consequence of a program, it may be considered a desirable end in itself or simply an intervening variable that is expected to result in other, more distal outcomes. The more precisely the concepts are understood and defined, the more likely it is that the researcher will choose measures appropriate to his or her research objectives.

The many definitions of social support offered in the literature will not be reviewed here. Rather, I will identify and discuss a number of dimensions on which most definitions and measures vary. These dimensions are: (a) whether a complex or simple definition of network structure is used; (b) the degree of emphasis on function or quality of relationships; *(c)* whether available or perceived support is of primary interest; *(d)* whether the availability or use of support is most important; and *(e)* whether social support is thought of primarily as a characteristic of the individual or of the environment. These distinctions among the dimensions of social support can generate useful guiding questions for the researcher engaged in program evaluation. The nature of the program, the purposes of the research, and the time and money available for the research will determine the final choice of measures.

Because the dimensions of social support are relatively abstract, I will offer illustrations of them utilizing two hypothetical program evaluations. The first is a parenting-skills class for middle-class parents to teach them how to care for a newborn child. The second is a more complex program designed to improve outcomes in high-risk, single, pregnant women.

Structure. Historically, the study of the relation between social support and health has focused on social networks: "the web of social ties that surrounds an individual" (Berkman, 1984, p. 414) and has utilized social network analysis (Barnes, 1954; Bott, 1957; Coleman, Katz, and Menzel, 1957; Hammer, Makiesky-Barrow, and Gutwirth, 1978; Henderson, 1977; Israel, 1982; Mitchell and Trickett, 1980; Wellman, 1981). Social network analysis assesses such characteristics as size, strength of ties, density, homogeneity of membership, and dispersion of membership. Mueller (1980) distinguishes between first order, second order, and extended networks. He argues that the important dimensions of social support are the source of support, the type of support given, and the intensity of the relationship. He hypothesizes that lack of strong support from, or a confiding relationship with a spouse appears to be more problematic in a marriage characterized by joint roles and a loose-knit external network. Dean and Lin (1977) focus on expressive social support as the most important stress buffer and identify several important dimensions of social networks such as intimacy and adaptation, size of the support group, reachability of the group, density, content, directedness, durability, and intensity of relationships and interactions.

Cochran and Brassard (1979) provide an excellent example of an application of network analysis to family studies. They have developed a theoretical model for understanding the possible relationships between parents' personal social networks and a child's development. The social network of interest includes people outside the household who "engage in activities and exchanges of an affective and/or material nature with members of the immediate family" (p. 601). Their model has five basic components: The network itself, the lines of influence transmission, network-related developmental processes, the child's stage of development, and network-related developmental outcomes. Examples of network-related developmental outcomes include independence behavior, perceptions of social roles, conceptions of child rearing, self-concept formation, perceptual differentiation, task completion, representational thinking, and cognitive receptivity. It is also possible to think of structure in relatively simple terms. For example, instead of defining social support in terms of how dense a person's social network is, one might simply be interested in how many friends that person has. Thus, depending on the needs of the researcher, simply assessing the existence and quantity of social relationships within the network may be adequate.

In the parenting-skills class, the assessment of social structure could probably be simple and straightforward, particularly if one wanted to measure social support as a program component. Measuring the number of classes attended would be the most obvious means of assessment. However, if the class taught parents about other resources, one might also want to assess knowledge and use of other sources of support. For example, Gottlieb (1981) found that the group experience convinced some participants of the value of informal support and social comparison, and that those participants then became more likely to utilize their own natural networks.

The program for high-risk mothers would demand a more complicated strategy. If it were designed to mobilize resources, one would want to know about significant others who could help with child rearing, the availability of medical and social services in the community, and the client's knowledge of those services. One might also want to know about the structure of the person's social network. For example, the program might be more successful for participants with strong, unrelated support sources than for those with closed, nonsupportive networks.

In selecting measures, one must keep in mind that assessing many features of the person's social network is not only time consuming and expensive, but also likely to be a burden to the respondent. A careful and detailed assessment of the structure of a person's social network probably will be justified only when the researcher has very specific hypotheses about the differential impact.

Function. The importance of social relationships depends on the quality of those relationships and the functions they serve. House (1981) identifies four major types of support: *instrumental, informational, appraisal,* and *emotional.* Instrumental support involves assistance, such as helping with a baby or household chores. Informational support might involve teaching child care skills. Appraisal support involves, for example, assurances that certain feelings or events are "normal," and that problem behaviors of a child will not last. Emotional support is the expression of love and concern. In a study of the effects of stress and social support on mothers and infants, Crnic, Greenberg, Ragozin, Robinson, and Basham (1983) found that emotional support had the most general positive effects on maternal attitudes.

Social scientists have employed a number of typologies of social support, but many differ only slightly from those just described. Cohen and Wills (1985), for example, describe four types: esteem support, instrument support, information support, and social companionship. Other researchers have used terms such as expressive support, self-esteem support, ventilation, and close support (Cohen and Wills, 1985). Cobb (1976) describes the main functions of social support as providing information about being cared for, esteemed, and being part of a network of communication and mutual obligation. Weiss (1973; 1974) describes six functions of social support as providing a sense of attachment or belonging, companionship, a sense of being needed, reassurance of worth, a sense of reliable alliance, and the opportunity of obtaining guidance. Lin, Dean, and Ensel (1981) differentiate primarily between instrumental and expressive support, and in a similar vein, Caplan (1979) distinguishes tangible from psychological support. Wortman (1984) describes six functions of social support: acknowledgment of the appropriateness of a person's beliefs; positive affect; encouragement of expression of beliefs and feelings; provision of advice or information; provision of material aid; and indications that a person is a member of a social network.

While there are many ways of defining the functions of social support, the distinctions among them are much less pronounced than the similarities. Whichever typology is chosen, it can guide the program evaluator in clarifying program goals and evaluation strategies. The program evaluator might ask: "Which definitions describe the functions that I think the program should serve?" The answer to this question will serve as a guide to instrument selection.

In the parenting-skills program class, the primary function is most likely to be informational. The program for high-risk mothers would undoubtedly have numerous functions. An important mechanism for improving the care that their children received might be to help the women deal emotionally with their situation, as these mothers often feel isolated, hopeless, and despondent. For such women, emotional, appraisal, and informational support would be most useful. Also, it might be critical to provide transportation to medical care facilities and to assist with access to other resources.

Perceived versus Available Support. Regardless of whether one is concerned primarily with a complex or simple description of social structure, and irrespective of the functions that those relationships are hypothesized to serve, it is useful to differentiate between perceived and available support. The importance of measuring available support is self-evident. If relatives living within 5 miles of a person are considered an important source of support, then the researcher might simply wish to ask about and count the number of such relatives. However, this approach is inherently limited in that it cannot measure the individual's experience of being supported by others (Turner *et al.*, 1983). A number of researchers have found that perceived support is related to certain outcomes. For example, Crockenberg (1981) assessed perceived affective and material assistance available to mothers and found that these were related to secure infant–mother attachments. Crnic *et al.* (1983) found that satisfaction with support as measured by the Interview Schedule for Social Interaction was related to mothers' attitudes toward their children. Crockenberg (1984) found that the availability of financial and social support as well as the adolescent mothers' satisfaction with the support were related to proper care-giving to children.

In the parenting-skills class, one might differentiate between perceived and actual support to determine if the program is providing appropriate information. For example, it might be that such a program failed to have an impact because most of the participants already had access to the information presented in the class. In that case, even though the program actually provided a great deal of information, the participants would not perceive it as useful. Similarly, the designers of a program for high-risk mothers may think that the primary obstacle to better child care is poor attitudes on the part of mothers. In reality, however, the main barrier to better care might be inadequate financial resources to obtain food and medical care. Discrepencies between actual and perceived support are so common and important that it is wise to always assess both aspects of a program. This approach will enable researchers to better understand program success and failure and will help program directors design more effective interventions.

Availability versus Use. Clearly families cannot benefit from programs that they do not attend: Yet focusing only on attendance will not help program designers understand factors related to program participation. For example, persons with a low sense of self-efficacy may be less likely to participate and may require special outreach strategies. Similarly, knowing that a mother lives in a neighborhood with a number of close relatives nearby is probably less important than knowing whether she asked those relatives for help and whether they were able to provide support.

Characteristics of the Individual or Environment. Rook and Dooley (1985) have noted that one can think of social support as an environmental variable with causes that are external to the individual (Leavy, 1983) or, at least partly, as a function of the characteristics of the individual (Heller and Swindle, 1983). In the second view, the individual is seen as playing an active role in creating and maintaining a network of supportive relationships; some people may have more social resources because they are more skilled at identifying and mobilizing those resources. This distinction is reflected in the ways programs define their goals. Some programs focus on changing the environment; others focus on modifying how people mobilize and/or evaluate the support available from others. Although this distinction may at first appear self-evident, it is important for applied researchers to be explicit about what it is they wish to measure and/or modify. For example, if an environment-oriented agency wishes to help parents cope more effectively with the demands of early parenting, they might offer support groups, provide information and training, and help young parents deal with problems as they arise via some mechanism such as a "hotline." To evaluate such a program one might simply count the number of sessions attended and/or the number of resources used.

An alternative strategy, more oriented toward individual coping skills, would be to teach participants about the problems they are likely to encounter, train them to assess and evaluate different types of problems, and help them develop general strategies for coping with problems as they arise. Part of the training might include assessing the kind of support they needed, the types of people most likely to be able to provide that support, and ways of eliciting help from others. In evaluating this second intervention one would want to measure participants' appraisal of events, the coping strategies they use, the types of support that they seek, and how successful they are in obtaining help.

Choosing between these approaches to program design is problematic given the current state of intervention research. For example, Gottlieb (1984) has pointed out that when planning interventions for children of divorced parents, there is little evidence to guide the choice between an intervention that emphasizes the development of a network of children with similar experiences and one that directly develops a confidant relationship. Research on these types of issues would help improve interventions, and tests of different types of interventions would stimulate further theoretical work (Rook and Dooley, 1985).

MEASURING SOCIAL SUPPORT

Once an evaluation strategy has been formulated, the researcher should review the work of others who have attempted similar evaluations and consider using scales that have been used and validated in other similar studies. While it is often necessary to develop a new measure of social support, it is generally advisable to use an existing scale (if appropriate and well designed) as its use will allow for comparisons across studies. The review of measures offered here is representative but certainly not exhaustive. Detailed descriptions of many social support measures can be found in the literature (Cohen and Wills, 1985; Donald and Ware, 1984; Donald, Ware, Brook, and Davies-Avery, 1978; House and Kahn, 1984; Tardy, 1985; Wallston *et al.*, 1983).

Measuring the Structure of Social Networks

There has been a great deal of research on how social network analysis can help to explicate the nature and role of social relationships (e.g., Wellman, 1981); the methodological and substantive work underlying social network analysis is quite sophisticated. However, a number of easy-to-use scales have been developed based upon this work.

Multiple-Item Measures. A good example of the application of network analysis to family studies is the Psychosocial Kinship Network Inventory (Llamas, Pattison, and Hurd, 1981; Pattison, Llamas, and Hurd, 1979; Pattison, DeFrancisco, Wood, Frazier, and Crowder, 1975). This instrument attempts to determine the psychodynamic social system of the individual. The subject first lists family, relatives, friends, co-workers, and social organizations, then draws the connections among them and rates them on five aspects of the relationship (interaction, emotional intensity, positive emotion, instrumental support, and symmetry). Another measure was developed by Berkanovic, Telesky, and Reeder (1981) for their study of social networks and health care utilization (Granovetter, 1973; Horwitz, 1977; 1978). Using the Salloway Social Network Inventory (Salloway and Dillon, 1973), they constructed scales measuring frequency of contact, consulting support, and role support (e.g., whether they would help with shopping if the respondent were ill) for other relatives and friends. A number of other variables were also used, such as network size and type of health advice usually given by network members. Comparable information was collected in relation to specific symptoms. [See Cohen and Wills (1984) for an excellent review of the studies in which these scales were used.]

The advantages of this approach to social network analysis are that it can provide a complex picture of the many social relationships that may have a direct impact on an individual or family and that may influence the effectiveness of a family intervention program. However, there are several disadvantages to this approach; one is respondent burden. The most sophisticated social network scales require substantial time and effort on the part of the respondents. Also, it is not clear that these approaches have been more useful in understanding the effect of social relationships on health, for example, than much simpler techniques that assess only the existence or quantity of social relationships (House and Kahn, 1984).

A number of simpler scales and single items measure the existence and/or quantity of a person's social relationships. One is the Social Network Index developed by Berkman and Syme (1979) for their study of mortality and social support. They found that persons with the lowest scores had higher mortality rates than those with many social contacts, even when adjustments were made for other risk factors such as initial health, socioeconomic status, positive health behaviors, and use of preventive health services.

Another measure assessing the objective characteristics of social environments is Rand's Health Insurance Experiment (HIE) (Donald and Ware, 1984). Representative population data is available for the Rand instrument. The Social Network Index has the advantage that its relationship with mortality and morbidity are known. These two scales and the Traditional Social Support Index, used by Holahan and Moos (1982), contain similar questions.

Single-Item Measures. In some situations, it is possible to use single items that tap the aspect of the social network thought to be most important. Single-item measures most frequently used include number of friends nearby, number of close friends, and frequency of talking to close friends. The measure of social relationships most frequently studied with respect to health is marital status. Other single-item measures include number of relatives nearby, frequency of church attendance or church membership, number of parents in the home, living with parents, presence of older sibling, ethnic congruence with the community, and participation in social groups. Donald and Ware (1982) found such measures to be quite reliable; the test–retest correlations over a 1-year period for church attendance was .80. The comparable figure for groups membership and activity was .64–.66, and reports of social contacts had a stability of .4 to .6 (see also House and Kahn, 1984). Moreover, they are straightforward, unobtrusive, and entail very little interviewer or questionnaire time. However, they are obviously limited as they fail to assess the functions that different sources of social support serve, the participants' perceptions of those sources, whether those sources were used, and if they were used, whether they served the intended function.

Measuring the Functions of Social Support

Cohen and colleagues (1985) developed the Interpersonal Support Evaluation List (ISEL) to measure tangible support, appraisal support, self-esteem support, and belonging support. It consists of 40 statements about the perceived availability of potential social resources. Respondents are asked to indicate whether statements such as "There is at least one person I know whose advice I really trust" are "probably true" or "probably false." Seven studies employing the student version of the ISEL and five studies employing the general population version found the responses to be moderately correlated with responses to several other widely used measures of social support. Furthermore, respondents gave similar responses when asked the same questions 6 months later, indicating that the responses were quite reliable (Cohen *et al.*, 1985).

Schaefer, Coyne, and Lazarus (1981) developed a similar scale, the Social Support Questionnaire, measuring tangible, informational, and emotional support. Tangible support is measured by asking respondents in which of nine situations they can count on help from another person. Respondents rate their spouse, close friends, relatives, co-workers, neighbors, and supervisors in terms of whether they are caring, confiding, reliable, and whether they boost their spirits.

The Interview Schedule for Social Interaction, a 50-item interview schedule developed by Henderson and colleagues (Henderson and Byrne, 1977; Henderson, Duncan-Jones, and Scott, 1980) assesses the availability and perceived adequacy of two dimensions of support: *social integration* (essentially, the number of relationships a person has) and *attachment* (the extent to which those relationships provide different types of social support). Crnic *et al.* (1983) used this scale in their study of the effects of stress and social support on mothers and their children.

Turner *et al.* (1983) argue that social support should be regarded as a personal experience rather than a set of objective circumstances or interactional processes. The scales that they developed focus specifically on perceived support. Among them are the Shortened Kaplan Scale and the Revised Kaplan Scale which measure dimensions of love, esteem, and network support described by Cobb (1976). They also developed a Provisions of Social Relations (PSR) scale to assess perceptions of the five functions of social support described by Weiss (1974). Turner *et al.* (1983) evaluated both the Kaplan Scale and the PSR scale and found that they were moderately associated with measures of reflected esteem and reflected love. In addition, they found a positive association between the experience and availability of social support.

Confidant Measures

One of the most studied variables in the social support literature is confiding relationships. For example, Pearlin, Lieberman, Menaghan, and Mullan (1981) ask: "Among your friends and relatives, excluding your husband/wife, is there someone you feel you can tell just about anything to, someone you can count on for understanding and advice?" Also, respondents are asked to indicate how strongly they agree or disagree with the statement that their spouse is someone . . . "I can really talk with about things that are important to me."

In a classic study of the social origins of depression, Brown and Harris (1978) found that among women in their sample who had experienced stressful life events, 32% without a confiding relationship experienced depression, whereas only 10% of those with such a relationship became depressed. Lowenthal and Havens (1968) found that elderly persons reporting a confidant relationship experienced less psychiatric impairment. These studies and others suggest the importance of a close, confiding relationship. However, a confidant cannot provide all types of support in all types of circumstances. Once again, the choice of measures must be informed by the research task. For example, a researcher investigating the impact on a family of a life-threatening disease may well focus on the sharing of emotional support and the development of a sense of attachment (Weiss, 1974), while a researcher concerned with facilitating use of services for a disabled child will opt for more instrumental measures.

Family Measures

Many researchers will want to consider the family rather than the individual as the unit of analysis. Unfortunately, measuring family-level variables is as difficult as it is appealing. One approach is to measure a variable for each family member and then aggregate the values in some way. Another approach is to assume that family interactions reflect integrated phenomena and to measure those phenomena.

Dunst (1983) has reviewed scales used in family studies and grouped them according to the type of support they measure. His categories include intrafamily support, kinship support, and extrafamily support. Intrafamily support is provided by nuclear family members and relatives. Kinship support includes support provided by kin, friends, neighbors, and other acquaintances. Dunst uses the term extrafamily support to refer to support provided by social groups, professionals, and professional agencies.

Wahler and colleagues (Wahler, 1980; Wahler, Berland, Coe, and Leske, 1977; Wahler, Leske, and Rogers, 1979) used the Community Interaction Checklist to measure intrafamily, kinship, and extrafamily support in their family studies. The Community Interaction Checklist elicits parents' recall of extrafamily social interactions in the preceding 24 hours. Each parent is interviewed separately and asked to recall several characteristics of those interactions, such as the identity of the person contacted, who initiated the contact, and how the person evaluates the interaction. Next, the parent is asked to estimate the total number of hours during which the parent had direct caretaking responsibility for the child.

Lewis, Beavers, Gossett, and Austin-Phillips (1976) have developed the Family System Rating Scales for the study of family systems. Trained raters observe from 10 to 50 minutes of videotaped interaction and rate the family on 13 9-point scales. These scales are designed to measure the power structure of the total family system, the degree to which the family's self-concept was congruent with rater's appraisal, the effectiveness of family negotiations, characteristics of the family system involved in the production of autonomous individuals, and various aspects of family affect. When used by professionals experienced in working with families, these scales tend to be quite reliable.

The Family Relationships Index is a qualitative index of social relationships derived from the Family Environment Scale (Moos and Moos, 1981). This index (Billings and Moos, 1981) is based on three subscales of the Family Environment Scale (Holohan and Moos, 1981). The subscales measure the extent to which the family members are helpful and supportive of each other, the extent to which family members are encouraged to act openly and to express their feelings directly, and the degree to which the open expression of conflict is characteristic of the family. Shamgar and Leslau (1975) have also developed a social support questionnaire that assesses intrafamily and kinship support.

Wilcox (1981) elicited the names of network members by asking a series of 12 questions about people who provided emotional and tangible support. His variables represented the range, diversity, and the number of connections between support networks. He used these data to examine the extent to which the network variables differentiated women who were successful and unsuccessful in adapting to divorce.

The Home Maternal Social Support Index (MSSI) was developed to assess a home visit program associated with the neonatal intensive care unit at the North Carolina Memorial Hospital (Pascoe, Loda, Jeffries; and Earp, 1981). The index consists of items scattered throughout an interview lasting approximately 1 hour. The items assess subjective and objective aspects of social support, as well as task-oriented and affective components. The scale also contains one item about community involvement and another about interactions with community helping professions.

Procidano and Heller (1983) have developed measures of perceived social support from friends and perceived social support from family. Each of these scales contains 20 items to which the respondent must answer "YES", "NO", or "DON'T KNOW." The scale measuring perceived support from friends contains items such as "I rely on my friends for emotional support," and the family scale contains items such as "My family is sensitive to my personal needs." Results from several studies indicate that the two scales are internally consistent and appear to be valid measures of constructs that are distinct from each other and from other network measures.

Other family measures that are discussed in more detail in other chapters of this volume include the Family Adaptation and Cohesion Scales (Olson, Russell, and Sprenkel, 1979a, 1980; Olson, Sprenkel, and Russell, 1979b; the Family Functioning Index (Pless and Satterwhite, 1973, 1975) (see Walker and Crocker, Chapter 6, this volume), and the Questionnaire on Resources and Stress (Holroyd, 1974; Holroyd and Guthrie, 1979; Holroyd and McArthur, 1976; see Krauss, Chapter 7, this volume).

DEVELOPING A MEASURE

Given the number and diversity of measures available, it might seem unreasonable to develop other scales. However, there are so many important dimensions along which social support may be conceptualized and measured that no single existing measure may be applicable for a particular program. For example, consider a program designed to increase contraceptive use by teenage girls. Social support will be critical to such an endeavor. The girls will probably learn how to gather information from others, compare program-delivered information to that provided by their friends and family, and rely on others in their social environment for evaluation of information, for transportation, etc. The evaluators of this program may want to know the ways in which others in the girls' social environment enhanced or hindered the achievement of program goals. However, probably none of the scales reviewed in this chapter would be suitable for such a study.

What steps ought to be taken in developing a new scale? First, collect detailed information about the process of intervention that is being considered and develop a natural history of how the intervention works. For example, in the program for teenage girls, a logical first step simply would be to interview the girls about what they know about contraception, who they rely upon for advice, who's opinions they value highly, and who they consider to be an "opinion leader." Such interviews could be conducted with a small group of participants before the program began and/or after the main intervention had been implemented. These interviews would be helpful in developing working hypotheses. A related task would be to identify the components of the intervention. After dimensions of primary interest have been identified, available scales can be considered. If available scales are not appropriate, then the researcher can write questions to cover the domains of interest, pretest the questions to make sure that they are understood as intended, assess the reliability of the scales constructed, and assess how valid the measures are. An excellent example of these steps is provided by Donald and Ware (1984). If one selects a subset of items from available instruments, standard psychometric techniques (Cleary, 1983) should be used to develop new scales.

CONCLUSION

Rook and Dooley (1985) have observed that two almost independent research traditions have developed with respect to social support—the analytic tradition of theorists and the more applied tradition of program evaluators. If these two traditions are to develop in a symbiotic way, it will be necessary to develop program evaluation instruments that take into account the theoretical distinctions that have emerged in the literature. Similarly, applied researchers must make basic researchers aware of the issues confronting them.

The work described in this chapter should provide a useful starting point for the fruitful integration of these two traditions. There are obvious limitations in our current ability to assess social support. It is incumbent upon family researchers to carefully conceptualize what they mean by support and what the exact function and hoped outcome of a program will be. For example, it should be decided very early in the study whether actual support, perceived support, or the process giving rise to support are of greatest interest. Similarly, distinctions between availability, structure, and function of relationships should be carefully considered when choosing an instrument to be used in a study. If the theoretical issues outlined here are taken into account in the design and implementation of family programs, both theoretical and applied work in this area should benefit.

ACKNOWLEDGMENTS

Work on this chapter was supported by a grant (MH 15783) from the National Institute of Mental Health.

REFERENCES

Barnes, J. A. (1954). Class and committees in a Norwegian Island Parish. *Human Relations, 7,* 39–43.

Berkanovic, E., Telesky, C., and Reeder, S. (1981). Structural and social psychological factors in the decision to seek medical care for symptoms. *Medical Care, 19,* 693–709.

Berkman, L. F. (1984). Assessing the physical health effects of social networks and social support. *Annual Review of Public Health, 5,* 413–432.

Berkman, L. F., and Breslow, L. (1983). *Health and ways of living: The Alameda County Study.* NY: Oxford University Press.

Berkman, L. F., and Syme, S. L. (1979). Social networks, host resistance and mortality: A nine-year follow-up study of Alameda county residents. *American Journal of Epidemiology, 109,* 186–204.

Billings, A. G., and Moos, R. H. (1981). The role of coping resources in attenuating the stress of life events. *Journal of Behavioral Medicine,* 7(2), 139–157.

Blazer, D. G. (1982). Social support and mortality in an elderly community population. *American Journal of Epidemiology, 115,* 684–694.

Bott, E. (1957). *Family and social network.* London: Tavistock.

Boyce, W. T. (1985). Social support, family relations, and children. In S. Cohen and S. L. Syme (Eds.), *Social support and health* (pp. 151–173). San Francisco, CA: Academic Press.

Broadhead, W. E., Kaplan, B. H., James, S. A., Wagner, E. H., Shoenbach, V. J., Grimson, R., Heyden, S., Tibblin, G., and Gellbach, S. H. (1983). The epidemiological evidence for a relationship between social support and health. *American Journal of Epidemiology, 117,* 521–537.

Brockington, I. F., and Kumar, R. (Eds.). (1982). *Motherhood and mental illness.* NY: Grune and Stratton.

Brofenbrenner, U. (1979). *The ecology of human development: Experiments by nature and design.* Cambridge, MA: Harvard University Press.

Brown, G. W., and Harris, T. (1978). *Social origins of depression.* London: Tavistock.

Bruhn, J. G. (1965). An epidiemiological study of myocardial infarctions in an Italian–American community. *Journal of Chronic Diseases* 18, 353–365.

Bruhn, J. G., Wolf, S., Lynn, T. N., Bird, N. B., and Chandler, B. (1968). Social aspects of coronary heart disease in a Pennsylvania German community. *Social Science and Medicine, 2,* 201–212.

Caplan, R. D. (1979). Patient, provider and organization: Hypothetical determinants of adherence. In S. J. Cohen (Ed.), *New directions in patient compliance.* Lexington, MA: D. C. Health.

Caplan, R. D., Cobb, S., French, J. R. P., Van Harrison, R., and Pinneau, S. R. (1975). *Job demands and worker health.* Washington, DC: DHEW (HIOSH), 75–160.

Carveth, W. B., and Gottlieb, B. H. (1979). The measure of social support and its relation to stress. *Canadian Journal of Behavioral Science, 11,* 179–188.

Cleary, P. D. (1983). Multivariate analysis: Basic approaches to health data. In D. Mechanic (Ed.), *Handbook of health, health care, and the health professional* (pp. 776–790). NY: Free Press.

Cobb, S. (1976). Social support as a moderator of life stress. *Psychosomatic Medicine, 38,* 300–304.

Cobb, S., Kasl, S. V., French, J. R. P., and Norstedbo, G. (1969). The intrafamilial transmission of rheumatoid arthritis VII: Why do wives with rheumatoid arthritis have husbands with peptic ulcer?. *Journal of Chronic Diseases, 22,* 279–293.

Cochran, M., and Brassard, J. (1979). Child development and personal social networks. *Child Development, 50,* 601–616.

Cohen, S., and Syme, S. L. (Eds.) (1985). *Social support and health.* NY: Academic Press.

Cohen, S., and Wills, T. A. (1985). Stress, social support, and the buffering hypothesis. *Psychological Bulletin, 98,* 310–357.

Cohen, S., Mermelstein, R. J., Kamarck, T., and Hoberman, H. M. (1985). Measuring the functional components of social support. In I. G. Sarason and B. Sarason (Eds.), *Social support: Theory, research, and applications.* The Hague, Holland: Martines Nijjhof.

Coleman, J., Katz, E., and Menzel, H. (1957). The diffusion of an innovation among physicians. *Sociometry, 20,* 53.

Crnic, K. A., Greenberg, M. T., Ragozin, A. S., Robinson, N. M., and Basham, R. B. (1983). Social support measures. In K. A. Crnic et al., Effects of stress and social support on mothers' and premature and full-term infants. *Child Development, 54,* 209–217.

Crockenberg, S. B. (1981). Infant irritability, mother responsiveness, and social influences on the security of infant–mother attachment. *Child Development, 52,* 857–865.

Crockenberg, S. B. (1984). Support for adolescent mothers during the postnatal period: Theory and research. In Z. Boukydis (Ed.), *Research on support for parents and infants in the postnatal period.* Norwood, NJ: Ablex.

Dean, A., and Lin, N. (1977). The stress-buffering role of social support: Problems and prospectives for systematic investigation. *The Journal of Nervous and Mental Disease, 165,* 403–417.

DiMatteo, M. R., and Hays, R. (1981). Social support and serious illness. In B. H. Gottlieb (Ed.), *Social networks and social support.* Beverly Hills, CA: Sage.

Donald, C. A., and Ware, J. E., Jr. (1984). The measurement of social support. In J. R. Greenley (Ed.), *Research in community and mental health* (Vol. 4, pp. 325–370). Greenwich, CT: JAI Press.

Donald, C. A., Ware, J. E., Jr., Brook, R. H., and Davies-Avery, A. (August 1978). *Conceptualization and measurement of health for adults in the health insurance study: Vol. IV, social health.* Santa Monica: The Rand Corporation.

Dunst, C. J. (1983). *A bibliographical guide to measures of social support, parental stress, well-being and coping, and other family-level measures.* Family, Infant, and Preschool Program. Western Carolina Center. Morganton, NC.

Gottlieb, B. H. (1981). Preventive interventions involving social networks and social support. In B. H. Gottlieb (Ed.), *Social networks and social support* (pp. 201–232). Beverly Hills, CA: Sage Publications.

Gottlieb, B. H. (1984). Theory into practice: Issues that surface in planning interventions which mobilize support. In I. G. Sarason and B. R. Sarason (Eds.), *Social support: Theory, research, and application.* The Hague: Martines Niijhof.

Granovetter, M. (1973). The strength of weak ties. *American Journal of Sociology, 78,* 1360–1380.

Hammer, M., Makiesky-Barrow, S., and Gutwirth, L. (1978). Social networks and schizophrenia. *Schizophrenia Bulletin, 131,* 185–190.

Heller, K., and Swindle, R. W. (1983). Social networks, perceived social support, and coping with stress. In R. D. Felner, L. A. Jason, J. N. Mortisugus, and S. S. Farber (Eds.), *Preventive psychology: Theory, research, and practice.* NY: Pergamon.

Henderson, S. (1977). The social network, support and neurosis: The function of attachment in adult life. *British Journal of Psychiatry, 131,* 185–191.

Henderson, S., and Byrne, D. (1977). Towards a method of assessing social support systems. *Mental Health Sociology, 4,* 164–170.

Henderson, S., Duncan-Jones, D. G., and Scott, R. (1980). Measuring Social Relationships: The interview schedule for social interaction. *Psychological Medicine, 10,* 723–734.

Hinkle, L. E., and Wolff, H. G. (1958). Ecologic investigations of the relationship between illness, life experiences and the social environment. *Annals of Internal Medicine, 49,* 1373–1380.

Holahan, C. J., and Moos, R. H. (1981). Social support and psychological distress: A longitudinal analysis. *Journal of Abnormal Psychology, 49,* 365–370.

Holahan, C. J., and Moos, R. H. (1982). Social support and adjustment: Predictive benefits of social climate indices. *American Journal of Community Psychology, 10,* 403–13.

Holroyd, J. (1974). The questionnaire on resources and stress: An instrument to measure family responses to a handicapped family member. *Journal of Clinical Psychology, 2*, 92–94.

Holroyd, J., and Guthrie, D. (1979). Stress in families of children with neuromuscular disease. *Journal of Clinical Psychology, 35*, 734–739.

Holroyd, J., and McArthur, D. (1976). Mental retardation and stress on the parents: A contrast between Down's syndrome and childhood autism. *American Journal of Mental Deficiency, 80*, 431–436.

Horwitz, A. (1977). Social networks and pathways to psychiatric treatment. *Social Forces, 56*, 86–105.

Horwitz, A. (1978). Family, kin and friend networks in psychiatric help-seeking. *Social Science and Medicine, 12*, 297–304.

House, J. S. (1981). *Work stress and social support*. Reading, MA: Addison-Wesley.

House, J. S., and Kahn, R. L. (1984). Measures and concepts of social support. In S. Cohen and S. L. Syme (Eds.), *Social support and health*. NY: Academic Press.

House, J. S., Robbins, C., and Metzner, H. L. (1982). The association of social relationships and activities with mortality: Prospective evidence from the Tecumseh County Community Health Study. *American Journal of Epidemiology, 116*, 123–140.

Israel, B. A. (1982). Social networks and health status: Linking theory, research, and practice. *Patient Counseling and Health Education, 4*, 65–79.

Kessler, R. C., and McLeod, J. D. (1985). Social support and mental health in community samples. In S. Cohen and S. L. Syme (Eds.), *Social support and health* (pp. 219–240). NY: Academic Press.

Leavy, R. L. (1983). Social support and psychological disorder. *Journal of Community Psychology, 11*, 3–21.

Lewis, J., Beavers, W. R., Gossett, J., Austin-Phillips, V. (1976). Family system rating scales. In J. Lewis *et al.* (Eds.), *No single thread: Psychological health in family systems*. NY: Bruner/Mazel.

Lin, N., Dean, A., and Ensel, W. M. (1981). Social support scales: A methodological note. *Schizophrenia Bulletin, 7*, 73–89.

Llamas, R., Pattison, E. M., and Hurd, G. (1981). Social networks: A link between psychiatric epidemiology and community mental health. *International Journal of Family Therapy, 3*, 180–192.

Lowenthal, M., and Havens, C. (1968). Interaction and adaptation: Intimacy as a critical variable. *American Sociological Review, 33*, 20–30.

Mitchell, R. E., and Trickett, E. J. (1980). Task force report: Social networks as mediators of social support: An analysis of the effects and determinants of social networks. *Community Mental Health Journal, 16*, 27–44.

Moos, R. H., and Moos, D. S. (1981). *Family Environment Scale manual.* Palo Alto, CA: Consulting Psychologists Press.

Mueller, D. P. (1980). Social networks: A promising direction for research on the relationship of the social environment to psychiatric disorder. *Social Science and Medicine, 14A,* 147–161.

Oakley, A. (1985). Social support in pregnancy: The "soft" way to increase birthweight?. *Social Science and Medicine, 21,* 1259–1268.

Olson, D. H., Russell, C. S., and Sprenkle, D. H. (1980). Marital and family therapy: A decade of review. *Journal of Marriage and Family, 42,* 973–993.

Olson, D. H., Russell, C. S., and Sprenkle, D. H. (1979a). Circumflex model of marital and family systems I: Cohesion and adaptability dimensions, family types, and clinical applications. *Family Process, 18,* 3–28.

Olson, D. H., Sprenkle, D. H., and Russell, C. S. (1979b). Circumflex model of marital and family systems II: Empirical studies and clinical applications. In J. Vincent (Ed.), *Advances in family intervention assessment and theory.* Greenwich, CT: JAI Press.

Pascoe, J., Loda, F., Jeffries, V., and Earp, J. (1981). The association between mothers' social support and provisions of stimulation to their children. *Developmental and Behavioral Pediatrics, 2,* 15–19.

Pattison, E. M., DeFrancisco, D., Wood, P., Frazier, H., and Crowder, J. A. (1975). A psychosocial kinship model for family therapy. *American Journal of Psychiatry, 132,* 1246–1251.

Pattison, E. M., Llamas, R., and Hurd, G. (1979). Social network mediation of anxiety. *Psychiatric Annuals, 9,* 56–67.

Pearlin, L. I., Lieberman, M. A., Menaghan, E. G., and Mullan, J. T. (1981). The stress process. *Journal of Health and Social Behavior, 22,* 337–356.

Pless, I. B., and Satterwhite, B. (1973). A measure of family functioning and its application. *Social Science and Medicine, 1,* 613–621.

Pless, I. B., and Satterwhite, B. (1975). Family function and family problems. In R. J. Haggerty, K. J. Roughman, and I. B. Pless (Eds.), *Child health and the community.* NY: Wiley.

Procidano, M. E., and Heller, K. (1983). Measures of perceived social support from friends and from family: Three validation studies. *American Journal of Community Psychology, 11*(1), 1–24.

Rook, K. S., and Dooley, D. (1985). *Applying social support research: Theoretical problems and future directions. Journal of Social Issues, 41,* 5–26.

Salloway, J. C., and Dillon, P. B. (1973). A comparison of family networks and friends networks in health care utilization. *Journal of Comparative Family Studies, 4,* 131–142.

Schaefer, C., Coyne, J. C., and Lazarus, R. S. (1981). The health-related functions of social support. *Journal of Behavioral Medicine, 4,* 381–406.

Shamgar, L., and Leslau, A. (1975). Social support/Life events questionnaire. In B. H. Kaplan and J. C. Cassell (Eds.), *Family and health: An epidemiological approach.* Chapel Hill, NC: Institute for Research in Social Science, University of North Carolina.

Tardy, C. H. (1985). Social support measurement. *American Journal of Community Psychology, 13,* 187–202.

Turner, R. J., Frankel, B. G., and Levin, D. M. (1983). Social support: Conceptualization, measurement, and implications for mental health. *Community and Mental Health, 3,* 67–111.

Wahler, R. G. (1980). The insular mother: Her problems in parent–child treatment. *Journal of Applied Behavior Analysis, 13,* 207–219.

Wahler, R. G., Berland, R., Coe, T., and Leske, G. (1977). Social systems analysis: Implementing an alternative behavioral model. In A. Rogers-Warren and S. Warren (Eds.), *Ecological perspectives in behavioral analysis.* Baltimore, MD: University Park Press.

Wahler, R. G., Leske, G., and Rogers, E. (1979). The insular family: A deviance support system for oppositional children. In L. Hmerlynck (Ed.), *Behavioral systems for the developmentally disabled: I School and family environments.* NY: Bruner/Mazel.

Wallston, B. S., Alagna, S. W., DeVellis, B. M., and DeVellis, R. F. (1983). Social support and physical health. *Health Psychology, 2,* 367–391.

Weiss, R. S. (1973). The study of loneliness. In R. S. Weiss (Ed.), *Loneliness: The experience of emotional and social isolation.* Cambridge, MA: MIT Press.

Weiss, R. S. (1974). The provisions of social relationships. In Z. Rubin (Ed.), *Doing unto others.* Englewood Cliffs, NJ: Prentice-Hall.

Wellman, B. (1981). Applying network analysis to the study of support. In B. Gottlieb (Ed.), *Social networks and social support.* Beverly Hills, CA: Sage.

Wilcox, B. L. (1981). Social support, life stress, and psychological adjustment: A test of the buffering hypothesis. *American Journal of Community Psychology, 9*(4), 371–386.

Wortman, C. B. (1984). Social support and the cancer patient: Conceptual and methodological issues. *Cancer, 53,* 2339–2360.

Zigler, E., and Weiss, H. (1985). Family support systems: An ecological approach to child development. In R. Rappaport (Ed.), *Children, youth, and families: The action–research relationship* (pp. 166–205). NY: Cambridge University Press.

part III

EVALUATION EXPERIENCES: CASE STUDIES
FROM THE FIELD

In Part III, the evaluators of 10 family support and education programs discuss the difficulties inherent in examining complex, individualized, community-based preventive programs for families with young children. The 10 evaluations are well-funded, flagship efforts with innovative research strategies designed to test and give greater specificity to the ecological principles underlying these programs. While they differ in many ways, they adopt the ecological premise that various kinds of support and education for parents can enhance both child and adult development.

We chose case studies as a vehicle to explicate the complexities of family support and education program evaluation for several reasons. First, while understanding of the importance of studying *program* implementation has grown considerably (i.e., it is no longer assumed that the program on paper reflects a program in reality) understanding and analysis of *evaluation* implementation is less advanced. Therefore these authors deemphasize program description and evaluation results (available in other publications) in favor of discussion of how decisions about design, measurement, and analyses were made and how problems were handled. Second, these studies illustrate the point that while every program and hence evaluation is different, most confront common problems. Their experiences therefore hold lessons for other programs. Third, each of the evaluators have adopted innovative approaches in response to critiques of previous evaluations of human service programs. For example, all employ a more subtly differentiated (and often more policy-relevant) set of program outcomes than just the child's cognitive development, most examine implementation and treatment issues, and several probe the use and availability of various types of social support.

These chapters, as a set, can be read as a debate among the authors about some of the key decisions confronting evaluators. While there is considerable agreement on some issues (e.g., such as the need to plan for attrition and the length of time it takes to state program goals in measurable terms), there is disagreement about other issues including: the ethics and feasibility of random assignment; how and whether to take into account individualized treatment; and how ambitious to be in exploring the causal processes underlying program effects.

In his discussion of the implementation of the Brookline Early Education Project's quasi-experimental evaluation design, Tivnan (Chapter 9) discusses some of the problems involved in recruiting and maintaining an adequate control group and in achieving a sample size large enough to afford the statistical power necessary to identify differential effects by subgroups. He also illustrates the utility of developing and using new as well as standardized measures to assess program goals related to school competence.

An experimental design with random assignment of participants to treatment and control groups is arguably the research design of choice in order to eliminate many threats to internal validity. However, random assignment does not remove all possible sources of bias that may occur as an evaluation is implemented. In his discussion in Chapter 10 of the Prenatal/Early Infancy Project, Olds describes how he and his colleagues handled several biases, including: horizontal diffusion; reactivity of measurement; nonequivalence of treatment and control groups on social and psychological factors likely to interact with the treatment; and the use of comparable services by the control group. He also argues for and illustrates the importance of analyzing evaluation data to detect unanticipated negative side effects of the program.

Individualization of program services in accord with each family's needs, rather than adherence to a standard, uniform treatment, is the hallmark of many family support and education programs, yet this is rarely taken into account in their evaluations. In his process study of patterns of participation and of ways in which they are affected by selected aspects of a parent's socioecological context, Powell (Chapter 11) shows how essential it is to move beyond the assumption of uniform treatment and simple counts of participation. Employing a rich, differentiated, and longitudinal set of measures of participation, and several measures of the parents' dispositional tendency, environmental stresses, and other nonprogram social support, he examines the complex interrelationships among these factors and discusses their theoretical and practical implications.

From their experience with the evaluation of Avance, a community-based organization providing parent education and family support to low-income Hispanic families, Rodriguez and Cortez describe in Chapter 12 the benefits of program evaluation and discuss how to select an evaluator and integrate evaluation into an ongoing program. Their examination of the sociocultural, economic, and contextual factors that relate to child abuse and their subsequent investigation of how Avance participation changed attitudes and knowledge about disciplinary practices suggested new program components for adults and led to more widespread recognition for the program.

Evaluation has costs as well as benefits, particularly for a developing program with volunteer staff. Ellwood describes in Chapter 13 some of those costs in her account of Minnesota Early Learning Design's (MELD) odyssey through three evaluations. Attempts to evaluate MELD, a peer/self-help parent education and support program, were complicated by a number of factors including pressure to evaluate prematurely, lack of adequate measures of good parenting, and conflicts between the staff, evaluators, and funders about what information would be most useful to collect. Ellwood's experiences with both external and internal evaluators demonstrate the difficulties involved in balancing program and evalution needs and in shaping a successful partnership between the program and evaluator.

Employing an ecological and social systems framework, Dunst and Trivette (Chapter 14) have redefined early intervention to include a range of sources of support for handicapped children and their families. In their experimental evaluation of the Family, Infant, and Preschool Program, they examine the direct and indirect effects of many types of support on parent, child, and family functioning. In the process, they elaborate and refine the conceptualization and measurement of social support. Their chapter illustrates one approach to designing program evaluation to contribute to both theoretical development and programmatic improvement.

The last four case studies describe different strategies for cross-site evaluation of multisite programs. Each struggles to balance the need for common measures and cross-site comparisons with respect for different programs and their individual evaluation needs. In Chapter 15, Bond and Halpern argue that the limited state of knowledge about home visit program effectiveness warrants a more flexible approach than that afforded by traditional summative evaluation; for their evaluation of the Child Survival/Fair Start infant health and development programs, they developed an action research approach. Not as internal or external evaluators but in a new role as brokers and synthesizers, they worked with program staff in a joint technical assistance process. Their chapter identifies the practical and methodological problems, mid-course corrections, and complex trade-offs that occurred as they helped the programs to define measurable goals, choose appropriate research designs and measures, capture program processes and implementation, and plan analysis strategies.

In Miller's case study (Chapter 16), an evaluation of an adaptation of the MELD Young Moms Program for low-income, urban, minority teenagers, she describes the difficulties that arose in implementing the program and in devising an acceptable evaluation strategy. She then examines the consequences of these difficulties for the overall evaluation, cautioning others about investigating too wide a range of variables in a developing program and underestimating the time and resources necessary to carry out a cross-site evaluation.

The Head Start experimental Child and Family Resource Program (CFRP) began with the assumption that one program, created to couple child development and family support services, could be carried out uniformly across 11 sites. This was called into question by the descriptive implementation substudy Nauta and Hewett describe in Chapter 17 as part of their case study of CFRP's evaluation. This comprehensive evaluation was designed to assess program implementation, processes, and participation as well as several child and parent outcomes. Their case study illustrates how important it is for external evaluators to have a clear understanding of how a program operates and how a careful ethnographic substudy of program processes can help to explain the pattern of quantitative outcomes.

In Chapter 18, Walker and Mitchell discuss their impact evaluation model as applied with the Too Early Childbearing Network, a group of teen pregnancy programs. This model emphasizes partnership with programs to transfer and build evaluation skills in order to empower local programs to conduct their own relatively simple and low-cost evaluations. It stresses the collection of formative data for ongoing program improvement as well as summative data to document effectiveness. They analyze the factors that make such a cross-site approach work, including: the choice of simple behavioral indicators, provision of technical assistance, and attention to presentation of data to the local community.

Together, these studies portray evaluation as a continuously challenging enterprise from start to finish, one requiring an ambitious, but not overly ambitious scope, a good research design and measurement strategy, and flexible evaluators able to make mid-course corrections. Bond and Halpern's description in Chapter 15 of action research–evaluation aptly characterizes the process of implementing most of these evaluations: "[It] is like navigation at sea, which relies heavily on repeated readings with a sextant to approximate position and chart a reasonable course."

chapter 9

LESSONS FROM THE EVALUATION OF THE BROOKLINE EARLY EDUCATION PROJECT

Terrence Tivnan

PROGRAM HISTORY AND GOALS

The Brookline Early Education Project (BEEP) began in November 1972 as a research and demonstration project delivering services to families with preschool children. The project was planned in collaboration with local school personnel, community representatives, and professionals from the fields of education, health care, evaluation methodology, and social policy. We sought to formulate a program that would demonstrate the effects of an array of early education services on children and their families and to provide a model for public school systems or other community agencies interested in developing similar programs. The local school system administered BEEP; major funding from the Carnegie Corporation of New York and the Robert Wood Johnson Foundation subsidized the Project's planning and evaluation and delivery of project services. The Project's main goals were to identify the strengths and weaknesses of a wide variety of possible services and to make this information available to program planners throughout the country.

These were ambitious goals. Numerous studies carried out during the 1950s and 1960s had direct bearing on the planning for BEEP. Influential studies and reviews, for example, by Hunt (1961), Bloom (1964) and Hess and Shipman (1965) stressed the crucial role of early experience and portrayed the early years as a time of opportunity for potential educational interventions. The most direct impetus for BEEP stemmed form the work of Burton White and the Harvard Preschool

221

Project. White's studies of young children (White, 1971; White and Watts, 1973) indicated that experiences during the first 3 years of life had a profound impact on development. In addition, this work identified different patterns in the ways that mothers acted as "teachers" of their young children and suggested that education programs for parents could have an important and lasting impact on childrens' subsequent performance. White was influential in developing the initial proposal for BEEP and played a key role in the early phases of the project.

Propelled by the findings of White and other researchers and by political timing in favor of large-scale social reform, Project Head Start was initiated in 1965 as a major strategy of the federal government's War on Poverty (Zigler and Valentine, 1979). But the early results from the formal evaluations of these preschool programs were rather discouraging. Typically either no effects were found or initial gains seemed to evaporate by the end of second grade (Jensen, 1969). A particularly controversial report by the Westinghouse Learning Corporation (1969) indicated that Head Start programs across the country—including both short-term "summer only" and longer term programs—were not so effective as had been anticipated. The report became the center of controversy and criticism (Cicirelli, Evans, and Schiller, 1970; Smith and Bissel, 1970; Zigler, 1973), and it also influenced some educators to abandon or alter early education efforts. Others undertook extensive reexamination of the pilot programs, often concluding that many were poorly designed, ineptly executed, or improperly evaluated. By the mid-1970s, Rivlin and Timpane (1975) suggested that few conclusions could be drawn about the effects of early education because there were so few well-planned and well-evaluated programs.

Many educators were impressed with the research evidence on the importance of early education efforts, however, and were convinced that more resources could be profitably invested in early education programs. Certainly it was clear that many children enter school with learning problems already established. Despite the controversy surrounding the early evaluation efforts, there was also optimism that well-designed and well-implemented studies could be carried out that would demonstrate the benefits of early intervention. The hope was that the common problems of the large-scale studies such as Head Start, which had relied primarily on *ex post facto* approaches to evaluation, and the generally unsophisticated approaches to evaluation carried out in many of the small-scale programs, could be overcome with new approaches to program planning and evaluation.

The planning for BEEP was initiated in this context of optimism and caution. In the early 1970s, the principles of scientific experimentation and method—the use of randomization, studying different levels or amounts of treatment, using carefully controlled field trials—that had long been used extensively in other fields of inquiry were advocated to improve knowledge about social and educational programs (Campbell, 1969). Robert I. Sperber, then the Brookline Superintendent of Schools, Burton White of Harvard, and their colleagues from Children's Hospital Medical Center in Boston, designed BEEP to incorporate the best prevailing ideas on child development and on programs for young children and their parents. The chief characteristics of the program were as follows:

1. It was public-school based to explore how well the public schools could coordinate the provision of early childhood services and to provide the opportunity for continuity of experience and support from the preschool years into the elementary grades.
2. It was a birth-to-kindergarten operation, spanning the entire preschool period.
3. It was family oriented, on the premise that the family is the primary educational influence on the child. Thus, the Project attempted to provide programs for parents as well as a network of family support services.
4. It was multidisciplinary in approach, involving educators, pediatricians, psychologists, and other specialists.
5. It was racially and economically heterogeneous in its enrollment. Unlike many other contemporary programs, there were no special eligibility restrictions. Recruiting strategies were designed to attract a diverse group of families.
6. It was carefully evaluated.

PROGRAM COMPONENTS

Based on the prevailing wisdom concerning the types of services that were likely to be effective and on the nature of the Project's overall goals, three sets of interrelated components or services were developed: parent education and support, diagnostic monitoring, and education programs for children.

Parent Education and Support

The major approach in this part of the project was to increase parents' knowledge and confidence by providing information on normal child development and by counseling about effective child management. The aim was to help parents take responsibility for their own behavior and decisions. In the first 2 years of the child's life, the parent education services took place primarily through teacher visits to the home and/

or family visits to the BEEP center. Informal discussion groups also were scheduled, and families could drop in at the center to meet friends, chat with staff, or borrow books or toys.

The amount of parent education offered to each family was controlled by random assignment of families to one of three levels of program intensity. The most intensive level involved frequent home visits, meetings, and limited child care. The moderate level involved the same offerings but on a less frequent schedule. The least intensive level involved no outreach through home visits, meetings, or child care. Information and support were available, but parents had to exert initiative to take advantage of the opportunities. These three levels of services were provided in order to determine whether the more intensive and expensive programs would indeed be more beneficial or cost effective. The implications of this decision will be discussed later.

As the children became involved in programs of their own from 24 months on, home visits were largely supplanted by less expensive modes of parent–staff interaction: parent–teacher conferences, small discussion groups, and classroom observation. Throughout the project, a nurse and social worker were available in person and by telephone to assist families who needed help in locating and using community services. Advocacy work on behalf of BEEP families included proper use of hospital emergency facilities, management of chronic illness, finding high-quality child care, and obtaining improved housing.

Diagnostic Monitoring

All children enrolled in BEEP received frequent health and developmental exams, which were administered both for research purposes and in an effort to ensure that children would not progress through the preschool years with undetected health or developmental conditions that would hinder their abilities to function successfully in school. A multidisciplinary team consisting of a pediatrician, a developmental psychologist, and a nurse conducted vision, hearing, physical, neurologic, and developmental exams. Parents were encouraged to observe the exams, and results were shared with them verbally and in writing. A copy of each written report was also sent, with parent permission, to the child's primary-care physician, since BEEP did not offer primary medical care.

One of the goals of the intensive schedule of diagnostic testing (carried out at age 2 weeks, 3, 6, 14, 24, 30, and 42 months, and entry into kindergarten) was to identify the most important or optimal times for a program such as BEEP to assess the health and developmental status of young children. For the diagnostic programs within BEEP there was no division of families into subgroups.

Education Programs for Children

Weekly play groups for groups of six to eight children from age 2 followed a routine geared to the developmental levels of the children. Parents observed the sessions frequently and discussed their observations with the teachers.

All 3- and 4-year-old BEEP participants had the option of attending a daily morning prekindergarten program. Classes typically consisted of 15–20 children and three staff teachers; several classes were bilingual. The curriculum was based on other preschool programs being developed during the 1970s, particularly the High/Scope Program (Hohmann, Banet, and Weikart, 1979), and emphasized structuring space and materials to help children develop skills essential for school (Hauser-Cram and Pierson, 1981). Teachers and parents jointly determined individual goals for the children. An interdisciplinary diagnostic team was available to advise appropriate action for children who needed special attention.

EVALUATION PLAN

A major concern during the planning period was to devise a rigorous and credible scheme for evaluating the impact of BEEP. Planners and funding agencies alike recognized the importance of having well-documented results and convincing evidence if BEEP were to serve as a model for other programs. The decision was made, therefore, to have an "impact" or "outcome" evaluation with both experimental and quasi-experimental components. As Bryk described in some detail (1975), the overall evaluation effort was also to be guided by input and process models of evaluation that were becoming more prominent at that time (Bernstein and Freeman, 1975; Scriven, 1972; Weiss, 1972). For example, the goals included assessing how well the program was actually delivering its services. Plans were also developed to conduct outcome or summative evaluations by studying parents and teachers as well as the children who participated in BEEP. I will review here primarily the design and implementation of the outcome studies that focused on the children. Several key components of the overall plan deserve mention.

Control Group

An early decision was made that no families would be randomly assigned to a no-treatment condition, in part because local agencies were often unenthusiastic about helping to recruit families for a no-treatment or comparison group. Furthermore, anticipating an issue that would become widely discussed in the evaluation literature (e.g., Cook &

Campbell, 1979), concern was also expressed over treatment diffusion from participants to control families.

Thus, BEEP was to be available to all families residing in Brookline or adjacent areas of Boston who had children born during the enrollment period (most of 1973 and 1974). Two approaches were used to generate comparison groups of children. First, families residing in the same geographic regions but who had children born during the year preceding enrollment were recruited to take part in the examinations that took place at the key evaluation checkpoints during the preschool years. It was felt that the use of these "noncontemporaneous controls" would reduce the bias that would be associated with the use of a comparison group drawn from among those families who had been eligible but had not taken part in BEEP. Presumably, the volunteer bias associated with BEEP families would be at least partly controlled by comparing them to children from families who might have been interested if BEEP had been available when their children were born.

Second, for the evaluation checkpoints at kindergarten and second grade, information was also collected on children who were classmates of BEEP children but who had not been enrolled in BEEP. Some of these came from families who had not enrolled in BEEP initially; others were from families who had moved in after BEEP enrollment closed. The inclusion of these several different groups made possible some assessment of cohort-specific effects or changes related to shifts in school policies or expectancies over time.

The problem of obtaining appropriate comparison groups was ongoing. In 1977, almost midway through the Project's lifetime, issues concerning comparison children were a major topic of discussion at a conference held with an advisory panel of evaluation consultants (BEEP Notes for Advisory Conference, 1977). Some of those issues had been anticipated by the original architects of the evaluation; others were new or posed greater difficulties than anticipated. For example, BEEP's recruiting success was impressive. The demographic profile of BEEP participants revealed that a heterogeneous set of families had been attracted—exactly what the planners had intended. Some children were being raised by young mothers who had not completed high school; other children were from families in which both parents held advanced degrees and were working professionals. But there had not been nearly so much early success in recruiting comparison subjects. For the first evaluation checkpoints at 14 and 30 months, most of the comparison families were middle-class English-speaking families, and relatively few minority children were available. (The problem was not so severe for the kindergarten and second grade checkpoints; comparison groups there were quite similar to the BEEP participants on most key variables.)

The difficulties encountered in obtaining comparable groups were raised repeatedly in discussions concerning the impact evaluation.

From an evaluation perspective, the problem was a complex and interesting one. Superficially it appeared that the direction of any bias introduced by the characteristics of the comparison group would tend to favor the comparison group; it would not be easy for critics to argue that the deck had been stacked in favor of BEEP. On the other hand, as the project proceeded and the high expectations and optimism of the planning phase gave way to more realistic projections of the likely impact of BEEP's services, other possible implications of f this bias problem began to be considered. If the effects of the program were to be small or moderate in size, then the lack of exact comparability between the BEEP and comparison groups could serve to obscure the program effects or even make the impact of BEEP seem negative—a major concern to the evaluation staff. Moreover, if the benefits were concentrated on certain subgroups of families, then the lack of adequate comparison families could complicate the analysis and make the identification of program impact more difficult. These difficulties arose not so much from flaws in the original evaluation design as from unanticipated difficulties in recruiting comparison families. The lesson to be learned is that practical difficulties in recruitment should be considered in any plan for establishing an appropriate comparison sample where a randomized trial is not possible. Furthermore, the evaluation design should, from the beginning, include a search for differential effects on subgroups of participants.

Problems Related to Attrition

Attrition rates, arising from families moving out of the area, also created two main concerns over time: the prospect of differential attrition leading to noncomparability of the BEEP and comparison groups, and the overall reduction in the size of the sample of families participating in BEEP. As the Project continued, staff members involved with families worked very hard with those families who displayed greater needs. Every effort was made to provide the services need to keep these families enrolled in the Project. Desirable from a service perspective, this raised a concern about influencing the evaluation. Specifically, it was important to consider the possibility that BEEP might lose some of its less needy families through moves to suburban locations, while retaining more of its families with greater needs. Further, because similar efforts could not be extended to members of the comparison group, and because it was more difficult to attract and retain comparison group families, it seemed that a different process might be at work for these families. In particular, it seemed more likely that families with greater needs would be less likely to stay involved as comparison families. Thus the long-run effect of the attrition process at least during the preschool years might be to increase the differences between BEEP and comparison families.

A second aspect of the attrition problem—the effect on the ultimate sample sizes—did not receive so much attention during the project (although, in retrospect, perhaps it should have). BEEP originally enrolled 320 families. By the close of the enrollment period, some attrition had already taken place—the final enrollment level was 285 families. The initial sample size was justified partly by the expectation that attrition would yield a sample of 100 to 150 families for the evaluation checkpoints when the children were in school. The early estimates of attrition rates proved to be quite accurate. For the kindergarten evaluation there were 132 children who entered the Brookline schools (BEEP families who lived in Boston were eligible for the Brookline schools) and who had been enrolled in BEEP from infancy to kindergarten (Pierson, Bronson, Dromey, Swartz, Tivnan, and Walker, 1983). By the end of second grade the number had dropped to 104, and the evaluation was expanded to include children who had participated in BEEP but had moved to nearby communities (Bronson, Pierson, and Tivnan, 1984; Pierson, Walker, and Tivnan, 1984).

The result was limited statistical power of the study's analyses, particularly in making comparisons across the three service levels within BEEP and in looking for subgroups of families who might have demonstrated particularly large or small effects. Especially regarding outcomes expressed in terms of rates (or percentages) of children who showed difficulty in various areas of school competence, the sample sizes for many analyses made detection of significant effects very difficult.

This aspect of the attrition problem was not a surprise; in fact, progress reports and other in-house documents clearly identified potential limitations (Bryk, 1975; Pierson and Nicol, 1977). But the issue of statistical power and the importance of considering likely effect sizes, which have received considerable attention in the evaluation literature in the later 1970s and 1980s (e.g., Cook and Campbell, 1979; Gilbert, Light, and Mosteller, 1975; Rosenthal, 1979), were not so carefully considered when the original plan for the BEEP evaluation was developed. Thus the BEEP experience holds some important lessons for future evaluators. First, the direction of any bias introduced by attrition from treatment and control groups may be difficult to anticipate in planning for an evaluation. Second, the effect of likely attrition on the statistical power of the analyses should be given considerable attention, particularly when the anticipated effect sizes are likely to be small or moderate or when the effects may be unevenly distributed across the participants—likely possibilities in most settings.

Service Levels

As noted previously, while diagnostic monitoring and direct education programs were provided equally for all children, the third component, the parent education and support programs, was offered at three different levels to which participants were randomly assigned. In line with this, the early program plan prescribed in some detail the amount and frequency of contacts between BEEP staff and parents. For example, it was initially planned that Level A families would receive one home visit every 4 weeks; Level B families would receive one visit every 6 weeks; Level C families would receive no home visits. However, this plan for implementing delivery of services proved unworkable and had to be revised. Ultimately, the average amount of contact with families did differ across the cost levels, but there was also considerable variation within a level. Increasingly, individualization of services was allowed and encouraged, and the Project moved away from a rigid model of service delivery. The rigidity was not only administratively difficult, but unrealistic as a model for future "real-life" implementation.

Assessment Measures

We were aware from the outset that reliance on traditional measures of achievement and behavior would not necessarily be appropriate for assessing all competence areas of interest to BEEP. Thus, we sought to develop innovative approaches to measurement more in line with our educational goals for the children. For example, BEEP was designed to improve children's competence in school. Because there was no one accepted definition of school competence, work began very early in collaboration with local school personnel to develop measures of school competence appropriate for the school settings in which BEEP children would later function. A variety of assessment tools were eventually used, ranging from standardized measures of development, intelligence, school readiness, and academic achievement, to measures designed or adapted to fill gaps in the standardized assessment batteries. These included teacher rating scales and instruments for directly observing children's behavior in classroom settings. Teachers were asked to rate children's success in performing adequately in a number of key areas that had been identified by school staff as important to the local school system. Carefully trained observers who were not informed about the specific purposes of the study made the observations of children's behavior in school (Bronson, 1975, 1978, 1981).

Our efforts to develop new ways of assessing child outcomes were important and successful. Findings at the kindergarten and second grade levels indicated that some important effects would not have been identified without the development of new measures sensitive to BEEP's educational goals.

HIGHLIGHTS OF RESULTS

The major evaluation findings available to date focus on impact on children's performance in kindergarten and second grade (Bronson *et al.*, 1984; Pierson *et al.*, 1983) and on parent interactions with school personnel (Hauser-Cram, 1983). Classroom observations of the kindergarten revealed significant advantages for BEEP children, particularly in social behavior and use of classroom time. These differences were consistent across subgroups of children with different characteristics and family backgrounds (Pierson *et al.*, 1983). At second grade, observations indicated that BEEP children had benefited particularly in mastery skills or academic learning behaviors. Table 9.1 illustrates some of these results. In addition, at the end of second grade there were relatively fewer BEEP children who were unable to decode or comprehend stories in a 2-2 level basal reader (Pierson *et al.*, 1984).

In many of the other analyses of possible program impact, few across-the-board differences were found between BEEP and comparison children, but some interactions with background characteristics were revealed. For example, analyses of the ratings obtained from the kindergarten teachers suggested that there were some advantages for BEEP participants in subgroups traditionally judged at-risk for school problems. No differences, or slight differences favoring the comparison groups, were found for subgroups where the overall incidence of problems was lower. For example, among families where the father had less than a high school education, kindergarten teacher ratings showed some advantages for BEEP. Among the remaining families there were typically no differences or slight advantages for the comparison group (Pierson *et al.*, 1983).

Further evidence of differential impact emerged in some of the results obtained at second grade, for example, in patterns of success in reading at the expected level during the spring of second grade. For well-educated families the benefits of BEEP participation appeared regardless of the level of parent-education services to which they had been assigned. But for less well-educated families there were indications

TABLE 9.1. Results of Observations of Children in Kindergarten and Grade 2: Percentages of Children Having Difficulty

Observation variable	Kindergarten		Grade 2	
	BEEP	Comparison	BEEP	Comparison
Mastery Skills Concerns				
Tasks not completed successfully	5	11	14	27*
Inadequate task attack strategies	13	13	18	32*
Time distracted	9	10	18	29*
Social skills concerns				
Time in cooperative interaction	8	18*	6	8
Rate of cooperative strategies	3	12*	18	21
Success in influencing others	3	12*	2	7
Use of language	3	10*	3	7
Use of time concerns				
Inadequate time in mastery tasks	3	16*	11	11
Inadequate time in social tasks	5	12*	17	18
Inadequate rate of social acts	13	14	2	2
Time not involved	2	15*	1	2

*Statistically significant differences.

(although not completely consistent) that the more intensive service levels were necessary; benefits were not so clear with the lowest level of parent-education services (Bronson *et al.*, 1984; Pierson *et al.*, 1984).

Disappointing, although not unexpected, was the lack of statistically significant differences on some of the standardized traditional cognitive measures (the McCarthy Scales of Children's Abilities given just prior to kindergarten; the California Achievement Tests given in second grade); it had been recognized early in the Project that such findings were very unlikely, and that reliance on such standardized measures had hindered efforts to evaluate other early education programs (Butler, 1974; Raizen and Bobrow, 1974; Smith and Bissell, 1970; Walker, Bane, and Bryk, 1973). The Project's early lack of enthusiasm for standardized measures was also based partly on skepticism about their sensitivity in measuring the educational goals of the local school system, and partly on the realization that there were relatively rich resources available for preschool children and their families in the Brookline–Boston community during the time BEEP was in operation. Thus, the comparison in BEEP's evaluation was really between families who had received services coordinated and administered through the local school system and families who often received similar services through other means. Therefore, large differences on standardized measures of cognitive performance seemed unlikely. Without the use of teachers' ratings and observations of children's behaviors in actual classroom settings the impact of the BEEP intervention would have been very difficult to detect, and criticisms concerning reliance on traditional tests (e.g., McClelland, 1973; Scarr, 1981; Seitz, Abelson, Levine, and Zigler, 1975; Zigler and Seitz, 1980) could have been applied to BEEP.

In summary, then, the evaluation has indicated that positive effects emerged and lasted through second grade. Children who took part in BEEP had relatively fewer problems in important aspects of classroom competence. Both in social interactions and in their approaches to learning and mastery behaviors they were doing relatively well. This reduction in classroom behavior problems may have important practical implications for elementary schools. Even when behavior problems are not so severe as to require special services, they do require teacher attention and reduce the amount of productive teacher time and energy available to all children for important learning tasks. As indicated by follow-up studies of other preschool programs, the long-term benefits, in both educational quality and reduced costs for special services (e.g., Schweinhart and Weikart, 1980; Weber, Foster, and Weikart, 1978), should be substantial.

Summary of Important Lessons

There are many lessons to be learned from a project like BEEP, some in the form of identified pitfalls, others in the form of benefits that might be incorporated into other programs. This section presents some of the major pitfalls and benefits of the BEEP program and its evaluation.

Pitfalls

Too Many Goals. While it is important to be ambitious, having too many goals can make it difficult for program evaluators to focus resources on the most important issues. BEEP was very ambitious in its goals. Each of the several different audiences was interested in slightly different aspects of the Project: educational, medical and health, and community-impact outcomes; outcomes expected for parents, children, and teachers; and others. The broad scope of Project activities made it difficult to carry out a comprehensive evaluation, to set up a study that would be rigorous from many different perspectives, and to summarize and explain it clearly. Even in a project as well funded for evaluation as BEEP, the effort required was daunting. Coordinating and allocating the resources required for different components of the overall evaluation was also difficult. Local and small-scale projects would be well advised to identify a few key issues as a focus of their evaluation efforts, rather than attempting to try many things simultaneously.

Limitations of Traditional Outcome Measures. This problem has been known for some time and still plagues efforts to assess the impact of early education programs. In the case of BEEP, we were able to minimize this pitfall by investing large amounts of time and resources in developing or adapting ways of measuring outcomes considered important by BEEP staff and local school personnel. After several years of pilot work, these new approaches gained substantial credibility as measures of children's functioning in school. Other programs might not have the capacity to develop techniques of their own, but they should consider the usefulness of classroom observations, teacher ratings, and parent reports as ways of supplementing traditional assessment measures.

Expectation of Big Effects. Given the limitations of assessment methods and the difficulties inherent in running a support program, the actual measured effects are likely to be small, difficult to detect, and unevenly distributed across participants. They are also likely to vary across different outcome areas.

These ideas about small effects and uneven impact, while part of the current conventional wisdom among evaluators, were not discussed in the evaluation literature of the late 1960s. During the 1970s, systematic evaluation of public programs became more widespread, and statisticians and data analysts began to focus on combining and accumulating results from different studies, but the procedures did not receive widespread attention until fairly recently (see, e.g., Gilbert *et al.*, 1975; Glass, 1976; Rosenthal, 1984). One of the main justifications for combining results from different studies has been the realization that in many cases the actual effects or benefits will be relatively small (Cook and Campbell, 1979; Light and Pillemer, 1984); the importance of anticipating this possibility in a well-designed evaluation is now very clear.

Expectation of Main Effects. Especially for programs offering individualized services to heterogeneous groups of participants, it is very likely that the benefits will not be spread evenly across those who participate; families will have different needs and will participate in different ways. Adjusting to meet these different needs may present special challenges to program evaluators. During the formulation of the evaluation plan careful attention should be given to the search for differential impact on various subgroups of participants, rather than focusing only on overall main-effects analyses, particularly in programs enrolling heterogeneous groups of families.

Benefits

The Benefits of Long-Term and "Inside" Evaluation. The BEEP evaluation was not only a long-term effort, but one based almost entirely on site. Although the evaluation team was not directly involved in the delivery of the education programs, the team members were part of the Project, not an outside agency contracted for the evaluation. While this arrangement can have drawbacks, in this instance there are reasons to believe that the on-staff evaluation was useful and helpful. The evaluators had a very complete and sophisticated understanding of the Project's goals and actual operation. The evaluation efforts could be directed toward areas BEEP staff and local school personnel considered most important. Outcome measures could be tailored to the particular needs of the local setting. Project staff could be consulted about service delivery. Records were available on how families actually participated.

The BEEP staff's willingness to cooperate in collecting data for the evaluation was also a major benefit. Despite the potential difficulties of occasionally conflicting goals of service providers and evaluators, the benefits of close-up and long-term commitment were considerable. The success of other projects that have operated in this way is further evidence in favor of this approach (e.g., Schweinhart and Weikart, 1980; see also, Lazar and Darlington, 1982).

Collaboration Across Professions. The collaboration of health-care professionals, psychologists, social workers, educators, and other professionals benefited the development of Project services and strengthened the evaluation. Sharing ideas, approaches to service delivery, and perspectives on impact assessment were important to the Project's overall success.

Realistic Views of How Families Participate. The experience at BEEP, where a comprehensive array of services was offered to a heterogeneous group of families, has provided useful information on the many different ways in which families will participate in and benefit from programs of early education and family support. BEEP has demonstrated that it is possible to avoid the rigid imposition of prespecified "treatments" or levels of service and to develop a program in which services can be individualized to meet a variety of needs.

Role of Local Schools. Finally, BEEP has demonstrated that a local school system can play a major role in coordinating the provision of services to families with preschool children. Rather than requiring new institutions or agencies, local schools and school systems can help co-ordinate health care services, education, and family support and make them available to residents in their local communities. While this is not a completely new role for schools, programs like BEEP have shown that it is appropriate for public schools to make stronger efforts during the preschool years to reduce the incidence of later problems. The advantages of this approach include the opportunity for school systems to make high-quality services available to a wide variety of families—not just those who can afford them or those who are most needy—and to allow for continuity of services to children from the preschool years on into the elementary grades. If locally based programs of family support and early education are organized with these goals in mind, and if they are carefully monitored and evaluated over extended periods of time, they can enhance our knowledge of what services to provide and how to assess the impact of those services. These programs will help to improve quality and promote equity in our schools and in society; the benefits will accrue at all levels of education.

References

BEEP Notes for Advisory Conference (1977). Brookline, MA: The Brookline Early Education Project.

Bernstein, I. N., and Freeman, W. E. (1975). *Academic and entrepreneurial research.* NY: Russell Sage Foundation.

Bloom, B. (1964). *Stability and change in human characteristics.* NY: John Wiley & Sons.

Bronson, M. B. (1975). Executive competence in preschool children. Presented to the annual meeting of the American Education Research Association, Washington, D.C., April. ERIC Document Reproduction Service ED 107 378.

Bronson, M. B. (1978). The development and pilot testing of an observational measure of school-related social and mastery skills for preschool and kindergarten children. Doctoral dissertation, Harvard Graduate School of Education.

Bronson, M. B. (1981). Naturalistic observation as a method of assessing problems at entry to school. Presented to the annual meeting of the Society for Research in Child Development, Boston, April.

Bronson, M. B., Pierson, D. E., and Tivnan, T. (1984). The effects of early education on children's competence in elementary school. *Evaluation Review, 8,* 615–629.

Bryk, A. S. (1975). *Evaluation primer and related documents.* Brookline: Brookline Early Education Project.

Butler, J. A. (1974). *Toward a new cognitive effects battery for Project Head Start.* Santa Monica, CA: Rand Corporation.

Campbell, D. (1969). Reforms as experiments. American Psychologist, 24, 409–429.

Cicirelli, V. G., Evans, J. W., and Schiller, J. (1970). The impact of Head Start: A reply to the report analysis. Harvard Educational Review, 40, 105–129.

Cook, T. D., and Campbell, D. T. (1979). Quasi-experimentation: Design and analysis issues for field studies. Chicago, IL: Rand-McNally.

Gilbert, J. P., Light, R. J., and Mosteller, F. (1975). Assessing social innovation (Eds.). Evaluation and experiment. NY: Academic Press.

Glass, G. V. (1976). Primary, secondary, and meta-analysis of research. Educational Researcher, 5, 3–8.

Hauser-Cram, P. (1983). A question of balance: Relationships between parents and teachers. Doctoral dissertation. Harvard Graduate School of Education.

Hauser-Cram, P., and Pierson, D. E. (1981). The BEEP prekindergarten curriculum: A working paper. Brookline, MA: The Brookline Early Education Project.

Hess, R. D., and Shipman, V. C. (1965). Early experience and the socialization of cognitive modes in children. Child Development, 36, 869–886.

Hohmann, M., Banet, B., and Weikart, D. P. (1979). Young children in action: A manual for preschool educators. Ypsilanti, MI: High/Scope Press.

Hunt, J. M. (1961). Intelligence and experience. New York: Ronald Press.

Jensen, A. (1969). How much can we boost IQ and scholastic achievement? Harvard Educational Review, 39, 1–123.

Lazar, I., and Darlington, R. (1982). Lasting effects of early education: A report from the Consortium for Longitudinal Studies. Monographs of the Society for Research in Child Development, 47 (2–3, Whole No. 195).

Light, R. J., and Pillemer, D. B. (1984). Summing up: The science of reviewing research. Cambridge, MA: Harvard University Press.

McClelland, D. C. (1973). Testing for competence rather than for "intelligence." American Psychologist, 28, 1–14.

Pierson, D. E., and Nicol, E. H. (1977). The fourth year of the Brookline Early Education Project: A report of progress and plans. Brookline, MA: The Brookline Early Education Project.

Pierson, D. E., Bronson, M. B., Dromey, E., Swartz, J. P., Tivnan, T., and Walker, D. K. (1983). The impact of early education measured by classroom observations and teacher ratings of children in kindergarten. Evaluation Review, 7, 191–216.

Pierson, D. E., Walker, D. K., and Tivnan, T. (1984). A school-based program from infancy to kindergarten for children and their parents. *Personnel and Guidance Journal, 62,* 448–455.

Raizen, S., and Bobrow, S. B. (1974). *Design for a national evaluation of social competence in Head Start children.* Santa Monica, CA: Rand Corporation.

Rivlin, A. M., and Timpane, M. P. (Eds.). (1975). *Planned variation and Head Start: Should we give up or try harder?* Washington, D.C.: Brookings Institution.

Rosenthal, R. (1979). The "file drawer problem" and tolerance for null results. *Psychological Bulletin, 86,* 638–641.

Rosenthal, R. (1984). *Meta-analytic procedures for social research.* Beverly Hills, CA: Sage.

Scarr, S. (1981). Testing for children: Assessment and the many determinants of intellectual competence. *American Psychologist, 36,* 1159–1166.

Schweinhart, L., and Weikart, D. P. (1980). *Young children grow up.* Monographs of the High/Scope Educational Research Foundation, No. 7. Ypsilanti, MI: High/Scope Press.

Scriven, M. (1972). The methodology of evaluation. In C. H. Weiss (Ed.), *Evaluating action programs: Readings in social action and education.* Boston, MA: Allyn and Bacon.

Seitz, V., Abelson, W. D., Levine, E., and Zigler, E. F. (1975). Effects of place of testing on the Peabody Picture Vocabulary Test scores of disadvantaged Head Start and non-Head Start children. *Child development, 45,* 481–486.

Smith, M. S., and J. S. Bissell (1970). Report analysis: the impact of Head Start. *Harvard Educational Review, 40,* 51–104.

Walker, D. K., Bane, M. J., and Bryk, A. S. (1973). *The quality of the Head Start Planned Variation data,* 2 Vols. Cambridge, MA: The Huron Institute.

Weber, C. U., Foster, P. S., and Weikart, D. P. (1978). *An economic analysis of the Ypsilanti Perry Preschool Project.* Ypsilanti, MI: Monographs of the High/Scope Educational Research Foundation, No. 5.

Weiss, C. (1972). *Evaluation Research.* Englewood Cliffs, NJ: Prentice-Hall.

Westinghouse Learning Corporation (1969). *The impact of Head Start: An evaluation of the effects of Head Start on children's cognitive and affective development, Vol. 1.* Washington, DC: Clearinghouse for federal scientific entific and technical information, Department of Commerce, National Bureau of Standards.

White, B. L. (1971). *Human Infants: Experience and psychological development.* Englewood Cliffs, NJ: Prentice-Hall.

White, B. L., and Watts, J. C. (1973). *Experience and environment: Major influences on the development of the young child,* Vol. 1. Englewood Cliffs, NJ: Prentice-Hall.

Zigler, E. F. (1973). Project Head Start: Success of failure. *Learning, 1*, 43–47.

Zigler, E. F., and Seitz, V. (1980). Early childhood intervention programs: A reanalysis. *School Psychology Review, 9*, 354–368.

Zigler, E. F., and Valentine, J. (Eds.). (1979). *Project Head Start: A legacy of the war on poverty.* NY: Free Press.

chapter 10

COMMON DESIGN AND METHODOLOGICAL PROBLEMS ENCOUNTERED IN EVALUATING FAMILY SUPPORT SERVICES: ILLUSTRATIONS FROM THE PRENATAL/EARLY INFANCY PROJECT

David Olds

The problems of design and methodology that my colleagues and I encountered in evaluating a program of pre- and postnatal nurse home visitation are, for the most part, inherent in all intervention research. In this chapter I will discuss our experiences with these problems in the hope that evaluators of other family programs can profit from them.

The program that Charles Henderson, Robert Tatelbaum, Robert Chamberlin, and I evaluated was established to improve the outcomes of pregnancy and early childrearing among socially disadvantaged families bearing first children (Olds, Henderson, Tatelbaum, and Chamberlin, 1986a, b). Our study, known as the Prenatal/Early Infancy Project (PEIP), began in 1977 with a 6-year grant from the Bureau of Community Health Services, including an initial year to plan the program and research activities. Supplemental funding was later provided by the Robert Wood Johnson Foundation and the William T. Grant Foundation to help complete the evaluation of the nurse-home visitation program ending at the child's second year of life. Subsequently, the Ford Foundation joined the original funding sources to support a study of the long-term impact of the program on the health and development of the children and the life-course development of their mothers through the child's fourth birthday.

The study was carried out in a semirural community of approximately 100,000 residents in the Appalachian region of New York State. Although the community was well served with health and human services, it exhibited the state's highest rates of reported and confirmed child abuse and neglect (New York State Department of Social Services, 1973–1982).

In 1980 it was rated the worst Standard Metropolitan Statistical Area (SMSA) in the United States in terms of economic conditions (Boyer and Savageau, 1981).

The aim of the program was to prevent a wide range of childhood health and developmental problems by improving the life-course development, social resources, health habits, and caregiving skills of the children's parents. The specific problems targeted for prevention included prematurity and low birth weight, growth and nutritional problems, accidents, ingestions, selected illnesses associated with stress and quality of caregiving, cognitive delays, behavioral problems, and child abuse and neglect.

Early intervention studies addressing such problems often have been difficult to interpret because of problems with either research or program design. Those that have been rigorously designed typically focus on single-variable interventions, such as encouraging a reduction in prenatal smoking (Donovan, 1977; Sexton and Hebel, 1984), providing nutritional supplementation (Rush, Stein, Christakis, and Susser, 1974; Rush, Stein, and Insoln, 1980), or encouraging parents to childproof their homes (Dershewitz and Williamson, 1977). These narrow interventions, however, are unable to address the full range of stressful family and community circumstances that often interfere with optimal maternal health habits and caregiving.

The objectives of our project were to create a program sufficiently comprehensive, structured, and individualized to have significant impact on the problems outlined above and to carry out its evaluation in a way that would meet the highest standards for field experimentation.

The first and major portion of this chapter is concerned with difficulties in planning the evaluation. Much has already been written on these topics, usually under the rubric of ensuring the "internal validity" of the study (Campbell and Stanley, 1966), but because rigorous standards for field experimentation are so infrequently applied, I have noted some of the difficulties my colleagues and I met in trying to achieve those standards in our own work. The second section deals with issues of implementation. Finally, the major findings of the study are reported and issues of data interpretation are addressed.

PLANNING THE EXPERIMENT

Defining the Problem

Frequently, interventions are applied to relatively heterogeneous populations, and massive amounts of data are gathered to determine effectiveness. Tukey (1977) calls this kind of trial a "clinical inquiry," as opposed to a "focused clinical trial." In the latter case, both the class of individuals and relevant outcomes are clearly stated when the problem is formulated. The clinical inquiry, on the other hand, is composed of myriad research questions, increasing the chance that statistically significant "program" effects uncovered will be accidental. As the number of dependent variables and subsamples of interest increases so does the probability of detecting these sampling artifacts.

In our case, we identified the objectives of the program after reviewing literature that implicated stressful family living conditions and certain parental behaviors as common factors in the development of a variety of family and child dysfunctions. Our literature review suggested that women who are teenagers, unmarried, and poor all exhibit a higher incidence of suboptimal pregnancy outcomes and subsequent caregiving dysfunctions than their older, married, middle-class counterparts. We reasoned that first-time mothers would derive greater benefit from the program than women who had already experienced childbirth and early motherhood, so we registered only women who had no previous live births. Because we had no way of knowing which of these particular at-risk groups (the teenagers, the unmarried, or the poor) would benefit most from the service, we enrolled anyone who had at least one of these risk characteristics.

In order to avoid creating a program that was known in the community as being only for the poor or for people with problems, however, we decided to accept anyone who asked to participate, as long as they were having a first baby (statistical modeling procedures allowed us to separate this nonrisk group from the rest of the sample for data analysis, when it was appropriate to do so). Of the women who enrolled, 78% had at least one of the risk characteristics, and 89% were white. By working with a sample with varying degrees of risk, we planned to test whether the program would be more effective with women who were at higher risk. We hypothesized that the beneficial effects of the program, in general, would be greater for families at greater risk, but we reasoned that severely emotionally disturbed parents probably would be too incapacitated to take advantage of the service. Unfortunately (or perhaps fortunately), we did not have a sufficiently large number of severely emotionally impaired parents to test the latter hypothesis.

Moreover, as discussed later, we examined a wide range of outcome variables. We did this because the program was designed to influence a complex biosocial system. Measuring numerous aspects of that system increased the problem of multiple comparisons; we attempted to handle this at the stage of data analysis by examining the extent to which the findings had theoretical coherence and the extent to which they could be validated by data from more than one source. Our study thus fell somewhere between Tukey's clinical inquiry and a focused clinical trial: The identification of families most likely to benefit was focused, although nonrisk families were registered as well; we examined a wide range of outcomes, but they were tied theoretically to the content of the home-visit program.

The Absence of Theoretical Foundations

Many of the problems with specifying the class of families likely to benefit and the probable outcomes of family support programs stem from failure to ground the investigation in a theoretical framework. Studies frequently have been based more on the investigators' clinical judgments than on explicitly stated theories, in part because no single integrative theory is capable of simultaneously capturing the complex interrelations of environmental and biological influences on health and development. Nevertheless, as noted in a recent report by the National Research Council (Travers and Light, 1982), intervention research with children and families might be strengthened if a larger number of studies were based on ecological theory (see Weiss, Chapter 1; Walker and Crocker, Chapter 6; Dym, Chapter 22; this volume).

Both the program and evaluation procedures employed in PEIP were generated from an ecological theoretical framework. Influences on the health and development of the child were viewed from the standpoint of social systems that operate at varying levels of proximity to the child. The elements of this system interact with one another to shape the context in which the fetus and child develop. As indicated in Figure 10.1, this framework highlights commonalities in the origins of the pregnancy and child-rearing problems frequently found in socially disadvantaged families. For example, social class differences in the incidence of preterm delivery and low birth weight can be accounted for largely by maternal health habits and behaviors during pregnancy (Miller and Merritt, 1979). Once the baby is born, social class differences in health and development can be traced to differences in caregiving (Elardo, Bradley, and Caldwell, 1975; Miller, Court, Walton, and Knox, 1960). The general ecological model represented in Figure 10.1 emphasizes that differences in maternal health habits and behaviors are strongly influenced by individual differences in the mothers themselves, their immediate families, the availability of informal and formal social support, the resources and values of the larger community in which they function, and the many stressful life circumstances with which socially disadvantaged families must contend. The quality of maternal health habits and caregiving is determined, in part, by the balance between stressful and protective characteristics of these elements. In Fig-

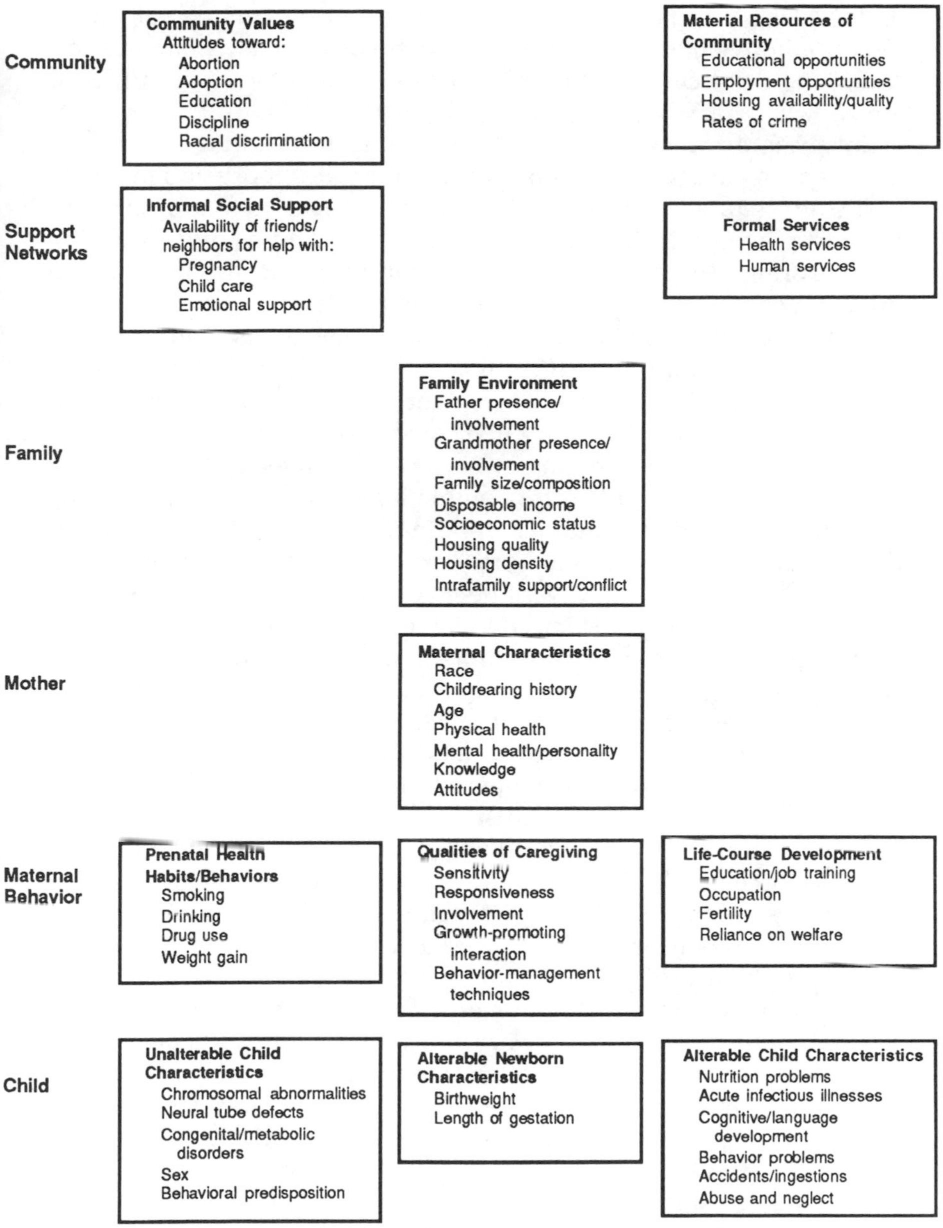

Community	**Community Values** Attitudes toward: Abortion Adoption Education Discipline Racial discrimination		**Material Resources of** **Community** Educational opportunities Employment opportunities Housing availability/quality Rates of crime
Support **Networks**	**Informal Social Support** Availability of friends/ neighbors for help with: Pregnancy Child care Emotional support		**Formal Services** Health services Human services
Family		**Family Environment** Father presence/ involvement Grandmother presence/ involvement Family size/composition Disposable income Socioeconomic status Housing quality Housing density Intrafamily support/conflict	
Mother		**Maternal Characteristics** Race Childrearing history Age Physical health Mental health/personality Knowledge Attitudes	
Maternal **Behavior**	**Prenatal Health** **Habits/Behaviors** Smoking Drinking Drug use Weight gain	**Qualities of Caregiving** Sensitivity Responsiveness Involvement Growth-promoting interaction Behavior-management techniques	**Life-Course Development** Education/job training Occupation Fertility Reliance on welfare
Child	**Unalterable Child** **Characteristics** Chromosomal abnormalities Neural tube defects Congenital/metabolic disorders Sex Behavioral predisposition	**Alterable Newborn** **Characteristics** Birthweight Length of gestation	**Alterable Child Characteristics** Nutrition problems Acute infectious illnesses Cognitive/language development Behavior problems Accidents/ingestions Abuse and neglect

FIGURE 10.1. Ecological model of influences on pregnancy and child-rearing outcomes.

ure 10.1, the direction of effect is thought to operate generally from top to bottom (although bottom-up effects such as child influences on caregiving do occur); for the sake of simplicity, no lines of influence are shown.

Following this conceptual model, the program was designed to meet the needs of parents for information, emotional support, and the relief of life stress to address simultaneously those factors that undermine parents' personal achievements, health habits, and care of their children. During the pregnancy phase of the program, the nurses' two primary goals were (1) to help women improve their diets, cut down on smoking, and avoid alcoholic beverages and drugs, and (2) to enhance parents' and other family members' psychological adjustment to the pregnancy, birth, and the demands of early childrearing. Once the baby was born, the primary goals were (1) to help parents engage in sensitive, growth-promoting interaction with their children, and (2) to help mothers clarify plans for completing their education, returning to work, and bearing additional children. The women's husbands or boyfriends and their own mothers were encouraged to participate in the home visits, since they were believed to play decisive roles in determining the extent to which the women would be successful in the areas of concern. Moreover, the nurses recognized that the extent to which parents adapt to the pregnancy and to their roles as parents is determined, in part, by the extent to which the stresses of poverty and limited social resources existed in their lives. A key ingredient of the program, then, was to link families with formal community services. A detailed protocol guided the nurses in their home-visit activities, but they adapted the content and timing of the program to the individual needs of each family. Sensitivity to parental concerns and an emphasis on family strengths were essential elements of the nurses' work.

Ecological theory also guided the research design. We hypothesized that the influence of the program on children, in general, would be mediated by improvements in maternal health habits and caregiving. To the extent that the nurses were successful in encouraging women to reduce the number of cigarettes smoked during pregnancy, for example, the newborn would be less likely to be of low birth weight. Since smoking is linked to anxiety and stress, however, we reasoned that it was important to determine whether the nurses were successful in enhancing informal social support, linking families with needed community services, and decreasing maternal psychosocial stress.

As Figure 10.1 illustrates, an ecological orientation directs the investigator's attention to social systems that influence both children and parents. Our interest in measuring influences at all levels of the ecological system led to a research design that required complicated statistical models and a large sample—essential to obtaining a relatively unbiased assessment of the influence of the program. Because families are inevitably complex, studies of family support programs will require complex research designs to yield the most useful information on their effectiveness.

Establishing Control Groups

Until recently, most studies of comprehensive family support services during pregnancy and infancy (Evrard and Gold, 1978; Klerman and Jekel, 1973; McAnarney, Roghmann, Adams, Tatelbaum, Kash, Coulter, Plume, and Charney, 1978; Osofsky, Osofsky, Kendall, and Rajan, 1973; Provence and Naylor, 1983) have employed nonrandomly assigned comparison groups that received routine services in other nonprogram settings. This made it especially difficult to interpret evaluation results, because program participants often differ from nonparticipants in unmeasured psychological characteristics (such as the motivation to participate in an educational/support program) that may influence the pattern of results obtained. Having no assessment of these characteristics limits the extent to which one can determine the comparability of the two groups, and, if necessary, statistically adjust for the differences. Random assignment virtually eliminates differences between the experimental families and those assigned to the control group at the start of the program. With random assignment, subsequent differences observed between those in the experimental program and the control group can be attributed, with greater confidence, to the influence of the program. Therefore, random assignment, including appropriate stratification (assignment within groups based on important background characteristics), should be employed whenever possible. This does not eliminate all possible sources of bias, nevertheless, as my discussion of statistical modeling will indicate.

Only a few investigations in the study of family support programs that have an emphasis on child health have employed random assignment (e.g., Dawson, van Doorninck, Butterfield, and Alexander, 1979; Gutelius, Kirsch, MacDonald, Brooks, and McErlean, 1977; Larson, 1980; Olds *et al.*, 1986a; 1986b; Seigel, Bauman, Schaefer, Saunders, and Ingram, 1980). In part, this lack of experimental work derives from considerations of ethics. For some people, randomly assigning families to receive services thought to be helpful while "depriving" other families is objectionable. In our own research, we attempted to minimize these objections. First, families were divided into four treatment groups. All groups were provided sensory and developmental screening and referral to the routine health care system for potential problems detected in the children at ages 1 and 2; those in Treatments 2, 3, and 4 were also provided free transportation for regular prenatal and well-child care; those in Treatments 3 and 4 were provided the foregoing services and nurse home-visitation during pregnancy; and those in Treatment 4 were provided both pre- and postnatal nurse home-visitation, in addition to the screening and transportation services. In other words, all families were provided some service that they otherwise would not receive.

For the pregnancy phase of the study, we compared families in Treatments 1 and 2 with those in 3 and 4 to create a contrast between those families who had the nurse during pregnancy and those who had no nurse. For the postnatal phase of the study, we compared families in Treatment 4 with those in Treatments 1 and 2, again creating a nurse versus no-nurse contrast. By providing some services to all families— as opposed to using a no-treatment control group—we risked undermining our ability to detect the effect of the nurse. We reasoned, however, that the screening and transportation services would have a relatively minor impact on the outcomes of the study, while greatly reducing the feeling on the part of the participants and members of the community that the control group was being deprived. Enough of a major difference in experience existed between the nurse-visited families and those in the comparison groups to justify this minor reduction in contrast. Further, all project services were paid for with research dollars. Without the experiment, these additional services would not have been available.

Finally, to create an additional hedge against possible charges of unethical practice, we prepared a list of serious family problems (health, social, emotional, and developmental), which our data gatherers used to identify participants in apparent imminent danger. These individuals were referred for further assistance through the routine health and human service system despite the contamination this created for the research. This contamination, like most other procedures employed in the study, was conservative, in that it too reduced the contrast in services received by the families in the nurse-visited and comparison groups.

Even those who argue that random assignment is a cornerstone of rigorous research design sometimes find it necessary to compromise this standard to maintain methodological rigor in other areas. In our case, two such trade-offs occurred. First, with about 80% of the sample already enrolled, we calculated that we could substantially increase the statistical power of the design (discussed later) to detect the effects of the postpartum nurse home-visitation service (Treatment 4) in comparison to the two no-nurse conditions (Treatments 1 and 2), if we changed the assignment ratios to include a higher portion of the remaining families in Treatment 4 than in the other three treatments. Therefore, during the last 6 months of sample enrollment, 34 families were assigned to Treatment 4, 16 were assigned to Treatment 3, 15 to Treatment 2, and 15 to Treatment 1. In doing this, we altered the pure randomization of the design by creating a minor confounding of treatments with time, insofar as women enrolled later had a greater chance of being assigned to Treatment 4 than did earlier enrollees. We reasoned, and analyses of selected dependent variables later confirmed, that the increase in statistical power would outweigh the possibly confounding influence of time differences on the treatment contrasts.

Second, concern about horizontal diffusion led us to make another trade-off with the originally planned randomization procedure. Horizontal diffusion, discussed in greater detail later, involves the unintended transference of the experimental intervention from families involved in the program to the comparison-group families. In our case, six women who were recruited for the study lived in the same households as other women already participating. As a result, we were concerned that if one were assigned to a nurse-visited condition and another were assigned to a condition that did not provide a nurse, the contrast would be reduced if the nurse-visited women shared their program-derived experience and knowledge. To avoid taking the chance that the new enrollees might be assigned to a different treatment group, and thus possibly contribute to horizontal diffusion, the six new enrollees were put into the same treatment as their housemates. The only other viable alternative would have been to exclude the six women from the study altogether.

With the qualifications outlined previously, families enrolled in the program were randomized to the four treatment conditions as follows. First, they were stratified by marital status, race, and seven geographic regions within the county. At the end of the intake interview, the women drew their treatment assignments from a deck of cards. The stratification was executed by using separate decks for the groups defined by the women's race, marital status at intake, and, for white women, geographic region. To ensure reasonably balanced subclasses, the decks were reconstituted periodically to overrepresent those treatments with smaller numbers of subjects, a procedure similar to Efron's (1971) biased-coin designs. Thus randomization was preserved while ensuring that the subgroups defined by various risk factors were reasonably balanced (had proportional numbers of cases) during most of the time that the enrollment of the sample was taking place. This was especially important, since the enrollment period lasted thirty months; if

funding for the study had become unavailable or some other problem
had occurred, we still would have enrolled families well distributed
across treatments and risk-factors. Women in Treatments 3 and 4 subsequently were assigned on a rotating basis, within their stratification
blocks, to one of five home visitors, so that we could control and test
for differences in nurse effectiveness.

Statistical Models

Even with random assignment, the possibility remains that treatment
conditions and other influences may be biased unless appropriate statistical adjustments are made for confounding variables. As noted before, we grouped participating women according to maternal background characteristics and then randomly assigned families within those
groups to the treatment conditions. Despite these efforts, at the time
of enrollment the groups were not perfectly equivalent with regard to
other important characteristics. Although the treatment groups were
equivalent on all standard demographic characteristics, the women assigned to Treatments 3 and 4 tended to have less social support than
women assigned to Treatments 1 and 2 (Olds et al., 1986a), and unmarried women assigned to Treatment 4 had a greater sense of control
over their lives than unmarried women in Treatments 1 and 2 (Olds et
al., 1986b). Had we not assessed maternal psychological characteristics
and social support at the outset, these important sources of nonequivalence would have been undetected.

More generally, our ecological framework posits that child health
and development need to be analyzed simultaneously in terms of influences operating at the level of parental psychological characteristics,
family functioning, and the community (see Figure 10.1). Our experience shows that unless these influences are measured and taken into
consideration in the design and analysis, results may be biased in unknown ways. Typically, investigators check the equivalence of treatment
and control groups on a few demographic characteristics at the beginning of a study to ensure that preexisting differences in the composition
of the sample do not account for differences observed subsequently.
But unless other potentially important influences on child health and
development (such as parental psychological characteristics, aspects
of the family environment, and level of social support) are examined
and, if necessary, statistically controlled, bias may result even with random assignment. The inclusion of additional variables of theoretical
importance in the statistical model minimizes this possibility; moreover,
it can reduce the amount of error variance so that outcomes of interest
can be discerned with greater power and precision (Keppel, 1973).

We measured a large number of theoretically significant variables, so that some subset could be entered into the statistical model for data analysis. We assessed aspects of the mother's physical stature, health, psychological status, social situation, as well as biological characteristics of the child, as part of our effort to rule out competing explanations for the influence of the program on the outcomes of the study. In general, the variables that we assessed for purposes of statistical control were those on which the program could have no impact, either because they were in existence prior to program participation or because they were relatively impervious to its influence. While all were not included in any one model at the same time, all were available for possible inclusion in the analysis—depending on the outcome under examination. Maternal prepregnant weight, for example, has a strong and unique bearing on birth weight, while it has little influence on child abuse and neglect. Conversely, maternal sense of control over life circumstances can help predict child abuse and neglect, even after controlling statistically for sociodemographic variables but it has no unique influence on birth weight. Thus, maternal prepregnant weight was included in the statistical model when we analyzed birth outcomes, and maternal sense of control was included in the model when we analyzed child outcomes, but these two background variables were not included in any one statistical model at the same time.

An additional advantage in gathering data on a range of background variables is that it creates a data base with which the investigator can begin to examine properties of the ecological system in which families are embedded. This strategy for minimizing bias is not without pitfalls, however, since the process of measuring so many variables, in itself, may alter the attitudes and behaviors of the participants, and thus introduce the problem of reactivity.

Before turning to this problem I would like to stress the importance of involving a statistician at all stages of evaluating family support programs, including the earliest stages of planning. This becomes especially important if the investigator decides to analyze the program within the context of the complex ecological system in which programs and families are inevitably embedded (Henderson, 1977, 1982).

Reactivity of Measurement

Reactivity of measurement is the alteration of the program participants' behavior as a result of the measurement process (Nunally, 1967). Because of the participants' sensitization to the objectives of the research and the possible change in their behavior, many have argued against employing a pretest/posttest design (Campbell and Stanley, 1966; Nunally, 1967). The problem, however, probably has been overstated. In a series of experiments, Lana (1969) found that few differences existed in the attitudes and opinions of experimental subjects who had been pretested and then posttested versus those who were posttested only. Indeed, in some instances pretesting contributed to smaller changes. So, while logically reactivity of measurement might seem problematic, the evidence suggests that it is less so than anticipated. Nevertheless, it is wise to consider the possibility of testing-reactivity, and where possible to select measures that are nonreactive. A measure of the number of appointments scheduled for childhood immunizations following a media campaign on the topic is an example.

The problem of reactivity was intensified in our research by our interviewing and testing families at frequent intervals over a 2½-year period; but it was minimized, we believe, by our combining relatively nonreactive measures (behavioral and health outcomes) with measures that potentially were more reactive (reports of attitudes and sentiments). By examining the degree to which these interview, behavioral, and record-review data converged, we were able to weigh the validity of the findings. Our reactivity problem was further minimized because we had a disadvantaged sample. The life circumstances of parents in the PEIP program frequently were so overwhelmingly difficult that it seems highly unlikely that several interviews or an infant-testing program in themselves would have a discernible impact on the outcomes of the study. If such minimal intervention were all that were required, we would hardly need the intensive interventions included in most comprehensive programs for disadvantaged families.

The problem of reactivity raises the related concern that interviewing and testing may interact with the treatment to intensify its effects. This problem may also be overstated. Insofar as interviewing and testing are integral parts of the family support program, the research data gathering in itself probably adds little to treatment effects. The possibility of such effects should be seriously considered in the interpretation of results, however, and again, corroborating evidence should be sought from sources of information where it is less likely that the result obtained is due to the interaction between the processes of measurement and the content of the program.

Sample Size and Statistical Power

When design complexity increases, so do sample size requirements. Studies often report no significant differences between program and control families because of Type II errors resulting from samples that are too small (Cohen, 1977; Freiman, Chalmer, Smith, and Knebler, 1978). Research plans must therefore consider both what is a clinically useful indication of program effect and the number of families required in the relevant groups for which estimates of program effect are to be made.

Because our program had a variety of outcomes, the determination of sample size was not straightforward. Outcomes differ in the extent to which they are amenable to intervention, so it may be reasonable to expect the program to have a moderate or even large effect (in standard deviation units) on one variable, and a small effect on another. We expected the PEIP program to have a relatively small effect on birth weight and a moderate effect on the children's mental development. Similarly, we reasoned that some outcomes such as child abuse and neglect occurred too infrequently to enable us to detect even a moderate reduction in incidence; a much larger sample would be required for such variables than for more frequently occurring variables, such as emergency room visits. After many power calculations, with different representative variables, we decided that an initial sample of 400, allowing for attrition, would provide us with a reasonably powerful test of treatment main effects on most outcomes of interest.

These power calculations, however, did not take into consideration the large sample required to test program effects that might be conditioned by the risk status of the families. We expected that our sample size—limited by constraints on time and money—would be inadequate to detect positive effects on the smaller groups of women and families at greater risk for the particular problem under investigation. Nevertheless, the program has been shown to have effects that, in general, were greater for families at greater risk (Olds et al., 1906a, b), in part because the impact of the program on the high-risk families was greater than anticipated. In the next round of preventive-intervention and family support studies, it will be important to take into consideration our findings and those of others (Anisfeld and Lipper, 1983; Peoples and Siegel, 1983) suggesting that the positive effects of intervention are likely to be concentrated on families at greater risk.

Cost–Benefit Issues

In this age of decreasing fiscal resources, determining the financial costs and benefits of family support services becomes increasingly important (see White, Chapter 19, this volume). Many of these services have been justified on the grounds that they ultimately save the public money because they prevent later disability and family dysfunction, which require costly public services to treat. With the exception of the

Perry Preschool Project (Berrueta-Clement, Schweinhart, Barnett, Epstein, and Weikart, 1984; Weber, Foster, and Weikart, 1978), and the Hazard Infant Care Project (Cowen, Culley, Hochstrasser, Briscoe, and Somes, 1978; Hochstrasser, Sonnes, Cowen, and Culley, 1980), however, few of these services have been analyzed thoroughly from the standpoint of costs and benefits. In part this may be because such studies present a number of self-contained conceptual and methodological issues that are best handled with the assistance of an economist.

The dearth of well-designed and well-executed cost analyses of family-support programs is especially unfortunate because services for children and families are frequently the first to be eliminated whenever local, state, and federal budgets are cut. We therefore included a cost–benefit study in our overall research plan, designed to compare the costs of the four treatments and to assess the financial benefits derived, such as reduced foster-care placements, fewer hospitalizations and emergency room visits, increased employment (leading to increased government revenue in the form of taxes), decreased reliance on public assistance, and reduced Medicaid expenses associated with reductions in subsequent pregnancy.

IMPLEMENTING THE PROGRAM AND EVALUATION

Verifying the Treatment

Before the presence or absence of program effects can be interpreted properly, it must be demonstrated that there was a clear program plan and that the service providers followed it faithfully. If one were working with a single-variable treatment, such as nutritional supplementation, treatment validation might be easier. Rush and his colleagues, for example, employed riboflavin markers in their prenatal nutritional supplementation beverage that, through urinalysis, could be used to quantify the amount of beverage ingested (Rush *et al.*, 1974, 1980).

Since the present treatment consisted of a complex education and social support intervention, we did not have the equivalent of biochemical markers to determine whether the program was delivered in accordance with the program plan. We attempted, instead, to handle the problem by closely monitoring the provision of the nurse home-visitation program. With a year of grant-supported planning, we piloted and revised the program protocol, including methods of monitoring its implementation, before beginning it with main-study families. We developed computerized forms for the nurses to report the extent to which they adhered to the program plan and achieved specific program objectives. Problems were documented in narrative form so that we might learn from the nurses' experience. Our preliminary analyses of the home-visit report forms indicate that because the needs of families differed so much, the amount of time that the nurses spent on particular topics varied tremendously from family to family. This type of variation was consistent with the plan, however, since the nurses were supposed to adapt the content of the educational program to the parents' needs and concerns. The nurses also differed in their affective qualities, which undoubtedly contributed to subtle variations in the way the program was carried out and experienced by families. Nevertheless, our analyses of the report forms reassured us that the content of the program was delivered in accordance with the program plan and in a reasonably uniform way across nurse home-visitors.

Horizontal Diffusion. A number of investigators have suggested that the apparent effectiveness of a program may be blunted because the details of the experimental intervention are communicated (either directly or indirectly) to members of the control group. Larson (1980), for example, used a historical control group rather than one that was randomly assigned in order to avoid possible horizontal diffusion. Potentially, this is a serious problem for any family-support research project, especially if carried out in a community where families are part of tightly knit social networks. Unfortunately, to our knowledge, no intervention study has systematically evaluated the extent of horizontal diffusion. If this factor can be monitored, the investigator can judge whether it has undermined the treatment contrast.

To help us assess the integrity of the PEIP research design, we asked women at each assessment period whether they knew others enrolled in the program and how frequently they discussed pregnancy or child care matters with them. We were particularly concerned about non-nurse-visited women discussing pregnancy or child care matters with nurse-visited women. Preliminary results of our analysis indicate that 20–25% of the women (whether nurse-visited or not) reported discussing pregnancy or child care matters with nurse-visited women. Most of the latter group of young women were enrolled in a new in-school program for pregnant adolescents. The potential influence of this and other programs on the research design is discussed in the next section.

Our approach to monitoring horizontal diffusion suffers from two problems: *(a)* It does not account for contacts with women who are participants, when the respondents do not know they are; and *(b)* it does not account for indirect effects mediated through individuals not enrolled in the program. Most important, our approach does not tell the investigator *at what point* the treatment comparison is no longer valid. Perhaps a greater accumulation of experience in measuring horizontal diffusion across studies will help determine that point.

Although this approach to measuring horizontal diffusion is far from perfect, it has proved useful. For example, even though teenagers in the nurse-visited and comparison groups had an opportunity to share information about the content of the home-visitation program, the effect of the program on the weight of the newborn was concentrated on those babies born to young adolescents (Olds *et al.*, 1986a). These positive program effects occurred despite the teenagers in the nurse-visited groups and the comparison groups having an opportunity to share information about the content of the home-visitation program.

Use of Other Services. Unfortunately, with the exception of the evaluation of the Child and Family Resource Program (described in Nauta and Hewett, Chapter 17, this volume), it is rare for investigators of family-support programs to designate the other services parents and children receive that may have effects comparable to the program under investigation. As a result, fully informed interpretations of intervention results are difficult to make. In our study, we monitored families' use of other services because the intervention plan called for the nurses to link families with other, needed services. Information was collected through interviews with participants and through reviews of agency records. By measuring each family's use of these other services, we were able to describe, more completely, the nature of the treatment contrasts embodied in the study.

Analysis of the pregnancy data revealed, for example, that although nurse-visited women were aware of more community services, attended childbirth classes more frequently, and made more extensive use of the nutritional supplementation program for women, infants, and children (WIC), a large portion of the women in the comparison conditions (Treatments 1 and 2) were visited by public health nurses and made use of these other community services. Moreover, during the first 10 months after delivery, teenagers in the comparison group were visited by a public health nurse more frequently than were the PEIP nurse-visited teenagers. The difference was only about one visit—approximately 0.5 compared to 1.5 public health visits—so the extra visit probably did not attenuate the treatment contrast very much given that the PEIP nurses visited their families about 18 times during the same period. Nevertheless, the rather high utilization of services among comparison-group women forced us to consider carefully the nature of the treatment contrasts in this study.

When the PEIP program was first offered in the community, few high-risk mothers were referred to childbirth education classes, and the classes made few accommodations for the special needs of these parents. As PEIP focused attention on their needs and enhanced the community's awareness of the potential benefits of childbirth classes for this group, the primary care providers began referring more of these women to childbirth education. Childbirth education instructors, accustomed to teaching middle-class couples, began to adjust their classes to the needs of unmarried teens. During the first 6 months of PEIP operation, 64% of the nurse-visited mothers attended childbirth education while only 36% of the comparison-group mothers attended; during a 6-month period assessed toward the end of the study, 58% of the comparison group and 56% of the nurse-visited group attended these classes. Enrollment in childbirth classes in itself may be of relatively minor importance for the overall outcome of the research, but the possibility of increased awareness of the needs of high-risk families on the part of the health and human service community and better services for the control group is of particular concern if the positive effects of the program are to be discerned. From the standpoint of community development, of course, the enhancement of other services for the target population is an indication of program success. One of the major findings of the Kirschner Associates' national survey on the impact of the Head Start Centers (1970), for example, was that the implementation of Parent–Child Centers administered through Head Start programs stimulated the improvement of other local services.

We wanted to determine the extent to which utilization of other services created a problem for the pregnancy phase of our study. Interviews were carried out with public health nurses and administrators, local obstetricians, nurses working in the offices of private obstetricians, childbirth educators, and WIC staff members to determine changes made in their health-education practices and in other services provided to women during the 30-month period in which the prenatal phase of the study was carried out. The analysis of these interviews is not complete, but one preliminary finding is worth noting: Both the public health nurses and the office nurses reported significant increases in the amount of time that they spent counseling patients about prenatal health habits; the private obstetricians, on the other hand, reported virtually no change at all in the amount of time spent on such matters. Since much of the educational material presented to pregnant women comes from nurses, one might expect a diminution of program effects on maternal health habits over time (as the control-group women received additional counseling on appropriate health behaviors), an issue we plan to address in future analyses. With the interview data that we have gathered on this topic, however, it is difficult to separate the influence of the experimental program on the teaching behaviors of the local nurses from the natural shifts and improvements in health awareness that constitute progress in the field.

Blind Assessment

In medical research, the most rigorous design is a double-blind trial, where neither subjects nor evaluators know which subjects received the experimental treatment. In family-support research, it is often difficult to hide the treatment from those who receive it. It is more reasonable to try to ensure that those conducting the assessment of child and family functioning are unaware of treatment status, thus minimizing bias in data-gathering.

We took great pains to conceal from staff members involved in data-gathering which families received the nurse. We asked parents not to reveal whether they were visited, but they sometimes inadvertently did so. At the end of the project, we asked interviewers to indicate whether they had learned the family's treatment status and found that interviewers did not know the treatment assignment of any of those women assigned to Treatments 1 and 2, but that they were aware of the family's treatment assignment for 18% of the women assigned to Treatment 3 and 35% of the women in Treatment 4. Fortunately, many of the interview data are relatively impervious to interviewer bias; moreover, in the case of PEIP, the data on program effectiveness are derived from a variety of sources, including medical and social service record reviews. For example, corroborating evidence of the effectiveness of the program in reducing child maltreatment came from a variety of sources, including state records of verified cases of child abuse and neglect and hospital emergency room records, in addition to parental interview data and observations of parental caregiving in the home (Olds *et al.*, 1986b). We therefore believe that the overall validity of the general finding was threatened only minimally by this erosion of blind assessment.

Attrition

Random assignment improves the chances of creating equivalent treatment and control groups at the outset, but it cannot assure equivalence at the completion of the study. Attrition can reduce group equivalence in either size or background characteristics. In the past, investigators themselves have been known to contribute to this bias. In the very earliest round of federally sponsored programs aimed at parent education, for example, individuals who did not participate fully in the program were dropped from some studies, leading to an investigator-induced selection bias (White, Day, Freeman, Hantman, and Messenger, 1972). In a social experiment, the failure of subjects to participate often amounts to program failure and needs to be considered as such in the analysis. If low-participation program families are excluded from the analysis, while their counterparts in the control group, who require less participation, are included, the results could inflate the appearance of positive program effects. Fortunately, this problem has been more adequately handled in more recent parent-support studies. In our study, once a subject was assigned to a treatment condition, data on that case were gathered (to the extent possible) and analyzed, regardless of the amount of subject participation.

Even if the dropout rate is equal across treatment groups, those who drop out of the program may have different background characteristics from those who drop from the comparison group, further compounding the attrition problem. To monitor this, we carried out analyses of treatment by drop-status interactions, using background characteristics as the dependent variables. The presence of such an interaction poses special problems that have to be handled on an ad hoc basis, depending on the nature of the interaction and the distribution of subject characteristics remaining in the sample. We found that women who dropped out of the nurse-visited condition had greater sense of control over their lives than women who dropped out of the comparison conditions. We determined that this differential dropout pattern was not due to the program itself, since virtually all of the low-risk nurse-visited dropouts stopped participating because of either miscarriage or moving from the study area. In some respects, this attrition was beneficial. As noted before, a preintervention bias existed among unmarried women that favored the nurse-visited group: At the start of the program, they had a greater sense of control over their lives than their counterparts in the comparison groups. After some of the more advantaged women dropped from the nurse-visited group, this preintervention bias was no longer present for the sample on which follow-up interviews were carried out, and the treatments remained essentially equivalent in other respects (Olds et al., 1986b).

ISSUES OF INTERPRETATION

Our analysis of the primary outcomes of the study are reported thus far in two publications (Olds et al., 1986a, b) and in a final report on the study (Olds, Henderson, Birmingham, Chamberlin, and Tatelbaum, 1983), but they are summarized briefly here. In general, the positive effects of the program were greatest for those women who were at greatest risk for the problem under investigation.

During pregnancy, the women randomly assigned to the nurse home-visitation conditions (Treatments 3 and 4) made better use of health and human services, experienced greater support from family members and friends, made greater dietary improvements, and had fewer kidney infections. The positive effects of the program on birth weight and length of gestation were concentrated on smokers and young adolescents (17 years of age). The nurse-visited smokers reduced smoking by 4 cigarettes per day and experienced a 75% reduction in the number of preterm deliveries; the nurse-visited young adolescents experienced a 395-gram improvement in the weight of their newborns ($p < .05$ for all findings) (Olds et al., 1986a).

During the first 2 postpartum years, according to state records, 19% of the comparison-group women at greatest psychosocial risk abused and neglected their children, as opposed to 4% of the highest-risk women who were nurse visited ($p = .07$). This reduction in verified case reports of child abuse and neglect was corroborated by (a) the women's reports of their babies' temperament and crying behavior; (b) the women's reports of conflict with and scolding of their babies; (c) interviewers' observations of the mothers' treatment of their children in the home; and (d) emergency-room records (Olds et al., 1986b). Significant improvements also were detected in the life-course development of the young women themselves and were reflected in outcomes such as reduced subsequent pregnancy and increased labor-force participation. These effects were concentrated among the women in greatest need of help in these areas (Olds et al., 1983).

Our interpretation of these results has, of course, taken into consideration the issues covered here. We found generally positive program effects even when most of the threats to the validity of the findings operated against the hypothesis of nurse effectiveness.

Generalizability

Even if family support experiments are designed in ways that minimize threats to internal validity, and even if they demonstrate positive effects for participants compared to control group members, the usefulness of the findings for the development of social programs and policy can be challenged. A common criticism leveled against social experiments is that the results have limited generalizability because the subjects are volunteers. To be sure, it is incorrect to generalize results beyond the characteristics of a sample, and voluntary participation is indeed an important sample characteristic. But since many, if not most, family support programs are voluntary, this presents little problem for most studies. The use of volunteers does limit the generalizability of results, however, if a substantial number of families refuse to participate in the experimental program because of the research and would have participated if no research were associated with it. Under these circumstances the results can be generalized only to the population that would volunteer for both an experimental program *and* a research project. In the PEIP case, only 3 women (out of 500 interviewed) declined participation because of the research; this creates only a slight restriction on the population to which the results can be generalized.

In designs that involve comparison services, a related threat emerges when participants prefer one service over another and those preferences are allowed to be expressed in whether the individuals participate in the study, such as, when prospective participants decline to enroll unless they receive the service they prefer. Such a scenario could lead to the more assertive members of the sample being concentrated in the service condition that was viewed as being more attractive. In order to minimize the possibility of this selective volunteerism among treatment and comparison groups in our study, we obtained consent *before* participants knew which services they would receive. Only one dropped out of the project after receiving a set of services with which she was dissatisfied. Overall, more than 80% of the women meeting the sample characteristics and living in the area were contacted, and about 80% of the women who were contacted agreed to register. Since most of these women came to us through the health and human service referral system, we have reasoned that the results can safely be generalized to most women who obtain routine care in the target community.

Even if the study participants are representative of their community, the question remains as to whether the program could be successfully carried out with staff members who are not so highly motivated and trained as the individuals who implemented the original experimental service. This problem was minimized in PEIP by the preparation of manuals that, eventually, will guide future service providers wishing to set up similar programs. The manuals describe the methods used (a) to screen, hire, and train nurse home-visitors; (b) to establish co-operation among other health and human-service providers; and (c) to work with families in the field to meet specific program objectives. Common problems in developing community cooperation and working with families in their homes are given special attention. In terms of special staff characteristics, it is our position that ability, enthusiasm, and commitment are essential ingredients for any successful nurse home-visitation program. Although this may limit the number of appropriate candidates for the job, we believe that nurses with these characteristics can be found in virtually any community in the country.

Modest Results, Negative Results, and Program Implications

The immediacy of the policy implications of intervention research often makes it difficult for the investigator to maintain the same level of objectivity found in research with fewer immediate consequences (Ricciuti, 1981). The cost of such research and the perceived effect of the results on similar programs can result in a drive to produce positive findings. As a result, individuals often either overstate the meaning of a particular positive finding or downplay the significance of a negative side effect. As an antidote to these tendencies, intervention researchers should continually remind themselves of the distinction between their roles as investigators and as social advocates (see also White, Chapter 19, this volume).

In our study, we found several indications that the program might have a negative impact for certain subgroups. During pregnancy, we found a greater incidence of preterm delivery in the group at lowest risk for poor birth outcomes—the older ($>$ 16 years at registration) women who did not smoke. At first we thought that the nurses' efforts to help might have interfered with the natural coping mechanisms of women who do not need help; but close examination of the characteristics of these women before they registered in the program showed that those in nurse-visited group had less social support and were older than their counterparts in the comparison group. For technical reasons (nonhomogeneity of regressions) we were unable to adjust statistically for these preintervention differences. Although we found no medical explanations for the higher rates of preterm delivery in the nurse-visited older nonsmokers, because there were no postregistration differences in health habits, social support, or levels of anxiety, we concluded that the difference in preterm delivery was due to factors present at registration that predisposed the nurse-visited older nonsmokers to deliver prematurely (Olds *et al.*, 1986a). We came to this conclusion, however, only after seriously considering the possibility that the program produced unexpected negative side-effects.

After delivery of the child, we also uncovered some indications that the nurse-visited married teenagers might have been harmed by the nurses' intervention. Specifically, during our in-home observations at 10 and 22 months of the child's life, we noted trends for the nurse-visited married teens to give poorer quality care than married teens in the comparison group (Olds *et al.*, 1983). During our follow-up evaluation, this same nurse-visited subgroup reported that they had more marital problems than their comparison-group counterparts (Olds, Birmingham, and Henderson, 1984). We became concerned that the nurses might have interfered with the fragile spousal relationships that often exist in teenage marriages by inadvertently competing with husbands for the attention and respect of their wives, despite explicit efforts to minimize this kind of problem.

We tested this interpretation by examining interviews completed at the end of the study in which we explicitly asked women whether the nurses created any problems between them and members of their family or friends. Without exception, the nurse-visited married teenagers denied any intrusiveness or interference in their spousal relationship. Since participant reports are notoriously biased in favor of programs, we reasoned that it was important to find additional sources of information that would corroborate these reports. A careful analysis of the background characteristics of the sample showed that at the time that they registered in the study, the nurse-visited married teens smoked a great deal more and that there were nonsignificant trends for them to report less support from their husbands than their counterparts in the control group. Although we have not yet carried out analyses to determine whether statistical control will remove these apparently negative effects of the program on caregiving and the spousal relationship, there are reasons to believe that they will; smokers are more anxious and irritable than nonsmokers (Matarazzo and Saslow, 1960; Schneider and Houston, 1970), and maternal smoking during pregnancy is associated with child maltreatment (Pascoe, 1985).

The two preceding examples are presented to illustrate the importance of explicitly looking for negative side-effects, so we can have greater assurance that our efforts to help will do no harm and that positive effects are interpreted in the context of possible negative effects.

Implications for Future Research and Policy Making

Even with the best designed investigations, it may be argued that the findings are due to some peculiar configuration of local circumstances or may be the result of random events—Type I error. I suspect that the success of the PEIP program had to do with careful program planning and supervision and considerable attention to issues of research design and measurement. Given the cost of this type of program, however, more work should be carried out to determine its effectiveness and generalizability before large investments of public or private funds are made. There are enough unsuccessful home-visitation studies with this population (Barkauskas, 1983; Seigel et al., 1980) to make us pause before running head-long into an expensive new program initiative in this area. Moreover, proposals to use paraprofessionals or volunteers to do the kind of work carried out by the nurses in our study are even less solid, since good evidence regarding their effectiveness is sparse and inconsistent (see, e.g., Gray, Cutler, Dean, and Kempe, 1979; Seigel *et al.*, 1980; van Doorninck, Dawson, Butterfield, and Alexander, 1980).

The results of our study will naturally serve as a guidepost, and to a certain extent, as a source of hope for those working with socially disadvantaged families. The only way to resolve whether the program should serve as a basis for governmental programs and policies, however, is to replicate the experimental program in varied settings, such as, inner cities and communities with a scarcity of other community services. Some may argue that the program should also be tested using paraprofessionals rather than more costly professional nurses but I would contend that such a test should await evidence that the general program model is effective in a variety of settings. At this stage it is important to ensure that the programs being tested are the best we can possibly design. After we have a better sense of the extent of their impact, we can begin to search for less expensive ways of achieving the same result.

Such a strategy, of course, requires a commitment of funds and planning that, unfortunately, is not characteristic of family policymakers to date. As the quality of intervention research improves and promising services are identified, however, it makes sense to begin supporting a strategy of planned replications of successful family-support services.

REFERENCES

Anisfeld, E., and Lipper, E. (1983). Early contact, social support, and mother–infant bonding. *Pediatrics, 72,* 79–83.

Barkauskas, V. (1983). Effectiveness of public health nurse home visits to primiparous mothers and their infants. *American Journal of Public Health, 73,* 573–580.

Berrueta-Clement, J. R., Schweinhart, L. J., Barnett, W. S., Epstein, A. S., and Weikart, D. P. (1984). *Changed lives: The effect of the Perry Preschool Program on youths through age 19.* Monograph of the High-Scope Educational Research Foundation. Ypsilanti, MI: High-Scope Press.

Boyer, R., and Savageau, D. (1981). *Places rated almanac.* NY: Rand McNally.

Campbell, D., and Stanley, J. (1966). *Experimental and quasi-experimental designs for research.* Chicago, IL: Rand McNally.

Cohen, J. (1977). *Statistical power analysis for the behavioral sciences.* NY: Academic Press.

Cowen, D., Culley, G., Hochstrasser, D., Briscoe, M., and Somes, D. (1978). Impact of a rural preventive care outreach program on children's health. *American Journal of Public Health, 68,* 471–476.

Dawson, P., van Doorninck, W., Butterfield, P., and Alexander, H. (November 1979). *Family support by lay home visitors*. Paper presented at the meeting of the American Public Health Association, New York.

Dershewitz, R. A., and Williamson, J. W. (1977). Prevention of childhood household injuries: A controlled clinical trial. *American Journal of Public Health, 67*, 1148–1153.

Donovan, J. W. (1977). Randomized controlled trial of anti-smoking advise in pregnancy. *British Journal of Preventive Social Medicine, 31*, 6–12.

Efron, B. (1971). Forcing a sequential experiment to be balanced. *Biometrika, 58*, 403–417.

Elardo, R., Bradley, R., and Caldwell, B. (1975). The relation of infants' home environments to mental test performance from six to thirty-six months: A longitudinal analysis. *Child Development, 46*, 71–76.

Evrard, J. R., and Gold, E. M. (1978). A one-year study of teenage pregnancy at Women and Infants' Hospital of Rhode Island. *Journal of Reproductive Medicine, 21*, 95–101.

Freiman, J., Chalmer, T., Smith, H., and Knebler, R. (1978). The importance of beta, the Type II error and sample size in the design and interpretation of the randomized control trial. *New England Journal of Medicine, 299*, 690–694.

Gray, J., Cutler, C., Dean, J., and Kempe, C. (1979). Prediction and prevention of child abuse and neglect. *Journal of Social Issues, 35*, 127–139.

Gutelius, N., Kirsch, D., MacDonald, S., Brooks, M., and McErlean, T. (1977). Controlled study of child health supervision: Behavioral results. *Pediatrics, 60*, 294–304.

Henderson, C. R., Jr. (August, 1977). Analysis of covariance in models for research in the ecology of human development. Presented at the Conference on Research Perspectives in the ecology of Human Development, Cornell University.

Henderson, C. (1982). Analysis of covariance in the mixed model: Higher-level nonhomogeneous, and random regressions. *Biometrics, 38*(3), 623–640.

Hochstrasser, D., Sonnes, G., Cowen, D., and Culley, G. (1980). Follow-up study of the impact of a rural preventive care outreach program on children's use of medical services. *American Journal of Public Health, 70*, 151.

Keppel, G. (1973). *Design and analysis: A researcher's handbook*. Englewood Cliffs, NJ: Prentice-Hall, Inc.

Kirschner Associates, Albuquerque, N.M. (1970). A National Survey of the Impact of Head Start Centers on Community Institutions. (ED045195) Washington, D.C.: Office of Economic Opportunity.

Klerman, L. V., and Jekel, J. F. (1973). *School-age mothers: Problems, programs, and policy*. Hamden, CT: Shoe String Press, Inc.

Lana, R. E. (1969). Pretest sensitization. In R. Rosenthal and R. Rosnow (Eds.), _Artifact in behavioral research_ (pp. 119–141). NY: Academic Press.

Larson, C. (1980). Efficacy of prenatal and postpartum home visits on child health and development. _Pediatrics, 66,_ 191–197.

McAnarney, E. R., Roghmann, K. J., Adams, B. N., Tatelbaum, R. C., Kash, C., Coulter, M., Plume, M., and Charney, E. (1978). Obstetric, neonatal and psychosocial outcome of pregnant adolescents. _Pediatrics, 61,_ 199–205.

Matarazzo, J. D., and Saslow, G. (1960). Psychological and related characteristics of smokers and nonsmokers. _Psychological Bulletin, 57,_ 493–513.

Miller, F., Court, S., Walton, W., and Knox, E. (1960). _Growing up in Newcastle Upon Tyne._ London: Oxford University Press.

Miller, H., and Merritt, A. (1979). _A fetal growth in humans._ Chicago, IL: YearBook Publishers.

New York State Department of Social Services. (1973–1982). Annual Report of Child Protective Services in New York State. Albany.

Nunally, J. (1967). _Psychometric theory._ NY: McGraw-Hill.

Olds, D., Birmingham, M., and Henderson, C. (November, 1984). Final report: Prenatal/Early Infancy Project. A follow-up evaluation at the third year of life. Final report to the Robert Wood Johnson Foundation (grant no. 6729).

Olds, D., Henderson, C., Birmingham, M., Chamberlin, R., and Tatelbaum, R. (November 1983). Final report to Maternal and Child Health and Crippled Children's Services Research Grants Program, Bureau of Community Health Services, HSA, PHS, DHHS, grant no. MCJ-36040307.

Olds, D., Henderson, C., Tatelbaum, R., and Chamberlin, R. (1986a). Improving the delivery of prenatal care and outcomes of pregnancy: A randomized trial of nurse home visitation. _Pediatrics, 77,_ 16–28.

Olds, D., Henderson, C., Chamberlin, R., and Tatelbaum, R. (1986b). Prevention of child abuse and neglect: A randomized trial of nurse home visitation. _Pediatrics, 78,_ 65–78.

Osofsky, H. J., Osofsky, J., Kendall, N., and Rajan, R. (1973). Adolescents as mothers: An inter-disciplinary approach to a complex problem. _Journal of Youth and Adolescence, 2,_ 233–249.

Pascoe, J. M. (1985). Child maltreatment and smoking during pregnancy. _American Journal of Public Health, 75,_ 1452.

Peoples, M. D., and Siegel, E. (1983). Measuring the impact of programs for mothers and infants on prenatal care and low birth weight: The value of refined analyses. _Medical Care, 21,_ 586–608.

Provence, S., and Naylor, A. (1983). _Working with disadvantaged families: Scientific and practice issues._ New Haven, CT: Yale University Press.

Ricciuti, H. (1981). Early intervention studies: Problems of linking research and policy objectives. In M. J. Begab, H. Garber, and H. C.

Haywood (Eds.), *Psychosocial influences in retarded performance: Volume 2, Strategies for improving competence.* Baltimore, MD: University Park Press, 293–302.

Rush, D., Stein, Z., Christakis, G., and Susser, M. (1974). The Prenatal Project: The first 20 months of operation. In M. Winick (Ed.), *Nutrition and fetal development.* NY: Wiley.

Rush, D., Stein, Z., and Insoln, M. (1980). A randomized controlled trial of prenatal supplementation in New York City. *Pediatrics, 65,* 683–697.

Schneider, N. G., and Houston, S. P. (1970). Smoking and anxiety. *Psychological Reports, 26,* 941–942.

Seigel, E., Bauman, K., Schaefer, E., Saunders, M., and Ingram, D. (1980). Hospital and home support during infancy: Impact on maternal attachment, child abuse and neglect, and health care utilization. *Pediatrics, 66,* 183–190.

Sexton, M. S., and Hebel, J. R. (1984). A clinical trial of change in maternal smoking and its effects on birthweight. *Journal of the American Medical Association, 251,* 911–915.

Travers, J., and Light, R. (Eds.). (1982). *Learning from experience: Evaluating early childhood demonstration programs.* Washington, D.C.: National Academy Press, 1982.

Tukey, J. (1977). Some thoughts on clinical trials, especially problems of multiplicity. *Science, 19,* 679–684.

van Doorninck, W. J., Dawson, P., Butterfield, P. M., and Alexander, H. I. (March 1980). Parent–infant support through lay health visitors. Final report to Maternal and Child Health Service, Bureau of Community Health Services, PHS, National Institute of Health, Department of Health, Education and Welfare, grant no. MC-R-080390-03-0.

Weber, C. U., Foster, P. W., and Weikart, D. P. (1978). *An economic analysis of the Ypsilanti Perry Preschool Project.* Monographs of the High/Scope Educational Research Foundation, No. 5.

White, S., Day, M. C., Freeman, P. K., Hantman, S. A., and Messenger, K. P. (1972). *Federal programs for young children. Volume II: Review of evaluation data for federally sponsored projects for children.* Washington, D.C.: National Technical Information Service, U.S. Department of Commerce.

chapter 11

TOWARD AN UNDERSTANDING OF THE PROGRAM VARIABLE IN COMPREHENSIVE PARENT SUPPORT PROGRAMS

Douglas R. Powell

In 1978 my colleagues and I undertook a study of a comprehensive educational support program for parents in a low-income neighborhood. The study differed from most investigations of parent programs in at least three major ways. First, it focused on program *processes*, not on parent and child outcomes. The intent was to investigate participant experiences rather than to assess program effectiveness. Second, the goal was to illuminate the existing *patterns of participation*, with a particular interest in differences across individuals. Thus, our study differed from most process studies in that we were not "checking" to see whether the program was being implemented according to plan, with an eye toward remediation or elimination of nonstandardized elements. Third, the study placed participants within their *socioecological* context by examining parent characteristics as predictors of program participation. We aimed to uncover baseline predictors of different modes of program involvement over time.

This chapter is a case presentation of how one research project approached the conceptual and methodological problems of measuring the nature and predictors of participation in a long-term program for parents. To set the study in the context of current evaluation practices I will begin with a discussion of program process and the treatment variable. I will then provide a brief description of the program and discuss selected major findings. Finally, I will note implications for future process research.

PROGRAM PROCESS AND THE TREATMENT VARIABLE

In evaluations of comprehensive education and support programs for parents the program or treatment is typically viewed as a single static variable, either present or absent. Conventional comparisons of treatment groups with control groups generally ignore differences in the quantity or quality of participation. In practice, a nonuniform treatment is dispersed across program participants in a nonrandom manner. It is impossible to standardize the treatment in a program responsive to diverse participant needs. In a home-based program, for instance, a worker is likely to introduce ideas and resources most relevant to the interests and needs of the family (Lambie, Bond, and Weikart, 1974). Even in a group-based program, parents may have remarkably diverse experiences. For example, some parents may form significant ties with fellow participants while other parents may relate more consistently to staff (Powell, 1985). These participation processes are the essence of program life, yet rarely come under the scrutiny of evaluation researchers. In neglecting to gather such information, evaluators lose opportunities to explain program effects precisely, and program designers lose opportunities to improve services.

Concern about the degradation of the treatment variable in program evaluation studies has been expressed in the literature for some time (Sigel, 1975). Boruch and Gomez (1977) have suggested that treatment labels may be meaningless or misleading. Extensive disregard for the complexity of early childhood education programs has led Zimiles (1977) to argue that the primary method of evaluating early childhood programs should be to describe program components and operations and hypothesize their effects.

Some evaluation studies have acknowledged variability in program experiences. Lambie *et al.* (1974), for instance, reported that mothers involved in a home-based parent intervention study varied considerably in their relationship with program staff and in their perception of the program curriculum's relevance, yet these differences were not explored in the quasi-experimental design used to compare all program participants with control and comparison groups. Several analyses have approached the question of differential program effects from a program (not participant) perspective. Within-program (Kessen, Fein, Clarke-Stewart, and Starr, 1975) and across-program (Goodson and Hess, 1976) comparisons have uncovered no relationship between curriculum content and program outcome. There is a need for detailed investigations of the ways in which parents are involved in family-centered programs and the correlates of participation over time (Wandersman, 1983). Research on parents' experiences in intervention programs may contribute to an understanding of how programs work or fail to work (Travers and Light, 1982). A desire to do so motivated our own study.

THE CHILD AND FAMILY NEIGHBORHOOD PROGRAM

The intervention program that we studied—the Child and Family Neighborhood Program—was established in 1978 in a white, suburban Detroit neighborhood identified by local school officials as having a large number of children with low academic achievement and socially isolated low-income families. Early intervention with families was seen as a means to improve school performance. Mothers were eligible if they lived in the neighborhood and had an infant 6 months old or younger. The program goal was to enhance the young children's development; the focus was on conditions of parenthood and parent–child relations. Specifically, we sought to strengthen mothers' informal and formal support systems and to increase their knowledge of how children develop, with particular attention to parent–child relations. Theoretically, the program reflected a socioecological perspective, linking quality of child rearing to the mothers' interactions with their immediate social environment (Bronfenbrenner, 1979).

At the core of the program were long-term discussion groups of 5 to 10 mothers who met twice weekly for 2 hours. Mothers were encouraged (but not required) to continue with the program until the "target" child was 3 years old (and hence eligible for Head Start or a similar program). Paraprofessionals trained in child development and group processes led the meetings.

There was no structured curriculum; topics were selected on the basis of stated or perceived parent interests. Periodic structured observations of group meetings indicated that discussion focused on four major areas: parenting (e.g., child development, feelings about parenthood, parent–child relations); home and family (e.g., marital relations, extended family, money, neighborhood, crime, community services, cooking); self (e.g., medical care, birth control, nutrition); and group (e.g., routine business, member relationships, evaluation of group activities). During the first 12 months, the average amount of time devoted to the four major topic areas was 35, 20, 24, and 24%, respectively. Over time discussion of parenting topics decreased significantly, while discussions of topics related to family, community, and homemaking increased (Eisenstadt and Powell, 1985).

Staff members were strongly committed to the belief that the program should "belong" to the members. In practice, however, observational data indicated that dialogue between staff and parents, with the staff person asking questions, dominated formal discussions. This pattern occurred about 46% of the time during the year, with little change across time. Other patterns, for the first year, were: staff monologue (22%); give and take primarily among group members (16%); group members asking questions of the staff member (10%); and no group focus (e.g., multiple conversations) (6%) (see Eisenstadt and Powell, 1985).

Children accompanied mothers to the program. About two-thirds of the mothers had preschool children who used a preschool staffed by program workers. The preschool used a traditional nursery school curriculum and was directed by a specialist with a graduate degree in early childhood education. The head teachers had specialized training in child development or early childhood education. While the preschool operated only during parent group meeting times, it did not function as a custodial care drop-off center for children. Its aim was to provide an enriching environment for young children, adhering loosely to the Bank Street model (Biber, 1977). No formal attempt was made to coordinate the preschool with the parent groups substantively, however, because the mother–infant pair (not mother–preschooler) was the primary client in the program. Infants remained with their mothers during the meetings for about the first 6 months. Subsequently the infants spent about one-half of the formal meeting time in the care of community paraprofessionals in a nearby room enabling group discussions to proceed without the distractions of increasingly mobile infants.

In addition to the group meetings, several special events (e.g., picnics) were held for the entire family. Optional weekly evening sessions usually addressed personal development topics (e.g., dieting) and were typically organized and led by mothers. Along with periodic family gatherings, they provided an opportunity for participants to meet participants from other groups. The family gatherings also offered fathers a direct yet subtle way to "check out" the program and its people. The evening sessions were a response to the mothers' interest in "having some place to go to at night that didn't involve money."

In addition to the paraprofessional group facilitators, the staff included a part-time social worker, a part-time public health nurse, and a specialist in child development who could be consulted about child rearing, health, or social service needs. They sought to provide limited direct assistance for serious problems and to help participants connect with the appropriate community agency or service provider. They also encouraged participants to share concerns and problems. Staff members did not provide therapy.

The program first operated in a community center and later at a former HUD house renovated for the purpose. Program participation was voluntary and free. Mothers were recruited through contacts made from hospital records, responses to printed announcements, referrals by lay persons familiar with the program, door-to-door canvassing by program staff, and referrals from public health programs, schools, and other agencies. Transportation was provided to and from program activities. The program enrolled an average of 40 new families each year. Generally, incoming mothers would form a new group; occasionally a new mother would join an existing group. The program was initially funded by the W.K. Kellogg Foundation. The Merrill–Palmer Institute (and later Wayne State University) operated the program in cooperation with the Wayne-Westland Community Schools in suburban Detroit. In 1981, when the Kellogg grant terminated, administrative responsibility for the program was assumed by the YWCA of Western Wayne County. The program continues today under the direction of a staff member who joined the project in its first days as a parent group leader. The main source of funding is a federal community development grant administered by the city of Westland.

Data Collection Methods

The aim of the study was to examine differences in program participation within the same program over a 24-month period and to identify baseline predictors of participation processes. Data were collected at baseline and every 6 months. As discussed in this section, several levels of participation were measured. Predictor variables focused largely on contextual factors, including environmental stress, social network ties, and number of children. Also examined as a predictor variable was a dispositional tendency regarding impulse control. Sources of data included systematic observations of group discussions; structured home interviews with mothers; observations of mother–child interaction; and staff records.

Measures

The most difficult measurement decisions involved identifying participation variables. The need to do this before the program began gave the task a speculative character; we did not know whether the phenomenon to be measured actually would occur. Since a major goal of most parent support programs is to facilitate supportive interactions and relationships among participants (Weissbourd, 1983), we expected an important dimension to be the quality of interpersonal ties with program peers. We anticipated that self-disclosure might play an important role in the development of these ties (Duck, 1981) and that relations with staff might be a major factor in participation (Hasenfeld and English, 1974). Data were collected in four areas: attendance (at regular groups meetings, special events, and the optional evening sessions), verbal behavior in group meetings, use of staff services, and interpersonal ties with program peers.

Verbal behavior in the regular group discussions was observed by evaluation workers familiar to the mothers. A total of 101 2-hour meetings were observed over a 3-year period. The observer worked with a record sheet covering the 2-hour period. Each 15 seconds during the formal part of the meeting the observer noted who was speaking and coded the comment according to a system modified from the Bales (1950) system. One of the most useful observation codes, developed by project staff, was labeled "narrative behavior," to refer to an individual's reporting of experience (not opinion). This behavior could be quite appropriate in a discussion group where a major goal is social comparison surrounding the parenthood experience. A running record of topics discussed also was kept. As noted earlier, we viewed verbal behavior in the discussion group to be a salient aspect of program involvement. We also wondered whether verbal behavior might be a mechanism through which other types of participation (e.g., relations with program peers) was established and, if so, what specific kind of verbal behavior might be involved. We were attracted to Bales' system of interaction process analysis because of its underlying theoretical ideas. We envisioned the parent groups as broad-based problem-solving groups that would continually face the two sets of issues inherent in the Bales system: instrumental or task-oriented concerns, and expressive or social–emotional concerns. Our interest was less in phases of group development, however, and more in the individual or personal level of analysis.

Participants' relations with staff focused on one-to-one interactions surrounding specific concerns or problems (e.g., contact with the program nurse about child illness). Records were kept of interactions with mothers outside of the normal program time (e.g., home visits, telephone calls). We found the telephone call records to be the most reliable measure of use of staff services. For most of our analyses, we included service calls where the mother was asking for service or receiving help and calls made on behalf of the mother to other persons or agencies in the community, but excluded all calls regarding logistics (e.g., transportation to program site). A score was computed to show the average number of calls per week for each participant for each time period.

The fourth area of participation, mothers' relations with each other, was measured in two ways. First, during interviews with the mothers (at 6-month intervals) we administered a questionnaire on which the mother indicated how well she thought each person in the group knew her, which showed how close she felt to others with whom she acknowledged some connection. Second, information from the self-disclosure questionnaire and from interview data was used to classify other members of the group as friends, acquaintances, or unrelated. To increase the reliability of such self-report measures, we required multiple-perspective agreement; both parties had to indicate in separate interviews that they were friends, for example, in order for the relationship to be classified as a friendship. Data came from questions asked in interviews with mothers about contact with participants outside of group meetings: Did she see any other members? How often did they share meals? Did they share rides? Did they talk on the telephone?, etc. Also during the interview, the respondent was asked to list all of her friends, in or out of the program.

We devoted considerable attention to social networks and life stress, because little research has been done in this area (see Krauss, Chapter 7; Cleary, Chapter 8, this volume). For example, mothers with high stress might be less able to participate in the program due to logistical problems, whereas those with minimal network ties outside of the program might perceive participation as highly advantageous. We also examined the relation between number of children and program involvement.

Traditionally, most parents have received significant assistance with child rearing from social network members (Sollie and Miller, 1980; Sussman, 1970). A frequent argument for the existence of family support programs is that such informal assistance has decreased considerably in recent years, and hence parents are in need of supportive programs (Weissbound, 1983). Yet, there has been little research on the relation between informal social network support and participation in a parent program. Is a low level of informal support, for instance, associated with a high use of program services? Many studies of networks and the utilization of formal services have measured structural properties of social networks such as density (Freidson, 1960, 1961; McKinlay, 1973). We used an alternative approach, examining the actual functions of social networks that are likely to be found in an intervention program (e.g., socialization, instrumental aid), especially in regard to stressful events and everyday needs. Whether a program is a substitute for or a supplement to an existing social network may be better understood by examining specific network functions than by developing inferences on the basis of the network's structure.

To measure social network support, we collected detailed information in baseline interviews about contact with friends and relatives. Each mother was asked to list her friends and to report how often she saw each person, how often they talked on the telephone, and where the person lived. The same information was obtained about relatives.

We developed an inventory of everyday coping to obtain information about instrumental help given or received during the previous 12-month period in relation to needs for food, clothing, housing, medical care, pet care, car care, and laundry. Four social network measures were derived in this manner: reciprocity (level of help given and/or received); supportive contact with relatives; supportive contact with unrelated peers; and parent support.

Environmental stress factors (e.g., inadequate income, unemployment) have been suggested as major reasons for low attendance levels and ineffectiveness of many parent education programs for low-income populations (Chilman, 1973). Yet, little research has been done to support these suggestions. A family's transactions with the community surrounding the management of stress has received limited consideration in research and theoretical work (McCubbin, 1979). The family stress literature has tended to emphasize adaptation to stress as an intrafamily process. We measured stress using the Holmes and Rahe (1967) life-event inventory and the Ilfeld (1976) current social stressors scale. With the latter scale, we found items pertaining to the financial and marital stress subscales to be the most useful.

First-time parents are commonly thought to be in the greatest need of parent programs. Yet at least one study has found that parents of one child were more likely to drop out (Lambie *et al.*, 1974). Therefore, we assessed the relation between number of children and longevity and type of program participation.

Our original research plan did not include consideration of dispositional tendency, since our interest was in contextual factors as predictors of program participation. As we came to know the participants informally, however, personal characteristics appeared to play an important role in program involvement. Simultaneously, the research literature on parent groups and social support increasingly noted that personality factors may contribute to the kind and amount of participation in a discussion group (e.g., Gottlieb, 1981). An assessment of maternal child-rearing attitudes using the Maternal Attitude Scale (MAS) (Cohler, Weiss, and Grunebaum, 1970) included an assessment of individual's dispositional tendency toward expression or inhibition. This scale is a 233-item Likert-type instrument with items written to measure Sander's (1964) theory of the issues or tasks confronting the mother during the first 3 years of a child's life. A major theoretical premise of this instrument is that attitudes determine aspects of an individual's adjustment to the social environment (Cohler *et al.*, 1970). The measure has been used in studies of normal and emotionally disturbed mothers (Cohler *et al.*, 1970), mother–infant attachment (Egeland and Farber, 1984), and high-risk mothers (Brunnquell, Crichton, and Egeland, 1981). Items on the scale of impulse expression were taken from the MAS *a priori* scales for curiosity, sex play, and anger; they asked the mother to agree or disagree with statements indicating that the child should be allowed/encouraged to show curiosity and express anger. The value of alpha for the 12-item scale was 0.809.

In addition to the program participation and predictor variables discussed previously, we collected extensive data on mother–child interaction (see Howrigan, Chapter 4, this volume), including the home environment. We used Carew's (1980) TIES observation system, which required 2 hours of naturalistic observation time in the home every 6 months, the HOME scale (Caldwell and Bradley, 1984), and a maternal teaching style measure developed for our study.

Participants' Reactions to Data Collection

The data collection schedule was demanding of participants. The baseline interview required about 2 hours. Each of the follow-up data collection points (every subsequent sixth month) involved two separate sessions of at least 2 hours each. One of these follow-up sessions involved a detailed structured interview. The other session was used for observing mother–child interaction (by two observers). All sessions were held in the mother's home. In addition to these visits, group meetings were periodically observed.

When mothers were contacted about participation in the program, they were told of the evaluation component; it was made clear as a part of informed consent procedures that refusal to participate in the evaluation did not result in a denial of any program services. A vast majority of mothers were receptive to involvement in the data collection sessions. Most exhibited eagerness and excitement about the home visits, at least in the first to second year. Only one mother during the 3-year period of data collection refused to participate in the data collection home visits; her refusal took the form of passive resistance (i.e., agreeing to participate, but failing to be present or to open the door).

Most mothers appeared to appreciate the opportunity to talk with the interviewer about their parenting and child-rearing experiences. Numerous instances occurred of mothers reminding evaluators of an anticipated session (e.g., "My time for you to come to the house is getting close"). The data collection sessions may have been viewed as a way to reciprocate or "repay" the program for services received without financial charge. Not uncommonly mothers indicated that a home visit was "the least I can do for the program."

Evaluators were familiar to the mothers because of their presence at the program site, and their periodic observations of group discussions. A high level of staff continuity was also a factor; two of the three data collectors remained with the program through the 3 years. All of the evaluation workers were women similar in age to the mothers in the program. Participants were approached as informants, not experimental research subjects.

Throughout the project, the evaluators encountered a problem familiar from other field studies involving high-risk populations: a high rate of canceled interview and observation sessions. During a 21-month period, for instance, 38% of scheduled home visits were canceled by mothers on the day of the visit, usually because of illness, pressing personal matters, or family crises. This represented 121 visits or 330 staff hours (the observations required two staff persons). Cancellations came about through "no shows," a mother initiating a call to the program site, or a mother responding to a call confirming the appointment. These figures do not include visits canceled 24 hours or more before the visit; generally staff were able to fill these times with other visits. Massive energy was expended in efforts to schedule visits with some mothers. Those with sporadic attendance patterns and no telephone were the most difficult to schedule.

Toward the end of the data collection period some signs that the evaluation work was "wearing thin" appeared among mothers who had joined the program in its first year. Some expressed boredom and/or frustration with repeated interview items (now the fourth, fifth, or sixth time a similar item was being asked over a 2- or 3-year period). In isolated cases a few mothers indicated that they felt like "guinea pigs."

The expected termination of the initial grant prompted considerable change within the program, in terms of several staff departures, planning for reorganized services, a new organizational context, and a new location. "Anticipatory grief" at the prospect of separations proved to be difficult for some parents and staff. No doubt some of these unsettling experiences were translated into negative responses to the interviews. It is also possible that after the novelty of program participation wore off, some mothers found the time involved in the data collection work an irritating burden.

Relations between Evaluation and Program Staff

The evaluation workers enjoyed excellent relations with the program staff; no noticeable researcher–practitioner tension was present. In addition to strong interpersonal skills among project staff, at least four factors appeared to be operating. First and probably foremost, as a process study, we were not judging the program's effectiveness or determining its future. Moreover, the absence of a treatment-control group design eliminated difficult issues like random assignment and withholding of services.

Second, the intervention was designed and implemented with evaluation as an integral component. The development of the program was motivated by research interests as much as by the desire to experiment with a comprehensive neighborhood approach to early intervention in a low-income setting. Several months before program workers were employed, two evaluation staff members were on the scene, working on instrumentation. Thus, staff members joined an enterprise clearly committed to evaluation. Also, from the beginning, all staff members maintained records (e.g., of attendance and telephone calls) that contributed to the evaluation data. Third, program and evaluation staff members were not separated physically. The data collection staff had offices at the program site, attended weekly staff meetings with program workers, and initially served as substitute staff in the preschool classroom.

Fourth, the evaluation staff contributed substantially to the delivery of program services. For example, before the program began, one evaluator produced a detailed ethnographic description of the community, including particulars about social and educational services; this information proved highly valuable to program staff. The data collection coordinator also provided in-service training to the preschool teachers, and, at the request of program staff and parents, evaluators carried out special developmental assessments when child behavior and growth were in question.

During the data collection years, descriptive evaluation data were shared with program staff at their request. Detailed reports of telephone calls and attendance patterns were described quantitatively. Generally these reports were viewed by the staff as useful documentation. Unfortunately, analyses of the data on patterns and predictors of program participation were not complete until the program was operating at a dramatically reduced funding level. Thus a programmatic response to the information was not possible.

While our study was carved out in a context of cordial working relations, its findings were ultimately of limited use to program staff in their funding efforts. By design, the data permit no statements about program effectiveness. Although staff members might have preferred an outcome study, the program has been able to attract and sustain financial support without such an evaluation report.

DATA ANALYSES

We collected an extraordinary amount of data on a limited number of mother–child participants. A central problem of the data analyses was how to use a small number of cases to yield good information about a large number of variables. We relied heavily on correlations for data reduction. Composite measures were created where strongly correlated variables were related conceptually. Many variables were discarded because of skewed distributions or failure to show a significant relationship with other predictor or criterion variables.

For several of the major sets of analyses there was a sufficient number of cases to block the sample and compare groups. For instance, we used discriminant function analysis to compare characteristics of early terminators ($N = 21$) and long-term participants ($N = 34$) of the program. Analysis of variance was used to examine differences in patterns of program participation over time. For all other analyses, however, the number of cases was too small for sophisticated analysis techniques such as path analysis. There are data on 42 cases who remained in the program through the first year; some cases have incomplete data. Correlations were used to generate a picture of the relationships existing within our sample. These analyses, while detailed and carefully executed, are viewed as exploratory; the small sample size limits conclusions or generalizations.

Some of the predictor variables showed relationships in which the two extreme positions resembled each other and differed from a middle position. For instance, both mothers with no involvement and mothers with relatively high involvement in community activities prior to program enrollment participated in the current intervention in similar ways (e.g., they formed ties with peers); those with a medium level of community involvement functioned in the intervention in a different manner. Accordingly, we made a systematic search for nonlinear relationships between predictor variables and program participation. In cases where such relationships were found, statistical significance was assessed using analysis of variance; statements of association utilized eta, the correlation ratio, instead of Pearson product moment correlations. After completing the analysis of zero-order relationships among variables, we computed partial correlations for each predictor variable, with other predictor variables held constant. In most cases this analysis did not extend information beyond the zero-order correlation analysis. An effort was made to identify variables that modified relationships between other pairs of variables. Several were found; that is, when the sample was dichotomized on one of the modifying variables (e.g., stress), relationships were found in one part of the sample but not in the other.

Summary of Findings

Analyses have been carried out in the following areas: dynamics of group life over time (Eisenstadt and Powell, 1985), stability and change in patterns of program participation (Powell, 1985), predictors of length of program participation (Powell, 1984), and processes and predictors of program participation (Eisenstadt and Powell, 1987; Powell, 1983); analyses of mother–child interaction data are in progress. Only a cursory and selected review of findings is presented here; additional information is available in articles cited previously.

A typology of program participation was developed based on a mother's orientation to staff versus peers, amount of change in participation indexes over time, and overall level of involvement. For some mothers, a major program dimension appeared to be interaction with peers; the program may have been viewed as a voluntary association akin to a church or social club. For other mothers, a major program source was staff help with medical and everyday living needs; in these instances, the program appeared to function as a social service agency. Some patterns of participation remained relatively constant during the first 12 months, while others showed increases or decreases (e.g., a gradual increase in connections with peers). Further, some mothers seemed to move quickly to establish ties with peers or staff, whereas others took a considerably longer time to use program resources at a moderate or high level.

Verbal behavior was the primary means for establishing involvement in the discussion group. Attendance at group meetings and level of verbal participation were positively correlated. The relationship proceeded from verbal participation to subsequent attendance or appeared within a single time period. No significant correlations were found between early attendance and subsequent verbal participation. For example, level of verbal participation at Time 1 was correlated with attendance at group meetings at Time 1, 2, and 3, there were no significant relationships between attendance at Time 1 and verbal participation at Time 2 and 3. Verbal participation of a particular kind— narrative behavior—was the means to establishing interpersonal connections with peers in the program.

Mothers with acute stress used staff services most extensively and attended fewer group meetings. While this is not surprising, it is important to note that high-stress mothers exhibited a delayed integration into group life that followed by about 6 months the modal patterns of low-stress mothers. For them, early narrative behavior (Time 1) was related to subsequent formation of interpersonal ties with program peers (Time 2); for the high-stress mothers, narrative behavior at Time 2 was correlated with peer ties at Time 3.

Program participation related to family and friend networks in different ways. Support from parents and other relatives was associated with the development of ties with fellow group members. Early terminators of program participation received less instrumental help from parents than long-term participants. There is no support, then, for the notion that frequent contact with one's parents inhibits participation in a parent program; on the contrary, we found supportive kin ties provided a context for the development of meaningful interpersonal ties with program peers. Friendship networks seemed to function in a different manner, however. It appears that extracurricular program activities compensated for limited nonfamilial peer ties outside of the program. Mothers who had fewer supportive friendships outside of the program at the time of program entry were more likely to attend evening and extra sessions, typically dominated by peers. Reciprocal helping relationships with relatives and nonfamilial peers before program entry seemed to help mothers more rapidly establish relationships with staff or peers in the program. For instance, reciprocity was related to early narrative behavior in group discussions.

Mothers with only one child were more likely to terminate involvement in the program within 6 months of joining than mothers with two or more children. Mothers with two children were high in attendance at regular group meetings and special events; mothers with three or more children were intermediate; and those with only one child were low in attendance. However, mothers with three children received the most staff service through telephone calls, those with two children were intermediate, and mothers with one child made the fewest calls.

With regard to impulse control, the controlled subsample showed more sensitivity to preprogram predictors of participation (e.g., family ties, number of children) than the expressive subsample. Preexisting needs seemed to influence the program participation of the controlled subsample; unlike the expressive subsample, behavior in one aspect of the program did not generalize to behavior in other aspects of the program. Expressive persons talked most during the early period of program involvement and were more likely to engage in narrative behavior than controlled persons.

Our findings have several implications for the operation and design of early intervention programs aimed at low-income parents. First, they suggest that participants "take" from a program what they need, thus calling into question program policies and staff practices that prescribe a modal or ideal pattern of participation; perhaps program staff should not attempt to change individual differences in patterns of program participation. Second, the findings appear to support the usefulness of comprehensive programs for low-income populations. Our study suggests that ancillary services were major sources of assistance to many mothers. Third, the delayed integration of parents with relatively high stress into the parent groups seemed to disrupt group functioning (for further discussion, see Eisenstadt and Powell, 1987). In such cases it may be wise to postpone group involvement until stressful dimensions of the parent's life have been addressed on an individual basis. For high-stress mothers, one-to-one exchanges may be easier to tap and more relevant to a specific problem than the more diffuse resources of a discussion group.

REFLECTIONS AND IMPLICATIONS

Throughout the research project we struggled with the problem of having so many data on so few cases. We opted for depth instead of breadth, and thus limited our selection of statistical approaches; but had we chosen a larger sample, it would have been necessary to use less labor-intensive measures than we did. For example, the mother–child observational data we collected were too detailed and micro-analytic for a large-scale evaluation study. Detailed codes and long observation sessions are not always necessary to answer most questions related to a program evaluation study, however. A combination of rating scales and observations based on a small number of key variables would constitute a more efficient measurement strategy for large-scale studies. Similarly, the Bales interaction process analysis system requires observer reliabilities that would be expensive to achieve in a large-scale study. Moreover, in the present investigation, most of the Bales codes did not correlate with other aspects of program participation or with the predictor variables. The narrative behavior code, originated by one of our observers and added 1 year into our study, was the most useful in our analyses.

Investigators of parent support programs face a measurement dilemma: There are few good existing measures relevant to anticipated parent and program functioning, yet it is not wise to generate new measures while undertaking a full-fledged evaluation study; the adoption or adaptation of valid and reliable measures saves time and money, permits comparability of findings across studies, and provides greater assurance of a measure's ability to discriminate across individuals. For instance, good measures of social support are not readily found (see Cleary, Chapter 8, this volume); many existing measures confound social support and life stress (Rook and Dooley, 1985) and are based on imprecise definitions (Thoits, 1982). While the construction of new measures has been recommended when novel programs are tested on small and idiosyncratic populations (e.g., Boruch and Gomez, 1977), we developed measures only when necessary because of the lack of adequate time and resources to engage in measurement work. The result was a mixture of tailored and existing measures.

Evaluators planning to do work with low-income and/or high-risk samples should keep our high rate of "no show" appointments in mind when developing budgets, timelines, and plans for staff time. Data collection staff in our study had to remain flexible.

Our experience prompts a strong recommendation that pilot work be conducted before a full-fledged evaluation of program processes is launched. This permits the identification of variables that seem to be operating in a program and the development or refinement of sensitive measures. As noted earlier, we found ourselves identifying process variables and measures before the program was operational and then needing to make modifications when the study was in progress. Pilot work with an existing program would have avoided the loss of data and the need to modify our measures.

Our findings have direct implications for the design of evaluations of comprehensive parent programs. First, it may be useful to approach the treatment as a multidimensional variable rather than a unidimensional construct. In our study, there was no single pattern of participation. Second, there is a need for longitudinal measurement of the treatment; characterization of participation at one point may not be representative of another point. Third, a focus on the interpersonal structure of a program setting may be a productive way to conceptualize the treatment; in our study, important differences were found between peer and staff orientations. While attendance is one of the most visible and easily measured indexes of program participation, our work prompts us to question its use as a primary measure. A focus on the *substance* rather than the *form* of participant involvement may lead to better understanding.

With regard to parent characteristics, we recommend that future research consider both personal and contextual variables. The focus in recent decades on situational (Mischel, 1968) and socioecological (Bronfenbrenner, 1979) determinants of behavior has overshadowed the role of dispositional tendencies in influencing individual functioning. Yet our findings indicated that dispositional tendency was a significant predictor of behavior, apparently serving as a major element in an individual's ability to use social support in a formal program setting. As Belsky (1984) has suggested, personality shapes parent behavior indirectly by first influencing the broader context (e.g., the social network) in which the parent functions.

This study has left us with a healthy respect for individual differences in program participation, as well as a commitment to evaluation research paradigms that consider interactions between program participation and parent characteristics. Parents and programs do not function in a social vacuum. Studying interactions between these systems may not make for a clean approach to research, but in the long run, the necessary "noise" in the data may well yield the best understanding of life in family support programs.

ACKNOWLEDGMENTS

The intervention study and research reported in this chapter were supported by a grant from the W.K. Kellogg Foundation. I wish to recognize Donna Cahill, Julie Kusiak, and Diane McCallum for their contributions to the development of measures and collection of data; without their energies and excitement, the study would not have been completed. Jeanne Watson Eisenstadt played an important and major role with data analyses.

REFERENCES

Bales, R. F. (1950). *Interaction process analysis: A method for the study of small groups.* Cambridge, MA: Addison-Wesley.

Barker, R. G. (1968). *Ecological psychology: Concepts and methods for studying the environment of human behavior.* Stanford, CA: Stanford University Press.

Belsky, J. (1984). The determinants of parenting: A process model. *Child Development, 55,* 83–96.

Biber, W. (1977). A developmental–interaction approach: Bank Street College of Education. In M. C. Day and R. K. Parker (Eds.), *The preschool in action: Exploring early childhood programs* (pp. 423–460). Boston, MA: Allyn and Bacon.

Birkel, R. C., and Reppucci, N. D. (1983). Social networks, information-seeking, and the utilization of services. *American Journal of Community Psychology, 11,* 185–205.

Boruch, R. F., and Gomez, H. (1977). Sensitivity, bias and theory in impact evaluations. *Professional Psychology, 8,* 411–434.

Bronfenbrenner, U. (1979). *The ecology of human development: Experiments by nature and design.* Cambridge, MA: Harvard University Press.

Brunnquell, D., Crichton, L., and Egeland, B. (1981). Maternal personality and attitude in disturbances of child rearing. *American Journal of Orthopsychiatry, 51,* 680–691.

Caldwell, B. M., and Bradley, R. H. (1984). *Home Observation for the Measurement of the Environment.* Little Rock, AR: University of Arkansas, Center for Child Development and Education.

Carew, J. V. (1980). Experience and the development of intelligence in young children at home and in day care. *Monographs of the Society for Research in Child Development, 45*(Serial No. 187, Nos. 6–7).

Chilman, C. S. (1973). Programs for disadvantaged parents. In B. M. Caldwell and H. N. Ricciuti (Eds.), *Review of Child Development, Vol. 3* (pp. 403–465). Chicago, IL: University of Chicago Press.

Cohler, B., Weiss, J., and Grunebaum, H. (1970). Childcare attitudes and emotional disturbance among mothers of young children. *Genetic Psychology Monographs, 82,* 3–47.

Duck, S. W. (1981). *Personal relationships and personal constructs.* NY: John Wiley & Sons.

Egeland, B., and Farber, E. (1984). Infant–mother attachment: Factors related to its development and changes over time. *Child Development, 55,* 753–771.

Eisenstadt, J. W., and Powell, D. R. (1985). *Life in parent discussion groups: An observational study.* Paper presented at the biennial meeting of the Society for Research in Child Development, Toronto, Canada.

Eisenstadt, J. W., and Powell, D. R. (1987). Processes of participation in a mother–infant program as modified by stress and impulse control. *Journal of Applied Developmental Psychology, 8,* 17–37.

Freidson, E. (1960). Client control and medical practice. *American Journal of Sociology, 56,* 374–382.

Freidson, E. (1961). *Patient's views of medical practice.* NY: Russell Sage.

Goodson, B. D., and Hess, R. D. (1976). The effects of parent training programs on child performance and parent behavior. Unpublished manuscript, Stanford University School of Education.

Gottlieb, B. H. (1981). Preventive interventions involving social networks and social support. In B. H. Gottlieb (Ed.), *Social networks and social support* (pp. 201–232). Beverly Hills, CA: Sage.

Hasenfeld, Y., and English, R. (1974). *Human service organizations.* Ann Arbor, MI: University of Michigan Press.

Holmes, T. H., and Rahe, R. H. (1967). The social readjustment rating scale. *Journal of Psychosomatic Research, 11,* 213–218.

Ilfeld, F. (1976). Characteristics of current social stressors. *Psychological Reports, 39,* 1231–1247.

Kessen, W., Fein, G., Clarke-Stewart, A., and Starr, S. (1975). *Variations in home-based infant education: Language, play, and social development* (Final Rept., No. OCD-CB-98). New Haven, CT: Yale University.

Lambie, D. Z., Bond, J. T., and Weikart, D. P. (1974). *Home teaching of mothers and infants.* Ypsilanti, MI: High Scope Educational Research Foundation.

McCubbin, H. E. (1979). Integrating coping behavior in family stress theory. *Journal of Marriage and the Family, 41,* 237–244.

McKinlay, J. B. (1973). Social networks, lay consultation and help-seeking behavior. *Social Forces, 51,* 275–292.

Mischel, W. (1968). *Personality and measurement.* NY: Wiley.

Powell, D. R. (1983). Individual differences in participation in a parent–child support program. In I. Sigel and L. Laosa (Eds.), *Changing families* (pp. 203–224). NY: Plenum Press.

Powell, D. R. (1984). Social network and demographic predictors of length of participation in a parent education program. *Journal of Community Psychology, 12,* 13–20.

Powell, D. R. (1985). Stability and change in patterns of participation in a parent–child program. *Professional Psychology: Research and Practice, 16,* 172–180.

Rook, K., and Dooley, D. (1985). Applying social support research: Theoretical problems and future directions. *Journal of Social Issues, 41,* 5–28.

Sander, L. (1964). Adaptive relationships in early mother–child interaction. *Journal of the American Academy of Child Psychiatry, 2,* 141–166.

Sigel, I. E. (1975). The search for validity or the evaluator's nightmare. In R. A. Weinberg and S. G. Moore (Eds.), *Evaluation of educational programs for young children: The Minnesota Round Table on Early Childhood Education II.* Washington, D.C.: The Child Development Associate Consortium.

Sollie, D., and Miller, B. (1980). The transition to parenthood as a critical time for building family strengths. In N. Stinnet and P. Knaub (Eds.), *Family strengths: Positive models of family life* (pp. 149–169). Lincoln, NE: University of Nebraska Press.

Sussman, M. B. (1970). Adaptive, directive and integrative behavior of today's family. In N. W. Ackerman (Ed.), *Family process* (pp. 223–234). NY: Basic Books.

Thoits, P. A. (1982). Conceptual, methodological and theoretical problems in studying social support as a buffer against life stress. *Journal of Health and Social Behavior, 23,* 145–159.

Travers, J. R., and Light, R. J. (1982). *Learning from experience: Evaluating early childhood demonstration programs.* Washington, D.C.: National Academy Press.

Wandersman, L. (1983). New directions for studying the interaction between parent education and family characteristics. In D. Powell (Chair), *Variations in the effectiveness of parent–child support programs.* Symposium conducted at the biennial meeting of the Society for Research in Child Development, Detroit, Michigan.

Weissbourd, B. (1983). The family support movement: Greater than the sum of its parents. *Zero to Three, 4,* 8–10.

Zimiles, H. (1977). A radical and regressive solution to the problem of evaluation. In L. G. Katz (Ed.), *Current topics in early childhood education* (Vol. 1). Norwood, NJ: Ablex.

chapter 12

THE EVALUATION EXPERIENCE OF THE *AVANCE* PARENT–CHILD EDUCATION PROGRAM

Gloria G. Rodriguez
Carmen P. Cortez

Gloria G. Rodriguez
Carmen P. Cortez

THE *AVANCE* PROGRAM

History and Philosophy

The *Avance* Educational Programs for Parents and Children is a private, nonprofit, community-based organization serving Hispanic families in San Antonio, Texas. The program was first implemented in Dallas in 1972 by two graduate students of Urie Bronfenbrenner—Ann Willig and Bonnie Park—with funds from the Zale Foundation. In the fall of 1973, it was implemented in San Antonio, where it has been developed under my (Gloria Rodriguez's) directorship.

I became involved in the field of parent education/family support in a desperate attempt to find a solution to the academic problems faced by many Hispanic children. I first became aware of this, and other issues affecting low-income Hispanic families, when I attended Our Lady of the Lake University from 1967–1970 with the assistance of a federally subsidized program entitled Project Teacher Excellence. The purpose of this program was to train low-income students from various San Antonio barrios to become bilingual teachers with the understanding that they would return to the barrio to teach.

Upon graduating from college I became a bilingual teacher of first grade children who were considered to be so far behind the other children in their class that retention had already been determined. Ac-

cording to the principal, the children had been labeled by their teachers
as "retarded," "slow learners," and "uneducable." Initially, I felt
strongly that the problem was one of language. Eventually, I came to
realize that it was this and much more. It was evident that the children
were proficient in neither Spanish nor English. They lacked the necessary foundation to help them meet with academic success. Extensive
work with these children resulted in the promotion of all but five. But
while they did learn to read and write in both languages, it appeared
that they could never "catch up" to the level of the children who entered school more prepared. They would continue to be classified as
slow and the labeling would continue.

The establishment of *Avance* was in large part prompted by these
experiences with children's educational deficiencies and with parents
who traditionally had not perceived themselves as academic teachers.
The concept of parents as educators is central to the philosophy of
Avance, which provides support and education to parents to help them
to raise competent, independent, and productive members of society.
Through strengthening the family, *Avance* aims to prevent or alleviate
a wide range of problems including illiteracy, poor school performance,
a high drop-out rate, teenage pregnancy, child abuse and neglect,
mental health problems (poor self-esteem, isolation, depression), substance abuse, crime and violence, poverty, and government dependence.

While parent education goes a long way toward achieving these
goals, the *Avance* experience, including lessons learned through evaluation, testifies to the importance of intervention on multiple levels.
Avance initiates and supports community development and the academic and economic advancement of individuals; *Avance* also works
directly with children through the provision of on-site day-care for parents while attending class.

Services Provided

In 1984–1985 the agency offered the following programs: *(a)* two Parent–Child Education Programs serving a minimum of 120 parents and
150 children on a monthly basis; *(b)* an Educational Opportunities and
Economic Development Program serving 395 individuals; *(c)* the *Avance*
Homebound Child Abuse Project serving 27 families; *(d)* two Parent/
Teen Projects funded by the National Center on Child Abuse and Neglect and the National Office on Adolescent Pregnancy Prevention
through COSSMHO serving 100 families; and *(e)* classes in Exercise
and Arts and Crafts serving 141 individuals. The Parent–Child Education
Program will be described in the most detail, as that was the primary
component when the evaluation was initiated in 1980.

The Parent–Child Education Program familiarizes participants with the basic social, emotional, physical, and cognitive needs of young children in a practical and supportive manner. It also provides assistance, information, and support to parents for the purpose of alleviating problems and obstacles that may impede effective parenting. Parents form their own social support network that provides reinforcement for desirable behaviors. A 3-hour, center-based activity is attended by parents weekly for 9 months. Classes are held between 10:00 A.M. and 1:00 P.M., Tuesday through Friday with each class consisting of approximately 15 mothers and 45 children. The weekly classes include 30 bilingual lessons in child growth and development, toy-making classes emphasizing learning through play, and outside speakers representing other community resources.

Special holiday celebrations and field trips (e.g., picnics and trips to the public library) are planned for parents and children. These activities strengthen the parent–child relationship; the social support network improves their self-concept and teaches them how to enjoy life with their children. These activities also give the parents a sense of belonging and a desire to participate in and complete the program.

Transportation is provided to and from the center for clients residing within assigned census tracts, and child care for their preschool children is offered at the facility. Each parent volunteers at least 12 times to assist with day care, as part of the required child-care practicum. During the 9-month program, parents are visited in their homes twice a month for 30 minutes for observation and videotaping of parent–child play interactions. These tapes are discussed in the third hour of center activities. One-to-one counseling is also offered to parents.

The Educational Opportunities and Economic Development Program, available to parenting program graduates and others in the community, is designed to foster self-sufficiency among a low-income minority population. *Avance* promotes economic stability and personal growth by providing on-site classes for the General Equivalency Diploma (G.E.D.), and in English As A Second Language (ESL). College courses are first offered on-site; later, students are assisted in filling out financial aid forms for studies on campus and are assisted in job placement.

The Avance Homebound Parenting Education Program is a support program for abusive parents with young children. Its goals are to provide a support system for families confirmed as child abuse and neglect cases through an individual program in the home and to prevent the recurrence of abuse and neglect by developing more effective parenting practices and positive parental role attitudes. Services include: weekly visits, individualized parenting education classes in the home, social activities to break isolation, and a comprehensive program for meeting needs through service integration. The parents are mainstreamed to the center-based program when the family situation is stabilized.

The Avance Concerned Parents National Demonstration Project addresses youth-related problems, especially teenage pregnancy. The goal of the project is to help prevent or reduce the incidence of adolescent premarital sexual activity by organizing and informing parents of adolescents.

The Parent–Teen Shared Interactions Model brings together teenagers and their parents, rather than working with either group in isolation. Group discussions are structured to alleviate familial and social stresses commonly occurring during adolescence (dating, smoking, drinking, drugs, premarital sexual activity, etc.). Opportunities are provided to enhance social skills and to promote values clarification.

The Community Served

Avance serves predominantly low-income Hispanic families on the south and west sides of San Antonio, Texas. The primary participants are mothers and their children. Services are provided in three centers located in or adjacent to a federally funded housing project. Of the population, 93% is Mexican–American, the majority being third-generation immigrants from Mexico. A survey undertaken in 1980 as a part of the *Avance* evaluation indicated that 53.8% of the women were either separated, widowed, divorced, or single; 85% of the respondents reported having no occupation. The remaining 15% held unskilled or semiskilled positions. The average monthly income for the families surveyed was $473.00. Many parents were abused as children, lacked knowledge and skills in child growth and development, had few support systems, and experienced continuous economic and social pressures. There was a 77% high school drop-out rate among the parents. The program serves two-parent families, single parents, teenage parents, AFDC (Aid to Families with Dependent Children) recipients, high-risk and abused/neglected children. The age range of the participants is from 15 to 69; the average family has 6.1 members.

In order to qualify for the parenting program, families must have a child under 4 years of age and be a resident of the community; both parent and child must participate. Although no fees are charged, families must contribute volunteer hours in clerical, craft, fundraising, or child-care activities. Participants learn of the program by word-of-mouth and through a biannual door-to-door outreach campaign. *Avance* accepts referrals from other service providers, and case management for "Priority 1" child abuse cases is coordinated with the State Department of Human Services.

THE EVALUATION EXPERIENCE

The Need for Evaluation

During the first half of *Avance*'s 12-year history, the agency became well-established in the community as a provider of parenting education. "Evaluation" was performed informally and intuitively, with revisions and adaptations occurring on a regular basis according to the needs and responses of clients.

The impetus to seek out a formal program evaluation came from three sources. First, we understood that we could not insulate ourselves from the world of facts and figures. Although we had been successful in winning community support from parents, we sought the kind of professional credibility that would be required for continued public and private support. Second, we recognized that there were conditions in the community and family which presented a number of obstacles to effective parenting. If we were to expand our program to meet multiple needs we would need to expand our sources of support. The importance of our mission and its difficulty underscored the need for evaluation. Third, we sought to replicate the *Avance* parenting education model in a second site and evaluation was needed to justify funds for replication.

These three goals were interrelated. Replication would require additional funding, which would, in turn, require documenting the effectiveness of the program and the need for it in the community. Yet, ironically, successful replication is itself proof of the soundness of program design. Contributing to the urgency of replication and evaluation was the need to formalize the curriculum. This task required assessing current problems and practices in the community in the areas of parenting, early childhood development, and the quality of life. Such an assessment would help us to determine the highest priorities for prevention and/or intervention services.

Opportunity Knocks

Funding for expansion became available in 1979, and the parenting education model was successfully replicated in another San Antonio community. The process began with a Grants Program Announcement for "Community and Minority Group Action to Prevent Child Abuse and Neglect," issued by the National Center on Child Abuse and Neglect (N.C.C.A.N.). It appeared as though the demonstration and collaborative research project being called for in the announcement was customized for *Avance*; although *Avance* had been developed to prevent academic problems and the high drop-out rate, it could also be considered as addressing the prevention of child abuse and neglect. The N.C.C.A.N. project would accomplish several goals for the agency: it would *(a)* establish professional credibility with the research community; *(b)* substantiate the need for and validate the impact of services; and *(c)* facilitate our involvement with a specific issue negatively impacting children and families, heretofore not formally dealt with by the agency. Our project, known as "Project C.A.N. Prevent," was one of three funded for urban, minority populations and one of a total of nine national demonstration projects. As the funding agent the N.C.C.A.N. was outstanding in providing useful literature and technical support regarding the evaluation design.

The Design of the Study

Two major questions guided the study: *(a) Which sociocultural, economic, and contextual factors and conditions can predict physical child abuse?* and *(b) how can participation in a parenting education program (such as Avance) result in lowered severity of discipline among participating parents?* Project C.A.N. Prevent, then, was designed as an effort that would incorporate research, development, and evaluation processes, and that would contribute not only to increased theoretical understanding but also to the development of appropriate primary prevention strategies.

The project was conducted in three phases: the survey phase, the program development phase, and the program evaluation phase. During the survey phase, demographic data, as well as information on child rearing and associated practices, were collected, analyzed, and interpreted in order to identify salient sociocultural, economic, and contextual factors and conditions associated with child abuse. In addition, the survey phase would provide the agency with an accurate population profile to substantiate the need for services. Furthermore, the data would enable the agency to prioritize its services. During the program development phase, survey data were utilized to address questions of program design (e.g., to determine where emphasis should be placed) and to identify gaps in the curriculum. Heretofore all changes and revisions had been conducted according to observational and felt needs determined by the staff.

During the program evaluation phase, the program was implemented in parenting education class settings, and its effectiveness assessed via a controlled pre/post test design. Curriculum material generated during the program development phase was used with parents on a weekly basis at the two *Avance* sites. In addition to receiving the parenting education curriculum, parents also participated in a toy-making class and extracurricular activities that reinforced and supported the themes of the curriculum. It was hypothesized that parenting knowledge and skills would be significantly greater after participating in the *Avance* Parenting Education Program. It was assumed that altering the conditions that contribute to child abuse and neglect (e.g., increase in knowledge, change in attitudes and skills, strengthening of support systems, increase in bonding, hopefulness toward the future) would lead to behavior changes.

Two instruments were developed. The *Avance*–San Antonio Parenting Needs Assessment Survey (hereafter, Survey) was utilized to identify the factors and conditions that are effective in predicting physical child abuse and to identify factors in which the parenting program could effectively intervene. The second instrument, the *Avance*–San Antonio Parenting Education Project Pre/Post Test (hereafter, Pre/Post Test), was composed of a subset of items from the Survey and was based on the content of parenting classes. The Pre/Post Test was designed to gauge changes in knowledge, skills, and attitudes as a result of participation in parenting classes. We were concerned about the self-report nature of the data collection instrument, but we were not in a position to study behavior directly. Our concern was somewhat mitigated by the inclusion of several questions that could reveal conflicting answers.

Survey data were collected by means of individual interviews with each subject. Three bilingual interviewers conducted the survey after intensive training. Interviewing techniques and instrumentation were pilot tested; pilot data were not included in the analyses. A total of 105 subjects, 35 from each of the three target communities, completed the Survey administered during Phase I of the study. Because the three communities are relatively small, we decided at the outset to utilize interviewer saturation rather than a sampling technique. Interviewers knocked on every door in a particular area until 35 eligible respondents agreed to be interviewed. Eligibility was determined by the presence of a mother of Mexican descent in the home with one or more children under the age of 5 years. Survey data were analyzed using forward multiple regression techniques, with severity of discipline as the dependent variable.

Upon completion of the survey phase, the program development phase was initiated with the construction of a pre/post test instrument. Technical consultants advised that the instrument be limited to those items that pertained to factors thought to contribute to, or cause, severe punishment. A clear, definitive focus of the test was established. The first draft of the pre/post test was field-tested with 160 residents from both sites. The field testing of the pre/post test instrument yielded constructive criticisms as to the appropriateness, clarity, and usefulness of the items. Modifications were made accordingly.

The Pre/Post Test was administered to program participants and to control group subjects (who were paid a $10.00 stipend). Pre/post data were analyzed using analysis of covariance, testing for differences between the study and control group posttest scores after controlling for the effects of age, education, number of children, and the pretest score on each variable.

Implementation: Roles and Reactions

The Role of the Administrative Staff. The administrative staff assumed leadership roles and in many instances performed the tasks of the evaluation process. These tasks included: *(a)* writing the grant proposal; *(b)* determining the layout of the activities in scope and sequence; *(c)* selecting a statistical consultant; *(d)* establishing an advisory board; *(e)* writing and selecting items for the survey questionnaire and for the pre/post test of the curriculum; *(f)* participating in the review of the data, statistical analysis/interpretation; *(g)* determining the implications for programmatic activities; *(h)* implementing the practical applications of the findings; and *(i)* assuming the primary role in dissemination activities. Every aspect of the evaluation process was closely tied to the program's service components. Furthermore, the ability to disseminate and present the project findings has been facilitated by the intense role of the administrative staff.

The Role of External Evaluators. Although the administrative staff was intensely involved in the evaluation, the evaluation was not conducted without external evaluators for two reasons. First, the staff of *Avance*, like most nonprofit organizations, had relatively little time to devote to activities other than service delivery. Second, since one of the goals of the evaluation was to establish credibility, we welcomed the objectivity that would be attributed to external evaluators.

In selecting an external consultant to review our design and to play a central role in data analysis, we adopted two major criteria. First, we required a well-trained and experienced professional with the sophisticated research and evaluation skills required of the project. Second, and equally important, was the ability of the individual to patiently understand and relate to the needs and desires of our community-based, grass-roots organization. The professional coming from the purist researcher milieu would have to assimilate the needs of this project, staff, clients, and agency in a nondemeaning and nonpatronizing manner. The ability to translate and communicate the formal process of research and evaluation, in ways which could be understood, appreciated, and applied at the practical level, was thus a major criterion in the selection process.

We selected as our external statistical consultant, Alan Holden, who played the principal role in the analyses of the data. He wrote a report on the survey data and analyzed the data generated from the pre/post testing. Upon completion of the data analysis, he discussed findings with the administrative staff and with the advisory board. He also prepared a draft of the preliminary final report, which was reviewed and critiqued by the administrative staff and advisory board, and from which the final report was gleaned.

The final report, authored by a second research consultant, Maria Robledo, presented an analysis and interpretation of the pre/post testing for the *Avance* Parenting Education Curriculum, along with a summary of the needs assessment survey. Discussions and implications of these findings involved the administrative staff, special consultants, and the advisory board.

Reaction of the Staff. The design, evaluation measures, and implications of the study were thoroughly discussed with the staff, and the role of each staff member was clearly defined. Staff members were eager and supportive; they carried out their roles as prescribed for the treatment group and contributed valuable observations and recommendations. For example, staff gave input on the development of child-development activities as well as on the form and content of efficient data-collection instruments such as home-visitor checklists.

Reaction of the Participants. Participants were informed of the questions they were to answer and the purpose of the study. Signed statements of confidentiality were provided. During the course of data collection, those participants who were administered instruments displayed little emotion; there were no visible observations or reports of reactions, either positive or negative, to the questionnaire. During the pre/post testing, although genuinely interested in helping *Avance* and willing to cooperate and assist in whatever they could, the participants were unimpressed with the research aspects and more eager to proceed with the services and other activities.

Results

Demographic, socioeconomic, and assistance indicators were analyzed within and across groups in order to profile the Survey sample. The selection of profile indicators was grounded in previous research, which identifies specific variables or sets of variables as predictors or mediators of child abuse.

A summary of the data collected through the Survey is presented in Table 12.1. It was clear that few households were able to subsist independent of outside financial assistance. The economic dependence and stress in this population were very acute, coinciding with the eco-

TABLE 12.1. Summary of Demographic, Socioeconomic, and Assistance Charisteristics by Group

	Sample (N = 105)	Westside (N = 35)	Southside (N = 35)	Control (N = 35)
Age in years ($\bar{x}$)	31.7	29.6	31.0	33.9
Mexican-born (%)	24.0	22.9	43.3	17.1
Education in years ($\bar{x}$)	8.0	7.6	8.4	8.0
High school graduates (%)	20.0	18.8	21.2	20.1
Dropped out due to pregnancy/ marriage (%)	29.9	33.1	28.2	28.4
Currently married (%)	41.9	36.9	44.5	42.3
Unemployed (%)	93.3	98.2	85.6	96.1
Household size ($\bar{x}$)	6.1	6.9	5.7	5.6
Number of children ($\bar{x}$)	3.5	4.2	3.1	3.1
Monthly income ($\bar{x}$)	$473	468	479	474
Income from wage sources (%)	45.5	18.4	88.6	28.7
Receiving welfare income (%)	55.2	85.7	40.0	40.0
Receiving food stamp income (%)	69.2	97.1	40.0	68.6
Monthly per capita income ($\bar{x}$)	$77	$68	$84	$85
Renting/buying home (%)	15.2	8.6	32.4	5.7
In federal housing (%)	55.0	74.3	23.5	68.6
Living with parents (%)	14.4	14.6	14.4	14.2

nomic stressor/child abuse connection suggested in other studies. People living in poverty are more at-risk of having economic stressors or crises, such as not being able to make ends meet, not having a means to receive psychological assistance with family problems, or not having the skills to obtain employment. And even though child abuse crosses ethnic and social barriers, the majority of the child abuse cases reported are from people living in poverty. These individuals have a greater likelihood of being reported because of crowded conditions, the visibility at public clinics and other social institutions (as opposed to private doctors' offices), and the means to conceal problems (e.g., bigger homes and yards, mobility). The Survey also collected data on levels of parenting knowledge and skills as well as the degree of conservative/liberal attitudes (see Table 12.2).

A series of analyses was conducted in order to examine the factors and conditions potentially predictive of child abuse. The dependent variable in the analysis consisted of respondents' self-reported frequency of physical punishment of their children. Approximately 78% of our sample believed in physical punishment. When asked how severely they physically punished their children, the entire group scored 4.78 on a 10-point scale of severity. More than 15% of the group reported physically punishing their children "often" and "always" regardless of

TABLE 12.2. Respondent Knowledge and Skills, Attitudes, and Stress-Response Levels

	Mean score	Ideal score[a]	Deficient[b] (%)
1. Attitudes toward parenting	17.4	25.0	48
2. Attitudes toward sex roles	29.2	50.0	67
3. Attitudes toward discipline	8.8	10.0	86
4. Attitudes toward education	17.8	25.0	69
5. Self–concept	18.1	50.0	84
6. Knowledge of child cognitive needs	76.1	150.0	79
7. Knowledge of child social needs	34.6	50.0	54
8. Knowledge of mother–child bonding	60.4	100.0	63
9. Knowledge of child growth and development	1.7	7.0	99
10. Knowledge of parenting skills	12.4	25.0	74
11. Knowledge of emergency procedures	8.1	20.0	83
12. Knowledge of child health	2.2	5.0	61
13. Social service agency utilization	5.5	28.0	88
14. Isolation/(social network use)	230.3	250.0	91
15. Internal emotional stress response (depression, nervousness, keeping worries to self)	8.5	10.0	84
16. External emotional stress response (crying, screaming)	5.4	10.0	61
17. Internal physical (suicidal) stress response	3.2	10.0	23
18. External physical stress response (hitting out)	5.0	10.0	51
19. Substance use and abuse stress response (alcohol consumption or taking medication for worries)	3.9	10.0	31
20. Illness and disability stress response	7.0	10.0	82

[a]High knowledge and skill levels; liberal attitudes, "high" isolation, stress-response level.
[b]Deficiency = <70% of ideal (Items 1–13) or >30% of the ideal (Items 14–20).

the nature of behavior infraction. Factors associated with the severity of physical punishment were determined through the use of forward multiple regression analysis. Background characteristics traditionally indicative of child abuse, such as having been abused as a child, accounted for a large percentage of the variance. It appeared that knowledge, attitudes, and skills also contribute substantially to predicting severity of punishment. Knowledge of child needs in several areas (cognitive, social, bonding), liberal attitudes toward parenting and education, and parenting skills predicted milder, fewer punishments; these were generally associated with higher levels of social service agency utilization. Analysis of the pre- and posttest data demonstrated that participation in the *Avance* Parenting Program resulted in significant increases in knowledge and skills, more positive attitudes, and greater ability to negotiate social support in times of stress or crisis (see Table 12.3).

There was some concern that the women who participated in *Avance* were self-selected in the sense that they, as a group, may have been more motivated to succeed. Our statistical consultant chose to address this question through an analysis of the pretest scores of program graduates (the study group), program-participant drop-outs (heretofore ignored), and the control group. If self-selection existed as an indicator of success in the program, and if participants selected themselves in, rather than drop-outs selecting themselves out, a test for the homo-geneity of variance would demonstrate the pretest scores of program drop-outs to be much more similar to the control (nonparticipant) than to the experimental (participant–graduate) group. The results of a Scheffe analysis between the three groups indicated that two groups were different from the third. The data demonstrated that there were similarities between program drop-outs and controls, as contrasted with

TABLE 12.3. Results of Pre/Post Test Analysis of Parenting-Education Curriculum Variables

Dependent variables	Unadj. x̄ Study group	Unadj. x̄ Control group	Adj. x̄ Study group	Adj. x̄ Control group	P-value adjusted for covariate
Knowledge of cognitive needs	51.4	45.7	51.5	45.4	.00
Knowledge of emotional needs	34.4	28.7	34.6	28.9	.00
Knowledge of social needs	42.7	38.19	42.9	37.6	.01
Knowledge of child health care	8.1	5.4	8.0	5.4	.00
Knowledge of teaching	16.2	14.7	16.3	14.3	.01
Attitudes toward punishment	30.1	26.8	30.1	27.0	.00
Hopefulness	16.4	15.6	16.4	15.4	.01
Knowledge of child growth and development	7.1	5.0	7.0	5.0	.01
Knowledge of birth control	5.3	3.3	5.2	3.1	.01
Pregnancy and prenatal knowledge	7.7	6.3	7.7	5.4	.00
Knowledge of social service agencies	2.3	1.2	2.2	0.2	.04
Social support for problems	15.0	13.4	15.0	12.1	.03
Social support for child care	15.8	13.7	15.9	14.5	NS
Social support on special occasions	19.4	19.9	20.3	19.9	NS
Severity of punishment	2.1	2.7	2.1	2.8	.06

program participants, particularly in areas of attitudes and social support, but in a puzzling direction. Drop-outs and controls, for instance, reported a more lenient attitude toward punishment than participants ($p = .02$), as well as a more hopeful outlook toward the future ($p = .02$). Two interpretations of this were possible: first, that the drop-outs and control members *were* more lenient and more hopeful than participants at the outset, and participants were more needful of the program and hence more motivated to continue in it; second, that drop-outs and controls overstated their leniency and hopefulness at the outset in contrast to participants who were more motivated to be self-critical (and self-improving).

A similar pattern was observed with the support variables (i.e., who is turned to for help with problems, child care, and on special occasions); controls and drop-outs reported higher levels of social support than participants. Again, greater need may have supplied the motivation for individuals to continue in the program. A variation of this explanation was that participants may have been more critical of their support networks at pretest, even if these supports were not, in fact, inferior or less available; thus, their perceived lack of support (see Cleary, Chapter 8, this volume) may have been correlated with motivation in some way. In any case, the participants improved significantly in their reported levels of social supports after being in the parenting program.

Presentation of the Results

Our external statistical consultant followed a time-line to produce, present, and explain to the administrative staff the data being generated. The advisory board was called in at regular intervals and presented with "blocks of information" for reaction. During these all-day meetings there were discussions of the content and reliability of the information presented. Recommendations of the advisory board were acted upon by the administrative staff and the external consultant. In addition, throughout the duration of the project, all compilations of findings were submitted for review to the National Center on Child Abuse and Neglect and the National Committee on the Prevention of Child Abuse and Neglect. Upon completion of the project, the results of the study were presented to program staff during a staff meeting.

Style and clarity of presentation of findings have been a major challenge, particularly to a mixed audience. When technical jargon and statistics are presented, lay people are bored, yet less informal presentations can be interpreted by researchers as representing deficiencies in the presentation and/or the project. Two types of audiences have shown great interest in our study: service-providers, and researchers. The first group has been extremely interested in replicating the model in their own communities and/or learning more from the *Avance* experience so that they can provide more efficient and effective services similar to those in this model. They are interested in *Avance* sharing its insights regarding how the community responds and learns, the causes and contributors to problems in families, and the determinants of a successful program.

Reaction from the research audience has been interesting and varied. Many researchers have been impressed with the accomplishments of *Avance* and its evaluation project and have been eager to learn the details of the evaluation experience in order to create additional models to test and measure the effect of prevention programs or similar treatment forms. *Avance* is now accepted as a full-fledged professional organization providing services based on a sound theoretical framework and creating significant change.

Lessons, Consequences, and Recommendations

The fact that the effects of the program proved to be positive was interesting, but not surprising. Of most interest were the data indicating where the program was strongest and where we had unknowingly been placing more emphasis. The data also demonstrated the severity of deficiency levels in parenting, and the severity of economic stress in the population which was not previously documented and which the program is now confronting. Debilitating economic conditions were consuming any potential for improvement and well-being in these families.

An unanticipated by-product of the research process was the creation of new service components. The data substantiated the need for the newer program components described in the first section, in particular, for the educational and economic development program. Operational for 2 years, this program provides classes in basic literacy skills, English, vocational-skills training, and professional-career training. There are now, on the average, 30 women enrolled at the college level each semester. The data demonstrated an expressed need for service, and the agency was obligated to respond.

The pre/post test instrument has continued to be of use with the parenting-education classes. The evaluation experience has made the agency keenly aware of the need to document not only the short-range effects but also the lasting effects of its impact. Case histories of the *Avance* graduates and children now stand as a research and evaluation need of the agency. Some steps are now being taken to address this requirement, including the establishment of the program for *Avance* graduate parents and their preteenagers and adolescents. Follow-up information is being gathered from this pool of 50 families.

Another noteworthy result of our project is the increased respect paid to us by potential funding sources, which we attribute in part to our attempts to combine research with program development. The agency foresees being called to provide technical assistance and training as a result of the evaluation experience.

Looking back, the administrative staff has come to the conclusion that the evaluation experience provided the impetus that thrust the agency into national prominence among family-support programs. A dual leadership role combining service provision and research has been placed upon the agency. The evaluation experience has also made the agency cognizant of the roles of self-evaluation and critical self-analysis. The clear directions that formal research can provide to a service-delivery model are now much more real. Its contribution is now recognized and appreciated at the practical application level.

We recommend to family-support programs embarking on evaluation that they follow three simple steps. First, get the best possible evaluation expertise that is also thoroughly familiar with your area of service. Second, seek an evaluator with whom you can effectively communicate at an equal level of mutual respect. Third, remain actively involved and informed in every aspect of the evaluation process.

If we could begin the evaluation process again, the evaluation design and procedures previously followed would remain constant, except that we would make use of computers and word processors. These would have made certain activities such as the typing of the instruments much more efficient. Also, the amount of statistics generated through this project merited the use of a computer on the premises to generate information more quickly.

ACKNOWLEDGMENT

Some information in this chapter has been extracted from *The Project C.A.N. Prevent FINAL REPORT, Avance*–San Antonio, Inc., San Antonio, Texas, June 1983; *Final Report Collaborative Research of Community and Minority Group Action to Prevent Child Abuse and Neglect, Vol. II, Culture-Based Parent Education Programs,* N.C.P.C.A., March 1983; and *Avance Educational Programs for Parents and Children: A Historical Perspective of its Twelve-Year Evolvement; Avance*–San Antonio, San Antonio, Texas, April 1986 (ERIC document ED-264034).

chapter 13

PROVE TO ME THAT MELD MAKES
A DIFFERENCE

Ann Ellwood

THE MELD PROGRAM

MELD—The Minnesota Early Learning Design—began in 1973 as an inquiry into ways in which families might be strengthened. It has evolved over the past 14 years into a family-support program implemented in 83 locations, 19 states, and 3 foreign countries. The program has gained a reputation—nationally and internationally—for its curriculum, its structure, and its process. The program name has come to connote a "melding" of the program's two primary components: information and support. The manner in which these are provided and the goals toward which they are employed will be discussed in this section. Later sections report on the program's evaluation at various stages in its development.

MELD offers support and education to parents in a variety of situations: first-time parents, single parents, married parents, teenage parents (see Miller, Chapter 16, this volume), Hispanic parents, and hearing-impaired parents. The program aims to help parents establish support networks involving not only other parents, but also various community resources, and to provide them with timely, accurate, age-specific, and unbiased child-rearing information.

The program philosophy places support and learning in the context of mutual help. It is well represented by such statements as: "We can support each other," "we can learn from each other," "we can make informed decisions." The purpose of this mutual help is not to gain approval or positive judgment, nor to promote a single style of parenting; rather, it is to promote cooperation while supporting individuality and a diversity of parenting styles.

The structure of the program reflects its philosophy: Parents learn with and from each other in peer/self-help groups. The groups are facilitated by experienced parents who have received over 60 hours of training and supervision but who are perceived primarily as peers, not as "experts" or professionals. Groups last 2 years, usually beginning during the mother's pregnancy and lasting through the child's second year.

Group leaders are volunteers who are trained and supervised by a site coordinator, a part-time professional who receives training over a 1-year period. Each MELD site maintains an ongoing but autonomous relationship with MELD's central office, which provides technical assistance and new program materials. Local agencies provide administrative and financial support to MELD groups. The MELD curriculum addresses issues of child health, child development and guidance, parent development, and family management.

During our initial outreach to funders we were advised to create a program that could be replicated in the future at other sites. This long-term outlook, they assured us, would eliminate unnecessary duplication of efforts in program development and would stretch funding. The result of this advice was a program that incorporated both standardized components and individualized features, making MELD well suited for replication in sites with diverse populations.

ERAS OF EVALUATION

Because our commitment to program replication emerged in the early years of the program, we acknowledged that our processes of experimentation and development would have to occur simultaneously with our process of evaluation, as evaluation data would be required to raise funds for replication. Of course, those of us who were involved with the program on a daily basis were intuitively evaluating all the time. We experimented with changes in structure and curriculum and asked parents to respond to those changes. Parents were our acknowledged collaborators. Our partnership enhanced the program and was emotionally rewarding for both parties as well. While this collaborative and informal evaluation process was fruitful and rewarding, we were urged by our consultants to begin formal evaluation. "No facts, no funds" was a reality we could not ignore if we were to expand. Thus, we entered our first era of program.

Evaluation Phase I

Getting Started (1973–1975). We began with little familiarity with evaluation. Foundation documents stressed the need for it but offered no guidelines, for example, concerning what ought to be evaluated, by which method, or for what purpose.

As a first step, we asked a group of academic and program consultants to help us create a request for proposals, which we submitted to five evaluation firms. We then formed a search committee to interview evaluators from each firm. During these interviews a discrepancy of goals between program staff and evaluators began to surface: Our goal was to explore the variety of *processes* by which we could best implement our program. For example, we wanted to ask such questions as: Will men attend parent group meetings? Will we be able to attract volunteers to facilitate the meetings? Will volunteers be able to provide quality services to parents? Will parents stay in the program for 2 years? While committed to our basic approach and structure, we were eager to refine the MELD concept and to further our understanding of how to make it work better.

Our funders and evaluation consultants, on the other hand, were interested in parental behavior *outcomes.* They wanted to prove that MELD made a measurable difference in the lives of the participants. We certainly understood the logic of behavioral outcome studies but felt that we were not at the appropriate point in our development to initiate such a study. However, we agreed to a parent behavior outcome evaluation, due largely to pressure from funders and concurrence from the five contending evaluation firms. We selected a local, private firm, known for its ability to evaluate "difficult to measure" programs.

One of the first tasks assigned to us by our evaluators was to define our program objectives. Writing a statement of objectives, even for a well-established organization, is a time-consuming and difficult task. In an organization such as ours, it required the participation of all staff and board members, as we recognized that each of these individuals could contribute valid ideas about current and future directions. In the early 1970s the task was particularly difficult: We were a new organization, guided more by a good idea and a dream than by quantifiable outcomes. We succeeded, however, in drafting a statement that not only served the purposes of our early evaluation effort, but also represented the kind of early groundwork and planning that yields long-term results both in the quality of a program and in the loyalty of the staff to its stated goals.

The Evaluation Design. With our program objectives defined, the evaluators proceeded to design a comprehensive study with measurable outcomes. Our consultants obtained opinions from experts in the field of child development regarding optimal behaviors, and we worked together to develop measurable objectives for the easier-to-measure aspects of parenting—safety, nutrition, health, language development, motor development. We hoped to collect data in all the major curriculum areas utilizing pre- and posttests, questionnaires, and a carefully designed baby book in which parents could record outcomes such as birth weights, immunizations, and developmental milestones.

The study design looked good on paper, but it seemed somewhat off-the-mark and required program activities that we were not willing or able to provide. For example, it was predicated on program stability and a uniformity of "treatment." Our evaluators were frustrated in this regard because we were in our early developmental phase and valued the flexibility that our program offered to participants with changing and diverse needs. While the program curriculum was well defined, individual parent groups were free to set their own agendas; at any one meeting, the component of the curriculum of most concern to the participants received the most attention. We were unwilling to impose uniformity in this respect. We were also unwilling to establish a control group, as that would require denying services to those who had requested them. To make matters worse for the evaluators, the composition of the parent groups changed during the 2-year period, as parents and facilitators came and went. Thus, in many ways, we were not able to stabilize our program components without jeopardizing the strengths and uniqueness of our program offerings.

Staff commitment to the evaluation process declined over time. Despite the fact that our volunteer facilitators were trained in the purpose and implementation of the evaluation design and had pledged their commitment to completing forms and executing evaluation responsibilities, they did not perform their evaluation duties. Their goal was to win the trust and confidence of the parents in their group. Our need to evaluate, to interrupt the group process with questionnaires and tests, was seen as an intrusion. We caused our evaluators further frustration because we were not willing to "demand" or "order" volunteer facilitators to complete evaluation forms.

While the intrusiveness of the evaluation process constituted one factor in the decline of commitment, perhaps a basic factor was that, over time, questions of interest to the staff became more clearly divergent from those of interest to the evaluators. The staff became increasingly interested in the process of positive parenting and in questions such as: How much support is available to new parents; what is the role of the father in the care of the child?; how can parents balance work with parenting responsibilities?; how much affection between parent and child is appropriate?

After 1 year of trying to modify our program to meet the needs of the evaluation design, we decided to abandon the design and its rigorous, time-consuming measures. In its place, we conducted extensive 2-hour interviews with each couple in the program, using the original evaluation design as our guide. For instance, the formal evaluation design required parents to log (on a weekly basis) their child's developmental achievements. We abandoned this and instead hired a consultant to administer developmental tests to a sample of MELD children at the end of the 2-year program. Although our approach was not as scientific as our evaluators would have liked, we felt we obtained the information we needed to carry the program forward.

Conclusions of Evaluation Phase I. From our attendance records, application forms, parent interviews, and developmental testing we learned that:

1. 81% of the families were present at each parent group meeting.
2. 100% of the mothers received prenatal care.
3. 42% of the participants were male.
4. 88% of the mothers did not smoke during pregnancy.
5. 72% of the mothers both breast- and bottle-fed their babies.
6. 100% of the children received well-baby checkups.
7. 89% of the children had updated immunizations.
8. 65% of the parents had not spanked their children by 2 years of age.
9. 97% of the children were free from accidents that required emergency room treatment during the first 2 years of life.
10. A sample (48%) of the children received the Bayley Scales of Infant Development. On the Motor Index, 62% of the children were ahead of other children of the same age. On the Mental Development Index, 81% of the children were ahead of other children the same age.

We concluded from these data that, indeed, the program was working. Both men and women were attending the meetings on a regular basis. And, from what we could observe, parents were providing for children's physical, emotional, and cognitive needs. However, at the conclusion of this first experience of evaluation, which included both the formal study and our own modified version of that study, we felt that we had learned more about the process of evaluation and its limitations than we had about the effectiveness of our program. Specifically, we had learned two lessons about evaluation.

The first was that it is extremely difficult to conduct a valid outcome evaluation of a program in its phase of self-definition and development (see Jacobs, Chapter 2, this volume). That genre of evaluation seems to require stability. Yet we were in a "catch-22" situation, as our development of a model program required funding, which in turn required evaluation.

The second lesson that we learned was that the current state-of-the-art in evaluation and family research seemed inadequate to the task of measuring the kinds of positive parenting behaviors that are of primary importance to programs like ours. The research offered data on behaviors that were easy to measure (e.g., birth weight and immunizations) but not on the more interpersonal parenting characteristics promoted by parent education and support programs. The research that was available on parenting was markedly negative in focus, addressing questions, for example, of why and how children were abused or why children had poor self-esteem, but saying little about positive parenting.

Evaluation Phase II: 1978–1981

After our "pilot" phase was completed, we expanded the program significantly in the Twin Cities, in other sites in Minnesota, and in Albuquerque, New Mexico. Our evaluation design during this second phase consisted of two parts: internal research and evaluation and external evaluation.

Internal Research and Evaluation (1978–1979). In order to explore questions of interest to the MELD staff and to lay the groundwork for an evaluation addressing these questions, we began a research project to identify positive parenting behaviors. We summarized our findings in a document entitled "The Positive Parenting Behaviors," which included 10 measurable behaviors with secondary objectives. When we circulated this document to experts in different areas, we discovered that they were hesitant to endorse it without supporting research studies, which, of course, did not exist at the time. Thus we abandoned our search for accurate positive parenting indicators and continued our efforts to collect the more common, gross indicators.

Since agreement on positive parenting behaviors proved so difficult to achieve, we conducted a literature search to identify *national norms* for parenting accepted by such groups as the American Academy of Pediatrics or the National Institutes of Health. We found that established norms were available, but only regarding birth weight, weight gain during pregnancy, immunizations, postpartum depression, and car and home safety. These were easy-to-measure behaviors but not behaviors of great interest to us. In fact they were quite distant from the kinds of positive parenting behaviors that our program sought to promote.

In an attempt to capture what we learned from the parent interviews we conducted during Phase I and from our Positive Parenting Behaviors and National Norms studies, we developed an extensive parenting questionnaire to address such areas as the child's physical, emotional, and cognitive development, parent roles and responsibilities, the couple's relationship, and the individual parent's level of satisfaction with his/her family life. We distributed the questionnaire to program participants at the end of their 2 years with the program.

External Evaluation. Although we were confident that the questionnaire would provide information needed to improve the program, we knew that funders and evaluators would question the credibility of our results because the questionnaire was neither designed nor executed within the parameters of a formal research design. We set out, once again, to find evaluators who could provide us with measurable, reliable data without interfering with our program operation.

The criteria we used in selecting an evaluator for the second phase were as follows:

1. *Experience* with other similar evaluation projects: We needed assurance that they could respond to new program ideas with innovative, appropriate evaluation measures, and sought this assurance from their other clients.
2. *Credibility* in the field of program evaluation: We assessed credibility through discussions with other evaluators.
3. A personal *work style* compatible with ours: The MELD philosophy influences the way we work together and the way we interact with consultants. We looked for evaluators who were good listeners, creative thinkers, and warm, personable human beings.
4. A feeling that we could *trust* the evaluator to present our successes and shortcomings in a professional way: The "trust" factor is an important one. The idea of someone always "looking over your shoulder" to see *what* you are doing and *why* you are doing it is not an easy one to accommodate. We needed assurance that our evaluators would be as committed to positive parenting as we were and would want us to succeed.
5. *Respect* for our program needs during the course of the evaluation: We sought to minimize conflicts between the evaluators' need to gather data and our need to modify the program as we saw fit to meet the needs of the participants.

Our research resulted in the selection of an evaluation team that would observe four MELD groups in the Twin Cities over a 2-year period and carefully document the observable impact of the program on its participants.

During our second phase of evaluation we shifted our objective from assessing behavioral outcomes to assessing the actual delivery of services. Put simply, we wanted to know whether we were, in fact, delivering to our participants what we saw ourselves as providing: support and education.

Conclusion of Evaluation Phase II. From our parent questionnaires we learned that:

1. 87% of the mothers did not smoke during pregnancy.
2. 50% of the fathers took paternity leave (or time off from work).
3. 83% of the mothers breast-fed their babies during the first 2 months of life.
4. 97% of the families owned and used car seats that met government safety standards.
5. 62% of the fathers said that the most important part of being a father was giving love and affection to their children.

In addition, our evaluation team provided us with results on the following dimensions:

• *Knowledge and information.* Comparing pre- and posttest scores, knowledge increased significantly in 24 of 36 areas of parenting and childrearing. Since no control group was surveyed, it cannot be concluded that these gains are solely due to the MELD program. However, when asked to indicate how much each of 10 resources (e.g., parents, other relatives, friends, pediatrician, books) contributed new knowledge about parenting over the previous 2-year period, participants ranked the MELD group meetings as the resource most responsible for gains in knowledge and information.

• *Support.* Participants rated MELD meetings as the second most important source of emotional support for parenting and child-rearing concerns; only "spouse" received a higher rating.

• *Qualities of group meetings.* MELD meetings were rated on six dimensions: content, style of presentation, suitability of material, facilitator enthusiasm, quality of discussion, and group enthusiasm. On a 4-point index of excellence, the average rating across all six dimensions was 3.5.

• *Group interaction and communication.* MELD meetings provided considerable amounts of information and support. Facilitators accounted for about 40% of the communication and parents about 60%. Fathers were active in giving both information and support.

Evaluation Phase III: 1981–1984

After engaging in program evaluation for 8 years, primarily with outside evaluators, we decided in 1981 to develop our own evaluation procedures utilizing the data sources and forms we found most useful during our previous evaluations of parenting behaviors and delivery of services, specifically, the application and attendance forms and the parent questionnaires. We compiled an easy-to-use evaluation manual and committed significant resources toward training for evaluation site coordinators. Their training covered *(a)* the design and purpose of the evaluation; *(b)* their responsibilities and facilitator and parent responsibilities regarding its implementation; and *(c)* procedures for administering and collecting evaluation forms. Site coordinators were responsible for collecting evaluation data from their site and sending it to MELD Central for analysis. We assumed MELD's new evaluation design would be widely used and result in the broadening of our data base. But while the site coordinators' enthusiasm for the evaluation was high initially, it began to fade within 6 months of their training. As a result we have collected very little data.

This experience has lent perspective to the issue of whether evaluations are best conducted internally or externally. Our previous experience with external evaluation suggested that discrepancies of goals and styles between program staff and evaluators were largely to blame for the decline in staff support. What became clear during our internal evaluation was that there are also benefits to having external evaluators. One benefit is increased credibility not only in the eyes of funding agencies, but also in the eyes of participants who felt a part of something "special" during the external evaluation. A second is that outside evaluators have chosen, professionally, to design and implement program evaluations. Program staff—whether site coordinators or volunteer facilitators—are more "people-oriented" than "paper-oriented." Moreover, paid staff tend to be overworked. In their time not spent with parents, they are eager to work in community relations and fund-raising, and it is often difficult to impose tasks upon volunteers, particularly in a nonauthoritarian organization like ours.

The attitude of many staff, facilitators, and site coordinators is that true program evaluation occurs during direct service; they observe problems and develop solutions as they occur. They often feel that evaluation results generated from questionnaires or tests only confirm what program staff already know and are therefore of interest primarily to funders and skeptics.

During this period, MELD participated in the Ford Foundation's Child Survival/Fair Start Initiative through a grant to the Child Welfare League of America (CWLA) (see Miller, Chapter 16, this volume). Specifically, we developed and implemented a new prenatal curriculum in five new sites for a new population—younger teen mothers. This experience reinforced our belief in the importance of allowing new programs to have a period of orientation and development before subjecting them to the additional demands of evaluation. We believe that such a period would have been beneficial not only to the procedural flow of the programs, but also to the evaluation process and its results.

Current Evaluation Efforts: 1985–present

Our most formal evaluation effort to date, the New Parents Project, is being conducted by the Department of Child Development and Family Studies at Purdue University. This study will follow a large sample of MELD families from the beginning of their involvement until 1 year after the "official" end of their MELD group (some groups continue to meet on an informal or purely social basis after the prescribed 2-year program). The study will investigate four main areas: the resources used by parents for child development and parenting information and support; stress and coping related to the parenthood role; relations with spouse, child, relatives, and friends; and feelings about one's self.

This evaluation is unlike our past efforts in three ways. First, it moves beyond examining whether MELD "makes a difference"—although this remains a critical emphasis—to a general exploration of the experiences and needs of first-time parents. This broader scope seems to help keep the interest and commitment of parents and staff at a high level. A second difference is the use of a comparison group consisting of families who are similar in background to MELD families but who are not part of a MELD group. Finally, the Project Coordinator of the New Parents Project is housed with MELD staff. This close proximity ensures a greater degree of communication between evaluation and MELD staff, which leads to a better understanding of each other's work and goals.

LESSONS AND SOLUTIONS

Our experiences have taught us that program evaluation is important. It helps establish a program's credibility, not only with funders, but also with staff and participants. It also serves to collect valuable data that balances facts against impressions, enabling program staff to keep in touch with the changing needs of parents.

We have experienced the strengths and weaknesses of both formal and informal evaluation and will continue to use both in a complementary fashion. The strength of our informal approach lies in its flexibility and its responsiveness to changing interests, circumstances, and opportunities. It involves collecting data during site visits, through phone calls, and from the written reports from site coordinators and participants. This type of evaluation effort is designed and carried out internally and benefits staff and participants in an ongoing and immediate manner.

Formal evaluation is essential to establishing credibility. Since it involves large-scale data collection, it is best carried out by outside consultants. This allows program staff more time for their work of choice: providing services to parents and evaluating "on-line" to improve those services. Thus, our solution to at least some of the problems discussed here is to "meld" the two approaches to maximize the benefit of their strengths while minimizing the costs of their weaknesses.

We have also begun to adopt a technical solution to facilitate the burdensome task of data collection and analysis. We hope to improve our ability to handle large amounts of data (e.g., attendance figures and numbers of parents in the program) by using the new, paperless technology. This will free us to devote more time to service provision.

Our experiences have taught us one lesson that, as already mentioned, is not easily translated into a solution: Program development and outcome evaluation do not mix. If possible, programs should wait until their goals and methods are well defined and established before initiating an outcome evaluation.

We now know that scientific evidence preserves and enhances our day-to-day program experiences. We know that a good program is insufficient unless it produces the evaluation data to show that it is a good program. And yet the final answer still eludes us. Will MELD's approach to parent support and education be effective in the long run? Will MELD babies of the 1980s be confident and competent adults and parents in the twenty-first century?

chapter 14

TOWARD EXPERIMENTAL EVALUATION OF THE FAMILY, INFANT AND PRESCHOOL PROGRAM[1]

Carl J. Dunst
Carol M. Trivette

This chapter describes an evaluation program being carried out at the Family, Infant and Preschool Program (FIPP) located in Morganton, North Carolina. FIPP is an outreach program of Western Carolina Center, a regional facility serving handicapped persons and their families. Since 1972, the program has provided early intervention services to over 1250 families of mentally retarded, handicapped, and developmentally at-risk children. It has four major components corresponding to the four missions of the program: comprehensive services, special projects, research and evaluation, and technical assistance and training. Our four interrelated program missions include:

1. The ongoing provision and mediation of support services to families of mentally retarded, handicapped, and developmentally at-risk children;
2. The development and dissemination of model-demonstration services designed to provide or mediate specific types of support;
3. The conduct of research and evaluation studies designed to identify intervention and nonintervention factors affecting parent, family, and child functioning.

[1]The work reported in this chapter was supported, in part, by grants from the National Institute of Mental Health (MH38862) and the North Carolina Department of Human Resources, Division of Mental Health, Mental Retardation, and Substance Abuse, Research Section (#83527). The authors extend their thanks and appreciation to the following individuals who have contributed to the work reported in this chapter: Johnna Clontz, Pat Condrey, Wayne deLoriea, Nancy Gordon, Pam Lowman, Debbie Smith, and Jean Young.

315

4. The provision of training opportunities related to both direct service and model-demonstration activities, and evaluation of the
   impact of support services.

The appendix provides descriptions of the types of activities conducted
within each of the four components.

We begin with a discussion of FIPP's conceptual framework and the
ways that framework has influenced the methodology used to evaluate
FIPP. We then describe the results of a number of studies demonstrating
the influences of social support on parent, family, and child functioning.
In the final section we discuss some of the conceptual, methodological,
and practical lessons learned along the way and suggest some implications for early intervention theory and practice.

New Conceptual Underpinnings for Research and Practice in Early Intervention

Early intervention programs have generally been child-focused and
implemented without reference to theory (Dunst, 1986a). The result
has been a failure to understand how events both within and outside
the family unit are related, and how they influence child, parent, and
family functioning. Our approach to early intervention is family- and
systems-oriented. It draws from several social systems and ecological
theories (described in the following section) and attempts to provide
and mediate the types of support services necessary to promote child,
parent, and family development. To test and continually improve our
approach to early intervention, we have integrated research and evaluation with direct service in an ongoing experimental evaluation model.
A basic premise of our program is that the goals, objectives, and methods of intervention should be derived from empirical evidence. Rather
than addressing the broad question "Does early intervention work?,"
we focus on identifying "intervention" variables that can be operationalized at the programmatic level.

An Integrated Social Systems Framework

Because we recognize the importance of the family in successful
early intervention, we looked to social systems theories to guide our
program design and evaluation. We adopted a model and approach to
early intervention (Dunst, 1985) that is rooted in the German–European
tradition of conceiving persons as whole, integrated organisms whose
behavior is affected by, and has meaning within, various ecological and
social contexts (Lewin, 1931, 1936; Reese and Overton, 1970). FIPP in-

tegrates and synthesizes theoretical formulations and empirical evidence from a number of social systems models, including social network theory (e.g., Bott, 1971; Cohen and Syme, 1985; Mitchell and Trickett, 1980; Mueller, 1980; Unger and Powell, 1980), human ecology (Bronfenbrenner, 1979; Cochran and Brassard, 1979), help-seeking theory (Gourash, 1978), and adaptational theory (Crnic, Friedrich, and Greenberg, 1983a).

Social network theory (a) describes social units and their linkages and *(b)* postulates how providing support by network members promotes individual, family, and community well-being. *Human ecology* involves the study of the interactions and accommodations between a developing person and his/her animate and inanimate environment, and how events in different ecological settings affect the person's behavior. *Help-seeking theory* examines the conditions that affect decisions to seek help and the sources from which help is sought. *Adaptational theory* explains how ecological influences affect reactions to the birth and rearing of an atypically developing child, and how different ecological forces, including social support, influence a family's ability to cope with and adapt to their child's handicap. To the extent that the complex relationships between the multitude of variables affecting family reactions can be statistically disentangled, the types of support that promote positive adaptations should be discernable. This information could in turn suggest ways of mobilizing social support networks to help families cope with a handicapped child (Trivette and Dunst, 1986c).

Collectively, these four theoretical orientations emphasize the importance of informal support from spouses, relatives, friends, parents, etc., for buffering negative reactions and promoting positive functioning around the birth and rearing of a handicapped youngster. The concept of social support is central to each of these four models and to the design and evaluation of FIPP. Each focuses on questions about how support from members of different social units affects the behavior of the person receiving support. Social support includes the "emotional, psychological, physical, informational, instrumental, and material assistance provided to others to either maintain well-being or promote adaptations to different life events" (Dunst & Trivette, 1985, p. 3).

The social support construct includes five components (Dunst and Trivette, in press [a]; Hall and Wellman, 1985; House and Kahn, 1985). These are relational, structural, functional, and constitutional support and support satisfaction. *Relational support* refers to the existence and quantity of social relationships, including such things as marital and work status, number of persons in one's social network, and membership in social organizations such as a religious institution. *Structural support* refers to the characteristics of social networks, including network density, stability and durability of relationships, intensity of feelings toward network members, and reciprocity of relationships. *Functional support* refers to the source, type, quantity, and quality of help and assistance. *Constitutional support* refers to an indicated need for help, the availability of specific types of support, and the type of support offered. *Support satisfaction* refers to the extent to which assistance and aid is viewed as helpful and useful.

Figure 14.1 shows the potential connections among the different components of the social support construct. This conceptualization is derived from our work and from that of Hall and Wellman (1985) and House and Kahn (1985). The existence of relational support is a necessary condition for, and hence a partial determinant of: *(a)* defining needs (constitutional); *(b)* the structural characteristics of one's social network; and *(c)* the types of assistance available from network members. Similarly, both constitutional needs and network structure may partially determine the types of support procured and offered. Finally, the types of support provided, especially the relationship between constitutional and functional support, will in part determine the degree to which one finds the assistance helpful.

Carrying out our research over extended periods of time afforded us an opportunity to assess the effects of different support components and dimensions and to develop a conceptual framework for defining the "social support domain." In retrospect, our initial attempts at measuring social support were rather crude and unsophisticated. Along the way, however, we discovered both the strengths and shortcomings of existing social support measures (Dunst and Trivette, 1985) and recognized the need to develop our own instruments and interview procedures if we were to fully capture the multidimensional nature of social support. For example, the notion of constitutional support evolved from the realization that no existing scales assessed the relationship between actual or perceived needs and availability of support to meet those needs.

A sizable body of evidence indicates that social support has positive influences on personal and familial health and well-being (e.g., Dean and Lin, 1977; McCubbin, Joy, Cauble, Comeau, Patterson, and Needle, 1980; Mitchell and Trickett, 1980; Cleary, Chapter 8, this volume). Recent work has demonstrated that the positive effects of social support go beyond mediation of intrapersonal and intrafamily physical and psychological health. A growing body of evidence shows that social support both directly and indirectly influences attitudes toward parenting (Crnic, Greenberg, Ragozin, Robinson, and Basham, 1983b); parental styles of interaction (Crnic *et al.*, 1983b; Crockenberg, 1981; Embry, 1980; Philliber and Graham, 1981; Weinraub and Wolf, 1983); parent attitudes, expectations, and aspirations for their children (Lazar and Darlington,

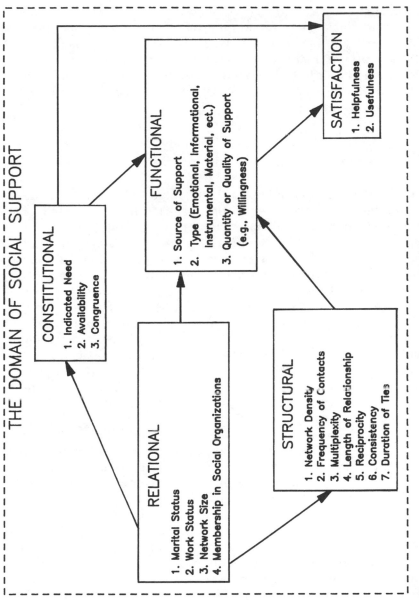

FIGURE 14.1. Conceptual framework for assessing the components of social support and the relationships among the five major components. (Modeled after House and Kahn [1985].)

1982); and child behavior and development (Crnic *et al.*, 1983b; Crnic, Greenberg, and Slough, 1986; Crockenberg, 1981). These findings had several implications for the design of FIPP's intervention and research program. First, the data strongly indicated that the behavior of a child and his/her siblings, parents, and other family members could be affected by provision of support; thus, support could be broadly conceived as a form of intervention. Second, the outcomes that support has been found to affect (well-being, attitudes, styles of interaction, etc.) tentatively suggested categories of behavior that could be taken as goals and outcomes of our intervention efforts.

A Social Systems Definition of Early Intervention

Our efforts to develop and test our integrated social systems model for both intervention and research purposes led us to a redefinition of early intervention. Traditional definitions have limited our understanding of how to effectively support and strengthen families of handicapped and at-risk children. They have also constrained the ways early intervention data have been collected and analyzed. For example, a traditional statistical analysis of an early intervention program considers the variance associated with a particular intervention a main effect due to the treatment. The remaining variance not accounted for is considered error variance (see Dunst, 1985, 1986a). Dunst (1985) found this assumption inaccurate. Multiple regression analyses examining relationships among different sources of support and child-, parent-, and family-level outcomes revealed that significant variance in the dependent variables was accounted for by sources of support beyond that attributable to early intervention.

Dunst (1985, 1986a) has proposed a broader based definition of early intervention as "the provision of support to families of infants and young children from members of informal and formal social support networks that impact both *directly* and *indirectly* upon parent, family, and child functioning." Stated differently, early intervention can be conceptualized as an aggregation of the many different types of help, assistance, services, etc. that individuals and groups provide to families with very young children. Involvement in a preschool special education program is one type of early intervention, but so is compassion from a friend, advice from a physician, respite care, counseling by a religious leader, and role-sharing between a husband and wife. FIPP considers early intervention to include all of these. This expanded definition has implications for direct-service activities as well as for research designed to assess the impact of different forms of support.

The Proactive Empowerment through Partnership (PEP) Approach to Early Intervention

FIPP's philosophy about families also distinguishes our program from more traditional ones. First, our program uses a *proactive* rather than a *deficit* approach in implementing interventions. A deficit model views behavior differences as indicative of deficiencies in the child, the parents, and/or their culture. In contrast, a proactive approach focuses on child and family *strengths*. That is, the things that children and families do well are used as a foundation for meeting family-identified needs. In addition, behavior differences are seen as variations in behavior resulting from ecological forces that affect the child and family. For example, the absence of certain interaction styles may be due not to poor parenting skills but to poor health or lack of social support (Dunst and Trivette, 1986b).

Second, FIPP differs from traditional programs in the locus of decision making. Traditional approaches often usurp the decision-making power of parents. In contrast, FIPP enables and *empowers* parents to make informed decisions and take control over their lives and the lives of their children by imparting information, skills, and knowledge to the families. One major focus of intervention, therefore, is promoting a sense of both intra- and interpersonal efficacy in families.

Third, in contrast to traditional approaches that are paternalistic in their treatment of children and their families, FIPP uses *partnerships* between individuals to achieve the goals the family selects. Partnerships avoid the client–professional dichotomy. Goals are based entirely on needs and are determined by assessment procedures conducted jointly by staff and families. Once goals are selected professionals and families work together to decide on an appropriate course of action.

The PEP approach to early intervention has one major implication for conducting and assessing the effects of *all* types of interventions. As Hobbs (1975) succinctly stated: "The goal is to strengthen normal socializing agents (the family, the school, the church, the neighborhood), *not to replace them*" (p. 114, italics added). Thus, early intervention efforts are considered successful to the extent that they help families mobilize their support networks.

BROAD-BASED PROGRAM EVALUATION

In addition to serving as a framework for conceptualizing early intervention practices, social systems theory has served as a theoretical base for designing evaluations of the impact of support provision and mediation. Over the past 6 years, we have been developing and implementing a research program designed to assess the impact of social support on families of mentally retarded, physically impaired, and at-risk children. (Detailed accounts of these efforts can be found in Deal, McWilliam, Cooper, and Trivette, 1986; Dunst, 1985, 1986a; Dunst and Trivette, 1984, 1985, 1986b, in press [a]; Dunst, Trivette, and Cross, 1986a, 1986b, in press; Dunst, Vance, and Cooper, 1986; Trivette and Dunst, 1986c, in press.) Here we briefly describe our methods.

Conceptual Framework

Our research focuses on the following: the description of changes in child, parent, and family functioning; the identification of factors associated with these changes; the study of these changes within and across ecological settings; and the translation of causal and mediational factors into interventions that optimize developmental change (Baltes, Reese, and Nesselroade, 1977). Because of increasing evidence that social support can buffer one from negative reactions to life events as well as promote positive functioning (Cohen and Syme, 1985), the major focus of our research is on the role of social support in promoting adaptations to the demands of rearing a child who is handicapped or developmentally at risk. Figure 14.2 depicts the direct and indirect influences of social support on parent well-being, family integrity, parent–child interactions, and child behavior and development. According to this model, support affects parent well-being and health; support and well-being affect family integrity; support, well-being, and family integrity affect styles of parent–child interactions; and support, well-being, family integrity, and interactive styles affect child behavior and development. Within this complex set of direct and indirect relationships, well-being, family integrity, and interactive styles can be both independent and dependent variables, depending on the juncture at which one assesses the influences of social support.

Other intra- and extrafamily characteristics are also examined as explanatory and moderating variables. Figure 14.3 shows an ecological map that (a) captures the complexities of factors affecting individual and family functioning and (b) unifies the various themes and notions central to the social systems models described before. Seven topologically nested settings and structures are specified, each embedded within the next highest level: (a) child; (b) family; (c) formal kinship network; (d) informal kinship network; (e) social organizations; (f) human service agencies and professionals; and (g) policymakers (exosystem). These particular groupings are derived from our research (Dunst, Jenkins, and Trivette, 1984) indicating that these different groups constitute discrete support sources. The bottom portion of Figure 14.3 shows the child, parent, and family characteristics; sources of support

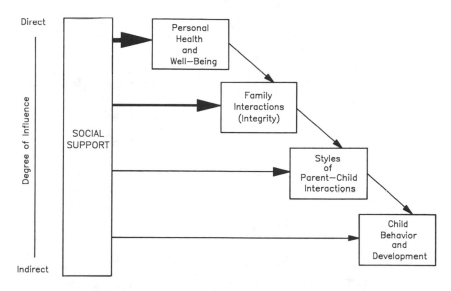

FIGURE 14.2. The hypothesized direct and indirect influences of social support on parent, family, parent–child, and child functioning.

(intrafamily, informal, and formal); and exosystem influences (Bronfenbrenner, 1979) that are likely to affect family development and functioning. The inverse relationship between help seeking from informal and formal sources of support is also depicted in this figure.

A Mediational Model of Social Support

Figure 14.4 shows the model we currently use to assess the effects of several major categories of variables on parent, family, and child functioning. The social support domain and relationships among the five components of support are as described previously (see Figure 14.1). Both parent and family characteristics (as shown in Figure 14.6) are considered partial determinants of support (Gore, 1985; Gottlieb, 1981; Heller, Amaral, and Procidano, 1978; Holohan and Wilcox, 1978; Mitchell and Trickett, 1980). Parent and family characteristics are seen as mutually dependent, although parental characteristics are seen as exerting a greater influence on family characteristics than vice versa (Duncan, Featherman, and Duncan, 1972; Sewell and Hauser, 1975). All three sets of variables (parent, family, and social support) are viewed

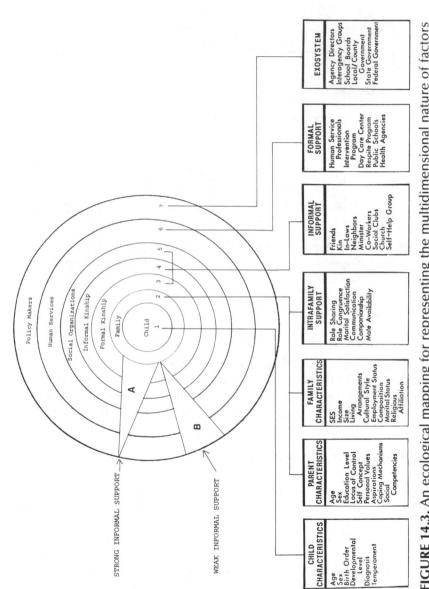

FIGURE 14.3. An ecological mapping for representing the multidimensional nature of factors influencing child, parent, and family functioning.

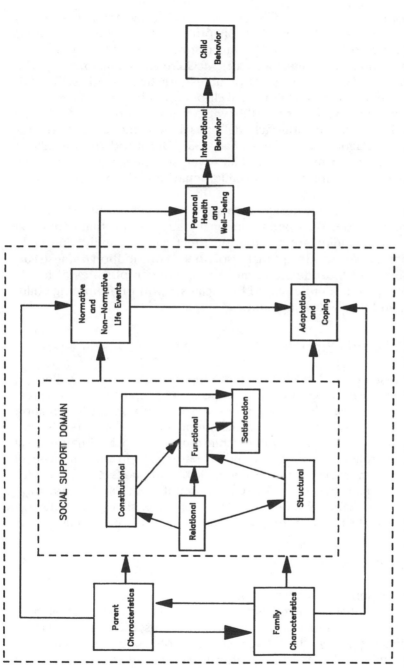

FIGURE 14.4. Conceptual framework for assessing the direct and indirect influences of parent and family characteristics, social support, and life events on personal well-being, interactional behaviors, and child behavior and development. (Modeled after Hall and Wellman [1985].)

as partial determinants of adaptation and coping mechanisms (Richman and Flaherty, 1985; Roskin, 1982; Shapiro, 1983; Tolsdorf, 1976) used in response to both normative and nonnormative life events (Mc-Cubbin, Cauble, and Patterson, 1982; McGuire and Gottlieb, 1979). The "combination" of all five sets of variables directly and indirectly influence parent and family health and well-being (Cohen and Syme, 1985). These five sets of variables together with well-being are seen as directly and indirectly affecting interactional behaviors (Crnic, Greenberg, Robinson, and Ragozin, 1984; Crnic *et al.*, 1986; Dunst and Trivette, 1986b; Philliber and Graham, 1981), and all seven sets of variables may have direct and indirect influences on child behavior and development (see Table 14.5).

Our research is not designed to support or refute the benefits of early intervention. We operate under the supposition that ecological influences, including social support, affect parent, family, and child functioning. We are attempting to isolate the contribution of these variables in order to understand more fully the complexities of family functioning and the role played by social support in promoting child, parent, and family development.

Data Collection Procedures

Our research and evaluation staff employ standard data collection procedures. Parents complete a number of self-report questionnaires, and they participate in home interviews so we can obtain information about various aspects of their social support networks. They also are videotaped interacting with their children in free-play situations. All families enrolled in FIPP are asked to participate in our family-level studies; the acceptance rate exceeds 90%. Data collection coincides with yearly FIPP transdisciplinary assessments that yield information about child behavior and development. Generally, all aspects of family-level data collection take no more than 1.5–2 hours per family.

Instrumentation Decisions

The independent variables in our research are grouped into five major sets: personal characteristics of the parents (education level, age, etc.), family characteristics (socioeconomic status, income), child characteristics (age, sex), child diagnosis (level of retardation, diagnostic group), and social support. The latter is measured in several ways: *(a)* the aggregation of different support components (see Figure 14.1); *(b)* separate sources of support (e.g., intrafamily, extrafamily, informal, formal [see Figure 14.3]); and *(c)* specific types of interventions (e.g., empowering of parents to operate their own preschool programs). Given methodological and logistical considerations (e.g., sample sizes), not every study examines each set of independent variables. However, we make every attempt to examine as many causal and mediational factors as possible across different studies in order to provide converging evidence regarding the cumulative and interactive effects of the different sets of independent variables.

The choices of which types and components of support to assess in the studies we have conducted thus far have been guided by the ecological map shown in Figure 14.3. We have systematically examined support from each of the six sources shown and have related types of support at each level to the same four categories of outcome measures (see later sections). As a result, we have developed a social support measurement "package" that assesses different components and types of support from each of the six different support sources.

Dependent variables are grouped into four major categories: parent (personal), family, parent–child, and child outcomes. Parent outcomes include physical and emotional well-being; coping; time demands children place on their parents; and attitudes, aspirations, and expectations for self and child. Family outcomes include family integrity and family adaptations. Parent–child outcomes include parental styles of interaction and shifts in the balance of power away from the adult toward the developing child during child–adult interactions (Bronfenbrenner, 1979). Child outcomes include behavioral and developmental gains, behavior engagement, perceptions of child behavior by the parents (e.g., temperament), and long-term placement outcomes (e.g., special education versus regular class placements, institutional avoidance).

Methods of Analysis

We use a number of strategies to analyze relationships between the various independent and dependent variables: (1) description of intraindividual changes and interindividual differences; (2) intergroup comparisons (e.g., mothers versus fathers); (3) multivariate analyses designed to establish systematic covariation among variables; and (4) causal modeling for estimating the effect sizes of the sets of variables temporally displayed in Figure 14.4. The latter has been accomplished using hierarchical multiple regression analyses by sets (Cohen and Cohen, 1983) to determine whether the different sets of independent variables *(IV)* account for significant variance in the dependent variables *(DV)*. In this type of analysis, the increments *(I)* in R^2 are determined sequentially where the sets of *IV*s are entered in a hierarchy dictated by our mediational model of support. A significant *I* indicates that a substantial amount of variance is accounted for in the *DV* by that *IV* set. To the extent that informal social support sets account for significant amounts of variance in the *DV* beyond what is attributable to parent and family characteristics sets, the unique effects of social support can be demonstrated. To the extent that informal social support accounts for a significant amount of shared variance with both child characteristics sets, we have established the "buffering role" of support. Selected findings are reported here to illustrate both our experimental approach to program evaluation and how our work contributes to theory building.

Social Support and Health and Well-Being

The roles that parent and family characteristics, social support, and coping abilities play in buffering negative reactions to both normative and nonnormative life events has been well documented (Cohen and Syme, 1985). We examined the plausibility of this "stress buffering" and "health promotion" model for explaining reactions to the rearing of a handicapped or retarded child with data gathered in a series of eight studies involving the parents of the children in our program.

The independent variables were parent characteristics (mother's and father's ages and education levels), family characteristics (SES and income), informal social support (two or more of the types of support shown in Figures 14.1 and 14.4), and child age and diagnosis (Developmental Quotients [DQ] and diagnostic group). Measures of social support included the Family Support Scale (Dunst *et al.* 1984), Family Resource Scale (Dunst and Leet, 1987), Maternal Social Support Index (Pascoe, Loda, Jeffries, and Earp, 1981), Parent Role Scale (Gallagher, Cross, and Scharfman, 1981), and Psychosocial Kinship Inventory (Pattison, DeFrancisco, Wood, Frazier, and Crowder, 1975). Each scale measures two or more components of support as shown in Figure 14.1. The dependent measures were several different scales of stress and well-being including the Questionnaire on Resources and Stress: Emotional and Physical Health Subscale (Holroyd, 1974, 1985), Psychological Well-Being Index (Bradburn and Caplovitz, 1965), and Personal Well-Being Index (Trivette and Dunst, 1986b). Hierarchical multiple regression analysis by sets was used to test the mediating influences of social support in response to the birth and rearing of a child with a poor developmental prognosis. Figure 14.4 shows the order the data were entered into the analyses.

The results are shown in Table 14.1. They are both clear cut and convincing. Social support was by far the most important mediating variable. In every instance, social support accounted for a significant amount of variance in the dependent measures. In addition, the more

TABLE 14.1. Multiple Regression Coefficients and Increments (I) in R^2 for Several Personal Well-Being Measures Used in Eight Investigations

Study	Sample size	Dependent measure	Type of support[a]	Parent characteristics (1) R^2	I	Family characteristics (2) R^2	I	Informal support (3) R^2	I	Child characteristics (4) R^2	I	Child diagnosis (5) R^2	I
Study 1	51	QRS Health	F,X	003	003	007	004	148	142**	149	001	161	012
Study 2	132	QRS Health	R,F,X	000	000	022	022	118	096**	159***	041*	162**	003
Study 3	106	WBI Well-Being	S,F,X	016	016	016	000	133**	117***	159***	026	167**	008
Study 4	40	PWI Well-Being	R,S,F	029	029	230**	201***	518***	288***	521***	003	—b	—
Study 4	40	QRS Health	R,S,F	019	019	072	053	289*	217*	331*	042	—	—
Study 5	65	QRS Health	R,F,X	109**	109**	137**	028	360***	223*	389***	029	399***	010
Study 5	65	PWI Well-Being	R,F,X	177***	177***	178**	001	385***	207***	402***	017	402***	000
Study 6	84	PWI Well-Being	R,S,F,X	045	045	067	022	281**	214**	286***	005	294***	008
Study 6	84	QRS Health	R,S,F,X	012	012	033	021	335***	302***	350***	015	351***	001
Study 7	35	QRS Health	R,S,F,X	000	000	091	091	467**	376**	505**	038	511*	006
Study 7	35	PWI Well-Being	R,S,F,X	028	028	051	023	650***	599***	664***	014	676***	012
Study 8	45	WBI Well-Being	R,S,C,F,X	013	013	013	000	317***	304***	332**	015	—	—

NOTES: The left-to-right progression of independent variables is the order in which they were entered into the regression analyses. QRS, Questionnaire on Resource and Stress Emotional and Physical Health Subscale; PWI, Psychological Well-Being Index, and WBI, Personal Well-Being Index. Decimal points have been omitted from the correlation coefficients.

*$p < .01$; **$p < .005$; ***$p < .001$.

[a]R = Relational, S = Structural, C = Constitutional, F = Functional, and X = Satisfaction (see Figure 14.1).

[b]Not measured in this particular study.

components of support that were measured, generally, the greater the variance accounted for. On the one hand, the findings demonstrate the importance of social support as a moderator of health and well-being. On the other hand, they show that support can "buffer" reactions to the rearing of a handicapped child. This questions the commonly held assumption that the more handicapped a child, the more stress the child will create for the parents. Our data simply do not support this contention. The fact that we have replicated the finding across eight studies, using different measures of support and well-being, makes our findings particularly robust.

Social Support and Parent, Family, and Child Functioning

The role that social support plays in affecting other aspects of parent, family, and child functioning was the focus of a recently completed study (Trivette and Dunst, 1986a). The subjects were 224 parents of preschool mentally retarded, physically impaired, and developmentally at-risk children. The parents completed a number of questionnaires, including the Family Support Scale (Dunst *et al.*, 1984), Questionnaire on Resources and Stress (Holroyd, 1974, 1985), Psychological Well-Being Index (Bradburn and Caplovitz, 1965), and Child Expectation Scale (Dunst and Trivette, 1986a).

The mediating influences of five categories of independent variables were examined: family characteristics (socioeconomic status and income), informal support, child characteristics (chronological age), child diagnosis (Developmental Quotient scores and diagnostic group), and formal support. The sum of the helpfulness ratings of the following Family Support Scale items was used as the measure of informal support: own parents, own relatives/kin, own friends, spouse/mate, spouse's parents, spouse's relatives/kin, spouse's friends, own children, co-workers, other parents, and a religious institution. The sum of the helpfulness ratings of the following Family Support Scale items was used as a measure of formal support: professional helpers, early intervention program, social agencies, child/family's physician, school/day care, social groups, clubs, and parent groups. Four categories of dependent measures were examined in relationship to the above five categories of independent variables: personal well-being (emotional and physical health, time demands, and well-being), family integrity, parent expectations, child behavior difficulty, child progress, and changes in developmental quotients.

Table 14.2 displays the results of the analyses. Taken together, the five independent variables produced multiple *R*s that were significantly related to the eight dependent measures. The results demonstrated

TABLE 14.2. Multiple Regression Coefficients and Increments (*I*) in R^2 for Seven Measures of Parent, Family, and Child Functioning

Dependent measures	Family characteristics (1)		Informal support (2)		Child characteristics (3)		Child diagnosis (4)		Formal support (5)	
	R^2	*I*	R^2	*I*	R^2	*I*	R^2	*I*	R^2	*I*
QRS Emotional and Physical Health	.020	.020	.095****	.075****	.095****	.000	.118****	.023	.118****	.000
PWI Personal Well-Being	.177****	.177**	.312****	.135****	.313****	.001	.341****	.028	.343****	.002
QRS Time Demands	.023	.023	.093****	.070****	.094****	.001	.162****	.068****	.163****	.001
QRS Family Integration	.041**	.014**	.083****	.042***	.083****	.000	.196****	.113****	.200****	.003
CES Parent Expectations	.001	.001	.020	.012	.096****	.076****	.414****	.318****	.417****	.003
QRS Child Behavior Difficulty	.025	.025	.093****	.068****	.094****	.001	.285****	.191****	.286****	.001
Child Progress Score[a]	.084****	.084****	.087****	.003	.097****	.010	.788****	.691****	.791****	.003
DQ Difference Score[b]	.003	.003	.006	.003	.050*	.044***	.241****	.191****	.270****	.029*

NOTES: The left-to-right progression of independent variables is the order in which they were entered into the regression analyses. QRS, Questionnaire on Resources and Stress; PWI, Psychological Well-Being Index; and CES, Child Expectation Scale.

*$p < .05$; **$p < .01$; ***$p < .005$; ****$p < .001$.

[a] Child progress was computed as the difference between the child's MA at the time the parents completed the questionnaires and his/her MA (mental age) 1 year earlier divided by the corresponding differences CAs (chronological age) $(MA_2 - MA_1) / (CA_2 - CA_1)$ multiplied by 100.

[b] Difference scores were computed as the child's DQ at the time the parents completed the questionnaires minus the child's DQ 1 year earlier.

that the parents' health and well-being, time demands placed upon the parents by the child, family integrity, and parent perceptions of child functioning were, in part, affected by the helpfulness of a family's informal social support network. Taken together, the results suggest that negative consequences often associated with the rearing of a child with developmental problems can be lessened or even alleviated when the members of a family's informal support network are mobilized to strengthen personal and familial well-being and buffer negative effects.

Social Support, Well-Being, and Interactional Styles

How the different sets of variables shown in Figure 14.4 were related to styles of parent–child interaction was the focus of a recently completed study (Dunst and Trivette, 1986b). The subjects were 102 mothers of retarded, handicapped, and developmentally at-risk infants and preschoolers. Participation in the study included: (1) the completion of a number of self-report measures; (2) an in-home interview; (3) a videotaping of a parent–child play episode; and (4) an assessment of child performance.

The mothers completed the Psychological Well-Being Index (Bradburn and Caplovitz, 1965) the Questionnaire on Resources and Stress: Emotional and Physical Health Subscale (Holroyd, 1974, 1985), Family Environmental Scale (Moos, 1974), and Maternal Social Support Index (Pascoe *et al.*, 1981). A modified version of the Psychosocial Kinship Network Inventory (Pattison *et al.*, 1975) was administered from which composite network characteristics measures (size of network, frequency of contacts with network members, durability of relationships, intensity of contacts, and network density) was derived. The total number of persons in the respondent's network who performed different support functions was used as a functional support measure.

The mothers were observed interacting with their children during a 20-minute play episode conducted at our Child Development Laboratory. The sessions were videotaped, and caregiver styles of interaction were coded using the Caregiver Styles of Interaction Scale (Dunst, 1986b). This scale includes a number of mutually exclusive categories of interactive styles ordered on a bipolar continuum. The five styles of interaction included: *passive* (caregiver observes but neither interacts nor responds to the child's behavior); *responsive* (caregiver responds contingently to the child's behavior); *engaging* (caregiver encourages the child to maintain ongoing interactions with people or objects); *elaboration* (caregiver encourages the child to elaborate upon his or her behavior competencies); and *imposing* (caregiver verbally elicits the child's attention and interrupts his or her ongoing play). The fre-

TABLE 14.3. Structural Coefficients and Multiple *R*s between the Independent and Dependent Measures

Measures	Maternal styles of interaction				
	Passive	Responsive	Engaging	Elaboration	Imposing
Maternal charcteristics	.13	.30	−.25	.58	−.54
Family characteristics	.22	.32	.03	.63	−.37
Child age	.42	−.36	−.20	.59	−.48
Child development quotient	.67	.42	.28	.16	−.24
Psychological well-being	−.10	.08	−.29	−.01	−.35
Emotional/physical health	.05	.33	−.06	.09	−.52
Family climate	.25	.38	.26		−.03
Maternal role accumulation	−.32	−.44	−.41	−.23	−.37
Satisfaction with support	.17	.32	.05	.22	−.19
Social network characteristics	.11	.26	.23	.13	−.25
Functional support	.09	.15	.59	.01	−.02
Caregiver styles of interaction:					
Frequency	.99	.96	.99	.99	.99
Duration	.61	−.22	.18	.84	.80
Multiple *R*	.51**	.57****	.46*	.48**	.53***

NOTES: Structural coefficients equal to or exceeding .20 ($p < .05$, two-tailed test) may be taken as evidence of a moderate relationship among the variables. Coefficients of .20 or greater have been underlined to indicate the variables that met this criterion.
*$p < .08$; **$p < .05$; ***$p < .01$; ****$p < .001$.

quency and duration of each style of interaction were used as dependent measures. Canonical correlation analysis was used to determine the extent to which 11 independent variables were related to these measures of mother–child interaction.

Table 14.3 shows the results. Our findings generally support the hypothesis that personal well-being and social support (but not family climate) have mediating influences on styles of maternal interaction, although there is considerable specificity with respect to both the particular measures that function as moderators and the interactive styles that are likely to be affected.

The most noteworthy finding concerned the relationship between maternal role accumulation and the manifestation of interactive styles. Mothers who reported less instrumental (intrafamily) support (e.g., help with household and childcare chores) were less likely to show any of the interactive styles. One possible explanation for this set of findings is that lack of instrumental support (i.e., role-sharing) decreased the sheer number of maternal opportunities to participate in interactions with the child, which, in turn presumably provided fewer opportunities to acquire parenting experience. The lack of parenting opportunities seemed to affect the mother's ability to display certain interactive styles.

If this interpretation is correct, then at least a portion of the variance in interactive styles seems to be affected by the broader based social context of the family (values, expectations, etc.). In particular, it is affected by the extent to which mothers receive assistance with household and childcare responsibilities (see Dunst *et al.*, 1986b).

The second set of particularly noteworthy findings were the relationships among family well-being and health and the interactive styles. Enhanced family well-being was related to increased contingent responding and increased use of engaging behaviors. Thus, well-being apparently functioned as a moderating variable influencing parenting behavior. More specifically, well-being and health seemed to set the occasion for increased sensitivity and parental assistance (see Dunst and Trivette, in press [b] for a detailed interpretation of these findings).

Social Support, Well-Being, Interactional Styles, and Child Development

The relationship between parent, family, and child characteristics, social support, well-being, and styles of interaction, and several dimensions of child behavior and development was recently examined with data collected in four studies. The independent variables included maternal and paternal age and education level; family SES and income; child age and sex; four components of support; parent well-being; and several different characteristics of parent–child interactions. In Studies 1 and 4, child progress was assessed by two measures: development measured by the Bayley mental scale and by a rating scale completed by the parents. In Study 2, the two dependent variables were goal directedness and child activity level (Simeonsson, 1979). In Study 3, the dependent variables were measures of both receptive and expressive language behaviors (Simeonsson, 1979). Canonical correlation analysis was used to determine the extent to which the independent variables were related to each set of dependent variables. As can be seen in Table 14.4, the health and well-being measures were significantly related to 3 of the 4 dependent measures and the interactional measures were related to 2 of the 4 outcome measures. Both sets of findings suggest that in addition to parent and family characteristics, both well-being and interactive styles are partial determinants of child behavior and development. It is worth noting that none of the support measures was related to any of the outcome measures. This indicates that support has indirect moderating effects on child behavior, since support has been found to be related to both well-being (see Table 14.1) and interactive styles (see Table 14.3) in our other studies.

TABLE 14.4 Structural Coefficients and Multiple *R*s for Four Sets of Child Behavior Data

Measures	Study 1 Child progress	Study 2 Behavior style	Study 3 Language	Study 4 Child progress
Mother's age	.06	.15	.06	.43
Mother's education	.39	.11	.23	.05
Father's age	.05	.17	.13	.36
Father's education	.53	.34	−.05	.05
Family SES	.29	.08	.37	.04
Family income	.15	.11	−.54	.27
Child age	−.06	.10	.46	.20
Child sex	−.11	.21	.17	—
Relational	.02	.07	.03	.21
Structural	—ᵃ	—	—	.15
Functional	—	—	—	.21
Satisfaction	.28	.12	.23	.14
QRS Health	.74	.39	.14	.40
PKI Well-Being				.31
Number of interactions	.46	.17	.33	—
Frequency of interactions	.44	.23	.41	—
Quality of interactions	—	.15	.39	—
Contingent responsiveness	—	—	—	.21
Elaboration	—	—	—	.01
Multiple *R*	.62*	.90**	.94**	.66*

ᵃ Not measured in this particular study.
*p<.05; **p<.001.

Summary and Implications

The results of the studies described here as well as those from our other investigations provide converging support for the theoretical and practical utility of our social systems perspective of parent, family, and child functioning. The hierarchical regression analyses showed that one can temporally enter variables in "order of causal priority" and estimate the mediational influences of variables. The canonical correlation analyses showed that the aggregation of a set of independent variables was related to different outcome variables in a complex but discernable fashion. Collectively, our results suggest a number of structural equation models that can be used for disentangling the complexities of family functioning and identifying the role social support plays in promoting positive functioning. In addition, our findings replicate those of other investigators who also have found that support plays a role in affecting parent, family, and child functioning (e.g., Cohen and Syme, 1985; Crockenberg, 1981; Crnic *et al.*, 1983b; Embry, 1980; Dean and Lin, 1977). Our studies add to a growing body of evidence that clearly indicates a need to take a family- and social-systems perspective for understanding family functioning. Procedurally, our results have had several major implications for our program. For example, we have used the findings that indicate that informal support is most likely to positively influence parent and family functioning to establish the following policy: To the extent possible, needs should be met by members of the family's social network closest to the family unit and should not be provided, replaced, or supplanted by formal support sources. In practice, this means, for example, that transportation should not be offered to a family if it can be provided by an informal support network member. We believe that this approach has the effect of mobilizing the family's natural support network and thus enhances and strengthens the family's ability to adapt to day-to-day demands and to address its own needs. This approach also helps to avoid dependencies upon professionals.

Retrospect and Prospect

The approach to program evaluation described in this chapter has evolved from experiences at FIPP over the past 6 years. A number of problems encountered in the conduct of our research have presented some unique challenges. A brief discussion of these problems should place our efforts in perspective. For heuristic purposes, we will address three general issues: conceptual, methodological, and pragmatic.

Perhaps the most important challenge that faced us when we initiated our research program was the selection of a conceptual framework. We needed a basis for characterizing the interdependencies among the ecological influences hypothesized to affect parent, family, and child functioning. As noted at the outset, early intervention programs, including FIPP, were for many years almost entirely child-focused and implemented in an atheoretical manner. Moreover, no explicit consideration was given to the possibility of the transactional effects of causal and mediating factors on different behavior outcomes. Consequently, we had to search outside the field of early intervention and child development to find a conceptual model with a broader based framework for studying the influences of different forms and types of intervention. Our initial attempts to characterize the myriad of factors affecting parent, family, and child functioning were modest at best. Through systematic investigation and validation of the causal and mediational influences of various ecological factors, however, we believe our current approach has theoretical and heuristic value for structuring early intervention practices as well as evaluating their impact.

There have been at least two major benefits from our conceptual approach to program development and evaluation. On the one hand, defining early intervention in social systems terms has led to considerable specificity in defining the treatment variables. Rather than consider early intervention in global terms, our strategy permits us to isolate the dimensions, types, and forms of support that influence parent, family, and child functioning. On the other hand, we believe our research has made and continues to make significant contributions to theory building. While it has long been recognized that support affects different aspects of family functioning, our data have begun to identify which types of support affect which types of functioning. Only through the systematic identification of the causal and mediational relationships between independent and dependent variables will we be able to discern the differential, cumulative, and interactive effects of ecological influences on behavior. The most formidable methodological task we have faced is the selection of analytical techniques that permit the proper tests of the hypothesized relationships between the inter- and extrafamily variables so central to our theoretical orientation. Although there are nonrecursive models for testing the bidirectional effects and transactional influences of variables upon one another (see, for example, Cohen and Cohen, 1983), we have thus far employed recursive techniques that permit only estimates of the causal and mediating influences of these various factors. Our methodological approaches, therefore, must be considered preliminary and indirect tests of our omnibus but differential hypotheses. Future efforts will require more sophisticated techniques if we are to discern the complexities of the relationships between different independent and dependent variables.

Programmatically and pragmatically, we have been fortunate that our research and evaluation efforts are so well integrated into FIPP that they have increasingly been viewed as part of the provision and evaluation of program efforts. However, this was not always the case, and staff resentment has occasionally surfaced. When we were first establishing our research program, direct service staff often saw the research as an evaluation of their performance. It required considerable discussion to convince people that the research findings could provide an empirical basis for making positive changes in the conceptualization and implementation of services.

The findings from our research efforts have formed the basis for significant changes in how we now provide and mediate support. Perhaps the most significant has been the way staff act toward families and children. Before we formulated our PEP approach, assessments and treatments focused on what families and children could *not* do. Parents often reported that the long lists of "can'ts" made them so depressed that they felt attending to their children's needs was hopeless. In contrast, parents now report that, for the first time, something positive is said about themselves and their children. One cannot but be struck by the positive effects this proactive approach has on the well-being of the parents. Indeed it is no coincidence that our research and the PEP approach focus on *promotion* of health and well-being and not on the reduction of stress. This is intentional, and is a direct result of the positive stance we take toward children and their families.

The way we define the roles of our staff members is a second major programmatic change that has resulted from our research efforts. Simply stated, a primary staff responsibility is "making a family's social support system work." This means neither replacing nor supplanting the functions that informal network members can perform, but a shift in emphasis from "doing" to "mobilizing." This is a direct translation of our research findings which indicated that provision of support from informal support network members is most likely to have the most positive influences on parent and family well-being. To the extent that a family's social network can be mobilized to provide support for meeting needs, family functioning should be enhanced, coping mechanisms strengthened, and health and well-being promoted.

A recurring pragmatic problem emerges whenever our data refute commonly accepted beliefs and practices. When results disconfirm what one intuitively believes (e.g., that stress level increases with degree of handicap), staff often accept the findings with skepticism. We have found that continuous dialogue with staff, pointing out the implications of the findings, is absolutely necessary in order to affect positive changes in staff attitudes, beliefs, and behavior. We suspect future research will uncover additional data that question accepted practices and beliefs, and we anticipate more program changes as a result. This will require continual reassurance for staff to understand the importance of the research and the significance of the findings for programmatic and policy decisions.

Prospectively, we believe our approach to program evaluation within the context of provision of direct services offers at least one set of techniques and strategies that might be used by others to document the impact of early intervention. Our biases are toward experimental evaluation of program efforts, and we strive to achieve rigor in our work. What we believe we have documented to date is that research, evaluation, and direct service need not be strange bedfellows.

REFERENCES

Baltes, P., Reese, H., and Nesselroade, J. (1977). *Life-span developmental psychology: Introduction to research methods.* Monterey, CA: Brooks/Cole.

Bott, E. (1971). *Family and social networks.* London: Tavistock Publications.

Bradburn, N., and Caplovitz, D. (1965). *Reports on happiness.* Chicago, IL: Aldine Press.

Bronfenbrenner, U. (1979). *The ecology of human development: Experiments by nature and design.* Cambridge, MA: Harvard University Press.

Cochran, M., and Brassard, J. (1979). Child development and personal social networks. *Child Development, 50,* 601–616.

Cohen, J., and Cohen, P. (1983). *Applied multiple regression/correlation analysis for the behavioral sciences* (2nd edition). Hillsdale, NJ: Erlbaum.

Cohen, S., and Syme, S. L. (Eds.). (1985). *Social support and health.* Orlando, FL: Academic Press.

Crnic, K., Friedrich, W., and Greenberg, M. (1983a). Adaptation of families with mentally retarded children: A model of stress, coping, and family ecology. *American Journal of Mental Deficiency, 88,* 125–138.

Crnic, K., Greenberg, M., Ragozin, A., Robinson, N., and Basham, R. (1983b). Effects of stress and social support on mothers of premature and full-term infants. *Child Development, 54,* 209–217.

Crnic, K., Greenberg, M., Robinson, N., and Ragozin, A. (1984). Maternal stress and social support: Effects on the mother–infant relationship from birth to eighteen month. *American Journal of Orthopsychiatry, 54,* 224–235.

Crnic, K., Greenberg, M. T., and Slough, N. M. (1986). Early stress and social support influences on mothers' and high-risk infants' functioning in late infancy. *Infant Mental Health Journal, 7,* 19–48.

Crockenberg, S. (1981). Infant irritability, mother responsiveness and social influences on the security of infant-mother attachment. *Child Development, 52,* 857–865.

Deal, A. G., McWilliam, R. A., Cooper, C. S., and Trivette, C. M. (1986). Strengthening families today for success tomorrow: The Family, Infant and Preschool Program. In J. M. Levy (Ed.), *Proceeding of the seventh annual National Conference of the Young Adult Institute.* NY: Young Adult Institute.

Dean, A., and Lin, N. (1977). Stress-buffering role of social support. *Journal of Nervous and Mental Disease, 165,* 403–417.

Duncan, O. D., Featherman, D. L., and Duncan, B. (1972). *Socio-economic background and achievement*. NY: Seminar.

Dunst, C. J. (1985). Rethinking early intervention. *Analysis and Intervention in Developmental Disabilities, 5,* 165–202.

Dunst, C. J. (1986b). *Caregiver Styles of Interaction Scales.* Unpublished scale, Family, Infant and Preschool Program, Western Carolina Center, Morganton, NC 28655.

Dunst, C. J. (1986a). Overview of the efficacy of early intervention programs: Methodological and conceptual considerations. In L. Bickman and D. Weatherford (Eds.), *Evaluating early intervention programs for severely handicapped children and their families* (pp. 79–147). Austin, TX: PRO-ED.

Dunst, C. J., and Leet, H. E. (1987). Measuring the adequacy of resources in households with young children. *Child: Care, Health, and Development, 13,* 111–125.

Dunst, C. J., and Trivette, C. M. (1984). *Differential influences of social support on mentally retarded children and their families.* Paper presented at the 86th meeting of the American Psychological Association. Toronto, Canada.

Dunst, C. J., and Trivette, C. M. (1985). A guide to measures of social support and family behavior. *Monograph of the Technical Assistance Development System* (No. 1). Chapel Hill, NC: TADS.

Dunst, C. J., and Trivette, C. M. (1986a). *Child Expectation Scale.* Available from Family, Infant and Preschool Program, Western Carolina Center, Morganton, NC 28655.

Dunst, C. J., and Trivette, C. M. (1986b). Looking beyond the parent–child dyad for the determinants of caregiver styles of interaction. *Infant Mental Health Journal, 7,* 69–80.

Dunst, C. J., and Trivette, C. M. (in press a). A family systems model of early intervention. In D. P. Powell (Ed.), *Parent education and support programs: Consequences for children and families.* Norwood, NJ: Ablex Publishing Company.

Dunst, C. J., and Trivette, C. M. (in press b). Determinants of caregiver styles of interaction used with developmentally at-risk children. In K. Marfo (Ed.), *Mental handicapped and parent–child interactions.* NY: Praeger Press.

Dunst, C. J., Jenkins, V., and Trivette, C. M. (1984). Family Support Scale: Reliability and validity. *Journal of Individual, Family and Community Wellness, 1*(4), 45–52.

Dunst, C. J., Trivette, C. M., and Cross, A. H. (1986a). Mediating influences of social support: Personal, family and child outcomes. *American Journal of Mental Deficiency, 90,* 403–417.

Dunst, C. J., Trivette, C. M., and Cross, A. H. (1986b). Roles and support networks of mothers of handicapped children. In R. Fewell and P. Vadasy (Eds.), *Families of handicapped children's needs and support across the lifespan* (pp. 167–192). Austin, TX: PRO-ED.

Dunst, C. J., Vance, S. D., and Cooper, C. S. (1986). A social systems perspective of adolescent pregnancy: Determinants of parent and parent–child behavior. *Infant Mental Health Journal, 7,* 34–48.

Dunst, C. J., Trivette, C. M., and Cross, A. H. (in press). Social support networks of Appalachian and nonAppalachian families with handicapped children: Relationship to personal and family well-beings. In S. Keefe (Ed.), *Mental health in Appalachia.* Lexington, KY: University of Kentucky Press.

Embry, L. (1980). Family support for handicapped preschool children at risk for abuse. *New Directions for Exceptional Children, 4,* 29–58.

Gallagher, J., Cross, A., and Scharfman, W. (1981). *Parent Role Scale.* Unpublished instrument, Frank Porter Graham Child Development Center, University of North Carolina, Chapel Hill, NC.

Gore, S. (1985). Social Support and styles of coping with stress. In S. Cohen and S. L. Syme (Eds.), *Social support and health* (pp. 263–278). Orlando, FL: Academic Press.

Gottlieb, B. H. (1981). Social networks and social support in community mental health. In B. H. Gottlieb (Ed.), *Social networks and social support* (pp. 11–42). Beverly Hills, CA: Sage.

Gourash, N. (1978). Help Seeking: A review of the literature. *American Journal of Community Psychology, 6,* 499–517.

Hall, A., and Wellman, B. (1985). Social networks and social support. In S. Cohen and Syme (Eds.), *Social support and health* (pp. 23–42). Orlando, FL: Academic Press.

Heller, W., Amaral, T., and Procidano, M. (1978). *The experimental study of social support: An approach to understanding the indigenous helper.* Paper presented at the 86th Meeting of the American Psychological Association, Toronto, Canada.

Hirsch, B. J. (1979). Psychological dimensions of social networks: A multimethod analysis. *American Journal of Community Psychology, 7,* 263–277.

Hobbs, N. (1975). *The futures of children: Categories, labels, and their consequences.* San Francisco, CA: Jossey-Bass.

Holohan, C. J., and Wilcox, B. L. (1978). Residential satisfaction and friendship formation in high and low rise student housing: An international analysis. *Journal of Educational Psychology, 70,* 237–241.

Holroyd, J. (1974). The Questionnaire on Resources and Stress: An instrument to measure family responses to a handicapped family member. *Journal of Community Psychology, 2,* 92–94.

Holroyd, J. (1985). *Questionnaire on Resources and Stress Manual.*

Available from Neuropsychiatric Institute, Department of Psychiatric and Biobehavioral Sciences, University of California, Los Angeles.

House, J. S., and Kahn, R. L. (1985). Measures and concepts of social support. In S. Cohen and S. L. Syme (Eds.), *Social support and health* (pp. 83–108). Orlando, FL: Academic Press.

Lazar, I., and Darlington, R. (1982). Lasting effects of early education: A report from the consortium for longitudinal studies. *Monographs of the Society for Research in Child Development, 47,* (2–3, serial no. 195).

Lewin, K. (1931). Environmental forces in child behavior and development. In C. Murchison (Ed.), *Handbook of child psychology.* Worcester, MA: Clark University Press.

Lewin, K. (1936). *Principles of topological psychology.* NY: McGraw-Hill.

McCubbin, H. I., Joy, C. B., Cauble, A. E., Comeau, J. K., Patterson, J. M., and Needle, R. H. (1980). Family stress and coping: A decade of review. *Journal of Marriage and the Family, 42,* 855–871.

McCubbin, H. I., Cauble, A. E., and Patterson, J. M. (Eds.). (1982). *Family stress, coping, and social support.* Springfield, IL: Thomas.

McGuire, J. C., and Gottlieb, B. H. (1979). Social support groups among new parents: An experimental study in primary prevention. *Journal of Clinical Child Psychology, 8,* 111–116.

Mitchell, R. E., and Trickett, E. J. (1980). Task force report: Social networks as mediators of social support. *Community Mental Health Journal, 16,* 27–43.

Moos, R. H. (1974). *Family Environment Scale.* Palo Alto, CA: Consulting Psychologists.

Mueller, D. (1980). Social networks: A promising direction for research on the relationship of the social environment to psychiatric disorders. *Social Science and Medicine, 40,* 147–161.

Pascoe, J., Loda, F., Jeffries, V., and Earp, J. (1981). The association between mothers' social support and provision of stimulation to their children. *Developmental and Behavioral Pediatrics, 2,* 15–19.

Pattison, E., Defrancisco, D., Wood, P., Frazier, H., and Crowder, J. (1975). A psychosocial kinship model for family therapy. *American Journal of Psychiatry, 132,* 1246–1251.

Philliber, S., and Graham, E. (1981). The impact of age of mother and mother–child interaction patterns. *Journal of Marriage and Family, 43,* 109–115.

Reese, H., and Overton, W. (1970). Models of development and theories of development. In L. Goulet and P. Baltes (Ed.), *Life span developmental psychology: Research and commentary.* NY: Academic Press.

Richman, J., and Flaherty, J. (1985). Coping and depression: The relative contribution of internal and external resources during a life cycle transition. *The Journal of Nervous and Mental Disease, 173,* 590–595.

Roskin, M. (1982). Coping with life change—A preventive social work approach. *American Journal of Community Psychology,* 10, 331–340.

Sewell, W. H., and Hauser, R. M. (1975). *Education, occupation, and earning: Achievement in the early career.* NY: Academic Press.

Shapiro, J. (1983). Family reactions and coping strategies in response to the physically ill or handicapped child: A review. *Social Science Medicine, 17,* 913–931.

Simeonsson, R. J. (1979). *Carolina Record of Individual Behavior.* Available from Carolina Institute for Research on Early Education of the Handicapped, University of North Carolina, Chapel Hill, NC.

Tolsdorf, C. C. (1976). Social networks, support, and coping: An exploratory study. *Family Process, 15,* 407–419.

Trivette, C. M., and Dunst, C. J. (in press). Characteristics and influences of role division and social support among mothers of handicapped preschoolers. *Parenting Studies.*

Trivette, C. M., and Dunst, C. J. (1986a). *Influences of social support on mentally retarded children and their families.* Paper presented at the second annual Parenting Symposium, Philadelphia, Pennsylvania.

Trivette, C. M., and Dunst, C. J. (1986b). *Personal Well-Being Index: Reliability and validity.* Available from Family, Infant and Preschool Program, Western Carolina Center, Morganton, NC, 28655.

Trivette, C. M., and Dunst, C. J. (1986c). Proactive influences of support on children and their families. In H. G. Linger (Ed.), *Family strengths (vol. 8): Positive and preventive measures.* Lincoln, NB: University of Nebraska Press.

Unger, D. G., and Powell, D. R. (1980). Supporting families under stress: The role of social networks. *Family Relations, 29,* 566–574.

Weinraub, M., and Wolf, B. M. (1983). Effects of stress and social supports on mother–child interactions in single- and two-parent families. *Child Development, 54,* 1297–1311.

APPENDIX: THE MAJOR COMPONENTS AND SECTIONS OF THE FAMILY, INFANT AND PRESCHOOL PROGRAM

Comprehensive Services

Child and Family Services. Needs are identified and services provided by two intervention teams, each including professionals from education, nursing, pediatrics, psychology, physical therapy, speech and language pathology, and social work. Services currently provided include: Transdisciplinary Child and Family Assessments, the development and implementation of Family and Child Intervention Plans (FA-

CIPs), Home-based Family Services, and Community Clusters (parent–child groups that provide children and other family members the opportunity to meet and learn from one another).

Community Resource Services. Designed to increase understanding, cooperation, and program planning between parents, professionals, and the general public and to improve provision of services to handicapped children and their families. Services are provided in three major areas: Public Awareness, Dissemination, and Follow-Along/Program Bridging.

Special Projects

Community Connection. A lending library and toy exchange program.

HOPE Network. The HOPE (Helping Other Parents through Empathy) Network is the FIPP parent-to-parent support program. Families with questions and concerns are linked with more experienced parents who provide emotional support and share knowledge.

Parent Advisory Board. Meets regularly to evaluate services, advise on the need for new services, and suggests ways to improve upon our service-delivery system.

Parent Co-op Project. Teaches parents to operate preschool programs for handicapped and nonhandicapped children. Parents receive training in basic classroom routines, intervention strategies, and behavior monitoring of child progress.

Project ASSIST. Project ASSIST (Accessing Social Support Interventions and Services by Teenagers) includes a work–study program, home-based support services, and life-skills classes to assist pregnant teenagers and teenage mothers to meet child and family needs through mobilization of their informal support networks.

Project ENHANCE. Project ENHANCE (Enhancing Handicapped and Nonhandicapped Childrens' Education) is a model demonstration classroom designed to optimize learning opportunities for both handicapped and nonhandicapped children.

Project HAPPEN. Project HAPPEN (Helping Agencies Promote Parent Empowerment through Networking) is a model demonstration project developing and implementing an empowerment model designed to optimize parent participation in decision making involving their children and families.

Project PROACT. A home-based respite program for families of severely handicapped children designed to reduce the time demands handicapped children place upon their families.

Project SHaRE. Project SHaRE (Sources of Help Received and Exchanged) is a barter and exchange program that mediates exchange of projects and provision of services.

Project STEP-UP. Project STEP-UP (Specialized Training Experiences Provided to Underserved Preschoolers) provides special education services to severely handicapped children. Emphasis is on initiating and sustaining interactions with the social and nonsocial environment.

Special Edition. A parent newsletter to keep families informed about FIPP happenings, new legislation, child development issues, etc.

Research and Evaluation Services

Applied Research Laboratory. Conducts studies that examine the efficacy of different intervention strategies and approaches.

Child Development Laboratory. Conducts studies that examine parent–child interactions and child behavior and development.

Early Intervention Efficacy Project. A large-scale, longitudinal study of the characteristics and determinants of behavioral and developmental change among the over 1000 children who have participated in FIPP during the past 12 years.

Institutional Avoidance Project. Examines the extent to which participation in both home- and center-based preschool programs for handicapped children prevents or delays subsequent long-term institutionalization.

Meta-Analysis Efficacy Project. Examines the extent to which different early intervention efficacy studies conducted during the past 20 years provide evidence that early intervention is effective.

Training and Technical Assistance

Consultative Services. Staff offers both case-specific and programmatic consultations in the areas of adaptive equipment, physical therapy, communications development, and behavior therapy.

Family and Infant Specialist Training Project. An intensive four-course sequence designed to train students to work with mentally retarded, handicapped, and developmentally at-risk infants and their families.

The PARENTS Project. The PARENTS Project (Parents Assisting Rural Educators through Networking and Teaching in the Schools) Project is designed to mobilize parent support networks, establish home–school partnerships, and empower parents to become more involved in their handicapped children's elementary school education.

Project SUNRISE. Project SUNRISE (Systematic Use of Newly Researched Interventions by Special Educators) provides training and technical assistance to preschool classroom staff. It is designed to promote the use of empirically based "best practices" for optimizing the learning capabilities of handicapped youngsters.

chapter 15

THE CROSS-PROJECT EVALUATION OF THE CHILD SURVIVAL/FAIR START INITIATIVE: A CASE STUDY OF ACTION RESEARCH

James T. Bond
Robert Halpern

CHILD SURVIVAL/FAIR START PROGRAM: HISTORY AND GOALS

In 1982 the Ford Foundation launched the Child Survival/Fair Start (CS/FS) initiative under which it sponsored community-based strategies to improve pregnancy outcomes, infant health, and infant development among low-income families. The Foundation has encouraged the development of programs relying on peer-to-peer support of prospective and/or new parents to achieve the following goals:[1]

1. Promoting simple health self-care practices
2. Encouraging appropriate utilization of formal medical care
3. Strengthening the parent–infant relationship
4. Strengthening parental skills in coping with other aspects of family life that impinge on childrearing, and helping families gain access to services and formal institutional supports

In initiating the CS/FS effort, the Foundation did not specify a particular intervention model. Decisions about how to intervene and what

[1]The Foundation also identified some of the component elements of these broad goals. Corresponding to the numbered goals in the text these included: (1) good maternal and infant nutrition, hygiene, home safety, managment of diarrhea, temperature taking, and so forth; (2) early identification of problems requiring care, appropriate help-seeking behavior, compliance with prescribed regimens, timely use of preventive prenatal and well-baby care, timely immunization; and (3) the sharing of information about infant developmental needs, demonstration of activities to stimulate cognitive, motor, and social development.

to evaluate were shaped by the needs and problems of the target populations, what was feasible under the circumstances, and the Foundation's desire to encourage peer-to-peer approaches. Of the seven projects funded, five utilized home-visiting models; those five will be considered here.

The CS/FS home-visit projects integrate health and child development concerns within the same program. However, as Table 15.1 shows, they vary significantly along a number of dimensions.

The Ford Foundation enlisted the authors to serve as cross-project evaluators of these programs. Neither *internal* nor *external* evaluators in the usual sense, we act as brokers, facilitators, technical assistants, and synthesizers. Our goals are to help each project develop its own research plan and to make the experiences of all five projects as additive and as mutually illuminating as possible.

THE CONTEXT OF EVALUATION

When we began in 1982, only one of the CS/FS home-based projects had a program in place. Three others were developing operational programs from the broad outlines sketched in their grant proposals. The fifth was not funded for some months. The established project received an initial 2-year grant; the others each received a 3-year grant, reflecting the Ford Foundation's understanding that they would require more development time before evaluation could begin.

Three-year grant cycles appear to have become the norm, placing considerable pressure on both foundations and grant seekers to make projects fit this time period. The history of home-based early intervention suggests that more than 3 years is often required to move a program from the drawing board into the field on a viable operational footing and to conduct an adequate summative evaluation. We were therefore concerned that the 3-year schedule for the CS/FS demonstration might stimulate a rush to full implementation and evaluation that would not serve any purpose well.

The grantees initially had different notions of what program evaluation would entail, a fact reflected in their budget allocations for evaluation activities and in their staffing plans. Indeed, two proposals were funded that did not earmark any funds or commit any staff time specifically to evaluation. Given the fact that each project, and not the cross-project evaluators, was responsible for conducting its own evaluation, the initial inattention to evaluation in grant applications was worrisome. Furthermore, our experience conducting research/evaluation within community-based service agencies led us to anticipate substantial competition for limited resources between evaluation activity and service delivery. Both researcher and practitioner would have to be willing to acknowledge each other's eligibility to compete.

From the outset, it was clear that CS/FS would be a multisite and multimethod demonstration in which methods were confounded with site and population characteristics. Within the broad framework of goals and approaches established by the Ford Foundation, individual projects were actively encouraged to develop interventions tailored to the specific needs of their client population and local communities. Further, each project brought to the program development task somewhat different theoretical perspectives, capacities for service development and delivery, and service priorities. These factors were bound to interact with cross-project variability, in client populations and communities, to produce significant unplanned and uncontrolled variation, both in intervention methods and in objectives. Clearly any assessment of the relative effectiveness of different CS/FS programs would have to be exploratory rather than confirmatory.

Despite this diversity, there was considerable overlap in the proposed means and ends of these interventions. Certain problems were universal among the economically marginal populations targeted by CS/FS. The programs also had a common commitment to promote both maternal and child health and early development, and all relied on paraprofessional home visitors to deliver all or most of the program's services. This common ground offered the possibility for measuring some features in the same way across all projects. The Ford Foundation hoped that doing this would yield valuable insights and hypotheses with external validity, but defining this common ground in operational terms would be one of our major challenges.

Our evaluation had to contend with a host of constraints and problems encountered in all field studies of ecologically complex home-based early interventions, including: inadequate theory to guide either intervention or evaluation; inadequate measures of many hypothetically important input, process, and outcome variables; practical difficulties in constructing research designs that incorporate adequate controls for obtaining unbiased estimates of program effects; and significant variability in the treatments received and benefits reaped by different infants and/or families. The last item in this list is particularly problematic for the evaluation of home-based programs that individualize their services. Customary approaches to determining program effectiveness may not be sensitive enough to capture the actual impacts of these individualized programs.

Finally, it was clear from the outset that we would be defining a new role as we went along, that of cross-project evaluator. Our own ex-

TABLE 15.1. Major Features of Child Survival/Fair Start Home-Visiting Programs

Location/sponsor	Target population	Community characteristics	Sample characteristics	Program model
South Dade County, Florida; Community Health Center, Martin Luther King Clinica Campesina	Mexican and Mexican–American migrant and seasonal farm workers	Two farm labor camps; pop. about 3500; over-crowded living conditions at height of season; legal problems for some families; services sketchy	All pregnant women in camps eligible	Four home visitors, all from present or former farmworker families; 12 home visits: 5 prenatal, 3 postpartum, and 4 more up to 12 months; also weekly mothers' groups
Austin, Texas; Center for the Development of Non-Formal Education CEDEN	Mexican and Mexican–American families	Two urban barrios of Austin; barrios somewhat isolated from larger community	All families, first come, first served, with infants 0–18 months at enrollment	Six paraprofessional home visitors; all work full time; weekly home visits for a minimum of 9 months from entry into program; occasional group meetings

Nashville, Tennessee; Center for Health Services, Vanderbilt	Rural families in six Appalachian communities, two each in Kentucky, Tennessee, and West Virginia; mixtures of black and white families	Generally small communities geographically and socially isolated; depressed economically; few services	All pregnant women in the communities but with an emphasis on psychosocially high-risk women	One professional in each community assisted by network of trained/supervised natural helpers, who gradually do most home visiting; monthly home visits during pregnancy through infant's first year; bimonthly during second year
Eutaw, Alabama, Community Health Center, West Alabama Health Services (WAHS)	Rural, black families in two contiguous west Alabama counties	Rural South; extremely depressed economically; high rates of out-of-wedlock birth and female-headed households	All pregnant women enrolled in prenatal care at WAHS; priority to first time pregnant teenagers	11 half-time home visitors, all community women; biweekly home visits during pregnancy up to 6 months of age; every 6 weeks till 18 months
Broward County, Florida; Broward General Hospital	Haitian immigrants and refugees	Several neighborhoods in Broward County where high concentrations of Haitians live; a second site in Immokalee, Florida, for Haitian farm workers; Haitian women isolated, stressed, limited English	All pregnant women but randomly assigned to treatment control conditions; first come, first served up to 50	Two home visitors in Broward, one in Immokalee; all home visitors Haitian but with longer U. S. residence; biweekly home visits during pregnancy to 12 months, then monthly to 18 months

perience and the literature provided numerous models for the roles of "internal" or "external" evaluator, but not for the role we were assuming. Each CS/FS project had or would have its own research team, responsible for designing and conducting its own program evaluation. We were not authorized to make decisions on design or methodology for CS/FS projects, nor to conduct independent evaluations. Rather, we were expected to advise, support, and synthesize—to "influence" project-level evaluations, but not to "direct" them.

CROSS-PROJECT EVALUATION STRATEGY

To chart a course for ourselves, we began by considering the overarching purpose of the CS/FS initiative: to explore the potential of community-based approaches for improving family health self-care, family utilization of medical care, maternal and infant health, and infant development. We interpreted "to explore the potential" to mean not only "to assess the impacts" of whatever interventions happened to occur, but also "to promote the development" of potential and "to increase understanding" of the intervention process.

Our first concern was to establish reasonable expectations regarding what might be learned. After two decades of enormous investment in social program evaluation, policymakers and seasoned evaluators alike have become much less sanguine about the potential contributions of evaluation research to public policy formation. Dreams of "conclusive findings" have been replaced by more humble aspirations of achieving "incremental clarification," with which we wholeheartedly agree. One of the preeminent voices in evaluation research addresses this issue:

> Disillusion is the bitter aftertaste of saccharine illusion. It is self-defeating to aspire to deliver an evaluative conclusion as precise and as safely beyond dispute as an operational–language conclusion from the laboratory. It is unreasonable to hope to tell the policy-shaping community all it needs to know. When the evaluator aspires only to provide clarification that would not otherwise be available, he has chosen a task he can manage and one that does have social benefits (Cronbach and Associates, 1980, p. 318).

Cronbach and his colleagues assume that ignorance cannot be defeated in a single, mannerly battle on an open field but only through repeated, opportunistic skirmishes that gradually wear it down. In the CS/FS case, we hoped only that the first 3 years might help to "clarify" the potential of home-based early intervention to ameliorate deep-seated problems of infant health and development among America's poor.

Next we sought balance between cross-project and within-project evaluation priorities. Our deliberations were directly influenced by program evaluations conducted during the 1970s, particularly of "planned variation experiments" that carried multimethod/multisite design to new lengths. The grand intentions of such well-known examples as Planned Variation Head Start (Datta, 1975) and Planned Variation Follow Through (Haney, 1977) were founded on inadequate research design, which confounded "planned variation" in intervention methods with differences in populations and contexts. Since CS/FS embodied the same design limitations plus cross-project variation in measurement and comparison/control strategies, we were eager not to treat its evaluation as a "horse race" pitting different intervention models against one another in a purportedly definitive test of strength.

At best, the cross-project evaluation would be *exploratory*—generating but not confirming hypotheses about the relative effectiveness of different interventions with different populations in different contexts. In order to maximize the potential for generating hypotheses, we opted to encourage the recognition and foster the construction of common objectives and common measurement of these objectives across projects. Responding to the Foundation's mandate to "synthesize CS/FS experiences," we decided not to attempt to pool inevitably incommensurate data from all projects for common analysis, but to plan for "qualitative integration" of findings from different CS/FS projects and possibly some degree of "quantitative integration" using meta-analytic procedures (see Hauser-Cram, Chapter 20, this volume).

The evaluation of complex programs in the last 20 years has revealed little about what sorts of intervention work in what ways for whom (Halpern, 1984). In fact, the field has not yet progressed beyond the point of having to demonstrate that home-based early intervention *can* work with at least some samples under some conditions. Therefore, if the "potentials" of CS/FS home-based early interventions were to be identified, it was imperative that project-level evaluations be sensitive to project-level processes and effects, and that pressures for cross-project evaluation not lead to compromises that might distort local interventions or mask their impacts.

Thus, we balanced our desire for common objectives and measurements across projects with support for the development of strong and coherent within-project evaluations. This balance was to be achieved, if necessary, at the expense of cross-project synthesis.

Our most radical strategic decision was to break the "summative evaluation" mold in which both we and within-project researchers initially had been cast by the language describing the CS/FS grant program and by our own grant proposals. We agreed with Carol Weiss's (1975) analysis that efforts to develop effective social policies and programs had suffered from too much summative evaluation of ill-conceived interventions and too little research into the causes of social problems and the obstacles to their solutions. We agreed also with Joseph Wholey (1979) that program "evaluability" assessments should be conducted before summative evaluations were undertaken. And we found Leonard Rutman's (1980) encouragement of collaboration between evaluators and practitioners to enhance program evaluability to be particularly compatible with the needs of CS/FS.

We feel these several perspectives are drawn together into a coherent research strategy by the underutilized paradigm of action research (Rapoport, 1985). This paradigm is defined by collaboration between researcher and practitioner to integrate basic research, program development, and program evaluation into an iterative cycle aimed at solving social problems. Action research places researchers in the field with practitioners, where evaluation decisions can be continuously monitored. Measures that are not working can be abandoned or modified before it is too late. If systematic differences are revealed between comparison group and program families, other strategies for experimental control can be devised. If environmental constraints appear to prevent the intervention from affecting important dependent variables, research efforts can be redirected from summative evaluation to basic research to increase understanding of the obstacles to intervention—perhaps pointing the way toward program improvements or changes in public policy. In short, action research encourages and permits the sort of flexibility that we believe is essential for effective research, development, and evaluation.

Our decision to embrace an action research strategy had several important implications. First, we should review and critique previous early intervention research for its application to program development efforts and evaluation planning. Second, we should stimulate each of the five home-visit programs to refine their definitions of the problems they faced, their models of problem etiology, and their understanding of the obstacles to successful intervention. Third, we should give as much or more priority to formative evaluation (with its emphasis on improving practice in the light of intermediate findings) as to summative evaluation (with its emphasis on finally judging the effectiveness of stable systems).

As we began implementing our strategy, we expected tension to arise from the different priorities of evaluators and practitioners. The former would seek to optimize research design and methodology for internal validity; the latter would seek to serve the vast unmet needs of poor children and families. Nonetheless, we believed that an action research strategy would mitigate the tension and would lead to a sensitive and credible evaluation of the CS/FS home-visit programs.[2] In the remainder of this chapter, we describe the first stages of implementation.

PROBLEMS AND TACTICS IN THE FIELD

Helping to Forge Evaluable Programs

Our first task was to learn what each CS/FS project hoped to accomplish and to help each determine whether it was developing plausible intervention strategies.[3] Our role varied significantly from project to project, depending upon the stage of program development, but we noted a common developmental process across projects: Focal problems were redefined, causal models were elaborated, vague goals took the shape of operational objectives, and (for the new projects) proposed intervention strategies were adjusted to fit new understanding of the problem and local constraints.

Although experience has convinced us that every new program will, and perhaps in some measure must, "reinvent the wheel," it is often possible to accelerate the program and evaluation development process by infusing relevant information and third-party insights that would not otherwise be available or considered. Some of the generic tactics we employed to facilitate the developmental process are described in the following list:

1. We conducted and shared a review of the literature on home-based early intervention (Halpern, 1984) with all participants. This

[2]Our activities in the field were not so sytematic as they may appear to be in this recounting, for the act of writing this chapter has made many implicit strategies explicit and has given new meaning to our experiences. Thus, what follows is a reconstruction of history, unavoidably altered and cleaned up by reflection and hindsight.

[3]Specifically, we asked ourselves and project staff the following sorts of questions: (1) What social/psychological/health problems will be addressed by the CS/FS intervention? What is their prevalance within the target populations? (2) What are the origins of these problems within the populations targeted for service, that is, what variables within individuals and their social/physical environments appear to cause the problems? Is it possible to identify persons most at risk? (3) What methods of intervention are proposed? Are these methods that have been demonstrated to or might logically be expected to affect variables in the presumed causal chains so as to ameliorate or prevent the problems of concern? Is it feasible to implement these interventions given available resources and probable environmental constraints?

history of the "wheel" helped to guide CS/FS's further work and
to clarify the project's potential contribution to the field.

2. We spent time on site participating in planning activities and being
   available to help when local staff showed the readiness and desire
   to rethink an aspect of their program or evaluation plan.

3. We encouraged cross-pollination through techniques such as periodic cross-project meetings and staff visits.

4. When focal problems were particularly vague or uncertain for the
   target population we encouraged projects to undertake "basic
   research" to assess the real needs for service and the actual prev-
   alence of supposed problems before rushing into implementation.

5. We used home visitors, drawn from the populations served, as
   important sources of information and insight and as a "reality
   check" for the professionals more socially distant from families
   being served.

6. We drew up "causal maps" to describe the individual, family, and
   community systems in which programs would intervene. An elaborated sample of such a map is illustrated in Figure 15.1. The content and organization of the maps were shaped by what we learned
   from CS/FS projects. Their purpose was to keep attention focused
   on the myriad factors that should influence decisions about intervention and evaluation strategy.

Deciding What to Measure

Deciding which aspects of program services, clients, and community
should be measured was a complex process; the scope and complexity
of possible measures are seen in Figure 15.1, where intermediate and
ultimate outcome variable domains are mapped in detail. Measurement
decisions were constrained by limited research budgets, field conditions, grantee priorities and sensibilities, and by considerations of client
tolerance. It was also necessary to consider the state-of-the-art of
measurement and instrumentation in the different domains, overall research design considerations, and the need for some common measures across all projects.

Deciding what to measure required juggling many considerations
simultaneously, trading off one against the other, until a satisfactory
compromise was achieved. To facilitate our collaboration with the individual projects, we did not discuss common cross-project measures
until the measurement batteries of each project were fairly well decided
and project staff had developed rationales for their decisions that were
strong enough to withstand unreasonable pressures for common

measurement. The individual projects had to take into account the unique characteristics of their communities and of the populations they served. Questions about knowledge of child development that can reasonably be asked of mothers who are high school graduates and have had previous child-rearing experience, for example, may not elicit meaningful responses from teenage primiparous mothers. Levels of literacy and cultural–linguistic differences further complicated the applicability of various measures. The understanding of questions, the willingness to share feelings, and the conditions that evoke and shape task performance (on infant measures) all had to be considered in choosing measures of important intermediate and ultimate outcomes. Finally, the available client data varied from setting to setting. One project, located within a rural health care agency, had direct access to extensive obstetric and pediatric medical records on members of the client population; other projects had to rely on parental self-report.

Questions of "client tolerance" were frequently raised in early discussions. Questions regarding reproductive behavior, personal income, venereal disease, and even citizenship in cases of illegal immigrants, for example, were thought to be too sensitive or embarrassing. Concern was also expressed that the inclusion of personal questions in pretreatment interviews might alienate potential clients.

Such objections were less frequent and vehement than we expected, perhaps because CS/FS practitioners were not only aware of the arguments for measuring each variable but actually participated in developing them. When objections were raised, we urged project staff to treat "objections" as "hypotheses" to test in pilot data collection studies. Consequently, practitioners generally discovered that clients were more tolerant of "prying" questions than they had imagined.

The state-of-the-art of measurement development placed severe constraints on all projects. The variables of interest ranged from quality of adjustment to parenthood, to parental coping, to infant feeding skills, to more subtle forms of the infant's failure to thrive. Discussion of one outcome domain, infant health, will serve to illustrate some of the difficulties posed for us by the underdevelopment of relevant measures.

"Good" health is typically defined as the absence of "bad" health— that is, reduced illness, injury, or morbidity. Among adults and school-age children fairly simple functional indexes of morbidity have been used with considerable success (e.g., illness-related absences from school and work). However, we were not able to identify or devise equally straightforward functional measures for infants. Although "normal" physical growth is sometimes used as a proxy for good health and nutrition among infants, it is difficult to obtain sufficiently reliable

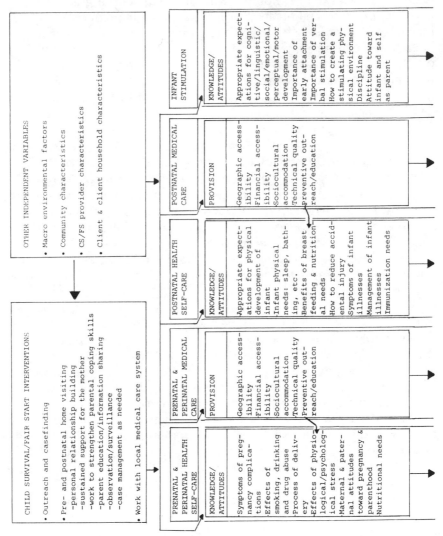

CHILD SURVIVAL/FAIR START INTERVENTIONS

• Outreach and casefinding

• Pre- and postnatal home visiting
   –personal relationship building
   –sustained support for the mother
   –work to strengthen parental coping skills
   –parent education/information sharing
   –observation/surveillance
   –case management as needed

• Work with local medical care system

OTHER INDEPENDENT VARIABLES

• Macro environmental factors
• Community characteristics
• CS/FS provider characteristics
• Client & client household characteristics

INTERMEDIATE OBJECTIVES

PRENATAL & PERINATAL HEALTH SELF-CARE	PRENATAL & PERINATAL MEDICAL CARE	POSTNATAL HEALTH SELF-CARE	POSTNATAL MEDICAL CARE	INFANT STIMULATION
KNOWLEDGE/ ATTITUDES	PROVISION	KNOWLEDGE/ ATTITUDES	PROVISION	KNOWLEDGE/ ATTITUDES
Symptoms of pregnancy complications Effects of smoking, drinking and drug abuse Process of delivery Effects of physiological/psychological stress Maternal & paternal attitudes toward pregnancy & parenthood Nutritional needs	Geographic accessibility Financial accessibility Sociocultural accommodation Technical quality Preventive outreach/education	Appropriate expectations for physical development of infant Infant physical needs: sleep, bathing, etc. Benefits of breast feeding & nutritional needs How to reduce accidental injury Symptoms of infant illnesses Management of infant illnesses Immunization needs	Geographic accessibility Financial accessibility Sociocultural accommodation Technical quality Preventive outreach/education	Appropriate expectations for cognitive/linguistic/social/emotional/perceptual/motor development Importance of early attachment Importance of verbal stimulation How to create a stimulating physical environment Discipline Attitude toward infant and self as parent

358

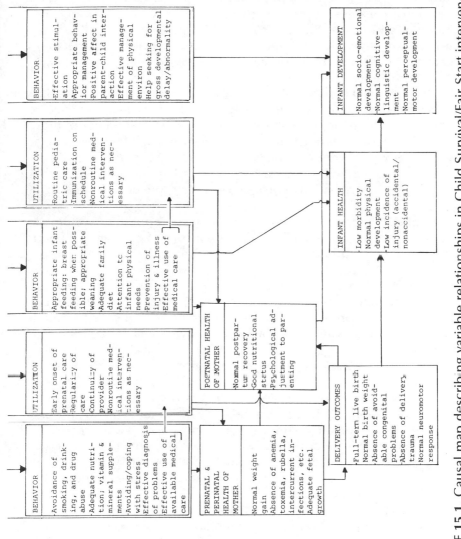

FIGURE 15.1. Causal map describing variable relationships in Child Survival/Fair Start interventions.

359

measurements under field conditions; stature and weight generally are not sensitive to the levels of morbidity and malnutrition found even among the most impoverished subpopulations of North American infants. Thus, we turned to more complicated measurement of illness: number of episodes, severity, and chronicity of illnesses during a defined period of time. Sources for this information included parents, providers of pediatric care, and observers (home visitors or data collectors). But each of these sources and measurement approaches presented problems.

First, we could find no fully acceptable procedure for reducing data to manageable proportions for analysis. Unless instances of specific types of illness and injury were collapsed into a small number of more general categories, if not a single "morbidity index," low frequencies within many categories and the large number of categories that would have to be considered would frustrate data analysis and interpretation—particularly the estimation of program effects in low-power, small-sample research.

Second, all approaches appeared to be susceptible to systematic measurement error that might bias comparisons of program with nonprogram infants. If program participation increased utilization of pediatric care, a larger proportion of illness/injury might be "discovered" and recorded in pediatric records for program infants than nonprogram infants. Program parents, being educated to "signs and symptoms," might become more sensitive to the occurrence of illnesses than nonprogram parents. Similarly, knowing their own behavior and their infants' health to be the subject of surveillance, they might report a higher or lower proportion of episodes than nonprogram parents. Because observers have far more access to program than to nonprogram families, they might underreport morbidity among nonprogram infants.

Other problems included local obstacles to obtaining pediatric records, logistical problems in reviewing pediatric records when individual children had multiple providers, variations in completeness of records among providers of pediatric care, limited diagnostic powers of parents and other amateur observers, and unreliable memories of parents in recollecting instances of morbidity.

Ultimately, projects made measurement decisions that reflected differences in project resources and emphases. All five opted for some form of surveillance and documentation of morbidity among program infants by home visitors for purposes of formative evaluation and case management. Three projects are experimenting with parent interviews in order to estimate morbidity among both program and nonprogram infants at one or more points. One project, with easy access to records and back-up from medical researchers, is attempting a full-blown pediatric record review, in addition to parental self-reports, in order to get multiple indicators of infant health outcomes. Although no one is confident that changes in infant health will be adequately measured, cooperative work on instrument design and shared results of preliminary analyses have led to perceptible progress beyond what any one project would have made individually.

Frequently in our consulting role, we have assisted project staff in deciding when to measure a simple "proxy" instead of the more complex variable of ultimate concern. Proxies can be good substitutes when it is prohibitively expensive to measure the "real thing" adequately, when there is no convincing way to measure it, or when the likelihood of finding program impacts is too small to justify the required investment in measurement. This is illustrated by the experience of the three CS/FS projects that intervene prenatally and are concerned with improving the nutrition of pregnant women. A review of available techniques suggested that affordable procedures (e.g., 24-hour recall) to assess nutritional intake might have formative evaluation utility, but that they were unlikely to produce data sufficiently reliable and reducible for summative evaluation purposes. In a cross-project meeting, which included health care professionals, several proxy variables for good prenatal nutrition were suggested. As a result, all but one project decided to rely upon measurement of such proxies as "weight gain during pregnancy" and "absence of anemia" as indexes for "good prenatal nutrition."

As noted earlier, evaluations of social programs typically have emphasized summative measures of program impact and slighted measurement of both the intervention process and the molar environmental variables that affect treatment outcomes (e.g., trends in the availability of medical care). Individual CS/FS projects are still deciding how far to go in unpacking the "black box" of treatment for both formative feedback and eventual insight into the results of the summative evaluation. Each project does some documentation of treatment by having home visitors keep records of the services provided to each family. Much of the information is descriptive and not easily reduced, but some of it (number of visits, curricular units completed, etc.) has already been or can be quantified easily. A few of the projects have developed protocols that supervisors use on periodic home visits to observe the home visitors' work, rating home visitors along different dimensions allowing narrative description of interactions. We have also worked with projects to design field procedures for developing selected family case histories that illustrate in rich detail the variable nature of transactions between programs and families with different kinds of support needs and problems. These case histories may capture many of the serendipitous interventions that underlie successful treatment but that are generally represented only by unsystematic anecdote.[4]

The relevant factors vary from site to site, but in every community there are important systemic or contextual variables that lie beyond the reach of CS/FS programs while significantly affecting the power of home-based early interventions to achieve their objectives. It seems to us critical that such factors be systematically documented over the life of the project. The policy significance of such observations may well be as great as that of whatever findings emerge about program impacts. We therefore urged each project to identify and track factors in the community and larger society that constrain and facilitate their program interventions. The process of attempting to document these environmental variables has been instructive in itself, revealing the variation in CS/FS communities and the programs' interdependence with other services.

For example, the availability of medical care facilities varies significantly from site to site, and use of those facilities was much affected by whether clients had health insurance—third party or Medicaid.[5] The communities in which CS/FS projects operate also vary substantially with respect to the availability of various social services and hence with respect to projects' referral options. Since the success of CS/FS interventions may be affected by access to medical and other social services, these factors must be documented. Moreover, external influences such as changes in macroeconomic factors and in immigration, health care, and welfare policies have also significantly affected intervention efforts over the short life of this demonstration project.[6]

We have encouraged project staff not to measure variables just because "they are there," but we have also encouraged them to measure some variables for descriptive or explanatory purposes. Too often, in

[4]This includes, for example, the mother who decides to breast feed her child after discovering, at the suggestion of a home visitor making an early postpartum home visit, that doing so relives the discomfort of engorged breasts; or the father who assumes new child-rearing responsibilities when, having been cajoled to participate in occasional home visits, he discovers the pleasure to be had and developmental contribution to be made by talking and playing with his infant child.

[5]The perversities of public policies that prevent many impoverished married women and their children from receiving Medicaid warrant careful documentation if we are to understand the dynamics of health care utilization within the CS/FS target populations.

[6]In one CS/FS community about 90% of heads of households in client families are unemployed due to a cessation of coal mining activities. As the CS/FS program begins its second year of operation, unemployment benefits, including health insurance, are running out, with dramatic impacts on family health and functioning.

our judgment, an emphasis on summative evaluation leads researchers to focus exclusively upon measurement of variables that will be used either to estimate treatment effects or to make covariance adjustments. By doing so they neglect whole realms of measurement that might further our understanding of the intervention process and the problems it addresses, and that might improve the effectiveness of intervention by providing feedback on treatment progress. For example, although CS/FS projects do not generally expect to make significant impacts on the physical growth of infants, given the fact that infants within the target populations typically exhibit normal rates of growth in the absence of treatment, all have decided to monitor infant growth in order to identify problems that may be indicative of "failure to thrive," extreme nutritional neglect, or illness.

Cross-Project Measurement: Toward a Core of Common Variables

Once each project had a firm grasp on its own measurement needs and priorities, we directly attempted to foster as much commonality in measurement across projects as we reasonably could. We began by listing variables of greatest cross-project interest, providing operational definitions when possible and indicating a need for operationalization when it was not. We then asked each project to go over the list and indicate: (1) whether the project intended to collect any information related to that variable; (2) whether it would measure the variable in the manner specified; and (3) (for dependent variables) whether any program impact was expected and what controls would be introduced to estimate treatment effects (e.g., pre/post on experimental subjects, historical controls from population, randomized controls, a nonrandom comparison group). We brought together representatives from all projects to consider the possibilities for common measurement and how to make those more nearly comparable before final versions of instruments were prepared.

A marathon 2-day meeting produced consensus about the operational definitions of some 25 background variables and another 25 or so dependent variables. The degree of consensus achieved surprised everyone. The seven domains of common measurement were: family/household characteristics; prenatal health self-care; prenatal, delivery, and neonatal status; postnatal health self-care; infant health; quality of home environment; and infant development. Each project made some direct contribution to operationalizing particular variables, and each project carried away some instrument, or piece of an instrument, developed by another. The occasion also provided an opportunity to build measurement development teams, bringing together projects that were particularly interested in measuring variables for which methods had not yet been identified. Examples of such variables included prenatal risk status, appropriate infant feeding practice, and infant health status. We also felt it was very important to document CS/FS interventions in ways that would subsequently facilitate cross-project comparisons. To achieve this, we developed an outline for describing home-visiting interventions to guide both general program description and the presentation of more detailed, quantitative treatment information.

Another component of our cross-project evaluation strategy was the development of a common approach to economic analysis of the projects. As a first step we developed a standard time-use log completed periodically by home visitors and their supervisors to record time spent in various activities related to service delivery. When these data (sampled over a 12-month period of full implementation) are combined with information from home visitor records about total number of visits made and number of completed treatments, it will be possible to describe the levels of effort in various activities required to produce (and ultimately, the cost of producing) an hour of direct service and a completed treatment.

Research Design Issues

Although in this presentation we have separated our decisions about measurement from decisions about research design, in reality these processes and final plans emerged together. As with measurement, decisions about design involved weighing the advantages, disadvantages, and feasibilities of many options and making trade-offs until we achieved an acceptable compromise. Although basic research concerns entered into these deliberations, primary attention focused on the difficult issue of summative evaluation design under field conditions, that is, how best to estimate the effects of CS/FS programs on parents and infants.

Both practical and ethical impediments to "true experimentation" were anticipated. Whenever one evaluates a program in which enrollment is voluntary and participation is demanding of the client (9–33 months of regular home visits in the five programs considered here), selection bias is likely to be a problem whether or not comparison groups are formed by random assignment. We asked ourselves two questions. First, if potential clients were randomly assigned to experimental and control pools, would persons actually agreeing to participate in experimental and control conditions still represent samples from the same population? Second, would attrition over time (9–33 months) from experimental and control groups be random or, if not random, similarly nonrandom? Our answer to both questions was "probably not." Even if initial randomization were possible, it seemed likely that experimental and control groups would become gradually nonequivalent over time, beginning with client decisions regarding participation. Under this assumption, true experimental design lost its singular advantage over other options—the potential of achieving unassailable internal validity.

Other practical and ethical impediments to randomization also presented themselves. Random assignment with its concomitant denial of services to some was felt to be morally unacceptable, especially on the part of home visitors who were members of the very communities they served and participants in the social networks they used for program recruitment. Even when the pool of potential clients exceeded service resources, neither practitioners nor researchers could condone strategies that denied services to persons they knew had real and potentially life-threatening needs.

Since, even if feasible, true experimental design under CS/FS field conditions did not promise unassailable internal validity, quasi-experimental designs of similarly threatened internal validity seemed to offer more value for the money. We felt that, given our limited understanding of how to help high-risk young families with crucial child-rearing tasks, research into home-based early intervention should be as much concerned with hypothesis generation as with hypothesis confirmation; with looking for possible signals of positive impact as with precisely measuring signal strength; and with understanding the nature of the human problems addressed and the dynamics of intervention as with rigorous estimations of its usually modest average effects. Regarding external validity, whatever designs were implemented would be limited, even for the one project operating in six fairly distinctive rural communities. The effect of client self-selection on sample representativeness would be operating in all the local projects.

In light of such threats to both internal and external validity, we aimed our sights at making assailable but plausible inferences about the occurrence of program effects on selected outcomes among persons served by the program. Within the constraints described previously, we encouraged an opportunistic approach to research design that capitalized on different local opportunities for quasi-experimental control in estimating effects on particular variables, and one that gave legitimacy to "patchwork" designs in which different effects are estimated using different controls or points of reference. In typical demonstration projects, monolithic evaluation plans are put in place at the beginning and then implemented mechanically through the final data collection point. We preferred an approach in the CS/FS instance that maintained flexibility and anticipated—in fact encouraged—midstream corrections. Having participated in several large-scale, federally funded evaluations where we were contractually bound to implement a priori evaluation plans to the bitter end (even when it became apparent early on that we were measuring the wrong things and losing all semblance of experimental control), we did not want the CS/FS projects to find themselves in similar straits.

Daily experience in the field constantly reinforced our decision to employ an action research strategy. For example, expectations of program impact have changed over time and will continue to do so. It has become apparent that some problems are more intractable than originally envisioned and may not be susceptible to amelioration by the sorts of interventions that CS/FS projects are able to mount in the field. In other instances, formal research or informal experience has indicated that a particular problem may be less prevalent or serious among the client group than originally thought; thus, there is little room for amelioration and low probability of achieving average effects large enough to be substantiated by statistical analysis.

When working with the staff of each project to establish priorities for estimation of program impacts, we took into account:

1. The real probability of affecting each dependent variable (rhetoric and wishful thinking aside)
2. The likely quality (completeness, reliability, validity) of data obtained from measures of each dependent variable
3. The potential for experimental control in estimating program effects on each variable
4. The data collection costs of obtaining adequate control
5. The sample sizes required to provide sufficient statistical power to detect effects of the magnitudes anticipated

Gradually, through this process, initial summative evaluation plans were reduced to manageable proportions.

The individualized nature of family needs poses a challenge to evaluation in most home-based early intervention programs. We employed several tactics to address the problem. First, each project was encouraged to focus recruitment to increase sample homogeneity. We did not want selectivity carried to the point of eliminating any basis for generalization to "real world" situations, but we did want to avoid chaos. (In one instance, "focusing recruitment" ultimately meant accepting into the program only women who were currently pregnant—in contrast to an initial recruitment plan that also would have enrolled any family with an infant under 1 year of age.) Second, we assisted projects to identify the most prevalent and serious needs/problems in their target populations and to adjust the focus of intervention accordingly. (Two projects conducted extensive surveys for this purpose and established baseline norms for later estimation of program effects.)

We also encouraged each project to capitalize on local opportunities for experimental control. This meant being open to the possible advantages of using different quasi-experimental designs for different questions, as well as multiple designs for the same question. The resulting evaluation designs have a "patchwork" appearance that may offend traditional summative evaluation aesthetics, but the strategy undoubtedly permitted projects to stretch their resources much farther than would otherwise have been the case.

Capitalizing on local opportunities involved, for example: using recent historical health records, for a target population served largely by a single clinic, to obtain norms for estimating program impacts; collecting data on parent–child interaction with younger siblings of index children and staging program implementation in two rural counties so that one county provides "wait-listed controls" for estimating program effects in the other. Often control data are drawn from different sources and samples for different dependent variables. When dependent variables were unlikely to be affected by maturation or historical factors that threaten internal validity, decisions were sometimes made to use program clients as their own controls.

Where dependent variables might be strongly influenced by maturational/historical factors, we encouraged projects to get "multiple fixes" on program effects. For example, changes in patterns of parent–child interaction represented important CS/FS goals. But patterns of parent–child interaction change dramatically as infants mature during the first year of life; thus program effects on parenting outcomes cannot be estimated persuasively by comparing interactional patterns at 12 months with those at 3 or 6 months among the same subjects. Different approaches to this problem included: constructing nonrandomized comparison groups from among families in the target population who were not recruited into the program because their infants were too old; drawing comparison families from very similar neighboring communities; and observing parental interaction with the older or younger siblings of index children.

NEXT STEPS

All five home-visit projects will not have analyzed final outcome data and reported their findings for another 2–3 years. There are many problems still to be encountered and many lessons still to be learned.

How satisfied we and others will be ultimately with the progress made remains to be seen.

At this juncture, the development problem that Lorion (1983) describes as "operationalizing the case" has become less urgent. All five home-visit programs have developed to a point where they might appropriately be called "models." They will continue to evolve, but at a much slower pace than before. Evaluation plans are being implemented with generally good success, though not without some problems of quality control in data collection and occasional changes of plan to improve measurement or experimental control. Participants and observers alike have refined their expectations about what can be learned from summative evaluation to what we consider reasonable dimensions. We believe that the CS/FS initiative will yield insights that contribute to the gradual clarification of important issues surrounding home-based early intervention. We also believe that a long-term commitment to research, development, and evaluation in this area will be necessary to build an adequate basis for public policy.

Our own plans for synthesizing project level research and evaluation results are still evolving. From the very beginning it was clear that we could not and should not pool data from different projects for common analysis. However, the appropriateness of applying quantitative meta-analytic techniques to site-level effects (5 projects, 13 sites) has been debated. Increasingly we feel that "qualitative" synthesis will be more feasible and useful at this stage of work than "quantitative" synthesis. Clear and careful thinking is likely to be more helpful than any amount of creative cross-project number crunching.

An exception may prove to be number crunching in connection with instrument development. One of the main barriers to home-based program evaluation has been measurement underdevelopment. Together with the research staff of various projects (including two non-home-visiting projects) we have begun to identify possibilities for further development of measures used in CS/FS research through secondary analyses of data, perhaps including data pooled from several projects that have employed the same instruments. If the limitations of measurement that plague research on home-based early intervention are ever to be overcome, more attention must be given to conducting serious measurement development research that sheds light on reliability and validity and points the way toward systematic improvement of measurement techniques.

LESSONS LEARNED ABOUT THE ACTION RESEARCH PARADIGM

As "cross-project evaluators," we have taken advantage of the CS/FS opportunity to clarify our own thinking about strategies for research and evaluation of complicated interventions under turbulent field conditions. Rediscovering the action research paradigm contributed to the process of clarification. We do not promote action research as a "theology" but as a practical approach to tackling social problems in field settings—one that integrates research, action, and evaluation persistently and systematically to develop solutions. In many respects action research is nothing more than a convenient name for what opinion leaders, concerned with research and evaluation in relation to social policy, are currently advocating in reaction to the "failed" social program development efforts of recent years. For the sake of convenience, we revive the name; for the sake of more effective social program development, we urge application of the approach regardless of nomenclature.

Why is it that action research has not caught on? First, it is difficult to implement. The different world views and value systems of key actors—researchers, practitioners, and evaluators—make the creation of effective action research teams a demanding and frequently unsuccessful enterprise. Academic researchers have little motivation, given current incentive systems within universities, to get involved in field-based program development; doing so might even have negative consequences for their careers. Nonacademic evaluators are perhaps more willing, but they have few opportunities; they are also not well-prepared to create opportunities, given their customary general-purpose and atheoretical approach to program evaluation. Practitioners, for their part, need to be convinced that research and evaluation are useful.

A second major obstacle to action research is that it is difficult to fund. With very few exceptions, governmental and private funding sources make no deliberate effort to stimulate action research by writing requests for proposals or establishing proposal review criteria that would encourage it. Moreover, current patterns of short-term funding and constantly shifting program emphases actively discourage the long-term commitments that serious action research demands. We hope that efforts of action researchers within the CS/FS initiative and elsewhere will begin to rectify this situation.

REFERENCES

Cronbach, L., and Associates. (1980). *Toward reform of program evaluation.* San Francisco, CA: Jossey-Bass.

Datta, Lois-ellin. (1975). Design of the Head Start Planned Variation Experiment. In A. M. Rivlin and P. M. Timpane (Eds.), *Planned variation in education: Should we give up or try harder.* Washington, D.C.: The Brookings Institute.

Halpern, Robert. (1984). Lack of effects for home-based early intervention? Some possible explanations. *American Journal of Orthopsychiatry, 54*(1), 33–42.

Haney, W. (1977). *A technical history of the national Follow Through evaluation.* Cambridge, MA: Huron Institute.

Lorion, Raymond. (1983). Research issues in the design and evaluation of preventive interventions. In J. P. Bowker (Ed.), *Education for primary prevention in social work.* NY: Council on Social Work Education.

Rapoport, Robert. (1985). Research and action. In R. Rapoport (Ed.), *Research and action: Innovations for children, youth, and families.* London: Cambridge University Press.

Rutman, Leonard. (1980). *Planning useful evaluations: Evaluability assessment.* Beverly Hills, CA: Sage.

Weiss, Carol H. (1975). Evaluation research in the political context. In E. L. Struening and M. Guttentag (Eds.), *Handbook of evaluation research.* Beverly Hills, CA: Sage.

Wholey, J. (1979). *Evaluation: Promise and performance.* Washington, D.C.: The Urban Institute.

chapter 16

THE CHILD WELFARE LEAGUE OF AMERICA'S ADOLESCENT PARENTS PROJECT

Shelby H. Miller

INTRODUCTION

Late in 1982, the Child Welfare League of America (CWLA) received a 3-year grant from the Ford Foundation under a new initiative called Child Survival/Fair Start for Children (CS/FS) (see Bond and Halpern, Chapter 15, this volume). The aims of this initiative were to improve birth outcomes for mothers and infants and to enhance children's later health and development. The CWLA was to implement and evaluate a long-term program of information and support for pregnant teenagers and young mothers in five metropolitan areas (Atlanta, Charlotte, Cleveland, Minneapolis/St. Paul, and Toledo) using a program model developed by the Minnesota Early Learning Design (MELD) (see Ellwood, Chapter 13, this volume).

The CWLA was the primary contractor on the project and was responsible for day-to-day program operations, including fiscal management, staff supervision, and process and impact evaluation activities. The author served as project director. MELD was the subcontractor and assumed the tasks of adapting the MELD's Young Moms (MYM) curriculum for a low-income, predominantly black sample, developing new materials, and training and supporting the program staff. The CWLA Adolescent Parents Project was designed to test the applicability and effectiveness of the MYM model for low-income, urban, minority pregnant teenagers and young mothers. Previously, the MYM model had been used almost exclusively with white teenagers.

The MYM program involves weekly group meetings of parents led by trained facilitators using curriculum resource materials. The model is based on several basic premises: *(a)* that pregnant adolescents and young parents can learn from each other and from mature women who have been through similar experiences; *(b)* that young mothers can generalize what they learn in a group to their daily experiences, especially in interaction with their babies; *(c)* that a program for pregnant adolescents and teenage parents must continue long after the babies' births because needs for information and support change over time; and *(d)* that receipt of information and support in a group setting should result in positive outcomes such as higher rates of continued education and fewer repeat pregnancies. The MYM model was selected for use in the project because it was one of the few available at the time that was both detailed and extensive in content.

The CWLA designed an evaluation to examine program implementation, as well as effects. The evaluation had to meet the needs of a variety of players including: the Ford Foundation; the CS/FS cross-site evaluators (the High/Scope Educational Research Foundation); the model initiators and curriculum developers at MELD: the administrators, program staff, and clients at the five individual program sites; and the CWLA evaluation staff.

This chapter will begin with a discussion of the adaptations made in the MYM model to increase its applicability to the project participants. This is followed by a description of the evaluation design and a review of the issues that had to be addressed in planning and carrying it out. The final section details some of the problems confronted in the data analysis, provides a summary of preliminary evaluation results, and notes lessons learned in the project that may be useful to others implementing and evaluating similar programs.

ADAPTING THE MELD YOUNG MOMS MODEL

In the original MYM model, groups of 10 to 15 young mothers met weekly over a 2-year period. These meetings were facilitated by pairs of mature, indigenous community women using a standard curriculum. It was MELD's intent that the characteristics of the program facilitators match to some extent those of the participants to promote the exchange of common experiences and support.

Several major adaptations were made in the original MYM model for the CWLA project. Most of these were necessitated by the following concerns: *(a)* most of the original participant population consisted of white, both low and middle SES, and older adolescent mothers in contrast to ours, which was predominantly minority, urban, poor teenagers of various ages; *(b)* the locations from which the teenagers could be identified and reached for services on our project were public welfare departments, hospitals, clinics, special schools, and day care centers, not primarily the social service agencies where MELD had piloted their MYM model in the past; and *(c)* unlike previous experiences with the MYM model, we sought both to implement the model for teenage mothers and to evaluate the program process and its impact. Adaptations of the MYM model for the CWLA project included: *(a)* addition of a prenatal curriculum component emphasizing early and regular medical care, adequate nutrition, and preparation for delivery (this extended the possible duration of the intervention from 2 to about 2¼ years); *(b)* added emphasis on school continuation or reentry, family planning, and preparation for future employment; and *(c)* a more systematic plan for program supervision entailing weekly telephone contacts with the site coordinators by the CWLA, biweekly calls by MELD, and 8–10 on-site visits over the Project period. The supervision plan was added to provide the programs with consistent support and information to insure effective and efficient implementation of the model; to enhance the evaluation process by collecting quantitative and qualitative data at various points in time during the project; and to allow the project director and MELD staff to coordinate their programmatic and evaluation responsibilities at the five sites.

More structure was also imposed on the model through the requirement that certain curricular topics be covered at specific times vis-à-vis the baby's birth. Unlike most previous MYM programs, additional services were not offered, (e.g., child care and transportation). Finally, prior to this effort, only a limited amount of descriptive data had been collected on the MYM model. Our plan to pursue the dual goals of process and impact evaluation thus marked a new stage in MELD. Therefore, one of the first tasks facing the CWLA and MELD staff was to agree upon the primary goals and objectives for the project.

PLANNING THE EVALUATION

Once funds were granted, staff members of the two contracting organizations (CWLA and MELD) convened to achieve agreement upon goals and objectives. A variety of factors were influential in this process including: MELD's interest in maintaining the MYM model's flexibility and adaptability; the author's and CWLA's desire for specific goals and objectives consistent with some of those emerging from the wider field of teenage parent intervention research; the sponsoring foundation's need for some points of comparison across all CS/FS sites; and the CWLA's and MELD's concerns that the evaluation would intrude extensively on program activities.

Written description of the MYM model, training materials, and reports regarding pilot efforts with MYM were first reviewed by CWLA and MELD staffs. The suggested goals, objectives, and possible effects of the program were discussed in sessions with both staffs present. These review and discussion activities were initiated by the project director to clarify program goals, to make sure that the MELD staff was confident that the program could be put into place and could affect the identified maternal and child behaviors, and to attempt to quantify the expected extent of program effect. The MELD staff, at this time in the Project's development did not have a set of agreed upon, measurable objectives for the MYM model but had instead a set of non-measurable goal statements. Some staff believed commitment to specific goals or objectives then could compromise the flexibility and adaptability of the model. MELD staff also expressed concern that committing to a set of measurable objectives might overwhelm or upset those attempting to start programs and otherwise inhibit the replication of the model. The author encouraged, and in some cases, pressed for, the inclusion of specific, measurable objectives with the belief that the program could influence them. She believed that the MELD staff needed to describe the model, the objectives, and the expected impact in fuller detail and in measurable terms, if the model was to be replicated beyond the pilot phase and evaluated.

The Ford Foundation's priorities for the CS/FS initiative also influenced the process of identifying objectives. These priorities emphasized outcomes such as prenatal care and adequate immunizations, not improved self-esteem, better school attendance, and increased knowledge of family planning methods which the MYM model also stressed. The external agenda of the Foundation initiatives was translated at the programmatic level into some pressure to affect some impacts about which the MELD staff did not feel particularly confident.

Apprehension regarding the impact of the evaluation on the implementation of the program also influenced the identification of goals and objectives for the model. This apprehension created a certain amount of tension between the program and evaluation staff, some of which was inherent in the nature of the effort. The MYM model was being adapted quite extensively and then was to be evaluated by an outside entity with a limited knowledge of MELD and the model.

A set of program objectives, more or less mutually agreed upon by project staff of the CWLA and MELD, were eventually defined (see Table 16.1) and incorporated into the evaluation strategy. Underlying the formulation of goals and evaluation design was the belief that receipt of

TABLE 16.1. Objectives for the Project[a]

For the young mother

The young mother will:

1. Increase her knowledge of child development, child health, nutrition, and child care, and increase the appropriateness of her expectations for her baby's development.
2. Integrate her knowledge of child care, child development, and appropriate expectations (No. 1 above) into her interaction and relationship with her baby.
3. Obtain adequate health care for herself and her baby, both prenatally and postnatally (including both routine care and responses to accidents or illnesses).
4. Increase her understanding of job possibilities and requirements for specific training and employment opportunities.
5. Make progress toward completing her education.
6. Take steps to plan her childbearing:
   a. Use family planning methods effectively (if sexually active).
   b. Increase her knowledge about contraceptives.
   c. Increase her knowledge about risks of pregnancy.
7. Increase her self-esteem.
8. Acquire or sustain positive attitudes and some knowledge about breast-feeding.
9. Set appropriate short- and long-term goals for the future in terms of education, childbearing, marriage, housing, and employment.
10. Provide a safe and stimulating environment for her child.

For the project

11. The group facilitators and/or site coordinator will make appropriate, timely referrals for services through the agency or hospital.
12. Determine the cost effectiveness of various aspects of the project, for example site coordinator training, group facilitator training, supervision of site coordinators, and recruitment of participants.
13. The project will be responsive to the specific needs and attitudes of the participants.
14. The project will provide information that is timely and related to the objectives—adhere to required topic plan.
15. The project will train site coordinators and project group facilitators in health care screening and conveying health care information in groups.
16. The site coordinator (with assistance from CWLA and MELD) will confer with child care workers in health care screening and use of an outline and curriculum for infant stimulation activities.
17. The child care providers will provide a safe and stimulating environment for infants who need care during project sessions.
18. Local professionals will be recruited and used in specific curriculum sessions.

[a]These were written as general statements and later translated into measurable terms.

appropriate and timely information, as well as assistance in a supportive environment, would affect the subsequent behavior of the young mothers. Having been informed and having received support, an adolescent mother would be able to procure the services she and her child needed and interact positively with her child to affect his or her development. Thus, the objectives concurred upon by the CWLA and MELD staffs emanated from the MYM curriculum components.

In retrospect, more time and attention should have been allocated early in the project for: (1) identifying the goals and objectives for the program; (2) translating the objectives into measurable terms; and (3) generating consensus on these objectives among project staff at CWLA, MELD, and the program sites. Time alone, however, would probably not have been sufficient to remedy the problems encountered. MELD's program staff were not fully prepared for the effort that such a replication and evaluation of the model entailed. Specifically, they lacked experience with impact evaluation procedures, had difficulty distinguishing between their goals and objectives for the MYM program, and were dissatisfied with the available measures. MELD's "democratic" program philosophy extended to decision making regarding the model. Much time in the early phases of the project was allocated to informing various staff members about the project, its timetable, and its proposed activities. Some individuals had trouble accepting what had been proposed to the Foundation, and these concerns had to be addressed.

Selection and Design of the Data Collection Instruments

Various factors were considered in the selection of existing measures and the design of new ones. These included: *(a)* the availability and appropriateness of measures used in other projects funded through the CS/FS initiative, past CWLA studies and other evaluations of long-term intervention programs with pregnant teenagers and adolescent mothers; *(b)* the limitations imposed by low levels of reading ability; *(c)* the potential for obtaining existing data from case records at hospitals, schools, and social service programs; *(d)* the desire to direct the majority of funds to program operations; *(e)* constraints imposed by the budget; and *(f)* the commitment to integrate evaluation activities into intervention activities as much as possible.

Guided by these factors, the author worked with the CWLA research analyst to review the evaluation plans, interview schedules, and instruments used in similar studies and program evaluations. Where possible, we identified and used previously developed scales whose reliability and validity had already been established and that were seen as appropriate for use with a primarily low-income sample. Several existing scales were used in their entirety; others were adapted extensively. The High/Scope Educational Research Foundation's Knowledge Scale (Epstein, 1980) measuring the appropriateness of mothers' expectations regarding child development, was shortened based on experiences with its use in an earlier CWLA study (Miller, 1983). To improve the scale's reliability and the range of content covered, the revised version included only the items on the first year of a baby's life. An observational measure of mother–child interaction was derived from the Home Observation for Measurement of the Environment (HOME) (Caldwell and Bradley, 1984; see Howrigan, Chapter 4, this volume). New instruments were also developed. Table 16.2 lists each measure, its origins, the program objectives to which it relates, and the time of its administration. Following the selection and design of the measures, the potential variables on which data were to be collected were organized according to program objectives. This was done to establish that sufficient data were being collected to determine whether the program objectives were met and to begin to arrange the format of the data collection procedures.

As Table 16.2 suggests, the process of designing and selecting the instruments resulted in a five-part data collection approach. First, participants completed forms regarding their own and their child's status at various times during the program. Second, data was extracted from agency or hospital records (on both participants and a comparison group). Third, child testing and home observations were conducted (for both groups). Fourth, attendance and content covered at meetings were recorded weekly. Finally, qualitative reports were prepared by staff.

This multifaceted approach to data collection was adopted for several reasons: It allowed for a balanced set of demands for data collection from participants, program staff, and others in the cooperating agencies; it permitted checks for validity; and it appeared to be the most efficient way of obtaining data on both the process and impact of the MYM program. The inclusion of qualitative reporting is not typical of evaluative efforts. We included it to document the richness of the program experience and to provide some explanation for both successes and problems encountered. This reporting was accomplished by having the local site coordinators and MELD and CWLA staff members respond verbally or in writing to specific questions at several points in the program implementation. These qualitative reports, with the weekly reports of program attendance and curriculum content covered, provided the formative data on whether the program was being implemented as planned, as well as a feedback mechanism for strengthening the intervention where possible.

TABLE 16.2. Measures Used on the CWLA Adolescent Parents Project

Measures	Origin	Related program objectives (numbers refer to Table 16.1)	Time of administration	Sampling
Case reading form	New	(Descriptive data)	At program initiation	Participants and comparison groups
Identification form	New	(Descriptive data)	At program initiation	All participants
My pregnancy	New with parts from Miller's (1983) earlier instrument	1, 3	At program initiation	Participants at four sites (all but Atlanta)
My family during my pregnancy	New with the Tennessee Psycho-social Screening Tool included (Simpkins, McMillian and Dunlop, 1980)	1, 3	At program initiation	Participants at four sites (all but Atlanta)
My baby's birth	New	3, 10	Following the child's birth (3–4 months after program initiation)	Participants at four sites (all but Atlanta)
How I feel about myself	Rosenberg's (1965) Self-Esteem Scale	7	At program initiation and follow-up interview	Participants at four sites (all but Atlanta) (to follow-up just home interview sites—Toledo and Minneapolis/St. Paul)
What I know about different ways to prevent pregnancy and the risks of getting pregnant	Adapted from Miller's (1983) earlier instrument and others	6	At program initiation and follow-up interview	Participants at four sites (all but Atlanta) (to follow-up just home interview sites—Toledo and Minneapolis/St. Paul)

Instrument	Source		Data collection point	Population
Inventory of the home environment	Caldwell and Bradley (1984)	2, 10	Home visits	Participants and comparison groups in two sites—Toledo and Minneapolis/St. Paul
Bayley Mental Scale	Bayley (1969)	2, 10	Home visits	Participants and comparison groups in two sites—Toledo and Minneapolis/St. Paul
Home interview	New	3, 5, 6, 9	Home visits	Participants and comparison groups in two sites—Toledo and Minneapolis/St. Paul
Parent, group facilitators log, cumulative attendance form, child care log	Adapted from MELD's original form	11, 13, 14	Throughout program	
	New	17	Throughout program	Child care workers, site coordinators and group facilitators
Participant exit form	New		Throughout program	Child care workers, site coordinators, and group facilitators
Time and expense forms	New	12	Throughout program	Child care workers, site coordinators, and group facilitators

(continued)

TABLE 16.2. (Continued)

Measures	Origin	Related program objectives (numbers refer to Table 16.1)	Time of administration	Sampling
What I know about child development	High/Scope Educational Research Foundation's Knowledge Scale (Epstein, 1980)	1	At program initiation and follow-up	All participants and comparison groups at two sites
What I know about jobs and what I am planning for my future	In part from MDRC's Project Redirection (Polit, Kahn, Murray, and Smith, 1982)	4, 9	At program initiation and follow-up	All participants and comparison groups at two sites
My life at school	In part from MDRC's Project Redirection	5, 9	At program initiation and follow-up	Participants at four sites (all but Atlanta) (to follow-up just home interview sites—Toledo and Minneapolis/St. Paul)
My health care	New	3, 6	At program initiation and follow-up	Participants at four sites (all but Atlanta) (to follow-up just home interview sites—Toledo and Minneapolis/St. Paul)

My baby's health care	New	2, 3	At program initiation and follow-up	Participants at four sites (all but Atlanta) (to follow-up just home interview sites—Toledo and Minneapolis/St. Paul)
My plans for my baby's care	New	1, 2	At program initiation	Participants at four sites (all but Atlanta) (to follow-up just home interview sites—Toledo and Minneapolis/St. Paul)
My baby's day	New	2, 10	At program initiation	Participants at four sites (all but Atlanta) (to follow up just home interview sites—Toledo and Minneapolis/St. Paul)

Selection of Participant and Comparison Groups

Initially, participants were those pregnant teenagers and young mothers who were younger than 20 years of age; delivered children after February 28, 1983; were known to the cooperating agencies at the sites either directly or through referrals; and were planning to rear their children themselves rather than relinquish them for adoption. The age criterion was later raised to 23. Comparison groups were composed of teenagers who met all of the participant selection criteria but the second; they had delivered their babies in the several-month period proceeding the participants' time of delivery. This procedure for selecting comparison group mothers was pursued because random assignment resulting in the withholding of services for some agency clients was neither feasible nor acceptable to local agency staff.

Issues in the Implementation of the Evaluation

The implementation of the evaluation plan was not without problems. The major problems involved the appropriateness of the data collection instruments for this particular population; the threats to reliability posed by reliance on data collected by self-report; and the difficulties posed by low attendance rates and high attrition. Each of these problems and our efforts to handle them will be described in turn.

First, the appropriateness of self-administered forms for adolescents with low levels of reading ability is questionable. Participants completed forms during program sessions. They required more assistance in completing them than we had expected, which necessitated additional staff time and a reduction in time allocated to program activities. Some additional requests for help on the evaluation forms may be attributable to the "peer support" atmosphere of the meetings and the general nature of activities taking place: sharing, problem solving, and discussion. While this group atmosphere may have threatened the validity of the data to some extent, care was taken in training and supervising the group facilitators administering the forms.

Second, larger than anticipated turnover of participants in the program over the 2¼-year period made it difficult to obtain all self-administered forms from all participants. Additional staff time for telephone and in-person interviews was necessary to reach some dropouts. At many sites, telephone calls and in-person interviews were also necessary to expedite the collection of follow-up data from the participants and to avoid detracting from the continuity of the program. The need for in-person interviews necessitated several changes in the evaluation plan. One was the elimination of several forms from the second administration (when the babies were 18–20 months old). These assessed knowledge of breast- and bottle-feeding and of self-esteem, on which participants showed quite high levels in the first administration. The collection of forms from the group facilitators regarding mother–baby interaction also proved problematic, and in fact was terminated both because the process proved intrusive to the group meetings and because the measure elicited few differences among mothers. Moreover, the irregular attendance of the infants at the group made observations of interactions difficult.

These additional data collection efforts created unanticipated demands on staff time and escalated competition between the program implementation and the evaluation components of the Project. From all checks and staff reports, the reliability of the data was quite high. The switch to individual interviews early in the process at most sites minimized the loss of group meeting time and may have resulted in unanticipated positive effects. Some participants and facilitators became better acquainted and identified unmet needs and possible sources of assistance. Still, the negative effects of the extensive data collection procedure cannot be underestimated. Some participants were deterred from attending the group meetings because they did not want to complete forms. Others refused to be interviewed after they had completed the initial round of data collection.

With hindsight, all of the data collection from the participants might have been more effective and efficient if it had been done individually and if the individual interviews at program intake and late in the intervention period had focused on fewer variables. If individual interviews are used exclusively, it is advisable either to have a person who knows the young mother well collect the data directly or to use a simply administered instrument. Incentives such as money or material items should be provided for the completion of interviews in order to maximize the compliance of both current participants and those who have dropped out.

Third, the heavy reliance on self-report, particularly regarding medical problems and use of health services, was a concern throughout the evaluation, even though checks for reliability were included. Direct measures obtained at routine check-ups or analysis of medical records might have been preferable. Yet these sources of data presume that young mothers receive routine care from the same or a limited number of care providers and presume easy access to medical records. Those data that were available from agency and hospital records about the participant and comparison group mothers' family backgrounds, their babies' fathers, their pregnancy histories, and prenatal care were collected quite easily. In fact, data on a wider than anticipated range of variables were available from most of the hospitals and social service agencies. Lack of comparability across sites was a problem, however, as not all sites utilized all sources of data. In retrospect, solutions to this problem would have been to request that the agencies add the missing data elements to their forms or that additional data be gleaned from other sources such as hospital files. Fourth, only one of four adolescents recruited had come to three or more of the group meetings, and generally, participants came to only 50% of the meetings that occurred between their first and last sessions. These relatively short and inconsistent patterns of attendance were difficult to change and consequently negatively influenced the plan for evaluation.

The greater than expected drop-out rate at the Atlanta site, particularly during its first year, required a substantial redesign of its data collection procedures. Rather than collecting information on the large numbers of new participants, hospital case-reading regarding prenatal and obstetrical variables and telephone interviews (or in-person sessions where necessary) regarding mother and infant status in the first year were conducted on a sample of program participants and comparison mothers during their babies' first year. This adaptation worked quite well despite the time-consuming tracking of mothers whose places of residence and telephone numbers changed frequently. The additional data from the Atlanta site has been used to elucidate the effects of a short-term intervention period with the MYM model.

Like the case-reading portion of the data collection, the home-visiting component proceeded nearly as planned. However, for budgetary reasons, its scope had to be restricted to two sites, Minneapolis/St. Paul and Toledo, where the groups began quite rapidly and attendance was maintained just about as expected over time. Careful documentation was kept when home visits were not possible. The young mothers enjoyed the home visits, particularly the infant tests where most observed their children's abilities with satisfaction and pleasure. Toys were given as incentives for completion of the home visits.

In retrospect, had funds been available or allocated differently, home visits would have been conducted in all the sites. These would have provided a more complete understanding of mother–child interaction and the children's developmental status, and perhaps a more reliable way of obtaining data from the mothers on their health and education status, and on their knowledge of child development and family planning methods. Total reliance on home interviews for the evaluation might have been a more efficient and cost effective plan.

Qualitative reporting of the successes and difficulties encountered in various phases of the programs' implementation also proceeded with few problems. Each site coordinator and the CWLA and MELD staffs organized their qualitative reports at the end of the first year of program operations using the same outline to facilitate cross-referencing and summary reporting. Items on the outline included participant recruitment strategies, group facilitator training, incentives for participation, and use of the required curriculum modules. Following receipt of the qualitative reports, questions specific to each site were posed verbally by the project director. This process of qualitative reporting continued through the second data collection and data analysis phases of the project. Problems such as the need for routine weekly phone calls to participants to ensure attendance and the need for elaborate transportation systems in some sites would not have been identified through other evaluation activities.

Issues in the Data Analysis. Data were first analyzed separately by site and then, when possible, aggregated. Those participants who attended the program for various numbers of sessions were compared with those who never attended, utilizing basic demographic, prenatal, and obstetrical variables obtained from the records at all five sites. Frequent, long-term users of the program were also contrasted with those who attended less frequently on a variety of outcome measures: their baby's health care status; the mother's health (including sexuality) and educational status; and knowledge of child development, family planning, and job preparation, using data collected near the initiation and termination of the programs at all five sites. In addition, data from the home interviews in Minneapolis/St. Paul and Toledo yielded direct measures of the baby's developmental status and mother–child interaction, as well as self-reports regarding utilization of health care and other services and the quality of the home environment when the babies were 18–20 months old.

Two major problems were encountered: the first with data reduction; the second with combining the data across sites. The number of variables being investigated was reduced substantially when most of the scales at the first data collections were found to be internally consistent, that is, scores on the individual scale items could be added together to form a composite measure. Scale and subscale scores were used whenever possible. However, the reliability coefficients (Cronbach's alpha) of several of the measures, specifically the one assessing knowledge of family planning methods and breast- and bottle-feeding, were not so high as preferred. Thus, the data on these scales were analyzed on an item-by-item basis, as well as for the total scale, on the assumption that a general body of knowledge was being reflected on each scale. The number of variables to be analyzed after the scales were developed was still extensive, but many were descriptive and pursued only if they helped to explain differences in outcome measures.

Differences across sites in the ages and races of participants were also identified. This necessitated some additional controls in the bivariate and multivariate analyses when site data were combined. Because of these differences, more effort was also directed toward within-site differences. The analysis plan was complex and more time-consuming than had been anticipated. However, such detailed analysis was important in so far as it helped to unravel the extent to which findings could be generalized to other populations.

While the data analysis is not complete, the results available to date suggest positive yet qualified answers to these questions. In all sites, coordinators and group facilitators were recruited, hired, and trained with few problems. There was little staff attrition during the Project period. Four groups of participants were initiated at each of the sites. Attendance stabilized only slowly, however, and unfortunately, this stabilization did not last at all sites. Prenatal attendance averaged 6.2 meetings and postnatal attendance averaged 12.0 meetings. The total number of weeks from the first to last meeting period varied from 3 to 83, but again, the mean was low, 20.2. These numbers indicate that many participants came to the program, tried it out, stayed for 4–5 months, and then dropped out. For most participants, the 4–5 months occurred in the immediate postpartum period, which can perhaps be viewed as a major transition time involving the greatest need for support. While the project was successful in implementing a part of the program, the extent of the intervention was much shorter than had been planned. The entire intervention (2–2¼ years) was received by only a small portion of the total sample. These results suggest that the MYM program can be staffed, initiated, and maintained for low-income, minority, pregnant adolescents and young mothers, but only for a limited time period. Curriculum content was delivered in the groups that took place; about half of the meeting time was allocated to sharing experiences and providing support, the other half to the required content. However, attrition and irregularities in attendance contributed to the need for some repetition of the curriculum modules already delivered.

The evaluation results regarding the impact of the intervention program received are also mixed. Many of the program objectives were not met and several were not pursued after the first data collection since the participants' scores on several scales approached the scales' ceilings. Several positive impacts were found, however, among the Atlanta participants when they were compared with a group of mothers who were not offered the program. When their babies were about 1 year of age participants reported fewer health problems for themselves and their children and had obtained more medical care for themselves. These findings are encouraging, although tentative.

There are also several findings from the data collected during the home interviews that look promising, but they are few and far between.

The participants were less likely than those refusing or never offered the program to use hospital emergency rooms for care of themselves or their babies, and they were slightly more knowledgeable about some aspects of family planning methods. Participants were also far more likely than those never offered the program to know the time in the month when they were most likely to become pregnant. Unfortunately, this knowledge did not seem to transfer to the behavior of using contraceptives and otherwise avoiding pregnancy. Apparently, lack of knowledge regarding family planning methods is not a primary obstacle to preventing pregnancies in this population (see Dym, Chapter 22; Slaughter, Chapter 21, this volume). Differences between the participant and comparison groups on their school status and the use of medical care and other community services were not significant.

While much analysis remains to be completed, it appears that the short-term program did not result in the extensive impacts for which we had hoped. Isolated impacts for certain groups of participants seem to be the pattern. Additional analyses should allow for a definitive answer regarding the program's impact, including the effects of varied lengths of program attendance.

RECOMMENDATIONS FOR EVALUATORS

At this time it is possible to draw some conclusions from this evaluation that have implications for the design of future interventions and evaluations. First, it is very difficult to investigate a wide range of variables effectively in a developing program. One must be very specific about the expected impacts of an intervention and direct the focus of the evaluation to those issues. Second, the literature on adolescent pregnancy and parenting is extensive, and the findings appear conclusive in several areas, such as obstetrical outcomes and use of health care. It seems unnecessary, therefore, to continue to collect data on these issues unless for descriptive purposes or when the planned intervention is believed to affect them directly. Third, there is a general lack of understanding of program evaluation methodology by service providers and thus a reluctance to commit to an evaluation plan tied to the clearly specified goals and objectives of the intervention. More staff training in evaluation methodology would be helpful, as would the dissemination of information on useful and promising evaluation models. Fourth, the amount of time required to design and implement an evaluation plan at several program sites should not be underestimated. Monitoring data collection activities from a distance contributes to that demand. Finally, the need for incentives to both staff and respondents to complete data collection forms must be addressed.

Whether monetary compensation, material reward, or other support, some incentives need to be provided in most evaluations requiring more than a minimal amount of time from program staff, clients, and a control or comparison group.

In sum, simpler, more easily implemented evaluation activities need to be incorporated into the operation of programs from their onsets with the full understanding and commitment of staff members. Funders should, in fact, require such efforts. Only through early incorporation of evaluation plans will data be available to inform program directors, policymakers, and funding agencies about the most effective and efficient ways to enhance the implementation and impacts of interventions.

REFERENCES

Bayley, N. (1969). *Bayley Scales of Infant Development*. San Antonio, TX: The Psychological Corporation.

Caldwell, B. M., and Bradley, R. H. (1984). *Home Observation for Measurement of the Environment (HOME)*. Little Rock, AK: University of Arkansas at Little Rock.

Epstein, A. S. (1980). *Assessing the child development information needed by adolescent parents with very young children*. Final Report, Grant No. 90-C-1341. Ypsilanti, MI: High/Scope Educational Research Foundation.

Miller, S. H. (1983). *Children as parents: Final report on a study of child-bearing and child rearing among 12- to 15-year-olds*. NY: Child Welfare League of America.

Polit, D., Kahn, J. R., Murray, C. A., and Smith, K. W. (May, 1982). *Needs and characteristics of pregnant and parenting teens: The baseline report for Project Redirection*. NY: Manpower Demonstration Research Corporation.

Rosenberg, M. (1965). *Society and adolescent self-image*. Princeton, NJ: Princeton University Press.

Simpkins, C., McMillan, D. W., and Dunlop, K. H. (1980). *Results of TIOP psychological screening for high risk of negative outcomes of pregnancy*. Nashville, TN: Center for Community Studies, George Peabody College, Vanderbilt University.

chapter 17

STUDYING COMPLEXITY: THE CASE OF THE CHILD AND FAMILY RESOURCE PROGRAM

Marrit J. Nauta
Kathryn Hewett

CONTEXT AND POLICY

In the early 1970s an extensive Head Start diversification effort was launched, partly in response to critics who claimed that the program did not have a lasting effect. Several innovative demonstration programs were initiated to promote the total development of young children through increased emphasis on parents and parent involvement, home-versus center-based education, and the extension of Head Start services to children from before birth to age 8. It became increasingly clear that a child is unlikely to benefit from cognitive stimulation if other factors such as hunger, illness, or disability in the family are ignored and that child development services are most effective when offered in the context of a full range of family support services.

This approach to promoting child development became the cornerstone of the Child and Family Resource Program (CFRP), a federally funded demonstration initiated in 1973 by the Administration for Children, Youth, and Families (ACYF). CFRP targeted services to low-income families with children not yet born through age 8, thus encompassing the prenatal, infant–toddler, and preschool periods, as well as the transition into the early years of elementary school. Our study focused on the infant–toddler component, in part because we hypothesized that earlier intervention would contribute to more lasting outcomes. Infant–toddler services were provided through periodic home visits and center-based activities. Family support services attempted to address the whole range of common problems that these families face—unemployment, inadequate housing, low self-esteem, single parenthood, and shortages of food and money, to name just a few.

A major CFRP goal was to work with representatives from different agencies to bring some cohesion to the fragmented system of public and private social services. Its mission was to become "advocates" for families with young children (Johnson and Nauta, 1980). CFRP's dual strategy for achieving enhanced child development was: (1) to strengthen families by providing social services and (2) to train parents to be more skillful in stimulating their children's social and cognitive growth. It implied that attention would shift from social-service provision to parent education and child development, once families learned to cope adequately with financial and personal problems.

This combination of family support and developmental services was expected to produce the lasting effects that Head Start had been unable to demonstrate at that time. Yet an inherent dilemma—a dynamic tension between child-development goals and family support—affected implementation of the program. Intervention and support were called for simultaneously. Both were mandated in the broad CFRP program guidelines and demanded local program resources. The dilemma posed by these two program philosophies had to be addressed in program implementation as well as in research designed to evaluate the CFRP impact (Hewett, 1982).

CFRP operated as a demonstration program at 11 sites around the country. Each site designed a program in response to local needs and available resources. Some of the variations in program approaches and philosophies were dramatic. For example, helping parents to become independent and self-reliant through employment or job training was an important objective at some sites, even when this meant mothers moving away from the program and its potential benefits. In contrast, other programs emphasized CFRP program participation above all else. There were numerous other differences across programs with regard to populations served and services offered. In fact, CFRP has often been characterized as having been "invented" eleven times (Nauta and Hewett, 1981).

CFRP recognized that each family is unique, despite common problems. Therefore, needs assessment, goal setting, and service strategies differed not only across sites, but across participants within a single site. These variations posed major challenges for the program's evaluation.

THE EVOLVING DESIGN OF THE EVALUATION

The 5-year evaluation, initiated in 1977 and carried out by Abt Associates Inc., of Cambridge, Massachusetts, had four basic research objectives:

1. To describe CFRP programs and their operations
2. To identify service delivery models
3. To link family outcomes to participation or nonparticipation in CFRP
4. To link family outcomes to particular aspects of CFRP treatment and to family characteristics.

Assessing the effectiveness of CFRP as a whole was an ACYF priority: Would the CFRP approach effect changes in children and families that were different from or greater than those provided by Head Start alone or by services obtained "piecemeal" from many other community resources? To address this question, a longitudinal outcome study was designed using randomly assigned treatment and comparison groups to assess CFRP's impact on families and children in a variety of domains at 5 of the 11 sites. The domains included child development and parenting skills, the primary focus of the program, and other areas of family life that might be influenced by CFRP participation: family independence and self-reliance, parental coping skills, and access to and use of community services.

Two other research strategies were employed to assess implementation in general and to provide a context for interpreting outcome study results and variations across and within sites. The descriptive study involved periodic site visits to document how programs were organized to provide services at each of the 11 sites. The process/treatment study assessed the CFRP "treatment" in all its variety. It identified the processes used to deliver services and the types of activities and services in which study families participated. Crucial family-level information was collected. Descriptive data at this level are often omitted from outcome studies. Thus, it frequently happens at the end of an external evaluation of a social program that both program staff and participants complain that the study missed important points and failed to see or report what the program "really" does. Although this complaint may be a defensive reaction to unfavorable study results, evaluators frequently share the uneasy feeling that their data somehow fail to convey the texture of the program.

After three waves of data collection, we reexamined our work and asked ourselves to what extent we had been able to capture the essence of the program and effectively measure impacts of CFRP on its participants. We realized that none of the three initial evaluation components offered a fully satisfactory account of what happens within CFRP to bring about changes. The descriptive and process/treatment studies provided a general picture of CFRP's operations, but they tended to adopt the perspectives of program staff far more than that of families. What we had failed to capture was the quality of CFRP as experienced every day by individual children and their families.

We were disappointed with the early quantitative results (after 18 months of family participation in CFRP) in the area of child development. We knew that participation in program activities was uneven and that contact with families was not frequent enough, but we could not explain why the children of active participants did not fare better than children of occasional participants or families in the comparison group. Did family need determine frequency or intensity of services provided? Did the most needy families receive the most attention from the program? In that case, the active families could not be expected to show greater gains than less needy, and perhaps less active, families.

The complexity and variability of CFRP suggested that CFRP was the kind of program for which supplementary use of qualitative techniques might be most revealing. Thus, we added an ethnographic study involving a small subset of families (7–9) at each of the five outcome study sites over a period of 6 months. Each local ethnographer spent half the time observing the program's staff and the families served. We hoped that the intimate familiarity and detailed description that are possible only in a study of this type would reveal unexpected, complex, or intangible program effects and give us a better understanding of program functioning. The endeavor paid off and enhanced the study's overall credibility. We learned about the day-to-day experiences of participants, the subtle but sometimes profound changes in their outlook and behavior, and the circumstances and events that bred frustration and failure (Travers, 1981).

The ethnographic study revealed some major flaws in the implementation of the program. First, the intensity (or frequency) of child development activities was extremely low; considerably more emphasis was placed on provision of social services. Second, there was great variation in the quality of the developmental activities. In some instances, there was didactic, mechanical use of predetermined exercises, with little attempt to capitalize on the interests of the child or mother, and at times with little apparent comprehension of the purpose of the exercise (Travers, 1981). The qualitative data enabled us to trace the program's failures in the area of developmental outcomes to specific and correctable problems of implementation.

ANTICIPATED AND UNANTICIPATED PROBLEMS: REALITIES IN THE EVALUATION OF COMPLEX PROGRAMS

We pursued the CFRP evaluation aware of the many and well-documented problems with such a design in a complex field setting (Cook and Campbell, 1979). Among the anticipated major problems were ethical and logistical difficulties in randomly assigning needy families to program treatment or comparison groups; attrition in sample sizes over the years; and the likelihood of comparison families receiving services similar to CFRP from other community agencies or of comparison families benefiting indirectly from CFRP efforts to change local service delivery. Lessons from previous evaluations with similar designs, for example, of Home Start (Love, Nauta, Coelen, Hewett, and Ruopp, 1976) and careful field procedures kept these problems within acceptable limits. We have described elsewhere many of the issues that arose (Travers, Nauta, and Irwin, 1982); we summarize some of the most important ones here.

Ethical considerations raised by the ACYF and by local program administrators dictated two decisions about random assignment. First, families considered at high risk were admitted to CFRP directly after special review by ACYF; in order to maintain group equivalency they were not included in the study sample. Second, families randomly assigned to comparison groups were assured preference for Head Start entry when the child reached the appropriate age.

Because significant attrition was expected, each site overrecruited for available slots in the program. There were an average of 40 CFRP and 42 comparison families per site. Over the 3-year data collection period the sample was reduced by 38%, which required a number of statistical adjustments to compensate for group nonequivalence. Attrition did not create serious statistical problems for comparisons involving the entire sample but did weaken the study's ability to detect different outcome effects within subgroups of families and within single sites. We describe our approach to this problem of analysis later in this chapter.

We recognized that maintaining a purely "nontreated" comparison group was an unrealistic goal. Most families in the program communities have available day care, social services, health screenings, and other services through local agencies (hospitals, churches, public and private groups), and data were collected from the comparison group to monitor the degree to which they received such services. These data were useful in explaining patterns of effects. For example, data on health care utilization helped to explain CFRP's modest effects on measures of preventive health care. Special efforts by comparison families and community health care agencies to arrange for health services reduced the advantage of the CFRP group. Furthermore, it was likely that CFRP's advocacy on behalf of families and its efforts to improve social service delivery in the overall community would benefit the comparison group as well. The ethnographic study provided some scattered hints of such a spill-over effect, but these effects were difficult to quantify.

Quantifying CFRP treatment itself at the family level proved difficult as well. The collection of descriptive treatment data began early with program staff recording information on needs, goal setting, and goal attainment on all families at the five sites. Our aim was to learn about the patterns of service delivery over time for specific families and to identify patterns that characterized the five programs. While goal attainment methodology (Kiresuk, Calsyn, and Davidson, 1978) had been used primarily in mental health settings and in educational programs where behavioral objectives could be explicitly set by staff and clients, its utilization seemed congruent with the CFRP approach of ongoing needs assessment, goal setting, and individualization of services.

We anticipated, although seriously underestimated, difficulty in capturing treatment data at the family level that would prove useful in relating treatment patterns to outcomes. It was clear from the start that similar treatment data could not be obtained from the comparison group (although a crude attempt was made to do so), which limited the data's use for group comparisons. For example, we could assess CFRP's effects in helping treatment families find work or enroll in job training, but we could not assess how comparison families with similar aims fared. There were other practical problems with the method. First, staff records were not always a valid reflection of the family's true goals and needs (such as the mother's need for adult socialization) or implicit staff goals for the family (such as relief of maternal depression or help for a child's low self-esteem). Second, it was difficult to distinguish short-term goals from long-term ones with many steps (such as completing a GED) and to differentiate family goals from regularly provided services such as health screenings. Third, defining goals and assessing progress on paper was not easy; staff who were excellent with families were not always good at this task and vice versa. This raised questions about the reliability of the records. Finally, and of importance, there was no way of "valuing" one set of goals over another, nor were there models of normative family development that would dictate what is desirable for a family (Hewett, 1982).

The needs assessment/goal attainment strategy as a result proved largely unsuccessful; the payoff of this costly effort was only minimal. Counts of needs, goals, and extent of goal attainment told us little about the everyday experiences of individual children and their families or the quality of those experiences. This was what led to rethinking the initial evaluation design and the addition of the ethnographic study.

TENSIONS AND INFLUENCES

Tensions existed and influences were exerted throughout the evaluation by actors at every level—by ACYF at the federal level, by local CFRP programs, by the evaluation team, and to some extent by enrolled parents. These tensions and influences are best understood in light of the background of the program and its stated goals. By the time the CFRP evaluation was initiated by Abt Associates Inc., CFRP had existed as a Head Start demonstration for 4 years, yet it had no data to justify continued federal expenditures. An earlier ACYF-sponsored study had produced inconclusive results of the program's impact, in part because of serious flaws in that study's design. The government's need for quantitative results in the area of child outcomes rather than outcomes in the broader perspective of family development became a major concern for local programs. ACYF's emphasis was justifiable given the Head Start mandate to "enhance child development."

The tension ensuing from the government's emphasis on child development deserves comment. As the demonstration matured, there seemed to be a divergence of opinion between ACYF and local programs about CFRP's mission and primary goals. While CFRP was premised on the belief that there is synergy between services that relate directly to children's development and services that support families more generally, there was actually some tension between social services and child development, created in part by constraints of time and resources. All too often social service provision preempted child development activities. Staff were often overworked and too busy dealing with families in crisis to spend time with those for whom parent education and child development activities were most likely to be effective. Social services and child development thus were competing, instead of mutually reinforcing activities.

A major contributing factor in this tension was a deliberate decision by the government not to impose much structure on local programs. In fact, CFRP was designed to allow and encourage local programs to adapt themselves to local conditions and to respond to perceived needs and concerns of the families served. In 1973, when CFRP began, this was a bold experiment in delegating program authority. To the extent that families themselves helped shape local programs, it is questionable whether they were choosing child development over other available services.

Local programs exerted considerable influence on both the evaluation and ACYF. Program administrators and staff were disappointed and upset with interim results, which showed no child development outcomes, particularly when continuation of the demonstration appeared to be at stake. They criticized the overemphasis on measures of child development and the study's inability to measure effects in important areas of family development and functioning. There was skepticism about the ability of any evaluation team to capture the essence and effects of CFRP's complex program efforts. Local program staff provided numerous and touching success stories of individual families who had benefitted greatly from CFRP. Quotes from a 1979 report to Congress by the General Accounting Office, based on a more qualitative and limited study of CFRP, were used to counter interim evaluation findings and to justify continued funding for the demonstration.

As mentioned earlier, this criticism led to the implementation of the ethnographic study, which became an important element in gaining credibility for the evaluation with local programs. Initially, federal policymakers questioned the payoffs of ethnographic research because of its lack of generalizability. But gradually, they too concluded that qualitative information on the actual experiences of families was needed to provide a better and more credible accounting of CFRP. CFRP national leadership and an advisory panel of evaluation experts played a major role in this shift in thinking.

Influences exerted on local programs by ACYF or by the study design concerned the nature of program services, the types of families recruited, and aspects of program participation. CFRP programs were pressured to emphasize infant–toddler activities and services, whether or not these had been a major program focus previously. Programs were included in the evaluation only if they could recruit substantial numbers of new families with infants. The evaluation also affected the length of time families stayed in the program. "After two years of participation," said one director, "we would ordinarily let a family have more say about how often we saw them and what services they received. To us, that was 'fostering independence' in families, which we were committed to do." But with evaluation families, CFRP staff often felt the need to make sure they continued to receive a high level of services.

These tensions and influences created some difficulties between evaluators and local program staff. To alleviate these difficulties, we met frequently with administrators and staff. We listened to their concerns, shared our uneasiness about the original study design, and, finally, redirected the study to include more qualitative data to supplement the quantitative results required by ACYF.

ANALYTIC APPROACH

Both the diversity across programs and variations in treatment within them necessitated a complex set of statistical analyses. Our general approach to assessing the program's impact involved a search for overall effects, followed by efforts to parcel out effects for subgroups of families (Travers *et al.*, 1982). We began by looking for overall program impact on each outcome measure—that is, for statistically significant differences between the CFRP and comparison group. Figure 17.1 depicts an overall group comparison on one outcome domain, that of maternal

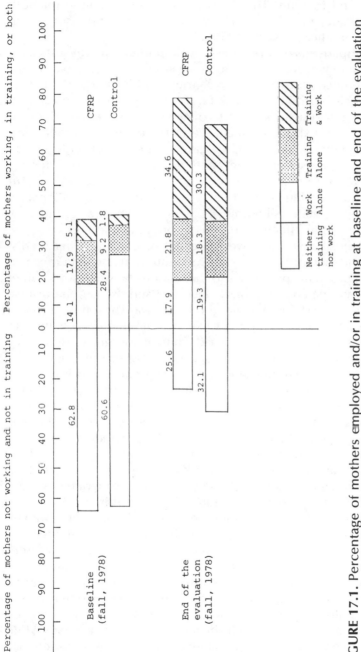

FIGURE 17.1. Percentage of mothers employed and/or in training at baseline and end of the evaluation (CFRP versus controls) (Travers *et al.*, 1982, p. 79).

employment and training. The dramatic increase over time for both groups was greater for CFRP mothers than for the comparison group (a marginally significant overall CFRP effect).

Overall comparisons of outcomes were important but not sufficient. Dramatic variations from site to site made it necessary to look for evidence of differences between the two groups within each site. In other words, we let each program "speak for itself" and looked at local outcomes in the context of local patterns of need among families. Because sample sizes were extremely small, we were concerned about overlooking small effects. Therefore, we gave a lot of attention to the direction and consistency of impacts and did not confine our interpretation solely to those that were significant at conventional levels. Our approach is illustrated in Figure 17.2. A positive effect for CFRP participants in changing maternal employment and training was found at all sites except one; the effects were most pronounced in two sites.

Using our qualitative data, we searched for corroborating or disconfirming evidence of the quantitative findings. Those data revealed different local program approaches to the tensions between work/career advancement and parental responsibilities. Not surprisingly, the reverse direction of effects in this domain at one site was caused by a strong emphasis on active participation in CFRP's developmental activities. In contrast, the site with the largest CFRP comparison group difference (which served many teenage mothers) aimed its efforts at tangible improvements in family circumstances, including continued schooling, job training, and employment. The qualitative data thus gave insights into reasons for observed patterns of effects. Furthermore, the ethnographic case studies contained many examples of success in areas where CFRP was generally weak, pointing to the program's unexploited potential. For example, the ideal case for CFRP would be one in which a mother "graduated" to school or work after having participated actively and having gained the full benefits of CFRP's program of parent education. Our data highlighted frequent cases of this sort.

Individualization of services within sites made it necessary to examine patterns of effects for different types of families. We partitioned the sample in a variety of ways to determine whether CFRP had different effects for different types of families with potentially different patterns of needs. Specifically, we compared effects for first-born children versus children with older siblings, families headed by single women versus two-parent families, families in which the mother had graduated from high school versus those in which she had not, and black versus white families. We compared effects for children with and without experience in day care to test the assumption that children in day care might have received services paralleling those of CFRP. Finally, we examined effects for mothers who showed different patterns on an attitudinal variable

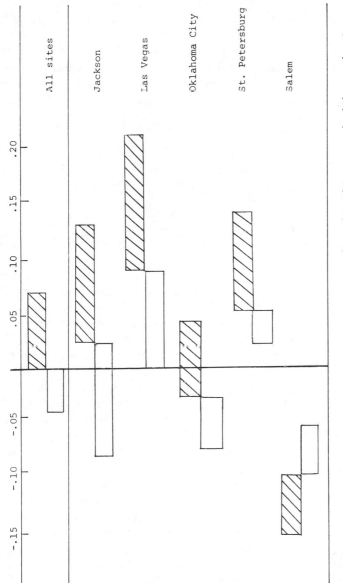

FIGURE 17.2. Change in mother's employment/training from baseline to end of the evaluation, by site (CFRP versus controls) (Travers et al., 1982, p. 82). Hatched box, CFRP; unfilled box, control.

called "coping," or locus of control, which assessed parents' feelings of efficacy.

From the outset we knew that there was wide variation in levels of program participation, which necessitated looking for differences in outcomes that might be linked to participation rates. Two approaches were taken to determine whether the program conveyed more benefits when more extensive "treatment" was actually received. First, within the CFRP group, we related outcomes to several different measures of treatment, such as parental teaching skills and children's developmental abilities linked to participation in home visits and center-based activities. Second, we compared all outcomes for the subset of families who were moderate-to-high participants to the comparison group. Again, we supplemented interpretation of results with qualitative insights from the ethnographic study.

LESSONS FROM THE EVALUATION

CFRP Effects

The findings on CFRP's effectiveness as a family-oriented child development program are not surprising given its general orientation (Nauta and Travers, 1982). The major emphasis was on providing needed support services to help low-income families become independent—both materially and psychologically. In material terms, the goal was to move families toward economic self-sufficiency through education and employment. In psychological terms, the aim was to help parents progress from feeling overwhelmed and incompetent to feeling not only secure in their abilities to provide for their families but also personally supported by families, friends, and informal networks. Barriers to independence, such as poverty, lack of employment opportunities in the surrounding community, chronic or unexpected illness, and personal problems, however, were often formidable.

The support services offered by CFRP had far-reaching effects on families. The staff marshalled services from multiple agencies in its efforts to work out comprehensive solutions to families' problems. One parent called CFRP an "ace in the hole," because it gave her one place to turn for help in times of need. CFRP staff were "advocates" for families and brought some measure of rationality, coherence, and personal concern to an otherwise confusing and impersonal system of social services, and CFRP always worked from the perspective of families. An important aspect of CFRP was that it established and maintained an integrated network of linkages to community agencies. The most obvious benefits were improved access to community agencies and increased use of social services.

Through extensive counseling and referral, the program demonstrably improved families' prospects for economic self-sufficiency: A higher proportion of CFRP mothers was employed and/or in school or job training than mothers in the comparison group after 3 years in the program, even in sites hardest hit by the recession of the late 1970s and early 1980s.

Another important consequence of CFRP was that the program increased parents' sense of control over events. Intangible but crucial shifts in attitude took place in parents who were often severely demoralized at the start. These attitudinal changes were often accompanied by striking changes in behavior. One single mother who was almost totally withdrawn when she entered the program became a community activist. The program helped her to see that she could "do something other than housework, watching soap operas, and chasing kids." It showed her that she could be independent and take responsibility in her life. The families that benefitted most from the program were those in which parents were distinguished by an attitude of determination and confidence.

For reasons cited earlier, the program's effects in the area of child development were disappointing. While CFRP's activities in parent education led to significant changes in parents and promoted child-rearing practices associated with positive social and cognitive development of children, these effects did *not* translate into measurable benefits for children. Possibly the documented improvements in parental teaching skills have led to changes that will manifest themselves later in the children's development, a question our study cannot directly address because it concluded when the children entered Head Start.

To realize the potential benefits of CFRP, a family had to participate actively for an extended period of time. Active families showed the greatest changes in child-rearing attitudes and practices, as well as changes in feelings of efficacy. These parents were also more likely to have obtained further education or job training. Participation in the program was thus an essential ingredient in CFRP effectiveness. However, CFRP on the whole did not seem well organized to serve working mothers or those who attended school full-time, because most program activities occurred during the day.

Program Goals and Management

CFRP clearly demonstrated that, at least in the case of the population served by Head Start, the provision of support services competes with other more child development-oriented goals for staff time and program resources. To effectively provide both support services and first-rate developmental services is costly, requiring a decrease in worker caseloads (from an average of 20 families), an increase in home-visit frequency (from once a month or less), more extensive child-development training for mostly paraprofessional workers, and increased staff supervision. In addition, the design and implementation of a complex demonstration such as CFRP may require better planning.

CFRP's mission was challenging. The requirements included services for families with infant–toddlers, services for those in transition from Head Start into public school, and the implementation of an inclusive approach to social-service delivery. Meeting these requirements all at once would test the abilities of even the most skilled program planner/administrator. In hindsight, overall program quality and effectiveness might have been enhanced had different aspects and components of CFRP been introduced in gradual, well-planned stages.

There are other lessons to be drawn from this demonstration that might guide other programs with similarly ambitious goals. When allowed local autonomy, programs will develop in unexpected ways that may not be fully consonant with national goals and expectations, even if they are well adapted to local needs and the desires of parents. While there are advantages to inviting local initiative and ingenuity, there is also a need to retain a measure of central (national or regional) control. This also applies to the management of local programs. The profile of service that grows out of give-and-take between families and staff, a major emphasis of CFRP through needs assessment and goal setting, will not necessarily reflect a program's stated goals. The preemption of child development by crisis management and social service referrals cited earlier is an example of what can evolve. There is often an understandable unwillingness on the part of program managers to encroach on the one-to-one relationship between family workers and parents, universally recognized as essential to program success. There are dangers of intrusion and regimentation. But by avoiding some degree of structure and central monitoring of services, one incurs the risk that program goals may be diluted or distorted in practice. Some structure and monitoring is needed to ensure that the services delivered are of acceptable quality and appropriate focus.

SUMMARY

This study provided lessons on the operation and effectiveness of complex, multifaceted social programs and on how to evaluate them. Our experiences, summarized briefly in this section, may help future evaluators of similarly ambitious and complex programs.

Some argue in favor of keeping evaluations as simple as possible. We concur provided that the evaluation design does justice to the program in all its complexity and variety. CFRP did not lend itself to a simple study design; it could not be treated as a "black box" that clients enter and leave, appropriately transformed or not. Posing the question "Did the black box do its work?" is appropriate only for programs that more rigidly specify or tightly control treatment, not for demonstrations or programs like CFRP so rich in variety, across and within sites. Questions of "why" and "how" are as important as questions of effect.

Designing a responsive study requires a basic knowledge of the program to be studied. Visits to solicit staff and parent views and to see the program in operation, before starting major design work, can be immensely valuable. Such visits tend to lessen tensions, but they are no substitute for rigorous field-testing of methodologies and measures to be used (particularly when new ground is being broken). The first-hand experience we advocate helps to avoid costly research with minimal payoff. For example, data collection on family goals might have been abandoned or scaled down earlier in favor of qualitative inquiry had our approach been better field-tested prior to full-scale implementation.

Our comments about simplicity concern selection of measures also. If the scope of an inquiry is too limited, some important benefits of the program and interactions among various outcomes may be undetected. For example, we would have done CFRP a grave injustice had we focused our inquiry solely on child-development effects rather than on outcomes associated with family development. On the other hand, one can cast the evaluation net too broadly, potentially leading to unsatisfactory results and superficiality. Few studies have the financial resources to cover all potential outcomes and do it well. Our advice is to focus on aspects that are measurable and to limit the number of complex and untested inquiries.

Launching one or more highly focused substudies involving a subset of the population under study can effectively supplement a basic research design. In the CFRP evaluation, a substudy involving in-home videotaped observations enabled us to examine the important relationship between parent–child interaction and child-development outcomes without collecting data on the entire sample (Nauta and Johnson, 1981). Similarly, the ethnographic substudy substantially enhanced our understanding of CFRP and increased the overall credibility of study results.

The attention given in this chapter to ethnographic research should not be interpreted to mean that we advocate qualitative research methods in all studies of social programs; it is appropriate only in dealing with a complex, multifaceted program such as CFRP. In less complex programs or studies with simpler research objectives, simple case studies will suffice to meet the descriptive needs of the study. Ethnographic or qualitative research is expensive. If used, it must be carefully designed to ensure maximum payoff. In our study, resource constraints precluded carrying out an anthropological field study, characterized by an atheoretical data-gathering approach and anthropologists typically spending considerable time before deciding what research questions to pursue. Our research effort was more structured. We provided ethnographers with a set of basic research questions to guide their work (Travers, 1981); we defined our expectations and communicated them clearly to our field researchers.

The overriding lesson we learned is that it is impossible to do a "quick and dirty" study that will do justice to a complex social program. Furthermore, a successful evaluator must be sensitive to complexity and responsive to local programs. What this implies is that evaluators must not start out with preconceived notions about a program and its impacts, but rather they should take the time to discover what the program is about. From this knowledge base, the inquiry can be fine-tuned. Our advice to evaluators is: Let your thinking, approaches, and evaluation strategies evolve.

REFERENCES

Cook, T. D., and Campbell, D. T. (1979). *Quasi experimentation.* Chicago, IL: Rand McNally.

Hewett, K. D. (with assistance from D. Deloria). (1982). Comprehensive family service programs: Special features and associated measurement problems. In J. Travers and R. Light (Eds.), *Learning from experience: Evaluating early childhood demonstration programs.* Report of the Panel on Outcome Measurement in Early Childhood Education Demonstration Programs. Washington, D.C.: National Academy of Sciences.

Johnson, L., and Nauta, M. J. (1980). *Evaluation of the Child and Family Resource Program: Phase III program study report.* Report to ACYF, OHDS, DHHS, Contract No. HEW-105-79-1301. Cambridge, MA: Abt Associates Inc.

Kiresuk, T. J., Calsyn, R. J., and Davidson, W. S. (1978). A critique of goal attainment scaling. *Evaluation Studies Review Annual, 3*:700–715.

Love, J. M., Nauta, M. J., Coelen, C. G., Hewett, K. D., and Ruopp, R. R. (1976). *National Home Start Evaluation Final Report: Findings and implications.* Report to ACYF, OHDS, DHHS, Contract No. HEW-105-72-1100. Ypsilanti, MI: High/Scope Educational Research Foundation and Abt Associates Inc. (Cambridge, MA).

Nauta, M. J., and Hewett, K. D. (1981). Features of Family Service Programs. Paper presented at the Society for Research in Child Development, Boston, Massachusetts.

Nauta, M. J., and Johnson, L. (1981). *Evaluation of the Child and Family Resource Program: Phase III research report.* Report to the ACYF, OHDS, DHHS, Contract No. HEW-105-79-1301. Cambridge, MA: Abt Associates Inc.

Nauta, M. J., and Travers, J. (1982). *The effects of a social program: Executive summary of CFRP's infant–toddler component.* Report to ACYF, OHDS, DHHS, Contract No. HEW-105-79-1301. Cambridge, MA: Abt Associates Inc.

Travers, J. (1981). *The culture of a social program: An ethnographic study of the Child and Family Resource Program* (main and summary volumes). Report to ACYF, OHDS, DHHS, Contract No. HEW-105-79-1301. Cambridge, MA: Abt Associates Inc.

Travers, J., Nauta, M. J., and Irwin, N. (1982). *The effects of a social program: Final report on the Child and Family Resource Program's infant–toddler component.* Report to ACYF, OHDS, DHHS, Contract No. HEW-105-79-1301. Cambridge, MA: Abt Associates Inc.

chapter 18

USING AN IMPACT EVALUATION MODEL WITH TOO-EARLY-CHILDBEARING PROGRAMS

Deborah Klein Walker
Anita M. Mitchell

INTRODUCTION

A review of the literature on evaluation of adolescent pregnancy programs reveals that the vast majority of studies are unsophisticated and provide little definitive information about the short- and long-term impacts of such programs. Most notably, the studies lack adequate control and comparison groups, longitudinal prospective designs, and realistic goals (Klerman, 1979). The most rigorous studies do reveal positive outcomes with respect to medical outcomes; in all controlled studies, poor clinical outcomes (e.g., anemia, prematurity, infant mortality, low Apgar scores) were reduced. However, evidence of impact with respect to repeat pregnancies and births, graduation from high school, employment, and economic independence is much less clear; to a large extent such outcomes have yet to be assessed by adequately designed studies.

Further, there are serious gaps in our knowledge about program components and procedures that are most effective in preventing teenage pregnancy and in assisting teenagers with simultaneous role transitions to adolescence and parenthood. An enormous amount of funds is expended each year on programs for these target populations with little assurance that the programs are having or will have the desired effects. While there is general consensus that programs for pregnant and parenting teenagers can produce short-term gains in crucial health and social areas, questions of long-term impact, and sustaining short-term gains are yet to be answered (Alan Guttmacher Institute, 1981; Baldwin, 1976; Chilman, 1979; Klerman, 1979; Mitchell and Walker, 1985; Phipps-Yonas, 1980).

Recognizing that policymakers, funding agencies, and program directors were in need of evidence of the effectiveness of teenage pregnancy programs, Dr. Marilyn Steele of the Charles Stewart Mott Foundation commissioned us to develop an impact evaluation model and to provide technical assistance for its implementation in all new adolescent pregnancy and parenting programs funded by the Foundation. Ten programs participated in the Too-Early-Childbearing (TEC) Network. The programs fell into three major categories—primary prevention, prenatal care, and postdelivery care—and were located in three major settings—schools, health institutions, and community agencies. Five programs entered the network in 1978, one in 1980, one in 1981, and three in 1982. The number of clients in a program year ranged from fewer than 50 to more than 1000. The programs used a wide range of strategies to accomplish their objectives, including instructional classes, home visits, newsletters, individual and group counseling, transportation, and public information techniques. Table 18.1 provides an overview of the characteristics of the eight programs in the TEC Network in 1984. While most of the programs continue to operate at the time of this writing, we will describe the programs and their evaluation during the 6-year period from late 1978 through 1984.

We saw networking among the programs as central to the success of the Foundation's overall evaluation and dissemination efforts. Networking would provide a mechanism for support and technical assistance as well as a forum for shared information about adolescent pregnancy and parenting programs. The TEC Network's Newsletter and annual reports of evaluation results served this function more broadly.

The evaluation team—the authors of this chapter—developed the impact evaluation model, assisted in the implementation of TEC Network programs, and is now in the final stages of data collection and analysis. The evaluation we designed was generated from the program's stated objectives and implemented by program staff with our technical assistance. This commitment and engagement assured that the data were collected conscientiously, and that the results would be used to improve programs and secure funding at the local level.

To describe our experiences, we will first present the eight steps of the impact evaluation model with examples drawn from 8 of the 10 programs, then discuss the implementation of the model, and finally make recommendations for family program development and evaluation.

TABLE 18.1. Characteristics of Programs in Too-Early-Childbearing Network (1984)

	New York	Sarasota	St. Louis	Oakland	Rochester	Corpus Christi	Seattle	Boston
Name of program	Comprehensive Adolescent Health and Education Dissemination Program	CYESIS Program for School-Age Parents	Parent/Infant Interaction Program	Teen Parent Assistance Program	Monroe County Adolescent Pregnancy Preventive and Supportive Services Program	Comprehensive Health and Education Program	Teen Indian Pregnancy and Prevention Services (TIPPS)	Teen Parent Family Support Project
Site	Columbia University Hospital, New York City	Sarasota County Schools, Sarasota	St. Louis Public Schools, St. Louis	Oakland Public Schools, Oakland	Monroe County Department of Health, Rochester	Gulf Coast Council of La Raza, Corpus Christi	Seattle Indian Health Board, Seattle	Alliance for Young Families, Boston
Date program began	Sept. 1978	Sept. 1978	Sept. 1978	Feb. 1980	Oct. 1981	Jan. 1982	Jan. 1982	Apr. 1982
Number of clients (last program year)	1000+	56	480	269	76	90	198	70
Program focus	Primary prevention	Prenatal	Prenatal/ postdelivery	Postdelivery	Postdelivery	Prenatal	Primary prevention Prenatal	Postdelivery
Program elements	Family life education Peer counseling Community health advocate Outreach Public education Health fairs Youth theater troup	Health, child development, and life skills classes Academic classes Bus transportation Free breakfast and lunch Day care Group counseling Individual counseling Case coordination of services Field trips	Peer support groups Individual counseling Home visits Case coordination of services Health, child development and parenting classes Day care Daily attendance monitoring	Outreach Case coordination of services Educational referral and placement Social services referral Career exploration and staff development	Home visits Individual counseling Case coordination of services Community newsletter Day care	Health, child development classes Academic GED program Transportation Individual counseling Case coordination of services	Outreach Individual counseling Health services Case coordination of services Family life education	Home visits Individual counseling Case coordination of services Day care

The Impact Evaluation Model

The purpose of impact evaluation is to provide evidence of the effectiveness or ineffectiveness of specific program components while the project is in progress (and at its termination) in order to facilitate decision making in program management. In addition to answering the long-term "so what difference does it make?" questions, the model encourages program changes and improvement based on short-term evidence. Thus it combines formative and summative evaluation. The major thrust is always program improvement—a commitment to making the program produce the positive changes in client behavior for which it was designed.

The programs funded by the Mott Foundation were contractually obligated to cooperate with the separately funded evaluation team to apply the model. The responsibility for the evaluation was placed with each program director. The evaluation team, on the other hand, was charged with providing whatever technical assistance was necessary to ensure faithful implementation of the evaluation model by each program and with helping program staffs develop or gain access to the required evaluation skills. We focused our efforts on helping staffs conduct their own evaluations, but with well-defined guidelines, timelines, and reporting procedures. Our challenge was to provide a flexible, low-cost evaluation model that could be implemented by staffs with minimal evaluation skills and that could provide useful guidance in decision making.

Steps in the Model

Step 1: Assessment of the Need for the Program. An assessment of needs is conducted to document the need for the programs/services in question. Included in this step are some combination of the following: an extensive literature review; an investigation of community resources, statistics, and reports; and a survey of appropriate persons and agencies. Data collection procedures are documented, and a rationale for using these procedures is stated.

When our study began, the programs in the TEC Network were already operating. Few had done adequate needs assessments; in most cases a need was presumed because of the incidence of teenage pregnancy in the community. Accepting the evaluation model and participating in the study compelled programs to make formal statements of need to justify their continued requests for support.

In Oakland, California, for example, the staff of the Teen Parent Assistance Program (TPAP) gathered pregnancy and parenting statistics from Alameda County, developed a directory of existing programs and services, and adjusted its focus to close gaps and avoid overlaps in services in the community. The program also looked closely at the postprogram activities of those parenting teenagers it had served. As a result, TPAP shifted direction from a stay-in-school program to a vocational skills development program for adolescent parents, with high school/GED completion as an intermediate step. Four programs (St. Louis, Missouri; New York City; Rochester, New York; and Sarasota, Florida) relied heavily on advisory boards of community representatives to help with community-wide needs assessment, using data from local health, education, and social service programs.

Step 2: Statement of Program Objectives. Important outcome, impact, product, and process objectives of the program are stated. Outcome objectives define the short-term results of the intervention; that is, how the target population will be changed (e.g., there will be a reduction in complications of pregnancy or more pregnant and parenting teenagers staying in school). Impact objectives are long-range and answer the "so what?" questions about the behaviors of the target population of the program (e.g., there will be a reduction in repeat pregnancies or an increase in high school completion). Product objectives define materials developed or produced by the program (e.g., an infant development curriculum, a poster, or client assessment form). Process objectives define the tasks the program staff will perform to achieve outcome, impact, and product objectives (e.g., provide prenatal group sessions, individual counseling, outreach to the community).

All objectives must be observable and/or measurable. Process objectives must be stated for each outcome, impact, or product objective; a single process objective may be directed toward more than one. For example, process objectives for reducing pregnancy complications might include provision of nutritional services, individual health counseling about habits such as smoking and drinking, or provision of breathing exercises and childbirth instruction. Process objectives for reduction in repeat pregnancies often include provision of instruction in reproduction and family planning and sometimes include direct access to contraceptives. Process objectives related to the development of a new curriculum might include reviews of the literature, the establishment of a task group, and presentation of selected units to similar groups.

Evaluators and staff must work together very early in the program's development to specify all four types of objectives and to ensure that they are realistic. This process is key to the success of both the evaluation and the program. We stress this step because even the most sophisticated evaluators often fail to specify clear objectives. No program in the TEC network had clearly written objectives at the beginning of the evaluation; in each case process objectives were confused with outcome and impact objectives.

We recommend an early consensus on objectives if a program is to be evaluated in a network. All programs can then use the same definitions of terms from the beginning, thus facilitating comparison and/or aggregation. The objectives agreed upon by all programs in the TEC Network are displayed in Table 18.2. In addition to this core set, several

TABLE 18.2. Common Outcome and Impact Objectives

Objectives	Primary prevention program	Prenatal care program	Postdelivery care program
Outcome objectives for teenage participants			
1. Reduction of incidence of complications of pregnancy.		X	
2. Reduction in incidence of low birthweight babies (under 2500 grams).		X	
3. Reduction in incidence of infant mortality.		X	
4. Increase in percentage in education/training programs 1 year after delivery (or completion of high school or GED requirements).		X	X
Impact objectives for teenage participants			
1. Increase in percentage completing high school or GED.	X	X	X
2. Reduction in incidence of repeat births.		X	X
3. Increase in percentage providing standard health care for the child.		X	X
4. Reduction in prevalence of child abuse and neglect.		X	X
5. Increase in percentage attaining economic independence.		X	X
6. Reduction in incidence of births to teenagers.	X		

programs tracked other outcome and impact objectives: increased academic performance as assessed by performance on standardized achievement tests (Sarasota); increased knowledge about family planning (New York); and enhanced self-concept (Boston).

Step 3: Statement of Information Needs. Decision makers—especially those responsible for determining a program's continuation as well as its direction—need information on which elements are most effective and therefore which funding sources are most likely to be supportive; whether one strategy works better than another; whether results justify the costs; which subpopulations benefit most from the program; what the costs are, etc. Management should formulate these questions before the program begins. Such questions demand specific information and therefore set the parameters of the evaluation.

The New York Comprehensive Adolescent Health and Education Project, for example, needed to know the relative effectiveness of peer counselors and professional adult counselors in order to target funding agents. Early findings caused them to direct resources toward provision of adult counselors. Similarly, other programs used early evidence from the evaluation process to make staffing and funding decisions. The Rochester program decided to use paraprofessionals instead of nurses at several follow-up check points in their monitoring process and to deliver services to all young mothers aged 16 and under; the Corpus Christi program decided to provide transportation to all program activities; and the St. Louis program decided to add day care and to discontinue the provision of transportation.

Step 4: Selection of Indicators. For each objective specified in Step 2 and for each information need specified in Step 3, the quickest and least expensive reliable indicator is selected. Indicators may include scores on standardized or locally developed tests, observations of performance, and unobtrusive measures (i.e., measures of behaviors that indirectly manifest the presence of the desired behavior). For example, Sarasota's Cyesis program focused on helping participants remain in school and graduate; consequently the Cyesis program needed to know the degree to which its educational program prepared the students academically. Their source for this information was scores on district achievement tests administered to all students in the regular school program. These scores enabled them to compare their students' performances with those of others in the district. Cyesis also used informal observations of participants' parenting skills or behaviors in the child care center to determine the adequacy of the parenting curriculum and to inform decision makers of possible needs for change. Examples of unobtrusive measures of participants' attitudes, mental health, and job readiness behaviors include the students' grooming, attendance, and level of participation. As can be seen, what decisions are important to the program must be determined (Step 3) before indicators can be selected that will inform those decisions (Step 4). These progressive steps appear to be absent in most evaluation models, which may help explain the lack of consistency and completeness in tracking results.

The scope and content of evaluation instruments vary widely as a function of many factors, including program objectives, the state of the art of measurement development, financial and other resources, and the measurement instruments available. The evaluator and program staff should agree on a core list of variables that assess the program objectives. In some cases, it may be necessary to forego assessment of a particular objective or use a proxy measure because it is too difficult to assess it with the available resources. For example, parenting behaviors are best assessed through observation of the behaviors in various environments (e.g., home, school). In the TEC Network, since the programs could not afford to use standardized observational measures, we agreed that an acceptable proxy measure of good parenting skills was whether the parent took the child for regular well-child health visits. We also agreed that an overall reduction in child abuse would serve as an excellent measure of program impact in the area of parenting skills; to date, however, only a few programs have been able to measure this successfully. In general, the best measures are those that can be reliably administered by gathering information directly from the client or client records. Simple counts of key behaviors (e.g., graduating from high school, repeat births, receiving welfare payments) are very important and fairly easy to obtain.

Finally, the use of individual, computer-ready client forms is encouraged so that various counts can be carried out later using several different combinations of variables. At a minimum—regardless of the level of funding—all programs should be able to describe the client population served and the program's activities using basic indicators (number of classes provided, number of outreach meetings, etc.).

Step 5: Selection of Comparison Standards. Program participants' ability to demonstrate the desired behavior at the end of the program (or at specified interim points) is not adequate evidence that the program has been successful; there may be other explanations for the behavior change. For example, one objective in the TEC Network was to reduce the incidence of repeat births. But if the entire community had taken this as an objective, so that concurrent with the program efforts there were numerous local efforts to discourage repeat pregnancies and births, it would be impossible to ascribe any change to the program alone without comparing the program participants to a similar group of young women who had also been exposed to the community efforts but were not program participants.

In order to present evidence that the program is responsible for any gains, there must be a comparison group equivalent to the program population on relevant variables. For objectives such as reduction in incidence of complications of pregnancy, low birthweight, and infant mortality, the comparison standard may be a similar group of young mothers in the community, if community health statistics are reported by appropriate variables (e.g., by age and race). Because of the existence of national and state vital health statistics systems (Walker and Richmond, 1984), local comparison standards in the health area (e.g., low birth weight, birth rates, infant mortality) are much more accessible to local programs than local comparison figures in education (e.g., dropout rates from school, attendance rates) or in social welfare (e.g., child abuse reports by adolescent parents, welfare usage by areas).

Because the creation of a control group via random assignment to treatment and control groups is very difficult for most programs to achieve, programs are encouraged instead to use a variety of comparison standard options. A review of recent major evaluation efforts (by the Urban Institute for the Office of Adolescent Pregnancy Programs [Burt, Kimmich, Goldmuntz, and Sonenstein, 1984] and by the Manpower Demonstration Research Corporation for the Ford Foundation [Polit, Kahn, and Stevens, 1985]) and discussions with experts on the evaluation of adolescent pregnancy and parenting programs confirm that there is no one acceptable option for using comparison groups or standards. The most acceptable comparison for a national audience has been national comparison standards (from vital statistics or other several-site studies), while officials and policymakers at the local and state level have preferred local comparisons (from local comparison groups or local comparison standards).

A few TEC programs (Boston, Corpus Christi, Sarasota, St. Louis) have successfully identified a comparison group within the community; in all cases, the comparison groups were biased in some measurable way, providing a look at another treatment group rather than a "no treatment" option. Obtaining data from a local comparison group can be time-consuming and expensive. Therefore, local programs are advised to use local and national comparison standards exclusively if they do not have the resources to collect data on a comparison group.

Step 6: Selection of the Evaluation Design. The measures of outcome and impact objectives identified in Step 4 are the dependent variables in the design; the measures of the process objectives that describe the program treatments become the independent variables. Other descriptive variables identifying clients at intake or during the program become controlling variables. Since no TEC program used a randomly assigned control group, all of the evaluations employ some type of quasi-experimental design (Campbell and Stanley, 1963; Cook and

Campbell, 1979). As a result of the network experience and additional funding from the Charles Stewart Mott Foundation, the TEC programs agreed to collect longitudinal follow-up data on all program clients using the same instruments at regular intervals based on the age of the client's baby.

Step 7: Data Collection and Management. A simple device for monitoring the implementation of the evaluation and ensuring that data will be collected on time and by the appropriate person(s) is the Task/Talent/Time analysis, a chart that lists all major evaluation activities, indicates who is responsible for the completion of each, and gives the date by which it can be expected to be completed. This prevents slippage in the time schedule and clarifies assignment of responsibility for each task.

Meticulous attention to data collection and to objectivity is imperative if the data are to be reliable and valid. If the data are to be derived from performance on tests, for example, the person(s) administering the test must be trained to follow appropriate procedures and to ensure that the subjects are motivated to do their best. Data reduction, aggregation, and analysis should be performed by the person designated as the project evaluator. In the TEC projects, data were collected by a staff person or designee; this was acceptable because no sensitive data (e.g., measures of satisfaction with the program, or drug use) were collected; thus there was no reason to suspect bias.

Step 8: Data Analysis and Processing. Careful data collection avails nothing if the data are not carefully processed and analyzed. Forms, whether for manual or computerized data recording, must be meticulously labeled (indicating date, population, types of data, etc.). The centralized examination of program data for a network of programs is facilitated by early agreement on common objectives, instruments, definitions, and reporting forms.

Responsible data maintenance presupposes rigorous efforts to include data either on the total sample or on a meticulously defined subsample from which performance of the total sample can be inferred. Attrition rates and analysis of respondent and nonrespondent characteristics are necessary to ensure the credibility and utility of the data. All TEC programs use a standardized format to report annually on descriptive characteristics of program participants and on comparison groups at each follow-up point in the longitudinal design.

Data analysis techniques must be carefully chosen. Unless an absolute standard is used as the unit of comparison, a test of significance will be needed to present evidence of program effectiveness. The specific data analysis strategy used will be determined by the type of design specified in Step 6. All TEC programs use one of two standard statistical software packages (SPSS or SAS) for their analyses.

In addition to outcome and impact data, programs need to collect, maintain, and analyze process data to determine whether programs have been implemented with fidelity and to document those aspects of the program that may be responsible for successes or failures on the level of outcome. The importance of linking process data to program outcome data is best illustrated by an example. The St. Louis program had several components; individual participants could participate in one or more of these components. Even within a single component there was considerable variation in participants' attendance, level of participation, etc. Without process data—that is, data on the degree of participation of each client in each program activity—it would be impossible to determine relative merits of different levels of participation and would therefore be difficult to determine whether participants should be required (or urged) to participate more fully. Decision makers need to review process data during program implementation and review interim results.

All of the TEC Network programs have used evaluation results to make program decisions. In St. Louis, evaluation results led to the addition of economic independence as an objective and the addition of a new program component. In Corpus Christi, the program was not doing as well as anticipated in keeping participants in school. Greater emphasis was placed on outreach to school dropouts, and an academy was established for participants wanting to pursue education at more convenient times. In Sarasota, results of the follow-up interview highlighted the need for follow-up intervention—now part of the social work component. Other programs have changed boundaries and eligibility criteria and have added or deleted components because of evaluation results. In all cases, the evaluation was used not only to prove but to improve.

As can be seen from the foregoing, evaluation is an integral part of the program; it must be considered at every stage of program planning, development, and implementation. Moreover, evaluation not only provides evidence of the effectiveness or ineffectiveness of programs and their components, but also provides program managers a tool for ongoing testing of the program. Needed modifications can be installed early enough to ensure attainment of objectives.

IMPLEMENTATION OF THE IMPACT MODEL IN THE TEC NETWORK

From the beginning of the evaluation project, strategies for networking and technical assistance included semiannual evaluation seminars in which project directors were trained to use the impact evaluation model and to perform various evaluation tasks; site visits for on-the-spot technical assistance; and technical assistance by telephone and mail. Site visits included at least one annual visit. They were initiated equally by the site staff and the evaluation team, and they varied greatly in focus and urgency. The first visit to a new member of the network included both members of the evaluation team. Problems, needs, and issues to be addressed were defined and communicated prior to site visits, so that meeting time could be devoted to problem solving. Assistance included defining program plans; establishing baseline data; selecting comparison groups or standards; gathering, analyzing, and interpreting data; validating locally developed instruments; modifying plans based on evaluation data; and documenting, reporting, and disseminating findings.

Getting Started—The First Three Years

The study began in 1978 with an evaluation seminar designed to establish a network among the original five programs. At the seminar, attended by all five program directors and the evaluator of the New York program (the only program that employed an evaluator at that time), the impact evaluation model was explained and technical assistance was provided individually to program directors. Technical assistance was continued during the first year through site visits to help program staffs strengthen their evaluation designs and implementation plans. This assistance typically focused on: refinement of objectives, modification/enhancement of strategies to support attainment of objectives, selection and/or development of instruments, establishment of consistent data management procedures, identification of comparison standards, and selection of appropriate statistical procedures.

When the study began, some programs had not adjusted program strategies to meet the changing needs of clients; some had no defined and documented programs with activities consistently sought out by clients; some had inadequate, inappropriate, or insufficient measurement instruments; none had comparison standards; and few had subjected data to statistical analysis. Even programs operational for several years had not collected data that would support continuance of their programs and procedures. With the exception of the New York program, systematic scrutiny of the effectiveness of program processes had not been undertaken or even seriously entertained. A full year of technical assistance in refining objectives, modifying strategies, and installing credible evaluation systems was needed before any of the other programs could be evaluated.

During the second year, December 1, 1979 to November 30, 1980, the evaluation team provided leadership, instruction, and technical assistance to the original five programs, plus one in Oakland, and monitored the establishment of baseline data for each program. Although by this time program staffs had developed considerably in terms of their evaluative ability, and the evaluation designs (including instrumentation, data collection, and data analysis) were being implemented with reasonable fidelity, most program staffs lacked the expertise, time, and perspective to accommodate changing populations, needs, and resources while maintaining the requisite evaluation standards. Continued monitoring and technical assistance by an independent and objective evaluation team ensured that early efforts to document program effectiveness would not be aborted. What was learned by the evaluation team during the first 2 years, both in working with the six programs and in pursuit of information about evaluation efforts in the field, was applied directly to ongoing programs, bypassing the usual lag between information generation and use. Ongoing technical assistance helped program directors and staff make decisions that were supported by the limited process and outcome data that were collected in the early stages of their evaluations. The third year, December 1, 1980 to November 30, 1981, was one of intensive data collection and analysis, and one in which the utility of this approach to evaluation and technical assistance became especially apparent. The evaluation team provided critical technical assistance and support as the individual programs wrestled with problems frequently encountered in human services programs, such as staff changes; changing populations; absenteeism; changes in delivery systems; inadequate resources for data aggregation, summary, and analysis; and lack of staff sophistication in statistical analysis. In some cases, the number of instruments being used was unrealistically high, creating a burden both for staff and program participants. In these cases, the evaluation team helped simplify the instruments and began standardization of instruments by encouraging programs to use similar forms.

Despite these and other difficulties, the evaluation team was able to help program managers develop credible data that not only could provide evidence of effectiveness, but also could guide programs in the use of emerging data to make management decisions while the programs were in progress. Some program elements and delivery systems that had been pursued for years because they had general acceptance were modified as mounting evidence cast doubt on their efficacy. Compelling evidence of the wisdom of other program choices was provided by the emerging data.

By the end of the third year, all of the programs had credible data on the clients they were serving and their program components, and three programs—St. Louis, Sarasota, and New York—had generated important evidence of the efficacy of various services and delivery systems. St. Louis and Sarasota documented positive birth outcomes and an ability to keep young mothers in school, while the primary prevention efforts in New York City demonstrated that sexually active teenagers could be encouraged to visit a family planning clinic.

Evaluation findings were shared each year at the semiannual TEC Network conferences and in the annual reports prepared by the evaluation team. By the end of this phase, the conferences were anticipated with great pleasure by many members of the network, as they became an important way of sharing ideas and friendship as well as support. Each semiannual meeting was hosted by a different member of the Network so that each program could be visited by other members and observed in its own milieu.

Consolidation of Evaluation Efforts—The Second Three Years

Year 4, December 1, 1981 to November 30, 1982, was one of consolidation, during which the programs became increasingly confident about their evaluations and their ability to demonstrate success in achieving their objectives. In fact, three of the original programs in the network (New York, Sarasota, and St. Louis) had used the information on their clients and short-term outcome objectives to solidify their positions in the community. During the fourth year four other programs joined the network. Two of the original programs (one for pregnant and parenting street youth in Boston, and the other a school-based program for pregnant youth in Flint) withdrew, as their funding periods had ended; the evaluation team could not recommend to the Foundation that these programs be continued unless adherence to the evaluation model improved. Fully cognizant of the evaluation team's concerns and the problems faced in implementation of the evaluation, each of the two programs chose to withdraw rather than make efforts to meet the guidelines.

The four new programs included one for Native American teenagers in Seattle; one for Hispanic teenagers in Corpus Christi; one for pregnant teenagers in Rochester; and one for school-aged parents in Boston. It was easier for these four programs to implement the evaluation model's early steps since the continuing programs shared lessons about program development (e.g., about forming advisory groups, outreach activities, curricula) and about implementation of the evaluation model (e.g., about evaluation instruments, procedures for data collection). This transfer of information to the new programs bolstered the confidence of the continuing three programs about the value of their efforts to date.

As the initial programs continued to gather data, it became evident that well-implemented prenatal programs did contribute to improved birth outcomes; program participants experienced fewer pregnancy complications and a lower incidence of low birthweight and infant mortality. School-based programs were also successful in keeping students in the educational system and reducing repeat pregnancies. Two of the programs showed success with prevention of pregnancies through outreach. Program efforts began to include follow-up studies to document evidence of long-range effects.

During the fifth year, December 1, 1982 to November 30, 1983, the network programs agreed to pursue a core set of common objectives appropriate for the focus of their programs (e.g., primary prevention, prenatal, postdelivery). These common outcome and impact objectives are listed in Table 18.2 along with their applicability for a particular program focus. The necessity for this type of standardization became obvious during this consolidation phase, as the newer programs asked the older ones for help; it also became increasingly clear that the programs in the network did share a common core of goals and objectives and were using many similar strategies (see Table 18.1). It also became clear to the evaluation team—which was obligated to report to the Mott Foundation on the overall TEC Network effort—that standardized instruments and data reporting procedures would be helpful in summarizing and disseminating findings.

During this project year two programs had primary prevention components, five had prenatal programs, and four had postdelivery programs. In addition to the common objectives, some programs also pursued unique objectives. The majority of programs were successful in meeting most of the short-term outcome objectives, and two programs (Sarasota and St. Louis) were successful on several of the common impact objectives (e.g., high school graduation and repeat births), using their own follow-up evaluation designs (Mitchell and Walker, 1984).

Recognizing that crucial evidence concerning impact objectives could not be collected without a longitudinal study design, the Mott Foundation funded a follow-up study during the fifth year of the evaluation project. At this point four programs were in their second year of funding, one in its fourth, and two in their fifth. All programs agreed to use the same follow-up evaluation design. At each data point, based on the age of the teenage mother's child, a core set of information relating to common objectives, descriptive client information, and program services delivered was collected. The dependent variables across sites included: high school graduation or GED completion; employment; economic independence; well-baby care; child abuse and neglect; and repeat pregnancies. This design allowed ongoing evaluation activities to be integrated into program and service activities.

Thus, it took 5 years of experience to generate a consensus among the program directors and evaluators that pursuing a common set of objectives using a common core of instruments would be productive. This early work helped to clarify the tools and approaches possible in implementing a low-cost evaluation at the local community level. The early struggles, successes, and findings of the TEC Network (as well as others) evolved into the standardized longitudinal approach that the programs in the original TEC Network and others (such as the National Urban League, the Massachusetts Department of Public Health) are now using.

During the sixth year, December 1, 1983 to November 30, 1984, technical assistance efforts via site visits and phone contacts focused on common data reporting and analysis formats. At this point, the study provided important information about short- and long-term effects of different types of pregnancy prevention and care programs (Mitchell and Walker, 1985). This information demonstrated that programs had made changes in their communities. For example, all four prenatal programs demonstrated statistically significant reductions in low birthweight babies as compared with local comparison groups and standards. In addition, there were improved outcomes on most other objectives (e.g., retention in school, repeat births, economic dependence, and health care access and use) for most program participants (Mitchell and Walker, 1985).

WHY THE MODEL WORKS: EVIDENCE OF SUCCESS

The most important component of this evaluation model is the provision of technical assistance at the program sites. Our site visits enabled us to work with the entire staff, including program supervisors, advisory committee members, and curriculum directors. Dialogue among and between these various individuals, all with some stake in the program, under the direction of the evaluation team member(s), proved very effective in generating support for the program directors and for the evaluation. All those present at these meetings developed considerable insight into the strengths and needs of the programs. Commitment was renewed, spurred by the promise of evidence.

One goal of the site visits was to ensure that the evaluation and service components were compatible and that needed services were being provided while evidence of effectiveness was being collected. In most cases, technical assistance centered around a review of the successes and problems in data collection and analysis. In some cases, instruments needed to be modified or new instruments selected or developed in order to provide the required information. In one case, the evaluation team prepared a coding manual for automated data processing and set up a coding process for the staff.

The technical assistance team also addressed several problems that were only indirectly related to the evaluation efforts, but that, if left unresolved, could have had deleterious effects upon the program evaluation. One of these problems was staff transition. Two of the programs experienced a staff change at the director level, and each of the programs experienced personnel changes at the programmatic level. In addition, four programs changed evaluators. Program staffs felt comfortable consulting with the evaluation team about these changes and their impact on the program and the evaluation.

The technical assistance team also helped program personnel prepare reports and proposals. Project directors were encouraged to use the information generated by the previous year's evaluation in order to refine their program plans and proposals for the following year. The project staffs were also encouraged to publish results in order to share their findings and successes and assist others interested in developing similar programs and evaluations.

One finding from the technical assistance effort is that local sites must have some financial and staff support—in addition to the technical assistance team—to design and implement a successful evaluation. Recognizing that the evaluation activities, including data reporting and analysis, required more effort than the program staff could manage, the evaluation team assisted program directors in locating supplemental funds and/or personnel to perform the evaluation tasks at their site.

Although success is difficult to quantify, several indicators can be used to judge the impact of the evaluation model itself. These criteria include program survival and longevity, use of the evaluation findings in program/management planning and policy development processes, products developed, dissemination of results, and program awards. Those that have been funded for 4 or more years have the most indicators of success in terms of use of findings, products developed, and dissemination of results. The program with the widest dissemination of results—New York—is one of the original programs, the only one based in a university, and the only one specifically funded for dissemination activities during its final year.

All of the programs have survived, have produced instruments and forms, and have made local presentations. Three programs (Sarasota, Rochester, and Boston) have received awards as model youth programs. Several programs have used evaluation findings in efforts to save, expand, or modify the program, and to advocate improved policies for pregnant adolescents or adolescent parents at the state and/or federal level. All the program directors have expressed positive feelings about the strategies used in this study and have indicated an interest in continuing to use them. All of the programs now have either evaluators on their staffs or contracts with consultants for evaluation services, and all, regardless of the level of evaluation sophistication, have used the technical assistance of the evaluation team.

Finally, one of the benefits of the Impact Evaluation Model is its cost. Overall, this model is relatively inexpensive to implement. During the first 5 project years, before the common follow-up data collection began, program spending averaged between $2000 and $5000 each year on evaluation activities. The overall evaluation and networking effort cost about $100,000 per year; this includes (approximately) $30,000 for technical assistance and travel, $20,000 for the costs of two conferences for all TEC Network programs, and $50,000 for local program evaluation activities.

IMPLICATIONS FOR FAMILY PROGRAM EVALUATION

Overall, experiences with the TEC Network have confirmed the usefulness of the impact evaluation model with local adolescent pregnancy and parenting programs in a variety of settings. Although the technical assistance and networking approach, combined with the impact evaluation model's procedures, has not been used with a variety of other social service and family programs, we feel that the lessons learned from the TEC Network programs can be applied to family programs in a variety of settings, and we encourage evaluators and program directors to do so.

In conclusion, we highlight three of these lessons. First, even for the smallest evaluation, money must be set aside for evaluation tasks, such as instrument development, and data collection and/or analysis. Second, the program should, ideally, participate in a network with similar programs that meet occasionally and should have some technical assistance available for evaluative and management issues. Finally, our efforts renewed our conviction that program evaluation should be viewed as a management tool that needs the full support and understanding of program directors. Again, we as evaluators sought not only to prove but also to improve. Our shared interest in understanding the failures and successes of the various program components formed the basis of our working relationship. Moreover, through this relationship we were able to demystify evaluation terms and empower program staffs to be involved in the evaluation process. Such empowerment is the key to successful evaluation and, ultimately, to the use of evaluation at the local level.

ACKNOWLEDGMENTS

The evaluation activities described in this chapter were funded by the Charles Stewart Mott Foundation. The authors wish to thank Marilyn Steele, Project Officer at the Charles Stewart Mott Foundation, and all the project directors and evaluators of programs in the Too-Early-Childbearing Program Network for their hard work and thoughtful comments throughout the evaluation process.

References

Alan Guttmacher Institute. (1981). *Teenage Pregnancy: The Problem That Won't Go Away.* NY: Planned Parenthood Federation of America.

Baldwin, W. H. (1976). Adolescent pregnancy and childbearing–growing concerns for Americans. *Population Bulletin, 31,* 1–33.

Burt, M. R., Kimmich, M. H., Goldmuntz, J., and Sonenstein, F. L. (1984). *Helping Pregnancy Adolescents; Outcomes and Costs of Service Delivery—Final Report on the Evaluation of Adolescent Pregnancy Programs.* Washington, D.C.: Urban Institute.

Campbell, D. T., and Stanley, J. C. (1963). *Experimental and quasi-experimental designs for research.* Chicago, IL: Rand McNally.

Chilman, C. S. (1979). *Adolescent sexuality in a changing American society: Social and psychological perspectives.* Washington, D.C.: Government Printing Office.

Cook, T. D., and Campbell, D. T. (1979). *Quasi-experimentation: Design and analysis issues for field settings.* Boston, MA: Houghton Mifflin.

Klerman, L. V. (1979). Evaluating service programs for school-age parents. *Evaluation and the Health Professions, 1,* 55–70.

Mitchell, A., and Walker, D. K. (1984). Evaluation report of the Too-Early-Childbearing Network. Los Alamitos, CA: Southwest Regional Laboratories.

Mitchell, A., and Walker, D. K. (1985). Evaluation report of the Too-Early-Childbearing Network. Los Alamitos, CA: Southwest Regional Laboratories.

Phipps-Yonas, S. (1980). Teenage pregnancy and motherhood: A review of the literature. *American Journal of Orthopsychiatry, 50,* 403–431.

Polit, D. F., Kahn, J. R., and Stevens, D. W. (1985). *Final Impacts from Project Redirection: A Program for Pregnant and Parenting Teens.* NY: Manpower Demonstration Research Corporation.

Walker, D. K. & Richmond, J. B. (Eds.) (1984). *Monitoring Child Health in the United States: Selected Issues and Policies.* Cambridge, MA: Harvard University.

part IV

CURRENT ISSUES IN THEORY AND POLICY

The chapters in this section focus on issues of broad relevance to theory and policy that we feel are likely to advance the thinking of program developers, policymakers, and researchers. Each chapter serves as a reminder that family programs must change and mature as they integrate new ideas about how children and families develop and new understanding of their role in larger family policy and research debates.

White's chapter (19) on cost analyses of family programs is an especially timely one in this era of cost containment and deficit reduction. Increasingly programs are being asked to conduct cost–effectiveness and cost–benefit studies, the results of which could have major effects on the availability and character of future family programming. White provides a clear presentation of these two approaches to cost analysis and identifies both the advantages and limitations of their application to family support programs. He also places the call for such studies in the larger context of social advocacy, national politics, and prevailing social values.

Hauser-Cram (Chapter 20) profiles another trend that may increasingly be applied to assessments of the effectiveness of family programs: that of using meta-analytic techniques to interpret program impact data. Meta-analysis is a hotly debated and relatively new analytic method which allows investigators to aggregate research findings across studies. Hauser-Cram argues that while these new techniques are themselves susceptible to pitfalls, and are not to be adopted as replacements for more discursive qualitative reviews, they allow for increased statistical power and greater sensitivity to relationships among findings not addressed in a single study.

Slaughter (Chapter 21) provides a thought-provoking exploration of the implications of racial and ethnic diversity for family program development. She challenges several assumptions concerning black children and families and argues that greater cultural consonance between programs and the populations they serve is critical. She highlights the issue of service modality, suggesting that cultural affiliations influence the desired mode, intensity, and content of programming and must be respected if programs are to be effective.

In the final chapter (22), Dym critiques and extends two popular ecological theories of human development: that of developmental psychologist Urie Bronfenbrenner, and that of family systems theorist Salvador Minuchin. Dym's perspectives on change in families, arising in part from his clinical experiences as a family therapist, suggest a more complex, recursive process than is often described by developmental theorists. While the more inclusive contextual model provided by family systems theory demands consideration of many aspects of family life and many foci of intervention, these demands may result, in our opinion, in a richer and more fruitful understanding of positive family functioning and of efforts to promote it.

Taken together, then, the chapters in this section present a sampling of issues and new directions that we feel need to be more fully integrated into the agenda of the family support movement. This movement cannot afford to pit commitment to serving families against the kind of self-critical inquiry promoted here; for it is only with such inquiry that the field can develop to respond better to the diverse needs of American families.

chapter 19

COST ANALYSES IN
FAMILY SUPPORT PROGRAMS

Karl R. White

As money for social service programs has become increasingly scarce, politicians, administrators, and evaluation specialists have begun to refer more frequently to the "cost–effectiveness" and/or the "cost–benefit" of a particular program or policy.

Although the terms are being used more frequently, very little good cost analysis work has been done (Barnett, 1986). As with many new ideas, present conceptualizations of cost analysis are overly simplistic, expectations are unrealistically high, and much of what is labeled as cost–effectiveness or cost benefit research suffers from serious conceptual and methodological inadequacies. After distinguishing between the types of cost analysis that are most applicable to the evaluation of family support programs, this chapter will outline some of the impediments to more widespread use of results from cost analyses and summarize the benefits that can be realistically expected from well-conducted cost analyses studies. In this presentation, it is argued that although cost analyses are useful, they are only one part of the decision-making process. And, as pointed out by Hayes (1982), other factors, such as constituency pressure, historical events, and societal values, will frequently and legitimately be given more weight in the decision-making process.

Differences between Cost-Benefit and Cost-Effectiveness Analyses

Although the terms are often used interchangeably, cost–benefit and cost–effectiveness studies address fundamentally different types of questions. Both types of studies require the simultaneous consideration of both costs and effects and similar techniques for calculating costs. The differences emerge in how the benefits or effects of the intervention are considered.

Cost–benefit analyses examine whether the outcomes of a particular program are worth more in pecuniary terms than the costs of the program. Generally, cost–benefit analyses are noncomparative—only a single program is considered,[1] and the only question addressed is whether the results of a program are worth more than it costs to obtain those results. While a cost–benefit analysis can be done for a single program, cost–effectiveness analyses must always consider two or more programs. By definition, cost–effectiveness analyses examine whether the unit of effect per unit of cost is greater for one program than for another.

A second important difference is that cost–benefit studies must be able to represent all program outcomes in monetary terms (no small task in many social programs), whereas cost–effectiveness studies need only to measure outcomes on a similar scale for two or more programs. The scale of comparison in cost–effectiveness studies can be anything from teenage pregnancy rates, to test scores, to incidences of reported abuse, to parental satisfaction with the program.

The differences between cost–benefit and cost–effectiveness analyses are best illustrated by a hypothetical example. Consider two alternative programs designed to decrease the high school drop-out rate of inner city youth. Historically, only 50% of those who begin high school have graduated. Program A enrolls 20 students and costs $20,000 with 15 of the 20 graduating from high school. Program B costs $15,000, but only 12 of the 20 students graduate from high school. Using the historically determined 50% graduation rate as a reference point, one could conclude that Program A resulted in an "effect of 5 additional graduates at a cost of $20,000, or one additional graduate for every $4,000. Program B was cheaper to implement but resulted in an "effect" of only two additional graduates for the $15,000 spent, or one additional graduate for each $7,500. In this case, Program A is the most cost–effective of the two.

Determining that Program A is more cost–effective than Program B does not require an estimate of the monetary value of graduating from high school as would be necessary for a cost–benefit analysis of Program A. Although difficult, it is possible to estimate the monetary value of high school graduation. For example, one could calculate the projected

[1] Obviously, cost–benefit ratios can be used to compare two programs by calculating cost–benefit ratios for each program and then comparing the results. The point here is that such analyses are usually done without such comparisons.

increase in earning capacity and decrease in social services associated with high school graduation based on historical information. However, such an analysis would ignore some other potentially important benefits of high school graduation on which it is almost impossible to place a monetary value (e.g., increased self-esteem and feelings of self-sufficiency, an intact peer support system, satisfaction at having completed a difficult task despite obstacles, and knowledge of others' willingness to help).

To a more limited degree, a cost–effectiveness study suffers from similar difficulties because it is not always clear how broadly or in what ways the "effects" of a program should be measured. For example, early intervention research has traditionally focused primarily on the effects of intervention on children's IQ test scores. In recent years, many have argued that some of the most important effects may be in such areas as the child's ability to adapt to a number of socially important environments, increases in the family's coping ability and satisfaction, and social–emotional growth for the child (Zigler and Balla, 1982). Even though it is admittedly difficult to measure the "effects" in such areas, it is dramatically easier to measure such "effects" than to estimate their monetary value. Furthermore, outcomes such as increased high school graduation rates, decreased divorce rates, and decreased child abuse are valuable as omnibus indicators of program impact even if we are unable to identify all of the components that have pecuniary value.

In summary, a cost–effectiveness comparison can be made by simultaneously considering the costs of two or more alternatives and the effects of the alternatives on whatever scale is available. In a cost–benefit study, however, the monetary value of both the costs and the benefits of the program must be estimated. A program is cost–beneficial if the dollar value of the benefits resulting from the program is greater than the dollar value of the resources required to develop, implement, and operate the program. Cost–benefit analyses do not require comparisons between two alternatives, whereas cost–effectiveness analyses can only be done if two or more programs are being compared. Finally, cost–benefit analyses become extremely complex in family support programs because the nature of the area in which such programs try to have an impact is very difficult to evaluate monetarily.

IMPEDIMENTS TO THE USE OF COST ANALYSES BY POLICYMAKERS

As budgets for social service programs become tighter, one might think that the logic of cost analysis would be so compelling that legislators and administrators would come to depend extensively on information from cost analyses to make decisions about whether to fund social service programs. In reality, there are a number of reasons why legislators and administrators have not made extensive use of such information and why it is unlikely that cost analyses will ever be the primary source of information for such decisions.

First, social service agencies have separate administrative structures and autonomous budgets, even though they serve overlapping constituencies. Thus, a director of health services is unlikely to be convinced that it is in his/her best interests to implement an expensive preschool nutrition program on the basis of evidence that such a program would reduce the incidence of learning disabilities in elementary school years and thus save the public schools more money than was necessary to implement the program. Although the health services director might implement the program for other reasons, the argument of dollar savings is not likely to be compelling because those savings have no impact on his/her budget.

In theory, bureaucratic inefficiency resulting from agencies protecting their own budgets and failing to coordinate with others for the common good can be corrected by legislator oversight. Unfortunately, legislators also have reasons for not using the results of cost analyses to make decisions. Benefits from family support programs often occur after many years and consequently cannot be documented until well past the next election. Even though we would like to believe otherwise, it is clear that elected officials are influenced primarily by factors that enable them to retain their elected positions.

Furthermore, although state legislators frequently ask about cost–benefit information, they usually vote for whatever they believe the majority of their constituency will support, regardless of whether it is cost beneficial. For example, neonatal intensive care units for very low birth weight babies are clearly not cost–beneficial (Butterfield, 1981; McCarthy, Koops, Honeyfield, and Butterfield, 1979; Walker, Feldman, Vohr, and Oh, 1984), yet every major hospital in the United States devotes hundreds of thousands of dollars to neonatal intensive care units. Alternatively, legalizing and selling marijuana, heroin, and cocaine under government sponsorship would probably be very cost–beneficial because of the reduced cost of enforcement, increased government revenues, and elimination of one of organized crime's most lucrative sources of revenue; yet the concept is not being seriously considered by any state in the country.

Problems with Cost Analyses of Social Programs

The use of cost analytical techniques is a relatively recent innovation in the evaluation of social programs. Like most new techniques, this has generated much discussion, high expectations, and only a few applications. Not surprisingly many of these applications have suffered from serious problems (Barnett, 1986). This is not the place for a complete methodological discussion of cost analytical techniques (a number of both introductory and advanced sources are available, e.g., Cohn, 1979; Levin, 1983; Mishan, 1976; Stokey and Zeckhauser, 1978; Thompson, 1980). However, it is useful to summarize some of the most frequently encountered problems in existing cost analyses of recent social interventions. As the following examples demonstrate, one of the most striking lessons of past cost analyses is the need for technical expertise in conducting such studies. While every program can and should do a better job of documenting the costs of service provision, conducting a cost–benefit or cost–effectiveness study requires technical expertise and experience in economic evaluation. Because this is such a new area, few program evaluators have such skills.

When a Dollar Is Not a Dollar

Measuring the value of program effects over a long period of time creates particularly difficult, and often undetected, problems for cost analysis. This is due to the difficulty of making objective estimates and judgments concerning such factors as inflation and the alternative use to which the money used to run the program could have been put. A program that cost $20,000 to implement in 1965 would have to return several times that amount in benefits by 1985 to be cost–beneficial.

For example, based on a recent survey of their alumni, Gallaudet College (the only college in the United States established specifically for deaf students) concluded that graduates of the college would earn $320,000 more during their lifetime than deaf persons without a college education. They conclude that, at current federal tax rates, this would amount to about $80,000 more in federal taxes paid as a result of a Gallaudet education. Since it currently costs the federal government about $45,000 for each Gallaudet student to complete a degree, the report concluded that students are repaying the government nearly $2 for each $1 spent (Gallaudet College, 1982).

Unfortunately, this conclusion is misleading. Even if inflation is ignored and it is assumed that the report's assumptions about tax rates are correct, the federal government does not even recoup the original investment when one considers the fact that the $45,000 spent on each student at Gallaudet could have been spent in other ways. Assuming that an average student graduates at age 22 and retires at 65, the return on the investment in the student accumulates over 43 years. As a hypothetical alternative, consider that if $45,000 were simply invested an interest rate of 8%, it would return $1,140,279.00 over 43 years. Compare this to the investment in the student. If taxes were paid in equal installments during 43 years of employment and invested at 8% interest as soon as they were paid, the value of the money repaid by the student would be $613,029 at the end of 43 years. This is $527,250 less than the straightforward financial investment, which, if converted to present value (at the time the student graduated) is $21,000 (Mishan, 1976). In other words, students are repaying a little less than half of the costs, rather than almost double as concluded in the report.

Another example comes from the analysis of the Yale Child Welfare Program reported by Seitz, Rosenbaum, and Apfel (1983). In their analysis of the benefits of a 2 ½ year day care program for disadvantaged children, Seitz *et al.* concluded that there were statistically significant and socially relevant differences on variables such as placement in special education classes, family income, and welfare receipt between experimental group children who received the intervention and control group children who did not. They concluded that "the financial implications of these results were considerable, totaling about $40,000 in extra estimated welfare costs and documented school service costs needed by the 15 control group families in the single year in which the follow-up data were gathered." The implication was that if benefits were aggregated over a longer period of time, the amount of savings to society would be much larger than the amount of money invested in the operation of the program.

The reported data were collected 10 years after the completion of the program. The annual cost of implementing the program in the early 1970s was $7500 per child. Assuming an 8% interest rate, the interest on the capital invested to operate the program in 1970 would have been worth 10% more than the alleged savings calculated by Seitz *et al.* in any given year. Thus, what appeared at first glance to be a substantial benefit is really a small but significant loss.

These examples are not intended to suggest that society should only support those programs that produce a net return on the original investment. There are many programs that we do and should support that are not cost–beneficial. However, the examples do point out that when extended time is involved, computing a rate of return can be somewhat complex, and unadjusted numbers can be very misleading.

The Robustness of Economic Assumptions

Every economic analysis is based on assumptions concerning future interest and inflation rates, what would have been done with the money had it not been used for the program in question, and how feasible it is for others to implement a similar program. Often, the specific data required to estimate both costs and effects are not readily available and so further assumptions are made. Every cost analysis should specify the assumptions made and the degree to which mistakes in those assumptions will alter the results. Unfortunately, few do.

For example, the initial[2] economic analysis of the Ypsilanti Perry Preschool Project (Weber, Foster, and Weikart, 1978) estimated the benefits of preschool intervention programs with disadvantaged children by comparing lifetime earnings for children who participated in the program to a randomly assigned group of children who had not participated in the program. At the time data were collected, the oldest children were in ninth grade and the youngest in fourth grade. Projections of lifetime earnings were made using some very strong assumptions of questionable validity. Although the process is too complex to explain in detail here, it basically involved using existing school records of the children's special education placement and retention in grade, assuming a similar pattern for each child for the remainder of their public educational experience, and using that to project how much schooling would be acquired by each child in the experimental and control groups. Since all the children in the experiment were black, the estimate of education attainment for each child was then referenced to the average annual income earned by blacks with corresponding levels of education in 1953. The resulting annual income was used to compute lifetime earnings for each child. The approach was not technically incorrect, but it did require some very strong assumptions. To the degree that those assumptions were wrong, the true results would be substantially different.

A standard economic technique used in such situations is known as "sensitivity analysis" (Stokey and Zeckhauser, 1978, pp. 233–236). Data are analyzed using different assumptions to determine whether the overall result changes dramatically depending on which assumptions are used. Typically, one would use one set of very conservative assumptions, another set of fairly liberal assumptions, and another set of moderate assumptions. If the conclusion is the same regardless of which assumptions are used, one can be more confident that the conclusion is correct.

Unfortunately, few cost analyses currently being done in social service programs perform sensitivity analyses. The results of such analyses are open to the criticism that anything can be proved if the appropriate assumptions are made. In many studies, it is difficult to determine whether such criticisms are justified, since the assumptions are often

---

[2] It should be noted that a more recent cost analysis of the Perry Preschool Project (Berrueta-Clement, Schweinhart, Barnett, Epstein, and Weikart, 1984) is exceptionally well done and improves substantially on the original work.

not explicit and little, if any, effort is given to testing the effects of alternative assumptions.

Defining Program Costs

Most cost analyses of social programs provide very little information about how program costs are determined. A common approach is to divide the total program budget by the number of people served and use that figure for an estimate of cost per person. Unfortunately, what appears at first glance to be a straightforward and logical way to compute costs can often be misleading. First, program budgets are often not accurate estimates of what the programs really cost. Oftentimes, facilities are donated, administrative costs are charged to other budgets, or "in-kind" contributions of staff are made by the sponsoring organization. In addition, contributed resources from outside the organization, such as parent transportation, use of student tutors, and donated equipment, are often ignored. Good documentation of actual costs of program implementation often requires more common sense than technical expertise.

If all resources needed to implement a program are not documented, findings may mislead those considering the implementation of a similar program; their ability to obtain donations, volunteers, shared resources, or in-kind contributions may differ significantly from that of the original program. For example, a program in a college town might have access to student volunteers, while a similar program in a large metropolitan area might have to pay all of its personnel.

Another important reason to identify all costs is to enable decision makers to consider the implications of using so-called free resources. Some decision makers may, for example, feel that contributing time to the program is a reasonable parental obligation, while others may believe that such services should be purchased by the program rather than being imposed on parents. Unless parent time is identified as an "ingredient" of the program, it remains a "hidden cost." Once all the "ingredients" of a program are identified, data can be analyzed according to who pays for which aspects of the project. For example, a cost–effectiveness analysis could be done of two alternative programs in terms of only those costs that are supported by the local municipality (excluding revenue from federal grants and the contributed time of parents); or the same analysis could be done with all costs included, regardless of source. Unfortunately, very few cost analyses of social programs collect enough information about costs to do such analyses.

Difficulties with Valuing Benefits and Costs

In many cases, important benefits and costs of a program are difficult to value and are consequently ignored. For example, consider a cost analysis of a program that reduces the number of profoundly mentally retarded children living in institutions by placing them back with their families. If only the obvious public costs are considered in comparing the costs of having the child live in an institution versus having the child live at home and be educated in a public school, the report might conclude that state and federal governments would save substantial amounts of money through deinstitutionalization. However, such an analysis would ignore a number of potentially important costs paid by the family and the government. Such costs might include the following:

- Reduced revenue to the family with concomitant decreases in taxes paid because one of the parents can no longer work.
- Deinstitutionalization of the children may contribute to increased stress and subsequent increases in divorce rates with concomitant increases in unemployment compensation and child support payments.
- The costs to the local municipality of creating additional sheltered workshops, group homes, or recreational opportunities.
- The cost to the family or the municipality of providing transportation for the child to the various programs in which he/she participates.

It is also very difficult to value the benefits of family support programs. For example, previous cost analyses of early intervention programs have translated increases in IQ or educational attainment into lifetime earnings. However, most people would agree that increases in IQ might also result in increased ability to appreciate art, music, and literature; more knowledgeable participation in the political process; and increased understanding about the requirements of daily living, such as traffic laws, banking regulations, and continuing educational opportunities. Such effects are extremely valuable, even though it is difficult to place a dollar figure on them. Although there are no easy answers to the valuation of such intangibles, it is important to recognize that such intangibles exist on both the benefit and the cost sides of the equation.

Confusing Societal and Private Benefits

Just as the costs of a program should be partitioned according to who is paying for which aspect of the program, benefits should be attributed clearly to various beneficiaries. In most analyses, it is par-, ticularly important to distinguish between public and private benefits. For example, the original cost analysis of the Perry Preschool Project concluded that the benefits of the project consisted of increased lifetime earnings, savings resulting from lower rates of grade retention and placement in special education programs, and reduced child care ex- penses (Weber *et al.*, 1978). Based on these data, it was argued that benefits of the program were nearly twice as large as the cost of the program. However, 88% of the total benefits were increased lifetime earnings. Increased earnings are essentially a private benefit. To argue that the program was cost–beneficial was technically correct but con- ceptually questionable because the only identifiable public gains from the program were the reduced costs to public education of lower rates or retention and special education placements and whatever portion of increased income would have been paid in taxes.

Although one can argue that societal benefit is merely the sum of all benefits accruing to individuals in the society, that is not the defi- nition of societal benefits most people have in mind when they are trying to determine whether a program supported by public funds is cost–beneficial. The point here is that cost analyses should specify who the beneficiaries are and how the benefits for each group balance with the costs contributed by different sources.

BENEFITS OF COST ANALYSES

Given all of the problems with cost analyses discussed in this chapter, is it worthwhile to bother with cost analyses? That depends in part on the purpose of the study. For example, Donald Campbell (1969) once made a useful distinction between "trapped administrators" and "ex- perimental administrators." Trapped administrators are those who have so committed themselves in advance to the efficacy of a specific pro- gram that they cannot afford an honest evaluation. Any failure of the program will be interpreted by themselves and others as a personal failure. Consequently, they simply cannot allow data to be collected that reflects poorly on their programs. For such people, well-conducted cost analyses are very dangerous. Experimental administrators, on the other hand, are committed to the importance of solving the problem, not to the efficacy of any particular approach. Such administrators are committed to systematically examining alternative approaches to de- termine which approach is best, and these administrators find cost analyses to be an extremely powerful tool. Examples of the ways in which cost analyses can be useful are given in the next sections.

A More Complete Picture

Most program evaluations focus only on benefits or only on costs. Much is to be gained by considering the two simultaneously. When such analyses are done, administrators will discover instances in which neither the most effective nor the least expensive program is the most cost–effective, and hence the program of choice. Consider three hypothetical programs, all designed to increase high school graduation rates of pregnant adolescents. Program A is the most effective, yielding 17 of 20 graduates at a cost of $20,000 per participant. Program B is the cheapest ($500 per participant), but only 2 of 20 girls graduate. Program C costs $2000 per participant, and 14 of 20 girls graduate. In a society with unlimited resources for such programs, Program A would probably be the method of choice because it is the most effective. However, in a more realistic situation where resources are limited, Program C would be preferred. Although graduation rates are somewhat lower, the cost for the program is a fraction of the cost of Program A. Thus, $500,000 could be used to help 175 girls graduate if Program C were chosen, but the same $500,000 would result in 100 graduates for program B and only 21 graduates for Program A. Thus, neither the most effective program nor the cheapest program is the most cost–effective program.

Improved Understanding of Program Operation

The process of identifying all ingredients that contribute to program costs often results in some surprising but useful findings. Taylor, White, and Pezzino (1984) recently conducted a cost–effectiveness analysis comparing two early intervention programs. Each program used the same curricula; policies and procedures for parental involvement, support services, and program administration were similar; and children came from similar socioeconomic backgrounds. It was believed by all concerned that the only significant difference between the two programs was the fact that one was half-day and the other full-day.

In the course of collecting data for the cost–effectiveness analysis, researchers discovered some important differences between the two programs that were not inherent in their classification as either half- or full-day programs. For example, although speech and physical therapy services were equally available to children in both programs, it was discovered that communication-disordered children in the half-day program received more than twice as much therapy as their matched pair–mates in the full-day program. This inequality probably arose because therapists had to travel further to children in full-day programs.

Consequently, scheduling was more difficult, and less therapy was given.

Similarly, program policies and guidance concerning the involvement of parents in both programs were identical. However, parents in the full-day program spent two to three times as much time assisting with their child's program as the parents in the half-day program. This was probably because teachers in the half-day program had two classes of children and, therefore, had to coordinate with twice as many parents.

Even though administrators were convinced that the only important difference between the programs was in the length of day that the children attended, the cost–effectiveness analysis revealed that there were many other factors that made the two programs different. One of the most valuable aspects of high quality, comprehensive cost analyses is a better, and sometimes surprising, understanding of program elements and activities and insight into how those activities might be related to program outcomes.

Discovering Unexpected Costs

Cost analyses often reveal that the program's real costs are very different from what was expected. For example, Pezzino (1984) recently reported the results of a cost–effectiveness comparison of providing speech and/or physical therapy to handicapped preschoolers with either certified professionals or with paraprofessionals who were supervised by a professional. The impetus for the study was the assumption that therapy services could be provided more economically with paraprofessionals. Surprisingly, it was discovered that even though both groups of people were about equally effective, very little money was saved in the total program budget through the use of paraprofessionals. This happened because physical therapy and speech therapy accounted for a relatively small part of the total program costs, and because professionals often voluntarily worked with two or three children at the same time, while paraprofessionals almost always worked one-on-one.

A similar phenomenon was observed in the half-day/full-day study referred to before (Taylor et al., 1984). The program's administrators assumed that full-day programs would be much more expensive than half-day—the only question for most people was whether half-day programs would be as effective. Surprisingly, if the contributed costs associated with parent involvement were ignored, the half-day program for communication-disordered children was actually 3% more expensive than the full-day program. These unexpected results were a function of the half-day program using much more of the centrally supplied speech and physical therapy (therapy accounted for 38% of the total instructional hours for half-day programs but only 11% for full-day programs) and having higher administrative costs.

THE USE OF COST ANALYSES IN FORMULATING PUBLIC POLICY

Historically, research and evaluation have been used primarily to attack someone else's program or defend one's own program rather than to determine objectively whether or not a particular program is successful, or which of two alternatives is best. Most programs are implemented by people who are deeply committed to that particular program for philosophical or self-protective reasons. In order to obtain money, such people often argue for specific programs as if they were certain to be successful. By overpromising in order to obtain money, it becomes almost impossible for administrators to conduct objective evaluations.

Research and evaluation, in general, and cost analyses, in particular, would be more credible and useful in the formation of public policy if advocates, politicians, and program administrators would shift from their advocacy of a particular program to advocacy of the seriousness of a particular problem and, hence, a commitment to systematically and dispassionately examining alternative solutions until the problem is solved or ameliorated. For example, one can argue that the incidence of child abuse in this country is unacceptably high without arguing for a specific program to ameliorate the problem. Having convinced people that child abuse is a serious problem, we should admit that there are at least half a dozen plausible ways to address the problem. By systematically examining the cost–effectiveness of those alternative approaches, valuable progress could be made in solving the problem.

However, instead of convincing policymakers and funding agencies of the seriousness of the problem, most advocacy efforts focus primarily on the advantages of a specific program for solving the problem. Having argued that the program is sure to be successful, administrators cannot allow data to be collected that show that the program is not completely successful. Such data would damage their credibility and suggest that the problem was not so serious as originally suggested.

As research and evaluation efforts become more committed to systematically evaluating alternative approaches for solving recognized problems, cost analyses will play an increasingly important role. It will demonstrate that the best program is not always the most effective or the least expensive and will often result in surprising and valuable information about program operation and costs. Such information is useful not only in selecting from alternatives, but also in improving ongoing programs.

ACKNOWLEDGMENTS

The work reported in this article was carried out in part with funds from the U.S. Department of Education (Contract No. 300-82-0367) to the Early Intervention Research Institute at Utah State University.

REFERENCES

Barnett, S. W. (1986). Methodological issues in economic evaluation of early intervention programs. *Early Childhood Research Quarterly, 1,* 249–268.

Berrueta-Clement, J. R., Schweinhart, L. J., Barnett, W. S., Epstein, A. S., and Weikart, D. P. (1984). *Changed Lives: The effects of the Perry Preschool Program on youths through age 19.* (Monograph No. 8.) Ypsilanti, MI: High/Scope Press.

Butterfield, L. J. (1981). Evaluation and economic exigency in the NICU. *New England Journal of Medicine, 305,* 518.

Campbell, D. T. (1969). Reforms as experiments. *American Psychologist, 24,* 409–429.

Cohn, E. (1979). *The economics of education* (rev. ed.). Cambridge, MA: Ballinger.

Gallaudet College (1982). *Survey of alumni, fact sheet.* (Available from Office of Alumni and Public Relations, Box S-12, Gallaudet College, Washington, D.C.: National Academy Press.)

Hayes, C. D. (Ed.) (1982). *Making policies for children: A study of the federal process.* Washington, D.C.: National Academy Press.

Levin, H. M. (1983). *Cost–effectiveness: A primer.* Beverly Hills, CA: Sage.

McCarthy, J., Koops, B., Honeyfield, P., and Butterfield, L. J. (1979). Who pays the bill for neonatal intensive care? *Journal of Pediatrics, 95,* 755–761.

Mishan, E. J. (1976). *Cost–benefit analysis.* NY: Praeger.

Pezzino, J. (1984). *A cost–effectiveness analysis of using professionals versus paraprofessionals in providing support services to handicapped preschoolers.* Unpublished manuscript, Utah State University, Early Intervention Research Institute, Logan, UT.

Seitz, V., Rosenbaum, L. K., and Apfel, N. H. (1983). *Day care as family intervention.* Paper presented at the biennial meeting of the Society for Research in Child Development, Detroit, Michigan.

Stokey, E., and Zeckhauser, R. (1978). *A primer for policy analysis.* NY: W. W. Norton.

Taylor, C., White, K. R., and Pezzino, J. (1984). Cost–effectiveness analysis of full-day versus half-day intervention programs for handicapped preschoolers. *Journal of the Division for Early Childhood, 9*(1), 76–85.

Thompson, M. S. (1980). *Benefit–cost analysis for program evaluation.* Beverly Hills, CA: Sage.

Walker, D-J. B., Feldman, A., Vohr, B. R., and Oh, W. (1984). Cost–benefit analysis of neonatal intensive care for infants weighing less than 1,000 grams at birth. *Pediatrics, 74,* 20–25.

Weber, C. U., Foster, P. W., and Weikart, D. P. (1978). An economic analysis of the Ypsilanti Perry Preschool Project. *Monographs of the High/Scope Educational Research Foundation, 5.* Ypsilanti, MI: High/Scope Press.

Zigler, E., and Balla, D. (1982). Selecting outcome variables in evaluations of early childhood special education programs. *Topics in Early Childhood Special Education, 1*(4), 11.

chapter 20

THE POSSIBILITIES AND LIMITATIONS OF META-ANALYSIS IN UNDERSTANDING FAMILY PROGRAM IMPACT

Penny Hauser-Cram

INTRODUCTION TO DISCURSIVE REVIEW

Those engaged in research on child development or family systems often are required to engage in the task of summarizing research studies. Such summaries have diverse goals. One is to document a gap—a set of important and intriguing questions that research has left unanswered. Such reviews may be used to support requests for research funds or, after completion of a study, to place the research in the context of major conflicts or trends in the field. A second type of literature review takes a more historical approach and examines changes in the conceptualization of a phenomenon over time. For example, Eleanor Maccoby (1984) describes how research on familial socialization has undergone a transition from a unidirectional view focusing on parental characteristics to a multidirectional emphasis on parent–child interaction. A historical perspective encourages researchers to reflect on the implications of theoretical changes. A third type of review integrates knowledge from several domains, culminating in the generation of a model to be tested in future studies. For example, in a review of research on child maltreatment, Jay Belsky (1984) posits a general model of parental functioning that may apply to all families. By discussing a few studies related to each element of the model (for example, social networks, developmental history, child characteristics) he diagrams the multiple influences on the determinants of parenting. Such a hypothesis-forming venture can stimulate research related to testing the validity of the model.

445

The kind of review that program evaluators and directors often find most useful summarizes knowledge of program successes and failures and relates program effectiveness to characteristics of children, families, and program components. Such reviews enhance evaluators' ability to respond to critical questions about program impact: Have those programs with a specific focus on conveying child development information been more or less successful than those that emphasize parent support functions? Are certain types of programs highly successful with adolescent parents but miserable failures with older populations? Do programs with a strong medical component result in outcomes for children that are different from those that are largely psychologically based?

The conventional way to respond to such questions is to produce a discursive review of the relevant literature. Reviewers using this approach often sort studies according to their theoretical constructs or models of program delivery and present the conclusions of each study in turn. The discussion highlights a pattern of results from the series of studies and develops a conclusion consistent with the pattern. Many times, however, a concise conclusion is not obvious, and reviewers need to wrestle with explanations for divergent findings. When findings conflict, reviewers frequently attempt to resolve the disagreement by providing reasons why certain studies should be given less weight (e.g., due to the inadequacy of certain measures, poor procedures, or design flaws). If the findings of even the most methodologically rigorous studies conflict, reviewers plead for more research.

Urie Bronfenbrenner's (1974) report on the effectiveness of early intervention programs is a fine example of a carefully executed discursive summary review that influenced the direction of future programs. In this report, Bronfenbrenner first specified, and then addressed, five critical questions about the relationship between program components and impact on children. He discussed the limitations of the data (e.g., the restricted range of measures) and methodological problems across studies (e.g., the lack of comparability between experimental and control groups). He then classified studies according to program characteristics and considered the results of each study in turn. His conclusion emphasized benefits that accrued to those in family-centered rather than child-centered programs and in programs that involve parents as the primary agents of intervention.

The discursive approach to synthesizing studies is both reasonable and persuasive. Readers not only get a sense of the general contradictions in findings but also are guided through arguments about specific inadequacies. These arguments shape an understanding of how the reviewers develop their final conclusions.

Criticisms of the Discursive Review

Some have questioned the conventional method of synthesizing information. Yin, Bingham, and Heald (1976) criticize the discursive review process as "more of an art than a science" (p. 140). Taveggia (1974) disapproves of the piecemeal fashion in which each study is analyzed and contends that reliable findings are often overlooked in this process. He claims that pleas for more research arise from a failure to cumulate findings systematically. Clarke-Stewart (1983) presents an example of the lack of scientific rigor evident in the discursive review process. She criticizes Bronfenbrenner's 1974 report, claiming his conclusion is based largely on the gains reported in a single program.

The discursive review, while yielding rich qualitative information about a study, is clearly vulnerable; in fact, it is a curious idiosyncracy of social science. The methods are not explicit and generally diverge from the standards established for synthesizing data within a single study. Before collecting data for the single study, investigators usually consider various design issues and methods of sampling. Researchers then test certain assumptions—such as homogeneity of variance and independence of errors—before they perform statistical techniques or interpret the data. In the discursive review process, there is no recognized procedure for aggregating information from various studies (Cook and Leviton, 1980; Jackson, 1980). Cooper (1979) and Glass (1976) argue that discursive reviews are especially susceptible to a reviewer's particular perspective or bias: A reviewer can be selective about which studies to include in a review and later claim that a particular study was excluded because of its methodological flaws.

Problems with Study Selection. The selection of studies for the review process thus raises several important questions. First, few reviewers report which data bases (e.g., Psychological Abstracts, Educational Resources Information Center) were used to locate studies for inclusion in the review. For example, in a study of the discursive review process conventionally used in psychology and education, Jackson (1980) found only 1 of 36 randomly selected reviews reported the population from which the studies were chosen for review. While he acknowledges that failure to report data bases does not necessarily imply inadequate selection procedures, he stresses that the absence of this information makes it difficult for the reader to assess the review's validity.

Second, few reviewers report how they select studies for their sample (Jackson, 1980). At worst, reviewers might base their summaries on samples that happen to be convenient, including only those studies with which they are familiar or to which they have easy access. In an analysis of 61 reviews of research on efficacy of treatment for hyperactivity, White (1982) found that 93.3% of samples were based on the "convenience" approach.

Another sampling procedure, perhaps used even more often is selection by some predetermined criterion. Using this method, an investigator includes "important" or "methodologically rigorous" studies. This practice is not without difficulties. First, reasonable differences exist over what constitutes "sound methodology." Studies do not always live up to the canons of empirical science, yet they may still contain much valuable information. Many studies exhibit tensions between internal validity (i.e., methodological rigor) and what Bronfenbrenner (1976) has called "ecological validity." Rigorous laboratory experiments may pass Campbell and Stanley's (1966) checklist of threats to internal validity but fail to produce important information about the real world.

In studies on peer relations among children enrolled in an early education project, for example, we may agree to include both laboratory and observational studies, though both types have often been criticized for a lack of methodological rigor. Reviewers predisposed toward observational research may discount the laboratory study because of its contrived setting, whereas those partial to laboratory studies may argue that even the best observational research lacks adequate control. Legitimate disagreements over which flaws should be tolerated may never be settled, but readers should be informed how selections were made.

Problems with the Aggregation of Findings. A second type of criticism of the discursive review process is that empirical findings are aggregated using imprecise and sometimes inaccurate procedures. Often the overall findings of many studies are pulled together, according to Light and Smith (1971), by "taking a vote." Reviewers who use this technique count up all the findings and categorize them by whether they favor the treatment group or the control group, or show no difference between groups. The "winning category" is assumed to be a good indicator of the true relationship between a treatment and an outcome.

While vote-counting is procedurally democratic, it is not an effective way to generate precise conclusions. One serious objection is that neither sample size nor size of the effect (the standardized difference between the treatment and control groups) is taken into account. By their nature, studies with small samples have less power to detect small differences in the population (Cohen, 1962). "To use a no difference result as evidence without reporting power is like reporting failure to observe mitochondria and not mentioning the magnification of the microscope" (Ladus, 1980, p. 604).

Vote-counting methods traditionally neglect the critical question of sample size, thereby treating large and small samples as if they have the same power or probability of rejecting the null hypothesis (i.e., the hypothesis that states the program had no effect) when it is false. Furthermore, with vote-counting, small samples that show the same form of the relationship, but with significance, are counted as votes against the null hypothesis. Statistical significance thus rests somewhat in the hands of investigators, since they can almost guarantee significance by using large samples. Carver (1978) and Hays (1973) emphasize that the odds of favoring significance for even trivial effects are greatly increased with a large sample. Well-funded investigators therefore need only select large samples and demonstrate significant effects to ensure that their studies will be counted as votes against the null hypothesis.

Hedges and Olkin (1979, 1980) contend that the vote-counting approach can result in a high probability of a Type II error—failing to reject the null hypothesis when it really is false and therefore overlooking the effectiveness of a program. They present tables illustrating that when 50 studies each with sample sizes of 30 or fewer subjects are being aggregated, vote-counting will fail to detect differences 86.2% of the time, even when the true effect is moderate—that is, when there is a half of a standard deviation difference between population means. Relying on statistical significance itself is thus an arbitrary, and often imprecise, criterion for drawing conclusions from a set of studies.

Another problem with vote-counting methods is that they ignore information about the magnitude of an effect. Without such information, readers never know whether a particular program or treatment "wins by a nose or a walk away" (Glass, 1977, p. 359). Policymakers often want to know if a program is highly or only moderately successful. They may want to withhold support from a program that is difficult and costly to implement unless the overall finding is one of more than moderate success. Moreover, they may want to compare the relative success of various programs, but significance tests alone do not provide information about the degree of success.

An additional criticism of vote-counting methods is that they fail to incorporate important information about interactions between treatment and outcome for different groups. Programs deemed successful in urban sites, for example, may fail in rural locations, yet vote-counters may still give the impression that those programs generally make "no difference." Systematic analyses of differences by site or population characteristics often provide valuable information that is overlooked in literature reviews (Light, 1979; Pillemer and Light, 1980a, 1980b). In fact, literature reviews are ideally suited for detecting interactions because they can incorporate information from a wide variety of settings and populations. Few single studies on their own, unless they are large-scale, are able to enlist such diversity.

META-ANALYSIS

Advantages of Meta-Analysis

Because of the weaknesses in conventional methods of review, several alternative ways of synthesizing research studies have been proposed (Glass, McGaw, and Smith, 1981; Light and Smith, 1971; Rosenthal, 1978) (see Green and Hall, 1984 for a review). Meta-analysis, a term coined by Glass (1976), is a method that uses summary statistics from primary studies to synthesize research findings. This form of aggregation relies on statistics often reported in journal articles, such as group means and standard deviations or specific statistical tests: *t*-tests, *F*-tests, or correlations. These summary data are used to calculate effect sizes *(d)*, defined as the difference between the treatment and the control group means divided by either the pooled standard deviation (Cohen, 1962) or the control group standard deviation (Glass, 1976).

The Benefits of Statistical Power. Meta-analysis offers several distinct advantages over the discursive approach and its frequent companion, the vote-counting method of aggregation. First, because quantitative aggregation of effects or studies enlarges sample sizes and, in turn, increases power, patterns of relationships can become apparent; the probability of detecting an effect, even a small one, is increased. In contrast, reviewers using vote-counting methods do not necessarily increase the probability of finding small effects by merely including more studies, because these effects may be buried in studies with small samples and nonsignificant findings.

The power issue becomes particularly important when aggregating studies using certain populations. For example, because the incidence of Down syndrome is relatively low, many studies that examine programs for children with this disorder use exceedingly small samples. Therefore, treatment programs involving this population usually need to demonstrate large advantages for program subjects in comparison to control subjects in order to produce significant effects. Vote-counting with statistical significance as the criterion may prevent reviewers from identifying the program models that have small but reliable effects. Aggregating these studies may highlight the modest gains frequently seen in this type of program.

Searching for Variation across Programs. Second, reviewers using meta-analysis can present a fairly comprehensive picture of results over a large range of subjects, programs, times, and measures (Pillemer and Light, 1980b). The reviewer using traditional methods can also develop a comprehensive picture, but meta-analysis provides a systematic method for examining similarities and differences across this range. If, for example, reviewers are interested in discovering whether early education programs are generally effective for all children, they will want to include studies with children from different kinds of families, enrolled in different program models. By aggregating a large number of studies, they can search for variation in outcome measures by population groups or program model. If there is little variation between groups or models then reviewers can make general conclusions more confidently. Reviewers can also determine whether findings are developed from a large range of measures, as the reliability of estimates is increased if similar findings are derived from multiple sources.

Reviewers using meta-analysis can often make statements about a large range of variables because they make use of more studies than are typically used in discursive reviews. Meta-analysis advocates, such as Smith (1980), stress that reviewers should include all obtainable sources. She demonstrates that there may be systematic differences in effect sizes by type of publication—journal, book, thesis, or unpublished report—and that if reviewers limit their sources to only certain types of publication, they bias their findings.

Responding to Broad Questions. Meta-analysis can use information from a wide variety of studies to answer broad questions about the general effectiveness of a program or treatment. For example, in the first published meta-analysis, Smith and Glass (1977) focused on a question about the general effectiveness of psychotherapy. Other reviewers using meta-analysis or related approaches to aggregation have asked similar questions about a wide range of domains, some of which have direct policy implications, such as: What are the effects of school desegregation on students' cognitive performance (Wortman, 1983)? Is class size related to student achievement (Glass and Smith, 1979)? Has the deinstitutionalization of mental health clients been effective (Straw, 1982)? These investigators amassed all obtainable studies on a topic with the goal of making a general statement about the success and magnitude of success related to a specific program or phenomenon.

Beyond these broad assessments, however, meta-analytic techniques can be employed to investigate systematically the relationship between a large range of descriptive variables and outcome measures. For this type of investigation, Glass and his colleagues (1981) recommend that certain types of variables be regularly coded.

These coded variables include:

- Attributes of the study's design (e.g., method of group assignment, internal validity)
- Characteristics of the population of subjects (e.g., age, socioeconomic group)
- Type of publication (e.g., journal, dissertation)

- Features of the treatment or program (e.g., the length of time, type of setting)
- Types of outcome measure (e.g., observational instrument, standardized test)

An investigator can then examine the relationship between each of these variables and the overall effect of the treatment. Some intriguing patterns have been revealed in such analyses. For example, in a reanalysis of Hall's (1978) literature on gender effects in decoding nonverbal cues, Eagly and Carli (1981) discovered that the sex of the authors of the primary studies was significantly related to the magnitude of sex differences reported.

An interesting feature of meta-analysis is that it gives reviewers an opportunity to examine the relationship between policy variables and program effects even when these relationships have not been explored in the individual study. For example, one potentially regulatable variable in preschool programs is class size. Suppose that no investigators in primary studies investigated the relationship between this feature and various outcomes, yet that a large proportion of studies report some information about class size in their descriptions. Reviewers could code the class size information and then systematically examine its relationship to cognitive and affective outcomes. They could also compare the relationship between class size and effect for different age groups. Although a significant correlation would not necessarily be grounds for policy making, it may suggest that variation in class size be built into future empirical studies where it could be examined rigorously.

In general, meta-analysis offers reviewers advantages similar to those gained by primary researchers who have the opportunity to move from a small pilot study to a large-scale investigation with a large sample and a wide range of subjects and measures. Investigators with large samples can develop more comprehensive pictures, generate more precise estimates of outcomes, and explore systematically the variation between certain variables and specific effects.

Controversies over Meta-Analysis

Despite its advantages over the discursive review process, meta-analysis has not been hailed universally as the best way to summarize research studies. Criticisms fall into three broad categories: technical shortcomings, the role of human judgment, and the tendency to mask important information.

Technical Shortcomings. One technical criticism leveled at meta-analysis involves the reliance on effects rather than on studies as the unit of analysis. For example, Smith and Glass (1977) calculated a total of 833 effects from 375 studies; effects clearly do not represent independent data points. This creates a problem of violation of assumptions for application of conventional statistical analysis. Furthermore, it requires reviewers to investigate several different distributions in generalizing the findings from their set of studies (Hauser-Cram, 1983). Although several resolutions to this dilemma have been proposed (Glass *et al.*, 1981)—such as using a jackknife approach to eliminate systematically the effects from each study in turn or employing a generalized least-squares analysis capable of dealing with correlated errors—none is entirely satisfying.

Another technical difficulty with meta-analysis concerns the opportunity for bias. Two types of bias can occur. First, all studies included in a synthesis may have a similar design flaw (Cook and Leviton, 1980; Slavin, 1984). For example, each study in a meta-analysis of early education programs may utilize a control group matched for demographic factors but that includes families less in need of services. Program staff may then show greater concern for program families and encourage sustained participation, while families in the control group with similar needs may drop out without notice. The effect of such a bias is that the program will not demonstrate as positive results as it should.

A second type of bias can occur because of imprecise measurement of poorly operationalized constructs. Cochran (1968) discusses how errors of measurement typical of social science indexes, such as instruments that measure attitudes or motivations, affect standard techniques of data analysis. Suppose we are interested in studying the relationship between years enrolled in an early education program (x_1) and achievement in first grade *(y)*, controlling for background factors (x_2). We can represent the relationship as the following: $y = b_0 + b_1 x_1 + b_2 x_2$. If x_2 is measured imprecisely, we get a corrupted measure of its effect. If x_2 is also correlated with x_1, the estimate of b_1 will be biased (Light, 1980); the direction of the bias will depend on the correlation between x_1 and x_2.

Neither type of bias is necessarily obvious to reviewers attempting to aggregate studies, nor are the problems unique to meta-analysis. Reviewers using any form of synthesis must face these potential obstacles. The reason that bias creates particular problems for those interested in meta-analysis, however, is that bias can greatly undermine the precision this method of aggregation aims at calculating.

Judgment Calls. Human judgment, of course, plays a significant role in all aspects of research, but it is open to more scrutiny with meta-analysis because the steps in the review process are made explicit and findings appear more precise. This allows readers to examine judgment calls carefully—an advantage for readers concerned with making the review process more scientific but a disadvantage for reviewers whose decisions may create criticism and controversy.

Judgment plays a unique role in meta-analysis in decisions made about the coding process of the set of primary studies. Deciding which variables to code, which analyses to perform, and how to interpret results all require decision making that is constrained by the limits of the studies under review. Light and Pillemer (1984) describe a set of studies on children's nutrition programs in which the programs are labeled similarly but the actual treatment varies from program to program. Meta-analytic techniques could be applied blindly based on program labels and a set of misleading analyses and conclusions about the program's effectiveness could be developed. Although a similar error could occur in a discursive review, it is less likely because such reviews typically contain case-by-case descriptions of programs.

Stock, Okun, Haring, Miller, Kinney, and Ceurvorst (1984) reported a related weakness inherent in meta-analysis. In a discussion of a meta-analysis of research on life satisfaction in American adults, they report reliability coefficients as low as 0.52 in coding a critical variable—study quality. Even with careful scrutiny of the coding process, reasonable individuals may disagree. Those undertaking a meta-analysis should be alert to the difficulty involved in attaining adequate estimates of reliability.

Masking Critical Information. The third type of criticism leveled against meta-analysis involves its tendency to overlook critical information. Meta-analysis allows consideration of interaction effects across studies but is less well suited to the analysis of interactions within studies. It may be that certain within-study interactions can guide future research and better explain aggregate findings.

If, however, certain variables have been considered in only a few studies, it is unlikely they will be included in a meta-analysis. For example, many studies have been performed on the relationship between mother's employment status and various child development indexes. Only a few studies have considered the interaction of variables related to mother's satisfaction with work and child outcomes—a relationship found to be significant (Farel, 1980; Hock, 1980). Unfortunately, a meta-analytic review of the maternal employment literature would most likely overlook the critical interaction effects simply because few primary studies have considered them. This would result in misleading findings and might divert readers' attention from the critical interactions.

Applying Meta-Analysis to Understanding Family Program Impact

While meta-analysis can lead to a better understanding of the impact of certain programs on children and families, it has limitations as well as advantages. Some examples that highlight both aspects are taken from a meta-analytic review that a colleague and I have undertaken of studies of early intervention programs for handicapped infants and toddlers (Shonkoff and Hauser-Cram, 1987). The review was limited by excluding studies in which two or more interventions were compared, major threats to validity existed (based on a reliable coding scheme), or "disadvantaged" children were the primary focus of intervention. Employment of meta-analytic techniques in our study allowed for precise measurement of program effectiveness. Based on analyses of 91 effects from 31 studies, we found disabled children enrolled in early intervention programs to demonstrate a 0.62 standard deviation superiority over comparison groups. Furthermore, higher effects were associated with outcomes tapping language development and lower effects for those measuring motor skills. Clearly, such analyses are valuable for those concerned with broad questions about overall program effectiveness.

Specific questions about the relationships between effectiveness and child, family, and program characteristics also can be investigated through meta-analysis. For example: Are programs more or less effective when they concentrate on one socioeconomic status group? Does program focus affect program outcome? Do early intervention programs benefit all children equally? In our study, we found that while most programs, in fact, served a mix of SES groups, few differences in effects appear to exist for those programs compared to others that concentrated on only one SES group. As for program focus, our findings suggest that programs with a structured curriculum that had extensive parent involvement were associated with significantly higher outcomes than other types of programs. We also found that, as a group, mentally retarded children displayed greater benefits than those with orthopedic impairments. This finding suggests the need to question whether intervention per se is more effective with mentally retarded youngsters or whether traditional outcome measures are inappropriate for the orthopedically impaired child. Policymakers and program directors will undoubtedly generate many sophisticated and specific questions to ask about the interactions of child, family, and program variables. Given sufficient data, meta-analytic procedures can be employed to respond to those questions.

Our meta-analytic review of studies on early intervention programs serves to clarify the limitations as well as the advantages of the method. One such limitation relates to the distribution of outcomes in the literature itself. For example, exceedingly few parent outcomes existed in our data set, and those few were generally highly specific program-developed measures. By necessity, therefore, our meta-analysis of early intervention programs concentrated on cognitive outcomes in children, neglecting parent measures. This is unfortunate, because the greatest effects of such programs may be on parents. In early intervention, the effect of such programs on children appears to be strong, and the results of a meta-analytic review will most likely enhance support of such programs. But if the effects on children had been weaker, publication of such results could have reduced support for such programs prematurely, that is, before the full array of appropriate outcomes had been considered. Because of the large number of effects analyzed in a meta-analysis, the results have an aura of credibility that can mask critical information.

Another drawback in employing a meta-analytic approach is the limited generalizability of findings. Because effects, not individuals, are the units of analysis, generalizations to individuals cannot be made. Therefore, knowledge that programs with both home-visiting and center-based components generally appear to be effective, for example, does not guide program directors in determining which families should receive both types of services. Furthermore, the analyses give no indication of the variability in the content of home visits or center-based groups. A qualitative analysis of the content of services would highlight important characteristics of these services and certainly complement a meta-analytic review. Together, discursive and meta-analytic approaches can provide a comprehensive picture of the effectiveness of a program, point out gaps in our knowledge of effectiveness, and offer some understanding of the range of the content of services provided.

Lessons from Meta-analysis on the Review Process

Although blind application of meta-analysis to the bulk of studies related to family programs would be hazardous, meta-analysis has encouraged valuable scrutiny of the review process. One important result of the introduction of meta-analysis has been thoughtful deliberation over the necessary components of any review, whether it takes discursive or meta-analytic form. Harris Cooper (1982), for example, suggests a set of guidelines for conducting a summary review. He delineates five stages of the review process: problem formulation, data collection, evaluation of data points, data analysis and interpretation, and presentation of the results. He encourages reviewers to consider the sources of variance and threats to validity inherent in each stage.

A slightly different approach to considering the review process is advocated by Light and Pillemer (1984). They have developed a checklist of 10 questions readers should answer in evaluating a review (pp. 160–161):

1. What is the precise purpose of the review?
2. How were the studies selected?

3. Is there publication bias?
4. Are treatments similar enough to combine?
5. Are control groups similar enough to combine?
6. What is the distribution of study outcomes?
7. Are outcomes related to research design?
8. Are outcomes related to characteristics of programs, participants, and settings?
9. Is the unit of analysis similar across studies?
10. What are the guidelines for future research?

Questions such as those posed by Light and Pillemer are valuable to those evaluating a review. At a minimum, reviewers need to consider the purpose and audience of the review, aggregate all available studies or reports, analyze findings systematically, and be explicit about the steps they have followed in determining their conclusions.

The advent of meta-analysis may not only encourage more discussion about the need for reporting standards and about the limitations of various review methods, but it may also stimulate technical advances. Meta-analysis is best suited to data sets with a large number of studies. But many types of family programs have perhaps too many studies to be managed adequately in a discursive format and too few to warrant the subgrouping commonly used in meta-analysis. Investigators working on this problem might develop new approaches for aggregation that are systematic and rigorous, in the spirit of meta-analysis, yet powerful enough to cope with only moderately large data sets.

Unfortunately, meta-analysis may be used detrimentally as ammunition for exacerbating the quantitative–qualitative split in the social and behavioral sciences. If reviewers using meta-analysis are pitted against those using discursive approaches, both camps will suffer. Instead, we need in the review process to value analytical and critical judgment as well as systematic and precise evidence. Presenting readers with findings only from a meta-analysis is rather like offering the "results" section of a journal article without the accompanying "discussion." Reviewers should provide information about the overall effect of a program and about the variation in effects across studies. But reviewers should also make explicit the theoretical perspectives that guided their analyses, describe the limits of the data base, and suggest hypotheses for future studies. Arguments about which approach to reviewing the literature is best—seeking one method to the exclusion of others—will hinder development of rigorous and comprehensive research methodologies that yield practical results. What we now need is more discussion about the assets and liabilities of the various review methods, with an eye toward using these methods in a complementary fashion. Only with a blend of richness and rigor can we achieve our most basic goal: understanding the impact of programs on children and families.

REFERENCES

Belsky, J. (1984). The determinants of parenting: A process model. *Child Development, 55,* 83–96.

Bronfenbrenner, U. (1974). *Is early intervention effective? A report on longitudinal evaluations of preschool programs.* Washington, D.C.: Department of Health, Education and Welfare.

Bronfenbrenner, U. (1976). A theoretical perspective for research on human development. In A. Skolnick (Ed.), *Rethinking childhood: Perspectives on development and society,* (pp. 108–127). Boston, MA: Little, Brown.

Campbell, D. T., and Stanley, J. C. (1966). *Experimental and quasi-experimental designs for research.* Chicago, IL: Rand McNally.

Carver, R. (1978). The case against statistical significance testing. *Harvard Educational Review, 48,* 378–379.

Clarke-Stewart, K. A. (1983). Exploring the assumptions of parent education. In R. Haskins and D. Adams (Eds.), *Parent Education and Public Policy,* (pp. 257–276). Norwood, NJ: Ablex.

Cochran, W. G. (1968). Errors of measurement in statistics. *Technometrics, 10,* 637–666.

Cohen, J. (1962). The statistical power of abnormal-social psychology research: A review. *Journal of Abnormal and Social Psychology, 65,* 145–153.

Cook, T. D., and Leviton, L. C. (1980). Reviewing the literature: A comparison of traditional methods with meta-analysis. *Journal of Personality, 48*(4), 449–472.

Cooper, H. M. (1979). Statistically combining independent studies: A meta-analysis of sex differences in conformity research. *Journal of Personality and Social Psychology, 37*(1), 131–146.

Cooper, H. M. (1982). Scientific guidelines for conducting integrative research reviews. *Review of Educational Research, 52,* 291–302.

Eagly, A. H., and Carli, L. L. (1981). Sex of researchers and sex-typed communications as determinants of sex differences in influencibility: A meta-analysis of social influence studies. *Psychological Bulletin, 90,* 1–20.

Farel, A. N. (1980). Effects of preferred maternal roles, maternal employment, and sociodemographic status on school adjustment and competence. *Child Development, 51,* 1179–1186.

Glass, G. V. (1976). Primary, secondary, and meta-analysis of research. *Educational Researcher, 5,* 3–8.

Glass, G. V. (1977). Integrating findings: The meta-analysis of research. *Review of Research in Education, 5,* 351–379.

Glass, G. V., and Smith, M. L. (1979). Meta-analysis of research on the relationship of class–size and achievement. *Evaluation and Policy Analysis, 1,* 2–16.

Glass, G. V., McGaw, B., and Smith, M. L. (1981). *Meta-analysis of social research*. Beverly Hills, CA: Sage.

Green, B. F., and Hall, J. A. (1984). Quantitative methods for literature reviews. *Annual Review of Psychology, 35*, 37–53.

Hall, J. A. (1978). Gender effects in decoding nonverbal cues. *Psychology Bulletin, 85*, 845–857.

Hauser-Cram, P. (1983). Some cautions in synthesizing research studies. *Educational Evaluation and Policy Analysis, 5*, 155–162.

Hays, W. L. (1973). *Statistics for the social sciences*. NY: Holt, Rinehart and Winston.

Hedges, L. V., and Olkin, I. (1979). *Three vote-counting methods for the estimation of effect size and statistical significance of combined results*. Paper presented at the annual meeting of the American Research Association, San Francisco, California.

Hedges, L. V., and Olkin, I. (1980). Vote-counting methods in research synthesis. *Psychological Bulletin, 88*, 359–369.

Hock, E. (1980). Working with non-working mothers and their infants: A comparative study of maternal caregiving characteristics and infant social behavior. *Merrill-Palmer Quarterly, 26*, 79–101.

Jackson, G. B. (1980). Methods for integrative review. *Review of Educational Research, 50*, 438–460.

Ladus, H. (1980). Summarizing research: A case study. *Review of Educational Research, 50*(4), 597–624.

Light, R. J. (1979). Capitalizing on variation: How conflicting research findings can be helpful for policy. *Educational Researcher, 8*(9), 7–11.

Light, R. J. (1980). Synthesis methods: Some judgment calls that must be made. *Evaluation & Education, 4*, 13–17.

Light, R. J., and Pillemer, D. B. (1984). *Summing up: The science of reviewing research*. Cambridge, MA: Harvard University Press.

Light, R. J., and Smith, P. V. (1971). Accumulating evidence: Procedures for resolving contradictions among different research studies. *Harvard Educational Review, 41*(4), 429–471.

Maccoby, E. (1984). Socialization and developmental change. *Child Development, 55*, 317–328.

Pillemer, D. B., and Light, R. J. (1980a). Benefitting from variation in study outcomes. In R. Rosenthal (Ed.), *New directions for methodology of social and behavioral science: Quantitative assessment of research domains*. San Francisco, CA: Jossey Bass.

Pillemer, D. B., and Light, R. J. (1980b). Synthesizing outcomes: How to use research evidence from many studies. *Harvard Educational Review, 50*(2), 176–195.

Rosenthal, R. (1978). Combining results of independent studies. *Psychological Bulletin, 85*(1), 185–193.

Shonkoff, J. P., and Hauser-Cram, P. (1987). Early intervention for disabled infants and their families—A quantitative analysis. *Pediatrics, 80*(5), 650–658.

Slavin, R. E. (1984). Meta-analysis in education: How has it been used? *Educational Researcher, 13*(8), 6–15.

Smith, M. L. (1980). Publication bias and meta-analysis. *Evaluation in Education, 4*, 22–23.

Smith, M. L., and Glass, G. V. (1977). Meta-analysis of psychotherapy outcome studies. *American Psychologist, 32*, 752–760.

Stock, W. A., Okun, M. A., Haring, M. J., Miller, W., Kinney, C., and Ceurvorst, R. W. (1984). Rigor in data synthesis: A case study of reliability in meta-analysis. *Educational Research, 11*, 10–14.

Straw, R. B. (1982). Meta-analysis of deinstitutionalization in mental health (Doctoral dissertation, Northwestern University). *Dissertation Abstracts International,* DDJ82-26026.

Taveggia, T. C. (1974). Resolving research controversy through empirical cumulation. Toward reliable sociological knowledge. *Sociological Methods and Research, 2*, 395–407.

White, K. (1982). *A meta analysis of previous research on the treatment of hyperactivity.* Final report. (ERIC Document Reproduction Service No. ED 224–218.)

Wortman, P. M. (1983). School desegregation and black achievement: An integrative review. Washington, D.C.: National Institute of Education. (ERIC Document Reproduction Service No. ED 239-003.)

Yin, R. K., Bingham, E., and Heald, K. A. (1976). The difference that quality makes: The case of literature reviews. *Sociological Methods and Research, 5*, 139–156.

chapter 21

PROGRAMS FOR RACIALLY AND ETHNICALLY DIVERSE AMERICAN FAMILIES: SOME CRITICAL ISSUES*

Diana T. Slaughter

INTRODUCTION

The greatest strength of American society is the diversity of its peoples. In the contemporary world, America is a relatively young nation, and we still welcome, to varying degrees, peoples from around the world. Whether as voluntary immigrants or political refugees, persons usually come in search of an economically better and more socially secure life for themselves and their children. The promise of American citizenship is that with hard work, dedication, and some talent, it is possible to achieve these goals. Even when entry into America is involuntary, as was the case with early black Americans, the dominant cultural value of economic and social justice is so embedded within the American social fabric that such aspirations have remained undaunted among black Americans despite generations of social deprivation and related racial barriers to opportunity. For better or worse, most black American families, like all American families, want their children to belong to American society and culture, to participate effectively and successfully in its institutions, and to derive benefits from that participation.

In Takanishi's (1978) historical account of the American approach to child and family policy, she argues that a late nineteenth-century emphasis on social reform led first to a focus on children's rights and then to attitudes sanctioning public intervention into the lives of low-income

*A slightly expanded version of this chapter was presented at the biennial meeting of the Society for Research in Child Development, April 23–26, 1987, Baltimore, MD.

families. In 1884 Jane Addams founded the first settlement house in America to serve newly arrived European immigrants. Intervention programs for similarly situated families have continued to appear since that time.

Perhaps nowhere is the American commitment to individuals more clearly demonstrated than in its historical approach to family policy. However, we have no explicit, written family policy, and the 1979 White House Conference on Families indicated we have little consensual ground upon which to build such a policy. American families are more diverse than uniform in their content, structure, and organization. This diversity is tolerated and supported by national policy. As a nation, we are very reluctant to initiate policies and develop programs that could infringe upon the right of individual persons to form families and rear children in those families as they see fit.

However, familial changes have been dramatic in the past 20 years. Given the rising divorce rates and the tendency of these adults to remarry, it is not uncommon for children to have two sets of parents and four sets of grandparents (Emery, Hetherington, and DiLalla, 1985). The number of single parent households is also rising. Pearce and McAdoo (1981) report that in America, generally, the proportion of female-headed households rose from 11 to 18% between 1970 and 1980; the comparable figures for black Americans are 30 and 44%. The ages of persons who become parents for the first time are more wide-ranging than ever before, because of the rise in teenage pregnancy rates on the one hand and the postponement of pregnancy and child rearing by women who pursue careers on the other. Stein (1983) reports 1980 U.S. Census data that reveal that the median age at first marriage for women increased from 20.8 years in 1970 to 22.1 years in 1980. In 1960, fewer than 30% of the women between 20 and 24 had never been married; by 1980 this figure had risen to 50%. Conversely, since 1970 there has been a dramatic increase in reported sexual activity among adolescents (Butler, Starfield, and Stenmark, 1985) and a 109% increase in teenage pregnancies (Pearce and McAdoo, 1981). A typical classroom may include children living in one or more of the aforementioned nontraditional (Macklin and Rubin, 1983) family situations.

I would characterize our traditional approach to family policy as one that deemphasizes racial and ethnic diversity and seeks to provide minimal intervention on behalf of developing children and/or dependent adult family members. We have stressed low-keyed services to individual family members, rather than services to families or communities as corporate, group entities. In this way, we have tried to intervene and service families without being prescriptive about their collective goals and rituals.

For many families, this approach has proved successful. Many ethnic communities have accumulated sufficient economic capital to address the needs of their member families. Over 20 years ago Glazer and Moynihan (1963) discussed how New York City Irish, Italians, and Jews had, along with Puerto Ricans and blacks, maintained distinctive ethnic group identities even though the first three groups had achieved the economic and political power to "assimilate" into broader American society. Further, within these ethnic communities a variety of special-interest institutions have been created and privately supported to help members with family-related problems.

However, capital resources have never been equitably distributed between racial and ethnic groups, and the rapidity of social change has left many families economically and/or socially vulnerable. Of the 41 million persons living below the poverty line, 11 million are members of American racial and ethnic minority groups (blacks, Native Americans, Hispanic-speaking peoples, and recent Asian immigrants); many are members of female-headed households containing several children (Norton, 1985; Pearce and McAdoo, 1981; Wilson, 1985). About 55% of black Americans live at or below the official poverty level. Collectively, black Americans have not accumulated enough capital to address the needs of such persons.

The challenge to service-oriented programs for this racial minority group is to enable their families to become truly economically and socially self-sufficient within American society, while simultaneously acknowledging not only that black families collectively have sociocultural integrity, but also that many individual members of these families have considerable strengths and adaptive coping skills. This is an extremely difficult position for any public or private benefactor to assume, since it involves providing and monitoring material resources while accepting the premise that the person's poverty is not entirely his/her fault. The American creed encourages us to believe that slothful work habits, lack of commitment to the job, and inferior talents and abilities are causes, rather than consequences, of individual poverty. As a young nation, we do not accept the proposition that racial and ethnic groups have unequal chances for economic advancement because it undermines one of our most fundamental premises: Regardless of racial, religious, or social background, every individual has equal opportunity for "life, liberty, and the pursuit of happiness," a phrase that in our materialistic society has all too often been identified as synonymous with economic and social advantage.

This chapter assumes *(a)* that American families are racially and ethnically diverse in ways that have great significance to family programs, and *(b)* that some racial and ethnic groups have more capital accumulation than others; therefore, family programs can rarely be solely financed and administered within these latter groups. Furthermore, *(c)* participants may be directly serviced by persons who are not members of their racial and ethnic groups. It argues that there are better and worse ways to render needed services, and that in the category of "better" ways is included sensitivity to the cultural ecology of participating families. Much of my child and family research has been conducted with black American populations. Therefore, in this chapter I restrict my examples to that group.

CULTURALLY CONSONANT FAMILY PROGRAMS: SOME DESIGN ISSUES

Historical Background

Following the prosperity of post-World War II years, the early family service programs (e.g., Auerbach, 1968) were designed primarily to service middle- and upper middle-income families. Child development research had burgeoned, particularly during the war years when married women worked and young children were available for study in nurseries and day care facilities. Although public funding for such facilities largely evaporated after World War II (Takanishi, 1977), middle- and upper middle-income parents were eager to take advantage of the latest "scientific" information about the physical, social, and emotional development of their children (Sears, 1975; Senn, 1975) and the perceived associated optimal child-rearing practices. Parent education programs were typically funded either by private sources or with local public tax monies.

About 20 years ago this emphasis shifted back to the poor. The shift occurred for several reasons. First, it was assumed that middle- and upper-income families could purchase established programs of their choice. If they were not available in their communities, they had the social and personal resources to create and sustain programs tailored to their needs. (The recent proliferation of "self-help" groups among the middle classes is an excellent example of the continued, less costly, use of this option.) Second, it was thought that family programs that supported educational, and therefore, occupational attainment would be a means of tackling social problems (Moynihan, 1965; Rainwater and Yancy, 1967) perceived to be afflicting the entire society (e.g., the higher rates of unemployment, underemployment, crime, and delinquency found in urban lower-income, particularly lower-income minority, communities). During this period of American social history, special family programs (e.g., Head Start) were developed and piloted with poverty-level families, regardless of their racial or ethnic background.

We have developed a collective, if too often unstated, wisdom about these family-oriented intervention programs. For example, we found program goals may be frustrated or defeated simply because program designers know little of the cultural–ecological context of the families to be served. Since the time of those early family service programs, for example, important differences between black and white families have been identified through basic research, differences that challenge the assumptions and beliefs about black American children and families upon which programs had been based.

Challenging Assumptions

The Assumption of Early Intellectual Deficit. It is frequently assumed that black children are intellectually inferior to white children. Yet, according to recent research, black infants are superior to white infants on early tests (0–18 months) of sensorimotor intelligence (Freedman and DeBoer, 1979). This is particularly true of infants whose mothers have experienced uncomplicated pregnancies and birthing conditions. Some have attributed this superiority to genetic factors, length of gestation, or early environmental influences. In the first year of life, black infants experience more human physical/affectional contact with a wider variety of persons composing their extended families (see Ward, 1971; Young, 1970). The greater social responsivity and diversity of caregivers may enhance their very early intellectual development. However, the social norms governing language production and usage differ for black and white infants and young children (e.g., Brice-Heath, 1982; Moore, 1985; Ward, 1971). Black adults less often individuate communication between themselves and children. They emphasize speech in immediate perceptual context. Play between parents and children is not typically viewed as an opportunity for teaching and learning (Slaughter, 1983). As traditional measures of intelligence and achievement become increasingly language-based with the children's advancing ages, without intervention black children fall further behind white children in their mean performance scores. Conventional definitions of "intelligence," therefore, contribute to societal perception of black children as less intelligent than white children.

The Assumption of Deviant Sex-Role Socialization. Black children differ from white children in their social, as well as intellectual, development. The arena of sex-role socialization (Lewis, 1975) is an illustrative example. In comparison with earlier studies of middle- and working-class white families, black parents appear to do less sex-typing. They are comfortable in encouraging young girls to be assertive, even aggressive, and black boys are not considered "unmasculine" if they share in domestic routines (e.g., Baumrind, 1972; Lewis, 1975). Generally, black parents have assumed a more relaxed view of sex and sexuality relative to developing children (e.g., Dougherty, 1978; Ladner, 1971; Young, 1970). In the past, pregnancy and childbearing were not automatically occasions for marriage. Black females and their family members consider the ability of the prospective child's father to provide for an independently established family. The young, and the two sets of families, might even enjoy continuing reciprocal relationships within the context of shared child care responsibilities.

The Assumption of Self-Hatred and Low Self-Esteem. Early researchers equated self-esteem and expressed racial attitudes of black children (Porter and Washington, 1979). A tendency for more young black children to express positive other-race views than young white children was thought to be indicative of black children's lower esteem. Today, we know that self-esteem and racial attitudes are independent personality dimensions (Cross, 1985; Spencer, 1982). Black children have as many positive conceptions of self as do white children (Hare, 1977; Rosenberg and Simmons, 1971). However, the racial group identifications of black children are more likely to vary than those of white children, who are consistently pro-white in their racial group identification. When black parents deliberately teach children about the positive aspects of their heritage, children are more likely to have positive, pro-black racial attitudes (Bowman and Howard, 1985; Spencer, 1983). Bowman and Howard (1985) indicate that adolescents whose reported academic grades were higher also reported experiencing more early parental attention to adaptive racial coping strategies.

The Assumption of Familial Weakness and Disorganization. Early attention to black family life (e.g., Moynihan, 1965) emphasized only weakness, disorganization, and pathology. A higher incidence of low-income, single-parent families in the black community, in comparison with the incidence of single parenting in the larger, predominantly white community, was considered the major cause. Today, we know that family structure is not a reliable indicator of family functioning (Harrison, Serafica, and McAdoo, 1984; Hill, 1972). Although single-parent, female-headed households are more at risk for the hardships associated with low income and poverty (Pearce and McAdoo, 1981; Wilson, 1985), these families need not be inherently weak, disorganized, or pathological. Since the Moynihan report, it has been found that, despite socioeconomic position, the extended and/or augmented family is an important and continuing influence in the black child's socialization (e.g., Martin and Martin, 1978; McAdoo, 1981; Peters, 1978; Stack, 1974). Fathers and mothers have historically been comfortable in sharing the nurturant, expressive dimensions of child care. However, indexes of marital dissatisfaction are higher for blacks than whites. Researchers (e.g., Hatchett and Jackson, 1983) have pointed to the importance of the extended family in buffering adult, and therefore child, members of black families from the impact of material deprivations, societal rejection, separation and/or divorces, and other manifestations of personal unhappiness or failures.

Implications of New Research Findings for Program Development

Each student of this new research finds some unexpected similarities between black and other children and families (e.g., self-concept results), some generally positive and adaptive differences (e.g., importance of extended and/or augmented kin), and some differences that could be maladaptive in mainstream institutions (e.g., teenage pregnancy is highly associated with dropping out of school).

What are the implications of these findings for family service programs? First, the extended and/or augmented family is an important factor in the children's and parents' lives. Its cooperation could determine the success or failure of a program that ostensibly intends only to serve the child and its primary caregiver. Second, the concerns of program developers might not be the concerns of the parents. For example, the long-term social consequences of teenage pregnancy might not be so immediately obvious to mothers and grandmothers who are accustomed to valuing and caring for children regardless of the circumstances in which they are conceived and delivered. The design of programs to reduce teenage pregnancy must include some equally compelling real-life options to "lure" young women into establishing alternative priorities for themselves. Furthermore, as indicated previously, black children are no less "intelligent" at birth than other children, and even under present conditions, they are as likely as other children to think well of themselves. In the black community, caregivers of children are particularly sensitive to stereotyping on the part of program developers and staff who would perceive them as intellectually and/or socially deficient or incompetent just because they are black or poor. However, parents appear to need assistance in continuing to provide positive role models and experiences for children. Parents particularly need help in learning how to support the continued intellectual development of their children beyond the first 18 months of life in ways which contribute to successful school achievement. When children are older, parents need to learn how to support the best efforts of schools and how to continue to monitor schools to ensure that high academic standards are held for their children (Slaughter, 1977).

The general lesson to be drawn is that an analysis of the cultural–ecological realities of racial and ethnic minority family life must precede the setting of program goals. Too often we have not asked ourselves what we know, historically and culturally, about the families we intend to serve and what we need to know in order to design programs effectively for them. At best, we have relied upon a few informants in the immediate community, rather than conducting systematic studies of research findings and literature about the group. It is only by virtue of the latter that program content can be built upon an informed synthesis of the best available information on the total group. Even after doing this, however, we have to keep in mind that there is considerable diversity within low-income racial and ethnic minority communities. Few families or children will exactly fit the profile of the normative child or family that we construct for purposes of program design. Beyond the study of the group, we will need to know more of the specific communities and neighborhoods in which the programs are to be implemented.

A cultural–ecological model for family program design would emphasize that even under conditions of exceptional stress family members have developed uniquely effective coping strategies, which have enabled the group culturally and historically to endure and at times even to prosper. The evidence for these strengths in the black community is that most black children do not have intellectual deficits and do have positive self-esteem, more "equitable" sex-role socialization experiences within their families, and a great variety of extended kin contacts to depend upon for social and affective support. At present, we need more basic research on child care and development within black families to learn more about how these competencies are optimally encouraged in urban settings. Clark's (1983) work on the family factors associated with achievement in black adolescents is an excellent example of one such approach.

The Structure and Organization of Culturally Consonant Family Programs

If program designers are to sustain and support family strengths in low-income minority populations, at least three minimal criteria must be met. First, parents must be respected for how they cope with mundane stresses; second, the families must be encouraged to express their beliefs about how a program can help them to improve their lives; finally, program content must be based upon the developers' considered judgment and knowledge of the group's cultural history and immediate social context. I cannot emphasize the phrase "considered judgment" enough. Parents cannot dictate program content, nor can uninformed prospective program developers. In most successful family service programs, there is an established channel for continuing dialogue between designers, developers, and participants as to the extent to which the service is meeting originally agreed upon goals.

Staff Attitudes and Structural Opportunities. Aside from cultural knowledge of the families one chooses to serve, staff attitudes can enhance effective family services. These staff attitudes include self-respect and enthusiasm, a belief that people can and do change for the better and desire to be part of instigating that change, and a genuine commitment and camaraderie among workers with a shared mission. These attitudes were typical of those I encountered at the New Orleans Parent Child Development Center (Andrews, Blumenthal, Bache, and Wiener, 1982) and the New York Nassau County Levenstein Toy Demonstration Program (Levenstein, 1970, 1977). These people sustained positive staff morale in the early 1970s during difficult financial times and were undoubtedly favorably perceived by program participants. The most well-designed family services programs may fail without suitable and enthusiastic people responsible for their administration and implementation.

One quality that may be particularly useful when modelled by staff is that of feeling in control of one's life. When staff feel and act in control of their work, participating program families are more likely to feel that they, too, can be in control of their own lives. Several researchers concerned with service delivery to low-income populations (e.g., Bronfenbrenner, 1975; Clarke-Stewart, 1978; Goodson and Hess, 1975) have suggested that a sense of potency (Slaughter, 1970) or agency with respect to one's life is a very important psychological factor associated with successful service delivery. This point is particularly relevant for racial and ethnic minorities. For example, black Americans have a long cultural history of experiencing powerlessness due to the impact of racism and discrimination in America (Blassingame, 1972; Comer, 1980; Gutman, 1976, Peters and Massey, 1983). Program structure, as well as staff attitudes, can promote fulfillment of a deeply felt cultural need for autonomy by providing significant opportunities for black staff and family involvement in highly visible leadership roles.

Identifying and Sharing Program Goals. Shared program goals between designers, developers, participants, and evaluators also enhance program effectiveness. In the Slaughter (1983) study, program developers and service providers were asked to describe the lifestyles of their own families before and after children (real or imagined), to describe their goals and role as developers, and to characterize how they would envision themselves as similar to or different from program participants. We found that most developers perceived their role as facilitating communication and enriching relationships, whether between primary caregiver and child or between primary treatment groups. One group participated in a home-based program in which the parent was used as a vehicle for "teaching" the child, with designated "lessons" for each visit. The structured curriculum did not directly stress maternal and family development. The other group participated in a peer maternal support group outside of the family setting. This program, which was more closely tailored to the goals of the developers as discussed before, proved more successful. We were able to document change on a wider range of behavioral measures, across a greater number of settings in which the two programs were implemented. We attributed its greater success in large part to the close parallel between program goals and organization.

Even the demonstration group, however, was not entirely unsuccessful. The staff goals that were articulated at the beginning of programs proved more potent than the incongruent program curriculum. One mother who had received home visits reported:

> [Before] I was just a blob until I got involved [in the program]. I didn't want to do nothing. I thought I knew everything about children and all the time he was just crying out for attention. I was just here. [Now] my activities are great; I joined the Advisory Board [in housing project site], joined social clubs and everything outside of the house. And I get along with the kids better because I sit and listen to them and talk, but mostly listen now, where before I thought I knew it all.

It is important to note that we only discovered the "real" aim of the programs by synthesizing our formal and informal conversations with, and observations of, program staff. In the future, it could be very useful to distinguish between the stated public goals of a family intervention program and how the staff understands and communicates those goals to program participants.

Communicating goals to program participants, whether directly or subtly, is a process that takes time. Our data indicated that most participants adopted a "wait-and-see" attitude at the onset of programs; trust was built gradually. Participants begin to trust program goals when they personally experience their implementation. When a mother experiences the growth of her abilities (e.g., to predict and identify a subtle impact upon her child's behavior following consultation with others) she comes to trust those who have helped her. She can see that others' approaches to childrearing, even if very different from her own, can have a positive effect.

Influence of Program Format. People come to feel close to people with whom they can effectively communicate. In our study, the discussion group members eventually became closer friends; they found in one another social support for experimenting with alternative ways of dealing with other extended family members and for comparing and evaluating the results of these efforts. In the nonjudgmental atmosphere deliberately and carefully cultivated by group leaders, members began to feel as if one another were "like family." This "family-simulated" support away from home enabled primary caregivers to develop additional internal resources.

However, I can imagine that in some cultures the peer support format would not be facilitating. For example, if adults within a culture use family membership as a primary source of competition between members, then much of the "discussion" in such a group would focus not on family problem-solving but on competitive judgments concerning whose family is best. Alternatively, if the culture or subculture demands exacting loyalty among defined family members, then encouraging participants to discuss family problems with outsiders could be seen as promoting disloyalty. Program content and format are best designed after having on-site input from potential participants and supporters and after studying their cultural–historical context.

Evaluating Programs with Racially and Ethnically Different Populations. Research with racially and ethnically different populations presents some unusual difficulties that require evaluators to be especially cognizant of the canons of good research. First, measures used should be normed with these populations. Second, if behavioral observations are to be made, representatives of the same race or ethnic group should be used as they are least likely to misinterpret culturally specific behaviors (Laosa, 1983). Third, if children are to be tested, same race/ethnic group examiners should be used. It has been documented that black children are more responsive to black, than white, examiners. Fourth, it is important to consider not only the need for family members' improvement, but also their strengths and resources—resources that are both cultural and individual. While these are simple prescriptions that stem logically from the dictates of quality research, these prescriptions are often not followed. The question is, why?

I believe that one of the major barriers is the reticence of program designers, developers, and evaluators to study the cultural backgrounds of the participants they wish to serve. Designers are interested in program elegance, developers in program implementation, and evaluators in program results. No one takes as a focal point of interest the life course and transitions of the participants themselves, as persons from families and communities that are highly significant to them. The tendency to perceive these persons as lacking in personal resources and skills contributes to this lack of attention to the strengths and adaptive coping resources that might be brought individually and collectively to the program.

CONCLUSION

In summary, to design, develop, and evaluate needed family service programs for American racial and ethnic minorities one needs a thorough, informed knowledge of their cultures. There is no shortcut to this knowledge, which results only from serious, systematic study, utilizing data from many sources. We must give our American minority families the same respect for their sociocultural integrity that we give to other nations and cultures in the world. At the same time, we do have a distinct advantage: These people are Americans and share the "American dream." Although many members of such groups are currently poverty-stricken, they want help to improve their own and their children's economic and social situation in American society. Keeping this dual perspective in view will enable staff to seek the necessary counsel to make wise programmatic and research evaluation decisions.

To be sure, not all persons want the particular help family service programs can provide; these persons account, in part, for the higher attrition rates in programs serving such communities, in comparison with those serving middle- and upper middle-income communities. To be successful, programs must convince those they wish to serve that what they offer will personally benefit them without at the same time alienating them from those adaptive, supportive, cultural–familial life styles that have endured despite societal misunderstanding and stereotyping.

The environmentalist position that behavior is infinitely malleable has recently been effectively challenged by research scientists with strong interests in behavioral genetics (e.g., Plomin, 1985; Scarr, 1982; Scarr and Weinberg, 1983). I would argue that culture is also an important limiting factor in behavioral malleability; over time it is often exceedingly difficult, if not impossible, to distinguish behaviors that are intransigent because of biological encoding from those dictated by cultural traditions. We must learn to appreciate that both human biology and human cultures change slowly; the primary mechanism of this change is intergenerational transfer through the family. In a society that prides itself on social engineering and rapid change, it is both humbling, and at times frustrating, for evaluators and policy analysts to have to remind themselves that racial and ethnic minorities have families and traditions that must be respected before services can be effective. In short, while program designers and developers play important roles as supporters, facilitators, and participants in a complicated process of social and psychological change, it is the program participants who must choose to change.

References

Andrews, S., Blumenthal, J., Bache, W., and Wiener, G. (1982). The skills of mothering: A study of Parent Child Development Centers. *Monographs of the Society for Research in Child Development, 47*(6, Serial No. 198).

Auerbach, A. (1968). *Parents learn through discussion: Principles and practice of parent group education.* NY: Wiley.

Baumrind, D. (1972). An exploratory study of socialization effects on black children. *Child Development, 43,* 261–267.

Blassingame, J. (1972). *The slave community.* New York: Oxford University Press.

Bowman, P., and Howard, C. (1985). Race-related socialization, motivation, and academic achievement: A study of black youth in three generation families. *Journal of the American Academy of Child Psychiatry, 24*(2), 134–141.

Brice-Heath, S. (1982). Questioning at home and at school: A comparative study. In G. Spindler (Ed.), *Doing ethnography: Educational anthropology in action* (pp. 96–101). NY: Holt, Rinehart, & Winston.

Bronfenbrenner, U. (1975). Is early intervention effective? In U. Bronfenbrenner (Ed.), *Influences on human development* (2nd ed.), (pp. 329–354). Hinsdale, IL: Dryden.

Butler, J., Starfield, B., and Stenmark, S. (1985). Child health policy. In H. Stevenson and A. Siegel (Eds.), *Child development research and social policy* (vol. 1, pp. 110–188). Chicago, IL: University of Chicago Press.

Clark, R. (1983). *Family life and school achievement: Why poor black children succeed or fail.* Chicago, IL: University of Chicago Press.

Clarke-Stewart, A. (1978). Evaluating parental effects on child development. In L. Shulman (Ed.), *Review of research in education* (pp. 47–119). Itasca, IL: Peacock.

Comer, J. (1980). *School power.* NY: Free Press.

Cross, W. (1985). Black identity: Rediscovering the distinction between personal identity and reference group orientation. In M. Spencer, G. Brookins, and W. Allen (Eds.), *Beginnings: The social and affective development of black children* (pp. 155–172). NJ: Erlbaum Associates.

Dougherty, M. (1978). *Becoming a woman in rural black culture.* NY: Holt, Rinehart, & Winston.

Emery, R., Hetherington, E., and DiLalla, L. (1985). Divorce, children, and social policy. In H. Stevenson and A. Siegel (Eds.), *Child development research and social policy* (vol. 1, pp. 189–266). Chicago, IL: University of Chicago Press.

Freedman, D., and DeBoer, M. (1979). Biological and cultural differences in early child development. *Annual Review of Anthropology, 8,* 579–600.

Glazer, N., and Moynihan, D. (1963). *Beyond the melting pot.* Cambridge, MA: MIT Press.

Goodson, B., and Hess, R. (1975). *Parents as teachers of young children: An evaluative review of some contemporary concepts and programs.* Stanford, CA: Stanford University, May 1975. (ERIC Document Reproduction Service No. ED 136 967).

Gutman, H. (1976). *Black family in slavery and freedom 1750–1925.* NY: Random House.

Hare, B. (1977). Black and white self-esteem in social science: An overview. *Journal of Negro Education, 46*(2), 141–156.

Harrison, A., Serafica, F., and McAdoo, H. (1984). Ethnic families of color. In R. Parke (Ed.), *Review of child development research: Vol. 7, The Family* (pp. 329–371). Chicago, IL: University of Chicago Press.

Hatchett, S., and Jackson, J. (June 1983). *Black extended kin systems: Correlates of perceived family solidarity, geographical propinquity of kin, interaction with kin, and aid from kin.* Paper presented at the meeting of the Groves Conference on Marriage and the Family, Freeport, Bahamas.

Hill, R. (1972). *The strengths of black families.* NY: Emerson-Hall.

Ladner, J. (1971). *Tomorrow's tomorrow: The black woman.* NY: Doubleday.

Laosa, L. (1983). Parent education, cultural pluralism, and public policy: The uncertain connection. In R. Haskins and D. Adams (Eds.), *Parent education and public policy* (pp. 331–345). Norwood, NJ: Ablex.

Levenstein, P. (1970). Cognitive growth in preschoolers through verbal interaction with mothers. *American Journal of Orthopsychiatry, 40,* 426–432.

Levenstein, P. (1977). The mother–child home programs. In M. Day and R. Parker (Eds.), *The preschool in action* (pp. 28–49). Boston, MA: Allyn & Bacon.

Lewis, D. (1975). The black family: Socialization and sex roles. *Phylon, 35*(3), 221–237.

McAdoo, H. (1981). *Black families.* Beverly Hills, CA: Sage.

Macklin, E., and Rubin, R. (Eds.). (1983). *Contemporary families and alternative lifestyles.* Beverly Hills, CA: Sage.

Martin, E., and Martin, J. (1978). *The black extended family.* Chicago, IL: University of Chicago Press.

Moore, E. (1985). Ethnicity as a variable in child development. In M. Spencer, G. Brookins, and W. Allen (Eds.), *Beginnings: The social and affective development of black children* (pp. 101–116). NJ: Erlbaum Associates.

Moynihan, D. (1965). *The Negro family: The case for national action.* U.S. Department of Labor: Office of Planning and Research.

Norton, E. (June 2, 1985). Restoring the traditional black family. *New York Times Magazine,* p. 43.

Pearce, D., and McAdoo, H. (1981). *Women and children alone and in poverty.* Washington, D.C.: National Advisory Council on Economic Opportunity.

Peters, M. (Ed.). (1978). Black families (Special issue). *Journal of Marriage and the Family, 40*(4).

Peters, M., and Massey, G. (1983). Mundane extreme environmental stress in family stress theories: The case of black families in white America. In H. McCubbin and C. Figley (Eds.), *Social stress and the family: Advances and developments in family stress theory and research* (pp. 193–218). NY: Haworth.

Plomin, R. (April 1985). Behavior genetics and intervention. In S. Scarr (Chair), *Malleability and intervention: Perspectives from developmental behavioral genetics.* Symposium conducted at the meeting of the Society for Research in Child Development, Toronto.

Porter, J., and Washington, R. (1979). Black identity and self-esteem: A review of studies of black self-concept, 1968–1978. *Annual Review of Sociology, 5,* 53–74.

Rainwater, L., and Yancy, W. (1967). *The Moynihan report and the politics of controversy.* Cambridge, MA: MIT Press.

Rosenberg, M., and Simmons, R. (1971). *Black and white self-esteem: The urban school child.* Washington, D.C.: American Sociological Association.

Scarr, S. (1982). On quantifying the intended effects of interventions: A proposed theory of the environment. In L. Bond and J. Joffe (Eds.), *Facilitating infant and early childhood development* (pp. 466–484). Hanover, NH: University Press of New England.

Scarr, S., and Weinberg, R. (1983). The Minnesota Adoption Studies: Genetic differences and malleability. *Child Development, 54,* 260–267.

Sears, R. (1975). Your ancients revisited: A history of child development. In E. Mavis Hetherington (Ed.), *Review of child development research: Vol. 5* (pp. 1–74). Chicago, IL: University of Chicago Press.

Senn, M. (1975). Insights on the child development movement in the United States. *Monographs of the Society for Research in Child Development, 40* (3–4, Serial No. 161).

Slaughter, D. (1970). Parental potency and the achievements of inner city black children. *American Journal of Orthopsychiatry, 40*(3), 433–440.

Slaughter, D. (1977). Relation of early parent–teacher socialization influences to achievement orientation and self-esteem in middle childhood among low-income black children. In J. Glidewell (Ed.), *The social context of learning and development* (pp. 101–131). NY: Gardner.

Slaughter, D. (1983). Early intervention and its effects upon maternal and child development. *Monographs of the Society for Research in Child Development, 48* (4, Serial No. 202).

Spencer, M. (1982). Personal and group identity of black children: An alternative synthesis. *Genetic Psychological Monographs, 106,* 59–84.

Spencer, M. (1983). Children's cultural values and parental child rearing strategies. *Developmental Review, 3,* 351–370.

Stack, C. (1974). *All our kin.* NY: Harper & Row.

Stein, P. (1983). Singlehood. In E. Mackin and R. Rubin (Eds.), *Contemporary families and alternative lifestyles* (pp. 27–48). Beverly Hills, CA: Sage.

Takanishi, R. (1977). Federal involvement in early education (1933–1973): The need for historical perspectives. In L. Katz (Ed.), *Current topics in early childhood education* (pp. 139–163). Norwood, NJ: Ablex.

Takanishi, R. (1978). Childhood as a social issue: Historical roots of contemporary child advocacy movements. *Journal of Social Issues, 34*(2), 8–28.

Ward, M. (1971). *Them children: A study in language learning.* NY: Holt, Rinehart, & Winston.

Wilson, W. (1985). *Cycles of deprivation and the underclass debate.* Paper delivered at the ninth annual Social Service Review Lecture, May 21, School of Social Service Administration, University of Chicago.

Young, V. (1970). Family and childhood in a southern Negro community. *American Anthropologist, 72,* 269–287.

Note Added in Proof

The APA recently adopted the convention of capitalizing "Black" and "White" when referring to race. Since this convention was instituted after this chapter was typeset, the Author would like to acknowledge this usage, although the actual change is not reflected in the text material.

chapter 22

ECOLOGICAL PERSPECTIVES ON CHANGE IN FAMILIES

Barry Dym

INTRODUCTION

A theory of human behavior is ecological if it locates behavior within patterns of relationships spanning the biological, psychological, and social realms (Bateson, 1972, 1979; Keeney, 1983b). In such a theory all parts are related and the whole is greater than the sum of the parts (von Bertalanffy, 1968). Ecological theories are also dynamic; the components and relationships are constantly changing and adapting to each other and to the broader environment.

An ecological theory of intervention, then, would have a number of requirements. First, it would incorporate and relate information from several levels of systemic organization (e.g., from person to family to culture) (Engel, 1977, 1980). Second, it would distill this complex organization to be simple and powerful in the hands of a clinician. Third, it would have as its base a model of "natural" processes of change, that is, change that proceeds without intentional human intervention. Only with such a base can the intervention be designed to respect and utilize the adaptive capacity inherent in human systems.

In this chapter, I will review two major attempts to apply ecological concepts to human behavior. One is by Urie Bronfenbrenner, who, in his book *The Ecology of Human Development* (1979), organizes research findings and proposes a general theory without offering explicit guidelines for clinical application. The other is Salvador Minuchin's structural family therapy, which emphasizes clinical application (1974). I will then discuss ways in which Bronfenbrenner's and Minuchin's ideas might

477

be carried further toward a more thorough-going ecological view of change and intervention. Finally, I will offer some programmatic suggestions consistent with an ecological perspective.

BRONFENBRENNER'S ECOLOGICAL PERSPECTIVE

According to Bronfenbrenner, development is a "lasting change in the way a person perceives and deals with his environment." It is "a person's evolving conception of the ecological environment and his relation to it, as well as a person's growing capacity to discover, sustain, or alter its properties" (Bronfenbrenner, 1979). Both child and context accommodate to one another, and the process of accommodation is profoundly influenced by the larger settings in which it is embedded. This familiar formulation, which locates individual behavior in its social context, is reminiscent of Piaget's (1954) dialectics of accommodation and assimilation and of Kurt Lewin's (1935) field theory.

In essence, Bronfenbrenner's concept of development focuses on the child's capacity to understand and shape the world in which she lives. His is as much a moral as a psychological theory. It is a call for alert, active citizens, capable of looking beyond their own narrow, immediate, and selfish interests. In this view, children not only help to shape and then accommodate to others' behavior, they actively participate in the "construction of reality" (Piaget, 1954; Bronfenbrenner, 1979) by which they live. The picture of the world that emerges will be more or less empowering for each child. Empowerment is a central concept for Bronfenbrenner, as it is the goal of human development and of those who aim to promote development through intervention.

The construction of an empowering reality depends on a number of qualities: The constructed reality must encompass the complexity of modern society; it must include many resources to meet the complex situations one will face; and a child must be confident that she can mobilize and use those resources. Hence a child who is able to move through many, varied settings will have an advantage. If she is guided by loving adults and is helped to develop good formal and informal skills and early opportunities to apply them successfully, her advantage is greater.

Children build complex mental pictures through a series of "ecological transitions" that "occur whenever a person's position in the ecological environment is altered as a result of a change in role, setting, or both" (Bronfenbrenner, 1979, p. 26). These transitional events include the arrival of a younger sibling, entry into preschool or school, being promoted, graduating, marrying, having a child, changing jobs, moving, and retiring. People accommodate to new behavioral expectations, and these patterns of accommodation are then assimilated into "molar" behavior that constitutes a lasting reorganization of the cognitive apparatus (Bronfenbrenner, 1979).

Bronfenbrenner's distinctive touch is most evident in his insistence upon the influence of larger social settings on the developing child. Some of these settings touch the child directly, like school systems. Some only touch her indirectly through her parents, such as work places and culturally patterned child-rearing practices. All "remote" and "near" systems are related to each other and to each child through a complex patterning comparable to that of the natural environment: The roots of trees are related to the composition of the soil, which is related to weather patterns, which is related to the larger topography, which is related to the type of vegetation that takes root in the area, and so forth.

Bronfenbrenner also may be seen as part of a tradition of moral or romantic protest against potentially destructive incursions into human systems by politicians and social scientists. Others in this tradition include Lincoln Steffens (1959) and Jane Addams (1961), who both wrote at the turn of the century, and Christopher Lasch (1979), a contemporary sociologist. Each of these authors argues against interventions by well-meaning reformers who fail to acknowledge the interconnectedness of community life. Similarly, Bronfenbrenner protests the way child development has been lifted out of its ecological contexts, implying that to try to help a child outside her context is not only impractical, but may do as much harm as good. It is possible, for example, to help a child learn a great deal in such a way that she is forever alienated from her family, relatives, and childhood friends.

While Bronfenbrenner has been helpful in broadening our lens, one wishes that he had been more consistent in his ecological perspective. Consider his idea of "reciprocity," which is a key concept in ecological thought. Bronfenbrenner defines it as a progressive, mutual accommodation between child and environment, but the preponderance of research he presents is so slanted in favor of the multifaceted influence of the environment on the child that one hardly sees the reciprocating impact of the child on the environment, the parents, and family (see Howrigan, Chapter 4, this volume). This slant is evident in research that measures environmental impact by changes in the child, such as an increase in child IQ scores (see Hauser-Cram and Shonkoff, Chapter 3, this volume). This one-directional approach suggests a linear causality that violates the more recursive, interactive ideas of causality in ecological science. A recursive view would look like this: A child is born; the couple reorganizes itself to accommodate the child; the child then accommodates herself, in part, to the parents' expectations; the new three-person configuration stabilizes until one of its members changes again and a new process of reorganization is initiated, followed by a new period of stability, etc. There is, in Bronfenbrenner's work, a peculiar paucity of research and thought about change in any system (or system-level) other than the child. If "reciprocity" is to be the guiding principle, then systemic change in several levels of the biopsychosocial field must be related and tracked, and research measurements must be broadened.

To do such tracking, one must know something about the internal organization of the systems in question. In Bronfenbrenner's work, only the child is treated as a system with an inside. His work fails to view families ecologically, as dynamic systems exhibiting a wide range of qualities. For example, some family organization is flexible and adaptive; some is rigid and unchanging. Families process information differently and families have different boundaries concerning outsiders and outside information, just as individuals and communities do. Without examining the internal organization of a child's family, or a community, one cannot understand the specific processes by which these systems change and develop. In order to advance Bronfenbrenner's proposed ecological perspective, we will have to conceptualize the relationship between what happens within various levels of a system—a child, a family, a community—and among the levels. This will be the goal of later discussion.

MINUCHIN'S STRUCTURAL FAMILY THERAPY

Bronfenbrenner offers a panoramic view of the developing child, but only implies what to do when development is slowed or blocked. Family systems therapy is a clinical discipline; it is applied ecological theory with clear implications for intervention. Just as Bronfenbrenner has challenged the conventional wisdom of developmental psychology, so family therapy has challenged the prevailing psychiatric focus on individual character, individual development, and individual treatment. For the past 25 years, family therapists have insisted that the emotional, behavioral, and cognitive problems of children should be diagnosed and treated in the family context. This shifts the focus of diagnosis and treatment from the intrapsychic world of the child to the patterns of interaction and thought in families. One concept basic to this approach is that the "problem" child may well develop naturally once free from disabling family patterns such as fusion and overprotectiveness on the one hand or neglect on the other.

Salvador Minuchin has been a pioneer in the developing field of family systems theory and is perhaps its most influential theoretician. His work is an explicit attempt to apply systemic and ecological theory to clinical practice. Like Bronfenbrenner, he borrows significantly from Piaget's dialectics of assimilation and accommodation.

In its early stages, Minuchin's structural family therapy (SFT) adopted a broad ecological perspective. For example, he and his colleagues established training programs in family therapy for primarily black and Hispanic residents of Philadelphia's inner city. The guiding concept was that the residents understood the cultures of the community far better than imported white professionals. Whereas traditional child therapy minimized the importance of cultural imagery, norms, institutions, and community networks and tried temporarily to isolate the patient from his environment, the Philadelphia Child Guidance Clinic saw family and community linkages as providing both understanding of the child's behavior and leverage for his treatment. Accordingly, white professionals in the program were required to make home visits and to keep in contact with school systems and community groups. Political involvement was considered integral to the Center's concept of psychotherapy.

Unfortunately, this broad ecological perspective has not been the most influential part of Minuchin's work. While some of his early collaborators (Aponte and Van Deusen, 1981; Auerswald, 1968, 1971, 1983) did create remarkably broad applications of the theory, much of its breadth died with the neoconservatism that emerged in the late 1970s. But the simple, powerful form of family therapy that Minuchin originated has endured and has been widely adopted and adapted by psychotherapists in the United States and abroad. It offers an excellent counterpoint by which to evaluate Bronfenbrenner's contribution.

According to Minuchin, both individuals and families develop through accommodation to internal and external stresses (or changes). Individuals develop a sense of belonging by assimilating general family patterns ("maps") and through membership in subsystems, for example, in an alliance with a father or a sibling. They develop individual identities by joining several subsystems within and outside the family. Problems arise when a child's sense of belonging is threatened. For example, a child who was particularly close to a now-divorced and absent father may be symptomatic.

In SFT, instead of treating the child, one treats the interactional pattern in which symptomatic behavior is embedded. Diagnosis consists of "mapping" the recurrent interactional patterns, called "structures," which interfere with individual development. The main structural components are boundaries and hierarchies. Boundaries regulate how people and information move from one subsystem to another. For example, when parents bring children between them to deflect their own conflicts, the parental subsystem is said to have porous boundaries. Hierarchies can be too rigid, as for example, when disciplinary rules do not change as a child matures.

A structural map of a typical "psychosomatic family," for example, is one in which the family structure is implicated in the failure of proven medical treatments to control a child's symptomatology. According to Minuchin, Rosman, and Baker (1978), psychosomatic families may be characterized by four common features: They are "enmeshed," that is, the boundaries between members are porous, leading to an absence of a clear sense of individual identity in family members; the family's hierarchy is rigid; parents are overprotective; and there is little or no conflict resolution in the family.

SFT focuses its efforts on restructuring families in order for individual members to develop appropriately. For example, in a psychosomatic family, we would try to firm up the boundaries around the parental subsystems, helping them to make decisions and resolve conflicts without including either the symptomatic or other child(ren). If the symptomatic child had become difficult to control, that is, was non-compliant in watching his diet or taking his insulin and increasingly truant at school—we would try to "repair" the hierarchy by helping the parents assert their authority effectively, appropriate to the age of the child. Mother and son may have formed an enmeshed pair in co-alition against father; in such a case, we would wish to break the enmeshment, helping the enmeshed individuals form alternative alliances, the mother closer to father, the child with siblings, friends, and father. The father may then encourage the development of independence and competence that had been retarded by the old family structure.

This description of restructuring is only skeletal and does injustice to the rich human drama that is reenacted in the course of SFT, but it should offer an idea of how symptoms are treated by treating the ecological family system. The internal experiences of the individual family members are altered and enriched by the changes of roles and settings that emerge. Here, then, is where Minuchin's method is a clinical analogue to Bronfenbrenner's key concept of "ecological transition." The new, more flexible family organization presumably keeps changing to keep pace with the developing child. Hence restructuring may be said to free development and make possible those reciprocally developing relationships of child and environment that Bronfenbrenner describes.

Structural family therapy has been applied in both broad and narrow ways, though the variation seems to be more a function of the practitioner, the community, and the political context than of the theory itself. From an ecological perspective, SFT is limited by its clinical emphasis on the present, in which Minuchin claims all that is relevant from the past is contained. While Minuchin talks of families as adaptive, developing, open systems, his clinical theory does not fully explore the dynamic strategies by which families organize to meet new challenges. This limitation is clearest in the clinical technique called "restructuring." One intervenes as if in a static environment, altering one structure and building another. No formal attention is given to changes in the family or to directions in which the family is already progressing. Perhaps most important, structure is imposed from without. An ecological approach must, first and foremost, devise methods of intervention that preserve the texture and integrity of the evolving ecology it addresses.

A CASE OF COMPLEXITY

In the second half of this chapter I will extend the ecological perspectives of Minuchin and Bronfenbrenner. Before doing so, however, I will present an illustrative case in order to ground the theories of change in more ordinary realities. The case is complex but not extraordinary; it is complex only because symptomatic behavior is viewed in broader context.

Lenny, at 9 years of age, can hardly read. His parents have called no attention to this problem. His teacher offers him a tutor; his tutor is frustrated by Lenny's lack of concentration and self-confidence. Since she cannot engage his parents, she calls in the school counselor. The school counselor is frustrated by Lenny's lack of responsiveness and refers him to a more "serious" therapist. The therapist believes that Lenny's parents subvert her efforts by failing to bring him regularly to his appointments. She also views them as alternately neglectful and domineering with their son. A family therapist is called. She claims she cannot do her job either. Lenny's unemployed father belongs to Alcoholics Anonymous, which seems to keep him self-absorbed; his mother's boss will not let her off the 4–11 shift at the factory. It is hard even to convene the family, much less to influence them. Furthermore, the Department of Social Services, which has threatened to take custody of Lenny's younger brother, makes recommendations that conflict with those of the family therapist, who also disagreed with the treatment plan of the individual therapist.

Then there is the busy, harried pediatrician, who bemoans his lack of opportunity to practice "medicine" (as taught in school). He sees Lenny's younger brother, Larry (age 4), who, like his uncle and grandfather, has asthma. The pediatrician is frustrated by many things: the constant family disorganization and stress that seem to exacerbate Larry's wheezing and hyperactivity; the parents' inconsistent administration of the "maintenance medication"; and the interference of Larry's maternal grandmother, who comes to his office to "fill him in" on family business.

There is nothing unusual about this case or about the professional responses to it. The symptomatic presentation of behavioral, cognitive, affective, or physiological disorders is just that—symptomatic presentation. Persistent symptoms are always embedded in larger patterns of biopsychosocial organization. When diagnosed and treated, these apparently discrete complaints overflow the orderly boundaries of professional disciplines. When this happens, clinicians frequently feel frustrated by their inability to succeed and by the elusiveness of the "real" problem. Is it cognitive or interpersonal? Is it biochemical or affective? The questions put to Officer Krupke in *West Side Story* are appropriate here: "What should we do, solve all the problems of society so one kid can learn to read?" In Lenny's case, is it neurological or emotional? When overwhelmed or frustrated, clinicians are apt to be annoyed at clients whose problems seem insoluble.

While complexity is the norm, the problem is that most clinicians treat complexity as deviant. Much clinical stress and confusion is attributable to a refusal to begin by viewing presenting problems in broader context. As a result, insufficient or inappropriate resources are mobilized toward solutions, professionals work at cross-purposes on the same case, and clients, passed from one helper to another, grow pessimistic. Relationships between those in need of help and those who provide it grow rigid and even antagonistic. For example, individuals and families known for the amount of attention they require and the lack of progress they make over the years (or even generations) are all too familiar in health care and social service systems, a situation symptomatic, in part, of the nonecological approach taken by many well-intentioned "helpers."

CENTRAL CONCEPTS OF ECOLOGICAL THEORY

Coevolution

Any one form of life evolves in relation to the evolution of other forms; they coevolve. For example, the birth of a child affects parental relationships, as does each of the child's developmental crises; patterns of parental relationship influence the shape of a child's development. Child and couple relationships can be said to coevolve. Similarly, herds of buffalo and the great plains are said to coevolve, and both evolve in relation to a broader environment. Gregory Bateson (1979) describes this as a circular or recursive relationship. The concept of coevolution is very similar to Bronfenbrenner's reciprocity, which he defines as a progressive, mutual accommodation (1979). In applying either we must resist the designation of one event as the "cause" and another as the "effect." Lynn Hoffman (1981) employs the analogy of species and their environments in coevolution to describe the coevolution of behaviors in families. For example, one cannot talk of buffalo causing the plains to evolve or of the plains simply shaping the buffalo. Similarly, parents do not cause childrens' actions any more than children cause parents' actions. The process is constantly interactive and changing.

This conceptual framework requires a different method of observing human problems. Let us take several examples from our illustrative case to see what coevolution in human relationships is like:

1. The more the parents fight about the father's drinking, the worse Larry's wheezing seems to become.
2. The worse the asthma becomes, the more stressed the family becomes and the more the father drinks.
3. The more commotion there is in the house, the more the grand-mother helps, and so the closer she draws to the nuclear family.
4. The more the grandmother enters the scene, the more the father suspects that she and his wife are ganging up on him. He leaves to go drinking.
5. The more commotion there is in the family, the more preoccupied Lenny is and the less he concentrates on reading.
6. The less Lenny concentrates, the more notices from school are sent home and the more the mother nags the father to help, which angers him.
7. The more the father drinks, the more difficult it is for him to find employment, making him more dependent on the mother's income. This makes her more dependent on her job and less able to challenge her boss, for example, about changing her 4–11 work shift, and thus she has less time for the children.

These, then, are some combinations of coevolving symptomatic behaviors and family patterns. The variety of combinations demonstrates how viewing these bio–psycho–social patterns as simple cause-and-effect is arbitrary and misleading.

Which problem is seen as most prominent depends on several variables, including the position and role of the observer. An agency concerned with alcoholism will find one cause, a pediatrician might see another, a school another, a family friend another. How much the family permits outsiders to see constitutes another variable. And finally, the observer's own system of values, expectations, and ideas will influence what is seen.

Recursive Cycles

Early family systems therapists promoted the concepts of circular causality and negative (closed system) feedback loops. According to this concept, when Mother nagged, Father drank and when Father drank, Mother nagged, *ad infinitum*. Or, when Mother nagged and Father drank, they fought, Larry wheezed, the parents' fight stopped, and Mother nagged, and so forth. While this circular formulation improved on the linear model of cause-and-effect, it was still too mechanistic. It treated human groups as closed systems, like machines, rather than open systems where variety and change are as normal as stability.

The idea of recursive cycles combines notions of stability and change. Like the feedback loop, it is a repetitive interactional sequence, in which symptomatic behavior is embedded and reinforced. Unlike negative feedback loops, however, the recursive cycle is always changing. Generally, the change is so gradual that it is imperceptible; at any given moment, feedback loops and recursive cycles may look alike, but the essence of the recursive cycle is its capacity to respond to internal and external pressures. Both the basic circular pattern and the elements that make it up keep changing over time. Since the change is gradual, adaptive, and evolving, it helps maintain the basic form of a system. Such a system is said to be in equilibrium. The term equilibrium is value-free; a system in equilibrium may be healthy or unhealthy for its members.

Let us return to our hypothetical case and observe the cycle changing. For example, it escalates in intensity until Larry wheezes, and then subsides as Mother refocuses her attention on Larry, and Father goes off by himself. The same sequence of behaviors may then repeat itself a few times each week. However, it may have taken years to build. Once the parental fighting had escalated until there was violence and was "capped" only by fear of serious injury. Over time, the parents learned to cap their fights by shifting focus to (or "triangling") another family member (Minuchin, 1974). This process of "detouring" parental conflict may become regular. One particular quality of dysfunctional systems is that they become rigid; the recursive cycles that characterize them look like closed system feedback loops. But even *they* change.

For example, at a certain developmental stage, Larry may refuse his mother's attention. Then the cycle might look like this: Father drinks, Mother nags, Larry wheezes. Mother attends to Larry. Father starts to go off. Larry objects. Father comes down hard on Larry. Mother protects Larry from Father. Father goes off. End of cycle. Still later in time, when Father punishes Larry, Mother, who has been pushed away by Larry too often, joins Father, and they punish Larry together. Now attention to Larry's chronic illness has been replaced by scapegoating the misbehaving son, but the function of defusing the parental fight has been preserved. Stability is maintained through change in recursive cycles. According to Brad Keeney, "the complementary relationship of change and stability is, in fact, the definition of cybernetic process" (1983a,

p. 377). Keeney illustrates the concept in a description of a tight-rope walker. "Remaining balanced on a high wire requires constant change of one's body position. Similarly, families must change to maintain stability or, as seen from the other direction, remain stable, in order to change" (Keeney 1983a, p. 377).

Let us look again at our family. There are times when the asthma attacks get out of hand, and Larry has to be taken to the emergency room. The severity of the attack may have to do with greater amounts of pollen in the air, with Larry's greater emotional vulnerability at a certain period, or some combination of physiological and psychological vulnerability. Larry's asthma now disrupts rather than stabilizes the system, and Grandmother may have to come in to help with the other children while Mother goes to the hospital with Larry. This upsets Father, and when Mother comes home they fight about Grandmother. Mother wants her to stay longer, until things are easier and more stable. Father wants her out. In order to remain stable, the system has brought in another member on whom to focus. This precarious balance permits the conflict between the parents to remain unresolved. Enlisting another family member to divert the parental fight allows Lenny, with his school failures, to become the focus of periodic scapegoating. Here, then, we may observe the basic family pattern of conflict–avoidant triangles being stabilized by constant changes in other aspects of family functioning. As Keeney notes, "A family, when defined as a cybernetic system, is therefore a social organism whose whole pattern of organization is stabilized through the change of its component parts" (1983a, p. 377).

Transformational Change

The kind of change we have discussed so far has elsewhere been called "fluctuation" (Prigogine, 1969) and "first order change" (Watzlawick, Weakland, and Fish, 1974). It represents small changes and adjustments that are well within the basic rules or patterns of a particular system. These changes not only fail to change a system, but work to stabilize it. For example, information generally creates first-order change. When a child is first diagnosed with asthma, his parents are informed about a maintenance regime, consisting, perhaps, of medication, a dust-free room, and a humidifier. Many families adjust to this regime with little basic change in their organization.

However there are at least two other possible scenarios: Family patterns may be so rigid or so chaotic that the family does not follow the maintenance regime and repeated use of hospital emergency rooms becomes the norm. In this case, first-order change is insufficient and a basic reorganization of the family—"second-order change" (Watzlawick *et al.*, 1974)—is required for the family to use its information. This is an occasion for professional intervention. As a second possible scenario, the child may need to stay home from school frequently because of debilitating respiratory infections, which require his mother to leave her job and remain at home full-time. This situation might generate a series of changes in roles and behavioral patterns. Here, then, is a spontaneous transformation of the family—second-order change. Systems are vulnerable to transformation when their ordinary coping strategies are no longer effective. This may happen as a result of a crisis—like a sudden illness or an accident—or when the small changes that are meant to stabilize a system fail. As von Forester notes, "Change that is only a fluctuation in a system at one time can suddenly become the basis for an entirely new arrangement of the system at another time" (quoted in Keeney, 1983b, p. 77). Think of the tightrope walker making a larger than usual adjustment just as a strong gust of wind blows. Transformational sequences can be precipitated by such random events.

To illustrate second-order change more fully let us return to our family. The father begins to drink, the mother nags, and a fight ensures; Larry's wheezing increases. This stable pattern includes a small fluctuation—Larry's wheezing—as a part of the stability, and it occurs regularly. His parents drop their fight and attend to Larry. When Larry has had a hard time with friends or schoolwork and this coincides with a bad cold, parental attention may not suffice to stop his wheezing. At this point, Grandmother, hospital emergency rooms, and other resources are enlisted. A recursive cycle with a broader social sweep acts as a kind of back-up for the cycle within the nuclear family. This, too, eventually becomes a familiar pattern with a larger fluctuation. But the size of the fluctuation makes the system less stable. It is now in disequilibrium. One day when Larry is wheezing uncontrollably, the car will not start (a random event), because Father had been neglecting its maintenance. Mother manages to get Larry to the hospital in time, but she is so frightened and enraged that she vows that her husband will not set foot in their house again until he attends to his drinking problem. Mother follows her vow with a court-ordered injunction. A series of changes lead to a reorganization of the family. Father joins AA, stops drinking, and finally engages in the court-ordered therapy in which he had long been passive and uninterested. The parental fighting precipitated by his drinking stops. Larry's exacerbated wheezing, which had followed the parental fighting, also stops. Occasions for Grandmother to intervene decrease, and so forth. The recursive cycle in which Larry's asthma was embedded no longer exists.

Moreover, a few days after the emergency room visit, Larry and his mother are back for a checkup. The physician insistently repeats instructions for Larry's maintenance medication. However this time, Mother is in a resolute frame of mind and hears the instructions more clearly than before, instituting them more firmly in the family routine, making Father's collaboration one part of the conditions for his return to the home. In effect, the medical instructions were random events that became integrated in the new family organization.

A few months later, it would be possible to identify patterned ways in which the family interacted around Larry's asthma, but it would not have been entirely possible to have predicted these new patterns based on the original patterns. According to theorists like Bateson (1972, 1979) and Prigogine (1969), second-order change is sudden, unpredictable in its timing and final shape, and discontinuous with past organization. Therapists and other agents of change have tried to make such events predictable and orderly. This, for example, is the bottom line of the medical model, with its oversimplified "magic bullet" theory of disease and cure: Each illness has a specific etiology, and therefore it is possible to develop a specific antidote to match a specific diagnosis. This is unidirectional, linear thinking.

Professionals who wish to document direct one-to-one relationships between their interventions and treatment outcomes often must rationalize and manipulate data with 20–20 hindsight. They think their interventions were helpful but cannot describe exactly how or why. Alternately, an intervention that worked for many similar families fails with the next. This troubles clinicians because their belief in linear causality (problem–intervention–outcome) offers no explanation for this failure. A shift toward a more complex ecological understanding is necessary. There, transformations follow their own logical course, integrating internal evolutionary or developmental principles with external stimuli—intentional and random.

Ecological Intervention

The theory of change presented here suggests a different approach to intervention from those that look for specific antidotes to resolve specific problems and focus only on the symptomatic person or behavior. Earlier I criticized SFT for imposing a static sense of organization on families, thus violating their ecological integrity. The aim of an ecologically based theory of intervention is to free a system to find its own (evolutionary or developmental) solutions to problems posed by internal or external stresses. A system is "freed" by moving it into a state of disequilibrium, in which the presently used adaptive techniques are inadequate. In disequilibrium, ecosystems are vulnerable to second-order change, with two possible results. First, the system may make a broader search through its repertoire of adaptive strategies and discover one, not previously found, applicable and use it in the present disequilibrating situation. Second, the system in disequilibrium may find no available coping strategy and therefore may have to reorganize itself to cope.

Interventions are generally directed at those adaptive strategies that have been rigidly applied in efforts to restabilize systems moving toward disequilibrium. According to Keeney, intervention should "facilitate a more adaptive pattern of organization for the troubled context. . . . To effect change of a cybernetic system, whether the system is punctuated as an individual, couple, family, neighborhood . . . requires an understanding of the change of change—*change of how a system's habitual process of change leads to stability*" (my emphasis) (Keeney, 1983a, p. 381). In other words, successful interventions are efforts to block those adaptive patterns that lead systems away from disequilibrium and back toward the dysfunctional state of equilibrium in which the symptom is embedded.

Let me briefly outline this idea of intervention (see Selvini-Palazolli, Cecchin, Prata, and Boscolo, 1978, for a detailed discussion of such intervention techniques). An agent of change identifies patterns of instability inherent in the ecosystem, for example, Larry's periodic severe asthma attacks, which initiate new adaptive strategies including hospitals and Grandmother. These strategies are more attenuated and more vulnerable to intervention and transformation than the day-to-day recursive cycles detailed earlier. The second step, then, is to intervene at the moment of maximum disequilibrium in order to disrupt the attenuated recursive cycle. The third step is to get out of the way, without helping to find solutions and create order, allowing the ecosystem to find its own solution. Once new patterns emerge—in this case, to cope with Larry's asthma—the clinician's support may be beneficial. However, if the adaptive pattern is gradually woven into the broader ecosystem, no professional support is required.

Context, Hierarchy, and Recursive Cycles

Now that we have sketched a theory of change, it is time to place it in broader ecological context. Bronfenbrenner portrays this context with the metaphor of nested structures (1979). George Engel, a family physician, emphasizes the interconnectedness of a biopsychosocial system, in which biological, psychological, family, and cultural system levels are arranged in hierarchical form (1977, 1980). These ideas have moved their respective fields toward more ecological and systemic paradigms. But they leave a gap for practicing clinicians who wonder how to relate one system level to another. How are psychological factors related to organ systems on the one hand, and cultural systems on the other?

While this chapter cannot answer this question in a very specific way—that would require empirical research—it can propose a speculative, heuristic model. The model takes Engel's biopsychosocial field as the starting point and is described in a series of propositions: (1) For any particular, enduring problem it is possible to identify a recursive cycle in which the problematic behavior is embedded; (2) that cycle passes through several levels of systemic organization; (3) within each level of systemic organization, recursive cycles may be identified; (4) the two cycles coevolve—changes in either the larger ecosystem (represented by the multilevel cycles) or in the component parts (represented by intrasystemic cycles) create changes throughout. Similarly, rigidities at any systemic level tend to support impasses throughout. Hence, these cycles tend both to move each other and, because adaptive change is usually slow, to hold each other in place (Dym, 1985).

To illustrate these propositions, let's return to Lenny's school difficulties. Remember, the cycle has no beginning, no "cause." We could as easily begin with his father's drinking or his parents' fighting. Since the reading problem is what brings the recursive cycle to professional attention, however, that is where we will begin.

1. Lenny does poorly in school.
2. Teacher and tutor agree that parental support for their assignments is the key to success or failure. They write to the parents.
3. The parents ignore the letter.
4. The teacher and tutor, in consultation with the guidance counselor, send a second letter (cosigned by the principal).
5. The parents come in, explain that they have been worried about Larry's wheezing, but promise to focus on Lenny.
6. For a week they do, and Lenny improves a little.
7. Then the fight over Father's drinking and unemployment begins anew; Larry's wheezing increases.
8. Lenny does poorly in school.

Now let us identify several systemic levels through which this recursive cycle passes: At the biological level, there is Larry's asthma, Lenny's dyslexia, and Father's alcoholism. On a psychological level, both Lenny's and Father's passivity and depression are evident. Within the family system, there is the recursive cycle regulating parental conflict, Father's alcohol use, and Larry's translation of psychological stress into somatic distress. In the community, the school system is narrowly involved in Lenny's reading, and the medical system helps maintain the rigidity of the cycle by responding almost exclusively to Larry's physiological problems. In the extended family, the maternal grandmother makes her contribution. Finally, there is the foreman at the factory where Mother works, who will not let her change shifts, keeping her unavailable to the boys after school. All of these forces tend to hold in place the large recursive cycle that we have identified.

To illustrate the third proposition, let us look at some recursive cycles within systems levels. The family cycle is as follows: Father drinks, Mother nags, the parents fight, Larry wheezes, Mother attends to Larry, Father goes off by himself, Lenny is alone—lost and unable to demand attention. At the psychological level, Lenny tends to move from feeling frightened and depressed (usually when his parents are fighting) to feeling lost, disorganized, and dreamy (usually when the family is organized around Larry's asthma). At school, there is another cycle: First there are individual frustrations when tutor and teacher work separately with Lenny, followed by mutually fueled anger at his parents, followed by efforts to convene their own resources and get others to take them off the hook (counselors, principal, family therapist, etc.), followed by hopefulness (after Lenny's parents make reassurances), followed by individual frustrations, and so forth.

The idea that these cycles coevolve with the broader cycle should now be clear. The smaller cycles, for example, are "triggered" by events in the larger cycle. The larger cycle cannot continue without the regular "firing" of the smaller cycles. The regular patterns of school personnel convening and separating emerged in response to Lenny's difficulties, the parental response to their concern, and the unseen (by them) cycles within the family. Changes in any of these cycles reverberate throughout the ecosystem. If the parents attended to Larry either more or not at all, there would be changes. Ironically, if the teachers simply gave up, Lenny might come more fully to his parents' attention.

Conversely, the rigidities of each phase of small and large cycles tend to counter changes in other parts of the ecosystem. For example, the professionals' responses may become so rigid that they fail to notice significant change, like Father's increasing sobriety, his attendance at AA meetings, and his efforts to help his children. If professionals confuse the awkwardness of his new efforts with his chronic avoidance and incompetence, they might deal with him in a scolding fashion. Such a response might well affect him much as his wife's nagging does. He may get upset and not attend the next meeting (school, therapy, etc.). Feeling betrayed, his wife will get angry at him. In such a case, the old cycles are reactivated for a different reason, and the possibility of adaptive change is lost.

IMPLICATIONS FOR FAMILY PROGRAMS

To illustrate the relevance of this ecological perspective to family support programs, I will leave behind the case of Larry's and Lenny's family and consider the broader case of teenage pregnancy programs. The predominant orientation of most adolescent pregnancy programs is a positive one, in that it does not condemn the young parents. Rather, it begins with the constructive question: What combination of information, support, and services should be offered to these teenagers so that they will take care of their own children and become productive citizens? A second crucial guiding question concerning the teenage mother is often unasked: Which forces in her immediate context will encourage her to use the information and support?

If the ecological perspective is to be embraced, more than a superficial acquaintance with the family and community is required (see Slaughter, Chapter 21, this volume). An ecological assessment would include asking such questions as:

- What is the cultural meaning of adolescent pregnancy and parenthood? What is the attitude of each teenager's mother to the program? Does she feel threatened or judged? (If so, she may subvert her daughter's participation.)
- Who are the other key players in the drama—a grandmother or an older sibling? (If, for example, an older sister has enthusiastically undertaken the hands-on parenting responsibilities in the past, the teenage pregnancy may be in keeping with the family tradition; a program that communicates implicit or explicit disapproval could meet with massive family resistance.)
- Does the pregnancy play a crucial role in family life? (Some families divert conflict—generally parental conflict—by scapegoating a child, by focussing on a child's troubles. Efforts to help such children or to bring them significantly outside their family and its influence are often met with great resistance.)
- How does the family currently relate with various community institutions, such as schools, churches, and social service agencies? (Their patterns of involvement with these community institutions— be they cooperative, adversarial, protective—will provide important information in developing an individual teenager's service plan.)

A teenage pregnancy may stabilize the girl's extended family, for example, in the case of the scapegoated child who diverts attention from parents in conflict. Changes—or programmatic intervention—may be unsuccessful. The same may be true in families with a tradition of adolescent pregnancies, although even in those families there may be ambivalent responses, and the pregnancy may stabilize some patterns while destabilizing others. For example, the same mother and grand-mother who feel at ease with their teenager's pregnancy may also feel disappointed. A careful family assessment by a skillful professional can attend sympathetically both to the family's tradition (thus gaining cred-ibility) and to their desire that the adolescent have a better life. The capacity to reach and mobilize those natural forces for change in the teenager's immediate context may well be the key to the success or failure of the program.

ISSUES OF TREATMENT AND TRAINING

Ecological notions of change require a capacity for a flexible response from professionals. Clinicians must be capable of intervening at the appropriate levels of systems in the biopsychosocial field and of doing so simultaneously or serially. They must be willing to work with other clinicians who claim particular domains in this field (e.g., the physician, the school tutor).

A second kind of flexibility implied by the ecological view has to do with timing. As I have suggested, systems are more vulnerable to change when in disequilibrium; professional efforts to help people in dise-quilibrium often meet resistance. The ecologically oriented change agent learns to observe and wait for "natural" opportunities for change to arise. When those opportunities arise, professionals should be po-sitioned to help so that individuals and families develop their own re-sources, in their own way, as much as possible. As maladaptive strat-egies begin to develop, or when systems at an impasse are temporarily unstable, the professionals will still be in a position to observe and intervene.

This approach to treatment requires coordinating the efforts of lay people and professionals—school counselors, psychotherapists, and medical doctors—each trained with different approaches to interven-tion. If the multidisciplinary approach advocated here is to be widely and successfully implemented, these professionals must be taught ecological theory and practice at the same time they are taught the particular view and techniques of their specialties. In that way, it will be adopted as a professional paradigm, and professional satisfactions can be experienced within its world view.

REFERENCES

Addams, J. (1961). *Twenty years of Hull House*. NY: Random House.

Aponte, H., and Van Deusen, J. (1981). Structural family therapy. In A. Gurman (Ed.), *Handbook of family therapy*. NY: Brunner/Mazel.

Auerswald, E. H. (1968). Interdisciplinary versus ecological approach. *Family Process, 7*(2), 202–215.

Auerswald, E. H. (1971). Families, change, and the ecological perspective. *Family Process, 10*(3), 263–282.

Auerswald, E. H. (Fall 1983). The Gouveneur Health Services Program: An experiment in ecosystemic community health care delivery. *Family Systems Medicine, 1*(3), 5–25.

Bateson, G. (1972). *Steps to an ecology of mind.* NY: Pallatine.

Bateson, G. (1979). *Mind and nature.* NY: Dutton.

Bronfenbrenner, U. (1979). *The ecology of human development.* Cambridge, MA: Harvard University Press.

Dym, B. (1985). Eating disorders and the family: A model for intervention. In S. Emmett (Ed.), *Theory and treatment of Anorexia Nervosa and Bulimia: Biomedical, sociocultural, and psychological perspectives.* NY: Brunner/Mazel.

Engel, G. L. (1977). The need for a new medical model: A challenge for biomedicine. *Science, 196,* 129–136.

Engel, G. L. (1980). The clinical application of the biopsychological model. *American Journal of Psychiatry, 137*(5), 535–544.

Hoffman, L. (1981). *Foundations of family therapy.* NY: Basic Books.

Keeney, B. (1983a). Cybernetics of brief family therapy. *Journal of Marital and Family Therapy, 9*(4), 375–382.

Keeney, B. (1983b). *Aesthetics of change.* NY: Guilford.

Lasch, C. (1979). *Haven in a heartless world: The family besieged.* NY: Basic Books.

Lewin, Kurt. (1935). *A dynamic theory of personality.* NY: McGraw-Hill.

Minuchin, S. (1974). *Families and family therapy.* Cambridge, MA: Harvard University Press.

Minuchin, S., Rosman, B., and Baker, L. (1970). *Psychosomatic families: Anorexia nervosa in context.* Cambridge, MA: Harvard University Press.

Piaget, Jean. (1954). *The construction of reality in the child.* NY: Basic Books.

Prigogine, I. (1969). Structure, dissipation and life. In M. Marois (Ed.), *Theoretical physics and biology* (pp. 23–37). Amsterdam: North Holland Publishing.

Selvini-Palazzoli, M. S., Cecchin, G., Prata, G., and Boscolo, L. (1978). *Paradox and counterparadox.* NY: Jason Aronson.

Steffens, Lincoln (1959). *The autobiography of Lincoln Steffens.* NY: McGraw-Hill.

von Bertalanffy, L. (1968). *General systems theory.* NY: George Brazilliar.

Watzlawick, P., Weakland, J., and Fisch, R. (1974). *Change.* NY: Norton.

Lessons
in Context

Francine H. Jacobs and Heather B. Weiss

Throughout this volume, the problems and promises of evaluating family programs have been illuminated from the varied perspectives of researchers, evaluators, and program directors. The chapters have raised and responded to some of the large questions about implementing sensitive family programs and responsible evaluations; they also have made practical suggestions about selecting outcome measures, solving common design dilemmas, and finding additional sources of advice and information. Though each chapter has told a unique part of this story, they share an appreciation for the power of context in determining the lives of children, the character of programs, and the success of evaluation. Therefore, we will use this cross-cutting theme of context in our conclusions.

CONTEXTS FOR CHILDREN

Over the past 20 years, ecological theories of child development have been integrated into mainstream thought, and clear consensus has emerged that a child's development is affected by her parents and her family's life circumstances. Bronfenbrenner, among others, has broadened the concept of environmental influences to include extended family, nonfamily neighbors or community members, formal and informal community services; the values, beliefs, and adaptive patterns of ethnic and cultural groups also have been identified as powerful influences on the developing child. We have come to view child development as a complex negotiation between external, contextual forces and innate capacities and temperament.

497

In the introduction to this volume, we have identified family support programs, in part, as practical expressions of this increasingly contextual understanding of how children develop. While the majority of programs grow out of the child development tradition and are focused primarily on promoting aspects of child development, they implement their services ecologically, for example, through parent education or attention to parent–child interaction. In addition, an increasing number are interested in enhancing family life and family development per se and, therefore, focus on the family unit. Others are interested in intervening in the relationship of families to the broader context of neighborhoods, schools, community service providers, etc. All these programs acknowledge the centrality of context in the lives of children and adults— a common sense position but a relatively new one nonetheless. As Weiss (1)* has documented, much of the available evidence of effects from family programs relies on measures of child outcomes. Jacobs (2) believes that this partly reflects a programming preference for focusing on children, but given the desire of many programs for impacts more broadly drawn, this also suggests shortcomings in theories of how to affect families and communities, and the absence of adequate measures of these broader effects.

The chapters in the first section of this volume have presented the current status of measurement along an ecological continuum and have identified promising approaches and techniques for those interested in evaluating impacts at these levels. Hauser-Cram and Shonkoff (3) have extended child measurement past cognition and achievement; Howrigan (4) has argued for multimeasure observations of parent–child interaction; Upshur (5) has offered methods and instrumentation for assessing parental or adult impact; Walker and Crocker (6), and Krauss (7) have discussed assessment of family-level impacts; and Cleary (8) has surveyed options for measurement of social supports.

The sparest information regarding the child's ecological environment, ironically, concerns the context in which children spend most of their time: The family largely has been neglected by child development researchers until recently, leaving a conceptual vacuum in which family programs, nonetheless, have striven to provide needed services. Concerns about the sketchiness of our present definitions of family and of our understanding of normal family process have surfaced throughout the volume.

Several authors have urged child development researchers toward a fuller, more inclusive, and less pathology-oriented definition of family: Howrigan (4), Walker and Crocker (6), Upshur (5), and Dym (22) noted that much of the current research and many existing programs consider

*Numbers in parentheses refer to Chapter number in this volume.

the mother–child dyad the "family," absenting fathers, siblings, and extended family members. Moreover, nonrelated individuals are considered family members within certain minority cultures and communities; since many intervention programs are targeted toward these populations, Slaughter (21) and Howrigan (4) have suggested a more culturally informed perspective on family membership. Those programs concerned with patterns of family health [e.g., Ellwood (13)] find a dearth of theory to support their attempts to design and evaluate health-promoting programs.

From his perspective as a family systems therapist, Dym finds that child development ecologists treat the family as a mysterious black box, a "shell without an inside." Ours is a limited understanding of how families operate, the processes by which they shape and educate their members, and the effects of individual development on family life. This situation at times leads to programs with "atheoretical" bases [Olds (10); Bond and Halpern (15)], that is, they operate without a clear sense of why their activities should affect certain children and families in particular ways. Alternatively, according to Walker and Crocker (6), Howrigan (4), Dym (22) and Cleary (8), programs and researchers fall back on shop-worn or incomplete theories of ecological influence, such as those assuming unidirectionality of influences from mother to child.

Family systems theory broadens our perspective by viewing the family as a living organism in which the development of an individual member has a reverberating, recursive, rather than linear, effect on others. Hence, the ways children develop influence parents, which in turn changes the child's experiences and milieu, which reinforces the parental behavior, etc. [see Dym (22); Walker and Crocker (6)]. Systemic thinking also can be applied to understanding social networks, the roles of formal and informal social support, and the organization of community services [see Cleary (8); Dunst and Trivette (14)].

Targeting the family in interventions, designing evaluations of family-oriented programs, and interpreting data from such evaluations all require more finely grained categorizations of families than are used presently. Upshur (5), Howrigan (4), Olds (10), Slaughter (21), and Hauser-Cram (20) have acknowledged that, while sociodemographics are often used to define a needy population and differentiate program effects, the variation within families similar along those dimensions are likely to be substantial. Data on the life cycle stages of families [Walker and Crocker (6); Dunst and Trivette (14)], familial patterns of coping and adapting to stressful life situations [Krauss (7); Slaughter (21); Rodriguez and Cortez (12)], cultural values and beliefs [Howrigan (4); Slaughter (21)], and personality traits of individual family members [Powell (11)] will be required if we are to understand what types of intervention are effective for whom.

PROGRAMS AND CONTEXT

We have spoken of programs and context from two perspectives: the internal environment of the program and the larger milieus in which programs operate. Both these contexts affect the ways programs are understood by participants, staff members, and communities, and the ways they are structured, delivered, and evaluated.

Inside the Program

According to Jacobs (2), the assumption that uniform interventions could be applied across programs and communities was one of the major shortcomings of the Great Society's early childhood program evaluations. Their approach neglected variations in program character that occur as individual programs evolve to best serve their particular set of clients with their particular constellation of staff within the political, cultural, and economic conditions of their communities.

Since those early evaluations were conducted we have increasingly acknowledged the influences of these program-related contexts. Rodriguez and Cortez (12), Nauta and Hewett (17), Miller (16), Ellwood (13), and Walker and Mitchell (18), among others, have presented their programs as systems: complex, dynamic organizations with distinctive internal lives. As such, programs predictably proceed through developmental stages, attempting on the one hand to accommodate to demands for change from clients, staff, funding agencies, while seeking to maintain a relatively constant set of services and assumptions about programming, on the other. This rich program process has been acknowledged as central to our understanding of why some programs succeed when other similar programs fail. Successful evaluations must contain methods to capture the essence of this program diversity [see, e.g., Nauta and Hewett (17); Bond and Halpern (15); Miller (16)].

The quality of staff interactions and the personal qualities of individual staff members are important components to this internal context [see Slaughter (21); Dunst and Trivette (14); Rodriguez and Cortez (12)]. Nauta and Hewett (17) portrayed the tension arising from a lack of consensus among staff members about whether child development goals or family service goals should take priority. Ellwood (13), Miller (16), and Nauta and Hewett (17) described varying stages in staff response to data collection and other evaluation-related activities. Olds (10), Dunst and Trivette (14), and Walker and Mitchell (18) spoke of program staff determination to make the programs and their evaluations "work." Information on these common internal characteristics of programs is critical for program developers and evaluators.

Family support programs are characterized by their individualized, rather than standardized, approach to providing services to families. Within any single program, the variation in treatment may be dramatic, as staff members differ among themselves in their perceptions of what services should be offered in what quantities [Nauta and Hewett (17); Tivnan (9)] and, given the choice, families differ in their perceived needs and use of program components [Powell (11); Cleary (8); Miller (16); Slaughter (21)]. The quality of services differs among individual providers, and sometimes families and staff members disagree with each other on needed services. Unless an evaluator can implement a design that adequately controls for all this potential variation [see Olds (10), for example), several authors have suggested that evaluators simply accept and document these differences. Within them may be clues to how, why, and when particular families and children change.

The potential variations in program practice and internal context in cross-site evaluation proceed exponentially, and again, the first lesson to take from these efforts is the inevitability of such heterogeneity. Miller (16), Nauta and Hewett (17), Bond and Halpern (15), and Walker and Mitchell (18) all have detailed the frustrations and promises of cross-site evaluation, attending to site differences, while at the same time moving programs toward consensus on at least some measurable objectives. An action-research model such as that suggested by Bond and Halpern (15) seems particularly well-suited to multiple-program evaluation.

Outside the Program

Programs are located in larger contexts, existing much as Bronfenbrenner describes the child in the family: as the core piece in a set of nested structures. Thus, an individual program's shape and ultimate impact are influenced by the community's beliefs about child rearing and healthy family functioning [Rodriguez and Cortez (12); Slaughter (21); Walker and Crocker (6)], by traditional community patterns of coping with life stressors [Howrigan (4); Krauss (7)], and by the place and strength of its supporters within the community [Tivnan (9)]. The availability and accessibility of other social services and informal social supports [Dunst and Trivette (14); Cleary (8); Olds (10)] also affect a program's success. These proximate influences on a program tell an important part of the story.

Programs also operate within the more mundane context of legislative and funding constraints, such as being allowed to serve only a certain population or to conduct a certain type of evaluation. They may be quite interested in evaluation but unable to pay for it, or they may know their clients need a particular service but be contractually con-strained from providing it (e.g., crisis intervention in a preventive pro-gram). Evaluators must be aware of these limitations.

Family support programs also exist within the context of the national policy debate about what constitutes appropriate public support for families [see Jacobs (2); Weiss and Jacobs). While many of these pro-grams are small, low budget, grass-roots operations, together they rep-resent an innovative, promising approach that should be documented, described, and studied in a serious manner. For their part, program advocates, family support movement spokespersons, and policymakers should resist making premature or unfounded effectiveness arguments until the "evidence is in."

EVALUATION IN CONTEXT

Several authors in this volume have recommended attention to these influences of context on programs and children in the design and ex-ecution of family program evaluation. Implicitly, however, they also have acknowledged that a contextual view makes the evaluator's job far more difficult. For example, it highlights the hazards of developing universal standards of "good parenting" or "healthy family functioning" that are necessary to implement some traditional evaluation designs [see Ellwood (13); Rodriguez and Cortez (12); Slaughter (21)]. Causal theories linking specific changes in children and families to specific family-oriented interventions are sparse and, at best, suggestive rather than definitive [Bond and Halpern (15); Olds (10)]. As one moves along the ecological continuum, the number and quality of outcome measures with sound technical properties decrease [Walker and Crocker (6); Krauss (7); Cleary (8)]. The field milieu within family programs rarely approximates desired laboratory conditions [Nauta and Hewett (17); Tivnan (9); Miller (16)]. Yet, some program funders and public officials persist in their demands for evaluations that deny many aspects of these contexts, as do gatekeepers to professional rewards for evaluators (such as journal article reviewers and academic promotion committees).

These complex factors, then, create part of the context for the eval-uation of family programs, and while retreat from them may seem more appealing than engagement, in fact we "can't go home again:" The insistently diverse nature of family-oriented programs and the devel-opment, however incomplete, of ecological theories of the child, family, and social network preclude the return to an earlier stage of evaluation practice. The authors of this volume urge that program design and evaluation be considered "in context" with the understanding that all issues cannot be attended to equally or simultaneously. However, if the field is to advance, we must first recognize that choices of focus are, in fact, made (e.g., between a child or family focus), and second, we must gain the insight and experience that will enable us to justify those choices.

Perhaps the most important contribution of *Evaluating Family Programs* is its insistence that the terms of discussion about what constitutes legitimate program evaluation and useful information be changed to reflect the complexities of context. A flawless evaluation design according to the abstract canons of social science research may be of limited value; indeed evaluations often must trade-off between neat scientific rigor and complex, but realistic, portrayal of programs. Such complexity derives in large part from the wide variations among programs. The age and stage of the program (pilot versus demonstration, in replication or not) the type of program (comprehensive versus targeted, preventive versus treatment, professional versus volunteer), financial and technological constraints on the evaluation, the disposition toward evaluation among staff members, the participants' ability to perform data collection tasks, the goals for participants and their "measurability," the potential impact on programs and participants an evaluation may have, and the audiences for evaluation all necessarily influence the design and implementation of evaluation.

Attempts to apply a single template to programs varying on all of these dimensions cannot successfully capture the essence of these programs; such attempts also antagonize program personnel who may feel misunderstood and burdened by the evaluation process. Evaluation models that can accommodate these differences, on the other hand, earn the respect and cooperation of program personnel. Such cooperation is essential if, in Walker and Mitchell's (10) terms, program evaluation is to be designed not only to *prove,* but also to *improve.*

Learning from the experiences of our authors, we can appreciate the costs of overlooking these factors. The early MELD evaluation efforts misgauged staff support and interest in the evaluation by assuming that service-oriented people would embrace research-oriented tasks [see Ellwood (13)]. Nauta and Hewett (17), and Olds (10), from different perspectives, have noted the potential for evaluation staff to become "inducted" into the program and the potential effects that situation can have on objectivity of observation or actual program operation. Miller (16) has concluded that the volume and complexity of data collection activities developed for the adolescent mothers in her programs did not reflect their literacy or motivational levels; they were good instruments in the abstract, but unsuitable for the program's population.

There are broader contexts into which any evaluation effort must be placed. Jacobs (2) described the chilling effects on public sentiment that early interpretations of Head Start evaluation results had in the

1960s and 1970s. Ellwood (13) discussed the pressures from funders to conduct a premature summative evaluation to insure continued funding. Weiss (1) cautioned that positive evaluation results from a well-funded demonstration are often transferred to replications with fewer funds and, therefore, probably fewer benefits: evaluators must be careful about their claims of external validity. White (19) has presented the call for cost-effectiveness and cost–benefit program studies within a public policy context, reminding evaluators of the difficulties in conducting sound cost studies and the potential for their misuse. Hauser-Cram (20) has focussed on the increasing sophistication of research methodology—in this case, meta-analysis—and has urged program directors and policymakers to become more discriminating consumers of evaluation and research. Evaluators must be mindful of these contexts as well.

RECOMMENDATIONS ON EVALUATION

Several specific recommendations to evaluators and evaluation researchers have emerged throughout these chapters. Risking repetition, we will note them briefly here:

1. Commitments must be made to the development and refinement of ecologically based measures and to the advancement of theory [Olds (10); Tivnan (9); Hauser-Cram and Shonkoff (3); Upshur (5); Walker and Crocker (6)].
2. Graduated approaches to evaluation, which reflect the needs of programs and the state of available methodology, must be implemented [Jacobs (2); Bond and Halpern (15); Walker and Mitchell (18); Ellwood (13); Powell (11); Rodriguez and Cortez (12)].
3. Family-oriented programs should be evaluated with a variety of measures and methods [Nauta and Hewett (17); Olds (10); Bond and Halpern (15); Howrigan (4); Krauss (7); Hauser-Cram and Shonkoff (3)].
4. Programs and funders should acknowledge that long-term and/or ongoing commitments to evaluation are often needed [Bond and Halpern (15); Nauta and Hewett (17); Walker and Mitchell (18)].
5. Successful evaluations are partnerships between programs and evaluators and must be entered respectfully from both perspectives [Rodriguez and Cortez (12); Powell (11); Krauss (7); Tivnan (9); Miller (16)].

Fvaluating Family Programs represents a modest step forward in our understanding of family program development and evaluation. We hope that the risks taken by its authors and editors in extending traditional practice and thought and in sharing their experiments with others will help consolidate progress in the field, thus encouraging other evaluators to help programs better support and nurture young families.

APPENDIX A: RESEARCH INSTRUMENTS AND THEIR SOURCES[1]

Activities Choice Probe (1975)
  Developer: W. Kessen, and G. Fein
  Source: Kessen, W., and Fein, G. (August 1975). Variations in home-based infant education: Language, play, and social development. (Final report No. DCD-CB-98). New Haven: Yale University Department of Psychology. (ERIC Document Reproduction Service No. ED 118 233.)

Adolescent Coping Orientation for Program Experience (A-COPE) (Form B) (1983)
  Developer: H. I. McCubbin, and J. M. Patterson
  Source: McCubbin, H. I., and Patterson, J. M. (1981). *Systematic assessment of family stress, resources and coping: Tools for research evaluation and clinical intervention.* St. Paul, MN: University of Minnesota.

  Family Stress, Coping, and Health Project, School of Family Resources and Consumer Services, University of Wisconsin-Madison, 1300 Linden Drive, Madison, WI 53706†

Adolescent–Family Inventory of Life Events and Changes (A-FILE) (Form B) (1981)
  Developer: H. I. McCubbin, J. M. Patterson, E. Bauman, and L. H. Harris

---

[1]Compiled by Charles L. Gerlach, Harvard Family Research Project.
Key: * Write for free copy; † write for ordering information; ‡ send the following amount to this address.

Source: McCubbin, H. I., and Patterson, J. M. (1981). *Systematic assessment of family stress, resources, and coping: Tools for research evaluation and clinical intervention*. St. Paul, MN: University of Minnesota.

Family Stress, Coping, and Health Project, School of Family Resources and Consumer Services, University of Wisconsin-Madison, 1300 Linden Drive, Madison, WI 53706 †

Arizona Social Support Interview Schedule (ASSIS) (1980)
Developer: M. Barrera
Source: Manuel Barrera, Jr., Department of Psychology, Arizona State University, Tempe, AZ 85281 *

Bayley Scales of Infant Development (BSID) (1969)
Developer: N. Bayley
Source: The Psychological Corporation, 555 Academic Court, San Antonio, TX 78204-0952 †

Beavers–Timberlawn Family Evaluation Scales also known as the *Family System Rating Scales* (1976)
Developer: J. M. Lewis, W. R. Beavers, J. T. Grossett, and V. Austin-Phillips
Source: Lewis, J. M., Beavers, W. R., Gossett, J. T., and Austin-Phillips, V. (1976). *No single thread: Psychological health in family systems*. New York: Bruner/Mazel.

The Behavioral Coding System (BCS) (1977)
Developer: G. R. Patterson
Source: Patterson, G. R. (1977). Naturalistic observation in clinical assessment. *Journal of Abnormal Child Psychology, 5*(3), 309–322.

Behavioral Style Questionnaire: 3–7-year-olds (1975)
Developer: S. C. McDevitt, and W. B. Carey
Source: Dr. Sean C. McDevitt, Devereux Center, 6436 E. Sweetwater, Scottsdale, AZ 85254 ‡ $10.00

The Box Maze (1974)
Developer: S. Harter, and E. Zigler
Source: Susan Harter, Department of Psychology, University of Denver, 2040 South York Street, Denver, CO 80208 *

The Caldwell HOME see *The Home Observation for Measurement of the Environment (HOME)*

California Achievement Tests (Forms E and F) (1950, most recent edition 1985)
Developer: CTB/McGraw Hill
Source: CTB/McGraw Hill, Del Monte Research Park, 2500 Garden Road, Monterey, CA 93940 †

Cattell Infant Intelligence Scale (1940)
Developer: P. Cattell

Source: The Psychological Corporation, 555 Academic Court, San Antonio, TX 78204-0952 †

Child Behavior Checklist (CBCL) (1981)

Developer: T. M. Achenbach, and C. S. Edelbrock

Source: Achenbach, T. M., and Edelbrock, C. S. (1981). Behavioral problems and competencies reported by parents of normal and disturbed children aged four through sixteen. *Monographs of the Society for Research in Child Development, 46*(1, serial no. 188).

Cincinnati Autonomy Test Battery (CATB) (1970)

Developer: T. J. Banta

Source: Banta, T. J. (1970). Tests for the evaluation of early childhood education: The Cincinnati Autonomy Test Battery (CATB). In J. Hellmuth (Ed.), *Cognitive studies*-I. New York: Bruner/Mazel.

Classroom Behavior Inventory: Pre-school to Primary (1966)

Developer: E. S. Schaefer, M. Aaronson, and B. Burgoon

Source: Dr. Earl S. Schaefer, Department of Child and Maternal Health, School of Public Health, The University of North Carolina at Chapel Hill, Rosenau Hall 201 H, Chapel Hill, NC 27514 *

Classroom Behavior Inventory—Preschool Form (Updated version of preceding research instrument, 1970)

Developer: E. S. Schaefer, and M. Edgerton

Source: Dr. Earl S. Schaefer, Department of Child and Maternal Health, School of Public Health, The University of North Carolina at Chapel Hill, Rosenau Hall 201 H, Chapel Hill, NC 27514 *

Community Interaction Checklist (1978)

Developer: R. G. Wahler

Source: Robert G. Wahler, Psychology Department, University of Tennessee, Knoxville, TN 37916 *

Confidant Measures (1981)

Developer: L. I. Pearlin, M. A. Lieberman, E. G. Menaghan, and J. T. Mullan

Source: Pearlin, L. I., Lieberman, M. A., Menaghan, E. G., and Mullan, J. T. (1981). The stress process. *Journal of Health and Social Behavior, 22,* 337–356.

Coping Health Inventory for Parents (CHIP) (Form D) (1983)

Developer: H. I. McCubbin, M. A. McCubbin, R. S. Nevin, and E. Cauble

Source: McCubbin, H. I., and Patterson, J. M. (1981). *Systematic assessment of family stress, resources and coping: Tools for research evaluation and clinical intervention.* St. Paul, MN: University of Minnesota.

Family Stress, Coping, and Health Project, School of Family Resources and Consumer Services, University of Wisconsin-Madison, 1300 Linden Drive, Madison, WI 53706 †

Denver Developmental Screening Test (DDST) (1967)

Developer: W. K. Frankenburg, J. B. Dodds, and A. W. Fandal

Source: Denver Developmental Materials, P.O. Box 20037, Denver, CO 80220-0037, (303) 355-4729 †

Developmental Expectations (1979)

Developer: C. Snyder, S. J. Eyres, K. E. Barnard, and S. Mitchell

Source: Snyder, C., Eyres, S. J., Barnard, K. E., and Mitchel, S. (1979). New findings about mothers' antenatal expectations and their relationship to infant development. *American Journal of Maternal and Child Nursing, 4,* 354–351.

Dual-Employed Coping Scales (DECS) (Form A) (1981)

Developer: H. I. McCubbin, and D. A. Skinner

Source: McCubbin, H. I., and Patterson, J. M. (1981). *Systematic assessment of family stress, resources and coping: Tools for research evaluation and clinical intervention.* St. Paul, MN: University of Minnesota.

Family Stress, Coping, and Health Project, School of Family Resources and Consumer Services, University of Wisconsin-Madison, 1300 Linden Drive, Madison, WI 53706 †

The EAS Temperament Survey for Adults

The EAS Temperament Survey for Children: Parental Ratings (1984)

Developer: A. H. Buss, and R. Plomin

Source: Buss, A. H., and Plomin, R. (1984). *Temperament: Early developing personality traits.* Hillsdale, NJ: Lawrence Erlbaum Associates, 100, 102.

Executive Skills Profile (1975)

Developer: M. Bronson

Source: Dr. Martha Bronson, 10 Kenway Street, Cambridge, MA 02138 †

Family Adaptability and Cohesion Evaluation Scales (FACES II) (1985)

Developer: D. H. Olson, J. Portner, and R. Bell

Source: David Olson, Family Social Science, 290 McNeil Hall, University of Minnesota, St. Paul, MN 55108 ‡ $30.00 (scales and manual)

Family APGAR (1978)

Developer: G. Smilkstein

Sources: Smilkstein, G. (1978). The Family APGAR: A proposal for a family functioning test and its use by physicians. *The Journal of Family Practice, 6*(6), 1231–1239.

Smilkstein, G., Ashworth, C., and Montano, D. (1982). Validity and reliability of the Family APGAR as a test of family function. *The Journal of Family Practice, 15*(2), 303–311.

For instructions on scoring and use, write to: Gabriel Smilkstein, M.D., Professor of Family Medicine, School of Medicine, University of Washington, Seattle, Washington 98195

Family Concept Assessment Method (FCAM)
Developer: F. van der Veen
Source: Dr. Ferdinand van der Veen, P.O. Box 73, Encinitas, CA 92024 †

Family Coping Inventory (FCI) (Form B) (1981)
Developer: H. I. McCubbin, P. G. Boss, L. R. Wilson, and B. B. Dahl
Source: McCubbin, H. I., and Patterson, J. M. (1981). *Systematic assessment of family stress, resources and coping: Tools for research evaluation and clinical intervention.* St. Paul, MN: University of Minnesota.

Family Stress, Coping, and Health Project, School of Family Resources and Consumer Services, University of Wisconsin-Madison, 1300 Linden Drive, Madison, WI 53706 †

Family Crisis Oriented Personal Evaluation Scales (F-COPES) (Form A) (1981)
Developer: H. I. McCubbin, D. H. Olson, and A. S. Larsen
Source: McCubbin, H. I., and Patterson, J. M. (1981). *Systematic assessment of family stress, resources and coping: Tools for research evaluation and clinical intervention.* St. Paul, MN: University of Minnesota.

Family Stress, Coping, and Health Project, School of Family Resources and Consumer Services, University of Wisconsin-Madison, 1300 Linden Drive, Madison, WI 53706 †

Family Educational Atmosphere Survey Instrument (1974)
Developer: J. B. Fotheringham, and D. Creal
Source: Dr. John B. Fotheringham, Ongwanada Medical Associates, Suite 314, 797 Princess Street, Kingston, Ontario K7L 1G1, Canada *

Family Environment Scale (1974)
Developer: R. H. Moos
Source: Consulting Psychologists Press, Inc., 577 College Ave., Palo Alto, CA 94305 †

Family Functioning Index (FFI) (1973)
Developer: I. B. Pless, and B. Satterwhite
Source: I. B. Pless, University of Rochester, School of Medicine, Rochester, NY 14620 *

Family Functioning Scale (1973)
Developer: I. B. Pless, and B. Satterwhite
Source: Pless, I. B., and Satterwhite, B. (1973). A measure of family functioning and its application. *Social Science and Medicine, 7,* 613–621.

Family Interaction Scales (FIS)
   Developer: J. Riskin, and E. E. Faunce
   Source: J. Riskin, M.D.; Mental Research Institute, 555 Middlefield
       Rd., Palo Alto, CA 94301 ‡ $14.00 (scales and manual)
Family Inventory of Life Events and Changes (FILE) (Form C) (1983)
   Developer: H. I. McCubbin, J. M. Patterson, and L. R. Wilson
   Source: McCubbin, H. I., and Patterson, J. M. (1981). *Systematic
       assessment of family stress, resources and coping: Tools for re-
       search evaluation and clinical intervention*. St. Paul, MN: Uni-
       versity of Minnesota.

   Family Stress, Coping, and Health Project, School of Family Re-
   sources and Consumer Services, University of Wisconsin-
   Madison, 1300 Linden Drive, Madison, WI 53706 †
Family Relationships Index (FRI) is composed of the cohesion, expres-
   siveness, and conflict subscales of the *Family Environment Scale* (1981)
   Developer: C. J. Holahan, and R. Moos
   Source: Consulting Psychologists Press, Inc., 577 College Avenue,
       Palo Alto, CA 94306 †
Family Support Scale (FSS) (1984)
   Developer: C. Dunst, V. Jenkins, and C. M. Trivette
   Source: Dr. Carl Dunst, Family, Infant and Preschool Program,
       Western Carolina Center, 300 Enola Road, Morganton, NC 28655 †
Family System Rating Scales see *Beavers–Timberlawn Family Evaluation
   Scales Feetham Family Functioning Survey*
   Developer: S. L. Feetham
   Source: Suzanne Feetham, Ph.D., R.N., Director of Nursing for Ed-
       ucation and Research, Children's Hospital National Medical
       Center, 111 Michigan Ave., N.W., Washington, D.C. 20010 ‡
       $5.00
Folkman–Lazarus Ways of Coping Checklist, Revised (1980)
   Developer: S. Folkman and R. S. Lazarus
   Source: Tests in Microfiche, Set K, Educational Testing Service,
       Princeton, NJ 08541-0001 †
Gesell Developmental Schedules (1925)
   Developer: A. Gesell
   Source: Gesell, A. (1925). *The mental growth of the preschool child*.
       New York: Macmillan.
*Griffiths Mental Development Scale for Testing Babies from Birth to
   Two Years* (1951)
   Developer: R. Griffiths
   Source: Test Center, Inc., 7721 Holiday Drive, Sarasota, FL 33581 †
Hassles Scale (1981)
   Developer: A. D. Kanner, J. C. Coyne, C. Schaefer, and R. S. Lazarus
   Source: Kanner, A. D., Coyne, J. C., Schaefer, C., and Lazarus,

R. S. (1981). Comparison of two modes of stress measurement: Daily hassles and uplifts versus major life events. *Journal of Behavioral Medicine, 4,* 1–39.

The Home Observation for Measurement of the Environment (HOME) (1984)

Developer: B. M. Caldwell, and R. H. Bradley

Source: Bettye M. Caldwell, Center for Child Development and Education, University of Arkansas at Little Rock, 33rd and University Avenue, Little Rock, Arkansas 72204 * ‡ $6.00 (for manual)

Index of Current School Adjustment

Developer: V. Seitz, N. Apfel, and L. Rosenbaum

Source: Victoria Seitz, Department of Psychology, Yale University, Box 11A Yale Station, New Haven, CT 06520-7447 * (Request teacher interview and school services forms.)

Infant Temperament Questionnaire (ITQ)—4–8 months (Revised 1977)

Developer: W. B. Carey, and S. C. McDevitt

Source: Dr. William B. Carey, 319 W. Front Street, Media, PA 19063 ‡ $10.00

Interpersonal Support Evaluation List (ISEL) (1983)

Developer: S. Cohen, and H. M. Hoberman

Source: Cohen, S., and Hoberman, H. M. (1983). Positive events and social support as buffers of life change stress. *Journal of Applied Social Psychology, 13*(2), 123–125.

Interview Schedule for Social Interaction (ISSI) (1977)

Developer: S. Henderson, P. Duncan-Jones, D. G. Byrne, and R. Scott

Source: Henderson, S., Byrne, D. G., and Duncan-Jones, P. (1981). *Neurosis and the social environment.* Sydney, Australia. Academic Press.

Inventory of Socially Supportive Behaviors (ISSB) (1981)

Developer: M. Barrera, I. N. Sandler, and T. B. Ramsay

Source: Manuel Barrera, Jr., Department of Psychology, Arizona State University, Tempe, AZ 85281 *

Iowa Tests of Basic Skills (Forms G and H) (1986)

Developer: A. N. Hieronymous, E. F. Lindquist, and H. D. Hoover

Source: The Riverside Publishing Company, 8420 Bryn Mawr Ave., Chicago, IL 60631 †

Manual for the Assessment of Performance, Competence, and Executive Capacity in Infant Play (1983)

Developer: J. Belsky, E. Hrncir, and J. Vondra

Source: Jay Belsky, Pennsylvania State University, Department of Individual and Family Studies, S-110 Henderson Human Development Building, University Park, PA 16802 *

Matching Familiar Figures Test (1964)

Developer: J. Kagan, B. L. Rosman, D. Day, J. Albert, and W. Phillips

Source: Kagan, J., Rosman, B. L., Day, D., Albert, J., and Phillips, W. (1964). Information processing in the child: Significance of analytic and reflective attitudes. *Psychological Monographs, 78*(1, whole no. 578).

Maternal Developmental Expectations and Child Rearing Attitude Scale
Developer: T. M. Field
Source: Tiffany M. Field, Mailman Center for Child Development, P.O. Box 01620 820, Miami, FL 33101 *

Maternal Social Support Index (MSSI) (1981)
Developer: J. M. Pascoe, F. Loda, V. Jeffries, and J. Earp
Source: John M. Pascoe, M.D., M.P.H., Pediatrics and Human Development, Michigan State University, B240 Life Sciences Building, East Lansing, MI 48824-1317 *

McCarthy Scale of Children's Abilities (1970)
Developer: D. McCarthy
Source: The Psychological Corporation, 555 Academic Court, San Antonio, TX 78204-0952 †

McMaster Family Assessment Device (FAD)
Developer: N. B. Epstein, L. M. Baldwin, and D. S. Bishop
Source: N. B. Epstein, Brown–Butler Family Research Program, Butler Hospital, 345 Blackstone Boulevard, Providence, RI 02906 *

Metropolitan Achievement Tests (1961, 6th edition, 1985)
Developer: G. A. Prescott, I. H. Balow, T. P. Hogan, and R. C. Farr
Source: The Psychological Corporation, 555 Academic Court, San Antonio, TX 78204-0952 †

Metropolitan Readiness Test (MRT) (1986)
Developer: J. R. Nurss, and M. E. McGauvran
Source: The Psychological Corporation, 555 Academic Court, San Antonio, TX 78204-0952 †

The Mutual Problem Solving Task (MPST) Maternal Interview
Developer: A. S. Epstein, and D. P. Weikart
Source: Epstein, A. S., and Weikart, D. P. (1979). *The Ypsilanti– Carnegie Infant Education Project,* Ypsilanti, Michigan: High/ Scope Press, 67–70.

Parent As a Teacher Inventory (PAAT) (1984)
Developer: R. Strom
Source: Scholastic Testing Service, 480 Meyer Road, P.O. Box 1056, Bensenville, IL 60106 †

Parental Attitude Checklist (1978)
Developer: R. D. Boyd, and K. A. Stauber
Source: Boyd, R. D., and Stauber, K. A. (October 5, 1978). Parental Attitude Checklist. In R. D. Boyd and K. A. Stauber, *Final report: Acquisition and generalization of teaching and child management behaviors in parents of children: A comparative study* (Ap-

pendix H). Portage, WI: BEH Research Project, Portage Project, Cooperative Educational Service Agency, no. 12.

The Portage Project, 626 East Slifer Street, P.O. Box 564, Portage, WI 53901 *

Parent Behavior Progression (PBP) (Forms 1 and 2) (1978)
    Developer: R. Bromwich
    Source: Bromwich, R. (Ed.), (1978). *Working with parents and infants: An interactive approach*. Baltimore: University Park Press, 341–359.

Parenting Stress Index (PSI) (1983)
    Developer: R. R. Abidin
    Source: Pediatric Psychology Press, 320 Terrell Rd. West, Charlottesville, VA 22901 †

Pattison Psychosocial Kinship Inventory (1981)
    Developer: E. M. Pattison, G. Hurd, and R. Llamas
    Source: Dr. E. Mansell Pattison, Department of Psychiatry and Health Behavior, Medical College of Georgia, Augusta, GA 30912-7300 *

Peabody Picture Vocabulary Test—Revised (PPVT-R) (1981)
    Developer: L. M. Dunn, and L. M. Dunn
    Source: American Guidance Service, Publishers' Building, P.O. Box 99, Circle Pines, MN 55014 †

Perceived Social Support from Friends and from Family (Pss-Fr) (Pss-Fa) (1983)
    Developer: M. E. Procidano, and K. Heller
    Source: Procidano, M. E., and Heller, K. (1983). Measures of perceived social support from friends and from family: Three validation studies. *American Journal of Community Psychology, 11*(1), 1–24.

Perry Preschool Assessment at Age 19 (1984)
    Developer: L. Schweinhart
    Source: Larry Schweinhart, High/Scope Educational Foundation, 600 North River Street, Ypsilanti, MI 48197 *

Play As a Cognitive Assessment Tool (1979)
    Developer: P. R. Zelazo, and R. B. Kearsley
    Source: Dr. Philip Zelazo, Montreal Children's Hospital, Department of Psychology, 2300 Tupper Street, Montreal, Quebec H3H 1P3, Canada *

Provisions of Social Relations Scale (PSR)
    Developer: R. J. Turner, B. G. Frankel, and D. M. Levin
    Source: Turner, R. J., Frankel, B. G., and Levin, D. M. (1983). Social support: Conceptualization, measurement, and implications for mental health. In J. R. Greenley (Ed.), *Research in community and mental health* (vol. 3, pp. 67–111). Greenwich, CT: JAI Press.

Questionnaire on Resources and Stress (QRS) (1974)
   Developer: J. Holroyd
   Source: Clinical Psychology Publishing Company, 4 Conant Square,
      Brandon, VT 05733
Questionnaire on Resources and Stress—Short Form (QRS-SF) (1982)
   Developer: J. Holroyd
   Source: Clinical Psychology Publishing Company, 4 Conant Square,
      Brandon, VT 05733
Questionnaire on Resources and Stress—F (QRS-F) (1983)
   Developer: W. N. Friedrich, M. T. Greenberg, and K. Crnic
   Source: William N. Friedrich, Department of Psychology, Mayo
      Clinic, Rochester, MN 55905 *
Rand's Health Insurance Experiment (HIE): Social Support Measures
   Developer: C. A. Donald, and J. E. Ware
   Source: Donald, C. A., and Ware, J. E. (1984). The measurement of
      social support. In J. R. Greenley (Ed.), *Research in community
      and mental health* (vol. 4, pp. 325–370). Greenwich, CT: JAI Press.
Revised Kaplan Scale
   Developer: A. Kaplan
   Source: Turner, R. J., Frankel, B. G., and Levin, D. M. (1983). Social
      support: Conceptualization, measurement, and implications for
      mental health. In J. R. Greenley (Ed.). *Research in community
      and mental health* (vol. 3, 67–111). Greenwich, CT: JAI Press.
Rosenberg Self-Esteem Scale (1965)
   Developer: M. Rosenberg
   Sources: Rosenberg, M. (1965). *Society and the adolescent self-
      image.* Princeton, NJ: Princeton University Press, 305–307.

      Robinson, J. P., and Shaver, P. R. (1973). *Measures of social psy-
      chological attitudes.* Ann Arbor, MI: Institute for Social Research,
      University of Michigan, 216–223.
Rotter Locus of Control Scale (1966)
   Developer: J. B. Rotter
   Sources: Robinson, J. P., and Shaver, P. R. (1973). *Measures of social
      psychological attitudes.* Ann Arbor, MI: Institute for Social Re-
      search, University of Michigan, 216–223.

      Rotter, J. B. (1966). Generalized expectancies for internal verses
      external control of reinforcement. *Psychological Monographs,
      80*(whole no. 609).
Salloway Social Networks Inventory
   Developer: J. C. Salloway
   Source: Jeffrey C. Salloway, Rush Medical College, Chicago, IL 60612 *
Shortened Kaplan Scale
   Developer: A. Kaplan
   Source: Turner, R. J., Frankel, B. G., and Levin, D. M. (1983). Social
      support: Conceptualization, measurement, and implications for

mental health. In J. R. Greenley (Ed.), *Research in community and mental health* (vol. 3, pp. 67–111). Greenwich, CT: JAI Press.

Social Network Index (1977)
Developer: L. F. Berkman, and S. L. Syme
Source: Lisa F. Berkman, Department of Epidemiology and Public Health and Institution for Social and Policy Studies, Yale University, New Haven, CT 06520 *

Social Network Scale (1975)
Developer: B. H. Kaplan
Source: Kaplan, B. H., and Cassell, J. C. (Eds.) (1975). *Family and health: An epidemiological approach.* Chapel Hill, NC: Institute for Research in Social Science, University of North Carolina (see Appendix A, pp. 101–103).

Social Support Index (1979) and *Social Support Questionnaires* (1979)
Developer: B. L. Wilcox
Source: Brian L. Wilcox, American Psychological Association, 1200 17th Street, N.W., Washington, D.C. 20036 *

Social Support Measure (1983)
Developer: K. A. Crnic
Source: Dr. Keith A. Crnic, Department of Psychiatry and Behavioral Sciences, CDMRC WJ-10, University of Washington, Seattle, WA 98195 *

Social Support Questionnaire
Developer: L. Berkman, M. Boyd, F. Cohen, J. Cohen, C. Schaefer, and B. VanDort
Source: Dr. Catherine Schaefer, Department of Epidemiology and Public Health, Yale University, 60 College Street, New Haven, CT 06510 *

Social Support Questionnaire
Developer: I. G. Sarason
Source: Irwin G. Sarason, Psychology Department, NI 25, University of Washington, Seattle, WA 98195 *

Stanford–Binet Intelligence Scale (Fourth Edition) (1986)
Developer: R. L. Thorndike, E. P. Hagen, and J. M. Sattler
Source: The Riverside Publishing Company, 8420 Bryn Mawr Ave., Chicago, IL 60631 †

The Sticker Game (1968)
Developer: T. M. Achenbach, and E. Zigler
Source: Thomas M. Achenbach, Department of Psychology, University of Vermont, 1 South Prospect Street, Burlington, VT 05401 *

Strange Situation (1978)
Developer: M. Ainsworth, and B. Wittig
Source: Ainsworth, M. D. S., Blehar, M. C., Waters, E., and Wall, S. (1978). *Patterns of attachment: A psychological study of the strange situation.* Hillsdale, NJ: Lawrence Erlbaum Associates.

Teacher Rating Scale for Use in Drug Studies With Children (1969)
  Developer: C. K. Conners
  Source: Conners, C. K. (1969). A teacher rating scale for use in drug
    studies with children. *American Journal of Psychiatry, 126,* 884.
Teaching Young Children Questionnaire (1978)
  Developer: R. D. Boyd, and K. A. Stauber
  Source: Boyd, R. D., and Stauber, K. A. (October 5, 1978). Teaching
    Young Children Questionnaire. In R. D. Boyd and K. A. Stauber,
    *Final report: Acquisition and generalization of teaching and child
    management behaviors in parents of children: A comparative
    study* (Appendix F). Portage, WI: BEH Research Project, Portage
    Project, Cooperative Educational Service Agency, no. 12.

    The Portage Project, 626 East Slifer Street, P.O. Box 564, Portage,
    WI 53901 *
Toddler Temperament Scale (TTS)—1–3-year-olds (1978)
  Developer: W. Fullard, S. C. McDevitt, and W. B. Carey
  Source: Dr. William Fullard, Department of Educational Psychology,
    Temple University, Philadelphia, PA 19122 ‡ $10.00
Traditional Social Support Index (1984)
  Developer: R. Moos, R. Cronkite, A. Billings, and J. Finney
  Source: *The Health and Daily Living Form,* available from: Rudolf
    H. Moos, Ph.D., Social Ecology Laboratory, Department of Psy-
    chiatry - TD114, Stanford University Medical Center, Palo Alto,
    CA 94305 ‡ $6.00
Training Manual for Classroom Observation
  Developer: J. Stallings
  Source: Jane Stallings, Chairman, Department of Curriculum and
    Instruction, University of Houston-University Park, 4800 Cal-
    houn, Houston, TX 77004 *
Vineland Adaptive Behavior Scales (1984)
  Developer: S. Sparrow, D. Balla, and D.Cicchetti
  Source: American Guidance Service, Publishers' Building, P.O. Box
    99, Circle Pines, MN 55014 †
Ways of Coping Checklist see *Folkman–Lazarus Ways of Coping
  Checklist, Revised*
Wechsler Preschool and Primary Scale of Intelligence (WPPSI) (1963,
  1967)
  Developer: D. Wechsler
  Source: The Psychological Corporation, 555 Academic Court, San
    Antonio, TX 78204-0952 †
Wide Range Achievement Test-Revised (1984)
  Developer: J. F. Jastak
  Source: Jastak Associates, Inc., 1526 Gilpin Avenue, Wilmington, DE
    19806 †

Your Baby and Average Baby Perception Inventories (1963)
Developer: E. R. Broussard, and M. Hartner
Source: Broussard, E. R., and Hartner, M. (1970). Maternal perception of the neonate as related to development. *Child Psychiatry and Human Development, 1,* 16–25.

APPENDIX B: GLOSSARY OF RESEARCH AND PROGRAM EVALUATION TERMS

Carole C. Upshur

ACTION RESEARCH: Research study conducted in an on-going service setting or demonstration program, as opposed to laboratory research. Research conducted to solve particular problems in specific settings, rather than to produce results generalizable to diverse populations.

ADAPTATIONAL THEORY: An ecological approach to understanding the various influences at work in a family with an atypical child. (See also ECOLOGICAL APPROACH; SOCIAL SYSTEMS THEORY)

ANALYSIS OF COVARIANCE: A more sophisticated analysis of variance in which subjects' scores on the outcome variable under study are adjusted by removing the influence of one or more other variables—the covariate(s)—already known to be correlated with the outcome variable and that could therefore be responsible for group differences if not controlled.

ANALYSIS OF VARIANCE (ANOVA): An inferential statistical technique used to compare the scores of three or more groups of subjects. When between group variability is significant, one concludes that differences among the groups occur not by chance but (probably) due to intervention.

ATTRITION RATE: The rate at which children or families drop out of a program or study before its completion.

BASE LINE: The level of behavior or the score on a test that is recorded before an intervention is provided or services are delivered.

521

BEHAVIORAL COUNTS: Measures of behavior that involve counting specific behaviors in specific contexts.

BEHAVIORAL GOALS/OBJECTIVES/MEASURES: Concrete and discrete behaviors that can be easily observed (e.g., obtaining a job, attending a parent support group, or learning to say 10 words). (Nonbehavioral goals or objectives—e.g., attitudes—can only be inferred from what a person says.)

BEHAVIORAL TAXONOMY: The classification and definition of types of behavior.

BIAS: An inaccurate understanding—either intentional or unintentional—of a situation. Bias occurs when incomplete data are collected, data come from only part of the target population, or collection methods are invalid.

BIOLOGICAL RISK: A term applied to infants and young children who have undergone a specific birth trauma, early medical problems, or diseases that are often related to later development problems.

BLIND RESEARCH/OBSERVERS: A study conducted so that those collecting data do not know what the treatment or intervention has been or who received it.

CASE STUDY: An in-depth study of a particular entity, designed to enhance understanding of that entity and to suggest more general hypotheses (see also CLINICAL INQUIRY).

CAUSAL SEQUENCE: The path or order in which an event or series of events (behaviors, attitudes, or knowledge) occurs, where each event is thought to cause the next. Much research in the area of child and family development seeks to identify causal sequences.

CHILD OUTCOME MEASURES: Methods of identifying changes that occur in children involved in a treatment or intervention program. Common child outcomes include scores on developmental tests, incidents of behavior problems, school attendance, and reading level.

CLINICAL INQUIRY, CLINICAL TRIAL: A research method involving detailed observation and in-depth analysis of a few individuals, as opposed to one that systematically examines larger numbers of individuals more superficially. Clinical inquiries can also generate questions or hypotheses for more systematic research (see also CASE STUDY).

CODING: The process of assigning information or observations to categories in order to organize, score, or tabulate the information.

COGNITIVE ASSESSMENT MEASURES: Tests, questions, or procedures designed to assess mental capacity or intelligence.

COHORT: A group of individuals who share broad demographic characteristics, such as age or year of entry into first grade.

COMPARISON GROUP: A group of individuals with characteristics (e.g., age, race, sex) similar to those of group in an intervention program. Data are collected from both groups to help researchers better estimate the likely effects of program participation. A comparison group often receives a standard intervention or alternative treatment to rule out the possibility that the changes observed in the experimental intervention or treatment group represent only a placebo effect (see also CONTROL GROUP).

CONCURRENT VALIDITY: See VALIDITY OF INSTRUMENTS

CONFOUNDING VARIABLES: Variables outside the focus of the study that may complicate one's understanding of what relationships are at work in a particular study or program evaluation. For example, if children of mixed income are enrolled in a special reading program and some children do much better than others, the result may be due to family income rather than to the variable under study (e.g., reading problems).

CONSTRUCT VALIDITY: See VALIDITY OF INSTRUMENTS

CONSTRUCT: A logical definition or ordering of concepts that together form the basis for understanding some abstract principle (see, e.g., LOCUS OF CONTROL; SOCIAL COMPETENCE).

CONTAMINATING VARIABLES: See CONFOUNDING VARIABLES

CONTEXTUAL VARIABLES: Variables that describe characteristics of children, families, or programs as background information for research study or evaluation.

CONTROL GROUP: A group of individuals not provided the same program as the one under study, but from which the same information is collected. Comparisons of information help determine what level of impact the special services produced. The term applies most often when group members are assigned randomly (see also RANDOM ASSIGNMENT; NONEQUIVALENT CONTROLS).

CONTROLLED SETTING: Setting (laboratory, residential program, or hospital) where treatments can be directly and exactly controlled by the researcher.

CORRELATION OR COEFFICIENT OF CORRELATION: A measure of the degree to which two variables change in relationship to one another. High correlations mean a high degree of predictability; low correlations indicate little relationship. The maximum positive correlation is $+1.00$; the maximum negative is -1.00.

COST–ANALYSIS STUDY: A study that examines the costs of delivering services and the economic benefits potentially gained because of those services. *Cost–benefit analyses* compare the financial costs of a program to the financial benefits of that program. *Cost-effectiveness analyses* are conducted on more than one program for the sake of comparison.

COST–EFFECTIVENESS ANALYSIS: See COST–ANALYSIS STUDY

COVARIANCE/COVARIABLES: Two or more variables that change in relationship to one another. For example, the effectiveness of a program component may co-vary with ethnicity, that is, the program is more effective with one ethnic group than another (see also CORRELATION; ANALYSIS OF COVARIANCE).

CRITERION REFERENCED INSTRUMENTS/MEASURES: Instruments or measures designed to determine whether an individual can perform at a specified level or meet certain criteria. Such instruments are often designed to determine whether a given program's specific goals have been met, as opposed to whether their participants compare favorably on "norm-referenced" instruments (see also NORMS).

CRITICAL PERIODS: Certain age ranges in child development thought important for developing particular skills.

CROSS-SECTIONAL STUDIES: Research or evaluation studies that collect information from groups of subjects at one point in time. (Usually used to describe characteristics of different groups rather than to evaluate effects of treatment or intervention.) (cf. LONGITUDINAL STUDIES)

CULTURAL ABSOLUTISM: Occurs when standards for "appropriate" child and family functioning are applied to other cultures and subcultures without accommodation to cultural differences.

DEFICIT MODEL: An approach to development that assumes a single standard of development and behavior. Individuals who fail to meet that standard are identified as having problems or delays. Model focuses on deficits as defined by such standards, rather than on positive attributes of groups not conforming to those standards (see also DIFFERENCE MODEL).

DEMONSTRATION PROGRAM: Program designed specifically to implement a new service delivery model. Usually well funded and incorporating extensive research or evaluation. The findings often are applied to the development of similar programs.

DEPENDENT VARIABLES/MEASURES: Goals or targets a program is designed to achieve, "dependent" for their change on other variables that are manipulated by the program. For example, providing day care may produce gains in prereading skills. The dependent variable is then prereading skills; the dependent measure is a reading-readiness test. "Day care" is an "independent variable" because it is controlled by the program or researcher (see also INDEPENDENT VARIABLES).

DESCRIPTIVE VARIABLES: Variables that describe the characteristics of a program or its participants.

DEVELOPMENTAL ASSESSMENT: Measurement of a child's abilities in a number of domains including cognitive, motor, communication, and social skills.

DEVELOPMENTAL PERSPECTIVE: A theoretical orientation to child and family development, which holds that children and families progress through predictable and identifiable stages of development and that success at one stage is required for successful mastery of subsequent stages.

DEVELOPMENTAL QUOTIENT/D.Q.: Score given when a child is assessed using a standardized developmental measure—a ratio of the child's skill level (usually expressed in age), divided by the child's chronological age, multiplied by 100.

DEVELOPMENTAL STATUS: A child's level of skill development in several areas.

DIFFERENCE MODEL: A model of child and family development/functioning that assumes different social and cultural groups have different but equally valid standards and values from a white, middle-class model (see also DEFICIT MODEL).

DIFFERENTIAL ATTRITION: See ATTRITION RATE

DISCRIMINANT FUNCTION ANALYSIS: A statistical procedure used to identify the combination of variables that best differentiates individuals on the basis of their membership in a particular group. For example, one might want to determine what characteristics best distinguish mothers classified as "low" on a stress measure from those classified as "high" on that measure (see also CORRELATION).

DISCRIMINANT VALIDITY: See VALIDITY OF INSTRUMENTS

DISCURSIVE REVIEW: A review of hypotheses tested, soundness of research designs, and results reported in research studies on a particular topic (see also META-ANALYSIS)

DISSEMINATION: Making known to other professionals, government agencies, or the general public the results of research or program evaluation.

DISTRIBUTION; SKEWED DISTRIBUTION: Statistical term used to describe the pattern of scores on a measurement instrument produced by a particular sample of individuals. Generally it is expected that some individuals in a group will score high, some low, and most somewhere in the middle. A skewed distribution means that this expected pattern is not evident.

ECOLOGICAL APPROACH: A theoretical model of human development that holds that context influences child development. Obstacles to, and opportunities for, change reside not simply in the child, but with the child in relation to the broader context.

EFFECT SIZE: A statistical calculation indicating how much a measured dependent variable has changed. Calculated by taking the difference between the treatment and control group mean scores and dividing it by the standard deviation of control group scores. An effect size of half a standard deviation (.50) is considered a moderately significant effect.

EMPIRICAL: Describes the results of direct observation. "Empirical data" is often contrasted with opinion, speculation, or theory.

ENUMERATIVE MEASURE: A direct count of the frequency of something (e.g., the number of single parent families or the number of parents attending a support group) (cf. METRIC MEASURE/PROPERTY).

ENVIRONMENTALISTS: See NATURE/NURTURE DEBATE

ENVIRONMENTAL RISK: Term applied to situation of infants and young children who have no immediate medical problems or history of specific prenatal or birth problems but who are "at risk" for developmental delays due to family problems and/or economic conditions.

ENVIRONMENTAL VARIABLES: Variables in aspects of a person's external environment (family, home, support group, or neighborhood) as opposed to variables in internal aspects (feelings, attitudes, knowledge, or behavior).

EQUIVALENCE: The extent to which comparison or control groups are the same as the treatment group, crucial to drawing clear conclusions about the effectiveness of the treatment or intervention.

ESTABLISHED RISK: Term applied to situation of infants and young children who have been identified as having a specific disease or disability known to cause developmental delays.

ETHNOGRAPHIC MEASURES/RESEARCH: Measures or research that focus on social, environmental, cultural, racial, or ethnic factors affecting children and families.

ETHNOLOGY: Anthropological study of cultural similarities and differences.

EVALUATION DESIGN: A plan for carrying out an evaluation, which specifies: the goals or objectives to be measured, the format for measuring or collecting information to determine whether the goals have been met, from whom information is to be collected, and how the information will be analyzed and used. Established evaluation designs have been developed to address concerns of validity and bias (see also EXPERIMENTAL DESIGN; QUASI-EXPERIMENTAL DESIGN).

EXPERIMENTAL DESIGN: A research design considered the most scientifically rigorous, in which data are collected from two groups of individuals, randomly assigned either to receive the services being evaluated (the treatment group) or to be a "control group." This process helps assure that differences (if any) found between the two groups are more likely due to the impact of services than to other factors (see QUASI-EXPERIMENTAL DESIGN).

EXPERIMENTAL MORTALITY: See ATTRITION RATE

EX POST FACTO RESEARCH/DESIGN: A research or evaluation plan that collects information only *after* services have begun or are completed. This design documents what participants achieved but does not allow inferences about the causes.

EXTERNAL EVALUATION: An evaluation carried out by consultants or researchers who are not members of the program staff (see also INTERNAL EVALUATION).

EXTERNAL VALIDITY: The extent to which the results of an evaluation or research study can be generalized to other similar programs or client populations (see VALIDITY).

F-TEST/F-RATIO: A statistical test utilized to calculate significant differences when performing an analysis of variance. It is a ratio of "between groups" variance divided by "within groups" variance and indicates the likelihood that differences among the means of three or more groups of subjects are likely to be chance. If the F-ratio obtains statistical significance, one can conclude that groups indeed perform differently (see also ANALYSIS OF VARIANCE).

FACE VALIDITY: See VALIDITY OF INSTRUMENTS

FACTOR ANALYSIS: A statistical technique that evaluates the concomitant variation among a large set of variables and indicates which groups of variables have the strongest interrelationships. Variables in these groupings presumably owe their interrelationship to the fact that they each relate to an "hypothesized underlying construct," the factor; most tests or measures tap more than one factor.

FACTORIAL EXPERIMENT: Experiment or evaluation study in which two or more programs or treatments are planned and evaluated to see which is most effective. For example, two early intervention treatments might be offered—one medical, one educational—each administered at both a full and partial service level. Such a study might reveal that a less expensive, less intensive service helps families just as much as a more expensive, intensive one.

FAMILY LIFE CYCLE: The different stages through which families progress from being newlyweds, to families with young children, etc. Each stage is associated with different family issues, problems, and changes in relationships.

FAMILY SYSTEMS THEORY: A theoretical perspective that views families as dynamic systems rather than as collections of independent individuals. Families are described in terms of structures and alliances, common patterns of behavior, and family "rules." The theory holds that therapeutic intervention with one family member will not succeed unless the family system's dynamics are considered.

FEEDBACK PROCEDURES: Mechanisms by which staff of a program and others are informed about evaluation results.

FIELD EXPERIMENTATION: Studies conducted in natural settings (in operating programs, schools, and family homes) as opposed to laboratories or contrived situations.

FORMATIVE EVALUATION: An evaluation study that provides regular feedback to staff while a program is in progress, so that it can be modified in order to increase positive outcomes (see SUMMATIVE EVALUATION).

FREQUENCY: The number or percentage of objects or events in a specific category. Anything that can be counted can be expressed as a frequency.

GENERALIZABILITY: The extent to which findings from one evaluation or research study can be applied to another situation.

GOALS: Broad statements of a program's purposes or expected outcomes, usually not specific enough to be measured and often concerning long-term rather than short term expectations (see also OBJECTIVES).

HALO EFFECT: Overall attitudes or opinions that influence how favorably or unfavorably a child or family is evaluated on specific measurement items.

HEREDITARIAN VIEW OF DEVELOPMENT: See NATURE/NURTURE DEBATE

HIGH-RISK FAMILIES: Families with characteristics known to lead to problems in a high percentage of cases.

HORIZONTAL DIFFUSION: The sharing of knowledge or experiences by program participants with nonparticipants who may have been purposely assigned to a different treatment or control group. Such "diffusion" blurs distinctions between treatment and nontreatment groups, thereby weakening assessments of program impact.

HYPOTHESIS: A causal statement providing the framework for a research or evaluation study.

IMPACT EVALUATION: Evaluation study designed to assess program effects on participants, focusing on long- and short-term changes in participants (see also INPUT/PROCESS EVALUATION).

INDEPENDENT VARIABLES/MEASURES: Variables under the control of the program or researcher, which can be manipulated to determine their effect on intervention outcomes. In a family-support program these may include the amount or type of service (e.g., support group, home visits, individual counseling) received. Child or family characteristics can also be considered independent variables, since the program might select certain children or families to participate—for example, families having their first child, or children under age 3. An independent measure is the particular scale, index, or other coding procedure used to determine the level, intensity, or amount of independent variables (see also DEPENDENT VARIABLES).

INDEX INFANT: The infant who is the primary subject of a research or intervention project.

INDICATOR: A specific piece of information (test results, specific behaviors, and child and family characteristics) used to "indicate" whether the objectives of the intervention have been achieved.

INFORMANTS: Individuals from whom data are collected.

INFORMED CONSENT: A research procedure whereby participants are informed of the types of information being collected and of the possible benefits and detriments to collection of the information or conduct of the study. Participants then must be allowed to accept or decline participation in the study.

INPUT/PROCESS EVALUATION: An evaluation or research study that focuses primarily on how a program operates or the extent and types of service participants receive. Often most appropriate for new and developing programs seeking to improve services (see also IMPACT EVALUATION)

INSTRUMENT: A questionnaire, checklist, test, observation protocol, or similar tools used to measure knowledge, attitudes, or behavior.

INTELLIGENCE QUOTIENT/I.Q.: A numerical score derived from tests that are designed to determine broad problem solving capability and the ability to think abstractly. For children, the score is usually calculated by dividing the child's mental age by his or her chronological age and multiplying by 100 (see DEVELOPMENTAL QUOTIENT/ D.Q.).

INTERACTIVE EFFECTS: Effects or "impacts" that occur only in specific treatment conditions for specific groups of program participants, rather than among all types of participants or in all treatment conditions.

INTERACTIVE MEASURES: Instruments designed to measure the interaction between two persons rather than focusing on an individual.

INTERNAL EVALUATION: An evaluation carried out by program staff or board members (as opposed to one carried out by an evaluator hired from outside the program).

INTERNAL VALIDITY: Characterizes evaluations or research studies where it is reasonable to infer that the results observed are due to the intervention or treatment and not to other influences and circumstances (see also MEASUREMENT ERROR; THREATS TO VALIDITY).

INTERVENTION VARIABLES: Characteristics of an intervention program (such as types and hours of services) that are being monitored in order to determine their effect on participants.

INTEROBSERVER/INTERRATER AGREEMENT: The degree to which independent observers or raters arrive at the same conclusion or score by observing or rating the same situation. High agreement (usually 80% or more) is needed on a consistent basis to ensure the reliability of the data.

INTRUSIVENESS: The degree to which the conduct of a study changes or interrupts normal program functioning or activities, typically by placing extra demands upon participants and staff (see also UNOBTRUSIVE MEASURES).

INTERVENING FACTORS/VARIABLES: See MEDIATING/MODERATOR VARIABLES

LIE SCALE: Questions included in a measure of attitude or opinion to determine whether the respondent is trying to "fake" (or "lie") on the test or questionnaire (usually minor modifications of questions asked elsewhere).

LIKERT SCALE: A format for obtaining responses to attitude questionnaires in which the respondent is asked to rate on a numerical scale strength of agreement or disagreement with a statement. For example:

1	2	3	4	5
Strongly agree	Agree	Not sure	Disagree	Strongly disagree

LINEAR CAUSALITY: A direct, one way relationship where one behavior or variable is seen to cause another.

LOCUS OF CONTROL: A psychological construct that describes the extent to which individuals feel their lives are controlled by their own actions (internal locus of control) or by outside events such as fate or luck (external locus of control).

LONG-TERM EFFECTS/OUTCOMES: Effects or outcomes expected to take a long time to develop or to occur after an intervention program is over.

LONGITUDINAL STUDIES: Studies that collect periodic information from a set of subjects over time (see CROSS-SECTIONAL STUDIES).

LOW POWER RESEARCH: Research or evaluation studies that collect data from small numbers of individuals (usually fewer than 30–35). Effects must be very large in order to be apparent (i.e., "statistically significant") through data analysis; the power to detect differences is low.

MEASURABLE OBJECTIVES: Goal statements that are made explicit enough to be measured, either directly (by counting) or with a measuring instrument.

MEASUREMENT ERROR: The extent to which the measures used in a research or evaluation study make a true indication of program impacts unobtainable.

MEDIATING/MODERATOR VARIABLES: Processed or factors that modify program impacts by intervening in the simple cause-and-effect relationship between program independent and dependent variables. (In a program using home visits to increase I.Q. scores, a mediating effect might be parent's income, as children from lower income families might make more gains than those from higher income families.) Mediating factors can be controlled statistically during data analysis.

META-ANALYSIS (META-ANALYTICAL TECHNIQUES): Statistical methods for compiling data across several independent research or evaluation studies so that general conclusions can be drawn about the effectiveness of the particular intervention being studied (see DISCURSIVE REVIEW).

METRIC MEASURE/PROPERTY: A scaled measure (e.g., child's height and I.Q.) (see ENUMERATIVE MEASURE).

MODAL: The most commonly occurring characteristic in a varied group. For example, if a program services 60 families of which 14 are low-income, 11 are high-income, and 35 are moderate income, the modal income is "moderate."

MOLAR VARIABLES: Variables in the society at large or in a specific geographic region that might affect how program participants fare in the program (e.g., unemployment rates, divorce rates, and shifts in health care funding).

MORBIDITY: Incidence or rate of disease.

MORTALITY: The rate of death (for a specific period or among a specific group).

MULTIDIMENSIONAL/MULTIFACTORIAL MEASURES: Questionnaires or tests that measure more than one developmental area. Usually provide subscale scores as well as an overall score.

MULTIPAROUS: Having given birth to more than one child.

MULTIPLE MEASURES: The use of several different measures or instruments to obtain more accurate information about a condition or impact for which there are no well-developed instruments.

MULTIPLE REGRESSION ANALYSIS: A group of statistical techniques that analyze the ability of several independent variables to predict the variation in a given dependent variable.

MULTIVARIATE CONTROLS: Various measures or characteristics held constant or "controlled" in a statistical analysis in order to understand better the relationship between other variables.

NATURAL VARIATION or NATURALISTIC SETTINGS: Where events happen without intervention or control by researchers, including homes and classrooms.

NATURE/NURTURE DEBATE: The debate about human development as represented by the hereditarians and the environmentalists. Hereditarians argue that the genetic make-up of a child at birth has more influence on the development and potential than environmental influences. Environmentalists believe an individual is shaped profoundly by life experiences (especially early ones).

NEEDS ASSESSMENT: Collection of data about a community or a defined group to determine what types of problems exist and what types of services or solutions might be needed.

NEONATAL: The period from birth through the first month of life.

NONCONTEMPORANEOUS CONTROLS: A control group that—because of age, geography, participation in other services, etc.—is ineligible for the intervention program.

NONEQUIVALENT CONTROLS: A control group similar to a group of program participants but not equivalent on all relevant dimensions (see also RANDOM ASSIGNMENT/RANDOM SAMPLING/RANDOMIZATION).

NONLINEAR RELATIONSHIP: A relationship or correlation between two variables that does not vary at a constant rate or progress in only one direction.

NORMS/NORMED/NORM-REFERENCED INSTRUMENT: Norms are defined by typical responses on a particular instrument or test. When new instruments are developed, they often are "normed" by administering them to a large number of "normal" individuals. Instrument users can then be provided scores that serve as points of comparison. An instrument for which norms have been established is norm-referenced.

NUMERICAL RATINGS: See LIKERT SCALE

OBJECTIVES: Statements indicating the planned goals or outcomes of a program or intervention in specific and concrete terms (see also GOALS; MEASURABLE OBJECTIVES).

OBSERVATIONAL MEASURES: Instruments or scoring systems that require the observation of behaviors. Based on precise definitions of what is to be observed and precise counting methods, including length of observation and number of intervals observed (see also INTER-OBSERVER/INTERRATER AGREEMENT).

OPERATIONAL DEFINITION/OPERATIONALIZED: A definition that includes precise information or criteria. For example, a general definition of "employed" might be "having a job"; an operational definition might define "employed" as having worked at least 20 hours per week for at least 10 of the previous 12 months.

OUTCOME EVALUATION/MEASURES/VARIABLES: Evaluation to assess the impact of a program or intervention on the participants. An outcome variable is a specific characteristic, trait, or behavior that is expected to change because of a program or intervention; an outcome measure is an instrument or format by which the outcome variable is measured (see also IMPACT EVALUATION).

PARAPROFESSIONAL STAFF: Staff members with less formal training than "professionals"; typically without a college degree.

PARTIAL CORRELATION/REGRESSION: A correlational or regression analysis conducted between two variables, holding a third variable constant. For example, a study examining the relation between mother's education and a child's developmental status might "statistically" hold family income constant (i.e., remove the effect of income on developmental status) because income is expected to influence this correlation.

PATH ANALYSIS: A statistical technique that attempts to determine the relative causal relationships, including direction of effects, among variables. For example, does a high score on a locus of control measure predict better success in a program, or does successful program participation lead to a high score?

PERCEPTUAL MOTOR SKILLS: Skills involving body movement as well as visual and auditory skills. Usually contrasted with "cognitive" or thinking skills.

PERINATAL: Occurring at birth.

PLANNED VARIATION EXPERIMENT: An evaluation study that sets up several different treatments of different intensity to be received by different groups of participants to determine which best achieved the desired goals or whether different treatments achieved different goals.

POLYADIC RELATIONSHIP: The variety of simultaneous influences on an individual.

POSTTEST: A test or other instrument given to program participants at the end of a program to measure how they have changed or what they have learned. These scores often are compared to those from pretests (see also PRETEST).

POSTTEST ONLY DESIGN: An evaluation design in which data are collected only after intervention services have been delivered. It does not describe the participants prior to the intervention. While it is useful for determining whether objectives have been met, it cannot determine whether or to what extent the intervention can be credited with promoting those objectives (see also EVALUATION DESIGN; EXPERIMENTAL DESIGN).

POWER CALCULATIONS/POWER TO DETECT DIFFERENCES: Statistical calculations carried out to determine how many children or families must participate in study to adequately detect modest but significant changes.

PREDICTOR VARIABLE: A variable that accurately predicts the value or characteristic of another variable (see also DEPENDENT VARIABLES; INDEPENDENT VARIABLES).

PRETEST: A test or instrument used with program participants before they enroll in or receive services to determine their level of knowledge, attitudes, behaviors, etc., before intervention. Information usually is compared to results on the same test or instrument administered at the end of the program (see also POSTTEST).

PRESENT VALUE: The current value of money available earlier, given the various ways it could have been invested or used. The calculation is often carried out in economic analyses of service programs to contrast financial investment (with compounded interest) with investment in human services or education.

PRIMARY PREVENTION: Prevention services aimed broadly at situations that sometimes cause problems rather than at problem solving ex post facto (see also SECONDARY PREVENTION; TERTIARY PREVENTION).

PRIMIPAROUS: Bearing a first child or having borne only one child.

PROCESS EVALUATION: See INPUT/PROCESS EVALUATION

PROGRAM EVALUATION: A planned review of a program. Attempts to answer questions of concern to the group that initiated or requested the evaluation. May seek to determine whether a program has met its stated goals or to provide feedback about the program's operation, participants' satisfaction with it, etc. (see also IMPACT, INPUT, FORMATIVE, AND OUTCOME EVALUATION).

PROJECTIVE TECHNIQUES: Indirect methods of collecting information about a person's beliefs, emotions, or opinions, in the assumption that people will attribute their own feelings to other people or objects. The best-known of these is the Rorschach "ink blot" test: A person describes what objects and relationships are seen in abstract shapes printed on cards. Other techniques include the use of word associations, story telling, and drawings.

PSYCHODYNAMIC THEORY: Theory of human development first proposed by Sigmund Freud. Describes early childhood needs and their resolution as the basis for all later mental, emotional, and behavioral development.

PSYCHOMETRIC PROPERTIES: Statistical characteristics of tests or instruments that indicate their validity and reliability regarding the particular psychological dimension they purport to measure.

PSYCHOMETRICIAN: A psychologist, statistician, or mathematician who designs and tests measurements of human behaviors and abilities.

Q-SORT: An instrument format that requires the subject to categorize or sort cards with different words or descriptions. (A Q-sort on self concept might have words such as "pretty," "helpful," "poorly dressed," "unworthy," etc.; the subject would be asked to sort the words into "most like myself" and "most unlike myself.")

QUALITATIVE MEASURES/DATA: Descriptions, comments, and observations that may be collected systematically but that are not usually scored numerically for statistical analysis. Many, nonetheless, produce useful descriptive information that could not be easily summarized by statistical analysis (see also QUANTITATIVE MEASURES/DATA).

QUANTITATIVE MEASURES/DATA: Tests or instruments used to report data in numerical terms (see also QUALITATIVE MEASURES/DATA).

QUASI-EXPERIMENTAL DESIGN: A research design using a comparison group or comparative data to determine whether the participants in a program have gained more than they might have through other interventions or on their own. Comparison groups are not created by random assignment; thus this design is open to more threats to internal validity than is an experimental design, but it is often more feasible to carry out in existing human service programs (see also EXPERIMENTAL DESIGN).

R^2: The result of a multiple regression analysis that indicates the relationship between a particular dependent variable and two or more independent variables. This indicates the proportion of variance in the dependent variables that is determined by the combined weights of the independent variables. The higher the R^2, the greater the relationship.

RANDOM ASSIGNMENT/RANDOM SAMPLING/RANDOMIZATION: Process by which assignment to treatment and control groups is done totally at random. Randomization insures that initial differences (i.e., prior to any intervention) among treatment groups, and between treatment and control groups, are attributable to chance variations and not to systematic bias or differences between groups. It can pose ethical problems if persons needing services are designated as "controls."

RATE SCORES: Scores reported in terms of frequency of a behavior in a specific time interval. Useful for purposes of comparison.

RATING SCALES: Instruments that, instead of counting behaviors, require an observer to assign an overall score to what is observed, based on specific directions. Can also be used in self-report questionnaires.

REACTIVITY: The degree to which participants in a research or evaluation study are influenced by the process of data collection.

RECURSIVE TECHNIQUES: Successive statistical manipulations applied in order to determine the directionality and interrelatedness of variables.

RELIABILITY/RELIABILITY COEFFICIENT: Accuracy with which an instrument measures what it is supposed to measure, extent to which a test or instrument can detect the true variance of a characteristic in a population with the least amount of error (or error variance). Reliability is important in selecting an instrument, test, or questionnaire; there are several approaches to determining reliability: *Test–retest reliability* is determined by giving the same questionnaire two or three times over a short period to the same individuals; in *split-half reliability* responses to half the questions are correlated to responses on the other half. Calculations of reliability involve analysis of the correlation of different scores for the same person or of scores obtained on two different halves of a questionnaire; this produces a "reliability coefficient" (see also STABILITY).

REPLICATE: To repeat or duplicate a program model or research study.

REQUEST FOR PROPOSAL (RFP): Statements issued by governmental or private agencies to make interested groups aware that funds for specific projects will be granted and that proposals written according to specific guidelines will therefore be accepted for review.

RESPITE CARE: Caregiving services provided to families with a handicapped or elderly member so that other family members can have relief from the constant burden of caregiving.

RISK FACTORS: Characteristics, of children or families, that are associated with a higher than normal frequency of later problems.

SAMPLE SIZE: The number of families or children participating in a research or evaluation study. For purposes of statistical analysis, a sample of at least 30–35 is preferred (see also POWER CALCULATIONS).

SCALING: Establishing an order or hierarchy of discrete units (such as abilities or attitudes).

SCIENTIFIC METHOD: A method of inquiry that seeks to determine causal relationships. Experimental techniques are used to hold some variables constant in order to detect the impact of other variables, which are manipulated purposefully. Through the use of these techniques, various possible explanations for observed impacts are eliminated until it is determined which variable is the most likely cause, thereby producing new knowledge. The scientific method is generally thought to be "objective" and "unbiased."

SECONDARY HANDICAPS: Additional disabilities or problems that result from a primary or initial disability or handicap.

SECONDARY PREVENTION: Services designed for children or families "at risk" for problems that are likely to occur. For example, a secondary prevention program for teenage mothers might attempt to prevent child abuse since there is an increased risk that child abuse will occur among this group (see also PRIMARY PREVENTION; TERTIARY PREVENTION).

SELECTION BIAS: The extent to which groups being studied are not fully representative of the population of interest. For example, families participating in a parent education program may be more inclined toward self-improvement than those choosing not to participate.

SELF-CONCEPT: A psychological construct that describes the opinion one has of oneself, in particular, the level of self-respect.

SELF-HELP: A service delivery model that uses mutual help (information sharing and problem-solving among peers) rather than, or in addition to, the delivery of professional services.

SELF-REPORT SCALES/MEASURES: Questionnaires or other tests on which participants in a study give their opinions or feelings about a topic or report their own behavior. Often felt to be less reliable than those involving direct observation, because participants will not always report information that depicts them unfavorably.

SELF-SELECTED SAMPLES: Participants in research studies who are volunteers or have chosen on their own to use services. Because these individuals are often more motivated than others who do not voluntarily participate in studies or programs, a bias may be created that could limit the generalizability of results.

SERVICE DATA: Information concerning the types and amount of services received by program participants in an intervention program.

SHORT-TERM EFFECTS/OUTCOMES: Effects or impacts from an intervention program that are expected to occur while participant is receiving services or shortly thereafter. Assumed to be an intermediate step to later, more long-term effects.

SIGNIFICANCE (STATISTICAL): Level of certainty that must be attained by statistical calculation to conclude that there is a relationship between two variables or, more generally, that something of importance has been found. The usual standard is that there must be less than a 5% chance of being wrong (the ".05 level"), or conversely, there must be a 95% probability that the conclusion is correct.

SKEWED DISTRIBUTION: See DISTRIBUTION

SLEEPER EFFECTS: Impacts from an intervention program not immediately apparent during or shortly after program participation, but that may become apparent later.

SOCIAL COMPETENCE: Skills that demonstrate an individual's appropriate interaction with others.

SOCIAL ECOLOGY/SOCIOECOLOGY: The study of the social and cultural context of an individual (including economic, religious, geographic, ethnic, racial, and class differences).

SOCIAL NETWORK THEORY: A perspective on human social behavior that focuses on the types of community, group, and individual contacts and interactions a person may have, and on how these contacts and interactions function.

SOCIAL RESPONSE BIAS: What is exhibited when participants in a study respond by indicating what they think most people would say, rather than indicating their true feelings.

SOCIAL SUPPORT: A complex concept that generally refers to the specific help provided to a person by family members or friends in response to a crisis or stressful event and to a sense of being loved and of belonging.

SOCIAL SYSTEMS THEORY: A perspective on human social behavior that focuses on each individual as a complex, integrated organism whose behavior results from simultaneous interactions in a multitude of physical and social contexts. Any attempt to change the individual must consider the impact that one intervention may have on the entire "system" in which the individual operates (see FAMILY SYSTEMS THEORY; ECOLOGICAL APPROACH).

SOCIODEMOGRAPHICS: Descriptive data indicating the social class or socioeconomic status of an individual or family.

SOCIOECONOMIC STATUS (SES)/SOCIAL CLASS: A family's or individual's economic, educational, and occupational relationship to others in the society. Economic status is based on individual or family income. Social status or "class" is based on factors such as level of education, type of job held, type of housing, and (sometimes) values a person holds. SES is the strongest predictor of child and individual development.

SOMATIC SYMPTOMS: Problems, pains, or diseases affecting the body (as opposed to behavioral or psychological symptoms).

STABILITY: The extent to which consistent results are found using an instrument over time (see also RELIABILITY).

STAKEHOLDER: A person or group with a particular interest in a program or its evaluation findings

STANDARD DEVIATION: A measure of the variability of scores, an essential statistical calculation for almost any level of data analysis in research. A large standard deviation indicates wide variability in how individuals score on a test and may indicate a lack of reliability.

STANDARDIZED MEASURES: Tests or instruments that have been administered to large numbers of "normal" children or adults and for which results have been reported. When such a measure is used by a new group, their scores can be compared to those of others (see also NORMS).

STATISTICAL CONTROL: The process of controlling for or "taking out" the influence of certain variables in order to determine the relationship of variables in which one is more interested.

STATISTICAL POWER/STATISTICAL SIGNIFICANCE: See SIGNIFICANCE; POWER CALCULATION

STRATIFICATION: A sampling technique that identifies various groups of the population a researcher wishes to study, specifies an unbiased method for selecting participants from each of those groups, and then sets a goal regarding how many should be recruited in each group.

SUMMATIVE EVALUATION: An evaluation study that attempts to provide a conclusive, definitive statement about program effectiveness at the end of the study. This usually requires holding program services constant and documenting them carefully (see also FORMATIVE EVALUATION).

SYSTEMS THEORY: See SOCIAL SYSTEMS THEORY; FAMILY SYSTEMS THEORY

TARGET POPULATION: The specific group of children or families a program intends to serve. A target population for parent training could be defined as "any first time parent," "families at risk of child abuse," "low-income families," etc.

TECHNICAL QUALITIES: The reliability and validity of a test or measure (see also PSYCHOMETRIC PROPERTIES; RELIABILITY; VALIDITY).

TERTIARY PREVENTION: Services designed to ameliorate a problem or to prevent its recurrence. A misnomer, "tertiary prevention" is actually *treatment* for a problem that has occurred (see also PRIMARY PREVENTION; SECONDARY PREVENTION).

THEORETICAL CONSTRUCT: See CONSTRUCT

THREATS TO VALIDITY: Problems that occur in conducting research or evaluation studies and that can interfere with determining whether the results found are valid. Common threats to validity include: history—concurrent events happening to a child or family outside of the intervention program that can influence behavior the evaluation is measuring; motivation—attitudes and behaviors that can make some children and families want to improve regardless of intervention; maturation—the natural growth and learning process does not stop when a child or family is enrolled in a program; selection bias—known or unknown differences in the groups studied that can make some groups look as if they performed better or worse than they actually did; test–retest effects—knowledge of desired behavior or questions on a pretest influence how a child or family performs on a posttest; and the "Hawthorne effect"—children and adults receiving services may improve because of the attention they get regardless of the services.

T-TEST: A statistical test of significance that is used to determine whether the means of two different samples or sets of scores are different enough to indicate an actual difference (see also SIGNIFICANCE).

TIMES SERIES TECHNIQUES: Procedures for collecting research or evaluation information in which the same data are collected at several different points in time.

TITLE I: Title I of the Elementary and Secondary Education Act (ESEA) of 1965 is a federal program that aims to help "educationally deprived children" who live in areas with high concentrations of low-income families. Its main goals are to raise student achievement (especially in the areas of reading, language arts, and mathematics) and to encourage parental involvement in the schools via local parent advisory councils.

TRANSACTIONAL INFLUENCE: The contribution made by both individuals where there is interaction between two.

TREATMENT/TREATMENT GROUP/TREATMENT EFFECTS: A treatment consists of the particular service(s) provided. A single program may offer a number of treatments. Recipients of the treatment(s) make up the treatment group. Treatment effects are specific outcomes or impacts expected to result from receipt of the services.

TYPE I ERROR: An error in statistical analysis leading to the conclusion that differences are significant when in fact they are not. Because statistical analysis is inferential, 100% certainty is impossible; a Type I error occurs when, despite 95% certainty that something has been found, the truth is that the results occurred by chance (i.e., the 5% chance of error has occurred) (see also SIGNIFICANCE; TYPE II ERROR).

TYPE II ERROR: An error in statistical analysis that occurs when the percentage of certainty required for significance is increased, making it difficult to detect a real difference that may be occurring. When analyzing data, researchers must balance the probability of Type II error against the probability of Type I error when choosing levels of significance. Exploratory research may choose a 5% or even 10% level of significance and then recommend that future research studies be designed for a more rigorous (1–5%) level of significance (see also SIGNIFICANCE; TYPE I ERROR).

TYPOLOGY: The classification or organization of items, programs, issues, etc., into groups of similar characteristics or types.

UNANTICIPATED OUTCOMES/UNINTENDED EFFECTS: Results or outcomes found to have occurred as a result of an intervention but that were not expected when the intervention was designed and implemented.

UNIDIRECTIONAL MODEL: A model of child development that sees the child as a *tabula rasa,* wholly molded by the environment.

UNOBTRUSIVE MEASURES: Measurements or data collection procedures in which the study participant is not directly involved. Unobtrusive measures minimize the possible reactions of people who know they are under scrutiny (see also INTRUSIVENESS; REACTIVITY).

VALIDITY: The extent to which a finding is well-grounded and justified (see also EXTERNAL VALIDITY; INTERNAL VALIDITY; THREATS TO VALIDITY; and VALIDITY OF INSTRUMENTS).

VALIDITY OF INSTRUMENTS: A valid instrument measures what it is supposed to measure. There are a variety of methods for determining validity; a single instrument rarely performs well on all methods. If a measure has *concurrent validity* its results correlate strongly with another already developed instrument measuring the same characteristics. If a measure has *predictive validity* a person's score on that measure can predict future behavior or future scores. If a measure has *discriminant validity* it yields different results from groups that are, in fact, different. If a measure has *construct validity* its subscales do not contradict one another. If a measure has *face* or *content validity* (the simplest type of validity) there is an obvious, logical connection between the method of measurement and what is purportedly measured (see also EXTERNAL VALIDITY; INTERNAL VALIDITY; and THREATS TO VALIDITY).

VARIABLES: Specific characteristics, behaviors, test scores, or other indicators that are studied in a research or evaluation project (see also DEPENDENT VARIABLE; INDEPENDENT VARIABLE).

VARIANCE: An important statistical concept that is an indication of the variability of test scores or other characteristics measured within a particular group. A high variance indicates a wide range and little predictability of scores, while a lower variance indicates a more uniform pattern of scores and the likelihood that the groups taking the test are similar on the dimension being measured. Low variance makes it easier to determine whether one group is significantly different from another on the tested dimension.

INDEX

543

DATE